# SAGE
# vantage

# SAGE Outcomes:
# Measure Results, Track Success

**FOR STUDENTS,** understanding the objectives for each chapter and the goals for the course is essential for getting the grade you deserve!

**FOR INSTRUCTORS,** being able to track your students' progress allows you to more easily pinpoint areas of improvement and report on success.

This title was crafted around specific chapter objectives and course outcomes, vetted by experts, and adapted from renowned syllabi. Tracking student progress can be challenging. Promoting and achieving success should never be. We are here for you.

## COURSE **OUTCOMES** FOR AMERICAN GOVERNMENT:

**ARTICULATE** the foundations of American government, including its history, critical concepts, and important documents and achievements.

**EXAMINE** the main institutions of American government, including their roles and interrelationships.

**DESCRIBE** the roles and relative importance of major entities and influences in American political life.

**ANALYZE** the development and impact of important governmental policies.

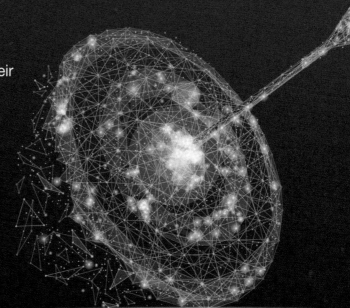

**Want to see how these outcomes tie in with this book's chapter-level objectives? Visit us at edge.sagepub.com/maltese for complete outcome-to-objective mapping.**

# Praise for

**AMERICAN DEMOCRACY IN CONTEXT**

JOHN ANTHONY MALTESE | JOSEPH A. PIKA | W. PHILLIPS SHIVELY

"I appreciate the blending of historical perspectives and cross-cultural approaches. This helps students better understand why and how governmental structures are the way they are and **WHY THAT MATTERS** for them. The book emphasizes for students that they are implicated in and have some claim over how those structures and rules constrain and shape policy outcomes."

—Brian M. Harward
*Allegheny College*

"The book is an accessible text for students that makes the subject matter and content **RELEVANT.** I like the contextual approach in helping students understand why these things are important, not just understanding how government works."

—Shannon Lynn Bridgmon
*Northeastern State University*

"I like the writing style and frequent examples and comparisons. The 'Picture Yourself' section is helpful, and I think **STUDENTS WILL LIKE IT.**"

—Amanda Friesen
*Indiana University – Purdue University Indianapolis*

"I like this comparative approach a lot and think that it helps when teaching the class to offer students **ALTERNATIVE VIEWS** of how politics in the United States could be relative to other systems. This is a book that places American politics in a comparative perspective. I would also add to my colleagues that teaching from this perspective is **VALUABLE,** as I think seeing contrasts in concepts can crystallize how exactly our American system works. I think the text reads nicely. To a novice, there is no jargon and the material is described in an intuitive way. I like the narrative to the text, as it is easy to follow."

—James Monogan
*University of Georgia*

# AMERICAN
# DEMOCRACY
# IN CONTEXT

Sara Miller McCune founded SAGE Publishing in 1965 to support the dissemination of usable knowledge and educate a global community. SAGE publishes more than 1000 journals and over 800 new books each year, spanning a wide range of subject areas. Our growing selection of library products includes archives, data, case studies and video. SAGE remains majority owned by our founder and after her lifetime will become owned by a charitable trust that secures the company's continued independence.

Los Angeles | London | New Delhi | Singapore | Washington DC | Melbourne

# AMERICAN
## DEMOCRACY
## IN CONTEXT

**JOHN ANTHONY MALTESE**
UNIVERSITY OF GEORGIA

**JOSEPH A. PIKA**
UNIVERSITY OF DELAWARE

**W. PHILLIPS SHIVELY**
UNIVERSITY OF MINNESOTA

**FOR INFORMATION:**

CQ Press

An Imprint of SAGE Publications, Inc.

2455 Teller Road

Thousand Oaks, California 91320

E-mail: order@sagepub.com

SAGE Publications Ltd.

1 Oliver's Yard

55 City Road

London, EC1Y 1SP

United Kingdom

SAGE Publications India Pvt. Ltd.

B 1/I 1 Mohan Cooperative Industrial Area

Mathura Road, New Delhi 110 044

India

SAGE Publications Asia-Pacific Pte. Ltd.

18 Cross Street #10-10/11/12

China Square Central

Singapore 048423

Printed in Canada

*Library of Congress Cataloging-in-Publication Data*

Names: Maltese, John Anthony, author. | Pika, Joseph August, author. | Shively, W. Phillips, author.

Title: American democracy in context / John Anthony Maltese, Joseph A. Pika, W. Phillips Shively.

Description: Los Angeles : SAGE, [2021] | Includes bibliographical references. | Summary: "American Democracy in Context uses a comparative approach to teach American Government and inspire students to understand, care and become active citizens. The narrative offers comparisons across nations and across time in the US so students understand the American system, how we got to this point and alternative views of what politics/policies would be if they lived in other democracies. The ultimate goal is to motivate students to understand why politics is relevant to their everyday lives and how they can bring about change to make their lives better. ADIC will be our first Vantage created from the ground up so leading with a strong digital message completes the story of this product"— Provided by publisher.

Identifiers: LCCN 2019030313 | ISBN 9781544345239 (paperback) | ISBN 9781544345208 (epub) | ISBN 9781544345215 (epub) | ISBN 9781544396200 (ebook)

Subjects: LCSH: Democracy—United States. | Representative government and representation—United States. | Political participation—United States.

Classification: LCC JK1726 .M35 2021 | DDC 320.973—dc23 LC record available at https://lccn.loc.gov/2019030313

This book is printed on acid-free paper.

Acquisitions Editor: Scott Greenan

Editorial Assistant: Sam Rosenberg

Content Development Editors: Scott Harris and Sarah Calabi

Production Editor: Andrew Olson

Copy Editor: Erin Livingston

Typesetter: Hurix Digital

Proofreader: Scott Oney

Indexer: Amy Murphy

Cover Designer: Janet Kiesel

Marketing Manager: Erica DeLuca

20 21 22 23 24 10 9 8 7 6 5 4 3 2 1

# BRIEF CONTENTS

**PART V PUBLIC POLICY**

CHAPTER 15: DOMESTIC AND ECONOMIC POLICY 381

# DETAILED CONTENTS

## CHAPTER 9: PARTICIPATION, VOTING BEHAVIOR, AND CAMPAIGNS

# CHAPTER 10: MEDIA AND POLITICS 243

# PART IV INSTITUTIONS OF AMERICAN DEMOCRACY

# PART V  PUBLIC POLICY

# PREFACE

## AMERICAN DEMOCRACY IN CONTEXT

**If this is the only course your students take in political science, it should matter. Put American politics in context for your students.** America's version of democracy is distinctive in some respects but also similar to others around the world. We can better understand the American version of democracy by comparing it with democratic practices elsewhere and by better understanding historically how it has become the way it is today. These two contexts will inspire students to develop a deeper and broader understanding of American practices and American institutions.

### PERSPECTIVE

These chapter-opening vignettes set the stage for the rest of the chapter discussion and help students see political connections by comparing a historical moment, current event, or policy in the United States to that of another country. For instance, students can picture how it would be to live in a country such as Canada that has short national election campaigns—about two and a half months from start to finish.

### PICTURE YOURSELF . . .

Students are invited to consider what it would be like to experience some aspect of the political system of another country or of the U.S. at another period of time or from a particular vantage point in order to fully understand and appreciate that aspect of government in the United States. Students can imagine, for example, being a citizen of Venezuela trying to figure out what to do when there are two persons claiming to be the lawful president.

### CONSEQUENCES FOR DEMOCRACY

These chapter-ending sections pull together the historical and comparative perspectives that help students understand the distinctive features of American politics as well as the common features of democracy. For example, U.S. political parties are more decentralized than those in many other nations—partly because of our electoral system and partly because of a long history of party reform, starting with the Progressive Movement—making it more difficult for Congress to take action on social and economic problems.

## DIGITAL RESOURCES

*A Complete Teaching & Learning Package*

*Engage, Learn, Soar* with **SAGE vantage**, an intuitive digital platform that delivers *American Democracy in Context* textbook content in a learning experience carefully designed to ignite student engagement and drive critical thinking. With evidence-based instructional design at the core, SAGE vantage creates more time for engaged learning and empowered teaching, keeping the classroom where it belongs—in your hands.

Easy to access across mobile, desktop, and tablet devices, SAGE vantage enables students to engage with the material you choose, learn by applying knowledge, and soar with confidence by performing better in your course.

## HIGHLIGHTS INCLUDE:

- **eReading Experience.** Makes it easy for students to study wherever they are—students can take notes, highlight content, look up definitions, and more!
- **Pedagogical Scaffolding.** Builds on core concepts, moving students from basic understanding to mastery.
- **Confidence Builder.** Offers frequent knowledge checks, applied-learning multimedia tools, and chapter tests with focused feedback to assure students know key concepts.
- **Time-saving Flexibility.** Feeds auto-graded assignments to your gradebook, with real-time insight into student and class performance.
- **Quality Content.** Written by expert authors and teachers, content is not sacrificed for technical features.
- **Honest Value.** Affordable access to easy-to-use, quality learning tools students will appreciate.

## FAVORITE SAGE VANTAGE FEATURES

- **3-step course setup** is so fast you can complete it in minutes!
- **Control over assignments**, content selection, due dates, and grading empowers you to teach your way.
- **Quality content** authored by the experts you trust.
- **eReading experience** makes it easy to learn and study by presenting content in easy-to-digest segments featuring note-taking, highlighting, definition look-up, and more.
- **LMS integration provides single sign-on** with streamlined grading capabilities and course management tools.
- **Auto-graded assignments** include:

  - formative **knowledge checks** for each major section of the text that quickly reinforce what students have read and ensure they stay on track;
  - dynamic, hands-on **multimedia activities** that tie real world examples and motivate students to read, prepare for class;
  - summative **chapter tests** that reinforce important themes; and
  - **helpful hints and feedback** (provided with all assignments) that offer context and explain why an answer is correct or incorrect, allowing students to study more effectively.

- **Compelling polling questions** bring concepts to life and drive meaningful comprehension and classroom discussion.
- **Short-answer questions** provide application and reflection opportunities connected to key concepts.
- **Instructor reports** track student activity and provide analytics so you can adapt instruction as needed.
- **A student dashboard** offers easy access to grades, so students know exactly where they stand in your course and where they might improve.
- **Honest value** gives students access to quality content and learning tools at a price they will appreciate.

## ⑤SAGE coursepacks

## SAGE COURSEPACKS FOR INSTRUCTORS

The **SAGE coursepack** for *American Democracy in Context* makes it easy to import our quality instructor materials and student resources into your school's learning management system (LMS), such as Blackboard, Canvas, Brightspace by D2L, or Moodle. Intuitive and simple to use, **SAGE coursepack** allows you to integrate only the content you need, with minimal effort, and requires no access code. Don't use an LMS platform? You can still access many of the online resources for *American Democracy in Context* via the **SAGE edge** site.

Available SAGE content through the coursepack includes:

- Pedagogically robust **assessment tools** that foster review, practice, and critical thinking and offer a more complete way to measure student engagement, including:

  - Diagnostic **coursepack chapter quizzes** that identify opportunities for improvement, track student progress, and ensure mastery of key learning objectives.
  - **Test banks** built on Bloom's taxonomy that provide a diverse range of test items.
  - **Activity and quiz options** that allow you to choose only the assignments and tests you want.

- Editable, chapter-specific **PowerPoint®** slides that offer flexibility when creating multimedia lectures so you don't have to start from scratch but can customize to your exact needs.
- **Instructions** on how to use and integrate the comprehensive assessments and resources provided.

## ⑤SAGE edge™

**SAGE edge** is a robust online environment featuring an impressive array of tools and resources for review, study, and further exploration, keeping both instructors and students on the cutting edge of teaching and learning. SAGE edge content is open access and available on demand. Learning and teaching has never been easier!

**SAGE edge for Students** at **http://edge.sagepub.com/maltese** provides a personalized approach to help students accomplish their coursework goals in an easy-to-use learning environment.

- **Learning objectives** reinforce the most important material
- Mobile-friendly **Flashcards** strengthen understanding of key terms and concepts, and make it easy to maximize your study time, anywhere, anytime.
- Mobile-friendly practice **quizzes** allow you to assess how much you've learned and where you need to focus your attention.

**SAGE edge for Instructors** at **http://edge.sagepub.com/maltese** supports teaching by making it easy to integrate quality content and create a rich learning environment for students.

- The **Test bank**, built on Bloom's taxonomy (with Bloom's cognitive domain and difficulty level noted for each question), is created specifically for this text.
- **Sample course syllabi** provide suggested models for structuring your course.
- Editable, chapter-specific **PowerPoint®** slides offer complete flexibility for creating a multimedia presentation for the course, so you don't have to start from scratch but can customize to your exact needs.
- An **instructor's manual** for each chapter includes a chapter summary, outline, multimedia links, discussion questions, and in-class activities.
- A set of all the **graphics from the text**, including all the maps, tables, and figures in PowerPoint formats are provided for class presentations.

## SAGE PREMIUM VIDEO

*American Democracy in Context* offers premium video, available exclusively in the **SAGE vantage** digital option, produced and curated specifically for this text, to boost comprehension and bolster analysis.

# SAGE COURSE OUTCOMES

Outlined in your text and mapped to chapter learning objectives, SAGE course outcomes are crafted with specific course outcomes in mind and vetted by advisers in the field. See how SAGE course outcomes tie in with this book's chapter-level objectives at **http://edge.sagepub.com/maltese.**

# A NOTE FROM THE AUTHORS

We write this book at a time when democracy seems under assault not only abroad but also at home. At no time in the last seven decades have there been so many challenges posed to fundamental political practices and institutions that have long gone unquestioned. Students need answers and a sophisticated understanding of how democracy works and why the nation adopted the practices now in place.

*Understanding* American politics involves much more than knowing the facts. It also requires understanding the causal connections in politics. From these connections, students can see how and why the decisions and actions of government officials matter to them. We have tried in this text to help students understand why politics and government institutions have developed as they have in the United States and to see the effects of our politics in things that they care about.

The three of us have been teaching American politics for more years than we want to count, and we have found that students are curious about the connections between things. They especially want to understand why we do the things we do and in the ways we do them. Our twin strategies to help students understand American politics include an analysis of its historical development and comparisons with the politics of other countries. We use both history and comparison as analytic devices—this book is neither a history of American politics nor a study of comparative politics, but both perspectives shed important light on American politics today.

In this spirit, causal connections run throughout the book. We use comparison and historical development to meet students' needs and to motivate them—not to fill a niche for comparativists or specialists in American political development. This is, at heart, a straight-ahead introduction to American politics, but one that adds essential context. In other words, we take seriously students' desire to understand why our system operates the way it does and its consequences for democracy.

Our experience is that many introductory American government texts are cluttered with boxes and features. This book minimizes all but the most important. We integrate most of our features—notably the bookends of each chapter, "Perspective" and "Consequences for Democracy"—into the text itself because they are so central to our presentation. In each chapter, "Perspective" and "Picture Yourself" present historical and comparative perspectives on the distinctive characteristics of American politics discussed in that chapter.

Students appreciate course materials that help them learn and truly understand difficult concepts. We have sought to write a book worth reading and not only cover the basics. We have challenged ourselves in writing *American Democracy in Context* and we want to challenge students, in the best sense of that word, to arrive at a better appreciation and a deeper understanding of how and why American politics matters. We have enjoyed working together on this project. We hope that you and your students will find similar pleasure from using it.

John Maltese, Joe Pika, and Phil Shively

# ACKNOWLEDGMENTS

The authors are grateful to the many people at CQ Press who have worked with us on this project. Monica Eckman lured us in (again) and saw us through the early stages of this project. We also thank those on the editorial and marketing side, on the production side, and on the digital side who helped us bring it to completion. Special thanks to Sarah Calabi for the countless hours she spent helping us revise the text, and to Erin Livingston for her expert copyediting. We are also grateful to the staff members at our respective universities who helped with the original edition. Above all, we are grateful to our families, who tolerated our long and erratic periods of work on this project. *American Democracy in Context* is a project we believe in that has lured even retirees back into the harness. We are proud of the results—written through sickness and health—and grateful to those who prodded us to make it better, even though we sometimes resisted. Most of all, we are grateful to our students, whose curiosity was and remains contagious.

The authors would also like to thank the instructors who have contributed their valuable feedback through reviews of this text:

Shannon Lynn Bridgmon, Northeastern State University

Amanda Friesen, Indiana University—Purdue University Indianapolis (IUPUI)

Brian M. Harward, Allegheny College

James Edward Monogan III, University of Georgia

Patrick Moore, Richland College

Noel A.D. Thompson, Tuskegee University

Laura Wood, Tarrant County College

John Maltese, Joe Pika, and Phil Shively

# ABOUT THE AUTHORS

JOHN ANTHONY MALTESE is the associate dean of the school of public and international affairs and the Albert B. Saye professor of political science at the University of Georgia. His books include *The Selling of Supreme Court Nominees* (winner of the C. Herman Pritchett Award), *Spin Control: The White House Office of Communications and the Management of Presidential News*, and, with Joseph A. Pika and Andrew Rudalevige, *The Politics of the Presidency*, currently in its tenth edition. He is a Josiah Meigs Distinguished Teaching Professor and was named a Georgia Professor of the Year by the Carnegie Foundation and the Council for Advancement and Support of Education (CASE). He writes about classical music in his spare time, for which he has won a Grammy Award from the National Academy of Recording Arts and Sciences.

JOSEPH A. PIKA is the James R. Soles professor of political science and international relations emeritus at the University of Delaware, where he was recognized for excellence in teaching, advising, and service, the latter including seven years on the State Board of Education. Professor Pika's areas of research include the American presidency and vice presidency, Delaware politics, and education policy. He has published multiple editions of *Politics of the Presidency* (the tenth edition, coauthored with John Maltese and Andrew Rudalevige, was published by CQ Press in Winter 2019), *Confrontation and Compromise: Presidential and Congressional Leadership, 2001–2006* (with Jason Mycoff, Rowman & Littlefield, 2007), and *The Presidential Contest* (with Richard Watson, CQ Press, 1996). He is an avid sports fan and political activist.

W. PHILLIPS SHIVELY is professor emeritus of political science at the University of Minnesota and has also served on the faculties of Yale University, the University of Oregon, and Oslo University, Norway. He has served as editor of the *American Journal of Political Science*, as program chair for the national meetings of the American Political Science Association, and as principal investigator and chair of the Comparative Study of Electoral Systems project (CSES). At the University of Minnesota, he has been inducted into the Academy of Distinguished Teachers for his work with students. His research centers on the comparative study of elections and statistical methods of research. Besides political science, Professor Shively's other main loves are natural history and classical music.

From left to right: Phil Shively, John Maltese, and Joe Pika.

# 1
# DEMOCRACY AND AMERICAN POLITICS

## After reading this chapter, you should be able to do the following:

- Understand the nature of politics, government, and citizenship.
- Differentiate among the types of democracies that exist in the world and identify the qualities that make a government truly democratic.
- Examine the functions of government as well as some of the challenges and controversies that affect its ability to perform each function effectively.
- Identify the four basic American values and describe how these values help to define the character of American politics.
- Explore the primary political ideologies that have helped to inform contemporary political discourse in the United States.
- Understand how comparison and historical analysis can deepen our understanding of American politics.

## Perspective: What Difference Does Democracy Make?

In the United States, trains covered with bright, fanciful graffiti are often seen rolling down the tracks. The graffiti constitutes vandalism, but while vandalizing property by painting graffiti is illegal in most states and cities, authorities do not usually enforce the laws against it very strictly. In fact, some Americans admire graffiti as an elevated art form, romanticizing graffiti artists as individuals who thumb their noses at the government.

It is different in Singapore. In 1994, 18-year-old American student Michael Fay ran afoul of Singapore's stringent laws protecting order and cleanliness. Singaporean police arrested Fay for stealing highway signs and vandalizing a car by scratching its paint. His court sentence: four months in jail, a fine of over $2,000, and four strokes with a cane. The caning—a common punishment in Singapore—was administered with a six-foot long, one-inch-thick cane that can cause serious injury. Other acts that are not necessarily considered crimes in the United States but can draw similarly serious punishments in Singapore include spitting in public, selling chewing gum, or failing to flush the toilet in a public restroom.

Singapore was a British colony until it became independent in 1965. Today, it is a prosperous financial center and technology exporter. Average incomes in Singapore are somewhat higher than those in the United States; crime rates are low; and the country is very clean, partly because of its stringent punishments for graffiti and similar offenses that other countries would consider minor. Its government is one of the least corrupt in the world.

Although efficient and prosperous, Singapore is not a democracy. Its government regulates citizens' behavior tightly. Elections are held regularly, but the People's Action Party, which has governed without interruption since it led the country to independence more than 45 years ago, does not allow a significant opposition party to develop or function. It requires all political organizations to register with the government, and organizers of any public gathering of more than five people must obtain a special permit. This allows the government to regulate opposition activity. The Party also controls the media, all of which are owned by government-linked companies. Such control includes the banning of all political films and political television programs. In the 2015 election, the Party got 70 percent of the vote, winning 83 of the 89 seats in Singapore's Parliament.

By contrast, the United States is less efficient and less tightly organized than Singapore, but it is a democracy. The media are not controlled by the government. The right of groups to organize and gather publicly is guaranteed in the First Amendment to the Constitution. And citizens who criticize public officials are protected against harassment. But the government in a democracy is not as free as a government like Singapore's to put laws in place that lack broad support. Harsh anti-littering laws with physical punishment and jail time would not be tolerated by the public, even though such laws might produce a very clean country.

Actually, Singapore probably presents the most attractive instance of a non-democracy that we can come up with, since most non-democracies are not particularly well organized or well run. Singapore's government avoids corrupt practices, it runs efficiently, and it has helped the country to prosper economically. But the lack of political freedom in Singapore has its costs. The people of Singapore are much more politically passive than Americans. While 17 percent of Americans discuss politics frequently, only 4 percent of Singaporeans do. Forty-one percent of them say that they never discuss politics at all. As far as political participation is concerned, 76 percent of Americans say that they would be willing to attend a lawful demonstration, whereas only 24 percent of Singaporeans would.[1] **«**

## GOVERNMENT AND POLITICS

When the people in a country need to consider changing the way things are done, they engage in **politics**, the process by which collective decisions—decisions that are binding for everyone in the country—are made for a country.[2] *Collective decisions* include such things as a law, a system of taxes, or a social program. We use *process* in this definition very broadly to include not only the actions of government officials but also all of the considerations that influence them, such as elections, public opinion, and the media. *Politics* consists of all the factors that contribute to collective decisions.

For example, in 2017, when President Trump called for repealing the Affordable Care Act (aka Obamacare), many voices contributed to that debate and to the political process that followed:

- policy schools, which provided scholarly assessments of various sorts of health care delivery systems
- the AARP (formerly the American Association of Retired Persons) and labor unions, which ran advertisements opposing the repeal
- insurance groups and business organizations that lobbied for or against the repeal
- the cable news channel MSNBC, which provided anti-repeal press coverage, and Fox News, another cable channel, which offered pro-repeal coverage

> **politics** The process by which decisions that are binding for everyone in the country are made, such as a law, a system of taxes, or a social program.

Republicans' attempts to repeal and replace the Affordable Care Act led to vigorous protest, including by disabled Americans, some of whom staged sit-ins at congressional office buildings.

- opponents of repeal, who conducted raucous protests at town hall meetings held by members of Congress
- ordinary citizens, who talked to one another about the merits of the proposals
- parents who brought disabled children to Washington to ask Congress to keep their health benefits intact
- members of Congress who engaged in arm-twisting, deals, and bargaining as they attempted to craft and pass, or persuade colleagues to vote for or against, the legislation

All of these voices were part of the politics associated with the decisions about whether, and how, to reform the U.S. health care system.

To facilitate the decision-making process, regardless of who participates (or is allowed to participate), every country has a **government**. A government helps a country to maintain internal order, to interact with other countries, and to develop laws and policies. What sets government apart from any other group is that only the government has the right to make decisions that are binding on everyone within the nation's borders and that the government has the right to use force (the threat of fines or jail) to ensure that the laws are followed and to implement its decisions.[3] Other groups can make more limited decisions, but they are prohibited from using force to implement them. A corporation such as Microsoft, for instance, can decide to design the Windows operating system for personal computers in a particular way, but that decision is binding only on those who voluntarily buy its product. Furthermore, Microsoft cannot use force to implement its decision. By contrast, the government of the United States can pass a law outlawing child pornography for everyone in the country and can use force to make sure everyone follows it.

Every person living in a country, then, is required to obey its laws—citizens and noncitizens alike. **Citizens** are people who are fully qualified and legally recognized as members of a country. However, not everyone living in a country at a given time is considered a citizen. Citizens of other countries who are visiting briefly or who have obtained permission to work or pursue their education in the country for a long or even indefinite period of time are not citizens. Also, several million undocumented immigrants live and work in the United States. But whether they are citizens or

**government** The set of people who make decisions that are binding for all people in the country and have the right to use force and coercion to implement their choices.

**citizens** Members of a country's population who are legally recognized as subjects or nationals of the country.

Naturalization ceremonies, in which noncitizens take an oath of allegiance to the United States and formally become American citizens, are held periodically around the country, usually in nondescript government offices but occasionally at special venues such as the Turner Field baseball stadium in Atlanta.

not, all who reside within a country's borders are both protected by the country's laws and required to obey them.

Various types of governments exist, and political scientists distinguish between them according to the basis of their power—in other words, where they get their right to rule. Many countries throughout the world have some form of nondemocratic government, in which a small group of people govern and the rest of the citizens of the country have no direct voice in what the government does. Important types of non-democracy include government by army officers (Thailand, for instance), government by a hereditary monarch (Saudi Arabia), government by a single party that allows no other parties to operate (Singapore), and government by religious leaders (Iran). In this chapter, however, we will focus on democratic government because that is the form of government in the United States.

## DEMOCRACY AS A FORM OF GOVERNMENT

In a **democracy**, all citizens can participate in the making of governmental policy, at least to some extent, even if indirectly. Though *democracy* is generally defined as "rule by citizens," this definition is more an ideal than a concrete, observable phenomenon. As we will see in this section, a variety of factors influence how fully and how directly citizens in a democracy share in the rule of the country. In fact, there is no country in the world where all citizens have precisely equal roles in making the decisions of the country. However, a number of countries approximate the ideal well enough that we call them democracies. As shown in Figure 1.1, 116 countries—more than half of all countries in the world—are democracies.

### DIRECT DEMOCRACY

The closest approximation to rule by all citizens is **direct democracy**, in which all of the citizens of a community gather to decide policies for that community. It was the mode of government in some ancient Greek city-states, and it still exists today in New England town meetings where all citizens come together to discuss and decide issues.[4] Direct democracy is possible only in a small community with relatively simple issues to decide. Even a direct democracy does not exactly accomplish "rule by the citizens," at least in the sense that all citizens contribute equally to the decision-making process. As in any group formed to accomplish assigned tasks, some people are more experienced or articulate than others, so not everyone is able to contribute equally. In fact, a direct democracy may actually express the will of only a fairly small group of leaders.

### INDIRECT DEMOCRACY

Direct democracy is impossible in a complex, modern country such as the United States. How could millions of U.S. citizens come together to make decisions? Faced with thousands of complex, detailed issues each year, how could all citizens participate adequately and still do anything else with their lives? Accordingly, almost all democracies today are **indirect democracies**, also called *representative democracies*. In an indirect democracy, all citizens vote to choose, from among alternative candidates, the people who will be in charge of making decisions and

**democracy** Rule by the people.

**direct democracy** Democracy in which all of the people of a community gather to decide policies for the community.

**indirect democracy** Democracy in which the people do not decide policies for the community themselves but elect representatives to decide the policies.

## FIGURE 1.1
## *Democracies of the World*

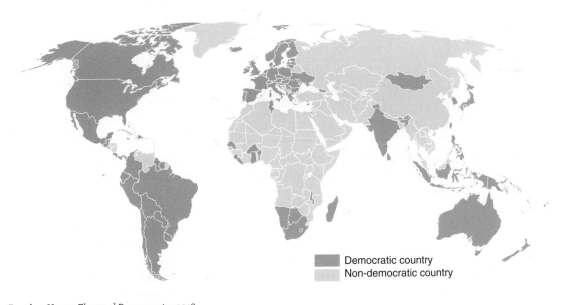

Democratic country
Non-democratic country

*Source: Freedom House, Electoral Democracies 2018.*

implementing policies. In the United States, for example, the people of a city may elect a mayor and members of a city council; residents of each state elect a governor and other statewide officials as well as members of the state's legislature. Every eligible U.S. citizen can vote to elect the president and members of Congress to represent them.

What is needed for indirect democracy to work well? Obviously, elections are a basic requirement. But are elections enough? Earlier in the chapter, we explained that Singapore holds elections regularly, but we noted that in the 2015 election, the People's Action Party, which has ruled the country since 1965, got 70 percent of the vote, winning 83 of the 89 seats in Singapore's Parliament. The government achieved this result by suppressing opposition. Such outcomes show that elections alone do not a democracy make. Thus, effective indirect democracy goes beyond merely holding elections; a number of other pieces must also be in place to ensure that the elections offer citizens a chance to affect decisions through their vote:

- open elections
- broad participation in the elections
- freedom of speech and media
- the right to organize
- majority rule . . . but with protection for minority rights

The first four requirements are discussed in this section. The twin requirements of majority rule and protection of minority rights are discussed later in this chapter in the section titled "The Challenges of Democracy."

The first requirement, of course, is that elections must be held regularly, and all qualified citizens must have an equal right to participate. Which citizens are considered "qualified" may evolve over time. Women's right to vote is viewed differently today than it was in the early nineteenth century, for instance, and in every country, there is some age below which citizens are not considered qualified to vote. But a democracy is limited if it denies the right to citizens who are widely regarded as qualified. Democracy in the United States was limited by the systematic denial of African Americans' right to vote in much of the South until 1965, when Congress passed the Voting Rights Act.

For much of the twentieth century, it was legal to require citizens to pay a poll tax as part of their qualification for voting. Rosa Parks herself paid $1.50 in 1957 for the right to vote in Alabama.

There should also be broad participation in the elections. This is a matter of degree—there is never 100 percent participation. But as we will see in Chapter 9, countries vary a good deal in how fully their citizens participate in elections. This is partly a function of citizens' own willingness to honor their responsibility to participate, but it is also a function of whether the government makes it easy for citizens to vote or sets up impediments to make it inconvenient for them to do so.

A third basic requirement of democracy, beyond the formal arrangements of voting and elections, is sufficient individual freedom to allow open debate. This in turn requires freedom of speech and a free, uncontrolled media. A country might hold regular elections and yet not be a democracy. Singapore is such a country. Another good example is Russia, which holds regular elections with alternative candidates but maintains such stringent governmental control over the media that the country cannot be considered a full democracy.

Finally, citizens of a democracy need to be able to organize independently into political parties and other organizations to pool their political efforts. Again, countries may hold elections yet fail to meet this requirement. For instance, China, which is ruled tightly by its Communist Party, holds elections in which individuals are allowed to run for office freely and sometimes can even win against the official candidate. But these independents are not allowed to form an organization to coordinate their efforts, which prevents them from having an effective voice. The Chinese system is not a democracy because isolated individuals—individuals who cannot combine with others—cannot challenge the sole legal political organization, the Communist Party, in any effective way.

For a democracy to function effectively, therefore, it needs more than just elections. A true democracy allows those with competing points of view to present their ideas in a lively and effective way through the following principles and structures:

- competing political parties
- freedom of speech and association
- equal access of voters to the process of selecting public officials
- equal access to those officials once they are elected

These requirements—the principles of democracy—as they apply to the United States are a central focus of this book. The United States was the world's first modern democracy, and over the years, aspiring democracies have measured themselves against the U.S. system, treating it as a standard. The extent to which the principles of democracy are realized in countries of the world today varies greatly, however. How does the United States' democracy compare with that of other governments around the world? Of the 116 democracies shown in the map in Figure 1.1, Freedom House, an organization that researches and promotes democracy, places the United States, along with only 47 other countries, in the highest category of democracies that meet most fully the requirements of a democracy.

For the first two hundred years after the first modern democracy was established in the United States at the end of the eighteenth century, the spread of this form of government was gradual. In a sudden spurt starting in the mid-1970s, however, many countries shifted from nondemocratic forms of government to democracy. Democracies represented only 31 percent of the world's states in 1977, a figure that had remained essentially unchanged since the 1950s. By the mid-1990s, however, about 62 percent of the world's states had become democratic, with the sharpest jump in the number of democracies occurring between 1989 and 1995.[5] Since the 1990s, however, there has been essentially no growth in the number of democracies. It was still the case in 2018 that 62 percent of the countries in the world were democracies.

Most democracies are found among the more prosperous countries of the world. In fact, the average per capita income of democracies is almost twice that of non-democracies.[6] The reasons why this is so are not fully understood, but it may simply be that people find it easier to work out their differences peaceably when they are reasonably well-off economically. The United States has been one of the world's most prosperous countries for two centuries.[7] This has helped it to cement its democratic form of government even during trying times, such as the nineteenth-century Civil War, when that government was severely tested.

## THE CHALLENGES OF DEMOCRACY

The widespread adoption of democracy in the later twentieth century probably stems ultimately from a basic human need for respect. Even if democracy is imperfect as practiced, the aspiration toward a more democratic form of government implies that all people are of equal worth and, at least in principle, have a right to be heard. Certainly, this aspiration has been present throughout American history and has led to a perception, both among Americans and worldwide, that the United States is a moral leader of the world. Translating the aspiration into practice, however, presents obvious difficulties. Democracies face two difficulties in particular—the problem of ensuring majority rule and the problem of protecting minority rights.

**ENSURING MAJORITY RULE** Representative democracy embodies the principle of majority rule—the idea that 50 percent plus one of the people should be able to choose a majority of the elected officials in a country and thereby determine its direction. Aside from many questions about the mechanics of elections (which we will explore in greater depth in Chapter 8), the fact that representative democracy makes people equal only in their right to vote also limits majority rule. The vote is a powerful resource in democratic politics, but other resources that are unequally distributed—for example, money, education, and social position (being a newspaper editor, for instance)—give some citizens more access to decision making than others. To the extent that these other resources affect the decisions that elected officials make, 50 percent plus one of the votes may not be the determining factor. According to surveys, for instance, for most of the period since World War II, strong majorities in the United States have favored prayer in the schools and stricter control of firearms, yet neither practice has become national law.

**PROTECTING MINORITY RIGHTS** Even if majority rule always prevailed, democracies would still face a second challenge—protecting minority rights, the basic freedoms of smaller groups within the general population. These may be racial, ethnic, or religious groups or individuals whose opinions differ from those of the majority. For example, what if a majority wanted to revoke a minority group's basic human rights, such as the right to equal treatment by the government or the right to speak freely? The principle of majority rule would seem to validate this decision, but most people would agree that it would be the wrong thing to do. In a telling example, in the late nineteenth and early twentieth centuries, white majorities in the Southern states passed many laws pushing African American minorities into inferior, segregated schools and other public facilities and denying them the right to vote. Overcoming the preferences of these majorities did not occur until the 1950s and 1960s, and doing so took rulings from the Supreme Court as well as congressional and presidential action. In the late twentieth and early twenty-first centuries, majorities of voters in many states voted to bar same-sex marriage—yet another example of the tension between majority rule and minority aspirations.

**majority rule** The principle that 50 percent plus one of the people should be able to elect a majority of elected officials and thereby determine the direction of policy.

**minority rights** Basic human rights that are considered important to guarantee for minorities in a democracy.

When studying a democracy such as the United States, we need to examine how the country deals with these two basic problems: How (and to what degree) is majority rule ensured? And how are minority rights protected under majority rule? These two questions will figure prominently in the succeeding chapters of this book.

## REPUBLICS

A concept that is often contrasted with democracy—and sometimes confused with it—is the **republic**. In the study of politics in general, a *republic* is simply a country not ruled by a monarch. But in the study specifically of American politics, we add another layer of meaning to the term. As you will see in Chapter 2, as the original founders of the United States considered how to design the new democracy and write its constitution, they used the term to denote government by the people's elected representatives, who—though they are ultimately responsible to the people—rule primarily on the basis of their own intelligence and experience. So, for them, a republic was distinguished from direct democracy as well as from monarchy. We will use the term *republic* to mean an indirect democracy that particularly emphasizes insulation of its representatives and officials from direct popular pressure. In political rhetoric today, the term *republic* is often used by people who favor democracy but do not favor intense and direct popular involvement in democratic government.

# FUNCTIONS OF GOVERNMENT

As we have seen, in the division of labor required by indirect democracy, some people serve as the elected representatives of the citizens and rule on their behalf. These people are the government, and they make decisions that are binding for all people in the country. Since most people, all other things being equal, would prefer not to be bound by rules, our views of government and its functions are generally characterized by some ambivalence: On the one hand, we do not enjoy being ruled; on the other hand, the alternative would result in chaos.

What sorts of functions do governments perform? What sorts of decisions do we *want* to have the government make for us? As a first answer to these questions, consider the Preamble to the United States Constitution, in which the authors laid out their reasons for establishing a central government:

> We the People of the United States, in Order to form a more perfect Union, establish Justice, insure domestic Tranquility, provide for the common defence, promote the general Welfare, and secure the Blessings of Liberty to ourselves and our Posterity, do ordain and establish this Constitution for the United States of America.

This Preamble alludes to two basic kinds of services that cannot easily be accomplished without government, and their provision accounts for two functions of every government of the world. The first function, captured by the phrase "[to] insure domestic Tranquility," is to provide basic security for people to live together and to deal with each other in financial transactions. The second function, exemplified by the phrase "[to] provide for the common defence," is to provide certain services called *public goods*—among them national defense—that can only be provided effectively by a government.[8] In addition to providing these two basic kinds of services, governments can and do perform a range of additional functions, as expressed by the phrase "[to] promote the general Welfare."

In other words, governments *have* to exist in order to provide a secure social and financial environment and public goods, but they can do other things as well. Governments often end up doing a variety of other things since, once a government exists, citizens often want it to perform additional services. Thus, government can shape the context of our lives in all sorts of ways. Let's look more closely at these functions of government.

## MAINTAINING ORDER AND SAFETY

Since the government is the sole entity with the right to use force and coercion to implement its choices, it is able to enact and enforce rules against crimes such as murder, burglary, and

**republic** An indirect democracy that particularly emphasizes insulation of its representatives and officials from direct popular pressure.

assault, thus ensuring our security. It can also provide a common currency for—and regulate—financial transactions and guarantee that contracts will be enforced, ensuring the security of our property. To ensure enforcement of the relevant laws, the government maintains agencies such as the police, the Federal Bureau of Investigation, and the Treasury Department. In effect, the government provides the basic social and financial network within which people can carry on their lives securely, functioning in the society and in the economy. This is true of every government in the world.

## PROVIDING PUBLIC GOODS

A **public good** may sound general but is in fact a very specific term. Public goods are more than "goods for the public"; they are, precisely, benefits that cannot possibly be given to some people while being withheld from others.[9] Public goods include national defense, space exploration, basic medical research, and public health programs to control the spread of disease. It is physically impossible to prevent any member of the community from using these goods. For instance, the U.S. government cannot defend its entire country's borders without also defending Phil Shively in Minneapolis, Minnesota.

Most importantly, the use of public goods cannot be restricted to only those who have helped to pay for them. Thus, public goods are dogged by the problem of **free riders**, who reason that since they will obtain the good in any case, they can get away without paying for its cost: "If I don't pay my share, the army will still be there, and I'll get all the benefits of it. Why should I pay?" Everyone could reason like this, so if a public good such as defense were left to private corporations or to organizations accepting voluntary donations, it would end up inadequately financed and everyone would lose out.[10] That is where government comes in. Since a government has the right to use force to implement its choices, it can require people to pay taxes and then use that tax money to pay for the public good. Mandating shared payment of a public good eliminates free riders.

Let's consider the case of public television, a public good that is largely funded by donations from viewers, not provided by the government in the United States and therefore suffers a serious free rider problem. Television signals that are broadcast on the air waves are a public good because no one in the community can physically be prevented from picking them up with a receiver, whether or not they have paid, so public television stations are

**public good** Something that benefits all members of the community and that no one can possibly be prevented from using.

**free riders** Those people who take advantage of the fact that a public good cannot possibly be denied to anyone by refusing to pay their share of the cost of providing the public good.

Public goods, such as clean air and water, benefit everyone, not only the specific people who paid for them.

faced with the problem of free riders. For this reason, every few months, the station's staff finds itself forced to interrupt their programming in the hopes of encouraging viewers to help defray the costs of running the station. They appeal to guilt: "Only one in ten of you who watch this station is a member; the rest of you are free riders." They appeal to acquisitiveness: "For the basic $35 membership, we offer this lovely ceramic mug, embossed with the station's logo." Perhaps the most effective pitch occurred a few years ago in Minneapolis, Minnesota, when the station staff promised that if they reached their goal early, they would cut off the fund drive at that point and return to regular programming. Contributions flooded in![11]

In short, through such actions as providing for the defense of the country, exploring space, protecting the environment, and developing public health programs such as immunization, the government is fulfilling its function of providing public goods. If the air quality is preserved, it is preserved for all of us. And so, preserving the air quality (a public good) raises the problem of free riders and is thus undertaken by government.

## PROMOTING THE GENERAL WELFARE

Beyond these two essential functions of providing a basic network of protective laws and security and providing public goods, however, government can also do more. Recall that in addition to establishing justice, ensuring domestic tranquility, and providing for the common defense (things only a government can do), the authors of the Constitution wanted the government to "promote the general Welfare." The general welfare can be promoted through various government services, and almost all governments do provide some benefits beyond the basic requirements. The American government performs each of the following services:

- providing infrastructure
- regulating the economy to ensure that it operates fairly
- providing support to people in vulnerable positions
- redistributing income to improve the lives of citizens with less wealth
- regulating behavior

**PROVIDING INFRASTRUCTURE**  Many other services that people feel are important as a basis for the economy and society, such as education, highways, and parks, are not public goods; in principle, they could be provided only to those who were willing to pay for them and withheld from those who don't. For example, all education could be offered by private schools and all highways could be offered to users on a toll basis (essentially the way railroads are). However, these are basic and important services that most people think government should provide because they constitute the underlying infrastructure for everything else; certainly, in the United States, the government provides such services.

**REGULATING THE ECONOMY TO ENSURE THAT IT OPERATES FAIRLY**  This function of government goes beyond maintaining order by enforcing contracts. As part of ensuring the fair regulation of the economy, the government regulates many financial transactions to make sure that everyone involved has enough information to make intelligent choices. The sale of stocks is regulated, for instance, to require companies offering stock to disclose full information so that those buying the stock know what they are getting. Drug companies must submit potential drugs to the U.S. Food and Drug Administration to make sure they are safe before they are offered for sale.

**PROVIDING SUPPORT TO PEOPLE IN VULNERABLE POSITIONS**  By providing money and services, the government can make sure that members of the society who are in an economically vulnerable position have reasonable support. The government provides support through the Social Security system to retirees, to children who have lost a parent, and to disabled people. The government also provides unemployment insurance, offers disaster relief, and in many other ways tries to help those who are either temporarily or permanently in a vulnerable position.

When Hurricane Maria devastated Puerto Rico in 2017, the federal government was accused of not fulfilling its duty to provide disaster relief and thus contributing to the death toll of more than 3,000 Americans.

**REDISTRIBUTING INCOME TO IMPROVE THE LIVES OF CITIZENS WITH LESS WEALTH**  Through the federal income tax system, and through the design of certain programs such as the pension system in Social Security, the government tries to lessen income inequalities in American society.

**REGULATING BEHAVIOR**  Beyond the need to maintain public order, the government also passes laws to regulate people's behavior (examples include laws against obscenity, public nudity, and the use of various drugs) and uses its police to enforce those laws.

## CONTROVERSIES ABOUT GOVERNMENT FUNCTIONS

We put the discussion of government functions in the previous sections in order according to how much public consensus exists for government action in each. Few dispute that the government should maintain social and economic order, though of course there are often lively disputes over *how* the government does this. (No one disputes the need for police forces, for instance, but people often disagree about how the policing should be done.) Certain public goods, such as national defense and diplomacy, are similarly uncontroversial, at least in the sense that people agree that the government should provide these public goods. There is a good deal of consensus around the need for government to provide for infrastructure as well—especially for elements such as education and highways. However, as we go down the list of functions, there is less consensus for a government-regulated economy.

Furthermore, within any of the areas of government function, people often disagree about *how* active the government should be, even if they generally concur that the government should be involved to some extent. How much is the right amount to spend on national defense? And what about environmental protection? Although considered a public good, it is surrounded by controversy: Should the government take actions to reduce human contributions to the warming of the earth's atmosphere? And of course, in areas such as redistribution of income or regulation of behaviors, the extent and nature of government activity is also often quite controversial, leading to questions such as whether the government should eliminate the tax on inherited wealth (the estate tax or "death tax").

## FIGURE 1.2

# Growth of Governmental Activity in the U.S., the United Kingdom, and Sweden

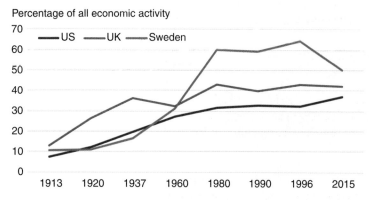

Percentage of all economic activity

Government's expenditures as a percentage of all economic activity grew in all three countries, but less in the United States than in Sweden or Great Britain.
Sources: Vito Tanzi and Ludger Schuknecht, Public Spending in the 20th Century: A Global Perspective (New York, NY: Cambridge University Press, 2000), 6; "General Government Spending," Organization for Economic Cooperation and Development (OECD), 2018, https://data.oecd.org/gga/general-government-spending.htm

Governments around the world differ in how active they are. In general, the United States government provides fewer goods and services, and spends less on them, than most other wealthy countries. National and local governments accounted for 37 percent of all expenditures in the United States in 2015 — evidence of a large and active government, it is true. But governments in the United Kingdom (also often called *Great Britain*) and Sweden account for more of their countries' expenditures—42 percent and 50 percent respectively.[12]

We see in Figure 1.2 that the United States, the United Kingdom, and Sweden all had relatively small government presences at the beginning of the twentieth century, but that their governments grew as a result of the two World Wars and the Depression in the first half of the twentieth century. In 1936, for instance, government spending in the United States accounted for only 16 percent of expenditures. The United States continues to have a smaller presence of government than the other two countries, however, despite its growth over several decades.

Governments also differ in how active they are in the different areas of government functioning. Although the United States spends more on national defense than most other wealthy countries, many of these other countries spend much more than the United States on social services and on protecting the vulnerable. For instance, in 2016, only 2 percent of all government spending in Germany went to national defense, compared with 61 percent for social programs and health; the figures were very different for the United States: 8 percent for defense and only 46 percent for social programs and health.[13]

The proper scope of government and the choices it should make are always controversial. Differences in the size of the government's presence and in what sorts of functions and policies the government emphasizes are due largely to differences in what the people of the country value. We explore Americans' values in the next section.

## AMERICAN VALUES

People derive their values from the general culture they inherit from past generations and also from their personal experiences. We will deal with Americans' "political culture" in detail in Chapter 6. For our purposes here, we can note that the Europeans who first settled the thirteen original colonies, most of whom came from England, brought with them from their home country many ideas about how government should operate. These ideas—passed from generation to generation and gradually modified by the ideas of newer cultures and immigrant groups as well—have helped to shape the values of Americans today. Historical experiences have also helped to shape these values. As we will explore in further detail in this chapter, the original migration from Europe, the continuing lure of an open frontier for much of the nineteenth century, and the modification of our values by newer cultures and ethnic groups have profoundly influenced Americans' ideas about the proper role of government.

Four basic American values have played a prominent role in determining the extent of government's involvement in people's lives and what the government does:

1. fairness based on contributions
2. freedom and individualism
3. support for the rule of law
4. religion

Let us look at each of these values separately.

## FAIRNESS BASED ON CONTRIBUTIONS

Fairness—treating people in the way they deserve—is a universal value found in all societies. Societies differ, however, in what they see as the basis for determining what people deserve. In the United States, fairness is often interpreted as getting what one deserves on the basis of what one has accomplished or contributed. In many other countries, fairness may more likely be interpreted in terms of equality—that is, as getting the equal treatment one deserves based simply on being a member of the society.

In a recent survey, people in 52 countries were asked a series of questions, including the following:

> Imagine two secretaries, of the same age, doing practically the same job. One finds out that the other earns considerably more than she does. The better paid secretary, however, is quicker, more efficient and more reliable at her job. In your opinion, is it fair or not fair that one secretary is paid more than the other?[14]

In almost all of the countries, a majority thought it was fair to pay the more efficient secretary the higher wage, but the size of the majority that believed this varied greatly. Fully 89 percent of Americans thought the difference in pay was fair—a higher percentage than in all but 4 of the 52 countries and a higher percentage than in any Western European country. Only 11 percent of Americans thought the difference was *un*fair, while about a quarter of the Italian and Spanish respondents felt it was unfair, as did about a third of the Indian and Brazilian respondents.

It's not that Americans don't believe strongly that they and others should be treated fairly—they do, as reflected by the public outcry over the government's decision to distribute bailout aid to banks during the financial crisis in 2009 after the banks made risky investments. But what these survey results demonstrate is that Americans base fairness on one's level of effort and one's contributions to society rather than on everyone being treated equally. Because of this view, government programs that are intended to help the vulnerable and make income distribution more equal tend to be controversial in the United States and usually face an uphill fight. When such proposals are made, arguments in favor of them tend to emphasize what the vulnerable or the poor have contributed through their own efforts rather than their neediness or the importance of treating everyone equally. Americans are much more likely to support programs for retired workers than for other at-risk populations, in large part because retired workers are thought to deserve support as a result of their earlier contributions.

This is not to say that the definition of fairness as treating everyone equally or according to their need lacks any support at all. In another part of the survey cited earlier, almost half of Americans stated that they believe, in general, that incomes should be made more equal. But overall, there is more emphasis on fairness as equal reward for equal accomplishment than in most countries.

## FREEDOM AND INDIVIDUALISM

In addition to fairness, Americans also regard freedom and individualism as important values. **Individualism** is the belief that people should be able to rely on themselves and be free to make decisions and act freely, with as little governmental or other societal control as possible. We value highly those who think for themselves. In 2016, for example, Donald Trump presented himself in the presidential campaign as a blunt "straight talker" who was not bound by ordinary rules of politeness. When John F. Kennedy wrote a book titled *Profiles in Courage*, he featured public officials who had taken stands that went against their parties or the opinions of their constituents, doing instead what they thought was right. Generally, Americans have always liked rebels and nonconformists, those who "march to a different drummer" or "color outside the lines."

The value of individualism has its roots in colonial times. Many of the early settlers from England and Scotland—Catholics in Maryland, Quakers in Pennsylvania, and Puritans in New England—had fled to the colonies to escape religious persecution and discrimination. Other colonists, such as convicted criminals and poor farmers, had emigrated to escape punishment

**individualism** The belief that people should have freedom to make decisions and act with as little government intervention or other control as possible.

The United States' status as a frontier society—and stories of the "Wild West" that made it back east—contributed to Americans' view of the nation as one that prized freedom and individualism.

and to start over after having their land confiscated. On some level, all of these colonists had sought freedom from government control.

Over the last two centuries, many waves of immigrants—including but not limited to Asians, Eastern Europeans, and Latin Americans—arrived in this country with little except their self-sufficiency and their willingness to work. Their primary goal was to build good lives for themselves and their children. Their experience of relying on their own labor and on their own determination to succeed reinforced the traditional American values of individualism and self-reliance.

For many years, America was considered a "frontier society," and this status encouraged the nation's disposition toward individualism.[15] Until the twentieth century, open land always beckoned. On the frontier, government ruled with a relatively loose hand and individuals had a good deal of independence. Indeed, this independence was one of the appeals of the frontier.

Finally, an important current in political thought that emerged around the time of the American Revolution further contributed to this affinity for individualism: classical liberalism. According to **classical liberalism**, a country's highest goal should be to allow all individuals in the nation to develop their intellectual and moral capacities to the fullest by making decisions for themselves rather than having decisions made for them by others. From this goal, it followed that the right of individuals to make their own decisions should be a basic principle of good societies and proper government. Classical liberalism is obviously different from what we call *liberalism* today. As we will see later in this chapter, today's liberalism argues for considerable central control in some areas such as the economy while arguing for individual freedom in others, such as abortion and free speech.

A major voice in classical liberalism at the time was John Locke; his writings influenced both the Declaration of Independence and the American Constitution (see Chapter 2).[16] The Bill of Rights, as the first ten amendments of the Constitution are collectively called, enshrines a number of protections for individual choice against government control—protections for freedom of speech, religion, press, and free association as well as protections against abuse by the government in criminal prosecutions.

## SUPPORT FOR THE RULE OF LAW

The **rule of law**, another basic American value, is the principle that laws, rather than the whims or personal interests of officials, should determine the government's actions. The Preamble to the Constitution refers to the rule of law in the phrase "[to] establish Justice." This principle

**classical liberalism**
The doctrine that a society is good only to the extent that all of its members are able to develop their capacities to the fullest and that to encourage this result, government should intervene as little as possible in people's lives.

**rule of law** The idea that laws, rather than the whims or personal interests of officials, should determine the government's actions.

deals not with what the government should do but rather with how the government should comport itself. According to the rule of law, government should be guided by basic principles and should follow fair procedures, as summarized in the statement, "Ours should be a government of laws, not of men."[17]

The rule of law embodies the idea that everyone should be treated the same way; thus, it is related to the value of fairness. It goes beyond simple fairness, however, in that it also maintains that careful procedures should be set up to limit what the government can do. Remember that the government is the one entity in a country with the right to use force to implement its decisions; the rule of law limits government so that it cannot abuse its power by treating people unfairly. For example, consider the many protections—some of which are stated in the Bill of Rights—that are designed to preserve the rights of accused persons in U.S. criminal trials. These include the right against unreasonable searches for evidence; the assumption that a defendant is considered innocent until proven guilty; and the right to not be held in prison for more than a short time without being charged with a crime, known as *habeas corpus*.

The Bill of Rights was included in the Constitution in order to guarantee Americans the same rights that English citizens had traditionally enjoyed. Thus, the United States established traditions of the rule of law earlier than most countries. It was not until after World War II, for instance, that France instituted the right of *habeas corpus* or the presumption of innocence. In general, the United Kingdom and its former colonies such as the United States, Canada, Australia, and India established strong traditions of the rule of law earlier than continental European countries and their former colonies.

## RELIGION

Americans are unusually religious. In one study, 49 percent of Americans—a far greater percentage than in any other prosperous country in the world—indicated that God is very important in their lives. Twenty-two percent of Australians responded in kind, but very few did from Japan, Germany, Sweden, or other prosperous countries (see Figure 6.5).[18]

Moral values rooted in religion have figured strongly throughout U.S. history, influencing both conservatives and liberals. For example, Christian denominations were partially

Barbara Davidson / Los Angeles Times / Getty Images

**Americans are more religious than citizens of any other prosperous nation. Many regularly attend services at temples and churches, like these members of Potter's House Church in Dallas.**

responsible for the nineteenth-century abolitionist movement. Many churches also supported a powerful temperance movement in the late nineteenth and early twentieth centuries; this movement led ultimately to a constitutional amendment banning the sale of alcoholic beverages (the Eighteenth Amendment, which was passed in 1920, before being repealed in 1933). The civil rights movement in the 1950s and 1960s drew strong support from both African American and white churches. Today, conflicts over abortion, same-sex marriage, proposals to ban pornography, and the teaching of creationism in public schools have strong moral/religious roots.

## VARIATIONS AND CONFLICTS IN VALUES

Fairness, individualism, belief in the rule of law, and religion are all basic American values, but this does not mean that every American holds these four values equally nor does it mean that every American views each of the values in the same way.

Sometimes values conflict with each other. Should the government set limits to executives' pay (fairness) or should they leave each executive free to earn whatever the market will bear (individualism)? Should homeowners have to build structures pleasing to their neighbors (fairness) or should they be free to build whatever they want, no matter how bizarre (individualism)? Should prayer be required in the schools (religion) despite the Constitution's ban on the government establishing a religion (rule of law)? Such conflicts between values form the underlying basis of American ideologies.

**FIGURE 1.3**

## *Value Conflict and Ideology*

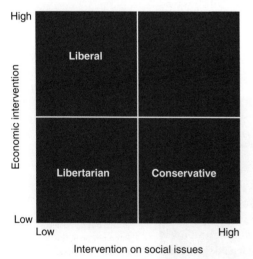

We have divided the grid into four quadrants here for the sake of simplicity. In reality, both dimensions are gradients; one person can be located higher or lower than another or farther left or right, even though both are located in the same quadrant. Each dimension is a matter of degree. Where do you think you would fall on the grid?

> **ideology** An interconnected set of ideas.

## AMERICAN IDEOLOGIES

An **ideology** is an interconnected set of ideas that forms and organizes our ideas and attitudes about politics. Our attitudes on gun control, on same-sex marriage, on appropriate levels of taxes, and on many other issues cluster and connect with each other. If we know whether certain individuals support gun control, for instance, that information may often help us to make an educated guess about whether they favor allowing same-sex marriage, though we would not be able to predict this perfectly. An ideology organizes our ideas and attitudes for us. It also adds emotional intensity to our views on issues, as our attitude on each issue is reinforced and strengthened for us by the issue's connection to the other attitudes in the ideological cluster.

In this chapter, we will present a brief overview of American ideologies. As indicated earlier, the four basic American values can sometimes conflict with one another. Not surprisingly, Americans' ideologies relate to different combinations of these basic values. Two particular lines of conflict between values form the primary basis of Americans' ideologies: the conflict between individualism and fairness and the conflict between individualism and moral beliefs.

The conflict between individualism and fairness, especially the broader interpretations of fairness, yields an economic left–right dimension or basis for ideology, with support for economic free choice at one end (the right) and support for government interventions (through regulations, taxes, and programs) to ensure economic fairness and equality at the other end (the left). Examples would include the dispute in 2017 over whether to provide tax cuts to people with large incomes and recurring disputes over whether to impose rules on banks to limit the fees they may charge customers.

The conflict between individualism and moral beliefs yields what is sometimes called a "social issues" dimension or basis for ideology, with support for free choice in such issues as abortion, sexually explicit entertainment, and drug or alcohol use at one end and support for government interventions to enforce moral values in such issues at the other. Moral issues do not only figure on the political right, of course. Those on the left have also sometimes favored moral imperatives over individual freedom of choice, as in liberals' desire to regulate hate speech. Currently in the United States, however, a constellation of moral values on the right is a major factor defining the political landscape.

As you can see in Figure 1.3, when we put these two dimensions together, we have a grid of possible ideologies. Individual Americans' ideologies can be located on the grid, depending on how they feel about government intervention to ensure economic fairness and how they feel about government intervention to enforce policies based on religious views. For instance, a person who opposes intervention in either case would be located in the lower-left part of the grid (low on economic intervention and low on social intervention). The quadrants on the grid serve as the basis for describing the major American ideologies.

## CONSERVATISM

**Conservatism** is represented in the lower-right part of the grid. It combines a desire for government intervention to reinforce moral views such as support for prayer in schools and opposition to same-sex marriage with a desire *not* to have the government intervene in the economic realm to bring about fairness through regulation of business, taxes, and other policies. Conservatives argue that fairness in economic settings is better accomplished by allowing free markets to work without government intervention.

## LIBERALISM

**Liberalism** is represented in the upper-left part of the grid. It combines a desire for governmental intervention to reduce economic inequality and inequalities between groups (especially between the majority and minority groups) with a desire *not* to have the government intervene to enforce policies based on religious views by regulating personal behaviors. Thus, liberals tend to favor higher tax rates for the wealthy than for the middle class and the poor and programs and policies to ensure equal treatment of women, members of ethnic and racial minorities, and gays and lesbians but tend to oppose, for example, prayer in schools or government bans on pornography.

## OTHER IDEOLOGIES

**Libertarianism** opposes government intervention of any sort, favoring maximum individual freedom for people to make their own decisions, and so it falls in the lower-left part of the grid. It is a minor ideology in terms of its numbers of supporters (the Libertarian Party received only 3 percent of the votes in the 2016 presidential election), but it has played a more significant role in our political discourse than those numbers suggest. Ron Paul, a libertarian, ran fairly strongly in the Republican presidential primary elections in 2012, getting as much as 30 percent of the vote in some states; his appearances on college campuses, especially, drew large and lively crowds. His son, Rand Paul, also a libertarian, has served in the United States Senate since 2010 as a Republican.

The libertarian ideology is simple: On the economic issues dimension, libertarianism coincides with conservatism, opposing the use of government programs to promote economic equality, but on the social issues dimension, it coincides with liberalism, opposing government restrictions on personal behaviors. Libertarianism is in fact the survival of classical liberalism, discussed on page 14, and as such, is deeply rooted in the history of American thought.

The upper-right part of the grid, characterized by support for government intervention in both dimensions, is unlabeled because there is no well-organized American ideology that falls in that part of the grid. In many European and Latin American countries, this part of the grid is filled by Christian–Democratic ideology; for instance, Angela Merkel, the chancellor of Germany, heads a Christian–Democratic party (see this chapter's "Picture Yourself" feature for more on values and ideology in Germany). Christian Democrats favor government

**conservatism** In the United States, the ideology that supports government intervention on behalf of religious values but opposes intervention in the economic sphere.

**liberalism** In the United States, the ideology that opposes government intervention on behalf of religious values but supports intervention in the economic sphere to reduce inequality.

**libertarianism** In the United States, the ideology that opposes government intervention in any area of people's lives.

Particularly since the 2016 election, some Americans on the left are identifying themselves as democratic socialists, including Alexandria Ocasio-Cortez, who was elected to the House in 2018.

intervention in support of religious values and also favor governmental economic and regulatory intervention to ensure fairness.

This combination of positions has never caught on strongly in the United States. There are, of course, some Americans who fall into this part of the grid; they often describe themselves ideologically as economically liberal but culturally conservative. However, no single term captures this combination of positions, and no structured organizations, think tanks, or political parties represent it. It may be that such an ideology has had difficulty taking full hold in the United States because of Americans' strong predisposition to individualism.

Two ideologies that originated in Europe but never took a strong enough hold in the United States to become significant are socialism and fascism. Because some American political figures are occasionally mislabeled as *socialist* or *fascist*, we will briefly introduce these ideologies here for the sake of clarification and to help you better understand how they are used in American political rhetoric.

**Socialism** developed out of conflicts between workers and employers in Europe in the nineteenth and early twentieth centuries—conflicts that were much more intense than similar conflicts in the United States. The socialist ideology at that time called for workers to take over the power of the state (either through elections or by revolution) and then use the state to control the economy by taking over and running all major industries. The end result was intended to be a society of equal citizens, with no economic or social distinctions among them. Socialism was a minor political force in the United States in the early twentieth century, reaching its high point in 1912 when its presidential candidate, Eugene V. Debs, received 6 percent of the vote nationally. Today, "socialist" parties in Europe have largely abandoned the goal of having governments take over industry but rather are democratic, free-market parties that favor policies to reduce economic inequalities. In the United States today, some politicians on the left, such as Bernie Sanders and Alexandria Ocasio-Cortez, use the term *democratic socialist* in this sense to describe themselves.

It has always been puzzling why there never was a large socialist party in the United States, given that throughout much of the twentieth century, socialism was a major political force in many other parts of the world. Perhaps the most succinct analysis was offered by Friedrich Engels, one of the founders of the international socialist movement, in a letter to an American friend. Engels attributed socialism's weakness in the United States to (1) the system of elections, which makes it harder to succeed with a new party than in most countries (we will look at this topic in detail in Chapter 8); (2) immigration and slavery, which had established a patchwork quilt of Irish, Germans, Czechs, African Americans, and others in which politics was dominated by disputes between ethnic groups rather than between workers and capitalists; and (3) the prosperity of the country, which gave workers a living standard better than anywhere else.[19]

**Fascism** was a nationalist, often racist ideology that flourished in Europe in the 1930s in the midst of the Great Depression and the devastation of World War I. Leaders such as Hitler in Germany and Mussolini in Italy adopted a showy, militaristic style of politics centered on a single, charismatic leader (themselves). A credible fascist movement in the United States has never come about, although some white power movements have adopted many of the symbols of fascism, such as the lightning bolt or the Nazi swastika.

**socialism** An ideology that favors having the government take over most businesses and run them in the interest of social and economic equality.

**fascism** A nationalist, racist ideology of the 1930s that centered power on a single charismatic leader.

**comparison** Comparing aspects of a country's government and politics to those aspects in other countries to better understand their causes.

**historical analysis** Examining the way politics has developed over time in a country in order to understand how its development has helped to shape its current form.

# COMPARATIVE AND HISTORICAL CONTEXTS

Our fundamental goal in writing this text is to help you understand how our particular form of democracy works and how it came to be. You may already know many facts about American politics—for example, about the separation of powers or the process by which a bill becomes a law. You will learn such facts from this book as well, but beyond learning what makes up American politics and government, you will also explore *causes* (what makes the U.S. system work as it does) and *effects* (what difference does that make, and why should we care?).

We chose to title our book *American Democracy in Context* because our main tool to help you understand American politics is to place it in a comparative and historical context. When we use **comparison**, we compare aspects of U.S. government and politics to those same aspects in the governments and politics of other countries. This comparative tool exposes us to possibilities beyond what we observe in the United States while offering insights into why various aspects of U.S. government and politics operate as they do. A second tool, **historical analysis**, allows us to investigate the roots and evolution of the U.S. system, allowing us to more knowledgeably evaluate how and why the U.S. system came to exist in its current form. The goal is to help you gain a more in-depth understanding of American democracy than you could acquire from a simple description of our politics.

As an example of how comparison and historical analysis may help us to understand American politics, consider the fact that Americans volunteer more for public purposes than people in many countries do (see Figure 1.4). In a survey of the citizens of 40 countries, U.S. citizens ranked near the top in volunteerism. When asked, for example, if they had volunteered to do charitable activities such as giving money or time or helping strangers in the last month, 62 percent of Americans responded in the affirmative.[20]

Why do Americans volunteer so much more readily than citizens of many other countries? Comparison may help us to some extent in answering this question. First of all, we notice from Figure 1.4 that in general, citizens of more prosperous countries tend to volunteer more than others. Of the top 10 countries in the figure, all but one are among the fifty most prosperous countries in the world; of the bottom countries, none are among the fifty most prosperous.[21] Of course, there are exceptions to this tendency. Indonesia is not a prosperous country and ranks just above the United States; and France and Japan, which *are* prosperous, rank low on the table. Nonetheless, the tendency is a strong one. We may hypothesize that in prosperous countries, people are secure enough in their own economic situations that they can more readily spare time or money to help others.

We also notice that six of the top ten countries share a common heritage as former parts of the British Empire: the United Kingdom and its former colonies (Ireland, Canada, Australia, New Zealand, and the United States). It seems likely that there is something in the culture all of these countries share that encourages helping others.

In addition to comparison, historical analysis may help us to understand why Americans volunteer so readily to help others. Volunteering has a long-established tradition in the United States. As early as 1832, Alexis de Tocqueville, a young French aristocrat who journeyed to the United States to study how the new democracy worked, commented on how willing Americans were to work voluntarily for the common good. American society at that time was made up mostly of farming communities with a great deal of social equality, in which neighbors helped each other more or less

FIGURE 1.4

## Americans Volunteer at a High Rate

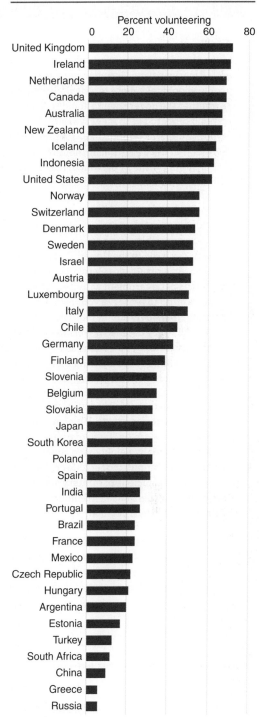

Sixty-two percent of Americans volunteered time, gave money, or helped strangers in a given month—more than the citizens of many other countries. In general, citizens of prosperous European and North American countries were more generous in this way than citizens of other countries. Why is this so?
Source: "Panorama de la Société 2014," OECD, 2014, 153.

As a German, how would your values compare with those of an American? In a survey conducted in 2006, both Americans and Germans were asked whether people should take more responsibility for themselves or whether the government should take more responsibility to see that everyone is provided for. The response gap was telling: Sixty-six percent of Germans thought that the government should take more responsibility while 41 percent of Americans agreed with this sentiment.[a] Why?

Classical liberalism, with its doctrine of giving individuals as much room for independent decision making as possible, never caught on as strongly in Germany as it did in the United Kingdom and its former colonies. As a result, as a German citizen, you are less suspicious of government activity and less anxious about wanting to preserve your own individual sphere of choice from government regulation. You are neither bothered by very detailed governmental supervision of people's lives nor by rules such as barring stores from opening on Sunday or requiring that all trash must be sorted into multiple categories.

Another value that is fairly distinctive comes from Germany's experience with Hitler and World War II in the 1930s and 1940s. Tired of tumult and defeat and knowing that many neighboring countries have blamed Germany for committing terrible crimes during that war, you are suspicious of military action. You are also wary of nationalism based in emotion, which was a hallmark of the Nazi regime.

This reluctance to pursue military options and suspicion of nationalism shows up in opinion surveys. Only 24 percent of you said you were "very proud" of your nationality compared with 56 percent of U.S.

citizens who were asked the same question. When asked whether you would be willing to fight for your country in the event of war, only 41 percent of you said "yes" compared with 57 percent of Americans.[b]

As you look across the Atlantic, you realize that though you have many things in common with the people of the United States, there are also differences, which sometimes condition the relations between your country and theirs. You find that Americans often do not understand why Germany will not contribute as much as the United States would like to common military efforts, for instance. But on the other hand, you yourself find it hard to understand why Americans are reluctant to be regulated by governments and international organizations in the cause of helping to slow down global warming.

## Questions to Consider

1. Free speech and other individual political rights are well protected in Germany, yet Germans are also very willing to allow the government to intervene in economic decisions. Is there any contradiction in this? Do you think support of economic intervention by the government makes it harder to ensure general freedom for people? Explain your response.

2. As noted in the discussion of ideologies, no well-organized political movement in the United States has ever supported high governmental intervention in *both* economic matters and social issues. (The upper-right quadrant of Figure 1.3 is empty, in other words.) In Germany, however, many religious citizens who want the government to reflect religious values in its policies also favor economic intervention. How might politics in the United States be different if that part of the political landscape were equally well populated?

[a]Inglehart, R., C. Haerpfer, A. Moreno, C. Welzel, K. Kizilova, J. Diez-Medrano, M. Lagos, P. Norris, E. Ponarin & B. Puranen et al., eds. 2014. World Values Survey: Round Six—Country-Pooled Datafile Version: www.worldvaluessurvey.org/WVSDocumentationWV6.jsp. Madrid: JD Systems Institute.

[b]Ibid.

as a matter of course. On the frontier, in fact, neighbors *had* to rely on each other, because the government had little presence there. The evolution of American society from these roots may have had a good deal to do with the high incidence of volunteering today.

These comparative and historical explanations work together to give us a richer understanding of volunteering in America than we could gain simply from an observation that Americans volunteer a lot.

# CONSEQUENCES FOR DEMOCRACY

Does it matter that the United States is a democracy with a strong emphasis on individual self-reliance and freedom? This may seem a strange question to ask. It is hard to imagine the United States being anything else, and the word *democracy* so purrs with respectability that it is a little hard to take the question seriously. Nonetheless, it is worth raising the question. After all, relatively few countries in the world have been democracies consistently for even the last few decades. As we saw, fewer than a third of the world's countries were democracies in 1977.

What would be different about the United States if it were *not* a democracy? Though it is difficult to speculate about such a broad question, there are some things we can probably conclude from comparisons with other countries. First of all, the United States would probably be just as prosperous if it were not a democracy. Most analyses of democracy and economic growth have concluded that it does not make much difference to the prospects for economic growth whether a country is democratic or not.[22] And we can see from many examples, such as China or Singapore, that a country can grow and prosper even though it is not a democracy.

Though democracy is not the source of countries' prosperity, however, it does affect how the fruits of that prosperity are distributed. In general, democracies are better than non-democracies at responding to the broad needs of their people. This makes sense, since in a democracy, the government is accountable to all of the people. A review of the well-being of people in democracies and in non-democracies concluded that democratic governments' policies in health and other areas were sufficiently better than those of nondemocratic governments that people in democracies had life expectancies that were three or four years greater than in non-democracies.[23] We can assume from this that if the United States were not a democracy, various policies of the government would be significantly less helpful to the broad range of people in the country.

But there is much more to it than this. In country after country around the world in the 1970s and 1980s, as people established democracy in their countries, they did not do it to improve their living standard or their health but because of deep aspirations for human dignity. The basic appeal of democracy is the individual dignity it confers on each citizen by giving him or her a small share of the power of government, and the protection its rule of law offers against arbitrary acts by the government. These are the values behind the movement toward democracy in other countries in the twenty-first century. And as we have seen, they are values deeply rooted in the American culture. Probably the greatest difference democracy makes to Americans is that it fulfills those values.

## *Critical Thinking Questions*

1. In the introductory comparison of Singapore and the United States, we saw that Singapore is cleaner, has less crime, and enjoys a slightly higher average income than the United States, but Singapore does not allow open competition between opposing values in its limited democracy. Which do you think would be the better country to live in? Why?

2. We introduced the concept of *public goods* on page 9 and along with defense spending, we used the space program and basic medical research as examples of public goods. Why do the space program and basic medical research, for example, qualify as public goods?

3. Germans are less willing than Americans to sacrifice (pay taxes, accept a lower income) to help prevent environmental pollution.[24] And yet Germans are much more active in recycling than Americans; they divide their recycling into several different categories, and Germany has drastically reduced its production of garbage and trash. How might you explain this paradox?

4. Can you think of reasons why Americans might be unusually religious compared with people in other prosperous countries?

# Key Terms

citizen, 3

classical liberalism, 14

comparison, 19

conservatism, 17

democracy, 4

direct democracy, 4

fascism, 18

free riders, 9

government, 3

historical analysis, 19

ideology, 16

indirect democracy, 4

individualism, 13

liberalism, 17

libertarianism, 17

majority rule, 7

minority rights, 7

politics, 2

public good, 9

republic, 8

rule of law, 14

socialism, 18

Visit edge.sagepub.com/maltese to help you accomplish your coursework goals in an easy-to-use learning environment.

# 2

# THE FOUNDING AND THE CONSTITUTION

## After reading this chapter, you should be able to do the following:

- Explain how the American colonies came into being and describe the influence of British tradition on the rights that the colonists came to expect.

- Describe the factors that led to the American Revolution and explain how the basic principles of the revolution shaped the governments that followed.

- Outline the structure and power of government under the Articles of Confederation and describe the weaknesses that ultimately led to their failure as a form of government.

- Describe the delegates to the Constitutional Convention, including the issues that united and divided them and the compromises among them that led to the final document.

- Identify the four core principles and major provisions of the U.S. Constitution as well as the ways in which it was undemocratic.

- Evaluate the arguments of those on both sides of the ratification battle and the roles of the Federalist Papers and the Bill of Rights in helping to secure ratification.

- Describe the formal process of amending the U.S. Constitution as well as the informal process of amendment through interpretation.

## Perspective: What Compromises Are Necessary for Ratifying a National Constitution?

It had been a long, hot summer, and the framers of the Constitution were growing weary. The process of drafting a constitution had led to passionate debates about issues ranging from the role of religion in government to how power would be shared between the national and local governments. Since convening in May, the framers had agreed that the national government would consist of three branches: legislative, executive, and judicial. The executive branch would be led by a president. A Supreme Court would enforce the Constitution, and the representative government would be elected by the people. Now, as the end of August approached, the framers remained deadlocked on several key issues. Nevertheless, they were determined to find compromises that would allow them to finish their work and send the Constitution on for ratification. Did this scenario take place in Philadelphia during the summer of 1787? No—Baghdad, summer of 2005.

Indeed, there are some significant similarities between the experiences of the framers in 1787 America and 2005 Iraq. Both were engaged in writing what scholars refer to as "post-conflict constitutions"—that is, constitutions written after winning a struggle for independence or overthrowing an existing government. Both the Constitutional Convention in Philadelphia and the Constitutional Drafting Committee in Baghdad (each with fifty-five delegates) were attempting to solve what appeared to be insoluble political problems. In 1787 Philadelphia, the framers, concerned with the weakness of the central government under the Articles of Confederation, were attempting to create a national government strong enough to ensure compliance with national law at a time when the core principles of the recently fought American Revolution had instilled in the populace a profound distrust of coercive government by distant rulers. How could they create a national government strong enough to keep the nation together but not so strong as to undermine core principles such as liberty or to excessively infringe on the autonomy of states? In 2005 Baghdad, the framers were similarly trying to balance a strong central government with regional autonomy. And both sets of framers consisted of rival factions that disagreed fundamentally about core issues. Could consensus be built under such circumstances?

Consider also the significant differences between 1787 Philadelphia and 2005 Baghdad. For one, the American framers were working in uncharted territory. Individual American states had created constitutions in the wake of the Declaration of Independence, but the concept of a written constitution governing an entire nation was new and untested. Moreover, there had never before been a republican (that is, representative) government on the scale of the United States. In contrast, constitution writing had become something of a cottage industry by 2005. In the past 50 years, some 200 new constitutions have been drafted for nations around the world; over 25 since 2005, ranging from Angola to Zimbabwe.[1] This has allowed observers to analyze which processes work best when creating a new constitution.[2] Another difference was that the Iraqi framers faced a nation much more deeply divided along lines of ethnicity, language, religious sect, and region than did the American framers. Moreover, the post-conflict situations were different: Whereas the American colonists had fought to win their independence from a colonial power, a tyrannical Iraqi government had been overthrown as a result of an invasion by outside forces, and the Iraqis drafted their constitution under the watchful eye of an occupying force.

The Iraq Constitution was ratified later in 2005 and remains in place. The fact that there are similarities between it and the U.S. Constitution is no accident. The U.S. Constitution has endured and become a model for many constitutions around the world. We now take for granted the success of the U.S. Constitution, but that success is really quite amazing. The American colonies were, as historian Joseph J. Ellis put it, "generally regarded as a provincial and wholly peripheral outpost of Western Civilization." Despite that, it became the breeding ground for a novel approach to governance that has endured the test of time and emerged as an archetype for success.[3] ◀◀

## THE AMERICAN COLONIES

In order to understand the factors that eventually led to the American Revolution, it is first necessary to understand how the colonies came into being and why they endured for so long. Europeans "discovered" America through Christopher Columbus in 1492. By then, North America had been populated for as long as forty thousand years and was already home to as many as ten million aboriginal or native people. France, Holland, and England led some explorations of the eastern seaboard of North America in the 1500s, but the road to English settlement did not really begin until 1606, when King James I issued charters to establish American colonies.

## MOTIVATIONS FOR COMING TO THE COLONIES

Several factors led to the migration of people from England and other European countries to North America. One factor was religion. As early as the 1560s, French Protestants (known as *Huguenots*) came to what is now South Carolina and Florida to escape religious persecution, and the New England colonies in particular were settled by people seeking religious freedom for themselves. Religious beliefs across the colonies varied considerably. The Pilgrims—a group of religious *separatists* (those who advocated a complete break with, or separation from, the Church of England)—sailed on the *Mayflower* in 1620 and settled the Plymouth colony in Massachusetts. The Puritans—a group of *nonseparatists* (those who sought to reform the Church of England rather than break away from it)—settled the Massachusetts Bay colony, soon outnumbering the Pilgrims. The Maryland colony was originally envisioned as a haven for English Catholics, though in the end, few Catholics settled there. Meanwhile, Huguenots were also drawn to the religiously tolerant Dutch colony of New Netherland (which later became the English colonies of New York and New Jersey) because the Dutch Reformed Church there reflected the Huguenots' Calvinist beliefs.

In addition to religion, economic incentives drew people to the colonies. This was especially true in colonies from Maryland southward, where colonists were lured by the opportunity to make money by growing tobacco. Virginia, for instance, began not as a religious refuge but as a corporate colony financed by a joint stock company. As a result, the southern colonies were more religiously and ethnically diverse than their northern counterparts.[4] The emphasis on growing crops for profit in the south led to the development of large plantations and inhibited urban development. Initially, these plantations lured young men from England and other European countries to work on them as indentured servants—laborers who entered a contract to work for no wages for a fixed period of time (usually three to seven years) in return for food, clothing, shelter, and their transportation to the colony. Some have suggested that as many as half of all white immigrants to the colonies during the seventeenth and eighteenth centuries may have come as indentured servants. Later, white servitude gave way to slavery when plantation owners resorted to buying slaves from Africa.

## BRITISH INFLUENCES ON AMERICAN POLITICAL THOUGHT

Two documents—the Magna Carta and the English Bill of Rights—greatly influenced American political thought. Each contained principles that the colonists eventually used to justify revolution. Later, those principles served as foundations for the new government they created. Likewise, two events in England in the 1600s—civil war and the Glorious Revolution—served in the short run to preoccupy the British and distract their attention from the colonies while in the long run serving as models for resisting the arbitrary power of kings.

**THE MAGNA CARTA**  The *Magna Carta* (which means "great charter" in Latin, the language in which it was written) dates to 1215, when King John (ruler of England from 1199 to 1216) was forced to sign it by English barons who had revolted after John had imposed heavy taxes, waged an unsuccessful war with France, and quarreled with the Pope. It is one of the great documents in Western civilization, and its articulation of rights strongly influenced the framers of the U.S. Constitution.

The Magna Carta was a practical document designed to remedy specific abuses of King John, so it includes many provisions (or "chapters") that are not so relevant today. Others, however, stand as a fundamental basis for the rule of law—the idea that even the most powerful leader of government is bound by the law. The most important of these is Chapter 39, which emphatically states the requirement of *due process of law*, or of fair procedures:

> No free man shall be seized or imprisoned, or stripped of his rights or possessions, or outlawed or exiled, or deprived of his standing in any other way, nor will we proceed with force against him, or send others to do so, except by the lawful judgment of his equals or by the law of the land.[5]

This provision of the Magna Carta limited the power of kings and later served as the basis for the guarantees in the U.S. Constitution that the government shall not take a person's life,

Mikael Karlsson / Alamy Stock Photo

This Miranda warning card, developed for Kansas City police officers, is intended to ensure Americans' due process rights.

liberty, or property without due process of law. Modern-day Miranda warnings are an outgrowth of this.

The fact that King John was forced to sign this document set an important precedent of free men standing up to the king. In 1297, the Magna Carta was placed in the statute books of England, where it remains to this day. By the end of the fourteenth century, the Magna Carta had come to be viewed not as any ordinary statute but as the fundamental law of the realm. Thus, opponents of King Charles I used it to justify rebellion in 1642.

**CIVIL WAR, THE GLORIOUS REVOLUTION, AND THE ENGLISH BILL OF RIGHTS** In 1642, 36 years after King James I had issued the first charters establishing American colonies, civil war erupted in England. James I (who ruled from 1602 to 1625) and his son and successor, Charles I, believed in the divine right of kings—that is, the idea that kings derived their right to rule from God and were not accountable to their subjects. They thus believed that they had absolute control over Parliament (the legislature in England) and could, for example, impose taxes without the consent of Parliament. Charles I took other unilateral steps as well, including arbitrary arrests and detentions, quartering troops in private homes, and even imposing martial law. He summoned and dissolved Parliament at will and claimed an absolute right to veto any legislation it passed. Increasingly angered, Parliament and its supporters waged a civil war against the king and his supporters.

In rising up against Charles I, Parliament invoked the Magna Carta and argued that the king was violating the rights of individuals. For example, opponents of the king argued that if he could tax without the consent of Parliament, then the English people and Parliament, their representative assembly, were in a state of servitude to the king. As we will see, concern about taxation without representation later became a key issue in the road to revolution in the American colonies.

The decades that followed were rocky times in England. Charles I was eventually beheaded. When his son, Charles II, tried to succeed him, another civil war ensued. Charles II fled to France, and Parliament declared England a "free state," to be governed as a commonwealth without a king. That commonwealth lasted from 1651 until 1659. Charles II returned to England and was restored to the throne in 1660. King Charles II was now careful not to oppose Parliament, but his brother, James II, who succeeded him in 1685, tried to reassert the divine right of kings and to rule without Parliament. As a result, he was run out of the country in what became known as the Glorious Revolution of 1688.

The action of James II led Parliament to enact the English Bill of Rights, a statute that spelled out the basic rights of Englishmen and limited the power of future monarchs. Among other things, the Bill of Rights declared freedom from taxation by royal prerogative: Only Parliament, the representative of the people, could impose taxes. Together, the Magna Carta and the Bill of Rights were considered to be part of the country's "unwritten" constitution, which came to be seen by British citizens as containing fundamental, inviolable principles.

## "NO TAXATION WITHOUT REPRESENTATION"

Some things never change: People hate taxes—or, at least, taxes that seem excessive or otherwise unfair. The colonists seethed at taxes imposed on them by Parliament because they considered them not only unfair but a flagrant violation of parliamentary power. Since the colonists had no elected representatives in Parliament, they believed that these taxes violated a fundamental principle of the English Bill of Rights: no taxation without representation. The Bill of Rights declared freedom from taxation by royal prerogative and instead gave Parliament the power to tax *because that body represented the people*. Anger over taxation without representation is, in no small measure, what led to the American Revolution.

**THE SUGAR ACT AND STAMP ACT** The first seeds of revolution were planted in 1764 when Parliament enacted the American Revenue Act, better known as the Sugar Act. People in

England had been complaining of too many taxes, and so Parliament used the act to shift some of the tax burden to the American colonists. The Sugar Act imposed duties on certain foreign goods imported into the American colonies—sugar and other goods, including coffee, some wines, and pimiento.

The timing could not have been worse, as the colonies were facing a bad economy. Not only did the new duties on imported goods increase prices for the colonists, but they also hurt American manufacturers of rum by making ingredients more expensive. As a result, the American rum trade was threatened to be priced out of the market; foreign buyers who had previously imported American rum now turned to other sources. Colonists reacted harshly to the Sugar Act. They quickly took up the rallying cry of "no taxation without representation." The Massachusetts assembly proclaimed that the act deprived the colonists of "the most essential Rights of Britons."[6]

Parliament made matters even worse for the colonists by imposing the Stamp Act the following March. From 1756 to 1763, the British had fought the French and Indian War in Canada and on the western frontier of the colonies; these battles were part of a larger struggle among a number of countries that transpired in Europe and elsewhere. British victory in the French and Indian War had left the country deep in debt, and the Stamp Act was an attempt by Parliament to raise money, ostensibly to pay for Britain's continued military presence in North America after the war. The act imposed a direct tax on a wide array of printed materials in the colonies, including everything from legal documents to newspapers to playing cards. Such materials had to either be printed on specially marked paper or have tax stamps affixed to them to indicate that the tax had been paid.

The Stamp Act galvanized the colonies. Several colonial assemblies adopted resolutions denouncing the tax. The first and most famous was a series of resolutions passed by the Virginia House of Burgesses on May 29, 1765. These Virginia Stamp Act Resolutions (also known as the "Virginia Resolves") stated that "the taxation of the people by themselves, or by persons chosen by themselves to represent them, . . . is the distinguishing characteristic of British freedom."[7] In so doing, the Virginia Resolves invoked the spirit of the Magna Carta and the English Bill of Rights.

The Stamp Act also provoked representatives from nine of the thirteen colonies to gather at Federal Hall in New York in October 1765.[8] This so-called **Stamp Act Congress** was the first official meeting of representatives from the various colonies, and it resulted in a Declaration of Rights. The declaration rejected the claim by the British Prime Minister, George Grenville, that as British subjects, the colonists enjoyed "virtual representation" in Parliament even if they did not formally elect representatives to Parliament. In direct defiance of Grenville, the declaration made it clear that "the only representatives of these colonies are persons chosen therein," adding that "no taxes can be constitutionally imposed on [the colonies] but by their respective legislatures."[9]

Representative bodies were not the only ones motivated by the Stamp Act to take action. Throughout the colonies, individuals formed associations known as the Sons of Liberty to attack British authority and resist taxation without representation by whatever means necessary. In some places, violent protests erupted. Those who distributed the hated stamps on behalf of the British government were hung in effigy, and in some cases, their homes were attacked. Defiant colonists refused to use the stamps and boycotted British goods.

**THE BRITISH RESPONSE** The reaction of the colonists to the Stamp Act alarmed the British, and in February 1766, Parliament repealed the act. But, in March, it also passed the Declaratory Act, stating that colonial bodies had "against law" claimed "the sole and exclusive right of imposing duties and taxes" in the colonies. Noting that "all [colonial] resolutions, votes, orders, and proceedings" that denied Parliament's power to tax (including the Virginia Resolves and the Stamp Act Congress's Declaration of Rights) were "utterly null and void," the act reiterated that the colonies were "subordinate unto, and dependent upon the imperial crown and Parliament of Great Britain."[10]

**Stamp Act Congress** The first national meeting of representatives from the colonies in 1765. In response to duties (taxes) imposed by Parliament on the colonies through the Stamp Act, this Congress passed a Declaration of Rights that denounced taxation without representation—an important step toward the American Revolution.

American newspapers bitterly opposed the Stamp Act. The Pennsylvania *Journal* showed its displeasure by marking the location where the stamp would be placed with a skull and crossbones in its October 24, 1765 edition.

Is Revere's depiction of the Boston Massacre—British soldiers firing point-blank into a small crowd of unarmed colonists and their dog—an accurate portrayal of the event? If not, what is inaccurate about it?

Then Parliament enacted the Revenue Act of 1767, the first of the so-called Townshend Acts, named after Charles Townshend, the chancellor of exchequer (treasury), who advocated them. Whereas the Stamp Act was a direct tax on goods in the colonies, the Revenue Act (similar to the earlier Sugar Act) was an indirect tax that placed duties on imported goods, including the paper, paint, glass, and tea the colonies imported from England. Townshend assumed that indirect taxes would be more palatable to the colonists than direct taxes, but he was wrong. The Massachusetts House of Representatives reiterated the now-familiar protest: no taxation without representation.

This time, Britain's response was harsh. It ordered the royal governor to dissolve the Massachusetts legislature. Soon thereafter, it sent regiments of British troops to Boston. The troops, known as "Redcoats" for their bright uniforms, became a hated fixture there. One cold night in March 1770, a group of several hundred men and boys pelted a small band of nine Redcoats with rocks, snowballs, chunks of ice, and oyster shells. Alarmed, the soldiers fired back, killing five men. The British soldiers had been provoked, but the incident was quickly dubbed the "Boston Massacre" and used to rally opposition to the oppressive force of the British. Nonetheless, John Adams—a future president of the United States—defended the British soldiers when they were tried for murder. He secured a verdict of "innocent" for the captain, who was tried first. In a subsequent trial of the remaining eight soldiers, six were acquitted and two were found guilty of the lesser charge of manslaughter.[11]

**THE BOSTON TEA PARTY**  As it had done with the Stamp Act, Britain backed down in the face of the colonial reaction to the Revenue Act. The colonists boycotted the imported goods that were subject to duties, and in 1770, Britain rescinded the duties for all goods except tea. Colonists evaded the remaining tea tax by buying smuggled tea from Holland, but Parliament foreclosed that option in 1773 when it passed the Tea Act. The primary purpose of that act was to save the nearly bankrupt East India Company by giving it a monopoly to sell tea in the colonies. Parliament lowered the price of tea so much that the tea from the East India Company— even after the tea tax—was cheaper than smuggled tea. Parliament assumed that the colonists would welcome the inexpensive tea. Instead, the colonists viewed it as a trick to get them to accept British taxation and tried to block British ships bringing the tea from the East India Company. In many cases, this blockade worked, but in Boston, a British ship refused to leave the harbor without unloading its cargo of tea and collecting the duty on it. The showdown led, on December 16, 1773, to the Boston Tea Party, in which a group of colonists disguised as Mohawk Indians boarded the ship and dumped all 342 chests of tea into the harbor. This act of defiance marked an important step toward revolution.[12]

Parliament responded to the Boston Tea Party by passing a series of measures in 1774 known as the *Coercive Acts* (or, as the colonists liked to call them, the *Intolerable Acts*), designed to punish Massachusetts. Among other things, the Coercive Acts closed Boston Harbor to all commerce until Britain received payment for the destroyed tea, brought the Massachusetts government under full British control, forbade most town meetings, and allowed British troops to be quartered in private buildings and homes in Boston.

## THE FIRST CONTINENTAL CONGRESS

Though aimed at Massachusetts, the Coercive Acts had potential ramifications for all of the colonies. As a result, representatives from all of the colonies except Georgia met in Philadelphia in September and October 1774 to decide how to respond. The delegates at these meetings of the First Continental Congress, in essence, represented twelve different nations. Although they came together in response to the common threat to their liberties posed by Great Britain, the colonies remained deeply divided on many issues. As historian Merrill Jensen put it, "The large colonies were pitted against small ones; colonies with many slaves were in opposition to those with fewer; colonies that had no western lines contended with those that did."[13] Despite these differences, the First Continental Congress resulted in an agreement by the colonies to engage in a total boycott of British goods.

The First Continental Congress also produced a declaration of rights and grievances. Among other things, the declaration—drawing on the language of the English philosopher John Locke—asserted the right to "life, liberty, and property"; denounced the keeping of British troops in the colonies in times of peace as "against law"; and reiterated that "the foundation of English liberty, and of all free government, is a right in the people to participate in their legislative council."[14] Since the colonists were not represented in Parliament, they claimed the right to a "free and exclusive power of legislation" in their own colonial assemblies, subject only to veto by the king.

The rallying cry of "no taxation without representation" had evolved into something far more significant: All legislation produced by a parliament in which the colonists were not represented was now considered suspect. And colonies with disparate interests and outlooks were uniting against Great Britain and around the cause of liberty. The liberty that the colonists sought was a direct outgrowth of rights espoused by the British tradition. England's failure to enforce those rights precipitated revolution.

## REVOLUTION AND INDEPENDENCE

Although some members of the First Continental Congress still hoped for reconciliation with Britain, war loomed. In anticipation of rebellion, British troops fortified Boston. Colonists also prepared for conflict by organizing small groups of armed militias known as *minutemen*. On April 19, 1775, fighting broke out in Massachusetts in the towns of Lexington and Concord.

### THE SECOND CONTINENTAL CONGRESS

After the violence in Lexington and Concord, the colonies quickly sent representatives to the Second Continental Congress to oversee steps toward independence and manage the impending war. By the time the Second Continental Congress convened in Philadelphia on May 10, 1775, full-fledged war had already erupted. The congress officially created the Continental Army and appointed George Washington to command it. But more than a year would pass before the Second Continental Congress voted to approve the Declaration of Independence. The congress then turned to writing the first, ill-fated national constitution: the Articles of Confederation.

The delay in formally declaring independence occurred because many colonists, who came predominantly from Britain, remained reluctant to make a full break with their homeland. Breaking their allegiance to the king—a powerful symbolic figure—proved especially difficult. Then, in January 1776, Thomas Paine anonymously published his 48-page pamphlet, *Common Sense*. Saying, "I offer nothing more than simple facts, plain arguments, and common sense," Paine provided a compelling justification for independence, and did so—as historian Joseph J. Ellis put it—"in language that was simultaneously simple and dazzling."[15] Paine took aim at King George III himself and sharply dismissed the institution of monarchy. The pamphlet's timing could not have been better: Colonists had just learned that the king had rejected any effort to resolve the dispute with them diplomatically and would instead seek to smash the rebellion with military force.[16] Breaking allegiance to the crown no longer seemed so difficult. And even though Parliament had been the source of the legislation that had prompted the dispute between Britain and the colonies, the king now became the symbolic enemy.

*Common Sense* was an instant best seller, with some 120,000 copies sold in the first three months alone and 500,000 copies sold within a year. This was at a time when the official population count of the colonies (excluding slaves and Native Americans) was only about 2.5 million.[17] A work would need to sell nearly *62 million* copies to reach a proportionate number of Americans today.[18] Clearly, Paine's rallying cry for independence had hit a nerve.

This British cartoon dismisses Thomas Paine as a radical revolutionary. His best-selling pamphlet *Common Sense* (skewered on the scroll he is holding as "Common Nonsense"), helped fuel the fight for revolution.

## THE DECLARATION OF INDEPENDENCE

In May 1776, only four months after the publication of *Common Sense*, the Virginia House of Burgesses instructed its delegates to the Second Continental Congress to propose independence—making Virginia the first of the colonies to call for such a resolution. That same month, the Continental Congress urged colonies to adopt constitutions in anticipation of impending independence and statehood. Then, on June 7, Virginia's Richard Henry Lee proposed before the Continental Congress "that these United Colonies are, and of right ought to be, free and independent States."[19] To implement Lee's resolution, the Continental Congress created a committee consisting of John Adams, Benjamin Franklin, Thomas Jefferson, Robert Livingston, and Roger Sherman to prepare what would eventually become the American **Declaration of Independence**.

> We hold these truths to be self-evident, that all men are created equal, that they are endowed by their Creator with certain unalienable Rights,[20] that among these are Life, Liberty, and the pursuit of Happiness.—That to secure these rights, Governments are instituted among Men, deriving their just powers from the consent of the governed,—That whenever any Form of Government becomes destructive of these ends, it is the Right of the People to alter or to abolish it, and to institute new Government.

In writing these words, Jefferson drew upon John Locke's *Two Treatises of Government* (1689). Locke believed that people enjoy certain natural rights, including "life, liberty, and property," that cannot be taken away without their consent. Through a **social contract**, people come together in a society under a government whose authority they agree to obey. If, however, a government deprives them of their natural rights without their consent, the social contract is broken, and the people have a right to rebel and replace that government with one that will honor the terms of the social contract. This concept of a social contract led the newly independent states, and eventually the new federal government, to adopt written constitutions. These constitutions served as contracts spelling out the powers of government and the rights of the people.

In making his case for rebellion in the Declaration of Independence, Jefferson listed a specific set of grievances against Britain. In doing so, he did not even mention Parliament but rather took aim exclusively at King George III: "The history of the present King of Great Britain is a history of repeated injuries and usurpations, all having in direct object the establishment of an absolute Tyranny over these States." Jefferson listed 27 specific grievances and, finally, declared that

> these United Colonies are, and of Right ought to be Free and Independent States, that they are Absolved from all Allegiance to the British Crown, and that all political connection between them and the State of Great Britain, is and ought to be totally dissolved.

Meanwhile, some delegates to the Continental Congress thought it premature to declare independence. South Carolina and Pennsylvania opposed independence in a preliminary vote on July 1, and New York abstained because its delegates did not have clear instructions from home about how to vote. (Each colony had a single vote in Congress determined by a majority vote of the delegates from that colony.) In an attempt to secure unanimity among the colonies,

**Declaration of Independence** A statement written by Thomas Jefferson and approved by the Second Continental Congress on July 4, 1776, that asserted the independence of the American colonies from Great Britain.

**social contract** The idea, drawn from the writings of John Locke and others, that government is accountable to the people and bound to protect the natural rights of its citizens. If the government breaks this contract, the people have the right to rebel and replace the government with one that will enforce it.

Congress delayed the final vote on Lee's resolution until the next day. The tactic worked. South Carolina reversed its vote and, as the result of strategic abstentions by two of its delegates, Pennsylvania now voted 3–2 in favor of independence instead of 4–3 against it. New York still abstained, but the New York Provincial Congress formally voted to support independence a few days later. Congress approved the final language of the Declaration of Independence on July 4, 1776, and the first public reading of the Declaration took place four days later in Philadelphia. The next day, July 9, George Washington ordered that the Declaration be read to members of the Continental Army in New York.

Independence had been declared, but the Revolutionary War dragged on for five years. The official peace accord, in which Great Britain recognized the independence of the United States, was not signed until 1782.

Popular uprisings, such as the Yellow Vest movement in France, which calls for economic justice for the working class, illustrate citizens claiming a broken social contract in the contemporary world.

## THE ARTICLES OF CONFEDERATION

With the Declaration, the colonies asserted their independence but still mostly lacked a formal government. In the months preceding the Declaration, would-be states had begun drafting their own written constitutions. By the end of 1776, all but three of the states had drafted and ratified constitutions. Georgia and New York followed suit in 1777, as did Massachusetts in 1780. These constitutions created state governments. However, a new national government to oversee the 13 states was also needed. The problem—similar to the one faced in Iraq in 2005—was how to balance regional autonomy with national power.

In the short run, the Second Continental Congress operated as the national government. The Continental Congress also took responsibility for writing a national constitution and, in fact, had appointed a committee for this purpose even before voting to approve the Declaration of Independence. But the process of drafting the constitution proved to be slow. The problem, above all, was that the new states were understandably wary of central authority. Furthermore, differences among the states led to heated debates. Large states wanted proportional representation in the national government, while small states wanted equal representation. Similarly, there was debate about whether states should supply funds to the national government in proportion to their population. If so, did the slave population count? Southern states, with large slave populations, said no. Later, during the Constitutional Convention of 1787, southern states would take a contradictory stance and argue that their slave population should count for purposes of representation in Congress. At this juncture, however, the issue did not arise because all states had equal representation in the Continental Congress and the states assumed that this practice would continue.

Debate also revolved around control of the land west of the colonies. The western boundaries for some states were not yet established. Should the new national government have the power to set those boundaries?[21] As a result of such debates, the drafting of the first national constitution, known as the Articles of Confederation, took well over a year; on November 17, 1777, the Continental Congress finally voted to approve the Articles. Ratification by the states was an even slower process, and the Articles of Confederation did not officially take effect until March 1, 1781.[22]

As its title indicates, the relationship that the Articles of Confederation established among the states was that of a confederation, a union of independent, sovereign states. In a confederation, the primary power, especially with regard to domestic affairs, rests with the individual states; the central government is limited to such functions as leading the nation's defense and foreign affairs. Confederations are relatively rare. A recent example is the State Union of Serbia and Montenegro, a confederated union of two former republics of Yugoslavia. Serbia and Montenegro maintained autonomous governments; they were united only for the purpose of defense. Their confederation lasted only from 2003 to 2006, when it was dissolved as the result of a referendum.

**Articles of Confederation** The first constitution of the United States (1781–1788), under which states retained sovereignty over all issues not specifically delegated to the weak central government, comprising a unicameral (one-house) legislature and no independent executive or judicial branch.

**confederation** A union of independent, sovereign states whose central government is charged with defense and foreign affairs but where the primary power—especially with regard to domestic politics—rests with the individual states.

## THE STRUCTURE AND POWER OF GOVERNMENT UNDER THE ARTICLES OF CONFEDERATION

The Articles of Confederation were designed to protect the power and autonomy of the states coming together in this confederation. The national government consisted solely of a weak *unicameral* (one-house) legislature; there was no executive or judicial branch. It had only those powers expressly delegated to it by the states, such as appointing army officers, waging war, controlling the post office, and negotiating with Indian tribes. Any powers not specifically given to the national government by the Articles of Confederation were reserved to the states.

Delegates to the Confederation Congress were appointed by state legislatures. To ensure equality among the states, each state—regardless of its size or the number of delegates it sent—had a single vote in Congress (as had been the practice in the First and Second Continental Congresses). A state cast its vote in accordance with the votes of the majority of its delegates; if a state could not achieve a majority among its delegates on a particular vote, it would abstain from voting.[23] Passage of legislation required at least nine of the thirteen votes, and amendment of the Articles of Confederation required a unanimous vote.

## WEAKNESSES OF THE ARTICLES OF CONFEDERATION

When drafting the Articles of Confederation, the delegates to the second Continental Congress focused more on the potential threats posed by a national government than on the benefits such a government might provide. After all, their bitter experience with Great Britain was fresh on their minds. Therefore, they were more concerned with limiting government than empowering it.[24] Moreover, people still thought of themselves as citizens of their particular state: They were Virginians or New Yorkers rather than Americans. Worse, states fundamentally mistrusted each other. They also had widely divergent economic interests and often saw each other as competitors. These factors led to the creation of a governing document with fundamental weaknesses.

The most obvious weakness of the Articles was that the national government had too little power. For example, Congress had no power to tax. This severely limited the ability of the national government to raise money to pay for debts incurred during the Revolutionary War. Congress requested money from the states, but payment was voluntary and compliance was poor.[25] To modern eyes, not giving Congress the power to tax seems strange, but if you remember that the American Revolution was a revolt against taxation by a distant government, then withholding of this power from the unfamiliar and distant national government (as opposed to familiar and near state governments) becomes more understandable.[26]

Congress also lacked the power to regulate commerce among the states. As a result, states jostled for economic advantage, routinely using protective tariffs (taxes imposed on imported goods) against one another as well as against foreign nations. Trade was further hindered by the fact that the new nation had no common currency. Although the new national government could, and did, print money to pay war debts, each state also produced its own currency. Since some states printed more money than others, currency from different states had different values, complicating trade and hurting the economy.

Significantly, Congress did not even have a permanent home. It originally sat in Philadelphia, but the delegates fled to Princeton, New Jersey, in June 1783 when a mutinous group of

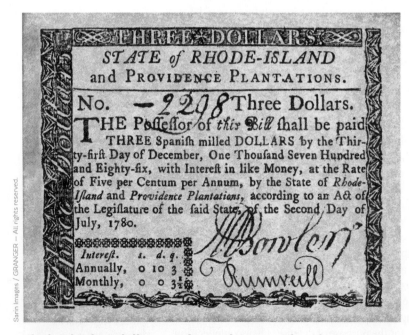

STATE of RHODE-ISLAND and PROVIDENCE PLANTATIONS.

No. — 2208 Three Dollars.

THE Possessor of this Bill shall be paid THREE Spanish milled DOLLARS by the Thirty-first Day of December, One Thousand Seven Hundred and Eighty-six, with Interest in like Money, at the Rate of Five per Centum per Annum, by the State of *Rhode-Island* and *Providence Plantations*, according to an Act of the Legislature of the said State, of the Second Day of July, 1780.

**Rhode Island's $3 bill came to be worth no more than the paper it was printed on.**

hundreds of Revolutionary War veterans mobbed Independence Hall, where the Confederation Congress was then meeting, to demand pay for their war service. After a little more than four months in Princeton, the Confederation Congress then moved to Annapolis, Maryland, before proceeding to Trenton, New Jersey, in 1784, and finally to New York City in 1785. Historian David O. Stewart has noted that Congress's homelessness was a potent symbol of its frailty, adding, "Vagabondage is not the hallmark of a great government."[27]

Another notable weakness was the fact that there was no separation of powers at the national level: All power, such as it was, lay in the legislature. The lack of a federal judiciary compounded the problems associated with trade wars among the states. For example, some states passed legislation cancelling their debts to other states. With no federal judiciary to turn to, those affected by such legislation sometimes had no legal recourse. Likewise, the lack of a federal judiciary made it difficult to resolve boundary disputes among the states. The lack of an executive branch meant that the national government had no real ability to execute its laws. Early attempts to administer laws through ad hoc committees, councils, and conventions were unsuccessful.

In short, the new national government had no power to lead, and often did not even have enough power to do what little it was supposed to. The national government seemed to be little more than a "rope of sand" holding the confederation together.[28] The states did not help the situation. They encroached on the authority of the national government by raising their own militaries, ignoring the nation's treaties with foreign powers, and waging war with Native Americans. Sometimes states did not even bother to send delegates to Congress, making it difficult to muster the necessary quorum for passing legislation.[29]

## SHAYS' REBELLION

By the mid-1780s, the new nation was in the midst of an economic depression. Farmers, in particular, had gone into debt to rebuild their farms after the Revolutionary War, in which many of them had served as soldiers. The combination of a bad growing season, high interest rates, and high state taxes to pay off the war debt made it impossible for many farmers to pay their bills. Foreclosures (losing one's property due to failure to pay a loan) skyrocketed, and imprisonment for debt was common. In Massachusetts, desperate farmers turned to the state for help. When help did not come, the farmers—led by Daniel Shays, who had been a captain in the Continental Army—banded together and tried, by force, to shut down the courthouses where foreclosures were issued. This armed rebellion by more than 2,000 farmers, which began in August 1786 and continued into 1787, came to be known as Shays' Rebellion.

Massachusetts appealed to the national government for help in restoring order. Congress requisitioned states for money to fund a national militia to quell the rebellion, but only Virginia complied. Without money, Congress was powerless to act. Massachusetts did not have enough money in its own state treasury to fund a state militia, and therefore had to rely on money from private donors. The whole event was unsettling, and it proved to be an important turning point. By highlighting the impotence of the national government, Shays' Rebellion galvanized the nation. Those who had long feared that the Articles of Confederation were deficient now had a dramatic example of Congress's inability to maintain order and protect the safety of the people.

# STARTING OVER: THE CONSTITUTIONAL CONVENTION

Before Shays' Rebellion, Virginia had already called for a convention to discuss a uniform regulation of commerce to remedy one of the primary defects of the Articles of Confederation. Only five states sent delegates to the convention, which convened in Annapolis, Maryland, in the fall of 1786. One of the delegates was Alexander Hamilton, who had previously served in the Confederation Congress; frustrated by the weakness of the national government, he had resigned in 1783. Long opposed to the Articles of Confederation, Hamilton now drafted a resolution that called on Congress to authorize a convention to examine the need either to amend the Articles of Confederation or to replace them altogether. Shays' Rebellion provided the

> **Shays' Rebellion** An armed rebellion by farmers in Massachusetts who, facing foreclosure, tried using force to shut down courthouses where the foreclosures were issued. The national government's inability to quell the rebellion made the event a potent symbol of the weakness of the Articles of Confederation.

impetus for the Annapolis Convention to support Hamilton's resolution. Congress now felt pressure to act. On February 21, 1787, it passed a resolution to convene a Constitutional Convention in Philadelphia for the sole and express purpose of revising the Articles of Confederation.

## THE DELEGATES AND THEIR MOTIVES

All of the states except Rhode Island (which opposed changing the Articles of Confederation) sent delegates to the Constitutional Convention. Of the 74 delegates the states had appointed, only 55 actually attended the convention, and far fewer stayed for the entire convention. The attendees included two of the most famous men in America, George Washington and Benjamin Franklin, and other luminaries such as James Madison and Alexander Hamilton. Notably absent were John Adams and Thomas Jefferson, who were abroad serving as ambassadors to Great Britain and France, respectively. Some passionate advocates of states' rights, such as Patrick Henry, also stayed away.

In 1913, influential political scientist and historian Charles A. Beard proposed a controversial thesis: In writing the constitution, the framers' primary goal had been to protect their property holdings and financial self-interest.[30] Beard argued that the framers were a group of wealthy elites who had been adversely affected by the type of government created under the Articles of Confederation (see Table 2.1 for an overview of the delegates' characteristics).[31] Beard argued that in establishing property rights and protecting the economic interests of elites, the framers had purposely limited the ability of the majority to exercise real power.

In the 1950s, historians such as Robert E. Brown and Forrest McDonald suggested that a rigorous analysis of the data debunked Beard's thesis. They pointed out that the framers were not as monolithic in their interests as Beard suggested (for example, some *opponents* of the Constitution also came from the privileged wealthy class, and not all supporters were wealthy creditors), and that a broader array of interests than Beard recognized had influenced the framers.[32]

Nonetheless, debate continues. Reality may rest somewhere between Beard's clear-cut assumptions and the views of critics such as Brown and McDonald. The framers, after all, were politicians influenced by a range of factors. Economics was undoubtedly one of them, but not the only one—or even, necessarily, the most significant one.

A bare quorum of delegates attended the opening session of the Constitutional Convention on May 25 in what is now called Independence Hall (the room where the members of the Second Continental Congress signed the Declaration of Independence). Thirteen tables—one for each state's delegation—were arranged in a semicircle. Rhode Island never sent delegates, and New Hampshire's arrived two months late. No more than 11 state delegations were ever in attendance at any one time. As had been the practice in Congress, each

TABLE 2.1

## *Characteristics of the Delegates to the Constitutional Convention*

| |
| --- |
| All were white and male. |
| Thirty-five were lawyers. |
| Almost three-fourths of them had served in the Confederation Congress. |
| Twenty-five had served in the Continental Congress during the Revolution. |
| Fifteen had participated in drafting their own state's constitution. |
| Eight had signed the Declaration of Independence. |
| At least one-third owned slaves (12 owned or managed plantations with slave labor). |
| Most were young, with many still in their twenties and thirties (Franklin, at 81, was a notable exception). |

state delegation had one vote. The group deliberated in absolute secrecy so that delegates could express their views without fear of outside retaliation or pressure. Despite the heat, they kept the large windows closed that summer and posted sentries outside to ward off eavesdroppers.[33]

## LARGE STATES VERSUS SMALL STATES: THE VIRGINIA AND NEW JERSEY PLANS

The Virginia delegation quickly took the reins after arriving in Philadelphia. Virginian James Madison issued a detailed critique of the Articles of Confederation entitled "Vices of the Political System of the United States," and further argued that confederations were, by their very nature, doomed to failure.[34] Most significantly, the group of Virginia delegates met every morning at a local boardinghouse to plot strategy for how to convince the other delegates to construct a new constitution rather than merely amend the Articles of Confederation. They also met each afternoon to greet arriving delegates.

The drafting of the Constitution was, after all, a distinctly political process, which involved consensus on some issues (such as the need for a limited, republican form of government) and conflict on others (such as what system of representation to adopt). Ultimately, compromise (on issues such as slavery, representation, presidential selection, and the court system) and creativity (the embrace of federalism, for example) led to success. Keep these "4 Cs" in mind—consensus, conflict, compromise, and creativity—as you read the rest of this chapter.

Once the convention formally assembled on May 25, Virginia's power became immediately evident. The delegates unanimously chose Virginian George Washington as its presiding officer. After the group had established the rules of the convention, Edmund Randolph, the head of the Virginia delegation, rose and introduced his delegation's proposal for a new constitution, the result of the daily strategy sessions they had held. This so-called **Virginia Plan**, primarily

> **Virginia Plan** A plan, favored by large states, to replace (rather than amend) the Articles of Confederation and create a strong national government consisting of three branches. It also called for replacing the one-state/one-vote system used under the Articles of Confederation with proportional voting power in the legislature.

**FIGURE 2.1**

## *Central Government Under the Virginia Plan*

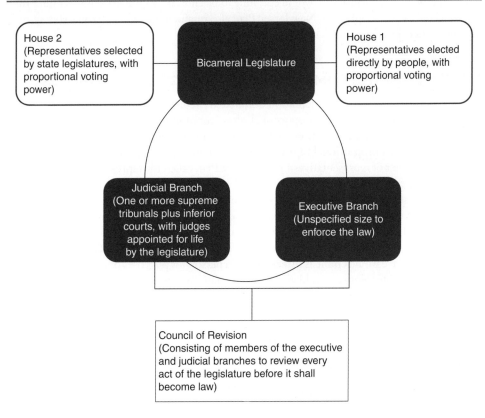

**FIGURE 2.2**

## *Central Government Under the New Jersey Plan*

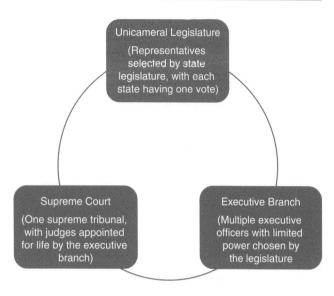

authored by Madison and consisting of 15 draft resolutions, was designed to replace rather than amend the Articles of Confederation and to establish a strong central government consisting of three branches: a bicameral legislative branch, an executive branch, and a judicial branch (see Figure 2.1).

The Virginia Plan called for members of the lower house of the legislature to be elected by the citizens of each state. Members of the lower house would, in turn, select members of the upper house. In addition to replacing the unicameral legislature that existed under the Articles of Confederation with a bicameral legislature, the Virginia Plan also called for the replacement of the one-state/one-vote system with proportional voting power in both houses: the number of representatives from each state would be based on the state's population, and each of their representatives would have one individual vote. This new voting plan would increase the power of more populous states at the expense of less populous states. It also raised a nasty question: Were slaves to be included when counting the population of a state? Bluntly put, were they to be counted as people or property?[35]

Small states strongly opposed the Virginia Plan. On June 9, William Patterson of New Jersey stood and proclaimed that he was "astonished" and "alarmed" at the Virginia Plan's proposal to base a state's voting strength on its population.[36] He then introduced an alternative set of proposals that came to be known as the **New Jersey Plan**, aimed at merely amending the Articles of Confederation. It, too, called for three branches, but unlike the proposals under the Virginia Plan, the New Jersey Plan called for maintaining a unicameral legislature, a weak executive branch comprising multiple officers (elected by Congress and subject to removal only upon majority vote of the state governors) rather than a single president, and a Supreme Court whose members would be elected by the executive officers (see Figure 2.2). Representatives to the legislature would continue to be chosen by state legislatures rather than being elected by the people. The New Jersey Plan also retained the one-state/one-vote system, thereby garnering support from small states.

## THE THREE-FIFTHS COMPROMISE AND THE GREAT COMPROMISE

The two questions of state representation dominated the next few weeks of discussion at the convention: (1) Should there be proportional representation in Congress, as called for in the Virginia Plan, or equal representation (one state/one vote), as called for in the New Jersey Plan? (2) In the event that proportional representation was chosen, who would be counted in determining the number of representatives? The Virginia Plan called for representation in Congress to be based on the "numbers of free inhabitants" in a state. This concerned smaller southern states because slaves made up such a large proportion of their populations (see Figure 2.3); if slaves were not counted, those states' power in Congress would be diminished.

To lure small southern states to accept the idea of proportional representation, James Wilson of Pennsylvania, a supporter of the Virginia Plan, introduced the so-called **Three-Fifths Compromise**: Each slave would count as three-fifths of a person for purposes of representation. This obviously deplorable solution would give southern states strong enough influence in Congress to prevent the legislature from abolishing slavery (a possibility that was already a concern to these states), but not as much influence as they would have if slaves were fully counted. (Of course, slaves did not have the right to vote and therefore would not be represented in Congress. Women did not have the constitutional right to vote either, but white women *did* count as full persons toward determining the number of representatives a state would have.) On June 11, the convention endorsed the Three-Fifths Compromise by a vote of 9–2, with only Delaware and New Jersey voting against it.[37]

**New Jersey Plan** A plan, favored by small states, to amend (rather than replace) the Articles of Confederation. It would have retained the one-state/one-vote system of voting in the national legislature, with representatives chosen by state legislatures.

**Three-Fifths Compromise** The decision by the Constitutional Convention to count slaves as three-fifths of a person for purposes of representation.

FIGURE 2.3

# Slaves as a Percentage of State Populations, 1790

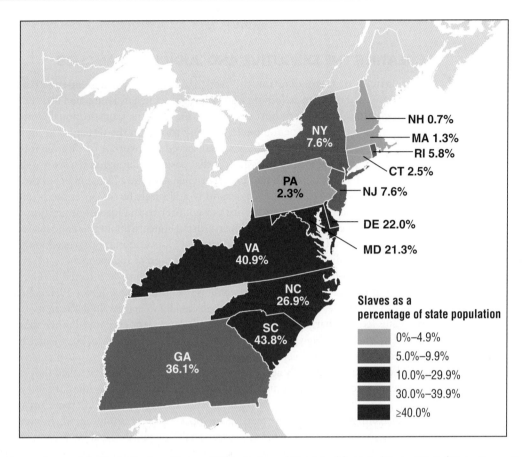

**Slaves as a percentage of state population**

- 0%–4.9%
- 5.0%–9.9%
- 10.0%–29.9%
- 30.0%–39.9%
- ≥40.0%

Source: "1790 Census: Return of the Whole Number of Persons Within the Several Districts of the United States," United States Census Bureau, accessed July 21, 2019, https://www.census.gov/library/publications/1793/dec/number-of-persons.html

It soon became clear, however, that even with the Three-Fifths Compromise, proportional representation was not a done deal. Quite to the contrary, that issue continued to dominate discussion for weeks and threatened to deadlock the convention. Finally, another compromise ended the impasse. Devised by Roger Sherman and Oliver Ellsworth of Connecticut, this so-called **Great Compromise** (sometimes referred to as the *Connecticut Compromise*) called for a bicameral legislature, as in the Virginia Plan, with a different method for determining representation in each house and different procedures for selecting representatives in each house.

In the lower house (which eventually became the House of Representatives), the Virginia Plan would prevail:

- Representation would be proportional.
- Representatives would be elected by the people.

In the upper house (which eventually became the Senate), the New Jersey Plan would prevail:

- Representation would be equal (each state would have two representatives).
- Representatives would be selected by state legislatures.

In keeping with the principle of "no taxation without representation," all legislation dealing with raising and spending money would originate in the lower house.

**Great Compromise** The decision by the Constitutional Convention to resolve the debate over equal versus proportional representation by establishing a bicameral (two-house) legislature with proportional representation in the lower house, equal representation in the upper house, and different methods of selecting representatives for each house.

The Convention debated the Great Compromise for 11 days, and, on June 29, finally passed it. The compromise ended the deadlock and resolved the fundamental question of representation in the legislature. Now the delegates shifted their attention to the other two branches of government.

## CREATING THE EXECUTIVE AND JUDICIAL BRANCHES

The Articles of Confederation did not provide for an independent executive branch. Furthermore, most state governors were selected by the legislature, had little or no veto power over legislation, and served short terms.[38] By the time the Constitutional Convention met in 1787, some believed the pendulum had swung too far in the direction of limiting executive power. For example, Thomas Jefferson had served as governor of Virginia for two years and experienced firsthand the powerlessness of that position. Though still wary of a strong executive (or governor), Jefferson wrote that his experience with the 173 members of the Virginia legislature had convinced him that "173 despots would surely be as oppressive as one."[39] This concentration of power in the legislature ran counter to the idea of separation of powers and resulted in unchecked legislative authority. Rising concern about this issue made arguments for a strong executive branch at the Constitutional Convention more palatable than they would have been immediately after finalizing the Declaration of Independence.

The Virginia Plan had called for an executive branch to be selected by Congress, without specifying its size or tenure or its specific powers. The New Jersey Plan called for a plural, rather than a single, chief executive to be selected by Congress. In discussions, some individual delegates led the charge for a stronger, more independent executive branch than that contemplated by either the New Jersey Plan or the original Virginia Plan, but the delegates remained divided on the issue of executive power through August.

The delegates eventually agreed to a single chief executive, to be called the *president*—a strategic choice to diffuse concerns about a strong executive. A derivation of the Latin word *praesidere*, *president* means "to sit at the head of" and "to defend." *President* therefore implied passive guardianship rather than aggressive leadership. George Washington, who served a mostly passive, ceremonial function at the Constitutional Convention, had been its president. Despite agreement on what to call the chief executive, the delegates remained divided over what powers to give, and how to select, the president.[40]

In a compromise that helped to establish our current system of checks and balances, the convention agreed to split a number of traditionally executive powers, such as declaring war, making treaties, and appointing officials, and allow the president and Congress to share them. Thus, Congress would declare war, but the president would wage it. Presidents would negotiate treaties, but those treaties were subject to ratification by the Senate. The president would nominate ambassadors and other officials, but they could serve only if the Senate confirmed them. Nonetheless, the question remained: Who would select the president?

No issue perplexed the delegates more than determining how the president should be chosen.[41] Additionally, how long should the president serve? Should he be eligible for reelection? Selection by Congress had been the default position throughout the summer. Advocates of a more powerful executive feared that this method of selection would perpetuate a model of executive subservience to the legislature. Popular election—a natural alternative—posed its own problems. First, it would give the large states an advantage over the small ones. The three most populous states had nearly as many eligible voters as the remaining ten states combined.[42] Small states thus feared that they would have little influence in the selection of a president. Second, the framers assumed that voters would be ill-informed and motivated more by local interests than the common good (an example of consensus among the delegates). George Mason scoffed that letting the people choose the president would be "as un-natural" as referring "a trial of colours to a blind man."[43]

The Committee on Postponed Matters finally proposed a compromise that won the support of the delegates: the president (and vice president—the first time this post had been recommended) would be chosen by an Electoral College consisting of electors from each of the states. The number of electors from each state would be equal to the combined total of that state's representatives and senators in Congress. Each state would select these electors according to rules established by its own state legislature.

Similar debates ensued about the federal judiciary. Most delegates agreed that some sort of federal judiciary was necessary. But should it consist of one court of last resort or a broader system of federal courts? How should judges be selected—by Congress or the president? If Congress had the power to select, should both houses of Congress participate or only one house? If only one of them participated, which one should it be?

Answers to these questions, as to others, came in the form of compromises and creative solutions. The Constitution created one Supreme Court but left it to Congress to decide whether to create other, lower federal courts. Judges for the court were to be nominated by the president, but the nomination was to be subject to confirmation by the Senate. (See Chapter 14.) The framers also embraced federalism (see Chapter 3)—a creative solution that gave some powers to the national government and others to the states. Federalism allowed proponents of a strong national government as well as proponents of states' rights to feel that they had won on some issues.

## THE CONSTITUTION

After almost three months of debate, the Convention completed a final draft of the Constitution. It consisted of a preamble followed by seven articles. When the Constitution came to a vote, 39 of the 55 delegates voted to support it. However, the supporters constituted a majority of each of the 12 state delegations in attendance and each state had one vote, so the final vote in favor of the Constitution was 12–0.[44] Thirty-nine delegates signed the document on September 17, 1787—the last day of the convention. Of the delegates in attendance, only three refused to sign the Constitution.

**republicanism** A form of government in which power rests with the people but where the people rule only indirectly through elected representatives bound by the rule of law.

### CORE PRINCIPLES

The establishment of the Constitution represented a significant break from the past. This break is evident from the first three words of the Preamble to the Constitution, "We the people," which stood in marked contrast with the Articles of Confederation's "We the undersigned delegates of the states," signifying that America was now one people rather than 13 individual states. No one could predict how successful and influential the Constitution would be, but more immediately apparent was how pathbreaking it was.

The governmental design created by the Constitution can be understood in terms of four core principles (see Table 2.2). Republicanism, the first of these principles, stands in contrast with both direct democracy and monarchy. A republican form of government is one in which power rests with the people (as opposed to a monarch or, as under the Articles of Confederation, the states), but the people rule only indirectly, through elected representatives bound by the rule of law. Rule by representatives was expected to temper the passions of public opinion associated with a direct democracy, while elections would assure that those representatives remained accountable to the people for their actions. Republicanism had never been tried in a country as vast as the United States, and some feared that elected representatives would be tempted to act tyrannically rather than according to the rule of law.

Second, the Constitution instituted a system of federalism. In contrast with both a *confederation*, where the primary power is left to the states, and a *unitary system*, where all areas of power belong to the central government, a *federation* is a system in which power is divided between the central

The Constitution was a work of compromise, but it was controversial even after being completed and only 39 of 55 total delegates signed the final document.

**TABLE 2.2**

## Four Core Principles of the U.S. Constitution

*Republicanism*: Power rests with the people, but the people rule indirectly.

*Federalism*: Power is divided between the central and state governments.

*Separation of powers*: Power is divided across all three coequal branches of government.

*Checks and balances*: Power is both divided and shared among the three branches, with each branch having some control over the other two.

government and the state (or other regional) governments. The Constitution listed the powers of the national government, and it also listed the powers denied to the states, implying that all other powers were retained by the states. The Tenth Amendment (part of the American Bill of Rights, ratified in 1791) later clarified this, stating: "The powers not delegated to the United States by the Constitution, nor prohibited by it to the States, are reserved to the States respectively, or to the people." Dividing powers between the national government and the states was another check designed to prevent tyranny.

As we will see in Chapter 3, debate continued even after the ratification of the Tenth Amendment about precisely what powers were reserved to the states and when, if ever, Congress could interfere with those powers. It was clear, however, that whenever it was exercising its constitutionally enumerated powers, the national government was supreme: If conflicts arose between national and state law in such cases, national law would always prevail. As the **supremacy clause** of Article VI, Clause 2 put it, the Constitution, as well as acts of Congress and federal treaties passed pursuant to the Constitution, were "the supreme Law of the Land; and the judges in every State shall be bound thereby, any Thing in the Constitution or Laws of any State to the Contrary notwithstanding."

Third, the Constitution instituted a **separation of powers** across branches of the national government. Similar to federalism, this was designed to prevent the concentration of power in any one part of government. Thus, the framers divided the national government into three coequal branches and gave each a separate function. The legislative branch was given the power to make the laws, the executive branch was given the power to enforce (or execute) the laws, and the judicial branch was given the power to interpret the laws. This stands in contrast with parliamentary systems such as the United Kingdom, where the prime minister and the cabinet, who together perform the executive function, are drawn from the legislature.

Finally, to further ensure that power would not become concentrated, the Constitution set up a system of **checks and balances** in which each of the three branches among which power was divided would have some degree of control over the other two. In other words, power is both divided and shared, as shown in Figure 2.4. We have already discussed how war powers, appointment power, and treaty power are each shared between the president and Congress. There are also other checks. For example, the president is given the power to veto legislation. Moreover, that veto can be overridden only by a two-thirds majority of both houses of Congress (as opposed to simply getting the most votes, which is required for passing legislation in the first place). Thus, the president has a check on Congress, but this check is itself limited. Similarly, courts have a check through their power to interpret laws passed by Congress, and—by means of judicial review—to strike down laws and executive actions that violate the Constitution. Though not specifically enumerated in the Constitution, judicial review—as discussed below—has become an accepted part of our constitutional system. And, Congress has the power to impeach—remove from office—the president, vice president, and other civil officers, including federal judges and Supreme Court justices.

## THE ARTICLES OF THE CONSTITUTION

The Constitution has only seven articles, preceded by a preamble and followed by the 27 amendments that have been made since its ratification. The preamble spelled out the justification for the

**supremacy clause** Article VI, Clause 2 of the Constitution specifying that federal laws and treaties passed pursuant to the Constitution trump contradictory state laws dealing with the same topic.

**separation of powers** The division of governmental powers among three separate and coequal branches—legislative, executive, and judicial.

**checks and balances** A method to protect against unrestrained governmental power by dividing and sharing powers among the legislative, executive, and judicial branches.

FIGURE 2.4

# System of Checks and Balances in the U.S. Federal Government

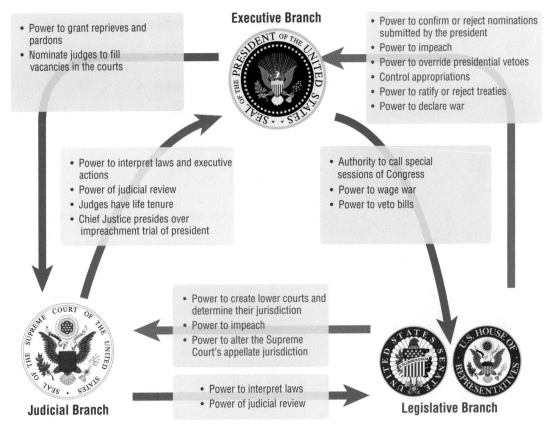

**Executive Branch**

- Power to grant reprieves and pardons
- Nominate judges to fill vacancies in the courts

- Power to confirm or reject nominations submitted by the president
- Power to impeach
- Power to override presidential vetoes
- Control appropriations
- Power to ratify or reject treaties
- Power to declare war

- Power to interpret laws and executive actions
- Power of judicial review
- Judges have life tenure
- Chief Justice presides over impreachment trial of president

- Authority to call special sessions of Congress
- Power to wage war
- Power to veto bills

- Power to create lower courts and determine their jurisdiction
- Power to impeach
- Power to alter the Supreme Court's appellate jurisdiction

**Judicial Branch**

- Power to interpret laws
- Power of judicial review

**Legislative Branch**

Arrows indicate the direction of a check that one branch exerts over the other.

Constitution ("to form a more perfect Union"), its fundamental goals (which included establishing justice and "securing the blessings of Liberty"), and made clear that the new Constitution and the government established by it were created by "We the people" (as opposed to being created by the states, as had been the case with the Articles of Confederation). The first three articles that follow the preamble each spell out the power of one of the three branches of government. The remaining articles are concerned with federal–state relations as well as with the relations among the states and provide procedures for ratifying the Constitution and amending it.

**ARTICLE I: THE LEGISLATIVE BRANCH** Because legislators are the representatives of the people, the framers thought of the legislative branch as being the most important and presented it first (see Figure 2.5). Article I opens by stating, "All legislative Powers *herein granted* shall be vested in a Congress of the United States, which shall consist of a Senate and House of Representatives" [emphasis added]. In other words, Congress is limited to those powers given to it by the Constitution. Those powers fall into two broad categories: enumerated powers and implied powers.

**Enumerated powers** are those powers specifically listed. Most enumerated powers are in Article I, Section 8, which contains a laundry list of specific powers given to Congress, including the power to impose and collect taxes, to borrow money, to regulate commerce, and to declare war. Some of these powers were lacking under the Articles of Confederation, notably the power to collect taxes and regulate commerce. Legislative powers not given to Congress, and not covered under implied powers, were presumably retained by the states, a presumption that was made explicit by the Tenth Amendment.

> **enumerated powers** Powers specifically listed in the Constitution, such as congressional powers outlined in Article I, Section 8.

FIGURE 2.5

# Confidence in Government and American Institutions

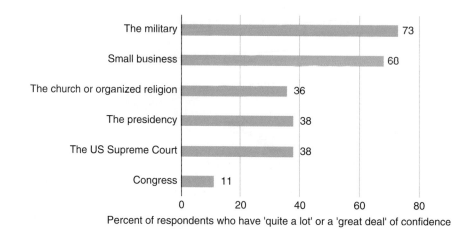

Percent of respondents who have 'quite a lot' or a 'great deal' of confidence

*The framers thought that Congress would be the most important governmental institution. How do people feel about it today, based on the findings shown here?*

Source: "Confidence in Institutions," Gallup, 2019, https://news.gallup.com/poll/1597/confidence-institutions.aspx

**Implied powers** are those authorized by the "necessary and proper clause" of Article I, Section 8, Clause 18. The necessary and proper clause (discussed in Chapter 3) expands the enumerated powers by saying that Congress has the power to "make all Laws which shall be necessary and proper for carrying into Execution the foregoing Powers, and all other Powers vested by this Constitution in the Government of the United States, or in any Department or Officer thereof." This clause is sometimes also referred to as the *elastic clause*, because it serves to expand Congress's power. The controversial question of how much the clause can—or should—expand Congress's power is discussed in more detail in Chapter 3 (see also Figure 2.6).

Article I, Section 9 places certain specific limits on the power of the national government. For example, it prohibits Congress from passing a bill of attainder (legislation declaring one or more people guilty of a crime) or ex post facto laws (those that retroactively criminalize behavior), limits when Congress may suspend habeas corpus (a recourse for unlawful imprisonment), and—in the so-called emoluments clause—prevents any government official (in any branch) from receiving any gift, payment, or items of value from a foreign state or its representatives without the consent of Congress.

Finally, Article I, Section 10 lists the powers that are withheld from the states. For example, states are forbidden to enter into treaties with foreign nations, coin money, or impose duties on imports and exports without the consent of Congress.

**ARTICLE II: THE EXECUTIVE BRANCH** Article II vests the executive authority in the president. In other words, it gives the president the power to carry out the laws. However, the ambiguity of the opening sentence of Article II has led to considerable debate about the precise scope of executive power. Unlike the opening of Article I, the opening of Article II does not limit powers to those "herein granted," even though Article II does contain enumerated powers. It simply says, "The executive Power shall be vested in a President of the United States of America." Does the omission of the words "herein granted" give presidents greater leeway than Congress? People disagree about the answer to this question. As we shall see in Chapter 12, three quite different interpretations of the scope of presidential power have emerged.

Article II, Section 2 enumerates specific powers of the president, such as serving as commander-in-chief of the armed forces, granting pardons, negotiating treaties, and appointing specified officials with the advice and consent of the Senate. In addition, Article II spells out the way in which presidents will be elected and eligibility requirements for the office (Section 1); it requires

**implied powers** Powers that are not specifically enumerated in the Constitution but are considered "necessary and proper" to carry out the enumerated powers.

that the president give information to Congress about the state of the union and recommend for its consideration such measures as he deems necessary and expedient and that he "take Care that the Laws be faithfully executed" (Section 3); and it provides guidelines for the president's impeachment and removal from office (Section 4).

**ARTICLE III: THE JUDICIAL BRANCH**  Article III is the shortest of the articles delineating the three branches of government. It creates a Supreme Court and says that the judges will hold office "during good Behaviour"—in other words, unless they are impeached, they will have life tenure (the method for selecting Supreme Court justices was spelled out in Article II). Life tenure was designed to promote judicial independence, as was a guarantee that justices receive a compensation for their services that would not be reduced during their tenure. No federal courts existed under the Articles of Confederation, and some members of the Constitutional Convention feared that a large federal judiciary with expanded jurisdiction would interfere with decisions that they felt should be left to the states. Therefore, the delegates postponed the decision about creating federal courts in addition to the Supreme Court by, in Article III, giving Congress the authority to establish lower federal courts if it chose to do so (which it quickly did, in the Judiciary Act of 1789; see Chapter 14).

**ARTICLES IV–VII**  The remaining four articles of the Constitution cover a wide range of issues. Article IV deals with the states and their relations. It requires states to give "full faith and credit" to the laws and judicial proceedings of other states, prohibits discrimination by one state against citizens of another state, guarantees a republican form of government in every state, and delineates procedures for admitting new states. Article V spells out the processes by which the Constitution can be amended. Article VI contains the supremacy clause, forbids the use of any religious test as a qualification for holding any office (in other words, candidates could not be disqualified because of their religious views or lack thereof), and guaranteed that debts incurred by the Confederation would be honored under the Constitution. Finally, Article VII spelled out the procedure for ratifying the Constitution.

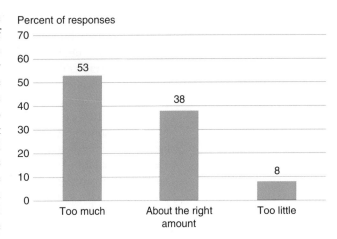

**FIGURE 2.6**

## Does the Federal Government Have Too Much Power, Just Enough, or Too Little Power?

Percent of responses

*What does this figure tell us about how Americans view the power of the central government today? Are the concerns expressed in this poll valid?*
Source: "Government," Gallup, 2018, https://news.gallup.com/poll/27286/government.aspx

# RATIFYING THE CONSTITUTION

The vote to approve the Constitution at the Convention was only the beginning of the battle. The document still had to be ratified by the states. Article VII of the Constitution spelled out the procedure: Each state would hold a ratifying convention. For the Constitution to take effect, at least nine of the thirteen conventions would have to vote in favor of approval. Once nine states voted to approve the Constitution, any states failing to vote for approval would exist as independent nations. The process ended up lasting more than two and a half years, during which time the Articles of Confederation remained in place. Unlike the deliberations at the Constitutional Convention, which were shrouded in secrecy, debate over the ratification of the Constitution was a distinctly public affair and the conventions were widely covered by the press.

### FEDERALISTS VERSUS ANTI-FEDERALISTS

Supporters of the Constitution and of the stronger national government it created quickly dubbed themselves **Federalists**. Opponents, who feared that the proposed national government would be too strong and who preferred that more power remain with the states, came to be known as **Anti-Federalists**. As Joseph J. Ellis has noted, however, both sides were really

**Federalists** Those who supported ratification of the Constitution and the stronger national government that it created.

**Anti-Federalists** States' rights advocates who opposed the ratification of the Constitution.

"Federalists," which literally meant favoring a federal system wherein power would be shared between a central government and state governments. The two sides simply disagreed over how power should be allocated in that system.[45]

Federalists started out with the upper hand in the debate. Their opponents lacked any substantive alternative to the Constitution except the Articles of Confederation, which were tainted with the stench of failure. Federalists were also aided by the fact that early ratifying conventions were in states that supported the Constitution; this would help to build momentum for ratification. Nonetheless, the Anti-Federalists probably reflected the sentiments of a majority of the American people, who remained deeply distrustful of a new and unfamiliar central authority and of its power to tax. Furthermore, many people still thought of themselves as citizens of their particular state rather than citizens of the United States. Indeed, ratification of the Constitution might well have failed had it depended on a national referendum (the method used by a number of countries in recent years, including Iraq in 2005).

A month after the Constitutional Convention ended, Federalists began publishing pro-Constitution articles in newspapers in New York, where ratification was in doubt. The articles appeared under the pseudonym "Publius" (Latin for "the people"), and in 1788, they were gathered together and published in two volumes as *The Federalist*. Now commonly known as the **Federalist Papers**, these 85 articles, written by James Madison, Alexander Hamilton, and (to a lesser extent) John Jay, provided not only a vigorous defense of the Constitution but also rich theoretical insights that still serve as a basis for understanding the Constitution today. In contrast with the populist tract *Common Sense*, which in 1776 helped to galvanize mass support for independence, the *Federalist Papers* failed to have a mobilizing effect among the general populace because they proved to be too dense and erudite for the average reader. They did influence and mobilize elites—Federalist delegates at the ratification conventions—but their greatest impact has been on subsequent generations who have used them as guides for interpreting the Constitution.

Those opposed to the Constitution penned their own articles under pseudonyms such as "Brutus" and "Cato" (the names of ancient Roman senators who decried tyranny when Julius Caesar took control away from the Senate and assumed power over the Roman Republic). These articles were written by a larger number of people than the *Federalist Papers*. The leaders of the Anti-Federalists included prominent individuals who had played important roles in the creation of the United States, such as George Mason and Patrick Henry. Their critique focused on the dangers of centralized power, which they worried would become despotic and infringe not only upon states' rights but also upon individual liberties. The fact that the Constitution lacked a bill of rights fueled their concern. Having so recently fought a war of independence to secure liberty, many readers shared these writers' wariness of a strong national government.

## ANOTHER COMPROMISE: A POST-RATIFICATION BILL OF RIGHTS

Delaware was the first state to ratify the Constitution in December 1787. Pennsylvania, New Jersey, Georgia, and Connecticut quickly followed suit. Massachusetts, however, derailed this momentum with a chief Anti-Federalist concern: that the new central government would run roughshod over the rights of the people.

During the Constitutional Convention, George Mason, a delegate from Virginia, had proposed that the Constitution include a bill of rights. The majority of the framers rejected this proposal, however, reasoning that since government was limited to those powers granted by the Constitution and the Constitution did not empower government to infringe upon those rights, a bill of rights was unnecessary. They further argued the potential danger of such a list: Failure to include a specific right might imply that that right was unprotected. These arguments did not convince Mason, who was so upset at the omission that he refused to sign the Constitution. Mason went on to become a leading opponent of its ratification.

As the debates played out, it became clear that without a bill of rights, the Constitution would not be ratified. But Federalists feared that calling another Constitutional Convention to modify the existing document would lead to new debates about issues far afield from a bill of rights. Therefore, Federalists conceded the issue by promising that if the Constitution was ratified, they would support an amendment to provide a bill of rights. This broke the logjam in Massachusetts, which voted for ratification in February 1788, followed by the required ninth state, New Hampshire, in June of that same year.

**Federalist Papers** Essays by James Madison, Alexander Hamilton, and John Jay supporting ratification of the Constitution. Originally published in newspapers under the pseudonym "Publius" (Latin for "the people"), they were gathered together in 1788 and published in two volumes as *The Federalist*.

Although approval by nine states led to ratification of the Constitution, four states still remained opposed and thus not part of the new nation. Not only would their failure to ratify leave the United States geographically split, but two of the four states were seen as key to the nation's success: Virginia and New York. The outcome was not clear in either state. Virginia, whose ratifying convention convened before New York's, became the focus of attention. At Virginia's convention, a debate between the Anti-Federalist Patrick Henry and the Federalist James Madison proved to be a defining moment. Indeed, Joseph Ellis argues that it might be "the most consequential debate in American history."[46]

Of the two men, Henry was, by far, the better orator. But Madison was, by far, the more prepared. In the end, Madison's soft-spoken, point-by-point rebuttal of Henry's theatrical criticisms of the Constitution won out. Virginia voted to ratify by a vote of 89 to 79 on June 25. Without this important turning point, Virginia would not have joined the United States, assuring a division between northern and southern states. Had the Anti-Federalists won in Virginia, the confidence of other states in the new national government might well have been shaken. Still, it is worth remembering that although Madison's position prevailed in the vote to ratify the Constitution, Henry's passionate defense of liberty strongly influenced the eventual decision to amend that Constitution to add a bill of rights.

## AMENDING THE CONSTITUTION

The Articles of Confederation had all but precluded amendments by requiring that they receive unanimous support from all the states. The framers now made the process easier, but not so easy that amendments would overwhelm the Constitution. Indeed, the U.S. Constitution stands out not only for its longevity but also for its relatively few amendments as compared with the constitutions of the states and many other countries. Plenty of amendments have been suggested (well over 10,000), but only 33 have been formally proposed to the states and only 27 of those have been ratified. The first 10 of these make up the Bill of Rights.[47] (See Table 2.3 for descriptions of the six formally proposed amendments that were never ratified.)

As a stark contrast, consider France, which has had 15 different constitutions since 1789 and has existed under monarchy and dictatorship as well as under various republics. France's current constitution was introduced in 1958 and, as of 2018, had already been amended 18 times. Or take an example from within the United States: The state of Alabama has had six constitutions since becoming the twenty-second state in 1819, and its current one—adopted in 1901—has been amended 928 times[48] as of 2018. The stability of the U.S. Constitution is partly attributable to its ambiguity. That ambiguity has allowed flexibility in interpreting the Constitution, and flexibility of interpretation has helped to ward off frequent amendments.

TABLE 2.3

## *The Six Failed Amendments*

| |
| --- |
| *Congressional Apportionment Amendment* (1789). More specifically delineated the number of people to be represented by each member of the U.S. House of Representatives. Ratified by 11 states. |
| *Anti-Title Amendment* (1810). Any U.S. citizen who received a title of nobility from a foreign power or who—without the consent of Congress—accepted any gift from a foreign power would be stripped of citizenship. Ratified by 12 states. |
| *Slavery Amendment* (1861). Prohibited Congress from passing laws that would abolish or interfere with slavery or other "domestic institutions" of the states. Ratified by 3 states. |
| *Child Labor Amendment* (1926). Granted Congress the power to regulate the labor of children under the age of 18. Ratified by 28 states. |
| *Equal Rights Amendment* (1972). Prohibited both the national government and the states from denying or abridging any rights on the basis of sex, thereby establishing the equality of men and women. Ratified by 35 states. |
| *District of Columbia Voting Rights Amendment* (1978). Granted the residents of the District of Columbia full representation in both houses of the U.S. Congress as well as full participation in the Electoral College. Ratified by 16 states. |

*Source: Mount, Steve. "Constitutional Topic: The Census." (http://www.usconstitution.net/constamfail.html).*

# Amidst Constitutional Change in Hungary

How can a democracy handle a democratically elected government that intends to change the constitution in ways that make the country a less viable democracy? After the fall of Communism in 1989, Hungary embraced democracy and capitalism. But in the country's April 2018 parliamentary election, the right-wing coalition government led by Prime Minister Viktor Orbán won its third consecutive two-thirds legislative majority since 2010. That two-thirds majority is significant, because that is what it takes to amend the constitution in Hungary. Orbán, who in 2016 had been the first global leader to endorse Donald Trump's candidacy for president of the United States, ran on a vigorously anti-immigration platform in 2018. In 2015, Orbán had built a wall along the border between Hungary and Serbia in the name of border security and to prevent asylum seekers from entering Hungary. Once reelected, he secured legislation in 2018 that criminalized any attempts by individuals or groups to help illegal immigrants claim asylum, as well as a controversial constitutional amendment that prohibited foreign nationals from outside Europe (any "alien population") from settling in Hungary.

That 2018 amendment was the seventh to Hungary's 2011 constitution (itself written by Orbán and his coalition), and Orbán promised more would come. Each had been secured by a two-thirds party-line vote of parliament. Earlier (equally controversial) amendments had weakened the power of Hungary's Constitutional Court (the equivalent of our Supreme Court) by limiting judicial independence and the Court's power to interpret laws; curtailed religious liberty by declaring

that the government has a fundamental duty to protect Christian culture and granting Parliament the sole power to decide which religious organizations count as churches; and helped to solidify Orbán's ruling coalition by banning political advertising in any venue except the state media (which happened to be controlled by Orbán's Fidesz party)—an action the Constitutional Court had previously declared unconstitutional when passed by ordinary legislation.

Such amendments were condemned by the opposition party within Hungary, and led to protests in the streets of Budapest, but—unlike amendments to the U.S. Constitution—Hungary's amendments did not require ratification beyond passage in parliament. Critics claimed the amendments were a threat to democracy and human rights, yet they were passed by super-majorities of Parliament whose ruling coalition had won resounding victories in three democratic elections.

## Questions to Consider

1. How important is the balance between majority rule and minority rights? Does Hungary's method of constitutional amendment achieve that balance?
2. What would be the consequences if the U.S. Constitution could be amended by a two-thirds vote of Congress without the need for ratification by the states?
3. What impact might Hungary's mode of constitutional amendment have on separation of powers? The rule of law?
4. Hungary's constitution has no separation of church and state. Is that good or bad? Why?

## THE FORMAL AMENDMENT PROCESS

As specified by Article V, the process of amending the Constitution consists of two stages: proposal and ratification. As shown in Figure 2.7, proposals can be made in either of two ways:

- by a two-thirds vote of both houses of Congress or
- by a request to Congress from two-thirds of the state legislatures to call a convention to propose amendments.

To date, all 33 amendments were proposed by Congress. The alternative route—a convention convened by a vote of the state legislatures—poses several problems. The Constitution does not specify how delegates to the convention should be chosen, how many delegates there should be, or what rules such delegates should follow. In addition, such a convention could presumably introduce as many amendments as it wanted. The last time we had a convention, in 1787, we ended up with an entirely new constitution. Fears that another convention could lead

FIGURE 2.7

# *The Constitutional Amendment Process*

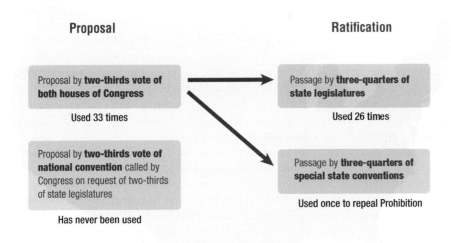

to similarly radical change, together with uncertainty about the mechanics of such a convention, make amendment proposals by Congress a safer and easier option.

Whether proposed by Congress or a convention, amendments must then be ratified by the states. Like proposals, ratification can come about in either of two ways (with Congress specifying the method for each amendment proposed):

- by a vote of three-fourths of the state legislatures or
- by a vote of three-fourths of specially convened state ratifying conventions.

As of 2019, only one of the 27 amendments ratified—the Twenty-First Amendment, repealing prohibition—was ratified by state conventions. In that case, Congress predicted that passage by state conventions was more likely than passage by conservative state legislatures.

## INFORMAL METHODS OF CONSTITUTIONAL CHANGE

In addition to changes to the Constitution through formal amendment, changes—subtle and not so subtle—have come about as a result of interpretation by the other branches of government. We usually think that such interpretation is done by federal courts, particularly the Supreme Court, but Congress and the president also share a role in interpreting the Constitution. The ambiguity of so much important constitutional language makes interpretation essential.

**JUDICIAL INTERPRETATION** The Supreme Court engages in judicial interpretation in the course of exercising its power of judicial review—that is, its power to strike down acts of government that violate the Constitution, the supreme law of the land. To decide whether an act violates the Constitution, the Court must, of course, interpret relevant constitutional language. For example, weighing the constitutionality of a law providing for the death penalty in serious criminal cases requires the Court to determine what is meant by the Eighth Amendment's ban on "cruel and unusual" punishment. Even if

Only one constitutional amendment has been passed to repeal another: the Twenty-First Amendment, which ended Prohibition. It was also the only amendment to be ratified by state conventions rather than state legislatures.

the Court determines that the death penalty itself is not cruel and unusual, other questions may arise: Is it cruel and unusual to execute children or the mentally disabled? Answers to such questions may change over time as the national consensus evolves and membership of the Court changes, even if the Constitution itself is not formally amended.

Judicial review is an important way of enforcing the rule of law—the idea that government is limited in its actions by the nation's constitution. Despite this vital function, judicial review was not a power specifically granted by the Constitution. Rather, it was established by the Supreme Court in the 1803 case *Marbury v. Madison*[49] (see Chapter 14).

Ambiguous constitutional language complicates the task of judicial interpretation. For example, the Fourth Amendment bans "unreasonable searches and seizures," but what exactly does that mean? Judges disagree not only about what the word *unreasonable* means but also about what constitutes a *search* (for instance, is a wiretap a search?). Similar difficulties extend to many of the most important clauses of the Constitution.

Even seemingly straightforward clauses, such as the First Amendment command that Congress shall make no law abridging freedom of speech, can lead to widely divergent interpretations. What, exactly, does constitutionally protected *speech* entail? Is every verbal utterance protected (including libel, obscenity, false advertising, and verbal threats to assassinate the president or overthrow the government)? Is speech even limited to verbal utterances, or does the First Amendment also protect symbolic speech, such as burning an American flag? And if it protects symbolic speech, what does *that* entail? (For more on interpretations of protected speech, see Chapter 4.)

Some argue that this ability of the Court to adjust its interpretation without the long and difficult process of constitutional amendment is a good thing. The ambiguity—and therefore the flexibility—of the Constitution allows phrases such as *cruel and unusual punishment* and *unreasonable searches and seizures* to evolve over time to comport with changing societal values and technological advances. This flexibility, they say, has helped the Constitution to endure. Others, however, fear that judges will exploit that flexibility and use it to "legislate from the bench." Why, they ask, should unelected judges be allowed to pick which interpretation of ambiguous clauses is correct? Won't their choices be based on their personal values and ideological predilections? Shouldn't such ambiguities be resolved by legislators who are accountable to voters? Those who favor judicial interpretation say no because they fear the "tyranny of the majority" and believe judges will be more dispassionate guardians of constitutional principle and minority rights precisely because they are unelected (and thus independent). This debate will be discussed in more detail in Chapter 14.

**COORDINATE CONSTRUCTION** Members of all three branches of government take an oath to uphold the Constitution. Even though neither Congress nor the president has the power of judicial review, both end up interpreting the Constitution. Such interpretation by Congress and the president is known as **coordinate construction**.[50]

Whenever Congress passes any law, it must be mindful of constitutional limitations on its power. Consider, for example, the First Amendment command that Congress shall make no law abridging the freedom of speech. Congress must interpret that language before enacting a law dealing with speech. The Supreme Court, of course, may disagree with Congress's interpretation and strike the law down, but since so few laws make their way to the Supreme Court, these initial determinations by Congress are important and can influence prevailing understandings of what constitutional clauses mean.

Once laws are passed, the president is charged by Article II, Section 3 of the Constitution to take care that they are "faithfully executed." However, Article II, Section 1, Clause 8 specifically directs presidents to "preserve, protect, and defend the Constitution of the United States." Based on that language, could presidents refuse to execute laws they believe are unconstitutional? Some argue that these clauses require coordinate construction: The president must interpret the Constitution to make sure that it is upheld and faithfully executed.

In recent years, presidents have attempted to use signing statements to do just that. The use of presidential signing statements, issued by presidents when they sign legislation into law, dates back to President James Monroe in 1822. Traditionally, such statements were ceremonial in nature, used to celebrate the passage of the law. More recently, presidents such as Ronald Reagan used signing statements to clarify how they believed executive branch officials should interpret ambiguous parts of the law.

**coordinate construction** Refers to constitutional interpretation by Congress or the president. Proponents of coordinate construction believe that all three branches of government (not only the judiciary) have the power and duty to interpret the Constitution.

Increasingly, however, signing statements have come to be used by presidents to identify portions of the law that they believe to be unconstitutional. Some laws passed by Congress are hundreds, even thousands, of pages long. The president cannot strike a particular line or clause from a bill before signing it. He must accept the full bill or use his veto power and reject the bill in its entirety. A signing statement allows the president to sign the bill but express his belief that one or more parts of it are unconstitutional. In using signing statements in such a way, a president would note the portion they believed to be constitutionally suspect but would enforce the law in its entirety unless the Supreme Court struck down that portion of the law.

George W. Bush used signing statements in a more controversial manner. He routinely used signing statements to express his intent not to enforce certain provisions of the law he was signing. In one famous example, Bush signed with much fanfare the so-called McCain Amendment banning the use of torture by U.S. officials, but quietly issued a signing statement claiming the power to disregard the law when he, as commander in chief, deemed it necessary to do so. After the *Boston Globe* publicized Bush's use of signing statements in an April 2006 article,[51] a report by a Task Force of the American Bar Association concluded that Bush had already used signing statements to challenge more than 800 specific provisions of laws he had signed. In one signing statement alone, Bush raised 116 specific objections involving almost every part of the Consolidated Appropriations Act of 2005 that he had just signed.[52] In short, Bush claimed the power to disobey portions of laws he had signed whenever he felt that those provisions conflicted with his interpretation of the Constitution. Critics claimed the president had exceeded his powers by imposing his own interpretation of the Constitution without waiting for a ruling from the courts.

Shortly after taking office, Barack Obama instructed government officials not to enforce Bush's signing statements unless they had clearance to do so from the attorney general. However, Obama indicated that he might use signing statements himself in some instances, and he did.[53] For example, in June 2009, President Obama issued a signing statement accompanying a war spending bill. In it, he said that he could ignore restrictions that Congress had placed on U.S. aid provided to the World Bank and International Monetary Fund. Some Democrats in Congress expressed concern that President Obama had used a tool that he and fellow Democrats had criticized President Bush for using.[54] However, Obama's use of signing statements was less frequent and less controversial than Bush's had been; by the end of his eight years in office, he had issued 37 signing statements challenging 114 specific provisions. In comparison, George W. Bush issued 161 signing statements challenging over 1,100 specific provisions during his eight years in office, and Donald Trump had—in only his first two years in office—issued 33 signing statements challenging 306 specific provisions.[55] For example, after signing the 2018 Defense Appropriations bill, Trump issued a signing statement challenging 52 provisions of the law.[56]

## CONSEQUENCES FOR DEMOCRACY

Drawing on John Locke's idea of the social contract, Americans embraced a written constitution to delineate the powers of government and the rights of its citizens. In contrast, Great Britain had an "unwritten" constitution that consisted of some written documents (such as the English Bill of Rights and Acts of Parliament) but also unwritten parliamentary conventions and royal prerogatives. Americans did not believe Britain's more amorphous constitution had done enough to protect the rights of its citizens, in part because Parliament could alter the constitution through simple legislation. The fact that we have a written constitution embodying a republican form of government designed to protect individual liberty and to prevent concentrations of power in government is, in no small measure, a direct outgrowth of the history and influences discussed in this chapter.

Today, written constitutions (largely based on the U.S. example) are the norm. Unwritten constitutions, such as those in the United Kingdom, Israel, and New Zealand, are now the exception. Yet the success of our Constitution depends not only on the strength and flexibility of its own structure but also on the convergence of other less-definable factors, including timing and luck, coupled with an underlying commitment to the rule of law. This makes it more difficult to determine how, when, or even whether the success of the U.S. Constitution can be duplicated in other countries.

We tend to take the success of our system of government for granted and forget that its structure was not preordained. As we have seen, the framers of the Constitution had fundamentally different views on many issues. Many aspects of our government could have been different if competing arguments had won at the Constitutional Convention, state ratifying conventions, or any number of other points in our history.

For example, think of how things might have been different if the United States had not approved a written Constitution and embraced judicial review as a mechanism to enforce it. We could have survived—and probably survived quite well—without either of them (the United Kingdom has), but the consequences to you and our democratic system would have been quite profound. We will see in future chapters how much judicial review touches all of our lives. School desegregation, abortion rights, and free speech protections—to name just a few things shaped by judicial review—would have had to come from political action rather than the courts. That means that some of the rights you now expect might have been delayed or never even granted. But it also means that politicians would have had to confront some issues on which they now defer to courts. The result would have been a system worse in some ways and perhaps better in others, but the result would have had a direct impact on your life.

As a final cautionary note, it is worth remembering that at the end of the day, the words of the Constitution are not enough to guarantee either liberty or the rule of law. Those words must be enforced. Many governments—including dictatorial regimes—have had constitutions with lofty but often meaningless language protecting basic rights. Even in our own country, African Americans were denied fundamental rights, such as the ability to vote, long after the Thirteenth Amendment to the Constitution had abolished slavery, the Fourteenth Amendment guaranteed the equal protection of the laws, and the Fifteenth Amendment proclaimed that the right to vote would not be abridged because of race, color, or previous condition of servitude. As the great twentieth-century American judge Learned Hand once wrote: "Liberty lies in the hearts of men and women; when it dies there, no constitution, no law, no court can save it; no constitution, no law, no court can even do much to help it."[57]

# Critical Thinking Questions

1. Constitution making often takes place in crisis-laden, post-conflict situations that provide disincentives to cooperation and make the creation of a successful constitution difficult. Remember that the first attempt to create a constitution for the United States—the Articles of Confederation—failed. What factors account for the successful drafting and ratification of the subsequent U.S. Constitution?

2. Imagine if round-the-clock cable news networks, attack ads, and the Internet had existed when our Constitution was written and ratified. How might they have changed the process? Would it have been harder for James Madison to prevail over Patrick Henry in today's media environment? Why or why not?

3. Identify ways in which the original Constitution was undemocratic. Assess the strengths and weaknesses of those provisions. How have amendments made the Constitution more democratic? What undemocratic features remain? Should any of these remaining features be altered or abolished? If so, which ones, and how?

4. Think about the four core principles of the Constitution discussed in this chapter: republicanism, federalism, separation of powers, and checks and balances. Each influences the way government operates and the policies it enacts. Now think about a policy issue that is important to you—for example, education, health care reform, or the legalization of marijuana—and assess how each of these principles affects the development and implementation of that policy.

## Key Terms

Visit edge.sagepub.com/maltese to help you accomplish your coursework goals in an easy-to-use learning environment.

RosalreneBetancourt 12 / Alamy Stock Photo

# 3
# FEDERALISM

## After reading this chapter, you should be able to do the following:

- Define federalism and explore the roots and functions, as well as the strengths and weaknesses, of the U.S. federal system.

- Differentiate between powers allocated to the national government and to the states as outlined by the U.S. Constitution.

- Compare dual and cooperative federalism and discuss how each affects the balance of power between the national government and the states.

- Explain how two landmark cases under the Marshall Court helped to establish a balance of power between the federal and state governments.

- Analyze the resurgence of states' rights in the period leading up to the Civil War.

- Discuss the evolution of federalism during the New Deal era.

- Understand the continuing evolution of federalism during the last half of the twentieth century and into the twenty-first century.

## Perspective: "Sanctuary Cities": What Are They and Why Does the U.S. Have Them?

Five days after taking office in January 2017, President Donald J. Trump signed an executive order to block so-called sanctuary cities from receiving federal funds. Describing the move as an effort "to ensure the public safety of the American people," the president characterized sanctuary cities as dangerous enclaves that "willfully violate Federal law in an attempt to shield aliens from removal from the United States"—adding that many of these aliens "are criminals" whose protection is "contrary to the national interest."[1]

What, exactly, are sanctuary cities? In fact, they are not necessarily cities but rather jurisdictional areas (which may extend to counties or even, in some instances, states) that have adopted policies designed to resist federal directives that local law enforcement aid federal officials in finding, arresting, and deporting undocumented immigrants. There are even "sanctuary schools" (both at the K–12 and college/university level) that have refused to share information with federal officials about students who may be undocumented.[2]

Supporters of sanctuary cities—relying on a fundamental tenet of states' rights—argue that the Tenth Amendment of the Constitution shields state and local governments from being compelled by the national government to use (or "commandeer") their resources—such as local jails and police officers—to enforce federal immigration laws.[3] For example, jurisdictions may decline to detain individuals suspected of being undocumented in local jails. Federal Immigration and Customs Enforcement (ICE) can only request that local authorities detain such individuals; it does not have the authority to compel such detainment. Some states and cities object to ICE policy that allows such individuals to be detained without a court warrant and so refuse to comply.

President Trump's executive order, however, was not explicitly directed at the refusal of sanctuary cities to detain individuals (even though Trump's rhetoric sometimes made it sound as though it was) but rather at a jurisdiction's refusal to convey certain information to ICE. For example, California policy prohibited local jail officials from sharing information about the immigration status of their inmates without a warrant signed by a judge. In issuing the Executive Order, the president pointed to federal law (8 USC 1373, Section B), which prohibits states or localities from implementing policies to prevent the sharing of such information.

Questions nonetheless remained about the constitutionality of the president's executive order. The Ninth Circuit Court of Appeals (which covers California) declared the executive order unconstitutional in August 2018 on separation of powers grounds, arguing that only Congress has the power to control spending under the Constitution. Thus, the majority concluded, the president could not unilaterally withhold funding, as threatened in the executive order. The Seventh Circuit Court of Appeals issued a similar ruling in response to Chicago's challenge to the executive order, although the Ninth Circuit Court of Appeals ruled in favor of the administration's policy in July 2019,[4] with the issue likely to be resolved by the Supreme Court. As of April 2019, there were nine sanctuary states and over 150 sanctuary cities and counties within a total of 27 states.[5]

The tension reflected in the debate between sanctuary cities and the Trump administration is a direct result of our system of federalism, where power is divided between the national government and the states. Germany, one of the few countries in Europe with a federal system, has also seen some local resistance to national immigration policy. For example, in 2017, some German states refused to deport individuals to Afghanistan whose asylum claims had been denied by the German national government. They did so using their legal right to issue a temporary moratorium on deportations.[6]

But what about the United Kingdom or the majority of European countries, which have unitary systems, where political power is concentrated at the national level? "Sanctuary cities" have sprung up there, too, but with a quite different meaning than the term has in the U.S. Sometimes called *refuge cities*, *cities of asylum*, and *cities of welcome*, these are municipalities that are committed to welcoming refugees and asylum seekers.[7] Such hospitality ranges from building a refugee reception center in Grande-Synthe, France, to efforts in Thessaloniki, Greece, to integrate refugees into the community rather than isolating them in a camp.[8]

Supporters of sanctuary cities argue that the federal government is inappropriately infringing on states' rights by requiring them to share information with immigration authorities.

While sanctuary cities in unitary systems may take charge of integrating migrants because of a perception that the national government is not living up to its responsibilities, they do not typically resist national directives in the way that U.S. sanctuary cities do. Italy is an exception. There, a group of mayors in several cities refused in 2019 to obey the Security Decree issued by Italy's populist interior minister that did away with humanitarian protections for asylum seekers, claiming the decree to be unconstitutional. But even in Italy, the question was not about the division of power between the national government and cities (as it is in the U.S.), but rather a disagreement about the constitutionality of a particular federal action.[9]

Understanding how different approaches to dividing governmental power leads to different conceptions of things such as sanctuary cities is what this chapter is all about. ◀◀

# UNDERSTANDING FEDERALISM

Issues involving federalism affect you daily, whether you realize it or not. They have provoked heated debate on a wide array of issues that range from sanctuary cities to education policy, health care reform, and same-sex marriage.

Except for a few tiny nations, all countries have more than one layer of government; they have not only a central, national government but also regional governments (called such things as *states*, *provinces*, *regions*, or *cantons*, depending on the country). *Federalism*—a defining characteristic of the U.S. Constitution—requires that power be divided between these two layers of government. In the United States, the duty of interpreting how the Constitution delineates these powers falls to the Supreme Court. Whether its members are cooperative federalists or dual federalists makes a huge difference. *Cooperative federalists* read constitutional clauses broadly to expand the power of Congress. *Dual federalists*, on the other hand, see such expansion as an invasion of states' rights. Congress's ability to enact Social Security, minimum wage laws, gun control legislation, child labor laws, and an individual mandate that requires everyone to purchase health care insurance are only some of the issues that hang in the balance of this debate. So, too, is the ability of states to pass more stringent environmental standards than the federal government, to allow the use of either medical or recreational marijuana, and to determine minimum drinking ages. To understand these debates, we must first explore the roots and functions of the U.S. federal system.

## THE FEDERAL SYSTEM

Unlike most other democracies in the world, the United States formally divides power between the national and state governments to form a **federal system** of government. The Constitution gives Congress the authority to legislate in certain specific areas while reserving other legislative powers to the states. Power is divided, with the national government having authority over some issues and states having authority over others. As such, two layers of government control the same geographic area and group of people, but each layer is responsible for different political issues. However, the delineation between these two layers is not always clear. The resulting gray areas, where reasonable people disagree about whether the national government or the states have authority to act, can make federalism somewhat difficult to understand. In addition to dividing certain powers, our federal system ensures that some powers are shared. For example, both states and the national government have the power to tax.

The first American attempt at self-governance, the Articles of Confederation, employed a very different governing structure: a confederal system. In a **confederal system**, ultimate authority rests primarily with regional entities (such as states) that have banded together to form a league of independent governments. A central government may exist, as it did under the Articles of Confederation, but it is created by the regional governments and has only limited powers, usually associated with defense and foreign affairs. No individual country today has a true confederal system, but the European Union (EU), which includes most of the countries of Europe, is a modern example of a confederation. The power ceded to the EU by its member countries, however, deals primarily with economic issues (the creation of a common market to guarantee the free movement of goods, capital, services, and labor among member countries), as opposed to defense and foreign affairs.

At the opposite extreme of a confederal system is a **unitary system**, which characterizes the vast majority of governments in the world today. In unitary systems, such as those of France or Japan, the central government has ultimate control over all areas of policy. The central government may delegate some of its power to regional or local governments, but unlike a federal system, a unitary system allows the central government to overrule any political decision made by local government. The central government is not, in other words, obligated to share power (as it is under a federal system); it can trump local action whenever it chooses to do so. (See Figure 3.1.)

After having fought and won a revolution to gain independence from Britain and its perceived tyranny, embracing a unitary system in America did not have much appeal. Therefore, the United States created a federal system, becoming the first nation to do so. Although a federal system now exists in a number of other countries, including Australia, Brazil, Canada,

**federal system** A system in which power is formally divided between the national government and regional entities such as states.

**confederal system** A system of government in which power rests primarily with regional entities that have banded together to form a league of independent governments.

**unitary system** A system of government in which the national government has ultimate control over all areas of policy.

## FIGURE 3.1

## *Three Systems of Government*

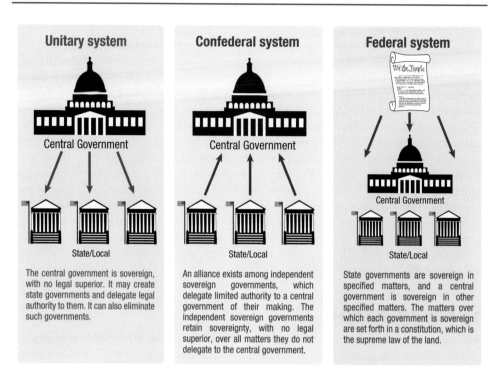

**Unitary system**

Central Government

State/Local

The central government is sovereign, with no legal superior. It may create state governments and delegate legal authority to them. It can also eliminate such governments.

**Confederal system**

Central Government

State/Local

An alliance exists among independent sovereign governments, which delegate limited authority to a central government of their making. The independent sovereign governments retain sovereignty, with no legal superior, over all matters they do not delegate to the central government.

**Federal system**

We the People

Central Government

State/Local

State governments are sovereign in specified matters, and a central government is sovereign in other specified matters. The matters over which each government is sovereign are set forth in a constitution, which is the supreme law of the land.

## FIGURE 3.2

## *Federations of the World*

*Source: Shively,* Power and Choice, *15th Edition.*

Germany, India, and Mexico, countries with a federal system remain a distinct minority. Federal systems tend to be found in larger countries (with some notable exceptions, such as Belgium). Thus, while federal systems make up only 10 percent of the world's countries, they encompass 38 percent of the world's people and cover 49 percent of the world's land area (see Figure 3.2).

In the United States, a division of power exists not only between the national government and the states but also between the state and local governments. This division varies from state to state, as does the number of governmental units within a particular state. Today, power in the United States is divided among more than 89,000 governmental units at the national, state, and local levels, resulting in a very complicated system of decision making.

## STRENGTHS AND WEAKNESSES OF A FEDERAL SYSTEM

The sharing of power between the national government and the states reflected the framers' belief in limited government. They feared that concentrations of power would breed tyranny. Thus, through separation of powers, they divided power horizontally at the national level between the three coequal branches of government—legislative, executive, and judicial—and established a system of checks and balances. At the same time, they used federalism to divide power vertically between the national government and the states. The resulting division of power not only gives individual states autonomy to deal as they see fit with policy areas over which they have control (such as education) but also increases the number of opportunities for people to influence and control different units of government.

This dispersal of power is thought to be one of the great strengths of federalism. In addition to protecting against dangerous concentrations of power and allowing a degree of autonomy to the states, federalism gives individual states the opportunity to experiment with different types of policy responses to public problems. As U.S. Supreme Court Justice Louis Brandeis once put it, "It is one of the happy incidents of the federal system that a single courageous state may, if its citizens choose, serve as a laboratory; and try novel, social and economic experiments without risk to the rest of the country."[10] Thus, individual states have been able to experiment with everything from educational policy to the legalization of medical usage of marijuana (currently permitted in over half the states). Federalism has also allowed states to give greater protection than the national government to issues such as the environment (something President Trump wanted to roll back).

Yet, as critics have noted, federalism also has its weaknesses. For instance, although dispersal of power may give citizens more opportunity to influence the political process, it also provides more veto points that can be used to stifle action on important issues. Likewise, state autonomy can translate into inaction; states may be unresponsive to policy problems that fall under their purview. And while federalism may allow states to experiment with different types of policy responses, variation among states can lead to inconsistencies in the way citizens are treated in different states. At its worst, states' rights can become a justification for policies that undermine social justice, such as racial segregation and Jim Crow laws (see Chapter 5).

# THE CONSTITUTIONAL ALLOCATION OF THE POWERS OF GOVERNMENT

Ever since the founding of the United States, a debate has persisted about how to divide power between the national government and the states. The Articles of Confederation came down decidedly in favor of the states. Then the U.S. Constitution created a federal system, with the national government and the states sharing power. However, the language of the Constitution leaves the precise balance of power between the two ambiguous. Such ambiguity was a compromise between those delegates who wanted a very strong national government and those who supported states' rights. Each side hoped their interpretation of this ambiguous language would prevail later on, but the result has been ongoing debate about the balance of power.

## NATIONAL POWERS

When states entered into the Constitution, they specifically delegated certain powers to the new national government. Chief among these are those given to Congress. Article I, Section 8

## TABLE 3.1
## *National Powers*

Congress's enumerated powers include but are not limited to the authority to do the following:

- Tax, borrow, and coin money
- Regulate interstate commerce
- Declare war
- Provide for an army and navy
- Make uniform naturalization laws
- Create a system of federal courts

**necessary and proper (elastic) clause** The last clause of Article I, Section 8 of the Constitution, which authorizes Congress to make "all laws which shall be necessary and proper" for executing the Constitution's enumerated powers; sometimes called the *elastic clause* because it allows congressional powers to expand.

**supremacy clause** Article VI, Clause 2 of the Constitution specifying that federal laws and treaties passed pursuant to the Constitution trump contradictory state laws dealing with the same topic.

**Tenth Amendment** The amendment to the Constitution that says, "The powers not delegated to the United States by the Constitution, nor prohibited by it to the States, are reserved to the States respectively, or to the people."

**reserved powers** The powers not delegated to the national government by the Constitution that are retained by states under the Tenth Amendment.

**police powers** The powers reserved to the states under the Tenth Amendment dealing with health, safety, public welfare, and morality.

of the Constitution includes a laundry list of specific congressional powers known as the *enumerated powers* (see Chapter 2 and Table 3.1).

In addition to these enumerated powers, the last clause of Article I, Section 8, known as the **necessary and proper clause**, gives Congress the power "to make all laws which shall be necessary and proper for carrying into Execution the foregoing Powers, and all other Powers vested by this Constitution in the Government of the United States, or in any Department or Officer thereof." The powers exercised by Congress under this clause are called *implied powers*, since (unlike the *enumerated powers*) they are not listed specifically in the Constitution. The necessary and proper clause is sometimes also referred to as the *elastic clause* because it allows the powers of Congress to expand like an elastic band. Just how elastic this clause should be has long been the subject of intense debate.

Starting with the Thirteenth Amendment, which abolished slavery, several constitutional amendments have included an enabling clause, which gives Congress the power to enforce the provisions of the amendment through appropriate legislation. Enabling clauses, therefore, allow Congress's power to expand. As with implied powers, however, determining what legislation is "appropriate" (and, thus, how much Congress's power can expand) has been the focus of debate.

Article VI of the Constitution contains the so-called **supremacy clause**. This clause states that the U.S. Constitution, all "Laws of the United States which shall be made in Pursuance thereof" (in other words, laws constitutionally enacted under Congress's enumerated or implied powers, or as a result of power derived from enabling clauses), and "all Treaties made . . . under the authority of the United States" are "the supreme Law of the Land." This means that states must obey each of these and that "the Judges in every State shall be bound thereby, any Thing in the Constitution or Laws of any State to the Contrary notwithstanding." At first glance, this seems very clear-cut: Anytime a state law or a provision of a state constitution conflicts with national power in the form of the U.S. Constitution, an act of Congress, or a treaty, it must give way to "the supreme Law of the Land." Yet, the ongoing debate about how much power Congress can legitimately derive from either the necessary and proper clause or the enabling clauses raises persistent contention: Precisely which laws are made in pursuance of the Constitution and are thus legitimately "supreme"?

## STATE POWERS

Those who opposed ratification of the Constitution did so because they felt it gave the new national government too much power—power that could be used to infringe upon both individual liberties (such as freedom of speech) and states' rights. Ultimately, ratification came as the result of a promise to add a Bill of Rights through the process of amendment (see Chapter 2). Among the first ten amendments that collectively form the Constitution's Bill of Rights, the **Tenth Amendment** serves as the major weapon in the arsenal of states' rights.

The Tenth Amendment says that any power that the Constitution has not delegated to the federal government, nor prohibited the states from exercising, is "reserved to the States respectively, or to the people." Among these **reserved powers** are states' **police powers**: those used by states to manage and maintain public order through laws designed to protect (police) the health, safety, morals, and public welfare of their people. Police powers also permit state regulation of things such as crime, education, marriage, and traffic. Since these powers are left to individual states, the resulting laws may—and do—vary from state to state. However, the ambiguity of constitutional language can make it difficult to draw a clear line between delegated powers and reserved powers. In fact, the exact parameters of the police powers have fluctuated across time due to the U.S. Supreme Court's changing interpretation of constitutional language.

For example, shifting interpretations of the commerce clause and the Tenth Amendment have allowed Congress to legislate in areas long thought to be the province of the states. Federal minimum wage laws were once routinely struck down by the Supreme Court as an unconstitutional infringement of state police powers under the Tenth Amendment. Now the Court upholds federal minimum wage laws as an acceptable exercise of Congress's commerce clause power. Neither the language of the Tenth Amendment nor the commerce clause changed—only the Court's interpretation of that language. We will examine specific examples of such changes later in this chapter.

In addition to their reserved powers, states have certain powers that are specifically listed in the Constitution (such as the power, enumerated in Article I, Section 4 to determine the "times, places, and manner" of holding elections for members of the U.S. House and Senate; and the power, enumerated in Article VII, to ratify amendments to the U.S. Constitution). A summary of the states' reserved and enumerated powers can be found in Table 3.2.

## CONCURRENT POWERS

Some powers belong exclusively to the national government (such as the power to declare war). Others belong exclusively to the states (such as the power to establish local governments within a state). However, some powers are shared between the national government and the states. These are known as the concurrent powers (see Table 3.3).

The power to tax is one example of a concurrent power. Although there are some limits on what types of tax each level can impose—states cannot impose a tariff (an import tax) without the consent of Congress and the federal government cannot impose a tax on real estate—both the national government and the states can impose excise taxes (non-property taxes, such as taxes on payrolls, estates, gasoline, and cigarettes). For example, Congress raised the federal tax on a pack of cigarettes from 39 cents a pack to $1.01 a pack in 2009.[11] In addition to this federal tax, individual states are free to add their own tax on cigarettes and to choose their own tax rate. As of 2019, the states of Connecticut and New York had the highest rate ($4.35 per pack) and Missouri had the lowest (17 cents per pack), with the District of Columbia having the highest rate of all ($4.50 per pack).[12] Thus, the cost of cigarettes—and gasoline and alcohol and many other goods and services—can vary considerably from state to state and even from county to county and city to city, since both can also impose taxes. For example, the tax rate on cigarettes in Illinois in 2019 was $2.98, but Cook County added another $3.00 tax, and the city of Chicago (which is in Cook County) added another $1.18, making Chicago the most expensive city in the country to buy cigarettes ($7.16 in state, county, and city taxes alone).[13]

Other concurrent powers include the ability to establish courts, borrow money, and charter banks and corporations. Once again, however, the precise line between exclusive powers and concurrent powers can change over time, largely because of changing interpretations of constitutional language by the Supreme Court.

## PROHIBITED POWERS

In addition to granting powers to the national government and the states, the Constitution also prohibits certain specific powers. Article I, Section 9 of the Constitution lists powers denied to Congress. For example, Congress is prohibited from passing a bill of attainder (a law declaring a person or group of persons guilty of a crime without a trial) or an ex post facto law (a law that makes an act a criminal offense retroactively, even though the act was not a crime

**TABLE 3.2**

## State Powers

Powers belonging to the states include the authority to do the following:

- Provide for public health, safety, and morality
- Regulate commerce within the state
- Establish local governments
- Ratify amendments to the U.S. Constitution
- Determine voter qualifications
- Conduct elections

**TABLE 3.3**

## Concurrent Powers

Concurrent powers include the authority to do the following:

- Levy taxes
- Borrow money
- Charter banks and corporations
- Establish courts

concurrent powers Powers shared by the national government and the states (both, for example, have the power to tax).

when it was committed). Among other things, Congress is also prohibited from granting titles of nobility and from favoring one state over another when exercising its authority to regulate interstate commerce.

Article I, Section 10 of the Constitution lists powers denied to the states. States, for example, are prohibited from entering into treaties, coining money, altering obligations of contracts, or issuing letters of marquee and reprisal (warrants authorizing what would otherwise be an act of piracy: the attack and capture of a ship). And, similar to Congress, states are prohibited from passing bills of attainder, ex post facto laws, and titles of nobility.

## RELATIONSHIPS AMONG THE STATES

States, of course, have to get along with each other. Bitter rivalries had existed among the states during the Articles of Confederation as they jostled for economic advantage. Mindful of this, the framers of the Constitution took effort to include provisions for states to resolve disputes and to assure that states recognize each other's contracts and judicial decrees. Article IV contains three clauses that focus on relationships among the states.

First, the **full faith and credit clause** requires each state to give "full Faith and Credit . . . to the public Acts, Records, and judicial Proceedings of every other State." As the Supreme Court has explained, each state existed under the Articles of Confederation as an "independent foreign entity" that was "free to ignore obligations created under the laws or by the judicial proceedings" of other states. The full faith and credit clause meant to change that by making states "integral parts of a single nation."[14] In particular, the clause ensures that things such as contracts and judicial decrees from one state are recognized and honored in every other state (thus preventing a contract made in one state from becoming void after crossing state lines). A primary purpose of the clause was to protect commerce and trade, since interstate business transactions depend upon enforceable contracts. Recently, however, some gun rights advocates have suggested that Congress use the full faith and credit clause to mandate "concealed-carry reciprocity." Such reciprocity would allow the resident of a state that allows the carrying of concealed weapons to obtain "non-resident" permits to carry them when they travel—even in states that prohibit their own residents from carrying concealed weapons.[15]

Second, the **privileges and immunities clause** forbids a state from denying citizens of other states the rights it confers on its own citizens. Thus, a citizen of one state cannot be precluded from traveling through or residing in other states or, while there, be prohibited from purchasing property or denied the protection of the law.

Third, the **extradition clause** deals with someone who is charged with a crime in one state but flees justice. If that person is found in another state, the extradition clause requires that state to return (extradite), upon request, that person to the state where the crime was committed.

In addition, Article I allows states, with the consent of Congress, to enter into **interstate compacts**. Interstate compacts are contracts between two or more states that create an agreement on a particular policy issue. Rarely used before the twentieth century, interstate compacts have become common since World War II. Over 200 such compacts are currently in operation, most of which have been created in the past 75 years. In general, there are three broad types of interstate contracts:

- border compacts, which establish or alter the boundaries of states;
- advisory compacts, which create a commission to study a problem and then issue a report offering advice to the respective states; and
- regulatory compacts, which establish an administrative agency to develop rules and regulations governing a particular issue.[16]

Interstate compacts cover a broad range of policy issues, including conservation, resource management, transportation, education, mental health, civil defense, and emergency management. A famous example of a regulatory compact is the Port Authority of New York and New Jersey, created in 1921 to build, maintain, and operate bridges and

**full faith and credit clause** The requirement of Article IV, Section 1 of the Constitution that requires states to recognize "the public Acts, Records, and judicial Proceedings of every other state."

**privileges and immunities clause** A provision of Article IV, Section 2 of the Constitution that forbids a state from denying citizens of other states the rights it confers upon its own citizens.

**extradition clause** A provision of Article IV, Section 2 of the Constitution that requires states to return (extradite), upon request, a fugitive who has fled the law to the state that has jurisdiction over the crime.

**interstate compacts** Contracts between two or more states that create an agreement on a particular policy issue.

tunnels between the two states. Over the next two decades, the Port Authority built, among others, the George Washington Bridge, the Goethals Bridge, the Holland Tunnel, and the Lincoln Tunnel. The Port Authority was also charged with building terminals, piers, airports, and even the World Trade Center in Manhattan—all designed to improve commerce and trade.[17]

Finally, Article III, Section 2 of the Constitution gives the Supreme Court the authority to resolve disputes among states, such as those involving water rights. Such disputes are among the few types of cases that can actually be initiated before the Supreme Court under its original jurisdiction (see Chapter 14) rather than coming to the Supreme Court on appeal.

The Bayonne Bridge, which connects Bayonne, New Jersey, with Staten Island, New York, is operated by the Port Authority of New York and New Jersey, an example of an interstate compact.

# COMPETING INTERPRETATIONS OF FEDERALISM

As we have already discussed, ambiguity in constitutional language dealing with federalism has led to much debate over the relative balance of power between the national government and the states. This disagreement is reflected in two competing interpretations of federalism: dual federalism and cooperative federalism.

## DUAL FEDERALISM

Dual federalism is an interpretation of federalism that favors states' rights. It views the Constitution as a contract among preexisting states. Under the Constitution, these states willingly delegated certain powers to the new national government, but dual federalists believe that states retain all powers not specifically delegated.

Dual federalists also believe that the Constitution is a fixed document (rather than a "living" document that is subject to changing interpretations). They emphasize the Constitution's clearly delineated express powers (such as Congress's enumerated powers) and believe that the Constitution should be interpreted consistently over time.

Thus, they reject the idea that judges can use ambiguous language in the Constitution to augment the powers of the national government at the expense of the states. Therefore, they embrace a very narrow interpretation of Congress's implied powers. To them, the necessary and proper clause allows only a very limited expansion of congressional power to do those things essential to carrying out the enumerated powers. There must, in other words, be a very direct link between enumerated and implied powers.

Dual federalists also firmly embrace the Tenth Amendment, which they believe stands as a significant limit on the power of the national government and an important protector of states' rights. They believe that any actions of Congress that go beyond the enumerated powers and a very limited interpretation of the implied powers violate the Tenth Amendment. They further believe that the Supreme Court should employ the Tenth Amendment to rein in the national government and protect the prerogatives of the states.

When considering the relationship between the levels of government, dual federalists view the national government and the states as dual sovereigns—two relative equals, each of which is supreme in its own sphere.

Finally, dual federalists believe that the proper role of the Supreme Court is to act as an umpire between these two equals. It should uphold the right of the national government to exercise its express powers but strike down attempts by the national government to use broad readings of constitutional language to intrude upon the reserved powers of the states. They consider such attempts to be power grabs that violate the Tenth Amendment.

**dual federalism** An interpretation of federalism that favors states' rights and regards states and the national government as "dual sovereigns" (two relative equals).

## COOPERATIVE FEDERALISM

**Cooperative federalism** is an interpretation of the Constitution that favors national supremacy. Although the term *cooperative federalism* was coined in the twentieth century, its basic tenets can be used to describe earlier eras, such as the national supremacy associated with the Supreme Court in the early 1800s.[18]

Cooperative federalism views the Constitution as a contract among the people rather than a contract among the states. The dual federalists' belief that the Constitution was a compact among the states allowed for the possibility that states could secede—leave the Union—as the Confederacy did during the Civil War. The cooperative federalist perspective rejects that possibility and puts ultimate authority with the people rather than with the states.

Rather than viewing the Constitution as a fixed document, cooperative federalists view the Constitution as an organic—"living"—document. They believe that the Constitution contains ambiguous language for a reason: to allow the document to adapt to changing times. Thus, rather than emphasizing the fixed nature of the express powers of the Constitution, as dual federalists do, cooperative federalists emphasize the ability to expand the power of the national government through a very broad interpretation of the necessary and proper clause. This broad interpretation allows Congress a wider range of implied powers than a dual federalist interpretation would allow: Congress can do anything that is useful or helpful to carry out its enumerated powers. There need only be, in other words, a very tangential link between the enumerated and implied powers.

In stark contrast with dual federalists, cooperative federalists minimize the significance of the Tenth Amendment. Rather than seeing it as a meaningful limit on the power of the national government, they dismiss the Tenth Amendment as a mere "truism."[19] In other words, the Tenth Amendment simply states the obvious: Powers that do not belong to the national government belong to the states or the people. Cooperative federalists do not believe that powers of the national government have to be expressly delegated but instead assert that they can include implied and even inherent power (in other words, powers that any sovereign government must hold, whether or not they are expressly enumerated or implied, such as defending its borders or acquiring new territory).

Quite simply, under a cooperative federalist view, the national government has whatever power it is able to derive—be it from narrowly defined enumerated powers or from broadly construed implied or inherent powers. Unlike the dual federalists, cooperative federalists do not believe the Tenth Amendment can be used to prevent these broad interpretations of implied and inherent powers. This interpretation is what reduces the Tenth Amendment to the truism that states simply have whatever power is left over.

When considering the relationship between the levels of government, cooperative federalists view the national government as supreme. They see the relationship as strictly hierarchical (as opposed to the system of dual sovereignty that dual federalists espouse).

Finally, rather than viewing the Supreme Court as an umpire between two dual sovereigns, cooperative federalists consider the Supreme Court to be a player on the national team. Thus, the Supreme Court should uphold broad interpretations of constitutional language (such as the commerce clause or the necessary and proper clause) that can be used to expand the power of the national government at the expense of the states.

**cooperative federalism** An interpretation of federalism that favors national supremacy and assumes that states will cooperate in the enforcement of federal regulations.

# EARLY PRECEDENTS: NATIONAL SUPREMACY PREVAILS

John Marshall, appointed chief justice of the Supreme Court in 1801 by President John Adams, was the longest-serving chief justice in the history of the Supreme Court. He presided over several landmark cases that expanded the power of Congress at the expense of the states. Chief among these are *McCulloch v. Maryland* (1819) and *Gibbons v. Ogden* (1824), both of which reflected the views of cooperative federalism.

## McCULLOCH V. MARYLAND (1819)

At issue in *McCulloch v. Maryland* was whether Congress had the authority to create a national bank. The enumerated powers did not specifically give such authority to Congress. Those who said that Congress had the authority anyway, such as Alexander Hamilton, the first secretary of the treasury, embraced a broad cooperative federalist interpretation of the elastic clause and argued that creating a national bank was "necessary and proper" (that is, useful or helpful) to carrying out Congress's enumerated powers. After all, the Constitution specifically gave Congress the power to collect taxes, borrow money, coin money, and regulate the value of money. Surely, he argued, a national bank would facilitate these enumerated powers.[20] Dual federalists who believed Congress did not have authority to create a national bank, such as Thomas Jefferson, argued that a national bank was not absolutely necessary or essential for these enumerated powers to be carried out.

Congress embraced Hamilton's position and created the First Bank of the United States in 1791 and the Second Bank of the United States in 1816. To express its opposition, the state of Maryland then passed legislation to tax all banks operating in the state that were not chartered by the state. James McCulloch, the head of the Baltimore branch of the Second Bank, refused to pay the tax. This led to a lawsuit between McCulloch and Maryland that ended up in the Supreme Court.

The Court confronted two legal questions when deciding *McCulloch v. Maryland:* Did Congress have the authority to create a national bank? And if so, did the state of Maryland have the authority to tax the Baltimore branch of that bank? The Court unanimously decided that Congress did have the authority to create a national bank. It concluded that creating the bank was a legitimate exercise of Congress's implied powers. In so doing, the Court embraced Hamilton's broad, cooperative federalist interpretation of the necessary and proper clause. By assuming that the necessary and proper clause allows Congress to do those things that are appropriate (as opposed to essential) to carrying out its enumerated powers and consistent with the *spirit* (as well as the letter) of the Constitution, the ruling paved the way for Congress to significantly expand its powers and to do so at the expense of the states.

With regard to the second question, the Court concluded that the state of Maryland could not tax the Baltimore branch of the national bank without violating the supremacy clause. As Marshall stated, "the power to tax involves the power to destroy."[21] States "have no power, by taxation or otherwise, to retard, impede, burden or in any manner control the operations of the constitutional laws enacted by Congress."[22] Since Congress has the authority to create a national bank, a state cannot punish that bank, discourage its operation within its borders, or seek to destroy it through taxation. To do so would violate the supremacy of national law.

The Supreme Court's answers to these legal questions had profound consequences. Its broad interpretation of the necessary and proper clause remains, to this day, an important source of congressional power. In addition, the limit on the power of states to tax the national bank became an important precedent that continues to prevent states from retaliating against or otherwise impeding other entities created by Congress, such as regulatory agencies, that operate within states.

## GIBBONS V. OGDEN (1824)

In *Gibbons v. Ogden*, the Marshall Court again ruled in favor of broad national power, this time in relation to the **commerce clause** of the Constitution (Article I, Section 8). Now the debate focused on how broadly to read the enumerated powers of the commerce clause, which gives Congress the authority to regulate interstate commerce. But what, exactly, does this authority entail?

Dual federalists believe the commerce clause gives Congress only those powers essential to regulating the trade of actual goods and commodities among the states. Therefore, Congress's power is largely limited to regulating the transportation of these goods and commodities across state lines. Cooperative federalists believe the commerce clause gives Congress the authority to regulate anything that has even an incidental effect on interstate commerce. Thus, in the twentieth century,

> **commerce clause** Article I, Section 8 of the Constitution, which gives Congress the authority to "regulate Commerce with foreign Nations, and among the several States, and with the Indian Tribes."

Even in the nineteenth century, the waterways around New York City were bustling, making control of ferry service across the Hudson a contentious issue.

cooperative federalist interpretations of the commerce clause expanded Congress's power to include regulation of the workplace (including the passage of minimum wage laws and maximum hour laws), which dual federalists insist should fall to states under their police powers.

*Gibbons v. Ogden* set an early precedent for a broad reading of commerce clause power. The case dealt with whether navigation and the transportation of people (rather than of goods and commodities) across state lines were subject to regulation by Congress. Why did this become a question? Aaron Ogden operated a steam-powered ferryboat between New Jersey and New York. The state of New York controlled who could navigate in those waters, and Ogden operated his boat with a state-sanctioned license (part of a steamboat monopoly). Soon thereafter, he faced competition from another ferryboat operated by Thomas Gibbons. Instead of a state-sanctioned license, Gibbons had a federal license granted to him by Congress. Unhappy with the competition, Ogden obtained an injunction from a New York state court to prevent Gibbons from operating his steamboat without a state-sanctioned license. Gibbons appealed, arguing that a license from Congress trumped a state-sanctioned one.

In an opinion again written by Chief Justice Marshall, the Supreme Court embraced the broad interpretation of Congress's commerce clause power and determined that Congress did have the power to issue the license.[23] Having concluded that Congress had the power to regulate navigation—not only the transportation of goods and commodities—and thus to issue the license to Gibbons, the Court then used the supremacy clause to conclude that New York State could not grant a steamboat monopoly that would render that license void. To do so would interfere with Congress's commerce clause power.

Again, this broad interpretation of the commerce clause has had profound long-term consequences. It paved the way for post-1937 rulings by the Supreme Court that allowed Congress to use the commerce clause to pass legislation dealing with everything from minimum wage laws to racial discrimination in restaurants.

## THE RESURGENCE OF STATES' RIGHTS

Although the Supreme Court under John Marshall solidly embraced the idea of national supremacy, the debate over federal power versus states' rights was far from settled. Indeed, it remained one of the most significant and divisive political issues of the 1800s. John Marshall's successor as chief justice, Roger Taney, moved the Supreme Court in a decidedly dual federalist direction. The most notorious ruling of the Taney Court—and possibly the most notorious Supreme Court ruling of all time—came in the infamous *Dred Scott* case of 1857 (see Chapter 5). Embracing dual federalism, the Court concluded that Congress had exceeded its powers when it abolished slavery in the territories. By insisting that the issue of slavery be left to individual states, the Court effectively ruled out a national legislative solution to the issue. In so doing, the ruling helped to precipitate the Civil War.

### NULLIFICATION, SECESSION, AND THE CIVIL WAR

**nullification** The concept that states can invalidate federal laws that they believe to be unconstitutional.

The debate over slavery was the overriding political issue in the days leading up to the Civil War, and states' rights came to be used as a justification to maintain it. Andrew Jackson's vice president, John C. Calhoun, an outspoken proponent of states' rights, proposed that states should be able to invalidate federal laws that they believed to be unconstitutional through the process of **nullification**.

In contrast with Calhoun, President Jackson—sympathetic to states' rights but convinced that nullification would destroy the Union—rejected the idea of nullification. Undeterred, Calhoun continued to advocate his nullification doctrine. As a result, South Carolina issued a formal Ordinance of Nullification in 1832.[24] Jackson's continued opposition to nullification led Calhoun to resign as his vice president the next month. Congress went on to pass legislation that authorized the use of military force against states that refused to enforce federal law.[25] Advocates of nullification lost the battle, but the seeds of Southern discontent had been sown.

In the decades that followed, slavery further inflamed relations between the national government and the Southern states. The election of Abraham Lincoln as president in 1860 proved to be the last straw. He had made it clear in the campaign that he supported efforts at the national level to prohibit slavery. Building on the concept of nullification and the ideas of coequal sovereignty inherent in dual federalism, Southern states now claimed the right of secession, the ability to withdraw from the Union. South Carolina formally exercised that right on December 20, 1860, and eleven others quickly followed suit. Together, the states that seceded formed the Confederate States of America.

The defeat of the Confederacy in the Civil War seemed to establish once and for all that states cannot secede, a view endorsed by the Supreme Court in *Texas v. White* (1869).[26] Nonetheless, fringe movements at both ends of the political spectrum continue to embrace the idea of secession. Today, the Texas Nationalist Movement calls for the secession of Texas.[27] As of 2009, it claimed that more than 250,000 Texans had signed up in support of that goal.[28] Vermont's secessionist party, called the Second Vermont Republic,[29] ran a slate of nine candidates in statewide elections in 2010. If you think such candidates never win, look to Alaska. There a candidate representing the Alaska Independence Party,[30] Walter Joseph Hickel, drew enough support to be elected governor in 1990. That party's 2006 attempt to place an initiative on the ballot calling for Alaska to secede from the United States was blocked by a ruling of the Alaska Supreme Court, which held that any attempt at secession violated the U.S. Constitution.[31]

Matthew Whitaker, who served as the acting attorney general in the Trump administration after Jeff Sessions resigned, was among those who had earlier advocated a controversial proposal to use the now-discredited doctrine of nullification to invalidate the Affordable Care Act (Obamacare).

## THE RISE AND FALL OF NATIONAL POWER IN THE WAKE OF THE CIVIL WAR

The so-called Civil War Amendments to the Constitution—the Thirteenth (1865), Fourteenth (1868), and Fifteenth Amendments (1870)—greatly expanded the power of the national government. They prohibited slavery, prevented states from abridging the right to vote on account of race, and prohibited states from depriving any person of due process of the law or the equal protection of the laws. Each contained an enabling clause, which expanded Congress's power to enforce the provisions of these amendments.

The modern Texas Nationalist Movement depicts the federal government as an oppressive force and calls for the secession of Texas.

Although it did not happen immediately, the Fourteenth Amendment also paved the way for the incorporation of the Bill of Rights—in other words, making the provisions of the Bill of Rights binding upon states as well as the federal government (see Chapter 4). Thus, the long-term effect of the Fourteenth Amendment has been to restrict the power of states by preventing them from passing legislation that would violate the First Amendment or other specific provisions of the Bill of Rights.

**secession** The act of withdrawing from membership in a federation.

Universal History Archive / Getty Images

In the early twentieth century, child labor was commonplace in factories, mines, and mills like this one in Macon, Georgia. The dual federalist Supreme Court struck down attempts by Congress to regulate the practice. These cases were later overturned after the emergence of a cooperative federalist majority on the Court in 1937.

The Civil War also expanded the role of the national government in other ways. For example, the cost of the war led to the first federal income tax. The war also led the federal government to become involved in a form of social welfare: creating and maintaining a vast pension system for war veterans and war widows. Nonetheless, the debate between dual federalists and cooperative federalists was far from over, and dual federalists soon began to win important victories from the Supreme Court.

As early as 1873, the Supreme Court began to limit the scope of the Fourteenth Amendment.[32] Ten years later, the Court sharply limited the enabling clause power that Congress derived from the Fourteenth Amendment.[33] But the biggest boost to states' rights came in *Plessy v. Ferguson* (1896). By ruling that state-imposed "separate but equal" facilities (such as schools) for whites and blacks did not violate the equal protection clause of the Fourteenth Amendment, the Court gave great leeway to states to impose racial segregation.[34] This laid the groundwork for a broad interpretation of states' rights that allowed states to pass Jim Crow laws and impose barriers to prevent blacks from voting (see Chapter 5).

The Court's narrow, dual federalist interpretation of the commerce clause from 1895 to 1937 also limited Congress's ability to regulate the workplace through such things as child labor laws and minimum wage laws. Starting in 1895, the Court embraced the so-called *direct–indirect* test to delineate congressional power under the commerce clause.[35] According to this test, Congress could only use its commerce clause power to regulate those things that had a direct effect on interstate commerce (such as the actual distribution of goods and commodities across state lines). It could not regulate those things that had only an indirect effect on interstate commerce (such as the production of items shipped in interstate commerce). Thus, Congress could not regulate manufacturing, mining, or agriculture, which the Court considered to be the province of states. Attempts by Congress to pass workplace regulations were mostly struck down by the Supreme Court as violations of the Tenth Amendment.[36] So, too, were attempts by Congress to regulate the economy.

## THE NEW DEAL AND THE RISE OF COOPERATIVE FEDERALISM

The stock market crash of 1929 and the ensuing Great Depression transformed politics in the United States. The Republican Party had dominated national politics since the Civil War, but the Depression led to a partisan realignment—a lasting shift in voters' partisan identification. Republicans, who had controlled the White House and maintained solid control of both houses of Congress since 1921, lost control of all three branches of government in the 1932 elections when Franklin Delano Roosevelt (FDR) won the White House and fellow Democrats took control of the House and the Senate. In contrast, the Supreme Court—given the lifetime tenure of its members—remained unchanged, standing as a dual federalist obstacle to Roosevelt's New Deal.

### THE SUPREME COURT THWARTS THE NEW DEAL

Roosevelt and his fellow New Deal Democrats greatly expanded the power of the national government. In stark contrast to the laissez-faire economic policies of their predecessors, which held that government should defer to the free market and intervene as little as possible in economic affairs, New Dealers believed government intervention in the economy was an essential step toward recovery.

A centerpiece of the New Deal was the National Industrial Recovery Act (1933), or NIRA, which authorized the federal government to regulate industry in order to spur recovery. The NIRA also established a national public works program to create jobs. In the process, the government created vast regulatory structures in the form of the National Recovery Administration and the Public Works Administration. Congress claimed that it had the authority to do this by embracing a broad cooperative federalist interpretation of its commerce clause powers. The Supreme Court, however, was still controlled by dual federalists, and it struck down the NIRA as unconstitutional in *Schechter Poultry Corp. v. United States* (1935).[37]

The Supreme Court struck down other major pieces of New Deal legislation, including legislation that gave the federal government the authority to regulate wages, working hours, and production standards in the coal industry. Continuing to embrace dual federalism, the Court again concluded that Congress did not have authority under the commerce clause to regulate production.[38]

Bettmann / Getty Images

President Roosevelt was furious about the string of defeats handed to him by the Supreme Court. After the Supreme Court invalidated the NIRA in *Schechter*, FDR held a press conference in which he criticized the decision by equating it with the Court's infamous ruling in *Dred Scott*.[39] The press dubbed the four members of the Court who most consistently voted against the New Deal the "Four Horsemen of the Apocalypse."[40] In the battle between the Four Horsemen and Roosevelt, the electorate seemed to come down squarely on the side of Roosevelt. While the Court continued to hand the New Deal more defeats, the president and his New Deal allies won landslide victories in the 1936 elections.

**By 1936, the repudiation of the Republican Party was clear: Democrats won a 333–89 majority in the House and a 75–17 majority in the Senate, and FDR was reelected in a landslide (523 electoral votes to Republican Alf Landon's 8).**

Emboldened, the newly reelected Roosevelt asked Congress to increase the size of the Supreme Court from nine to fifteen members. Several of the rulings against the New Deal had been by 5–4 or 6–3 votes, with dual federalists controlling the majority. Expanding the size of the Court would allow Roosevelt to appoint six new justices with a cooperative federalist perspective who would presumably uphold Congress's power to enact New Deal legislation.

## THE SUPREME COURT EMBRACES COOPERATIVE FEDERALISM

In opposition to the dual federalist "Four Horsemen" of the Supreme Court were three cooperative federalist justices who usually voted to uphold New Deal legislation. The press dubbed them the "Three Musketeers."[41] In addition, there were two decisive "swing" justices on the nine-member Court.[42] In 1937, these two centrist justices joined the Three Musketeers to form a new 5–4 cooperative federalist majority.

Even though the two centrist votes that prompted this shift to cooperative federalism took place before FDR announced his Supreme Court–packing plan, they have sometimes been called "the switch in time that saved nine" because the shift they precipitated undercut the justification for expanding the size of the Court. Cooperative federalists won another victory at the end of the 1937 Supreme Court term when one of the Four Horsemen retired and Roosevelt had the opportunity to replace him. The remaining Horsemen soon retired as well. By the time President Roosevelt died in office in 1945, he had appointed all nine justices on the Court—the result of natural attrition and a presidency unhindered by term limits.[43]

**Between 1935 and 1943, the Works Progress Administration (WPA) created almost 8 million jobs.**

The results of these membership changes were striking. In case after case, the Court went on to overturn dual federalist precedents. In April 1937, the Court upheld the National Labor

Relations Act in a broad cooperative federalist ruling that rejected the rigid interpretation of the direct–indirect test it had used the year before. Now Congress could use its commerce clause power to regulate the production of goods as well as the transportation of goods across state lines. The vote in that case was still 5–4.[44] But only four years later, the transformation was complete. The Court unanimously overturned *Hammer v. Dagenhart*, a landmark 1918 dual federalist ruling that had held that Congress could not use its commerce clause power to regulate child labor by stopping the shipment of goods produced by children across state lines. In its new embrace of cooperative federalism, the Court dismissed the Tenth Amendment as merely a "truism."[45]

### IMPLEMENTING COOPERATIVE FEDERALISM

The expansion of national power made possible by the "switch in time" led to a much more complex relationship between the national government and the states. The old dual federalist relationship has sometimes been described as "layer cake federalism," with each layer of government having clearly defined responsibilities. With the federal government becoming more active in telling states and localities what to do, the cooperative federalist relationship looked more like a swirled marble cake. States now cooperated with the federal government (hence the term *cooperative federalism*) by implementing its rules and regulations rather than having independent control as they did under dual federalism.

## PICTURE YOURSELF···
# Amidst California's "Anti-Okie" Panic of the 1930s

In the 1930s, a period of prolonged drought led to severe dust storms that devastated farms, particularly in the state of Oklahoma and the surrounding Great Plains region. This so-called Dust Bowl struck at the worst possible time—in the midst of the Great Depression. It destroyed millions of acres of farmland and forced tens of thousands of families to abandon their farms and relocate. In all, it is estimated that as many as two million people were left homeless by the Dust Bowl.[a]

Suppose you were one of these impoverished farmers who lost everything and went looking for a better life elsewhere. No matter what state you came from, you would have been derisively dubbed an "Okie" (because so many of the migrants came from Oklahoma). Let's assume you chose to go to California (a particularly popular destination in those days). Would you worry about California letting you in? Probably not, since today, we take it for granted that states cannot prohibit the entry of citizens from other states. But worry you should. Overwhelmed by the tremendous influx of impoverished people from other states, California reacted by trying to keep out their fellow Americans. There, you and your fellow Okies would have been marginalized as "'criminals,' 'troublemakers,' 'parasites,' 'enemies of society,' or, even worse, 'radicals'"—even if you had been a prosperous pillar of your community before the Dust Bowl destroyed your farm.[b]

Had you arrived at the California border in 1936, you would likely have been rudely turned away by armed officers of the Los Angeles Police Department (LAPD). The LAPD Police Chief, James Edgar ("Two-Gun") Davis, deployed 136 of his officers to 16 major points of entry into California to block the migrant caravan. Had you somehow gotten into the state, Davis—who once said that constitutional rights only benefited "crooks and criminals"—would have threatened you with arrest and a 180-day jail term with hard labor.[c] No one in California seems to have suggested building a wall at that time, but some might have welcomed it. In the spring of 1936, the *San Francisco News* commissioned John Steinbeck to write a series of articles about the plight of these migrants. Published in October 1936 as "The Harvest Gypsies," they led to Steinbeck's classic 1939 novel *The Grapes of Wrath*.

Then, in 1937, California passed legislation that criminalized bringing or helping to bring indigent people into the state. Thus, if you had friends or family in California who brought you into the state, they could have been punished, too. That is precisely what happened to a California resident named Edwards. He drove to Texas in 1940 and brought back to California his wife's brother, who was unemployed. For this act of charity, Edwards was tried, convicted, and given a six-month suspended jail sentence.

Is that constitutional? Existing Supreme Court precedent at the time suggested that the California law used to convict Edwards could, indeed, be a valid exercise of California's police power. In an 1837 case, *Mayor of the City of New York v. Miln*, the Court concluded that it is "as necessary for a State to provide precautionary measures against the moral pestilence of paupers, vagabonds, and possibly convicts as it is to guard against the physical pestilence, which may arise from unsound and infectious articles imported."[d]

Edwards, however, appealed his conviction all the way to the Supreme Court. There, despite the earlier ruling in *Miln*, he won—thanks, in no small part, to the Court's 1937 "switch in time" that led to its more expansive cooperative federalist reading of the commerce clause. In a unanimous decision in *Edwards v. California* (1941), the Supreme Court concluded that the law imposed an unconstitutional burden upon interstate commerce. In so doing, the Court also explicitly rejected the language of *Miln*: "Whatever may have been the notion then prevailing, we do not think that it will now be seriously contended that, because a person is without employment and without funds, he constitutes a 'moral pestilence.' Poverty and immorality are not synonymous."[e]

## Questions to Consider

1. Suppose you had lost your farm and had traveled to California in the 1930s in search of a better life. What would you have done if confronted by the LAPD at the border, or if a friend or relative of yours had been charged under the California law for helping you come to the state?

2. What are the similarities and differences between California's effort to secure its borders with Arizona, Nevada, and Oregon in the 1930s and today's efforts to secure the southern border between the United States and Mexico?

3. Is there ever an instance in which a state might be justified in using its police powers to exclude someone from entering the state? If not, why? If so, when?

4. It is easy to dismiss *Mayor of the City of New York v. Miln* and the 1937 California law as relics of their time. But what about more recent anti-vagrancy statutes enacted by some cities to counter their burgeoning homeless populations? Are they problematic?

[a]*The Dust Bowl*, directed by Ken Burns (2012, Washington, DC: Florentine Films), http://www.pbs.org/kenburns/dustbowl/about/overview/

[b]Thomas Conner, "The Anti-Okie Panic," *This Land*, November 10, 2016, http://thislandpress.com/2016/11/10/the-anti-okie-panic/

[c]Cecilia Rasmussen, "LAPD Blocked Dust Bowl Migrants at State Borders." *Los Angeles Times*, March 9, 2003, http://articles.latimes.com/2003/mar/09/local/me-then9

[d]Mayor of the City of New York v. Miln, 36 U.S. 102 (1837) at 142.

[e]Edwards v. California, 314 U.S. 160 (1941) at 177.

As Congress's power to regulate increased, it imposed more and more legal requirements on states (ranging from dictates to maintain the privacy of medical records to regulations designed to maintain clean air and drinking water). Money from the federal government to implement these requirements typically came in the form of **categorical grants**. These are grants for states to do very specific federally mandated things. Sometimes, in order to qualify for funds, states are required to match a portion of a grant with their own money. Categorical grants are used to pay for such things as Medicaid and food stamps, programs that were part of President Lyndon Johnson's so-called Great Society in the 1960s—a federal expansion agenda that also included "War on Poverty" initiatives such as Head Start (which offers preschool education for poor children) and Upward Bound (which helps prepare poor high school students for college). The Great Society also expanded the federal government's role in the arts, environmental protection, and motor vehicle safety.

Such programs, of course, cost money. Not surprisingly, the federal budget steadily increased as the federal government took on more and more responsibilities. Sometimes Congress imposed a legal requirement on states to administer these programs but offered no money to pay for them. These requirements are called **unfunded mandates**. The 1990 Americans with Disabilities Act (ADA) is a good example. This law mandates that public transportation be accessible to people with disabilities, but it does not pay states or localities to retrofit trains and buses to comply with the law. Paying for such unfunded mandates became a substantial portion of many states' budgets.

## THE NEW FEDERALISM AND BEYOND

After the federal expansion of Lyndon Johnson's Great Society (1964–1969), Republican president Richard Nixon (1969–1974) sought to shift some of the balance of power back to the states. President Nixon coined the phrase *New Federalism* to describe this new approach.

**categorical grants**
Funds from the national government to state and local governments that must be used to implement a specific federal regulation in a particular way, leaving recipients no flexibility regarding how to spend the money.

**unfunded mandate**
A legal requirement imposed on states by Congress to administer a program that comes with no federal money to pay for it.

## THE NEW FEDERALISM

One of the ways New Federalism tried to restore power to the states was by implementing the use of block grants to states. Unlike specifically targeted categorical grants, where the federal government tells states precisely how and where to spend funds, block grants give states more flexibility. Block grants are meant to be spent on some general area, such as education or transportation, but states are relatively free to spend the money as they wish within that broad parameter.

President Nixon proposed consolidating 129 different categorical grants into six block grants. Congress stymied this initial proposal but did begin to create some new block grants. President Ronald Reagan (1981–1989) had more success. At his urging, Congress consolidated 77 categorical grants into nine block grants in 1981. The move may have given more flexibility to the states in terms of how to spend the money, but states ended up with less money to spend as a result of the consolidation. Another expansion of block grants took place in 1996 when Democrat Bill Clinton (1993–2001) held the White House and Republicans controlled Congress.[46]

In his 1996 State of the Union Address, President Clinton famously stated, "The era of big government is over." He added, however, that "we cannot go back to the time when citizens were left to fend for themselves." Instead, he envisioned a leaner federal government working in partnership with state and local governments, as well as with religious, charitable, and civic associations.[47] Toward this end, Clinton and the Republican Congress limited the ability of the federal government to impose unfunded mandates on states, reformed the federal welfare system, and abolished federally imposed speed limits.

Appointments to the Supreme Court by Republican presidents starting with Nixon also had an effect on Supreme Court rulings dealing with federalism. In 1995, for the first time since 1936, the Court struck down a piece of legislation on the grounds that Congress had exceeded its commerce clause power. In *U.S. v. Lopez*, a 5–4 majority invalidated the Gun Free School Zones Act of 1990, in which Congress banned guns from "school zones": the grounds of a public, parochial, or private elementary or secondary school and the area within 1,000 feet of those grounds. Congress used its commerce clause power to do this; specifically, it prohibited any firearm in these zones "that has moved in or affects interstate or foreign commerce." The Court majority, however, concluded that regulating guns fell under states' police powers. Several subsequent rulings have extended this shift back toward states' rights—a trend that is likely to continue as a result of President Donald Trump's appointments to the Supreme Court.

## FEDERALISM IN THE TWENTY-FIRST CENTURY

Issues of federalism have been at the forefront of several important policy debates in the twenty-first century. Same-sex marriage proved to be the hot-button issue at the start of the century. Massachusetts became the first state to recognize same-sex marriage in 2004. Other states followed suit, prompting some states to pass constitutional amendments banning same-sex marriage or civil unions. With public support for same-sex marriage steadily growing, the Supreme Court invalidated such amendments in *Obergefell v. Hodges* (2015), declaring a constitutional right to same-sex marriage. By May 2018, a Gallup poll found 67 percent approval of same-sex marriage (roughly the same percentage that opposed it in 1996; see Figure 3.3).[48]

Health care reform quickly became another contentious issue. The Affordable Care Act (ACA), which President Obama signed into law in March 2010, required states to expand Medicaid coverage to all adults with an income up to 138% of the federal poverty level. States that failed to comply would lose all preexisting federal Medicaid funds. Prior to the law, the federal government only required states to provide Medicaid coverage to low-income children, pregnant women, parents of dependent children, people with disabilities, and qualifying individuals over 65.

The ACA initially provided full federal funding to support the expansion. Over time, however, federal funding would gradually decrease to 90% under the assumption that increased Medicaid funding would eventually pay for itself by reducing hospital costs for uncompensated care and by stimulating the economy through the influx of federal funds to the states (including new jobs associated with Medicaid expansion and tax revenue generated from health care providers).[49] But several states sued the federal government over the ACA's Medicaid expansion, arguing that compulsory Medicaid expansion violated states' rights and foisted an unacceptable financial burden on them.[50]

block grants Funds from the national government to state and local governments that are earmarked for some general policy area, such as education, while giving the recipients flexibility to spend those funds within that policy area as they see fit.

## FIGURE 3.3
# *Public Opinion on Same-Sex Marriage 1996–2018*

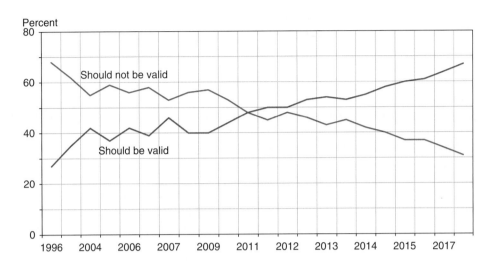

*How has public opinion about same-sex marriage changed since the Supreme Court's decision in Obergefell?*

*Source: "Two in Three Americans Support Same-Sex Marriage" Gallup, May 23, 2018, https://news.gallup.com/poll/234866/two-three-americans-support-sex-marriage.aspx*

## FIGURE 3.4
# *Marijuana Legalization as of June 2019*

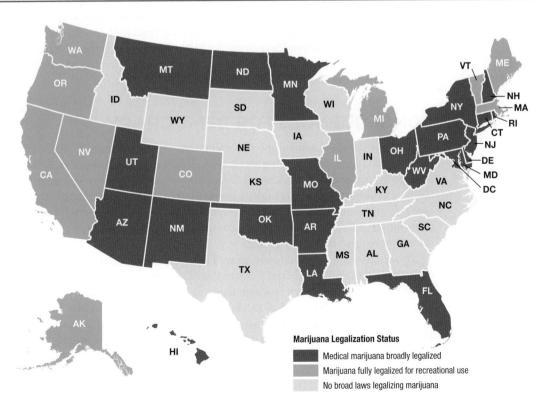

**Marijuana Legalization Status**
- Medical marijuana broadly legalized
- Marijuana fully legalized for recreational use
- No broad laws legalizing marijuana

*Source: Dan Bilefsky, "Legalizing Recreational Marijuana, Canada Begins a National Experiment," The New York Times, October 17, 2018, https://www.nytimes.com/2018/10/17/world/canada/marijuana-pot-cannabis-legalization.html*

In this instance, the Supreme Court ruled in favor of the states, concluding that they must be allowed to opt out of the Medicaid expansion requirement without losing their preexisting Medicaid funding. Although the Court, in *National Federation of Independent Business v. Sebelius* (2012), did uphold the rest of the ACA—including its controversial "individual mandate" (requiring individuals, with a few exceptions, to purchase health insurance)—the Court's holding on the Medicaid provision undermined the ACA's goal of expanding health insurance coverage for low-income individuals. As of 2018, 35 states plus the District of Columbia had expanded Medicaid, but 14 had not.[51]

Similar disputes arose over another Obama administration policy, the Clean Power Plan, which required states to submit plans for reducing carbon dioxide emissions. Under the policy, states that failed to develop their own plan would be compelled to comply with a plan imposed by the Environmental Protection Agency (EPA). In 2016, the Supreme Court, by a 5–4 vote, ordered the EPA to halt enforcement of the plan until a lower federal court had ruled on it. Before the lower court had an opportunity to do so, President Trump, who took office in January 2017, began efforts to scrap the Clean Air Plan, paving the way for litigation from progressive states and environmental groups who argued that Trump's alternative rules fall short of EPA standards mandated by the Clean Power Plan.[52]

With Trump as president, progressives and even some Republicans began to embrace other aspects of states' rights to counter Trump administration policies. This included the use of sanctuary cities discussed at the beginning of the chapter as well as opposition to President Trump's plan to allow oil and gas drilling off of most of the nation's coastline. Coastal states quickly proposed legislation to enact local bans on such drilling, paving the way for legal confrontations between states and the federal government.[53] Similar opposition arose in some quarters to Attorney General Jeff Sessions's January 2018 decision to rescind the Obama-era policy that the Justice Department not prosecute marijuana-related offenses under the federal Controlled Substances Act in states that had legalized the use of marijuana in some form. Despite the Attorney General's move, President Trump indicated that he might be willing to sign bipartisan legislation allowing states to determine their own marijuana policies. By June 2019, 11 states plus the District of Columbia had legalized the recreational use of marijuana for adults over the age of 21, while an additional 22 states have legalized marijuana for medical use (see Figure 3.4).[54] Still, the threat remained that the government could enforce the Controlled Substances Act through federal prosecutions for such use. In 2018, Canada became the first major world economy to fully decriminalize the sale and possession of marijuana for recreational use (the medicinal use of marijuana had been legal there since 2001).[55]

## CONSEQUENCES FOR DEMOCRACY

Most people do not initially think that federalism will be the most engaging topic they will cover when studying American government. They may even think of it as boring, but first impressions can be deceiving. After all, federalism was one of the most contentious issues, if not *the* most contentious issue, from the Constitutional Convention through most of the 1800s. Debates about national supremacy versus states' rights permeated the Constitutional Convention, influenced the development of our political parties, led to the Civil War, and shaped subsequent civil rights policies.

Those debates have never gone away. They were at the forefront of whether Congress, during the Progressive Era of the 1890s to the 1920s, could pass legislation protecting employees in the workplace through laws regulating things such as minimum wages, child labor, and maximum hours. Embracing dual federalism, the Supreme Court mostly said no.

As the United States struggled to emerge from the depths of the Great Depression in the 1930s, the debate turned to whether the New Deal legislation implemented by President Franklin Roosevelt and his fellow Democrats in Congress was constitutional. Until 1936, the answer was, again, mostly no. That changed with the "switch in time" in 1937. That switch not only meant that New Deal legislation designed to regulate the economy was upheld but also that workplace regulations that had been routinely struck down for decades were now deemed constitutional.

Today, many of the most controversial aspects of federalism deal with social issues such as same-sex marriage, gun control, health care reform, education, immigration, and the legalization of marijuana. Far from being uninteresting, we believe that federalism—throughout our history—has involved some of the most fascinating and relevant issues one can imagine. Certainly, these policies relate to you on a daily basis: what you studied in high school, who you can marry, at what age you can drink alcohol, how fast you can drive, whether or not there is a minimum wage, and whether you can be discriminated against in a hotel because of your race, to name only a few. Just as profoundly, federalism will shape your future. After all, things such as Social Security and Medicare would not have been possible without the "switch in time." Think about that the next time someone says that federalism is boring or unimportant. In fact, few aspects of our governmental system have a greater impact on your daily life.

## Critical Thinking Questions

1. As you follow current events, ask yourself: How do perspectives on federalism influence what policies can be implemented concerning those issues?

2. One's decision about whether to support states' rights or national supremacy sometimes varies according to the policy issue in question. For example, some conservatives who otherwise support states' rights balk at the idea of allowing states to recognize same-sex marriage or approve the use of marijuana. Can such discrepancies be reconciled?

3. Think back to the opening vignette of this chapter. What are the pros and cons of sanctuary cities? How do the actions of sanctuary jurisdictions illustrate federalism in action?

4. Did the framers make the right choice when they created a federal system in this country? Did the Supreme Court make the right choice with its "switch in time" in 1937?

## Key Terms

block grants, 69
categorical grants, 69
commerce clause, 63
concurrent powers, 59
confederal system, 55
cooperative federalism, 62
dual federalism, 61

extradition clause, 60
federal system, 55
full faith and credit clause, 60
interstate compacts, 60
necessary and proper (elastic) clause, 58
nullification, 64
police powers, 58

privileges and immunities clause, 60
reserved powers, 58
secession, 65
supremacy clause, 58
Tenth Amendment, 58
unfunded mandate, 69
unitary system, 55

Visit edge.sagepub.com/maltese to help you accomplish your coursework goals in an easy-to-use learning environment.

# 4
# CIVIL LIBERTIES

## *After reading this chapter, you should be able to do the following:*

- Explain the purpose of the Bill of Rights and the process by which its provisions came to be "incorporated."

- Define *prior restraint* and examine the various free speech tests devised by the Supreme Court to distinguish between actions that are constitutionally protected and those that are not.

- Explore the debate over what constitutes an establishment of religion and where to draw the line between constitutionally protected free exercise of religion and unprotected conduct.

- Discuss the arguments for and against the constitutional right of privacy and recognize the types of issues to which it applies.

- Understand the concept of procedural due process and other rights of criminal defendants and explain how the process of incorporation has affected those rights.

## *Perspective: How Much Government Control of the Internet Is Too Much—Or Too Little?*

The Internet has transformed the way that people communicate. It has also vastly increased access to information—and disinformation. The use of social media such as Facebook to spread disinformation ("fake news") during the 2016 presidential election has led to calls for government to regulate such platforms. But how would that square with the First Amendment and its guarantee that Congress shall make no law "abridging the freedom of speech, or of the press"? Would such regulation amount to government censorship?

Not all countries, of course, have qualms about censorship. China, for example, enacted a law in 2013 designed to curb "online rumors." Under the law, those who post online rumors that are viewed by 5,000 or more Internet users or that are reposted more than 500 times can be arrested and jailed. In China, *online rumors* are broadly defined to encompass any socially destabilizing content (that is, pretty much anything the government wants to censor). In 2018, China launched a mobile app that allows the public to report such rumors.[1]

China has a long history of censoring and restricting access to the Internet. It has developed one of the most sophisticated Internet filtering systems in the world. E-mail, websites, blogs, chat rooms, and bulletin boards are all filtered for content by the government. Both Google and Yahoo! controversially agreed to alter their search engines in China in order to comply with government censorship, and the Chinese government blocked Facebook, Twitter, and YouTube in 2009 and cracked down on microblogs in 2011.[2]

At the time of the crackdown, China had a population of 1.3 billion, with roughly 485 million Internet users. The government requires Internet service providers (ISPs) to track precisely who is online and what sites users visit, and the government holds ISPs legally accountable if their users violate laws regulating Internet use. Likewise, the government requires Internet content providers (ICPs) to verify the identity of those logging onto their sites and to track their online activity. Failure to do so can lead to revocation of their business license and even arrest.

After signing up for Internet service, Chinese citizens are required to register with the local police within 30 days. Those using Internet cafés must present an identification card, which the café keeps on file for 60 days, along with a detailed log of each patron's online activity. The café must cut off access to any patron who tries to access a forbidden website and must file a report with the government about such attempts. Forbidden websites have included Voice of America (a U.S. government-funded news radio service), foreign news outlets such as CNN and BBC News, and any site that deals with controversial topics ranging from Tibetan independence to democracy. Among the keywords that trigger filtering systems and block Internet access are *revolution, equality, freedom, justice, Taiwan, Tibet, democracy, dissident, STD,* and *human rights*.[3]

Many Westerners, including civil rights organizations, have criticized China's censorship.[4] But Chinese leaders have fought back, arguing that such criticism smacks of a double standard. Liu Zhengrong, deputy chief of the Internet Affairs Bureau in China, has pointed out that it is common practice around the world to remove "illegal and harmful" information from the Internet and claimed that China's Internet regulations were no different.[5]

U.S. citizens do not have to register with the police when they sign up for Internet service, of course. Nor does the U.S. government filter content the way the Chinese government does. Although it is a crime to post or download child pornography, there is little content regulation beyond that. Should there be more? And to what extent should the government be able to monitor what you see and do online? As part of the Bush administration's post–9/11 "War on Terror," the U.S. National Security Agency monitored, without court order, e-mails, text messages, and phone conversations in which at least one party involved in the communication was believed to be outside the United States. With a court order, all Internet activity can be monitored by the government. Is that acceptable? The answer largely depends upon how one believes that liberty and national security should be balanced—an issue we will return to later in this chapter. **«**

## THE BILL OF RIGHTS

**Civil liberties** consist of the basic rights and freedoms that citizens enjoy without governmental interference. These include not only the freedoms of speech, press, assembly, and religion but also the guarantee that government will not take one's life, liberty, or property without due process of law. These liberties are spelled out in the first ten amendments to the United States Constitution, collectively known as the **Bill of Rights**. In contrast with civil liberties, civil rights (discussed in Chapter 5) focus not on the freedoms from government interference found in the Bill of Rights but rather on the guarantee of equal treatment by the government found in the equal protection clause of the Fourteenth Amendment. In other words, *civil rights* refers to freedom from governmental discrimination (unequal treatment) based on some individual characteristic such as race, gender, or disability. Thus, the right to peaceably assemble is a civil liberty guaranteed by the First Amendment, but if the government were to arbitrarily discriminate in the enforcement of that right—by determining that people with green eyes can peaceably assemble but people with blue eyes cannot—we would call that discriminatory treatment a violation of civil rights.

The Bill of Rights is such a central part of the Constitution that it is hard to imagine the document without it. And yet, in the waning hours of the Constitutional Convention of 1787, the members of the convention—voting as state delegations—unanimously rejected a proposal for a Bill of Rights that was introduced by George Mason of Virginia, an ardent defender of individual rights who had drafted the famous Virginia Declaration of Rights in 1776.[6]

Many of the delegates, such as Alexander Hamilton, felt that a Bill of Rights was unnecessary. Seven of the states already had a bill of rights in their own state constitutions.[7] Hamilton also believed that the Constitution limited the powers of the national government to those enumerated. Therefore, he believed that the national government would be powerless to abridge rights. As he put it in *Federalist 84*, "Why declare that things shall not be done which there is no power to do?"[8] Moreover, enumerating specific rights could easily lead to the omission of others. Would the implication be that the national government was free to infringe upon rights that were not enumerated? Finally, confronting the issue of a Bill of Rights at this late stage might lead to another long round of debate and undermine fragile compromises that were already in place.

Mason disagreed, believing that the Constitution gave too much power to the national government. The lack of a Bill of Rights intensified the fear that the national government might subvert states' rights as well as those of individuals. But Mason had not been able to convince delegates to the Constitutional Convention to accept his position. His personality did not help. He was an impatient man who disliked compromise. His verbal jousting tended to alienate opponents.[9] In the end, a frustrated Mason famously refused to sign the Constitution, saying that he would sooner chop off his right hand than do so.[10] He then became a leading critic of the Constitution during the ratification debate.

James Madison, another delegate from Virginia, initially opposed a Bill of Rights, but—due in part to the persuasive efforts of Thomas Jefferson—changed his mind and became one of its strongest proponents.[11] His conversion was partly pragmatic. It came as he was running for Congress from a district in Virginia that strongly favored a Bill of Rights. But it also was a matter of timing and strategy. Before the ratification of the Constitution, its opponents were calling for a second Constitutional Convention to modify the proposed document. Madison knew that such a convention could lead to a radical transformation of the Constitution and undermine the goals of the Federalists. Therefore, the initial goal was to get the document ratified unscathed.

Once the Constitution was ratified, however, the dangers posed by amendments became less serious. At that point, a Bill of Rights could be used to defuse lingering opposition to the Constitution. As Madison put it in January 1789,

> Circumstances are now changed: The Constitution is established . . . and amendments, if pursued with a proper moderation and in a proper mode, will not only be safe, but may serve the double purpose of satisfying the minds of well-meaning opponents, and of providing additional safeguards in favour of liberty.[12]

Thus, acting on a proposal by Madison, the First Congress sent twelve amendments to the states for ratification. The first two, dealing with the size of the House of Representatives and the compensation of senators and representatives, were not ratified. As a result, the proposed

**civil liberties** The basic freedoms that citizens enjoy from governmental interference, such as the freedoms of speech, press, assembly, and religion, and the guarantees of due process and other specific protections accorded to criminal defendants.

**Bill of Rights** The first ten amendments of the U.S. Constitution, which form the basis of civil liberties.

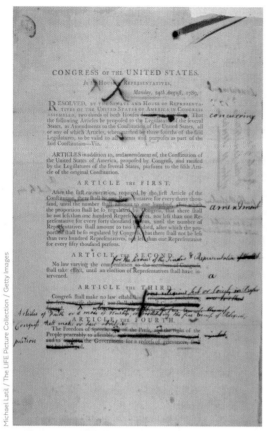

Similar to the Constitution, the Bill of Rights was a highly contested document. The version seen here includes a number of changes made by the Senate to the version passed by the House, as well as the first two Articles, which were not ratified at that time.

Third Amendment, dealing with the freedoms of religion, speech, and the press, became the First when the amendments that make up the Bill of Rights were ratified in 1791.[13]

## THE BILL OF RIGHTS AND THE STATES: THE ORIGINAL UNDERSTANDING

Just as it is hard to imagine our Constitution without a Bill of Rights, so it is hard to imagine our Bill of Rights not protecting individuals from state laws that infringe upon their liberties. And yet the Bill of Rights was originally thought to limit only the power of the *national* government—not the power of the states. States' rights advocates, in particular, had pushed for a Bill of Rights to prevent the new national government from encroaching not only on individual rights but also on the power of the states.

It is telling that James Madison's proposal that the Bill of Rights include an amendment that said, "No *state* shall violate the equal rights of conscience, or the freedom of the press, or the trial by jury in criminal cases" was rejected.[14] Instead, the First Amendment clearly states, "*Congress* shall make no law." And even though the remaining amendments seemed more general (the Sixth, for example, says, "In *all* criminal prosecutions, the accused shall enjoy the right to a speedy and public trial, by an impartial jury"), the common understanding was that these guarantees applied only to actions by the *federal* government, such as federal criminal prosecutions.[15] Thus, after the ratification of language in the First Amendment—"Congress shall make no law respecting an establishment of religion"—seven states (Connecticut, Georgia, Maryland, Massachusetts, New Hampshire, South Carolina, and Vermont) continued to maintain some form of religious establishment.

In the 1833 case *Barron v. Baltimore*, the U.S. Supreme Court reaffirmed the view that nothing in the Bill of Rights limited state action. Chief Justice John Marshall wrote the opinion in *Barron*. Given what we know about Marshall, his ruling might seem surprising. He was, after all, an ardent Federalist who did much in other cases to strengthen the national government at the expense of the states. Why would he write an opinion that vindicated states' rights? It may simply be that the answer was so obvious and the intent of the framers so clear that the outcome was preordained. As Marshall himself put it, the legal question presented was "of great importance, but not of much difficulty."[16] But there was another issue—one not directly raised in the case—that may have influenced the Court: slavery.

The reality of slavery is impossible to reconcile with the concept of liberty espoused by the framers. And yet many framers, including James Madison and Thomas Jefferson, owned slaves. As discussed in Chapter 5, the Constitution did not use the word *slavery*, but it nonetheless endorsed it in several ways. Madison himself had reassured the Virginia ratifying convention that nothing in the proposed Constitution would interfere with slavery in the states.[17]

By the time the Supreme Court decided *Barron v. Baltimore*, slavery had become a hot-button issue. Abolitionists were mobilizing. *The Liberator*, an important anti-slavery newspaper, had begun publishing in 1831. Fearful that the rising tide of abolitionist literature might lead to slave rebellion, southern states began around 1830 to adopt laws that restricted freedom of speech and of the press.[18] Discrimination against blacks had been taken for granted. Now it was spreading to whites who spoke out on their behalf. Had *Barron* extended the Bill of Rights to state action, these laws would have been called into question, possibly precipitating civil war. Thus, as the noted constitutional historian Michael Kent Curtis put it, the decision in *Barron* arguably promoted "the stability of the Union at the expense of liberty."[19]

In the coming years, state restrictions on civil liberties intensified. For example, Virginia made it a felony for abolitionists to enter the state and speak in favor of abolishing slavery or for anyone to circulate books that denied the right to own slaves. By 1859, Virginia had even banned the *New York Tribune*. Missouri not only imposed severe penalties for expressing anti-slavery views but required that state officeholders take an oath to assure that they supported slavery. In North Carolina, a man was convicted and sentenced to a year in prison for distributing to fellow whites an anti-slavery book that Republicans were using as a campaign document in 1858. Mob violence against abolitionists was also on the rise.[20] And through it all, the Bill of Rights of the United States Constitution offered no protection.

## THE INCORPORATION OF THE BILL OF RIGHTS

In order for the specific provisions of the Bill of Rights to limit state action, they needed to be *incorporated*. Incorporation simply means applying the Bill of Rights to the states. If you say that the First Amendment guarantee of free speech has been incorporated, you mean that the free speech clause not only limits actions by the federal government ("Congress shall make no law") but it has also come to limit state action (so that no state government shall make any such law either).

Some people have called for *total incorporation*: making every provision of the Bill of Rights applicable to the states. Others have called for *selective incorporation*: making only the most essential provisions applicable to the states. Still others have argued that there may be fundamental rights that are not specifically enumerated in the Constitution but that are so important that the Supreme Court should recognize them and use them to limit the actions of both the federal government and the states. When the Court discovers one of these unenumerated rights (such as privacy) and applies it to the states, the result is called *incorporation plus*. This could be either *total incorporation plus* (applying all the specifically enumerated provisions of the Bill of Rights to the states plus other rights deemed fundamental by the Court) or *selective incorporation plus* (applying only the most fundamental provisions of the Bill of Rights to the states plus other rights deemed fundamental by the Court).

But if the Bill of Rights was originally meant to limit only the actions of the national government, what justifies incorporation? Two clauses in the Fourteenth Amendment (ratified in 1868) provided opportunities for incorporation: the privileges or immunities clause and the due process clause. Using either of these clauses to apply the Bill of Rights to the states has proven to be controversial. Some argue strongly that these clauses were meant to incorporate the Bill of Rights and should be used to do so.[21] Others vehemently reject that contention.[22] This is yet another example of how reasonable people can disagree fundamentally over the meaning of the Constitution.

The privileges or immunities clause of the Fourteenth Amendment says, "No state shall make or enforce any law which shall abridge the privileges or immunities of citizens of the United States." Some, such as Rep. John Bingham (R-OH) who drafted this clause, used the words *privileges* and *immunities* as shorthand for the fundamental rights of citizens of the United States that states could not abridge: the Bill of Rights. After all, the words *rights*, *liberties*, *privileges*, and *immunities* were all used pretty much interchangeably at that time.[23] The Supreme Court, however, rejected that interpretation in the so-called *Slaughterhouse Cases* of 1873 and embraced a cramped interpretation of privileges and immunities that basically reduced it to protecting a narrow range of rights of U.S. citizens, such as the ability to travel through states and purchase property.[24] With that decision, the ability to use the clause to incorporate the Bill of Rights seemed to evaporate.

There the matter stood until the twentieth century, when a new set of Supreme Court justices turned to the Fourteenth Amendment's due process clause to accomplish what the privileges or immunities clause had not, even though that clause is not as clear-cut a means of incorporating the Bill of Rights as was the privileges or immunities clause. The **due process clause** of the Fourteenth Amendment says, "No state shall . . . deprive any person of life, liberty, or property without due process of law." This due process clause (similar to the other due process clause in the Fifth Amendment limiting federal action) was meant to guarantee fairness. It does not prevent government from depriving someone of life, liberty, or property, but it does require that the government employ fair procedures before doing so. This notion of applying fair procedures is known as *procedural due process*.

**incorporation** The process by which the Supreme Court has made specific provisions of the Bill of Rights applicable to state and local governments as well as the federal government.

**due process clauses** Clauses in the Fifth and Fourteenth Amendments that prevent the federal government (in the case of the Fifth) and states (in the case of the Fourteenth) from depriving people of life, liberty, or property without fair proceedings.

How, then, could the due process clause be used to incorporate provisions of the Bill of Rights? One way is to argue that states violate due process if they do not follow certain procedural guarantees in the Bill of Rights, such as the protection against double jeopardy. But it can also be argued that if the actual content or substance of a particular state law violates a basic right, such as the First Amendment right of free speech, then the law itself constitutes a violation of due process because it is fundamentally unfair. This latter approach is known as **substantive due process**.

Over time, the Supreme Court used the due process clause to incorporate most—but not all—of the provisions of the Bill of Rights through a long process of selective incorporation and has done so one clause at a time (see Table 4.1). Justice Benjamin Cardozo's majority opinion in *Palko v. Connecticut* (1937) offered a justification for selective incorporation: Those rights that are "implicit in the concept of ordered liberty" should be incorporated, but other provisions of the Bill of Rights should not be.[25] In other words, some rights are more important than others. But deciding which provisions of the Bill of Rights to incorporate is subjective. Justice Hugo Black tried to minimize that subjectivity by suggesting that *every* provision of the Bill of Rights be applied to the states through the process of total incorporation. To do otherwise, he argued, allowed Supreme Court justices to substitute "their own concepts of decency and fundamental justice for the language of the Bill of Rights."[26] Black's argument did not prevail. Thus, the Third and Seventh Amendments have not been incorporated, nor has a portion of the Fifth Amendment (see Table 4.2). But since the unenumerated right of privacy has been incorporated, it looks like the concept of selective incorporation plus ended up winning the incorporation battle.

The most recently incorporated provisions of the Bill of Rights are the Second Amendment right to "keep and bear arms" (2010) and the Eighth Amendment protection against "excessive fines" (2019). The decision to incorporate the Second Amendment, which came in a 5–4 ruling in *McDonald v. Chicago*,[27] marked a departure from long-established precedent. Prior to *McDonald*, the Supreme Court had held that the right to keep and bear arms was limited by the introductory

> **substantive due process** A judicially created concept whereby the due process clauses of the Fifth and Fourteenth Amendments can be used to strike down laws that are deemed to be arbitrary or unfair.

## TABLE 4.1
## *Chronology of Provisions Incorporated*

| Provision | Amendment | Year | Case |
|---|---|---|---|
| "Public use" and "just compensation" conditions in the taking of private roperty by government | V | 1896 and 1897 | *Missouri Pacific Railway Co. v. Nebraska*, 164 U.S. 403; *Chicago, Burlington & Quincy Railway Co. v. Chicago*, 166 U.S. 226 |
| Freedom of speech | I | 1927 | *Fiske v. Kansas*, 274 U.S. 380; *Gitlow v. New York*, 268 U.S. 652, 625 (1925) (dictum only); *Gilbert v. Minnesota*, 254 U.S. 325 (1920) (dictum only) |
| Freedom of the press | I | 1931 | *Near v. Minnesota*, 283 U.S. 697 |
| Fair trial and right to counsel in capital cases | VI | 1932 | *Powell v. Alabama*, 287 U.S. 45 |
| Freedom of religion | I | 1934 | *Hamilton v. Regents of University of California*, 293 U.S. 245 (dictum only) |
| Freedom of assembly and, by implication, freedom to petition for redress of grievances | I | 1937 | *De Jonge v. Oregon*, 299 U.S. 353 |
| Free exercise of religious belief | I | 1940 | *Cantwell v. Connecticut*, 310 U.S. 296 |
| Separation of church and state; right against the establishment of religion | I | 1947 | *Everson v. Board of Education*, 330 U.S. 1 |
| Right to public trial | VI | 1948 | *In re Oliver*, 333 U.S. 257 |

| Right against unreasonable search and seizures | IV | 1949 | *Wolf v. Colorado*, 338 U.S. 25 |
|---|---|---|---|
| Right to travel as an aspect of "liberty" | V | 1958 | *Kent v. Dulles*, 357 U.S. 116 (right to travel internationally); *Crandall v. Nevada*, 73 U.S. (6 Wall.) 745 (1867) (right to interstate travel) |
| Freedom of association | I | 1958 | *NAACP v. Alabama*, 357 U.S. 449 |
| Exclusionary rule as concomitant of unreasonable search and seizures | IV | 1961 | *Mapp v. Ohio*, 367 U.S. 643 |
| Right against cruel and unusual punishments | VIII | 1962 | *Robinson v. California*, 370 U.S. 660 |
| Right to counsel in all felony cases | VI | 1963 | *Gideon v. Wainwright*, 372 U.S. 335 |
| Right to vote | XIV | 1964 | *Reynolds v. Sims*, 377 U.S. 533 |
| Right against self-incrimination | V | 1964 | *Malloy v. Hogan*, 378 U.S. 1, 84 S.Ct. 1489; *Murphy v. Waterfront Commission*, 378 U.S. 52 |
| Right to confront and cross-examine witnesses | VI | 1965 | *Pointer v. Texas*, 380 U.S. 400 |
| Right of privacy | Implied by various | 1965 | *Griswold v. Connecticut*, 381 U.S. 479 |
| Right to impartial jury | VI | 1966 | *Park v. Gladden*, 385 U.S. 363 |
| Right to speedy trial | VI | 1967 | *Klopfer v. North Carolina*, 386 U.S. 213 |
| Right to compulsory process for obtaining witnesses | VI | 1967 | *Washington v. Texas*, 388 U.S. 213 |
| Right to jury trial in cases of serious crime | VI | 1968 | *Duncan v. Louisiana*, 391 U.S. 145 |
| Right against double jeopardy | V | 1969 | *Benton v. Maryland*, 395 U.S. 784 |
| Right to counsel in all criminal cases entailing a jail term | VI | 1972 | *Argersinger v. Hamlin*, 407 U.S. 25 |
| Right to keep and bear arms | II | 2010 | *McDonald v. Chicago*, 561 U.S. 3025 |
| Right against excessive fines | VIII | 2019 | *Timbs v. Indiana*, 586 U.S. ___ |

OTHER INCORPORATED PROVISIONS

| Right of petition | I | | Included by implication of other First Amendment incorporations |
|---|---|---|---|
| Right to be informed of the nature and cause of the accusation | VI | | Included by implication of other Sixth Amendment incorporations |

*Source: Reprinted with permission of Cengage from Craig Ducat,* Constitutional Interpretation, *9th ed. (Boston: Wadsworth, 2009).*

**TABLE 4.2**

## *Provisions of the First Eight Amendments Not Incorporated*

| Amendment | Provision(s) Not Incorporated |
|---|---|
| III | All |
| V | Right to indictment by grand jury |
| VII | All |

*Source: Reprinted with permission of Cengage from Craig Ducat,* Constitutional Interpretation, *9th ed. (Boston: Wadsworth, 2009).*

FIGURE 4.1

## *The Right to Bear Arms*

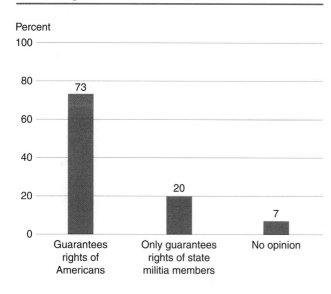

*Survey respondents were asked in 2008 whether they believe the Second Amendment guarantees the rights of individual Americans to own guns, or whether they believe it only guarantees members of state militias such as National Guard units the rights to own guns. How did public opinion square with the Supreme Court's interpretation of the Second Amendment prior to 2008? Did the Court do the right thing when it incorporated the Second Amendment?*

*Source: USA Today/Gallup, Feb. 8-10, 2008 https://news.gallup.com/poll/105721/public-believes-americans-right-own-guns.aspx*

clause of the Second Amendment, which indicated that the right was "necessary to the security of a free State" and related to a "well-regulated Militia." Thus, in rulings dating back to 1876, the Supreme Court maintained that the Second Amendment only limited the national government, not states, and that the limit on the national government only prevented it from abolishing state militias.[28] In other words, the amendment did not create an individual right of gun ownership.

By the late twentieth century, however, federal gun control legislation had become a controversial political issue. Polls showed that a solid majority believed that the Second Amendment protected private gun ownership (see Figure 4.1), and the National Rifle Association lobbied vigorously against gun control legislation, arguing that it violated the Second Amendment. Then, in 2008, the Supreme Court agreed, striking down a District of Columbia law that banned the ownership of handguns and regulated other firearms in the District.[29] Having recognized for the first time that the right to keep and bear arms is an individual right, the next step was incorporation—which came in the *McDonald* case. Nonetheless, the Court pointed out that gun ownership is not an absolute right. Like speech, it can still be regulated under certain circumstances.

This discussion illustrates how, as new issues become salient over time, Americans may expect the Supreme Court to reevaluate the incorporation of specific rights (see Tables 4.1 and 4.2). Whether the Court chooses to do so depends largely on an interchange between evolving American values and societal norms, past precedents set by the Supreme Court, and individual judgment of the Supreme Court justices currently sitting on the bench.

## THE FIRST AMENDMENT FREEDOMS OF SPEECH, PRESS, AND ASSEMBLY

Could a democratic system survive without the free exchange of ideas? The ability to report on the actions of government, to express support for or opposition to governmental policies, to engage in meaningful debate, and to be knowledgeable enough about current issues to cast an informed vote would seem to be central to the existence of democracy. All of these things presuppose freedom of speech and of the press. Americans rightly count these as some of their most precious freedoms. But how much freedom does the First Amendment really allow? How much *should* it?

The phrase "Congress shall make no law" sounds categorical, yet Congress has passed quite a few laws that restrict freedom of speech and of the press in one way or another, and the Court has upheld many of them. Indeed, the Supreme Court has consistently ruled that neither freedom of speech nor of the press is absolute. Nonetheless, the protection of free speech and the press is greater in the United States than most other liberal democracies. Hate speech, for example, is banned in Germany (where it is a crime to deny the Holocaust) and some other European nations (as well as Canada) but is protected in the United States under the first amendment.

### FREEDOM OF THE PRESS AND PRIOR RESTRAINT

**prior restraint** Censorship before publication (such as government prohibition against future publication).

In the common law tradition inherited from England, the principle of *freedom of the press* had a rather narrow meaning: no prior restraint on publication. Prior restraint means censorship before publication. Such censorship emerged very quickly after the invention of the printing press. England required prepublication licensing as early as 1534. To publish something, an author first had to submit the material to the government for approval. This meant that the government could squelch political criticism and control the content of what people read. Prior restraint provoked great opposition, and England abolished the practice in 1695. Thereafter, the principle of no prior restraint became a part of English common law.

The principle of no prior restraint may have been what the framers had in mind when they wrote the First Amendment, but it was not until 1931 that the Supreme Court, by a narrow 5–4 vote, held prior restraint to be unconstitutional in *Near v. Minnesota*. In that case, Minnesota had imposed an injunction against a newspaper, *The Saturday Press*, on the grounds that it created a "public nuisance" because of its "malicious, scandalous, and defamatory" content.[30] There is no doubt that the newspaper was anti-Semitic, but the Court majority ruled that the injunction—which prohibited future publication—violated the First Amendment. Despite its ruling, the majority held that in "exceptional cases," the government could still prohibit publication in advance. For example, the Court suggested that the government could use prior restraint to prohibit a publication detailing troop movements in times of war. The Court also suggested that obscene material was subject to prior restraint. And, despite the general presumption against prior restraint, the majority still held that certain types of punishment *after* publication were constitutional.

Forty years later, the Nixon administration tried to use *Near v. Minnesota* to justify imposing a prior restraint on *The New York Times* to prevent it from publishing a series of articles based on classified government documents related to Vietnam known as the "Pentagon Papers." The government argued that publication of the documents would harm national security. However, the Supreme Court ruled against the government in *New York Times v. United States* (1971).[31]

In addition to national security sometimes justifying prior restraint, some argue that the Sixth Amendment guarantee of a fair trial may sometimes justify prior restraint. "Gag orders" to prevent prejudicial publicity are commonplace in some countries. For example, the French Civil Code protects the presumption of innocence by restricting the media from depicting suspects in handcuffs or describing them as guilty prior to conviction.[32] There are no such constraints on the U.S. media, where courts protect even sensationalistic pre-trial coverage under the guise of freedom of the press.

A recent controversy related to prior restraint involves the nondisclosure agreements that President Donald Trump required White House employees to sign. The president and his legal team tried to use those agreements to prevent publication of books by former White House aides, such as Cliff Sims's *Team of Vipers*. Trump did not succeed in blocking publication of that or other critical books, but his lawyers filed an arbitration claim against Sims for violating the terms of the nondisclosure agreement. Sims, in turn, filed a lawsuit in February 2019, arguing that such agreements in that context violate the First Amendment.[33]

President Trump's frequent denunciation of the news media has also raised free speech concerns. He has repeatedly labeled much of the mainstream media (including ABC, CBS, CNN, NBC, and *The New York Times*) as "fake news" and the "enemy of the American people," as he did in a February 17, 2017 tweet (see photo at right).

Anti-media rhetoric became a consistent theme at Trump rallies before and after his election as president, raising concerns among some that the rhetoric encouraged violence against reporters and was designed to limit freedom of the press. In June 2017, Republican Congressman Greg Gianforte from Montana was convicted of misdemeanor assault for body-slamming a reporter during his election campaign.[34] Subsequently, President Trump praised Gianforte at a rally, saying, "Any guy that can do a body slam, he's my kind of— he's my guy."[35]

After a court battle, the Supreme Court ruled in favor of *The New York Times* and allowed the paper to resume publishing classified documents related to the Vietnam war.

**Donald J. Trump** ✓
@realDonaldTrump

Follow

The FAKE NEWS media (failing @nytimes, @NBCNews, @ABC, @CBS, @CNN) is not my enemy, it is the enemy of the American People!

1:48 PM - 17 Feb 2017

47,924 Retweets 148,206 Likes

74K    48K    148K

President Trump's repeated denunciations of the media have raised concerns about free speech as well as potential violence against journalists.

## WHAT DID THE FRAMERS MEAN BY "FREEDOM OF SPEECH"?

If the framers considered "no prior restraint" to be the principle behind freedom of the press, what principle did they have in mind for freedom of speech? It simply is not clear. When the First Amendment was ratified, Pennsylvania was the only state whose constitution specifically protected speech, but it did so by closely linking it to freedom of the press (other states, such as Massachusetts, protected only freedom of the press).[36]

The free speech clause of the First Amendment raises many questions. Does it guarantee more than prohibition against prior restraint? Is it limited to political speech? Did it simply mean that only states could regulate speech? The Supreme Court has consistently rejected the notion that freedom of speech is absolute. Still, the question remains: Where should courts draw the line? Is obscenity constitutionally protected? False advertising? Threats to overthrow the government? For that matter, is *speech* limited to verbal utterances and written words? Or are symbolic expression and other forms of nonverbal communication also protected? In short, even though the First Amendment language dealing with freedom of speech and of the press may, at first glance, seem clear-cut, it is anything but.

## THE ALIEN AND SEDITION ACTS OF 1798

James Madison expressed the fear that a Bill of Rights might serve merely as a "parchment barrier" against "overbearing majorities." There was justification for that fear. As the Pulitzer Prize–winning historian Leonard Levy has noted, "any member of the Constitutional Convention could have cited examples of gross abridgments of civil liberties in states that had bills of rights."[37]

Arguably, this is what happened when Congress enacted the Alien and Sedition Acts seven years after ratification of the Bill of Rights. These four separate laws were passed when the United States was under threat of war with France. One of them, the Sedition Act, allowed for the prosecution of anyone who "shall write, print, utter or publish" any "scandalous and malicious" statement against the government, either house of Congress, or the president. Since the Federalist Party controlled both the White House and Congress, this act effectively meant that critics of the Federalists—notably opposition newspaper editors representing the views of the Democratic–Republican Party—were subject to imprisonment for up to two years and a $2,000 fine if convicted.[38] Ten people, including a member of the U.S. House of Representatives, were convicted under the act before it expired in 1801.[39] The Supreme Court never ruled on the constitutionality of these laws, but President Thomas Jefferson later pardoned all of those who had been convicted. In fact, the Supreme Court did not rule on a free speech case until 1919.

## THE SUPREME COURT CONFRONTS RESTRICTIONS ON SPEECH

One month after the United States entered World War I, Congress passed the Espionage Act of 1917, which made it illegal to "willfully cause or attempt to cause insubordination, disloyalty, mutiny, or refusal of duty in the military or naval forces." A year later, Congress passed the Sedition Act of 1918 as an amendment to the Espionage Act. It kept the language quoted above but inserted "or incite or attempt to incite" after "attempt to cause." It also made it a crime to "willfully utter, print, write, or publish any disloyal, profane, scurrilous, or abusive language" about the United States government, Constitution, military or naval forces, flag, or the uniform of the Army or Navy or to "willfully advocate, teach, defend, or suggest the doing of any of the acts or things in this section enumerated" (such as obstructing the recruitment or enlistment of military personnel). Offenders were subject to a fine of up to $10,000, imprisonment for up to 20 years, or both. [40]

These laws led to the arrest of more than 6,000 people. Among those convicted were members of the Socialist Party of America, whose leader, Eugene V. Debs, ran for president in each election from 1900 through 1912, winning over 900,000 votes—roughly 6 percent of the popular vote—in 1912. The Socialist Party opposed U.S. entry into World War I. It believed that war in general amounted to government coercion of the working class by capitalist elites. As part of that opposition, Charles Schenck and other Socialist Party members prepared and mailed a leaflet to some

15,000 young men who had been drafted.[41] The leaflet did not directly encourage draft resistance, but it did argue that the draft violated the Thirteenth Amendment prohibition on "involuntary servitude" and it urged recipients to petition the government for repeal of the draft. Schenck was arrested and charged with violating the Espionage Act. Convicted and sentenced to 15 years in prison for distributing the leaflets, Schenck appealed to the United States Supreme Court, arguing that his First Amendment right to free speech had been violated. He lost: A unanimous Supreme Court upheld his conviction in *Schenck v. United States*.[42]

Justice Oliver Wendell Holmes wrote the decision for the Court. In it, he created the **clear and present danger test** to determine the limits of constitutionally protected speech. Over the years, that test has come to be associated with protecting free speech, but it was originally used to justify restricting speech. Holmes himself later came to be seen as a champion of free speech, but that stance is not so apparent in this initial case. The fact that the United States was at war influenced Holmes's decision. He admitted that "in many places and in ordinary times" the leaflet would have been constitutional. But, he added, "the character of every act depends upon the circumstances in which it is done." That reasoning led to one of the most famous lines in any Supreme Court decision: "The most stringent protection of free speech would not protect a man in falsely shouting fire in a theatre and causing a panic." The question that the Court must answer is whether "the words are used in such circumstances and are of such a nature as to create a clear and present danger that they will bring about the substantive evils that Congress has a right to prevent."[43]

The unanimity of the Supreme Court began to fragment by the end of the year, although a 7–2 majority still upheld the convictions of Jacob Abrams and several other Russian immigrants in *Abrams v. United States*.[44] Once again, the defendants—self-proclaimed anarchists and revolutionaries—were charged with violating the Espionage Act for distributing leaflets that called for workers to rise up against the "hypocritical," "cowardly," and "capitalistic" government of the United States by engaging in a general strike. Language in the leaflet specifically targeted munitions workers. Unlike the flyers at issue in *Schenck*, which were sent through the mail to young men who had been drafted, the flyers in this case were dumped out the windows of an apartment building in lower Manhattan. Although many factories in that area made clothes, shoes, buttons, and hats, none manufactured weapons of war. Abrams and his co-defendants were convicted and sentenced to 20 years in prison. The majority of the Court in *Abrams* used the clear and present danger test to uphold the convictions, but this time, Holmes and Louis Brandeis dissented. Like the majority, Holmes and Brandeis used the clear and present danger test, but they reached the opposite conclusion.[45]

The split grew in the ensuing years, with Holmes and Brandeis remaining lonely dissenters. By 1925, in *Gitlow v. New York*, the majority no longer claimed to use the clear and present danger test. Instead, the justices in the majority used the so-called **bad tendency test** to argue that government cannot be expected to measure the danger of every utterance in a "jeweler's scale" to determine its threat. "A single revolutionary spark may kindle a fire that, smoldering for a time, may burst into a sweeping and destructive conflagration." Why wait for the clear and present danger of the roaring flame when the government could easily put out the spark? It should be able to "suppress the threatened danger in its incipiency."[46] In contrast, Holmes and Brandeis continued to embrace the clear and present danger test and made it more protective of speech. According to their new interpretation, only speech that posed a grave threat of "serious evil"—one in which the danger was not only possible but imminent—could be punished by the government.[47]

The Socialist Party, led by Eugene V. Debs (pictured on the right on this 1912 campaign button), opposed U.S. involvement in World War I; some members advocated the view that the military draft was unconstitutional. Under the Espionage Act, this advocacy was considered a crime, despite their claim of free speech. How should the courts draw the line between protecting the public and protecting free speech?

**clear and present danger test** A free speech test that allows government to restrict only speech that poses a clear and present danger of substantive evil; over time, it has become increasingly protective of speech.

**bad tendency test** The least protective free speech test, which allows government to restrict speech that merely poses a tendency or possibility to do harm (as opposed to a clear and present danger).

The degree to which the Supreme Court is willing to protect speech—or any other part of the Constitution—depends in part upon who is sitting on the Court. From the late 1930s through the 1950s, the membership of the Court was profoundly transformed. Until 1937, corporate lawyers appointed by Republican presidents dominated the Court. But President Franklin Roosevelt eventually had the opportunity to appoint a new majority. His imprint on the Court not only led to the rise of cooperative federalism (discussed in Chapter 3) but also helped to spur the rights revolution of the twentieth century.

The move to incorporate the Bill of Rights began in earnest during the 1930s. And, as new cases came before it, the Supreme Court began to protect free speech rights more vigorously. Nonetheless, it took time to overturn some of the old free speech precedents—especially when the speech in question advocated the violent overthrow of the government. The fear of communism in the 1940s and 1950s led to renewed restrictions on speech. For example, the Supreme Court upheld the convictions of Eugene Dennis and other members of the Communist Party in 1951, even though some critics claimed that they were convicted for mere advocacy that posed no clear and present danger.[48]

Ironically, a Republican president, Dwight Eisenhower, helped to cement the rights revolution by appointing Chief Justice Earl Warren and other liberals to the Supreme Court in the 1950s. Still, it was not until 1969 in *Brandenburg v. Ohio* that the Supreme Court finally overturned a precedent that still employed the old bad tendency test in cases advocating violence against the government. The Court now ruled that the government could only punish advocacy that incites or produces "imminent lawless action."[49]

Although the Court unanimously rejected the bad tendency test in *Brandenburg*, new fractures were already emerging. Both Hugo Black and William O. Douglas agreed with the rest of the Court that Brandenburg's conviction should be overturned, but they argued that the Court did not do enough to protect speech. Both believed that speech is absolutely protected by the Constitution—a view that the majority of the Supreme Court has never embraced. However, Justice Black believed that only pure speech was absolutely protected. He was among those who had read the free speech clause literally to protect only speech—not conduct that may accompany speech (symbolic expression). The fact that Black was unwilling to go as far as some of his non-absolutist colleagues in protecting these other forms of expression is a reminder of the difficulty of determining precisely what the First Amendment protects.

> **symbolic speech** Communication that is neither spoken nor written but is nonetheless accorded free speech protection under the First Amendment.

**SYMBOLIC SPEECH**  The category of **symbolic speech** consists of forms of expression such as signs or symbols instead of pure speech. The Supreme Court first accorded First Amendment protection to symbolic speech in the 1931 case *Stromberg v. California*. In that case, the Court overturned the conviction of 19-year-old Yetta Stromberg for flying a red flag at a communist youth camp in California. In so doing, it struck down a California law that made it a felony to display a red flag "as a sign, symbol or emblem of opposition to organized government."[50] Since the 1960s, the Supreme Court has applied First Amendment protection to a number of other forms of symbolic expression. For example, it upheld the right of high school students to wear black armbands to class as a form of protest against the Vietnam War in *Tinker v. Des Moines Independent Community School District* (1969).[51] The majority did not recognize an absolute right to wear the armbands, but it claimed that in this case there was no evidence that the armbands had disrupted classroom routine and therefore First Amendment rights should prevail.

The issue of student speech continues to be controversial. In 2002, high school students in Juneau, Alaska, were allowed to miss their regularly scheduled classes in order to watch the Olympic torch pass by at a school-sponsored event across the street. One of the students displayed a banner at the event that read "Bong Hits 4 Jesus." The school principal seized the banner (school policy prohibited the

Mary Beth Tinker stands with her brother and mother after learning that the Supreme Court upheld her right to wear an armband signaling her opposition to the Vietnam War while at school. Should students' free speech rights be more limited than other citizens?

display of messages promoting drug use at school events) and suspended the student. Were the student's First Amendment rights violated? A 6–3 majority of the Supreme Court said no in *Morse v. Frederick* (2007).[52] Only one justice in the majority (Clarence Thomas) argued that students have *no* free speech rights and that *Tinker* should be overturned. The rest of the majority simply argued that the school's interest in deterring drug use by students justified its action in this case.

Symbolic speech cases often raise issues of *conduct*, which consists of actions rather than words. Conduct (such as trespassing, disturbing the peace, or destroying property) may accompany speech and can be punished by the government. However, speech and conduct can be intertwined so closely that it may be difficult to determine where one ends and the other begins. For example, Justice Black dissented in the *Tinker* case, arguing that students wearing armbands amounted to constitutionally unprotected conduct rather than constitutionally protected speech. His concern focused on the potential disruption to the learning environment.

Another symbolic speech case that raised the issue of conduct is *Texas v. Johnson* (1989), which involved burning the American flag. The Supreme Court voted 5–4 to overturn the conviction of Gregory Johnson for burning an American flag to protest the policies of President Ronald Reagan.[53] Johnson burned the flag outside the 1984 Republican National Convention in Dallas, Texas. President George H.W. Bush responded to the Court's controversial ruling by calling (unsuccessfully) for a constitutional amendment to protect the flag. In *Texas v. Johnson*, the majority emphasized that the Supreme Court had consistently rejected the idea that an "apparently limitless variety of conduct can be labeled 'speech' whenever the person engaging in the conduct intends thereby to express an idea" but added that there are some types of conduct—such as the burning of the American flag, in that case—that are "sufficiently imbued with elements of communication" to fall within the scope of First Amendment protection.[54] The challenge remains: How and where to draw that line?

Flag desecration laws vary around the world. Some advanced democracies, such as Israel, Italy, and Switzerland, ban it and provide harsh penalties (including hefty fines and jail time). Others, such as Denmark and Japan, do not forbid the burning of their own flag, but prohibit desecrating flags of other countries. In 2016, President-elect Trump tweeted, "Nobody should be allowed to burn the American flag—if they do, there must be consequences—perhaps loss of citizenship or year in jail."[55]

**OBSCENITY** A majority of the Supreme Court has never considered obscenity to be a form of constitutionally protected speech, and the Court has pointed to obscene publications as an exception to the general First Amendment rule of no prior restraint.[56] The problem has been *defining* obscenity. As Justice Potter Stewart famously proclaimed in 1964, "I know it when I see it," but defining it in concrete terms remains elusive.[57]

For many years, the Supreme Court used the *Hicklin* test to determine whether something is obscene. Derived from *Regina v. Hicklin*, an 1868 case from England, the test made it easy to restrict speech.[58] According to the *Hicklin* test, any material that had merely a *tendency* "to deprave or corrupt" a child could be outlawed. A publication, such as a book, did not have to be considered as a whole. A single, isolated passage could be taken out of context and used to suppress the book or punish its distributor.

The Supreme Court abandoned the *Hicklin* test in *Roth v. United States* (1957). The new *Roth* test was much more protective of speech. It no longer allowed isolated passages to be taken out of context, and it no longer used children as the baseline for judging whether material was obscene. Now the question was whether an *average* person "applying contemporary community standards" would find that the "dominant theme of the material, taken as a whole, appeals to the prurient interest." Thus, a novel that could have been banned using the *Hicklin* test because of an isolated paragraph that a child might happen to read would now be judged in its entirety by the standards of an average adult.

Still, questions remained. Are "community standards" national or local? How does one measure the "dominant theme" of a work? And what exactly is a "prurient interest"? Justice William Brennan, who wrote the opinion in *Roth*, tried to answer those questions in subsequent cases, but a majority of the Court could not agree on any single interpretation of the test. To Brennan, *community standards* meant the standards of "society at large" (a national community standard),

ATTA KENARE / AFP / Getty Images

**Iran's obscenity laws are much stricter than those in the U.S.; it is considered obscene for women to appear without a headscarf known as a *hijab*. Standards vary not only across the world but within the U.S. Is there anything you would outlaw as obscene that seems to be ordinary in other parts of the country?**

and material could be deemed obscene only if, taken as a whole, it was "utterly without redeeming social importance" and did not possess even a "modicum of social value."[59]

By the 1970s, the Supreme Court was moving in a more conservative direction. President Richard Nixon, who had criticized the Supreme Court's obscenity rulings during his 1968 presidential campaign, had the opportunity to replace four justices during his first three years in office, including Chief Justice Warren. The new Court, headed by Chief Justice Warren Burger, grappled with the issue of obscenity in *Miller v. California* (1973). The resulting *Miller* test kept some aspects of the *Roth* test: The relevant audience continued to be the average person, and the material in question still had to be considered as a whole. But *community standards* were now defined as local rather than national, and material had to lack "serious literary, artistic, political, or scientific value," thereby rejecting the contention that material had to be utterly without redeeming social importance.

Although the legal definition of obscenity now seems to be limited to hard-core pornography, the Supreme Court has ruled that the broadcast media can be regulated more stringently—partly to assure that scarce airwaves are used in the public interest. As a result, government can ban language and nudity on the broadcast media that may be offensive but is not obscene (for more about government regulation of the airwaves and the Internet, see Chapter 10).

In stark contrast to the lenient attitude toward obscenity in the U.S., Iran has some of the strictest obscenity laws. There, women are not even allowed to be out in public (or depicted on film) without a hijab (a veil that covers the head and most of a woman's skin). Merely removing a headscarf in public can be punished with up to ten years in prison.[60] Nor are women in Iran allowed to dance in public with members of the opposite sex. In 2018, Iranian officials arrested an 18-year-old girl for posting videos of herself on Instagram dancing alone to music (fully clothed, though sometimes without a head scarf) and forced her to deliver a confession on state television (a form of public shaming).[61]

**LIBEL AND SLANDER**  The First Amendment protects neither libel (written defamation of character) nor slander (spoken defamation of character), but the Supreme Court has set a high standard for government officials and other public figures who seek damages for defamation. In the landmark 1964 libel case, *New York Times v. Sullivan*, the Court held that public officials seeking damages for libel must prove not only that the statement is false and damaging but also that it was made with "actual malice"—that is, "made with knowledge that it was false or with reckless disregard of whether it was false or not."[62] In the absence of malice, falsity of the claim is not enough. Subsequent Supreme Court cases extended the actual malice standard to other public figures besides government officials.

Why such an exacting standard for public figures? President Trump, for one, has called the standard "a sham and a disgrace,"[63] because it makes it more difficult for him and other public figures to sue, and other liberal democracies such as Canada and Germany have rejected such a high standard.[64] But Justice Brennan, who wrote the opinion in *New York Times v. Sullivan*, defended it, arguing that there is a "profound national commitment" in the United States "to the principle that debate on public issues should be uninhibited, robust, and wide-open, and that it may well include vehement, caustic, and sometimes unpleasantly sharp attacks on government and public officials."[65] To allow anything less would interfere with a basic principle of the First Amendment: the free flow of ideas and opinion on matters related to the public interest. It could also interfere with the media's ability to act as a government watchdog.

The actual malice standard makes it difficult but not impossible for public figures to win libel suits. Private figures who neither hold public office nor fall into the categories of celebrity that make an individual a public figure are not bound by the actual malice standard and may recover libel damages more easily. Whether one is a public or private figure, certain types of material are generally immune from libel charges. These include the publication of opinion

**libel** Written defamation of character, which is not accorded First Amendment protection.

**slander** Spoken defamation of character, which is not accorded First Amendment protection.

as opposed to fact (such as a restaurant review) and parody (such as political cartoons).

**FALSE ADVERTISING** In 1943, the Supreme Court ruled that the First Amendment does not protect commercial advertising.[66] But what happens when political speech is part of a commercial advertisement? Faced with such instances in the 1970s, the Supreme Court has accorded some degree of First Amendment protection to commercial speech. For example, it struck down state laws that prevented lawyers from advertising and that banned advertising for abortion services.[67] It also struck down a federal law that prohibited the mailing of unsolicited advertisements for contraceptives.[68] Nonetheless, the Court has made it clear that the First Amendment does not prevent government from passing laws to prevent false, misleading, or deceptive advertising. In addition, government can require that warning labels be printed on products such as tobacco, alcohol, and pharmaceuticals.

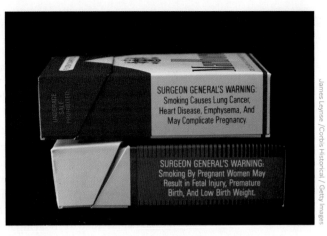

The Supreme Court has ruled that the First Amendment protection of free speech does not prevent the government from requiring warning labels on some products, including cigarettes. Do you think this infringes on the rights of the tobacco companies?

## CAMPUS SPEECH

In the 1980s and 1990s, many public colleges and universities implemented speech codes that were designed to combat discrimination and harassment on campus. These codes were intended to prohibit abusive language that attacks individuals because of characteristics such as their race, ethnic origin, religious beliefs, or sexual orientation.

Some argue that racist and sexist speech stifles intellectual exchange and that such codes actually increase free speech by removing intimidation. Others denounce such restrictions as "political correctness" and argue that the codes reflect a political agenda. For example, some conservative Christians have complained that codes have been used to vilify their views. When Roger Williams University in Rhode Island temporarily froze funding for a college Republican newspaper that ran a series of articles condemning homosexuality, Jason Mattera, the editor of the paper at the time, said, "You're not automatically a bigot if you don't agree with [homosexuality]. What they're essentially doing is silencing the only conservative voice here on campus."[69] Based on such concerns, President Trump signed an executive order in March 2019 to protect free speech on college campuses, although some—such as the University of California system—called Trump's proposal "misguided and unnecessary."[70]

The Supreme Court has not directly ruled on the constitutionality of campus speech codes, but some lower courts have. For example, a federal court struck down a University of Michigan code in 1989 that banned "any behavior, verbal or physical, that stigmatizes or victimizes an individual on the basis of race, ethnicity, religion, sex, sexual orientation, creed, national origin, ancestry, age, marital status, handicap, or Vietnam-era veteran status."[71] An "interpretive guide" of the code issued by the University Office of Affirmative Action included examples of conduct that could be sanctioned. One example read, "A male student makes remarks in class like 'Women just aren't as good in this field as men,' thus creating a hostile learning environment." A graduate student in biopsychology, who was studying the biological bases of individual differences in personality traits and mental abilities, challenged the law. He feared that discussion of controversial theories about biologically based differences between the sexes and races might lead to sanctions against him. Although the court struck down the University of Michigan's code on the grounds that it was overly broad and too vague, other campus codes still stand.

## FREEDOM OF ASSEMBLY

In addition to the freedoms of speech and of the press, the First Amendment guarantees "the right of the people peaceably to assemble." Such assembly is essential to the free exchange of ideas. It is at the basis of everything from political parties to protest marches. But like other First

Amendment freedoms, it is not absolute. As with speech, there are certain **time, place, and manner restrictions**. In other words, the freedoms of speech and assembly do not mean that people can assemble anytime, anywhere, and say whatever they want however they want. Just as students are not completely free to disrupt algebra class with political speech, the right of assembly must be balanced against other interests such as traffic safety, noise restrictions, and trespass laws.

For example, as part of the civil rights struggle of the 1960s, Harriet Adderly and other university students assembled outside a jail in Tallahassee, Florida, to protest racial segregation and the earlier arrest of fellow civil rights demonstrators. However, their assembly took place on restricted property. The county sheriff warned them to move their protest elsewhere, but the protesters refused and were arrested for trespassing. The Supreme Court upheld their subsequent convictions, noting that the trespass statute was designed to further the security of the jail. Moreover, the protesters had no lack of notice, the law was clear and uniformly applied, and the arrest took place not because of the *content* of the protesters' speech but because of their *conduct:* where they were saying it.[72]

In contrast, the Supreme Court overturned the convictions of civil rights protesters who were arrested on the grounds of the South Carolina state capitol. Unlike the jailhouse grounds, the area around the state capitol was open to the public and was considered a *public forum*: a place where people traditionally gather to express their views. And in contrast with the trespass ordinance in Florida, the breach of the peace ordinance that police used to arrest the protesters in South Carolina was vague and randomly applied. In fact, the breach of the peace was caused more by agitated onlookers than by the protesters themselves, who were peacefully singing hymns and songs such as "We Shall Overcome." In this case, the arrest *did* appear to be based upon the content of the protesters' speech and therefore violated the First Amendment freedoms of speech and assembly.[73]

Once again, it is sometimes difficult to determine when assembly is permissible and when it is not, especially in trying to determine precisely which locales constitute a public forum. Balancing public safety concerns with First Amendment rights can also be tricky. For example, the Supreme Court ruled in 1978 that the Chicago suburb of Skokie, Illinois—home to a large Jewish population—could not deny a permit for a march by the American Nazi Party.[74] Many in Skokie viewed it differently. They equated the Nazi march with constitutionally unprotected "fighting words" that would provoke a riot. In a 1942 case, the Supreme Court had suggested that some words are so inflammatory, so certain to provoke a violent response, that they are not deserving of free speech protection.[75] Others insisted that preventing the march would constitute a prior restraint; if a breach of the peace or riot ensued because of the march, the conduct should be punished after the fact. In the end, a federal court forced the City of Skokie to permit the Nazis to march.

Consider, too, the case of the Westboro Baptist Church, whose 75 members have staged hundreds of protests to highlight their belief that the ills of the United States—from the 9/11 terrorist attacks to Hurricane Katrina and other natural disasters—are God's punishment for a society that condones homosexuality. They first gained national attention by picketing the funeral of Matthew Shepard, a college student who was beaten to death in 1998 because he was gay. Their signs proclaimed that Shepard was in hell because "God Hates Fags." More recently, the church has targeted funerals and burials of American soldiers killed in Iraq—carrying signs such as "Thank God for Dead Soldiers" and "God Hates Your Tears"—because they believe that U.S. combat deaths are an example of God's just retribution for homosexuality in America.[76]

Such actions provoked the Southern Poverty Law Center to label the church a *hate group*. More than half the states have passed laws restricting graveside demonstrations. Congress also entered the fray by passing the Respect for America's Fallen Heroes Act (Pub.L. 109-228) to establish buffer zones around military cemeteries during burials; President George W. Bush signed it into law on May 29, 2006. Only three members of the House of Representatives voted against the bill. One was Ron Paul, a Republican from Texas who sought the Republican presidential nomination in 2008 and 2012. Another was Barney Frank, an openly gay Democrat from Massachusetts. Both questioned the constitutionality of the law and argued that it violated civil liberties. The Supreme Court has not directly ruled on the constitutionality of the law, but in 2011, it did reject a lawsuit brought against the Westboro Baptist Church by the family of a soldier whose funeral was picketed. The picketers stayed outside a 1,000-foot buffer zone from the church, and the Court upheld the picketing on free speech grounds.[77] In European countries

**time, place, and manner restrictions** The stipulation that the freedoms of speech and assembly do not mean that people can assemble anytime, anywhere, and say whatever they want, however they want.

that have laws regulating hate speech, regulating such demonstrations would be much easier; the free exercise rights (see below) of the Westboro Church would not be as much of an issue as it is in the U.S. Although Article 9 of the European Convention on Human Rights says that "Everyone has the right to freedom of thought, conscience, and religion," the Article goes on to say that the freedom of religion can be limited in the interests of "public safety ... the protection of public order, health or morals, or for the protection of the rights and freedoms of others."

# THE FIRST AMENDMENT GUARANTEE OF FREEDOM OF RELIGION

Much controversy has been generated by the two religion clauses in the First Amendment: the **establishment clause** and the **free exercise clause**. Incorporation has added fuel to the fire because it allowed the Supreme Court to use the First Amendment to strike down such customs as prayer in the public schools (which, if not for incorporation, would be a matter for individual states and localities to decide).

## THE ESTABLISHMENT CLAUSE

What does it mean to "make no law respecting an establishment of religion"? Should the establishment clause do nothing more than prevent Congress from interfering with the ability of states to establish religions? Or was it intended, as Thomas Jefferson famously put it in 1802, to establish "a wall of separation between church and state"? Even the framers disagreed about how to answer such questions.

The incorporation of the establishment clause in 1947 revived the debate. States were now prohibited from passing laws respecting an establishment of religion, but it remained unclear exactly what *establishment* means. At one extreme, so-called separationists argue that the establishment clause erects a high, impenetrable wall of separation between church and state that prohibits any governmental support of or financial aid to religion. At the other extreme, so-called accommodationists argue that the establishment clause only prevents the government from giving preferential treatment to one religion over another. Government aid or support to religion is acceptable as long as it is nondiscriminatory. In between are a variety of middle-ground approaches.

The battle between these two positions has played out in high-profile cases. In *Engel v. Vitale* (1962), the Supreme Court ruled on a case involving a prayer written by the New York State Board of Regents to be recited aloud each morning by students in New York's public schools: "Almighty God, we acknowledge our dependence upon Thee, and we beg Thy blessings upon us, our parents, our teachers, and our country."[78] The majority of the Court embraced a separationist view and held that any state-sponsored prayer in public schools violated the establishment clause, even if the prayer was nondenominational and participation in its recitation was voluntary.

The decision left students free to pray privately in school, and many religious organizations such as the American Baptist Convention, the American Jewish Congress, the American Lutheran Church, the Episcopal Church, the National Council of Churches of Christ, and the United Presbyterian Church initially supported the ruling on the grounds that religious training should be left to families and churches. Others, such as Senator Barry Goldwater (R-AZ), declared that the Court had "ruled against God."[79] Later, President Ronald Reagan expressed his opposition to the ruling in the 1980s, and his attorney general, Edwin Meese III, went even further. In a July 1985 speech to the American Bar

**establishment clause** The First Amendment provision that prevents government from imposing religion on citizens and is used to justify the separation of church and state.

**free exercise clause** The First Amendment provision that protects the right of citizens to practice their religion without governmental interference.

State-sponsored prayer in public schools was ruled unconstitutional in 1962 by the Supreme Court. Some schools replaced it with a moment of silence during which students were encouraged to pray if they wanted to. Does this satisfy the Court's ruling?

Association, Meese criticized the Supreme Court for ignoring the original intent of the establishment clause and called incorporation a "politically violent and constitutionally suspect" blow to federalism.[80] Over the years, several attempts to overturn *Engel v. Vitale* by constitutional amendment have failed.

Most countries around the world have also rejected the type of state-sponsored prayer at issue in *Engel v. Vitale*. A study by the American Civil Liberties Union concluded that only 11 out of 72 countries surveyed endorsed state-sponsored prayer. The countries that do so range from Saudi Arabia and Libya to Germany and Great Britain, and in the latter two countries, participation by students must be voluntary.[81]

Many establishment clause cases in the United States have involved disputes over some form of government funding. *Everson v. Board of Education* (1947), the case that incorporated the establishment clause, is an example.[82] Under New Jersey law, parents of schoolchildren were reimbursed for the cost of transportation to and from school, including parents of children who attended private religious schools. By a 5–4 vote, the Supreme Court ruled that such a reimbursement by the government did not violate the establishment clause.

In *Everson*, the money went to parents. What if government funds go directly to the religious schools? For instance, Pennsylvania had a program that reimbursed church-affiliated elementary and secondary schools for the cost of teacher salaries related to instruction in nonreligious subjects such as math and English. When the Supreme Court considered that program in *Lemon v. Kurtzman* (1971), it created a test to help determine when a law or program violates the establishment clause.[83] According to the three-part *Lemon* test, government laws and programs do not violate the establishment clause if the following conditions are satisfied:

1. They have a secular (nonreligious) purpose [the intent prong].
2. Their primary effect is neither to advance nor inhibit religion [the effect prong].
3. They do not lead to excessive government entanglement with religion [the entanglement prong].

The Pennsylvania program failed the *Lemon* test because it did not satisfy the last prong. Only "excessive and enduring entanglement" could guarantee that teachers were not interjecting religious beliefs into secular classes. The Supreme Court subsequently used the *Lemon* test to strike down an Alabama law that provided for a one-minute moment of silence in all public schools "for meditation or voluntary prayer."[84] The Court said that the law failed the first prong of the *Lemon* test: Its clear intent was to promote religion. The ruling implied that some moment of silence laws, if properly written and implemented, might pass the *Lemon* test. Likewise, the Supreme Court struck down a Louisiana law that required the teaching of "creation science" (a literal interpretation of the Biblical account of creation) alongside the teaching of evolution. The Court again said that the law violated the first prong of the *Lemon* test: The intent of the legislature was to promote religion.[85]

Compare those with a case that came before the Supreme Court in 2019 concerning a 40-foot-tall World War I memorial shaped like a Christian cross that stands on public land in Bladensburg, Maryland. The District Court concluded that the memorial had a secular purpose (to remember fallen soldiers), thereby passing the intent prong of the *Lemon* test, and that it also passed the effect and entanglement prongs. The Court of Appeals disagreed, however, saying that the memorial failed both the effect and entanglement prongs. A fractured 7–2 ruling by the Supreme Court ultimately held that the cross did not violate the establishment clause.[86]

The issue of separation of church and state is not unique to the United States. Article I of the French Constitution says that France shall be a "secular" republic, and since 1905, France has had a law requiring the separation of church and state.[87] In 2004, France passed a controversial law that banned the wearing of conspicuous religious symbols such as Muslim headscarves, Sikh turbans, Jewish skullcaps, and Christian crucifixes in government-operated primary and secondary schools.[88] Although the law was couched in the language of separation of church and state, many denounced it as a violation of religious freedom.

In the United States, the establishment clause and the free exercise clause are similarly apt to be at odds. The Supreme Court decided the *Everson* case the way it did partly because if the government had denied reimbursement of transportation costs to parents of children who went to religious schools while reimbursing parents of children who went to secular schools, the former group could feel that it was being penalized for its religious beliefs: a violation of the free exercise clause. Such tension between the establishment and free exercise clauses is not unusual. Whatever the tension, a majority of Americans seem to support the idea of a clear separation between church and state (see Figure 4.2).

## THE FREE EXERCISE CLAUSE

We take our right to worship for granted, but many countries restrict the free exercise of religion—sometimes brutally. For example, Eritrea—a small country in the northeastern part of Africa—bars many religious groups from practicing their faith publicly. Those who do are subject to arbitrary arrest and detention. Thousands of religious prisoners have been tortured or otherwise ill-treated, sometimes resulting in death. Members of the armed forces face severe punishment for the possession of any religious material, including Bibles. The government is especially fearful of Protestant Evangelical, Pentecostal, and other Christian denominations not traditional to Eritrea.

Among those persecuted in Eritrea are Jehovah's Witnesses. They are denied government-issued identity cards and therefore cannot get legal recognition of marriages and land purchases. Jehovah's Witnesses who, on religious grounds, have refused to serve in the military have been summarily imprisoned—sometimes for over a decade—without a trial. Children of Jehovah's Witnesses have been expelled from their schools for refusing to salute the flag (Jehovah's Witnesses believe that such salutes are forbidden by the Bible). And, like members of other unrecognized religious sects, Jehovah's Witnesses are regularly arrested without charge and imprisoned.[89]

Jehovah's Witnesses have also faced persecution in this country. Persecution of Jehovah's Witnesses was especially rampant during World War II because of their refusal to salute the American flag and their attempts to secure religious exemptions from military service—actions that led to charges that they were un-American. Some even claimed that Jehovah's Witnesses were Nazi sympathizers when, in fact, the Jehovah's Witnesses' campaign to do away with flag salutes had actually begun when Jehovah's Witnesses in Nazi Germany were sent to concentration camps for refusing to salute Hitler and the Nazi flag.[90]

Thousands of Jehovah's Witnesses were arrested in the United States during World War II for refusing to serve in the military, and the sect's members became targets of mob violence. Their door-to-door proselytizing and their harsh denunciation of organized religion, especially Catholicism, also fueled strong feelings against them. Between 1938 and 1946 alone, Jehovah's Witnesses were at the center of 23 Supreme Court cases. One of these cases, *Cantwell v. Connecticut* (1941), incorporated the free exercise clause of the First Amendment.[91]

*Cantwell* and many other free exercise cases rest on the distinction between religious *belief*, which is absolutely protected by the free exercise clause, and religious *action*, which is not. Similar to the distinction between speech and conduct, the so-called belief–action distinction was recognized by the Supreme Court in 1879 when it unanimously upheld an act of Congress that outlawed polygamy.[92] Mormons claimed that the law violated their free exercise rights, but the Court said that the law applied equally to everyone and restricted only action, not belief.

The Court also grappled with the belief–action distinction in *Cantwell*. Newton Cantwell and his two teenage sons traveled from state to state spreading the word of Jehovah. In New Haven, Connecticut, an overwhelmingly Catholic city, their proselytizing met harsh resistance. After several people complained to the police, the Cantwells were arrested and convicted for violating a state law that prohibited individuals from soliciting money for any cause without a license. They were also convicted of breaching the peace.

## FIGURE 4.2
## Separation of Church and State

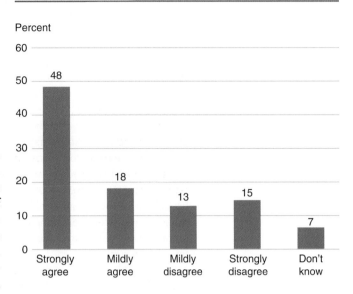

*How did those surveyed in this poll respond when asked whether they agreed that "The First Amendment requires a clear separation between church and state"? What do you think "a clear separation between church and state" means? Is the answer obvious?*
Source: First Amendment Center, State of the First Amendment Survey, 2010.

The Court unanimously struck down the Connecticut law because it allowed the government to pick and choose what causes were eligible for solicitation. The Court reaffirmed the belief–action distinction but concluded that the law violated the First Amendment because it allowed the same action to be treated differently depending upon the beliefs of those carrying out the action. The Court also overturned the breach of the peace conviction on the grounds that the Cantwells' actions were not "noisy, truculent, overbearing or offensive" nor did they draw a crowd or impede traffic. However, the breach of the peace conviction could have been upheld under the belief–action distinction if the Cantwells' actions had done any of those things.

Deciding when it is permissible for a generally applicable law to restrict free exercise rights can be tricky, as can deciding what exactly constitutes a protected religion. Do federal laws that criminalize drug use restrict the free exercise rights of Native Americans who use peyote as part of their religious worship services? Can a Muslim woman's driver's license be revoked if she refuses on religious grounds to remove her veil for a driver's license photo? Can localities use animal cruelty laws to prevent animal sacrifice when it is used as part of a religious worship service? The legal tests used to judge such cases have changed over time, but since 1990, the Court has held that generally applicable laws—those that apply equally to everyone, regardless of their religious beliefs—are presumed to be constitutional as long as they have a rational basis, even if they incidentally restrict some free exercise rights.[93] (For a full discussion of the rational basis test, see Chapter 14.)

Recently, the Court has considered cases involving the religious freedom of owners of businesses and public accommodations. In *Burwell v. Hobby Lobby Stores, Inc.* (2014), the Court ruled 5–4 that the provision of the Affordable Care Act requiring family-owned corporations to include, in opposition to their religious beliefs, contraceptive coverage as part of their health insurance plans violated the federal Religious Freedom Restoration Act (RFRA). Four years later, the Court ruled 7–2 in favor of the owner of a bakeshop in Colorado who refused, on religious grounds, to create a wedding cake for a same-sex couple.

## THE RIGHT OF PRIVACY

In addition to the specific guarantees of the Bill of Rights, such as freedom of speech, the Supreme Court has recognized one of the most controversial constitutional rights: the unenumerated right of privacy. This recognition has raised a whole host of questions. What is the basis for this right? After all, the word *privacy* never appears anywhere in the Constitution. Is it permissible for the Court to "discover" new rights and use them to strike down laws? Or do such discoveries amount to the Court impermissibly legislating from the bench? The right of privacy is especially contentious because it often involves highly controversial practices such as birth control, abortion, and consensual sex among adults as well as the right to die.

Unlike the U.S. Constitution's unenumerated right of privacy, the European Convention on Human Rights contains a specifically enumerated right of privacy, with Article 8, Section 1 stating, "Everyone has the right to respect for his private and family life, his home and his correspondence." Section 2, though, allows governments to restrict this right of privacy when that restriction is "in accordance with the law and is necessary in a democratic society in the interests of national security, public safety or the economic well-being of the country, for the prevention of disorder or crime, for the protection of health or morals, or for the protection of the rights and freedoms of others."

### THE NATURAL RIGHTS TRADITION

The United States has a long natural rights tradition. **Natural rights** are those basic, fundamental rights that all human beings are entitled to, whether the government recognizes them or not. The English philosopher John Locke identified life, liberty, and property as the quintessential natural rights. Thomas Jefferson borrowed from Locke when he wrote the Declaration of Independence. Some of those who opposed the addition of a Bill of Rights to the Constitution were afraid that an enumeration of rights would suggest that no unenumerated rights existed. Thus, the Bill of Rights ended up including the Ninth Amendment: "The enumeration in the Constitution, of certain rights, shall not be construed to deny or disparage

**natural rights** Basic rights that all human beings are entitled to, whether or not they are formally recognized by the government.

others retained by the people." Some people see this as a textual justification for the Supreme Court to recognize and enforce unenumerated rights. Others argue that the Ninth Amendment was only meant to allow states to go further in recognizing rights than the federal government: Lack of an enumerated right in the Constitution did not mean that it could not be recognized by a state.

Still others have asked a more fundamental question: Do natural rights exist at all? Even if they do, should a simple majority of the Supreme Court be entrusted with discovering them? To do so might open the door to judicial policy making. For example, in the early part of the twentieth century, a majority of the Supreme Court read economic rights into the Constitution and used them to strike down government regulations of business such as minimum wage laws, maximum hour laws, and child labor laws. Since 1937, when the Supreme Court overturned that line of decisions, the majority of the Court has viewed the decisions in those cases as misguided—an attempt by the Court majority to impose its policy judgments on everyone else.

Ultimately your enthusiasm (or disdain) for reading rights into the Constitution and then using them to strike down legislation may depend upon what you think about the legislation in question. If you like the legislation that is struck down, it is easy to accuse the Court of unjustifiable judicial activism. If you don't like the law, it is easy to praise the Court for vindicating natural rights.

## DISCOVERING THE RIGHT OF PRIVACY

The Supreme Court first established a constitutional right of privacy in *Griswold v. Connecticut* (1965).[94] By a 7–2 vote, the Supreme Court struck down a Connecticut law that made it a crime for anyone, including married couples, to use any form of birth control. In his opinion for the Court, Justice Douglas argued that this law violated the right of privacy of married couples (it took a future case to extend this constitutional protection to unmarried couples).[95]

Where did this right of privacy come from? Douglas argued that it was implied by specific language in the Bill of Rights. He noted that the First Amendment's guarantee of free speech and assembly protects the freedom to associate and implies a right of privacy in one's associations. The Third Amendment's prohibition against quartering soldiers in any house in time of peace without the permission of the owner suggests a zone of privacy against government intrusion. So, too, does the Fourth Amendment's ban on unreasonable searches and seizures and the Fifth Amendment's ban on self-incrimination. The Ninth Amendment clearly states that the failure to enumerate a specific right does not mean that it does not exist. Finally, the Fourteenth Amendment allows for fundamental rights to be incorporated. Taken together, Douglas argued that these specific provisions imply a zone of privacy broad enough to protect the marital bedroom from government intrusion and fundamental enough to apply to the state of Connecticut.

Not all the justices agreed with Douglas. Some thought the right of privacy was even more expansive than Douglas admitted, but signed on to his decision. Others strongly rejected any right of privacy. Hugo Black dissented even though he admitted that the Connecticut law was "every bit as offensive to me as it is to my Brethren of the majority."[96] But Black was a literalist, and he looked in vain for a specific constitutional clause that the law violated. "I like my privacy as well as the next one," Black wrote, "but I am nonetheless compelled to admit that government has a right to invade it unless prohibited by some specific constitutional provision."[97]

## ABORTION

*Griswold v. Connecticut* paved the way for *Roe v. Wade* in 1973.[98] *Roe* is one of the most famous and one of the most controversial of all Supreme Court decisions. It involved a Texas law that criminalized abortions. Was that law constitutional? By a 7–2 vote, the Supreme Court said no. But in so doing, it tried to balance two competing constitutional rights: the privacy right of a woman to control her own body versus the state's interest in protecting the life of the fetus.

Justice Harry Blackmun's majority opinion assumed that the right of privacy is fundamental and that any law interfering with that right triggers strict scrutiny. (For a more complete discussion of the strict scrutiny test, see Chapter 14.) Since the Texas antiabortion law interfered with a woman's right of privacy, the state of Texas had to demonstrate that it had a compelling reason to restrict that privacy right. The state claimed to have two compelling reasons: (1) protecting the health of the mother and (2) protecting the life of the fetus.

Blackmun assessed these claims in the light of medical technology as it existed in 1973. He relied on statistics showing that the abortion procedure was actually safer than childbirth until the end of the first trimester of pregnancy (each trimester represents three months of a pregnancy). Therefore, he concluded that the state did not have a compelling interest in regulating abortion procedures on safety grounds prior to that first "compelling point"—the end of the first trimester. However, he said that states did have a compelling interest in passing laws that regulated the abortion procedure in order to protect maternal health from that point forward.

Blackmun then asked, *When does a state have a compelling interest in protecting the life of the fetus?* At one extreme are those who argue that states have a compelling interest in doing so from the point of conception. Those at the other extreme argue that states do not have a compelling interest until childbirth because a fetus is not a person until then. Blackmun sought a compromise. When he was writing in 1973, a fetus could not survive outside of the mother's womb until the end of the second trimester, known as the *point of viability*. Using that as his second compelling point, Blackmun concluded that states have a compelling interest to regulate (and to ban completely, if they so choose) abortions in the last trimester.

This so-called trimester framework gave a woman's privacy right priority in the first three months of pregnancy but gave the state's interest in protecting life priority in the last three months of pregnancy. In the second trimester, states could regulate abortions in order to protect maternal health but could not ban the procedure altogether. In contrast, the two dissenters argued that laws banning abortions are a reasonable exercise of state police powers.

Like any middle ground position, the trimester framework came under attack from both sides. As time went by, advances in medical technology also eroded it. The first compelling point moved closer toward childbirth, while the second compelling point moved closer to conception. In other words, late-term abortions became safer, and premature babies born at earlier stages in their mothers' pregnancies began to survive with greater frequency. That change affected the second trimester, in particular. This development led some, such as Justice Sandra Day O'Connor, to suggest that the trimester framework should be abandoned.[99]

By 1992, the composition of the Supreme Court had changed dramatically since the 1973 decision in *Roe*, and many predicted that a new majority existed that would be willing to overturn it. The opportunity to do so came in *Planned Parenthood of Southeastern Pennsylvania v. Casey* (1992).[100] The resulting 5–4 decision abandoned the trimester framework but reaffirmed the "central tenet" of *Roe*. It also established a new "undue burden standard" (a middle ground between strict scrutiny and rational basis) that made it easier for some abortion restrictions to stand.

With President Trump's appointments of Neil Gorsuch and Brett Kavanaugh to the Supreme Court, there may be a new 5–4 majority willing to limit abortion rights further or even overturn *Roe v. Wade*. Although Chief Justice Roberts sided with the liberal wing of the Court in February 2019 to form a 5–4 majority to temporarily block a highly restrictive Louisiana abortion law from going into effect[101]—at least a short-term victory for proponents of *Roe*—it seemed certain that the Court would revisit the abortion issue soon.[102]

The availability of abortion varies across countries (see Figure 4.3). For example, a woman can go to prison for having an abortion in Chile. Abortion is illegal under all circumstances or permitted only to save the life of the mother in much of Africa and South America. On the other hand, since Ireland's historic 2018 referendum that overturned that country's long-standing ban on abortions, it is effectively allowed in all European countries, with some restrictions. For example, France requires a woman to undergo counseling before obtaining an abortion. And while Germany technically prohibits abortion, a woman will not be prosecuted for obtaining an abortion during the first trimester as long as she undergoes counseling that seeks to persuade her to carry the pregnancy to term. This compromise was forged after the reunification of East and West Germany in 1989. Abortion was one of the great debates of reunification because the people of East Germany had been accustomed to very liberal abortion laws whereas the people of West Germany had not.

FIGURE 4.3

## *Abortion Laws Around the World, 2019*

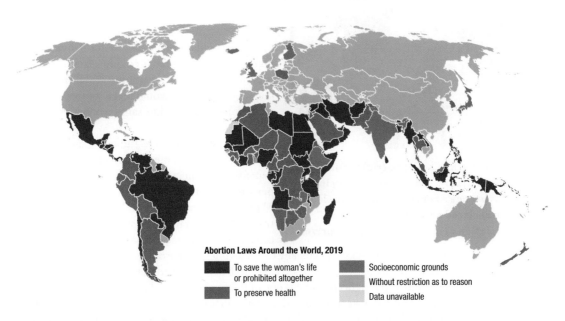

Abortion Laws Around the World, 2019

- To save the woman's life or prohibited altogether
- To preserve health
- Socioeconomic grounds
- Without restriction as to reason
- Data unavailable

*Source: Center for Reproductive Rights (www.worldabortionlaws.com).*

Abortion is a particularly contentious issue in the United States. As the political theorist Ronald Dworkin has noted, the controversy over abortion is in part a result of the explosive mix of religiosity and progressive women's movements in this country. The United States, he notes, is not only "among the most religious of modern Western countries" (and "by far the most fundamentalist") but also the home of a women's movement that has traditionally been more powerful than anywhere else.[103] Another important factor may be the way national abortion law came about in the United States. Instead of resulting from the normal process of political struggle and compromise worked out by Congress, it was established by the Supreme Court in *Roe v. Wade*. If *Roe* is ever overturned, each state legislature will need to decide whether or not to allow abortions, unless Congress chooses to enter the fray and establish a uniform policy for the entire country. Either way, political fights over the issue would be fierce.

## EXTENDING THE LIBERTY OF SAME-SEX COUPLES

How far does the right of privacy extend? *Griswold* gave married couples a limited privacy right to use contraceptives free from government intrusion. *Roe* then extended that right to cover aspects of bodily autonomy. But what about state laws that criminalize certain types of consensual sexual behavior among adults?

This issue came before the Supreme Court in *Bowers v. Hardwick* (1986).[104] The state of Georgia made it a felony, punishable by up to 20 years in prison, to engage in sodomy (defined by the law as oral or anal sex). The law applied equally to homosexual and heterosexual couples, including married partners. This case involved a gay Atlanta bartender named Michael Hardwick who was arrested for engaging in oral sex with another man in his own bedroom. A police officer accidentally discovered them when he came to serve Hardwick a warrant for not appearing in court for an open container violation. The district attorney did not prosecute Hardwick, but he did not drop the charges either. Therefore, Hardwick brought a civil suit challenging the constitutionality of the Georgia law in federal court. He argued that it violated the right of privacy. By a narrow 5–4 vote, the Supreme Court rejected that claim and upheld the Georgia law, claiming that it had a rational basis. The dissenters used strict scrutiny to conclude that the law violated the right of privacy.

REUTERS / Richard Carson

Tyron Garner (left) and John Lawrence (right) sued after sheriff's deputies discovered them engaging in consensual sex in Lawrence's home. The Supreme Court's decision in the case declared anti-sodomy laws an unconstitutional violation of individuals' right to privacy.

The Supreme Court overturned *Bowers v. Hardwick* in *Lawrence v. Texas* (2003).[105] This time, the majority concluded that laws criminalizing private, consensual homosexual conduct have no rational basis. Justice Antonin Scalia criticized this conclusion in dissent. If states have no rational basis to proscribe homosexual conduct, he asked, "What justification could there possibly be for denying the benefits of marriage to homosexual couples exercising '[t]he liberty protected in the Constitution'?"[106] His prediction that the majority's reasoning would make it more difficult for courts to uphold laws banning same-sex marriage proved to be correct.

In 2003, the Supreme Judicial Court of Massachusetts ruled 4–3 that "barring an individual from the protections, benefits, and obligations of civil marriage solely because that person would marry a person of the same sex violates the Massachusetts constitution."[107] Various states plus the District of Columbia followed suit, recognizing either marriage or civil unions/domestic partnerships of same-sex couples. However, other states specifically banned same-sex marriages. In 2015, the Supreme Court, in *Obergefell v. Hodges*, declared such bans to be unconstitutional. In a 5–4 ruling, the Court concluded that the right to marry is one of the fundamental liberties protected by the due process clause of the Fourteenth Amendment and that the equal protection clause prohibits same-sex couples from being treated differently than opposite-sex couples in the eyes of the law. By the time of the *Obergefell* decision, eighteen other countries (starting with the Netherlands in 2001) already recognized same-sex marriage. By 2019, twenty-seven countries sanctioned same-sex marriage, but consensual homosexual conduct remained illegal in over seventy countries.[108]

## THE RIGHT TO DIE

Courts have long recognized a common-law right of individuals to refuse most unwanted medical procedures. But does the right of privacy also extend a broader constitutional right—one that includes a right to die? May patients refuse invasive procedures that would extend their lives, such as the use of an artificial respirator, on privacy grounds? The issue is complicated because such patients are often incapacitated and are not able to express their wishes. Moreover, they may have left no written instructions, such as a living will. Can the patient's guardian make a substituted judgment for the patient in such a situation? This question is especially controversial because refusal of treatment under these circumstances often leads directly to the death of the patient.

Guardians sometimes argue that their loved one would not want to be kept alive with no hope of meaningful recovery—if, for example, the patient were brain dead. They offer the legal argument that forcing artificial life support on patients violates a fundamental right of privacy. But others argue that decisions to withdraw life support violate the patient's right to life and may even constitute murder.

The Supreme Court first confronted the right to die issue in *Cruzan v. Director, Missouri Department of Health* (1990).[109] As in *Roe v. Wade*, the Court balanced competing interests. The majority noted that patients have a constitutionally protected right to refuse medical treatment but argued that such a right must be balanced against the interests of states (such as their interest in protecting life). Thus, the Court upheld a Missouri law requiring "clear and convincing" evidence that a patient would want life support refused before granting a guardian's request to discontinue it. Seven years later, the Court ruled that a patient's privacy right does not include a constitutional right to commit suicide. Individual states are the ultimate arbiters of such decisions. By January 2019, seven states plus the District of Columbia chose to allow doctor-assisted suicide, either through legislation or court ruling.[110] Assisted suicide is legal in Germany and Switzerland, but some countries go even further. Active euthanasia is legal in Belgium, Canada, Colombia, Luxembourg, and the Netherlands.[111]

# THE RIGHTS OF CRIMINAL DEFENDANTS

Article I of the Constitution contains several specific rights of the criminally accused. For example, it provides for the **writ of habeas corpus,** a court order that allows a judge to release a prisoner who is being detained illegally. It also prohibits bills of attainder (laws that allow someone to be punished without a trial) and ex post facto laws (laws that make an action illegal retroactively). But most of the rights that we associate with the criminally accused are found in the Bill of Rights. Originally, of course, guarantees contained in the Bill of Rights applied only to federal criminal prosecutions. Incorporation made most of these guarantees applicable to the states as well, which, since most criminal trials take place at the state level, has had a profound effect on our criminal justice system.

## DUE PROCESS RIGHTS OF THE ACCUSED

We spoke earlier in this chapter about the concept of *procedural due process:* the idea that the government must follow fair proceedings before taking away a person's life, liberty, or property. The due process clause of the Fifth Amendment limits the actions of the federal government ("No person shall be . . . deprived of life, liberty, or property, without due process of law"). The Fourteenth Amendment added another due process clause that specifically limits state action ("[No] State shall . . . deprive any person of life, liberty, or property, without due process of law").

The Bill of Rights contains other specific guarantees that deal with the rights of criminal defendants. For example, the Fourth Amendment protects against "unreasonable searches and seizures." The Fifth Amendment requires grand jury indictment in capital or otherwise infamous crimes and protects against double jeopardy (being tried twice in the same court for the same crime) and self-incrimination. The Sixth Amendment guarantees the right to a speedy and public trial by an impartial jury in which the accused has the opportunity to confront witnesses against him or her and has the right to a lawyer. The Eighth Amendment protects against "cruel and unusual punishment" as well as "excessive bail" and "excessive fines."

Can the Fourteenth Amendment's guarantee of due process be met without incorporating these specific guarantees? Until the middle of the twentieth century, the Supreme Court often said yes. Most of the provisions of the Bill of Rights dealing with criminal defendants have only recently been incorporated, the majority of them in the 1960s and the prohibition of excessive fines as recently as 2019. Even today, some provisions—such as the Fifth Amendment right to grand jury indictment and the Eighth Amendment right against excessive bail—have not been incorporated. (See Table 4.2 on page 81.)

Before incorporation, states merely had to apply due process, and the Supreme Court often upheld convictions in cases where states did not follow other specific guarantees in the Bill of Rights—for example, convictions in cases where defendants were tried twice for the same crime or denied the right against self-incrimination.[112] As long as the overall criminal process seemed to be fair, a procedural error based on one of the specific guarantees of the Bill of Rights typically was not deemed serious enough to overturn a state court conviction.

Even after incorporation, the Supreme Court continues to recognize that there may be more than one way for states to prosecute accused criminals while still protecting their rights. Only those specific guarantees of the Bill of Rights that the Court has deemed "fundamental" have been incorporated. This has been done through the process of selective incorporation discussed earlier in this chapter. But some of the incorporated provisions are ambiguous, allowing the Court to give states some flexibility in the way they apply even some of the incorporated provisions.

A good example is the Sixth Amendment right to trial by jury in criminal cases. The Supreme Court incorporated that right in 1968.[113] But what exactly does *a right to trial by jury* mean? The Sixth Amendment says nothing about the specific size of the jury or whether the verdict must be unanimous. Nonetheless, all federal juries consist of 12 people and federal criminal cases require a unanimous verdict to convict. Does incorporation of the Sixth Amendment bind the states to juries of 12 people and unanimous jury verdicts? The Supreme Court has said no.[114] Nonetheless, the Court has held that juries that are *too* small (which it defines as any made up of fewer than six people) violate due process.[115] Likewise, it held that verdicts that are not

> **writ of habeas corpus** A judicial order requiring that a prisoner be brought before a judge to determine whether there is a lawful justification for incarceration.

# As a Prospective Juror in Japan

Throughout Japan, groups of people gathered to participate in more than 500 mock trials. Some took part in play-reading sessions of *Twelve Angry Men*, a 1954 television play about tense jury deliberations that became a classic 1957 movie. All of these events were staged in order to prepare citizens for a radical change in Japan's criminal justice system: the adoption of a system of trial by jury in 2009.

We take jury trials for granted, but 80 percent of Japanese opposed the change and said that they did not want to serve as jurors. Why not? The jury system violates several deep-seated cultural norms shared by Japanese: "a reluctance to express opinions in public, to argue with one another and to question authority."[a] The mock trials and play-reading sessions attempted to overcome those obstacles.

The new Japanese jury system is quite different from the one used in the United States. In Japan, six jurors sit with three professional judges. When weighing guilt or innocence and determining sentences, the jurors must arrive at a majority decision and have the support of at least one of the three judges.[b] Unlike American jurors, they can question witnesses.

Potential jurors were not the only ones nervous about the change. Lawyers were not used to making closing arguments or having to speak in terms that ordinary people could understand.[c] Experts expressed concern that randomly selected jurors would not be qualified enough to render verdicts in complicated criminal cases.[d] Prosecutors were afraid that conviction rates might fall.

In Japan, only those cases in which conviction is almost certain are brought to trial. The conviction rate for all prosecutions in Japan is over 99 percent, and failure to obtain a conviction can be a career setback. Jurors might also question the tools used by prosecutors, whose investigatory powers are largely unchecked.

Unlike the United States, where Miranda warnings and other procedural guarantees protect criminal defendants, suspects in Japan can be held for up to 23 days without access to a lawyer. Confessions of guilt are common during that time.[e]

The first case utilizing the new system took place in August 2009. More than 2,000 people lined up to watch the proceedings. Katsuyoshi Fujii, age 72, had already confessed to stabbing a neighbor to death; the jury was charged with determining a sentence. They questioned Fujii and the victim's son, and heard from Fujii's lawyers, who sought leniency. Prosecutors could have asked for the death penalty but suggested 16 years in jail; the jurors sentenced him to 15. This first case went smoothly, but a survey of potential jurors continued to show that one in four remained unwilling to serve— even though refusal would subject them to a fine of 100,000 yen (roughly $1,300).

Now, some years after the implementation of the new system, citizens are often still unhappy to be chosen to serve as jurors. Yet interviews with those who have served suggest that the overwhelming majority come away with a positive impression of the experience.[f] No significant reduction in convictions was noted in the first five years of the new system.[g] To the extent that the system contributes to the public's understanding of the judicial system and their confidence in it, the reform appears to be a success.

## Questions to Consider

1. Might the use of jurors in Japan lead to greater protection of civil liberties? If so, how?
2. What do you think of the concern that randomly selected jurors in Japan are not qualified to decide complicated cases? Is that a valid concern for American juries?
3. The right to trial by jury in criminal cases is a guarantee of the Sixth Amendment of the U.S. Constitution. Why is that right so important?

[a] Norimitsu Onishi, "Japan Learns Dreaded Task of Jury Duty," *The New York Times*, July 16, 2007.
[b] Justin McCurry, "Trial by Jury Returns to Japan," *The Guardian*, August 3, 2009, http://www.guardian.co.uk/world/2009/aug/03/japan-trial-by-jury-returns
[c] Richard Lloyd Parry, "Trial by Jury Returns to Japan and the Lawyers Aren't Happy," *The Times*, February 28, 2009, http://www.timesonline.co.uk/tol/news/world/asia/article5818123.ece
[d] "Japan's Landmark Jury Trial Ends," *BBC News*, August 6, 2009, http://news.bbc.co.uk/2/hi/8188447.stm
[e] Bennett Richardson, "In reform bid, Japan opts for trial by jury," *Christian Science Monitor*, June 4, 2004, http://www.csmonitor.com/2004/0604/p06s02-woap.html
[f] Dimitri Vanoverbeke, *Juries in the Japanese Legal System: The Continuing Struggle for Citizen Participation and Democracy* (New York, NY: Routledge, 2015), 159, 175.
[g] Ibid., 157.

unanimous may violate due process if the jury is too small: It ruled that even though 11–1 and 10–2 verdicts are constitutional, a 5–1 verdict violates due process.[116]

We take jury trials for granted, but they are largely a by-product of the common law system that originated in England. Many other countries with a civil law tradition (where law is codified in statutes rather than being based on legal precedents) do not have trial by jury. This includes countries such as France, Germany, and Italy. Others, such as Japan, have only recently instituted jury trials in some cases (see "Picture Yourself").

## JUDICIAL EXPANSION OF THE RIGHTS OF THE CRIMINALLY ACCUSED

In addition to specific guarantees in the Bill of Rights, the Supreme Court has used judicial opinions to expand the rights of the criminally accused. For example, it ruled in *Gideon v. Wainwright* (1963) that the Sixth Amendment right to legal representation applies to those who cannot afford a lawyer.[117] If the accused is too poor to hire one, the court must assign one. Many states have responded by creating a system of *public defenders*: lawyers whose full-time job is defending indigent criminal suspects.

The so-called *Miranda* warnings are another prime example of the Court expanding rights. After watching countless movies and television shows in which criminal defendants are read their rights, you can probably recite these warnings by heart:

> You have the right to remain silent. Anything you say can be used against you in court. You have the right to talk to a lawyer of your own choice before questioning. If you cannot afford to hire a lawyer, a lawyer will be provided without charge.

These warnings are the result of the 1966 case *Miranda v. Arizona*.[118] Prior to this case, the admissibility of confessions in state criminal cases was judged on a case-by-case basis using the basic standard of due process, with the Fifth Amendment right against self-incrimination not applying to police interrogations. *Miranda* required police to warn suspects, prior to questioning, that they had the right to remain silent and to request a lawyer. Absent such warnings, information obtained from suspects may not be admitted as evidence in court. Although some criticized the *Miranda* warnings as an example of the liberal Warren Court affording too many rights to criminal defendants, the conservative Rehnquist Court upheld the central holding of *Miranda* by a 7–2 vote in *Dickerson v. United States* (2000).[119]

Yet another judicially created principle is the **exclusionary rule**, which prevents evidence that was discovered by illegal means—for instance, through an improper search without a warrant—from being introduced in criminal trials. Created by the Supreme Court in *Weeks v. United States* (1914), the exclusionary rule was originally limited to federal cases.[120] Even when the Supreme Court incorporated the Fourth Amendment ban on unreasonable searches and seizures in 1949, it initially ruled that incorporation did not require states to apply the exclusionary rule.[121] That changed in 1961 with *Mapp v. Ohio*, which required states to enforce the exclusionary rule.[122] Similar to the Miranda warnings, the exclusionary rule has generated controversy. Some argue that it goes too far in protecting the rights of criminal defendants because it might allow a guilty person to go free if a police officer violates search-and-seizure guidelines. Others argue that it is an essential element of due process and an important deterrent against police misbehavior.

In the years since *Mapp* was decided, the Supreme Court has made some exceptions to the exclusionary rule. One of the most significant came in *United States v. Leon* (1984).[123] In that case, the Court ruled that evidence seized by police pursuant to an invalid warrant may be admissible because the error lies not with the police but the magistrate who issued the warrant. This is known as the *good faith exception*. Other countries also exclude certain evidence that has been tainted by police misconduct, but they are not as deferential to the rights of criminal defendants as we are in the U.S. Canada is a good example. Rather than assuming that all tainted evidence will be excluded, Canada calls for it to be excluded in those cases where it "is established that, having regard to all circumstances, the admission of it in proceedings would bring

*Miranda* warnings The list of rights that police must read to suspects at the time of arrest, including the right to remain silent and the right to request a lawyer. Absent such warnings, information obtained from suspects is inadmissible in court.

exclusionary rule The principle, created by the Supreme Court, that illegally seized evidence may not be introduced in criminal trials.

FIGURE 4.4

## Countries With the Highest Numbers of Executions, 2018

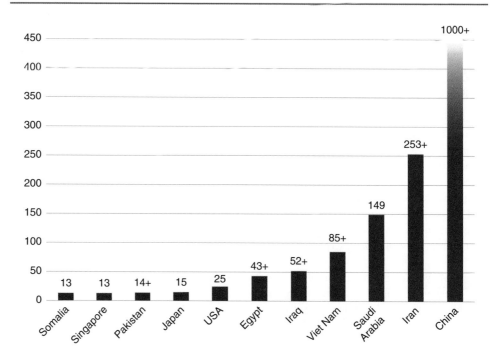

Note: Plus signs indicate that the figure calculated by Amnesty International is a minimum.

Source: "Death Penalty 2018: Dramatic Fall in Global Executions," Amnesty International, April 10, 2019, https://www.amnesty.org/en/latest/news/2019/04/death-penalty-dramatic-fall-in-global-execution/

the administration of justice into disrepute."[124] This provides a greater opportunity for tainted evidence to be admitted than would be the case under the U.S. system.

## THE DEATH PENALTY

Whether to administer the death penalty—and, if so, how—leads to great debate. The Eighth Amendment bans "cruel and unusual punishment." Does capital punishment violate that ban? If not, where does one draw the line between forms of execution that are constitutional and others that are not?

Some thirty-five years ago, lethal injections were introduced in the United States as a more humane alternative to electrocution, the gas chamber, hanging, and use of a firing squad. In 2008, the Supreme Court considered whether lethal injections cause unnecessary pain, thereby violating the Eighth Amendment. Typically, lethal injections consist of a three-drug cocktail administered intravenously. The first drug, an anesthetic, renders the condemned unconscious; the second drug paralyzes the body; the third drug causes cardiac arrest. Medical personnel do not administer lethal injections because to do so would violate the Hippocratic Oath they have sworn to "do no harm," and critics charge that the prison employees who typically administer these drugs are often poorly trained. If the first drug is not administered correctly, the inmate can experience excruciating pain that may not be apparent to onlookers because of the paralysis caused by the second drug. By a 7–2 vote, the Court upheld the use of lethal injections.[125]

As of March 2019, 30 states administer the death penalty. More than half the countries in the world have abolished the death penalty in either law or practice. It has been abolished completely in Canada, Australia, Britain, most of Europe, and parts of South America. The United

FIGURE 4.5

# *The Death Penalty and Public Opinion, 1937–2018*

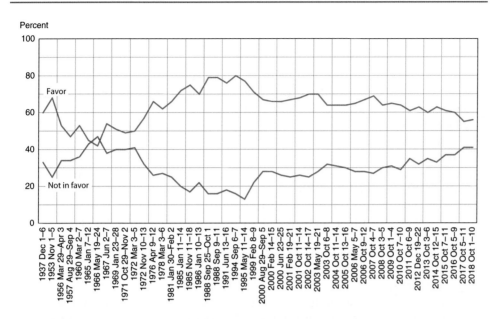

Percent

*Survey respondents were asked, "Are you in favor of the death penalty for a person convicted ot murder?"*

*Source: Gallup Poll (http://www.gallup.com/poll/1606/death-penalty.aspx)*

States is one of only five fully developed nations to retain the death penalty (the others are Japan, Singapore, South Korea, and Taiwan). According to Amnesty International, 20 countries carried out executions in 2018, with the United States having the seventh-highest rate of confirmed executions in the world.[126] (See Figure 4.4.)

Since the late 1960s, a majority of Americans have consistently supported the death penalty (see Figure 4.5). Support for the death penalty reached a high of 80 percent in 1994 and declined to 56 percent in 2018.[127] Only two Supreme Court justices have argued that the death penalty itself constitutes cruel and unusual punishment. However, a majority of the Court did rule in 1972 that random and arbitrary imposition of the death penalty may constitute both cruel and unusual punishment and a violation of due process.[128] It also ruled in 1977 that the death penalty may be an excessive form of punishment for certain types of crimes (such as rape of an adult).[129] In 2002, the Court ruled that executing mentally retarded offenders was unconstitutional.[130] The Court extended that ruling in 2005 to offenders who were under the age of 18 when they committed their crime.[131]

## BALANCING NATIONAL SECURITY WITH CIVIL LIBERTIES

Do the needs of national security justify restrictions on civil liberties? President Trump revived the debate when, in January 2017, he signed an executive order banning foreign nationals from seven predominantly Muslim countries from entering the United States. His stated purpose was to protect national security by keeping terrorists out of the United States. But given Trump's pledge during the 2016 presidential campaign for "a total and complete shutdown of Muslims entering the United States," some challenged the ban as a violation of religious liberty. Others challenged the ban on due process or equal protection grounds or as a violation of statutory guidelines. Although several lower courts overturned the ban, the Supreme Court ultimately upheld a revised version of the ban by a 5–4 vote in June 2018.[132]

Several Trump administration policies related to immigration (which the president formally declared to be a national emergency in order to build a wall along the southern border of the

United States) also raise civil liberties issues. The highest profile of these was perhaps the administration's family separation policy, which separated undocumented immigrants from their children as part of a zero-tolerance approach to deter migrants from entering the country. In yet another victory for the Trump administration, the Supreme Court voted 5–4 in March 2019 to uphold the government's authority to detain any immigrant awaiting deportation who had ever been convicted of a criminal offense—even if the conviction occurred long ago and the individual had completed their prison term for the conviction. In a strongly worded dissent, Justice Stephen Breyer argued that the ruling—which allowed individuals who had already paid their debt to society to "be deprived of their liberty for months or years without the possibility of bail"—raised serious due process concerns.[133]

Achieving a balance between national security and civil liberties was also hotly debated in the aftermath of the September 11, 2001, terrorist attacks on the World Trade Center and the Pentagon. As part of the "War on Terror," both Congress and President Bush took actions to limit civil liberties. Congress passed the USA Patriot Act in October 2001 to expand the government's power to collect phone records, monitor e-mail communications, and gather information from libraries and bookstores about what people were reading. It also contained "sneak and peek" provisions that allowed the government to seize information without informing the person involved. The government argued that such measures were necessary to combat the threat of terrorism and protect national security. In 2015, the USA Patriot Act was replaced by the USA Freedom Act, which still authorized government surveillance but with greater limits.[134]

Behind the scenes, President Bush secretly authorized the use of warrantless wiretaps by the National Security Agency on telephone calls between the United States and foreign countries in cases where one of the parties was suspected of links to al-Qaeda. When *The New York Times* revealed the program in 2005, critics charged that the Bush administration had ignored civil liberties and violated the 1978 Federal Intelligence and Surveillance Act (FISA), which allowed such wiretaps only if a special court issued a warrant for the tap either before or up to 72 hours after the start of the surveillance.[135] Although President Bush suspended the particular program uncovered by *The New York Times*, Congress validated his authority to wiretap foreign intelligence targets without a warrant, even if they were speaking to U.S. citizens, through amendments to FISA in 2007 and 2008.

Critics also raised concerns about the Bush administration's treatment of suspected terrorists. The administration claimed the right to detain terror suspects, including U.S. citizens, indefinitely without charge and without access to a lawyer. Several Supreme Court decisions limited the powers claimed by the Bush administration. For example, *Hamdi v. Rumsfeld* (2004) held that U.S. citizens, including terror suspects, have the constitutional right to consult a lawyer and to contest their detention before an independent tribunal.[136]

The Bush administration wanted any trials of these detainees to take place before a military commission rather than in federal court, and the president authorized the use of such military commissions by executive order. However, a 5–3 majority of the Supreme Court held in *Hamdan v. Rumsfeld* (2006) that military commissions were not authorized by Congress and violated international law.[137] The ruling was seen as a major setback for the Bush administration, but the Republican-controlled Congress subsequently passed the Military Commissions Act of 2006 at the urging of the White House. The Act authorized the use of military commissions. The Obama administration initially banned the use of military tribunals to try terror suspects but rescinded that ban in 2011.

Civil libertarians also expressed concern about the use of "enhanced interrogation techniques" (such as waterboarding) used against terror suspects by the Bush administration. The Bush administration denied that such techniques constituted torture and pointed to the broad prerogative powers claimed by presidents during war and other emergencies as a justification for such action, but critics disagreed. President Obama eventually revoked the executive order issued by Bush that had authorized enhanced interrogation.[138] Although Trump repeatedly endorsed such techniques during the 2016 presidential campaign (saying at one point that he would endorse the use of waterboarding "in a heartbeat" because "only a stupid person would say it doesn't work"), his Central Intelligence Agency director, Gina Haspel, promised during confirmation hearings not to resume the use of enhanced interrogation techniques.[139]

## CONSEQUENCES FOR DEMOCRACY

Constitutional language is the basis for our civil liberties, but it is important to remember that constitutional language alone is not enough to preserve them. The constitutions of many other countries, including China, offer similar guarantees that ultimately prove to be hollow. What makes the U.S. system different is its long-standing commitment to the rule of law—its willingness to hold the government accountable to the Constitution. Any retreat from that commitment to the rule of law would have profound consequences for the liberties we cherish and take for granted.

Even with a strong commitment to the rule of law, holding government accountable to the Constitution requires interpretation of that document. And, as we have seen throughout this chapter, the ambiguity of constitutional language gives the Supreme Court great power to determine the actual scope of civil liberties. Quite simply, the way that civil liberties are interpreted and enforced matters to our democratic system and to you. Your ability to protest the government, worship as you please, use birth control, marry a same-sex partner, and decide whether to refuse medical treatment all depend not only on what the Constitution says but also on how the Supreme Court interprets it.

That is why so many Americans pay attention to who sits on the Court. The large number of 5–4 decisions discussed in this chapter is a vivid reminder of the power of individual justices. It is undeniable that President Trump's appointments of Neil Gorsuch and Brett Kavanaugh have shifted the balance of the Court and will influence policy for years to come (just as Hillary Clinton's appointments would have done if she had won the 2016 election). That is why, as we will discuss in more detail in Chapter 14, judicial appointments are so important (and so highly contested).

Once they get on the Court, the tests justices choose to apply to individual cases have profound consequences. Being able to identify what kind of tests the justices use in particular cases may seem pedantic at first, but their choices affect everything from the regulation of your sexual behavior to whether an invocation is allowed at high school football games.

Incorporation has consequences, too. It has consequences for states, whose policy options are affected; for taxpayers, who may have to fund requirements such as jury trials in criminal cases; and for you, whose rights are extended.

Think about the consequences all of this has had for you and your friends. If you care about such things as prayer, guns, protest, sex, life, and death, civil liberties matter to you.

## Critical Thinking Questions

1. How would our system of government be different if the Supreme Court had not embraced incorporation, and how would that difference affect you?

2. When, if ever, would you be willing to allow the government to curtail your civil liberties?

3. To what extent should the Supreme Court be able to recognize rights that have not been enumerated in the Constitution?

## Key Terms

bad tendency test, 85

Bill of Rights, 76

civil liberties, 76

clear and present danger test, 85

due process clauses, 79

establishment clause, 91

exclusionary rule, 101

free exercise clause, 91

incorporation, 79

libel, 88

*Miranda* warnings, 101

natural rights, 94

prior restraint, 82

slander, 88

substantive due process, 80

symbolic speech, 86

time, place, and manner restrictions, 90

writ of habeas corpus, 99

Visit edge.sagepub.com/maltese to help you accomplish your coursework goals in an easy-to-use learning environment.

The Washington Post / Getty Images

# 5
# CIVIL RIGHTS

## After reading this chapter, you should be able to do the following:

- Identify how the U.S. Constitution and the U.S. Supreme Court addressed slavery prior to the Civil War.

- Examine the history of discrimination against African Americans and their struggle for equal treatment after the Civil War.

- Evaluate the role of the courts in expanding African American civil rights in the twentieth century.

- Review the history of gender inequality in the United States.

- Analyze the roots and ramifications of ethnic discrimination in the United States.

- Investigate how the fight for civil rights has moved beyond race, gender, and ethnic origins, including expanded rights for the lesbian, gay, bisexual, and transgender (LGBT) community.

- Explain the actions the federal government has taken toward redressing past discrimination and evaluate the effectiveness of these actions.

## Perspective: The Confederate Monument Debate

There has been a renewed debate recently about what, if anything, to do with Confederate monuments. There are more than 700 of them in 31 states across the United States, in public spaces ranging from city squares to state capitols and courthouse grounds. Most of the monuments were erected decades after the Civil War ended, during the height of the so-called Jim Crow era of racial segregation from the 1890s through the 1950s. Rather than honoring Confederate soldiers who died in the war, as most monuments did in the immediate aftermath of the conflict, these glorified leaders of the Confederacy.[1] Critics view them as symbols of white supremacy designed to defy civil rights. New Orleans mayor Mitch Landrieu agreed and ordered four such monuments to be removed in 2017.

One of the four New Orleans monuments that were removed did not even directly commemorate the Civil War. Instead, the Liberty Place Monument, erected in 1891, commemorated an 1874 Reconstruction-era uprising led by white supremacists. An inscription added to the monument in 1932 hailed that uprising as an important step toward the results of the 1876 elections, which—as the inscription put it—"recognized white supremacy in the South and gave us our state."[2] The other three monuments that were removed in 2017 honored leaders of the Confederacy. One was a bronze statue of Jefferson Davis (the only president of the Confederacy), which had been dedicated in 1911 at a "whites only" ceremony on the 50th anniversary of Davis's inauguration. Children wearing red, white, and blue formed a living Confederate battle flag and sang "Dixie" at the event. Another was a bronze statue of Confederate General G.T. Beauregard on horseback, unveiled in 1915 (the same year that the Hollywood film *Birth of a Nation* glorified the Civil War and the Ku Klux Klan). A time capsule in the giant marble base of the statue, put in place in 1913, contained Confederate flags, currency, medals, and a photo of Jefferson Davis.[3] The final monument (and the oldest) was a bronze statue, dedicated in 1884, of Confederate General Robert E. Lee standing high atop a 60-foot column, facing north with his arms crossed. Debate about whether to remove similar monuments in Virginia drew national attention and led to violence soon thereafter.

Although many aspects of the Civil War, the slavery issue, and race relations are distinctly American, many nations around the world have confronted similar questions about how to deal with monuments to former regimes. Understanding how they have dealt with the issue may offer guidance as we continue to struggle with how to resolve this contentious debate. In the aftermath of World War II, for example, the newly created Federal Republic of Germany (what we came to think of as "West Germany") banned the swastika, the Nazi party, and even publication of Adolf Hitler's book, *Mein Kampf,* and systematically removed Nazi-era memorials. In the years to come, it enacted laws against hate speech (*Volksverhetzung*—

literally "incitement of the people") and Holocaust denial, which remained in place after the reunification of East and West Germany. Thus, neo-Nazi marches are legal in the U.S., but not in Germany. No memorials to World War II generals grace the public squares of Germany nor is it legal to display the Nazi flag (though it is in the U.S.). Even Hitler's bunker in Berlin, where he killed himself in 1945, has been paved over for fear that it would be treated as a shrine for neo-Nazis. On the other hand, memorials to the victims of the Nazi regime have been erected—from the massive Memorial to the Murdered Jews of Europe (mere steps away from the Hitler bunker) to tiny brass cobblestones called *stolpersteine* ("stumbling blocks") on streets throughout Germany, providing brief biographical details of the men, women, and children deported from those locations to concentration camps during the war.[4]

The 1932 inscription on a Confederate memorial in New Orleans hailed the end of Reconstruction as recognition of white supremacy in the South.

**Brass markers called *stolpersteine* across Germany mark the last official address of thousands of victims of the Holocaust and are engraved with biographical details.**

Nazi Germany may seem like a particularly harsh comparison, but should any of the steps taken in postwar Germany be applied to the Confederate monument debate in the U.S.? Here, the display of the Confederate battle flag is a common sight. Until 2015, it flew over the state capitol of South Carolina, and it can still appear on special-order, state-issued license plates in several states as part of the Sons of Confederate Veterans logo. Should the battle flag be banned? Should there be more memorials to the victims of slavery and racial violence? Would something similar to *stolpersteine* make sense here—identifying spots where slaves were sold or where lynchings took place? Should we ban neo-Nazi marches and other forms of hate speech? Should Confederate monuments be removed? If so, all of them? Were all four of the New Orleans monuments equally offensive? Answers to these questions are not easy. **«**

# SLAVERY IN AMERICA

The struggle for **civil rights** in the United States—freedom from governmental discrimination (unequal treatment) based on age, gender, race, or other personal characteristics—has affected many groups in the United States. Slavery—sanctioned, however discreetly, by the U.S. Constitution—paved the way for decades of racial discrimination in the United States, and so we start there.

## SLAVERY AND THE CONSTITUTION

The U.S. Constitution did not contain the words *slave* or *slavery*, but debates about slavery—by then a firmly entrenched and legally recognized practice—greatly influenced the framers. Slavery, of course, does not comport with the framers' lofty rhetoric of rights, but the hard truth is that several sections of the Constitution not only recognized but indirectly sanctioned the practice of slavery.

For example, Article I, Section 9, in roundabout language, prohibited Congress from abolishing the importation of slaves until 1808 and empowered Congress to impose a tax or duty "on such Importation, not exceeding ten dollars for each Person." Article IV, Section 2 contained the so-called **fugitive slave clause**, which required the return of slaves (those "held to Service or Labour in one State under the Laws thereof") if they escaped to another state—even one where slavery was outlawed. And the so-called Three-Fifths Compromise of Article I, Section 2, discussed in Chapter 2, allowed each slave to be counted as three-fifths of one person for purposes of representation and taxation. Even the Bill of Rights originally did nothing to protect African Americans because the incorporation of the Bill of Rights—made possible by the ratification of the Fourteenth Amendment in 1868—is mostly a twentieth-century phenomenon (see Chapter 4).

Congress outlawed the importation of slaves in 1808, but the legality of slavery itself was a decision left to individual states. Early on, some states, such as Vermont (1777, before it officially entered the Union in 1781), Massachusetts (1780), and New Hampshire (1784) abolished slavery through

> **civil rights** Freedom from governmental discrimination (unequal treatment) based on age, gender, race, or other personal characteristics.
>
> **fugitive slave clause** A provision of Article IV, Section 2 of the Constitution that required the return of escaped slaves to their owners even if they fled to a state where slavery was outlawed. Repealed by the Thirteenth Amendment (1865).

## FIGURE 5.1
## *Timeline of the Abolition of Slavery*

|  |  |
|------|-------|
| 1444 | First public sale of African slaves in Lagos, Portugal |
| 1482 | Portuguese start building first permanent slave trading post at Elmina, Gold Coast (now Ghana) |
| 1510 | First slaves arrive in the Spanish colonies of South America, having traveled via Spain |
| 1518 | First direct shipment of slaves from Africa to the Americas |
| 1777 | State of Vermont, then an independent republic, becomes first sovereign state to abolish slavery |
| 1780s | Trans-Atlantic slave trade reaches peak |
| 1803 | Ban on import of slaves to Danish West Indies colonies takes effect |
| 1807 | United Kingdom outlaws British Atlantic slave trade |
| 1808 | End of slave trade in the United States |
| 1811 | Spain abolishes slavery |
| 1813 | Sweden bans slave trading |
| 1814 | Netherlands bans slave trading |
| 1826 | French ban on slave trading goes into effect |
| 1833 | Britain passes Abolition of Slavery Act, gradually ending slavery in all British colonies |
| 1819 | Portugal abolishes slave trade north of the equator |
| 1846 | End of slavery in Danish West Indies |
| 1848 | France abolishes slavery |
| 1851 | Brazil abolishes slave trading |
| 1858 | Portugal abolishes slavery in its colonies, though all former slaves are subject to a 20-year apprenticeship |
| 1861 | Netherlands abolishes slavery in Dutch Caribbean colonies |
| 1862 | Emancipation Proclamation declares end of slavery in the U.S. South |
| 1865 | 13th Amendment of Constitution bans slavery in the United States |
| 1886 | Cuba abolishes slavery |
| 1888 | Brazil abolishes slavery |
| 1926 | League of Nations adopts Slavery Convention abolishing slavery |
| 1948 | United Nations adopts Universal Declaration of Human Rights, including article stating, "No one shall be held in slavery or servitude; slavery and the slave trade shall be prohibited in all their forms." |

*Source: "Who Banned Slavery When?" Reuters, March 22, 2007, https://www.reuters.com/article/uk-slavery/chronology-who-banned-slavery-when-idUSL1561464920070322*

their state constitutions. But slavery continued to be legal in many states, and slaveholders in those states argued that slaves were property protected by the Fifth Amendment of the U.S. Constitution. (See Figure 5.1 for a chronology of slavery around the world.) Proslavery and anti-slavery forces in Congress agreed on the Missouri Compromise in 1820, which—with the exception of Missouri—banned slavery in new states north of the 36° 30' latitude line (see Figure 5.2). But Congress repealed the Missouri Compromise through passage of the Kansas–Nebraska Act of 1854, thereby allowing each territory to decide for itself whether or not to allow slavery.

## SLAVERY AND THE SUPREME COURT

Proponents of slavery generally embraced states' rights, but they did champion one aspect of national supremacy: the power of Congress to enforce the fugitive slave clause of the Constitution through legislation such as the Fugitive Slave Act of 1793. This, they argued, prevented states from passing laws, such as one enacted by Pennsylvania in 1826, to protect

## FIGURE 5.2
## *The Missouri Compromise, 1820*

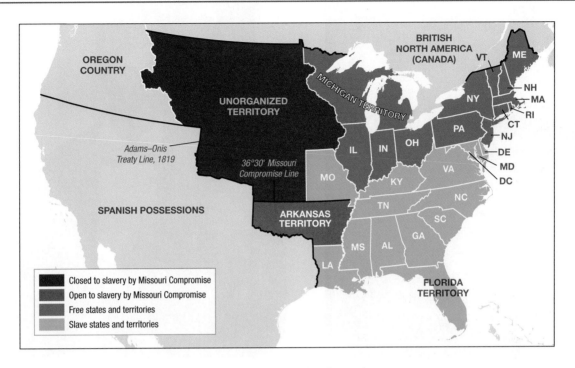

Legend:
- Closed to slavery by Missouri Compromise
- Open to slavery by Missouri Compromise
- Free states and territories
- Slave states and territories

*Source: https://teachingamericanhistory.org/static/neh/interactives/sectionalism/lesson1/*

the due process rights of African Americans. The Supreme Court invalidated the Pennsylvania law in 1842, arguing that the federal government had exclusive power to regulate the return of fugitive slaves.[5]

A year earlier, the Supreme Court had ruled in favor of 53 Africans who, on the slave ship *Amistad* bound for Puerto Principe, Cuba, had revolted, killed the captain, and tried to return the ship to Africa but ended up in the United States instead. There, proslavery advocates deemed the men slaves and wanted them tried for mutiny, murder, and piracy. Abolitionists, on the other hand, viewed the men as victims: freemen who had been kidnapped and therefore had a right to resist their captors. The Supreme Court sided with the abolitionists. It freed the Africans and allowed them to return to Sierra Leone.[6]

The *Amistad* case was a rare Court victory for abolitionists, who suffered a stinging defeat in *Dred Scott v. Sandford* (1857), one of the most infamous decisions ever handed down by the Supreme Court. The case involved Dred Scott, who had been born a slave in Virginia and had been sold to an army surgeon, John Emerson, in 1832. Emerson's military career took him to Illinois and the Wisconsin territory, where slavery was banned. Eventually, while serving in the Seminole War, Emerson left Scott with Emerson's wife in St. Louis, Missouri. Emerson died in 1843, and Scott tried to purchase his freedom from Mrs. Emerson. She refused, and Scott subsequently sued for his freedom, citing precedents in Missouri case law holding that slaves brought to Missouri after having resided in free states (such as Illinois) or territories were entitled to their freedom.

The Missouri trial court ruled in favor of Scott, but the Missouri Supreme Court overturned the ruling and abandoned earlier "once free, always free" precedents. The U.S. Supreme Court affirmed that ruling. In so doing, it could have simply declared that the Missouri Supreme Court had the final word on Missouri law. Instead, in an opinion written by Chief Justice Roger B. Taney, the Supreme Court issued a sweeping ruling that deemed African Americans a "subordinate and inferior class of beings" who were—even if they were free blacks—disqualified from U.S. citizenship and therefore unable to sue in federal court.[7] Moreover, the Court ruled that Congress had exceeded its authority when it passed the Missouri Compromise and explicitly held that slaves were property whose owners deserved constitutional protection.[8]

Chief Justice Roger Taney (left) ruled that Dred Scott (right) and all African Americans were a "subordinate and inferior class of beings" who did not have the right to sue in federal court.

Reaction to the *Dred Scott* decision was fierce. It crystallized attitudes on both sides of the slavery issue and, many argue, made the Civil War inevitable. That war was largely, but not exclusively, a battle over slavery. President Abraham Lincoln issued the Emancipation Proclamation in September of 1862 freeing slaves in all Confederate states that did not return to Union control by January 1, 1863. Notably, the Emancipation Proclamation did not free slaves in Union states. The complete abolition of slavery did not come until after the Union victory in the Civil War, with the ratification of the Thirteenth Amendment to the Constitution on December 6, 1865.

## CIVIL RIGHTS FOR AFRICAN AMERICANS AFTER THE CIVIL WAR

**Thirteenth Amendment** The constitutional amendment that abolished slavery and other forms of involuntary servitude.

**Fourteenth Amendment** The constitutional amendment containing the guarantees that no state shall deprive any person of the equal protection of the law nor deprive any person of life, liberty, or property without due process of law.

**Fifteenth Amendment** The constitutional amendment guaranteeing that the right to vote will not be denied based on race, color, or previous condition of servitude.

The period from 1865 to 1877, known as *Reconstruction*, saw various attempts by the Republican-controlled Congress to redress the inequities of slavery and promote the civil rights of African Americans. For example, the Civil War amendments to the Constitution—the Thirteenth, Fourteenth, and Fifteenth Amendments—did much to lay the groundwork for equal rights. The Thirteenth Amendment (1865) abolished slavery and other forms of involuntary servitude. The Fourteenth Amendment (1868) contained, among other things, the equal protection clause stating that no state shall "deny to any person within its jurisdiction the equal protection of the laws." It also, as discussed in Chapter 4, contained language that has made most provisions of the Bill of Rights applicable to the states through the process of incorporation. The Fifteenth Amendment (1870) guaranteed that the right to vote would not be "denied or abridged by the United States or by any State on account of race, color, or previous condition of servitude." Likewise, Congress passed sweeping civil rights legislation in the 1860s and 1870s. However, subsequent Supreme Court rulings neutered those laws and minimized Congress's power to enforce the Fourteenth Amendment. The end of Reconstruction allowed the passage of new laws that stifled voting rights, perpetuated the lingering effects of slavery, and promoted racial segregation.

## THE BLACK CODES AND THE CIVIL RIGHTS ACTS OF THE 1860S AND 1870S

Although Southern states were required to ratify the Thirteenth Amendment before being readmitted to the Union, they proceeded to pass laws known as the **Black Codes** that replaced Slave Codes that had existed before the Civil War. These new Black Codes, which varied from state to state, perpetuated legal discrimination and effectively "preserved slavery in form after it had been abolished in fact."[9]

Thus, South Carolina law required that African Americans who contracted to work for white employers be known as *servants*, and their employers be known as *masters*. All the codes allowed unemployed blacks to be arrested for vagrancy and then hired out to pay off their fine. For example, the Louisiana code required that "every adult freed man or woman shall furnish themselves with a comfortable home and visible means of support within twenty days after the passage of this act." Those who did not meet that requirement—which was almost impossible to fulfill in such short time—were to be "immediately arrested by any sheriff or constable" and hired out to "the highest bidder, for the remainder of the year."[10] The various codes also prohibited blacks from pursuing certain occupations, living in certain areas, marrying whites, and owning firearms. They excluded blacks from voting and authorized whipping as a form of punishment for blacks.[11]

Congress quickly intervened to invalidate the Black Codes through passage—over the veto of President Andrew Johnson—of the Civil Rights Act of 1866. The Black Codes also helped to precipitate passage of the Fourteenth and Fifteenth Amendments to the Constitution, and Congress passed additional Civil Rights Acts in the 1870s that were the most sweeping national efforts to protect African Americans until the 1960s. The Civil Rights Act of 1875 was particularly important because Congress outlawed discrimination in businesses such as restaurants, hotels, and theaters from which African Americans were frequently barred. Each of the Civil War amendments contained an enabling clause—that is, a provision that gave Congress the power to enforce the amendment through legislation. In passing the Civil Rights Act of 1875, Congress relied on its enabling clause power to enforce the equal protection clause.

## THE SUPREME COURT INTERVENES: THE CIVIL RIGHTS CASES AND *PLESSY V. FERGUSON*

The flurry of protection accorded African Americans by Congress proved to be short-lived. Soon the Supreme Court turned back many of the advances brought about by the Civil War Amendments and the Civil Rights Acts. In the *Civil Rights Cases* (1883), the Court ruled 8–1 that Congress did not have the authority to outlaw private discrimination in hotels, restaurants, and other business establishments because the equal protection clause only limited *state* action: "No *state* shall . . . deny to any person within its jurisdiction the equal protection of the laws." Thus, the enabling clause only empowered Congress to pass laws preventing state-sanctioned discrimination.[12]

The lone dissent came from John Marshall Harlan, a southerner from Kentucky. Harlan had previously owned slaves and had originally opposed the Emancipation Proclamation and the Civil War Amendments, but he later changed his mind and become one of the great champions of civil rights. He had, in 1877, been the first southerner appointed to the Supreme Court after the Civil War and his nomination generated some opposition from Republican stalwarts because of that, although he ended up being confirmed by voice vote.[13]

Thirteen years after the Civil Rights Cases, the Supreme Court took an even more significant step in *Plessy v. Ferguson* (1896). An 1890 Louisiana law required railroad companies to provide "equal but separate accommodations for the white and colored business" and made it a criminal offense for a person of one race to insist on occupying a seat in a railroad car designated for another race. An organization of black and white citizens proceeded to challenge the law. They recruited 30-year-old Homer Plessy, who was one-eighth black, to purchase a seat on

**Black Codes** Post–Civil War laws passed by states that perpetuated discrimination against African Americans.

*Civil Rights Cases* Cases wherein the Supreme Court ruled that Congress did not have the authority to outlaw private discrimination in business establishments.

*Plessy v. Ferguson* A Supreme Court ruling that established the "separate but equal" doctrine, upholding state segregation laws.

the railroad car for whites. Plessy was light-complexioned and could easily pass for a white man, but according to Louisiana law, he was considered black. Once Plessy took his seat, he announced that he was one-eighth black, refused to move, and was arrested. As such, he was able to challenge the Louisiana law. In a 7–1 ruling, the Court upheld the Louisiana law. It embraced the view that the equal protection clause of the Fourteenth Amendment allowed segregation of the races, thus establishing the **separate but equal doctrine**. Justice Harlan was once again the lone dissenting voice. In passionate and eloquent language, he chastised the majority for its ruling. "Our Constitution is color-blind," he insisted, "and neither knows nor tolerates classes among citizens. . . . The thin disguise of 'equal' accommodations for passengers in railroad coaches will not mislead any one, nor atone for the wrong this day has done."[14]

## THE RISE OF JIM CROW LAWS AND BARRIERS TO VOTING

The separate but equal doctrine embraced by the Supreme Court in *Plessy v. Ferguson* led to the proliferation of state and local laws requiring the segregation of the races. These came to be known as **Jim Crow laws** —named after a character in minstrel shows played by a white man in blackface. Laws such as those banning intermarriage among the races, requiring separate schools for black and white students, and preventing white female nurses from working in wards for black patients are all examples of Jim Crow laws. At the same time, states embraced a variety of discriminatory devices used to keep African Americans from voting. These included poll taxes, literacy tests, grandfather clauses, and white primaries.

*Jim Crow* was a character in minstrel shows portrayed by a white man in blackface.

**Poll taxes** required each voter to pay a tax in order to vote. Poll taxes had been common during the colonial period but had become rare by the mid-1800s. They were revived in the late nineteenth century as a way to prevent poor blacks from voting. The Supreme Court unanimously upheld the constitutionality of poll taxes in *Breedlove v. Suttles* (1937), but the Twenty-Fourth Amendment to the Constitution (1964) banned the use of poll taxes in federal elections, and the Supreme Court declared the use of poll taxes in state elections to be unconstitutional in *Harper v. Virginia State Board of Elections* (1966), thereby overruling *Breedlove*.[15]

**Literacy tests** were also administered as a precondition for voting. Although theoretically meant to determine whether a voter could read and write, complicated questions on literacy tests were really designed to prevent African Americans from voting. They frequently included arcane questions about the U.S. Constitution and state law. These tests prevented many literate blacks from voting, but they did not prevent illiterate whites from voting because **grandfather clauses** exempted voters from literacy tests and poll taxes if they could prove that their grandfathers had voted before a date that corresponded with the end of the Civil War. The Supreme Court struck down the use of grandfather clauses in *Guinn v. United States* in 1915.[16] Congress finally suspended the use of literacy tests through the Voting Rights Act of 1965.

The Democrats were the dominant party in the "solid South" after the Civil War—so much so that whatever candidate won a primary election for state and local office was all but guaranteed to win the general election. To further minimize the influence of black voters, southern states instituted **white primaries**. In other words, only white voters were allowed to vote in the primary election—the only one that really mattered because whichever Democratic candidate won the primary was assured of victory in the general election.

**separate but equal doctrine** Based on the *Plessy v. Ferguson* ruling that claimed that the equal protection clause of the Fourteenth Amendment allows the segregation of races.

**Jim Crow laws** State and local laws requiring the segregation of the races, including prohibition of interracial marriage and mandating of racially segregated schools.

**poll taxes** Tax payments required prior to voting; revived by states in the late nineteenth century as a way to prevent poor blacks from voting.

# AFRICAN AMERICAN CIVIL RIGHTS IN THE TWENTIETH CENTURY

The combination of Supreme Court rulings, Jim Crow laws, and voting restrictions had a devastating effect on the rights of African Americans. The Ku Klux Klan, a white supremacist vigilante group that had originally formed in the 1860s but mostly died out after Reconstruction ended, resurfaced with a vengeance in the twentieth century. By the 1920s, the Klan had become a major social and political force. Its symbol of intimidation was the burning cross, and over the years, the Klan came to be associated with the lynching of African Americans and with other mob violence.

The Ku Klux Klan gained strength during a period of massive immigration from Europe. In addition to white supremacy, it embraced harsh anti-immigrant, anti-Catholic, and anti-Semitic views. The Klan was so prevalent in some states, such as Alabama, that politicians felt they had to join it in order to win elections. This was true even of some progressive politicians, such as Hugo Black, who briefly joined the Klan in 1923, was elected to the U.S. Senate from Alabama in 1927, and went on to be appointed to the U.S. Supreme Court by Franklin Roosevelt in 1937.[17] Neither Black's tenure in the Senate nor his rulings on the Supreme Court reflected the views of the Klan; in fact, Black became a champion of civil rights.

## THE NAACP AND THE FIGHT FOR CIVIL RIGHTS THROUGH THE COURTS

In 1909, a coalition of blacks and progressive whites formed the **National Association for the Advancement of Colored People (NAACP)**, an organization devoted to promoting the civil rights of African Americans. Early in its history, the NAACP turned to the courts to accomplish its goals. It played an important role in the above-mentioned *Guinn v. United States* (1915), which struck down the use of grandfather clauses. The NAACP also brought legal challenges to segregation. For example, a case brought by the NAACP led the Supreme Court in 1917 to strike down a Louisville, Kentucky, ordinance that required residential neighborhoods to be segregated by race.[18] Involvement in these early cases was piecemeal and largely unorganized.

By the 1920s, however, the NAACP began planning a more systematic strategy to use legal challenges to fight segregation. It hired full-time legal staff and, in 1939, created a separate group—the NAACP Legal Defense and Education Fund (LDF)—to devote all of its energies to litigation. Thurgood Marshall, who had worked on the NAACP's legal staff since 1935, became the first director and chief counsel of the LDF. (He went on, in 1967, to become the first African American justice on the U.S. Supreme Court.) The NAACP timed the creation of the LDF well. The Supreme Court's "switch in time" in 1937 (see Chapter 3) led the Court to become more receptive to cases involving individual rights. As a result, the LDF's systematic court challenges led to a series of court victories over the next decade, notably in the area of segregated education.

Initially, the LDF won victories without directly overturning *Plessy v. Ferguson* and its separate but equal doctrine. *Sweatt v. Painter* (1950) is a good example. That case involved Heman Marion Sweatt, an African American who had applied to the University of Texas Law School in Austin. The school automatically rejected his application because Texas law prohibited integrated schools. When Sweatt sued, Texas hastily created a separate law school for blacks in Houston. The Supreme Court unanimously ordered the University of Texas to admit Sweatt to the Austin campus because the separate law school for blacks was clearly not its equal.

Although the Court did not overturn the separate but equal doctrine, its ruling was based on more than the physical inequities between the schools, such as the comparative sizes of their faculty and libraries. Significantly, it implied that separate law schools for blacks in Texas could never be equal to those for whites. A law school "cannot be effective in isolation from the individuals and institutions with which the law interacts," Chief Justice Vinson wrote, yet the separate law school for blacks excluded the 85 percent of the population that included most of the "lawyers, witnesses, jurors, judges and other officials" with whom Sweatt and other African American lawyers would inevitably deal.[19]

Based on that language, the NAACP decided that the time had come to challenge the separate but equal doctrine head-on. The LDF brought challenges to segregated primary and

**literacy tests** A precondition for voting in some states, purportedly to verify a voter's ability to read or write but actually designed to prevent blacks from voting.

**grandfather clauses** Exempted voters from literacy tests and poll taxes if they could prove that their grandfathers had voted before the end of the Civil War.

**white primaries** A Southern strategy for minimizing black voter influence that allowed only white voters to vote in the primary elections (the only ones that really mattered).

**National Association for the Advancement of Colored People (NAACP)** An organization devoted to promoting the civil rights of African Americans.

secondary schools in Delaware, Kansas, South Carolina, Virginia, and Washington, DC, on the grounds that such segregation violated the equal protection clause of the Fourteenth Amendment. At the Supreme Court level, these challenges were consolidated into one case: *Brown v. Board of Education*.

## BROWN V. BOARD OF EDUCATION

When *Brown v. Board of Education* was first argued before the Supreme Court in 1952, the justices were divided about how to rule.[20] Even Chief Justice Vinson, who had written the opinion in *Sweatt v. Painter*, was reluctant to take the next step and explicitly overrule *Plessy v. Ferguson*. The justices were still deadlocked in the summer of 1953 when Vinson unexpectedly died and was replaced by Earl Warren. Partly as a stalling tactic to buy time to gain greater consensus, the Court ordered the case to be reargued. An astute politician, Chief Justice Warren also convinced his colleagues to divide *Brown* into two cases. The first would focus on the merits of the case (whether segregated schools violated the equal protection clause), and the second would focus on the more difficult question of relief (how to implement school desegregation if they did).

Under Chief Justice Warren's leadership, the Court issued a unanimous decision in 1954 rejecting the application of the separate but equal doctrine to elementary and secondary schools. The decision effectively overturned *Plessy v. Ferguson*, although it technically applied only to segregated schools. Warren wrote the opinion in *Brown* himself and chose simple, non-accusatory language. He assumed, correctly, that the opinion would be printed in newspapers around the country, and he wanted average people to be able to read and understand it. He noted in the opinion that "education is perhaps the most important function of state and local governments" and that "it is doubtful that any child may reasonably be expected to succeed in life if . . . denied the opportunity of an education." Warren then turned to the central question: "[I]n the field of public education, the doctrine of 'separate but equal' has no place."[21] Having overturned the separate but equal doctrine in education, a more difficult problem remained: how to implement school desegregation. In *Brown v. Board of Education II* (1954), the Supreme Court unanimously ordered local school boards and the lower courts to handle the planning and implementation but allowed them to do so "with all deliberate speed"—a phrase that seemed to invite delay and obstruction. Indeed, much of the South mobilized against enforcement of school desegregation.

In 1957, Governor Orval Faubus of Arkansas ordered the Arkansas National Guard to block the entry of African American students at Little Rock Central High School, prompting a showdown with President Dwight D. Eisenhower. Eisenhower federalized the Arkansas National Guard, thereby taking control away from Faubus, and sent federal troops to Arkansas to enforce desegregation. In a measure of public sentiment at the time, Faubus was named one of the "Ten Most Admired Men in America" in a 1958 Gallup poll. As late as 1964—a decade after the initial ruling in *Brown v. Board of Education*—only about 2 percent of black children in the South attended elementary or secondary schools with white children.[22]

## THE CIVIL RIGHTS MOVEMENT

Although *Brown v. Board of Education* did not immediately bring about school desegregation, it did serve as a major catalyst for the ensuing civil rights movement. Buoyed by its success in *Brown*, the NAACP continued to fight segregation in other venues. When 15-year-old Claudette Colvin was arrested in Montgomery, Alabama, for refusing to give up her seat in the "colored" section of a crowded segregated bus to a white woman, the NAACP saw an opportunity. By custom, Montgomery bus drivers asked black passengers to give up their seats in the first row of the black section when the white section was full, thereby extending the number of seats available to white passengers. But this actually violated the law. Montgomery law said that segregation must be enforced. As part of that enforcement of segregation, the law also said that no black passenger in the "blacks only" section could be asked to give up a seat to a white passenger, just as no white passenger in a "whites only" section could be asked to give up a seat to a black person. Thus, Colvin's arrest violated a law that everyone had come to ignore. The NAACP enlisted Rosa Parks, whom they considered to be better prepared to endure a protracted legal battle, to challenge the

*Brown v. Board of Education* The Supreme Court decision that overturned the "separate but equal" doctrine and declared racially segregated schools to be unconstitutional.

practice that led to Colvin's arrest and to draw attention to segregation. Thus, just as Colvin had done, Parks refused to give up her seat in the black section of the bus to a white passenger and was arrested. The NAACP not only helped Parks win her successful legal battle but organized a boycott of the Montgomery bus system that lasted for 381 days. A 26-year-old black minister, Martin Luther King, Jr., came to prominence during that boycott. King embraced the philosophy of nonviolent civil disobedience taught by India's Mahatma Gandhi (1869–1948) and formed the Southern Christian Leadership Conference (SCLC) in 1957.

Bettmann / Getty Images

After a series of attacks on the buses carrying Freedom Riders, the National Guard was called in to stop the violence, but arrests continued for violations of Jim Crow laws.

Another group that embraced nonviolent resistance was the Congress of Racial Equality (CORE). Among CORE's activities were the Freedom Rides, begun in 1961 to test a 1960 Supreme Court ruling in *Boynton v. Virginia* that struck down racial segregation in interstate passenger transportation (such as interstate buses and bus stations) on the grounds that it violated the federal Interstate Commerce Act.[23] Freedom Riders were groups of black and white civil rights activists who rode Greyhound and Trailways buses through the South. At least one black Freedom Rider on each bus would sit with a white counterpart at the front of the bus—the area traditionally reserved for white passengers only—and at least one black Freedom Rider would sit in the back of the bus to avoid arrest, report back to CORE, and arrange bail for those who were arrested.

Tensions rose as the buses traveled into the Deep South. The first—a Greyhound bus on a route that was usually full—held only five regular passengers as it passed into Alabama, along with seven Freedom Riders and two journalists. When the bus pulled into the station at Anniston, Alabama, a mob of about 50 people led by the Ku Klux Klan attacked the bus, beating it with clubs, metal pipes, and chains, smashing its windows, and slashing its tires.

When the police arrived, they did not arrest anyone. Instead, they simply escorted the bus to the city limits. The police then turned back to town and let the bus go on its way, even though 30 or 40 cars carrying members of the mob had followed them. Finally, unable to go any further because of its slashed tires, the bus stopped and the mob attacked the bus again. Someone threw a flaming bundle of rags into the bus that then exploded and started a fire in the bus. The mob held the door of the bus shut, shouting, "Burn them alive!" Only when the gas tank exploded did the startled mob retreat, allowing the Freedom Riders to escape.[24]

After mobs attacked other buses, Attorney General Robert Kennedy told Alabama governor John Patterson that he would call in federal troops if the state could not maintain law and order. Patterson dispatched the Alabama National Guard to help protect Freedom Riders traveling through the state. Over the next few months, some 300 Freedom Riders were arrested in Mississippi. The arrests and savage attacks shocked people around the nation, including many southerners, and drew national attention to ongoing civil rights abuses in the South.

In 1963, Martin Luther King, Jr., and the SCLC used boycotts and nonviolent protests to bring attention to segregated businesses in Birmingham, Alabama. For example, they organized "sit-ins" in which African Americans would peaceably occupy seats at a "whites only" restaurant. Police arrested hundreds of protesters, including King. Then, at the direction of Police Commissioner "Bull" Connor, they used high-pressure water hoses, electric cattle prods, and police dogs to disperse a group of protest marchers that included women and children. Horrific images of police violence again shocked the nation and helped to propel the civil rights movement forward. That summer, King was among the organizers of the huge March on Washington for Jobs and Freedom.

## CONGRESS TAKES ACTION

Public outcry over the violent reaction to desegregation in the South and attention focused on the civil rights movement by the March on Washington put pressure on Congress to act.

## TABLE 5.1
## *Major Provisions of the Civil Rights Act*

1. It barred arbitrary discrimination in voter registration.
2. It outlawed discrimination in public accommodations associated with interstate commerce, such as motels, hotels, and restaurants.
3. It authorized the U.S. Justice Department to file lawsuits to force the desegregation of public schools.
4. It authorized (but did not require) federal funds to be withheld from programs that practiced discrimination.
5. It banned discrimination in employment based on race, color, religion, national origin, or sex and created the Equal Employment Opportunities Commission (EEOC) to enforce that ban.
6. It expanded the power of the U.S. Commission on Civil Rights, a watchdog group charged with investigating civil rights abuses and making recommendations to remedy them.

Congress had already passed civil rights acts in 1957 and 1960, but these acts produced little or no change. President John F. Kennedy was assassinated in November 1963, just months after Martin Luther King, Jr.'s "I Have a Dream" speech, and his successor, Lyndon Johnson, urged Congress to pass sweeping civil rights legislation to honor the memory of President Kennedy. The **Civil Rights Act of 1964** was the most sweeping civil rights legislation since the 1870s. It contained six major provisions, shown in Table 5.1.

A year later, Congress passed another landmark piece of legislation: the **Voting Rights Act of 1965**. The act was a response to ongoing efforts to keep blacks from voting in the South. In March 1965, Martin Luther King, Jr., who had joined a local voter registration campaign, helped to organize a 50-mile march from Selma, Alabama—where only 2 percent of eligible African Americans were registered to vote—to the state capital in Montgomery. The march was designed to draw attention to the struggle to achieve voting rights for blacks. Governor George C. Wallace ordered state troopers to stop the march. As the marchers approached the Edmund Pettus Bridge on Route 80, the troopers—some on horseback—used whips, nightsticks, and tear gas to break up the march. Televised images of the brutal attack yet again shocked the nation and led President Johnson to call out the National Guard to protect the marchers. As the marchers continued toward Montgomery, President Johnson addressed a joint session of Congress on March 15, 1965, to urge passage of the Voting Rights Act. Congress moved quickly, and the president signed the Voting Rights Act into law on August 6, 1965.

The Voting Rights Act contained two major provisions. First, it outlawed literacy tests. Second, it provided federal oversight of state and local elections in areas in which a pattern of discrimination had been established. Such areas could not make any changes to their election law or voting requirements without obtaining *preclearance*—approval in advance from the U.S. Department of Justice. The Voting Rights Act, coupled with voter registration drives in the South, led to an increase in the number of black voters registered to vote in the South from 29 percent of eligible black voters in 1960 to roughly double that by 1970.[25]

Then, in 2013, a narrow 5–4 majority of the Supreme Court struck down the preclearance provision of the Voting Rights Act in *Shelby County v. Holder*. Writing for the majority, Chief Justice John Roberts noted that the Voting Rights Act "employed extraordinary measures to address an extraordinary problem." While admitting that no one doubted that voting discrimination still took place, he argued that the conditions that originally justified such extraordinary measures no longer existed. Thus, he concluded, the preclearance provision was no longer necessary. In dissent, Justice Ruth Bader Ginsburg vehemently disagreed, arguing that "the evolution of voting discrimination into more subtle second-generation barriers is powerful evidence that a remedy as effective as preclearance remains vital to protect minority voting rights and prevent backsliding."[26]

Since then, Democrats have rallied around the issue of voter suppression. In her rebuttal to President Trump's State of the Union address in 2019, Stacey Abrams, who had recently lost a race in Georgia to become the nation's first black female governor, highlighted the problem. As she put it, "The foundation of our moral leadership around the globe is free and fair elections, where voters pick their leaders—not where politicians pick their voters."[27] Abrams and others argued that voter suppression runs the gamut from voter registration to ballot access to the counting of votes and is a long-standing problem. For example, the contested presidential election of 2000 and subsequent recounts in Florida highlighted the fact that predominantly black counties tended to have the least accurate voting equipment and often provided poor instructions to voters

**Civil Rights Act of 1964** The most sweeping civil rights legislation since the 1870s; expanded civil rights and increased protections against various forms of discrimination.

**Voting Rights Act of 1965** Landmark legislation that outlawed literacy tests and took other steps to guarantee the voting rights of African Americans.

at the polls. As one commentator recently put it, voter suppression today is "a labyrinth, not a wall"—"an accumulation of everyday annoyances, legal barriers and confusion."[28]

There remained disagreement between the parties, however, over what constitutes *voter suppression*. Republicans, for example, have championed voter ID laws that require a state-issued photo ID in order to vote. They argue that the measures prevent voter fraud. Democrats retort that there is no evidence of systematic fraud and that the measures are really designed to make it more difficult for minority voters— who tend to vote Democratic—to participate. Prior to *Shelby County v. Holder*, for example, the Obama Justice Department—exercising its preclearance function—rejected a South Carolina voter ID law because registered minority voters there were almost 20 percent less likely than registered white voters to have state-issued photo IDs (see Chapter 9).[29]

The "Unite the Right" rally in Charlottesville was a startling public display of white nationalism and praise for the Confederacy and Nazi party. How should the government balance free speech rights and the rights of minorities in cases such as this?

## BLACK LIVES MATTER AND WHITE NATIONALISM

Despite the election of America's first African American president in 2008 and speculation at the time of a post-racial America, ongoing concerns about racial profiling and police brutality spurred the #BlackLivesMatter movement in 2013. Events in 2014 involving police violence against African American men, including video of the death of Eric Garner from a choke hold in New York City and the fatal shooting of 18-year-old Michael Brown in Ferguson, Missouri, brought the movement to the foreground. It has expanded into a global network that campaigns against violence and systemic racism toward black people.

But it was not only the actions of police that brought the subject of racism back to the foreground. Recent years have seen the murder of nine African American worshippers by a 21-year-old white supremacist at the Emanuel African Methodist Episcopal Church in Charleston, South Carolina, in July 2015; heated debates about whether or not to remove Confederate monuments from public spaces; and an August 2017 "Unite the Right" rally organized by a coalition of white supremacists in Charlottesville, Virginia (including Ku Klux Klansmen, neofascists, white nationalists, and the alt-right), where a car driven by one of the white supremacists rammed a crowd of counter-protesters, killing a 32-year-old woman and injuring 28 others.

At the same time, far-right nationalist parties grew in power around the world (see Figure 5.3), and Donald Trump won the presidency amidst accusations from his opponent, Hillary Clinton, that he had "built his campaign on prejudice and paranoia" and was "taking hate groups mainstream and helping a radical fringe take over the Republican Party."[30] After the election, opponents continued to criticize the president for allegedly racist statements.[31] This included his response to the events at Charlottesville, when—after a wave of criticism for initially failing to condemn white nationalists for the violence there—he finally denounced hate groups, "including the KKK [Ku Klux Klan], neo-Nazis, [and] white supremacists," but added, "I think there is blame on both sides."[32]

A post-racial America still seems to be an elusive goal.

# WOMEN AND EQUAL RIGHTS

African Americans are not the only citizens who have struggled for equality and the right to vote in the United States. Throughout most of American history, cultural stereotypes perpetuated the widely held view that women were inferior to men. Similar to children and the feeble-minded, women were viewed as generally well-intentioned but, by nature, less capable and less responsible than men.[33] The men who drafted the U.S. Constitution debated the legal status of slaves in that document but never thought to discuss the legal status of women.[34] Women, after all, were not considered capable of engaging in politics. They were not only restricted from voting, serving on juries, and pursuing higher education but were also considered by common

**FIGURE 5.3**
## Rise of Nationalism in Europe

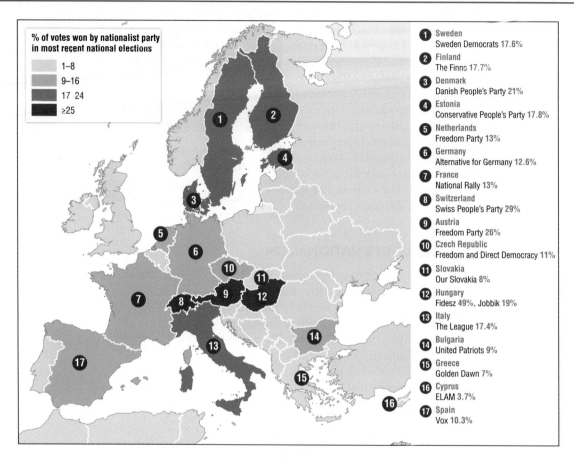

% of votes won by nationalist party in most recent national elections

- 1–8
- 9–16
- 17–24
- ≥25

1. **Sweden** — Sweden Democrats 17.6%
2. **Finland** — The Finns 17.7%
3. **Denmark** — Danish People's Party 21%
4. **Estonia** — Conservative People's Party 17.8%
5. **Netherlands** — Freedom Party 13%
6. **Germany** — Alternative for Germany 12.6%
7. **France** — National Rally 13%
8. **Switzerland** — Swiss People's Party 29%
9. **Austria** — Freedom Party 26%
10. **Czech Republic** — Freedom and Direct Democracy 11%
11. **Slovakia** — Our Slovakia 8%
12. **Hungary** — Fidesz 49%, Jobbik 19%
13. **Italy** — The League 17.4%
14. **Bulgaria** — United Patriots 9%
15. **Greece** — Golden Dawn 7%
16. **Cyprus** — ELAM 3.7%
17. **Spain** — Vox 10.3%

Source: BBC, "Europe and Nationalism: A Country-by-country Guide," April 29, 2019 (https://www.bbc.com/news/world-europe-36130006)

law to have no legal existence apart from their husbands. This meant that they could not sign contracts or even own or inherit property. Most states even allowed men to subject their wives to "reasonable" physical punishment.[35] When Arkansas extended property rights to women in 1835, it had nothing to do with women's rights. Instead, in a time of economic panic, it was designed to shelter the husband's property from creditors.[36]

Closed out of politics, women joined churches at higher rates than men and used religion as a pathway to social activism through charitable work, temperance societies, and abolitionism. Women of the nineteenth century were not expected to speak in public to audiences of men (middle-class Americans were shocked when the British radical Frances Wright dared to do so in the late 1820s), but some religious organizations—such as Quakers—encouraged women to give personal witness in church meetings. One Quaker, Lucretia Mott, became a leading figure in the women's rights movement.[37] Mott advocated the abolition of slavery, and—along with Elizabeth Cady Stanton—served as part of the American delegation to the World Anti-Slavery Convention in London in 1840. There, after much debate, the convention leaders barred women delegates from participating on the convention floor; they were only allowed to view the proceedings from the galleries. Furious at the slight, Mott and Stanton vowed to advocate for women's rights back home.[38]

## THE FIGHT FOR WOMEN'S SUFFRAGE

The Seneca Falls Convention—organized by Mott and Stanton and held in Seneca Falls, New York, in July 1848—is often viewed as the birth of the organized women's rights movement in the United States. Spanning two days, the convention attracted some 300 participants, mostly women, but the abolitionist and African American leader Frederick Douglass also attended (the convention advocated the abolition of slavery as well as the advancement of women's rights). The convention issued a Declaration of Sentiments concerning the rights of women that was modeled on the Declaration of Independence. Borrowing language from Thomas Jefferson, this Declaration made an important addition: "We hold these truths to be self-evident: that all men *and women* are created equal" [emphasis added]. The document then went on to catalogue a long list of grievances. For example, women were denied their inalienable right to vote, forced to submit to laws in which they had no voice, denied property rights, and "if married, in the eye of the law, civilly dead." Men had oppressed women "on all sides," the Declaration proclaimed, and "withheld from her rights which are given to the most ignorant and degraded men." To rectify this, the Convention—after much debate—used the Declaration to make a then-shocking vow: that it was "the duty of the women of this country to secure to themselves the sacred right of the elective franchise."[39]

In the years that followed, various groups were formed to fight for women's right to vote, including the National Woman Suffrage Association, founded in 1869. This fight became known as the **women's suffrage movement**. The Constitution originally left it up to states to determine voting requirements. Initially, no state allowed women to vote, and many states further restricted the franchise by requiring the ownership of property (a right typically withheld from women). Some sort of property qualification had existed in all of the colonies and was not abandoned by all of the states until 1856.[40] New Jersey briefly allowed women to vote from 1790 to 1807, but not until 1890—two decades after the Fifteenth Amendment prohibited the abridgement of voting rights "on account of race, color, or previous condition of servitude"— did another state, Wyoming, extend the franchise to women. By 1900, only three more states had joined Wyoming in allowing women to vote: Colorado (1893), Idaho (1896), and Utah (1896). For a global view of women's suffrage, see Table 5.2.

By the turn of the twentieth century, an organization called the Women's Christian Temperance Union (WCTU) had gained tremendous power and influence. Formed in 1873 by a group of evangelical Christian women, the WCTU quickly developed into a mass organization of women fighting for social and moral reform. Often associated primarily with the abolition of alcohol, the WCTU also embraced other social reform issues and became a powerful engine in the fight for women's suffrage.

That fight gained momentum during the early twentieth century. Starting around 1908 and continuing for a decade, women took to the streets in huge parades and mass gatherings to advocate for their right to vote. Those calling for women's suffrage came from a variety of backgrounds, classes, and races, and they wanted to be able to vote in order to accomplish different goals. Nonetheless, they stood united on the short-term goal of securing women's suffrage.

## TABLE 5.2

## *Years, by Select Countries, in Which Women Gained the Right to Vote*

| | | |
|---|---|---|
| 1893: New Zealand | 1902: Australia | 1913: Norway |
| 1918: United Kingdom | 1918: Canada | 1919: Germany |
| 1920: United States | 1930: South Africa | 1932: Brazil |
| 1944: France | 1945: Italy | 1945: Japan |
| 1947: Argentina | 1950: India | 1952: Greece |
| 1953: Mexico | 1956: Egypt | 1963: Kenya |
| 1971: Switzerland | 1984: Yemen | |

*Source: Data from Inter-Parliamentary Union (http://www.ipu.org/wmn-e/suffrage.htm)*

> **women's suffrage movement** The drive to grant women the right to vote.

The women's suffrage movement was a coordinated effort, with local headquarters all over the country that organized protests and marches to draw attention to their cause.

A constitutional amendment to guarantee women the right to vote had first been drafted by Susan B. Anthony and Elizabeth Cady Stanton and introduced in the U.S. Senate in 1878. Congress consistently failed to pass it in the years that followed, but President Woodrow Wilson (1913–1921) became a champion of the proposed amendment. After initial unsuccessful appeals to Congress, President Wilson called Congress into special session in 1919 to consider the amendment again. This time it passed, and Congress sent it to the states for ratification. After decades of hard work, women finally gained their constitutional right to vote through ratification of the Nineteenth Amendment in 1920.

## WOMEN'S RIGHTS IN THE WAKE OF THE NINETEENTH AMENDMENT

Despite securing the constitutional right to vote, women's social and economic rights still lagged far behind those of men. Women continued to be precluded from engaging in a wide range of professional activities. Long after the ratification of the Nineteenth Amendment, even highly educated women found themselves largely restricted to being elementary and high school teachers, nurses, or secretaries, and many colleges and universities continued to deny admission to women. Princeton and Yale did not admit women until 1969, and Harvard College did not admit women until 1972 (Harvard Medical School began admitting women in 1945 and Harvard Law School followed suit in 1953). As late as 1970, only about 8 percent of U.S. physicians were women, and only about 4 percent of lawyers were female. Careers in business and politics were also elusive.

Women had entered the workforce in large numbers during World War II because of the labor shortage created by men entering the military, but they were largely displaced after the war. By the 1960s, women still found it difficult to be hired for many occupations. When the EEOC (created by the Civil Rights Act of 1964) failed to enforce the law against sex discrimination in hiring, a group of women's activists formed the National Organization for Women (NOW) to fight for women's rights.

## THE EQUAL RIGHTS AMENDMENT

NOW lobbied for a constitutional amendment to guarantee equal rights to women. The Equal Rights Amendment (ERA) had first been introduced in Congress in 1923. The Republican Party included support for the ERA in its party platform beginning in 1940, followed by the Democrats in 1944, but Congress did not pass the ERA and submit it to the states for ratification until 1972.

The main text of the proposed ERA was straightforward. Section 1 stated simply, "Equality of rights under the law shall not be denied or abridged by the United States or by any state on account of sex." Section 2 gave Congress the power to enforce the amendment through legislation, and Section 3 said it would take effect two years after ratification. But ratification never came. Congress stipulated a seven-year deadline for ratification, which required support from 38 of the 50 states. By 1979, only 35 states had ratified the ERA. Congress granted a 39-month extension, but no additional states ratified the amendment by the 1982 deadline. Nonetheless, Nevada voted to ratify the ERA in 2017 and Illinois followed suit in 2018, leaving the amendment only one state shy of ratification. Although the deadline for passage has expired, Congress could vote to extend the deadline if another state votes to ratify.[41]

In the absence of the ERA, NOW and other organizations (such as the American Civil Liberties Union's Women's Rights Project, which Ruth Bader Ginsburg co-founded in 1972) followed the example of the NAACP and fought for women's rights through court cases. However, courts continue to apply the equal protection clause somewhat differently when ruling in

**Nineteenth Amendment** The constitutional amendment that guaranteed women the right to vote.

**Equal Rights Amendment (ERA)** A proposed constitutional amendment that would have guaranteed that the government could not deny or abridge the rights of women on account of their sex. It was not ratified.

cases based on gender than they do in cases involving racial or ethnic classifications. The Supreme Court set a high bar, known as *strict scrutiny* (see Chapter 14), when determining whether a law treats someone differently because of race or ethnicity. However, when dealing with classifications based on gender, it uses an intermediate standard, so the government need only demonstrate an important justification for classifications based on gender.

Although intermediate scrutiny gave women greater constitutional protection than they had previously enjoyed, some say it is not protection enough and have argued for the application of strict scrutiny to gender discrimination. The Supreme Court rejected that argument by a 5–4 vote in *Frontiero v. Richardson* (1973). Intermediate scrutiny is justified by its supporters on the grounds that gender-based classifications can be motivated by factors other than discrimination.[42] For example, state laws that restrict women from working in an area that may pose environmental hazards if they become pregnant are designed to protect women, not discriminate against them. But when do such protections cross the line and become outmoded paternalism? For example, should it be permissible to exclude women from the military draft? Is such exclusion a form of gender discrimination, or does the government have an important interest in protecting women from combat? Exclusion of African Americans from the draft would clearly be considered racial discrimination. But using the intermediate standard for classifications based on gender, the Supreme Court in 1981 upheld the restriction on drafting women.[43]

## SEXUAL HARASSMENT IN THE WORKPLACE

Title VII of the Civil Rights Act of 1964 made it unlawful to discriminate in the workplace. This included discrimination with regard to hiring, firing, financial compensation, and other terms and conditions of employment. Left unclear was whether sexual harassment constituted a form of sex discrimination in these contexts.

Until the late 1970s, most courts concluded that sexual harassment did not constitute discrimination under existing law. That changed in 1976, when a federal district court recognized that *quid pro quo* sexual harassment—that is, implicit or explicit requests for sexual favors in return for employment or advancement in the workplace—was, indeed, a form of sex discrimination under Title VII.[44]

In addition to quid pro quo harassment, the Supreme Court ruled in 1986 that sexual harassment that creates a hostile work environment also violates Title VII. A *hostile work environment* was defined as unwelcome physical or verbal conduct of a sexual nature that is so persistent or severe that it causes an intimidating, hostile, or offensive work environment. In the case that established this precedent, Mechelle Vinson was hired by Sidney Taylor as a teller trainee at a bank. Vinson quickly rose to teller, head teller, and then assistant branch manager. Although these advancements were based on merit alone, Taylor—Vinson's supervisor—engaged in a persistent pattern of sexual harassment. He made sexual advances to her, exposed himself, and raped her on several occasions. Fearful of losing her job, Vinson engaged in sexual intercourse with him 40 or 50 times over the course of four years. A unanimous Supreme Court agreed that this persistent pattern of sexual harassment by Taylor amounted to a form of discrimination based on sex.[45]

Today, a hostile work environment need not consist of the level of abuse endured by Mechelle Vinson. It can be established by persistently leering (staring in a sexually suggestive manner); making offensive remarks about one's looks, clothes, or body parts; inappropriate touching (including patting or pinching); telling lewd or sexual jokes; or sending sexually suggestive notes, e-mails, or pictures. The Supreme Court extended protection to cases of same-sex harassment in 1998.[46]

**Alyssa Milano** ✔
@Alyssa_Milano

Follow

If you've been sexually harassed or assaulted write 'me too' as a reply to this tweet.

Me too.

Suggested by a friend: "If all the women who have been sexually harassed or assaulted wrote 'Me too.' as a status, we might give people a sense of the magnitude of the problem."

1:21 PM - 15 Oct 2017

23,181 **Retweets** 51,682 Likes

💬 65K    ⟲ 23K    ♡ 52K

Alyssa Milano's October 2017 tweet spread the hashtag #MeToo, which had been created by the activist Tarana Burke in 2006 to highlight the pervasiveness of sexual harassment and assault.

The hashtag #MeToo began to spread virally on social media in October 2017 after allegations of sexual abuse and harassment by Hollywood film producer Harvey Weinstein came to light. More than 4.7 million people used the hashtag in the first twenty-four hours, generating more than 12 million posts, comments, and reactions.[47] Revelations of sexual harassment by a string of other high-power individuals helped to spur the #MeToo Movement, which also took flight—in varying degrees—in other countries. Some countries adopted a literal translation: #AnaKaman in Arab-speaking countries and #YoTambien in Spain. France adopted a more evocative hashtag: #BalanceTonPorc ("squeal on your pig").[48]

Over the next year, the movement toppled one U.S. senator, eight members of the House of Representatives, and at least thirty state lawmakers, and ended the campaigns of at least twenty-five candidates in the 2018 midterm elections.[49] Those elections also saw a record number of female

## PICTURE YOURSELF...
# As a Woman in Zambia

Zambia is a democratic republic—one of the most urbanized countries in sub-Saharan Africa and one of the poorest. Sixty percent of the population lives below the poverty line (jumping to 83 percent in rural areas).[a] Zambia's population is also one of the youngest in the world, with a majority of the population under the age of 18 as of 2015, and a median age of 16.7 years.[b] Picture yourself as a woman who lives in one of the rural areas there. You are 20 years old, married, and have two daughters and a son. Zambia has one of the highest rates of child marriage in Africa. Like almost one out of three women in Zambia, you were married before the age of 18 and experienced physical violence at a young age.

In theory, Zambia's constitution guarantees you equality with men. In fact, it contains significant exceptions in laws governing adoption, marriage, divorce, the inheritance of property, and other matters of "personal law." Moreover, Zambia—like the United States—has a dual court system (see Chapter 14). Statutory law is supposed to take precedence over local customary law, but there are more than 70 tribes governed by some 240 chiefs. Deep-seated tradition is difficult to overcome—especially in rural areas where tribal customs prevail. As a result, Zambia still recognizes both statutory marriages and customary marriages (such as yours). The rules of statutory marriage, such as property rights and the minimum age of 16 to marry, do not apply to customary marriages, where girls as young as 12 can marry.

Because discrimination against women is deeply rooted in Zambia's customary law, you are far from equal to your

male counterparts in many ways. For example, adultery is lawful for men but not for you. The law recognizes men as superior to you, giving your husband the authority to control your movements and those of your daughters. Under customary law, you are viewed as property belonging to your husband. This precludes you from owning or inheriting property.[c] Thus, you live in fear that if you are widowed or abandoned, as some of your friends have been, you may be evicted from your home.

Efforts have been made by both the government and nongovernmental organizations in Zambia to extend property rights to women married under customary law.[d] But even if a woman managed to retain land, she could not determine what crops to plant on it. That is considered to be a man's decision. The draft of a new constitution calls for equitable ownership of land by women, but almost ten years after that draft was written, it has still not been adopted. Even if it is, it must be enforced. And so, you do your best to feed and take care of your children, hope your husband won't leave you, and prepare for your next child, which is due in three months.

## Questions to Consider

1. What are the consequences of a dual court system in Zambia for women's rights?
2. In a deeply patriarchal society, how effective can law be in changing behavior toward women?
3. How different is the plight of women in Zambia today from that of women in the United States during the nineteenth century?

[a] "10 Facts About Poverty in Zambia," The Borgen Project, May 5, 2017, https://borgenproject.org/10-facts-about-poverty-in-zambia/
[b] "Children in Zambia," UNICEF, accessed July 20, 2019, https://www.unicef.org/zambia/children-zambia
[c] "Human Rights Violations in Zambia, Part II: Women's Rights," Shadow Report, UN Human Rights Commission, July 2007, 5, 10, and 12, http://www2.ohchr.org/english/bodies/hrc/docs/ngos/omct_zambia1.pdf
[d] Ibid., 28. See also "Protection for Women's rights in Zambia," Focus on Land in Africa, 2019, http://www.focusonland.com/countries/protection-for-womens-rights-in-zambia/

## FIGURE 5.4

## *The Gender Wage Gap, 1955–2018*

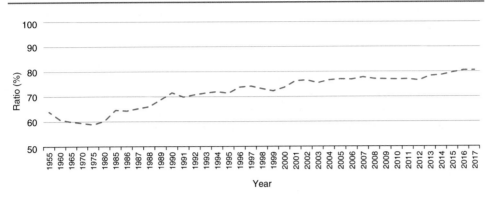

*Despite passage of the Equal Pay Act in 1963, a wage gap still exists in the workplace today. How might you explain this?*

*Source: "The Gender Wage Gap: 2018 Earnings Differences by Race and Ethnicity," Institute for Women's Policy Research, March 7, 2019, https://iwpr.org/publications/gender-wage-gap-2018/*

candidates for governor, U.S. House, and U.S. Senate, with a record number being elected to serve in Congress (100 Democrats and 17 Republicans) and nine winning governorships.[50]

## EQUAL PAY FOR EQUAL WORK

Another issue related to the workplace is the concept of *equal pay for equal work*. Women have typically earned less than men, even when performing exactly the same job. In 1963, Congress took action to redress that inequity by passing the **Equal Pay Act**. At the time, women earned an average of 59 cents for every dollar earned by men. The Equal Pay Act prohibited wage discrimination based on sex. Thus, employers cannot pay one gender a lower wage for equal jobs requiring equal skill, effort, and responsibility that are performed under similar working conditions.

> **Equal Pay Act** Legislation that prohibits wage discrimination based on sex.

The Equal Pay Act allowed women to sue employers who did not comply with its provisions, but women's salaries continued to lag behind those of their male counterparts. According to the Institute for Women's Policy Research, women still earned only about 81 cents for every dollar earned by men as of 2018 (see Figure 5.4). And a 2007 Supreme Court decision, *Ledbetter v. Goodyear Tire & Rubber Company*, made it more difficult for women to sue over discriminatory wages. In a 5–4 ruling, the Court interpreted the 180-day statute of limitations for filing claims as starting with the initial salary decision by an employer (rather than within 180 days of the most recent discriminatory paycheck). For example, a failure to give a raise to a woman performing the same job performed by a man could not be contested beyond 180 days of the salary decision itself—even if the female employee did not discover the discrepancy until after that 180-day period. Lilly Ledbetter found herself in such a situation, but the Court ruled that since she had filed her claim after her 180-day window of opportunity, she could not sue.

Since the *Ledbetter* decision was based on an interpretation of statutory law (rather than constitutional law), Congress overturned the decision through passage of the Lilly

Lilly Ledbetter (right), whose unsuccessful lawsuit over discriminatory wages was the inspiration for the Fair Pay Act, attended the ceremony where President Obama signed the bill into law.

Ledbetter Fair Pay Act, which President Obama signed into law in 2009. That Act clarified the statute of limitations and said that the 180-day statute of limitations resets with each discriminatory paycheck. The extended time period made it easier for women to file equal pay claims.

In 2011, the Supreme Court also made it more difficult for women to use a class action lawsuit to sue for discriminatory wages, promotions, and job assignments. In 2000, a 54-year-old employee filed a sex discrimination suit against Wal-Mart. This eventually turned into a class action lawsuit on behalf of 1.6 million women who had worked for the company since 1998. Women made up 70 percent of Wal-Mart's hourly workers but only 33 percent of management. In a 5–4 ruling, the Supreme Court concluded that those bringing the class action did not have enough in common to constitute a class because they had not provided convincing proof of a company-wide pattern of discrimination. The dissenters, including all three of the Court's female justices, disagreed and criticized the majority for disqualifying the class action suit at the starting gate.[51] The standard set by the Court will make large class action suits more difficult in the future. Some observers, including then–House Minority Leader Nancy Pelosi (D-CA), called the ruling a setback for the cause of women's equality.[52]

The principle of equal pay for equal work is common in many countries (to be a member of the European Union, for example, each country must embrace that principle), but Iceland became, on January 1, 2018, the first nation to go a step further and actually make it illegal to pay men more than women for the same work (women made up 48% of Iceland's parliament when the law was enacted). The law applies to companies with 25 or more employees. Violators are subject to a fine.[53]

## TITLE IX

While Title IX of the Education Amendments of 1972 is best known to the public for the effect it has had on high school and collegiate athletics, it had a broader purpose. It was intended to abolish all forms of sex discrimination in educational programs that receive federal funding and led to more women attending institutions of higher education. For example, the percentage of female law school students rose from about 8 percent in 1970 to 33 percent in 1980.[54] Passage of Title IX also led to women being admitted to previously all-male public institutions, including the four U.S. military academies in 1976. The Virginia Military Institute, a publicly funded school, continued to deny admission to women until the Supreme Court ruled in 1996 that its exclusion of women violated the equal protection clause.[55]

# DISCRIMINATION BASED ON ETHNICITY

The fight for civil rights has certainly not been confined to blacks and women. Many ethnic groups have faced discrimination at various points in the history of the United States.

## NATIVE AMERICANS

As we saw in Chapter 2, North America was already home to as many as 10 million indigenous people when Christopher Columbus "discovered" America in 1492. These Native Americans were deeply affected by European colonization. Their population fell prey to epidemic diseases brought from Europe (such as smallpox, measles, influenza, and cholera), warfare with white settlers, and forced migration. Early on, tens of thousands of Native Americans were enslaved by colonists, but the Native American slave trade mostly died out by 1730 when the African slave trade expanded.

As the European population expanded in the United States in the early 1800s, settlers began to move to the lower south of the U.S., where land was occupied by Native Americans. To facilitate this expansion, Congress passed the Indian Removal Act in 1830. The Act called for the relocation of Native American tribes in the southeastern United States, including the Cherokee, Chickasaw, Choctaw, Creek, and Seminole. The first to be moved was the Choctaw tribe, which was resettled from what are now the states of Alabama, Mississippi, and Louisiana to "Indian Territory" (present-day Oklahoma). Some 17,000 Choctaws embarked on the journey,

**Title IX** One of the Education Amendments of 1972 designed to abolish all forms of sex discrimination in public education.

but harsh weather and lack of food led to the deaths of as many as 6,000 en route—a journey that came to be known as the *Trail of Tears*. In Florida, the Seminoles refused to leave, resulting in a bloody war that lasted from 1835 to 1842.

*Manifest Destiny*—the nineteenth-century belief that the United States was destined to expand westward across the continent—had a particularly devastating effect on Native Americans. As Americans moved westward, more Native Americans were displaced and killed in battles. The Indian Appropriations Act of 1851 authorized the creation of Indian reservations where Native Americans could be relocated. Enforcement of the policy by the U.S. Army led to a series of conflicts including the Sioux Wars, which culminated in the massacre of women and children at Wounded Knee, South Dakota, in 1890.

Starting with the passage of the Dawes Act in 1887, U.S. policy toward Native Americans began to shift toward assimilation rather than separation—part of an effort to convert Native Americans to Christianity. This included coercing children from Indian reservations to attend boarding schools run by whites. The clear purpose of relocating children to these boarding schools was the weakening of the identity and culture of Native Americans. Reservations continued to exist, but under the Dawes Act, only those Native Americans who left their tribes were allowed to become U.S. citizens and vote. Not until 1924 did the Indian Citizenship Act grant citizenship to all Native Americans born within the United States, including those born on reservations. Despite their citizenship, many Native Americans were denied the right to vote by states and continued to face other forms of discrimination.

A coordinated civil rights movement for Native Americans has emerged only in the past 50 years or so, perhaps because tribes were small and scattered. The American Indian Movement (AIM), a radical Native American activist movement, formed in 1968. It drew publicity through organized protests, including the occupation of Mount Rushmore and protests at World Series and Super Bowl games in which participating teams used figures of Native Americans as mascots or team names (such as the Cleveland Indians or Washington Redskins). While AIM tried to generate publicity, the Native American Rights Fund (NARF), founded in 1970, followed in the tradition of the NAACP's LDF and NOW by using court cases to secure rights for Native Americans. This included efforts to recognize tribal sovereignty, guarantee the religious freedom of Native Americans, uphold voting rights, and protect sacred places such as Native American burial grounds. These efforts have had mixed results. For example, the Supreme Court held that government could restrict the use of peyote as a sacramental element in Native American religious ceremonies[56] and efforts to prevent the Dakota Access Pipeline from running through Native American lands, which prompted the Obama administration to reconsider the plan, failed when Donald Trump gained office.

After several years of effort by two U.S. senators—Sam Brownback (R-KS) and Byron Dorgan (D-ND)—Congress passed a formal apology to Native Americans in 2009. The apology was buried in the 2010 Defense Appropriations Bill. Little noticed at the time of its passage, it apologized "on behalf of the people of the United States to all Native Peoples for the many instances of violence, maltreatment, and neglect inflicted on Native Peoples by citizens of the United States." President Obama signed the bill into law on December 21, 2009.[57]

**Protests at the Standing Rock Sioux Reservation against the planned route of the Dakota Access Pipeline, which opponents said threatened the area's water supply and ancient burial grounds, lasted for nearly a year and prompted solidarity marches across the country before President Trump allowed the pipeline to proceed as planned. How should the government weigh the interests of minority groups?**

## IMMIGRANTS

The United States is a nation of immigrants, but at various times during its history, segments of the population have embraced *nativism*—that is, opposition to immigration. For example, the immigration of large numbers of Irish and German Catholics starting in the 1830s led to the so-called Know Nothing Movement in the 1840s and 1850s, an anti-Catholic group that opposed immigration.

The organization formed a national political party, formally known as the American Party, and scored some electoral victories—especially in Massachusetts—but quickly faded.

Later in the 1800s, large numbers of Chinese came to the United States in search of gold in California and jobs building the transcontinental railroad. Some labor organizations, such as the Knights of Labor, led opposition to the cheap labor provided by Chinese immigrants and called for their expulsion. Some of this opposition led to riots against Chinese laborers. Even Congress became involved. For the first and only time in its history, Congress passed legislation banning immigration on the basis of race: the Chinese Exclusion Act in 1882 banned further immigration of Chinese for 10 years. Many people spoke openly of the so-called Yellow Peril posed by this supposedly inferior race. Congress extended the Chinese Exclusion Act in 1892 and made it permanent in 1902. Not until 1943, when China was an ally of the United States in World War II, did Congress allow limited immigration of Chinese.

Despite the easing of immigration restrictions, widespread racism toward people of Asian descent continued. This was compounded by racist portrayals of the Japanese—an enemy of the United States during World War II. Fearing a Japanese invasion of the West Coast after Pearl Harbor, President Franklin Roosevelt ordered the forced relocation of some 117,000 people of Japanese descent who lived in that area—two-thirds of them native-born U.S. citizens—to concentration camps.

One such citizen, Fred Korematsu, was arrested when he refused to leave his home in San Leandro, California. The Supreme Court, in a 6–3 decision, upheld Roosevelt's order. In his dissent, Justice Murphy wrote that the policy that allowed Korematsu's arrest went over the brink of constitutional power and fell into "the ugly abyss of racism."[58]

In 1988, President Ronald Reagan signed congressional legislation that extended a formal apology to Japanese Americans who had been affected by the relocation policy and authorized reparations of $20,000 to each of the surviving detainees. Since those who were relocated had lost homes, businesses, and most of their property as well as their liberty, many considered this to be paltry compensation, and many of the survivors died before payment could be made. In January 1998, President Bill Clinton awarded Fred Korematsu a Presidential Medal of Freedom—the highest civilian award in the United States.

Immigration from Eastern and Southern Europe in the late nineteenth and early twentieth centuries also led to nativist movements. Immigrants from places such as Italy and Poland provided cheap labor but provoked fears that they were taking jobs away from Americans. Negative stereotypes were commonplace, as were extreme prejudice and even violence. In New Orleans, a mob of some 10,000 people lynched eleven Italians in 1891—one of the largest mass lynchings in U.S. history.[59] During this period, the Ku Klux Klan embraced anti-immigrant and anti-Catholic views as well as white supremacy.

## THE CURRENT CONTROVERSY OVER IMMIGRATION

It is estimated that there are some 12 million undocumented immigrants in the United States.[60] Many of these are Hispanics who have crossed the border from Mexico. How to deal with this has become a highly divisive issue, with President Trump determined to build a border wall and Democrats opposed. Earlier calls for immigration reform by George W. Bush and Barack Obama went nowhere in Congress.

Trump's rhetoric, as both candidate and president, has heightened the debate about immigration in general. When he announced his candidacy at Trump Tower in June 2015, Trump said,

> The U.S. has become a dumping ground for everybody else's problems. . . . When Mexico sends its people, they're not sending their best. . . . They're sending people that have lots of problems. . . . They're bringing drugs. They're bringing crime. They're rapists. And some, I assume, are good people.[61]

Almost four years later, in April 2019, President Trump said to migrants seeking refuge in the United States, "Our country is full."[62]

President Trump's policies also provoked controversy. A notable example is his "zero tolerance" approach that embraced family separation as a deterrent to unauthorized border crossings. In response to widespread criticism when it became apparent that the government did not have a plan for reuniting the families, Trump rescinded the policy in June 2018. During the two months the policy was in effect, at least 2,737 children were separated from their parents.[63] In March 2019, Trump threatened to close the U.S.–Mexico border altogether, but quickly backed off that threat after business groups and fellow Republicans warned of the dire economic consequences of such a policy.[64]

## HISPANICS

Hispanics are the largest and fastest-growing minority group in the United States. They made up 16 percent of the nation's total population according to the 2010 census. The U.S. Census Bureau has estimated that Hispanics will make up close to 30 percent of the nation's population by 2060.

Hispanics have also faced discrimination. Mexican Americans in the Southeastern United States and California confronted discriminatory laws and practices similar to those faced by African Americans. These included segregated schools, the use of poll taxes and other devices to discourage voting, and exclusion from service on juries. In 1928, the League of United Latin American Citizens (LULAC) formed to combat discrimination. It also engaged in voter registration drives, community education campaigns, and litigation to further the rights of Hispanic Americans. It successfully sued in 1945 to integrate the Orange County School System in California, where Hispanics had been compelled to attend segregated schools. The Federal District Court decision in *Mendez v. Westminster*, an important precursor to *Brown v. Board of Education*, concluded that requiring separate schools for children of Mexican ancestry violated the equal protection clause of the U.S. Constitution.[65] The subsequent ruling in *Mendez* by the Ninth Circuit Court of Appeals decided the case on narrower grounds but still struck down the segregation.[66] LULAC also brought an end to the exclusion of Hispanic Americans from juries through a landmark Supreme Court case, *Hernandez v. Texas*.[67] Another group, the Mexican American Legal Defense and Education Fund (MALDEF), was organized in 1968 to fight for civil rights through a combination of advocacy, educational outreach, and litigation. Since then, it has brought successful legal challenges to attempts by public school districts to charge tuition to children of undocumented immigrant parents and to redistricting plans that discriminated against Latino voters.[68]

Hispanics are now a significant voting bloc nationwide, with especially high populations in important swing states such as California, Texas, and Florida, which have a large number of electoral votes in presidential elections (see Figure 5.5). The 2018 midterm elections brought the number of Latinos in Congress to a record high (40 in the House and 4 in the Senate), but this remains far from representative of their share of the population, which is expected to almost double by the year 2060 (see Figure 5.6). So far, at least, there is a disparity between population and representation, but the increased numbers could affect the balance of political power (for now, at least, helping Democrats more than Republicans). Barack Obama appointed the first Hispanic justice to the Supreme Court in 2009, and presidents since Jimmy Carter

The Trump administration's family separation policy sparked widespread protest. In response to the outcry, the administration rescinded the policy but struggled to reunite children with their families. Should the U.S. treat noncitizens differently from citizens when it comes to civil rights?

**FIGURE 5.5**

## The Hispanic Vote, 2018

**Many of the Latino eligible voters in the U.S. lived in California and Texas in 2018**

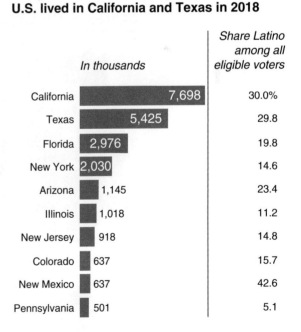

| In thousands | | Share Latino among all eligible voters |
|---|---|---|
| California | 7,698 | 30.0% |
| Texas | 5,425 | 29.8 |
| Florida | 2,976 | 19.8 |
| New York | 2,030 | 14.6 |
| Arizona | 1,145 | 23.4 |
| Illinois | 1,018 | 11.2 |
| New Jersey | 918 | 14.8 |
| Colorado | 637 | 15.7 |
| New Mexico | 637 | 42.6 |
| Pennsylvania | 501 | 5.1 |

*Source: Antonio Flores and Mark Hugo Lopez, "Key Facts About Latinos in the 2018 Midterm Elections," Pew Research Center, October 15, 2018, https://www.pewresearch.org/fact-tank/2018/10/15/key-facts-about-latinos-in-the-2018-midterm-elections/*

## FIGURE 5.6

### The Projected Hispanic Population in the U.S. Through 2060

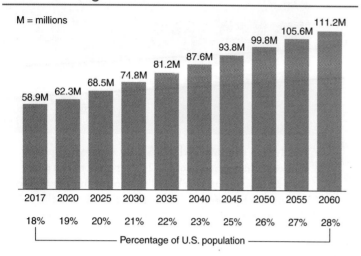

M = millions

| Year | Population | Percentage of U.S. population |
|------|-----------|------|
| 2017 | 58.9M | 18% |
| 2020 | 62.3M | 19% |
| 2025 | 68.5M | 20% |
| 2030 | 74.8M | 21% |
| 2035 | 81.2M | 22% |
| 2040 | 87.6M | 23% |
| 2045 | 93.8M | 25% |
| 2050 | 99.8M | 26% |
| 2055 | 105.6M | 27% |
| 2060 | 111.2M | 28% |

Source: "Hispanic Population to Reach 111 Million by 2060," U.S. Census Bureau, https://www.census.gov/library/visualizations/2018/comm/hispanic-projected-pop.html

have focused in varying degrees on appointing Hispanic judges to the lower federal courts. In contrast, during his presidential campaign, Donald Trump questioned whether an Indiana-born federal judge of Mexican descent who was presiding over a lawsuit filed by former students of Trump University could be impartial because "he happens to be, we believe, Mexican." "I have a Mexican judge," he added.[69] Once in office, President Trump's judicial nominees were predominantly white (87% as of August 2019) and male (77.7%). As of August 2019, only 2.7% (five of his judicial nominees) were Hispanic and 4.3% were African American (eight nominees).[70]

The growing use of Spanish in the United States as a result of the rising Hispanic population has led to debate. The United States has no official language at the national level, but some have pushed to make English the country's official language. In contrast to the federal government, 31 states have designated English as the official language (see Figure 5.7). The actual scope of these state laws varies from one state to another. While some simply declare English to be the official language, others prohibit or limit government from offering non-English language assistance or services (such as courtroom translation, multilingual emergency police lines, and multilingual election ballots). Is there anything wrong with that? At what point, if any, does insistence on English-only services violate individual rights? So far, the Supreme Court has not struck down such laws. Should it? Some groups, such as MAL-DEF and the American Civil Liberties Union, think so.

## FIGURE 5.7

### States With Official English Laws, 2019

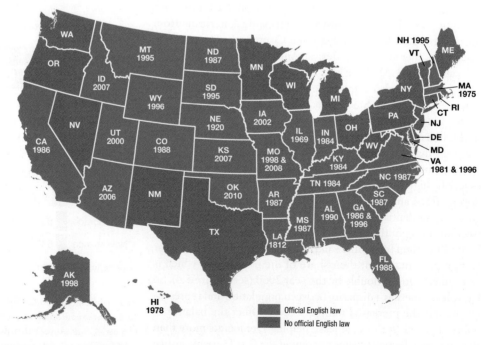

Source: U.S. English (https://www.usenglish.org/us-states-official-english-laws/)

# NEW FRONTIERS IN CIVIL RIGHTS

The civil rights movement for blacks, women, and ethnic minorities has a long history, even if advances have been recent and incomplete. Within the government, civil rights advocates have made great strides toward the equal treatment of individuals regardless of race and gender, and they have begun to work to achieve similar gains for other groups, such as members of the LGBT community and individuals with disabilities.

## LGBT RIGHTS

Advocating the rights of lesbian, gay, bisexual, and transgender (LGBT) individuals is a recent phenomenon. As we saw in Chapter 4, laws criminalizing private homosexual conduct between consenting adults were commonplace through much of U.S. history. Laws sentenced people to jail and hard labor for homosexual conduct. Illinois became the first state to decriminalize such conduct in 1962, but the U.S. Supreme Court did not strike down such laws until 2003. Around the world, some 70 nations still criminalized homosexual conduct as of 2019, with 11 still allowing the death penalty. (Brunei adopted a law in April 2019 that allowed those convicted of such conduct—including foreigners and children—to be stoned to death or whipped, but then backed down from enforcing it in the face of worldwide opposition.)[71]

Because of the stigma associated with homosexual conduct, advocacy groups for LGBT rights were relatively slow to form. The so-called Gay Liberation movement did not begin in earnest until the 1969 Stonewall Riots in New York City (which were precipitated by police raids of a gay bar in Greenwich Village called the Stonewall Inn). Those riots helped to galvanize LGBT political action, including the creation of advocacy groups such as the Gay Liberation Front, the Human Rights Campaign, and the Gay and Lesbian Alliance Against Defamation (GLAAD).

By then, the 1964 Civil Rights Act had banned discrimination in employment based on race, color, religion, national origin, or sex, but it did not ban discrimination based on sexual orientation. As a result, lesbians and gay men continued to face routine discrimination in the workplace, in securing housing, and in gaining custody of their children. Same-sex partners were denied privileges that were routinely granted to heterosexual partners, ranging from hospital visitation rights to employment benefits. Change came slowly. Wisconsin, in 1982, became the first state to ban employment discrimination based on sexual orientation, and since then, more than 20 states and the District of Columbia have followed suit. Efforts to enact federal legislation in the form of an Employment Non-Discrimination Act have so far been unsuccessful, as has passage of federal legislation to prevent housing discrimination, but in 2010, President Obama ordered hospitals that receive Medicare or Medicaid payments to grant visitation rights for same-sex couples.[72] Then, in 2019, the Supreme Court finally agreed to decide whether the 1964 Civil Rights Act bans discrimination in employment based on sexual orientation or transgender status.[73] Whatever the Court decides, the ruling will be historic.

The courts have already played a major role in extending gay rights. An early example is a 1996 case in which, by a 6–3 vote, the Supreme Court struck down Amendment 2 to Colorado's state constitution. Amendment 2 prohibited the state government from protecting individuals based on their "homosexual, lesbian, or bisexual orientation, conduct, practices, or relationships," including the enforcement of local ordinances that provided such protection. Writing for the majority, Justice Anthony Kennedy said that Amendment 2 seemed "inexplicable by anything but animus toward the class it affects."[74] Most significantly, the Supreme Court in 2015 guaranteed the right of same-sex couples to marry (see Chapter 4). In 2019, Pete Buttigieg, the openly gay mayor of South Bend, Indiana, announced his candidacy for president of the United States. Though not the first openly gay major party candidate for president (Fred Karger, who ran for the Republican presidential nomination in 2012, holds that distinction),[75] Buttigieg was the first presidential candidate married to another man, and the first to draw widespread attention and support.

Military service has also been an issue when it comes to LGBT rights. Gays were long banned from serving in the U.S. military. Amidst much controversy, President Bill Clinton implemented a compromise "Don't Ask, Don't Tell" policy in 1993 that prohibited the military from asking service members or applicants about their sexual preferences. But the compromise only protected closeted service members, not those who were openly gay, lesbian, or bisexual. Not until 2011, when Congress repealed "Don't Ask, Don't Tell," could gay people serve openly in the military. Then, in 2016, President Obama lifted the ban on openly transgender people serving in the military.[76] President Trump, however, announced a reversal of that policy on Twitter in July 2017, and subsequently directed his defense secretary to draft policies to implement that decision. That policy shift was quickly challenged in court, and two lower federal courts issued injunctions to stop its implementation. In January 2019, the Supreme Court, in a 5–4 decision, lifted those injunctions, allowing the ban to go into effect while the cases continued to make their way through the system.[77]

Another issue related to the rights of transgender people arose in 2016. The Department of Justice and the Department of Education issued joint guidance to educational institutions formalizing the view of the Obama administration that the law known as Title IX prohibits discrimination on the basis of gender identity and that students should be treated in school settings in a way that is consistent with their gender identity. This included things ranging from honoring the student's preferred name to permitting transgender students to use sex-segregated facilities (such as bathrooms) in accordance with their gender identity. In 2017, the state of North Carolina enacted (but subsequently repealed) a "bathroom bill" that rejected that guidance and required students to use sex-segregated facilities consistent with their sex assigned at birth.[78] Other states also considered enacting such legislation, and several filed suit against the federal government to overturn the guidance. The Trump administration responded by rescinding the guidance in February 2017 (see Chapter 12 for more on unilateral executive action).[79]

## DISABILITY RIGHTS

Efforts to protect the rights of the disabled are also relatively recent. Throughout much of our history, people with disabilities were shunned and discriminated against. Parents often hid children with disabilities and sometimes even killed them. Perspectives began to change in the wake of World War II, when many disabled veterans returned home. But even as social stereotypes began to recede, physical barriers remained. Few buildings or modes of mass transit were handicap accessible, and disability was not deemed a protected category in the Civil Rights Act of 1964.

The first legislation directly protecting the disabled came in 1973 with the Rehabilitation Act, which prohibited disability discrimination by the federal government in the hiring of federal employees and in programs that received federal aid. The act was amended in 1978 to require handicap access to federal buildings.

In 1990, Congress passed the Americans with Disabilities Act (ADA). The ADA defines *disability* as "a physical or mental impairment that substantially limits a major life activity." That definition has been subject to interpretation. The Supreme Court, for example, has ruled that conditions that can be corrected with medication or other corrective devices are not covered. Thus, blindness is covered but nearsightedness is not. Still, there are gray areas.

Most significantly, the ADA requires both public and private employers to make "reasonable accommodations" for employees with disabilities, and it requires that public buildings and services be accessible to people with disabilities. Although major obstacles remain, the ADA has made buses and trains more wheelchair accessible, and buildings have added ramps, handrails, and other accommodations for the disabled. There is also an expectation that rental car companies provide vehicles with hand controls for disabled drivers and that telecommunications companies accommodate the deaf and hard of hearing. For example, captions are provided on television shows, and telecommunications devices for the deaf are provided by telephone companies. Such accommodations required by the ADA can be expensive. As a result, the ADA was opposed by many members of the business community.

## REDRESSING PAST DISCRIMINATION

What should the government do to remedy and atone for violations of civil liberties, such as slavery and other forms of past discrimination? This is a difficult and often politically charged question. Are apologies appropriate? Are they enough? Should the government pay reparations, as it did to Japanese Americans who were interned during World War II? Many of the formal vestiges of discrimination have been removed in this country, but lingering harms remain in the form of a staggering wealth gap between blacks and whites (see Figure 5.8), together with so-called redlining in which various services (e.g., financial, banking, insurance, health care) are either denied—or, more subtly, cost more—for residents of low-income neighborhoods (figuratively marked off by a red line) that are often racially associated. Should policies be enacted to remedy past discrimination and its lingering effects by ensuring that certain groups are represented in college admissions and hiring? If so, how long should such policies stay in place? What else can be done to reduce the wealth gap?

## AFFIRMATIVE ACTION

President Lyndon Johnson introduced the idea of **affirmative action**—a policy intended to promote equal opportunities for members of previously disadvantaged groups in education and employment—at a commencement speech at historically black Howard University on June 6, 1965. Three months later, he signed an executive order that implemented affirmative action for the first time. Executive Order 11246 not only prohibited federal contractors from discriminating in employment on the basis of race but also required them to "take affirmative action to ensure that applicants are employed . . . without regard to their race, color, religion, sex, or national origin." The actual implementation of affirmative action has caused heated debate (see Figure 5.9). Opponents argue that it amounts to preferential treatment of minorities and women—"reverse discrimination"—which should be considered a violation of the equal protection clause.

**FIGURE 5.8**

## The Racial Wealth Gap

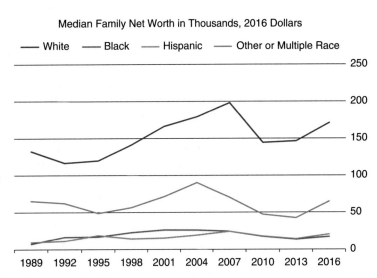

Source: "Survey of Consumer Finances (SCF)," Board of Governors of the Federal Reserve System, July 23, 2018, https://www.federalreserve.gov/econres/scfindex.htm

**FIGURE 5.9**

## Public Views on Affirmative Action

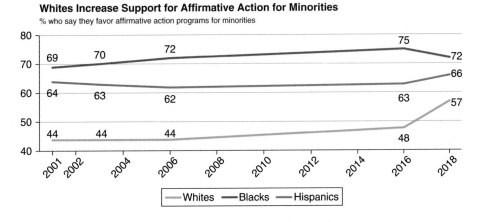

Source: Jim Norman, "Americans' Support for Affirmative Action Programs Rises," Gallup, February 27, 2019, https://news.gallup.com/poll/247046/americans-support-affirmative-action-programs-rises.aspx

> **affirmative action** A policy intended to promote equal opportunities for members of previously disadvantaged groups in education and employment.

In its first major ruling on affirmative action in *University of California v. Bakke* (1978), the Supreme Court, in a complicated 5–4 decision, struck down race-based quotas in the admissions process at the University of California Medical School, arguing that quotas in this instance—where race was the only criterion used by the University to fill its minority positions—were not the least intrusive means of achieving racial diversity among the student body. At the same time, the Court did not completely rule out the use of quotas in all circumstances. It recognized that achieving racial diversity is a legitimate goal and that race or sex can be one of many factors considered in the admissions process.

In the 1980s and 1990s, several Supreme Court decisions limited but did not abolish affirmative action. Most notably, the Court began to apply strict scrutiny to affirmative action cases. In early cases, the majority of the Court did not treat affirmative action as a violation of equal protection, but by 1995, it did.[80] This meant that the government had to demonstrate a compelling justification for a racial classification and that any necessary interference with a fundamental right to achieve that compelling interest must be the least restrictive means of achieving the end. Thus, it became more difficult for specific instances of affirmative action to withstand judicial scrutiny.

Nonetheless, the Supreme Court continues to uphold limited forms of affirmative action in areas such as law school admissions. In a 5–4 decision in *Grutter v. Bollinger* (2003), the Court—using a strict scrutiny test—concluded that the University of Michigan had a compelling interest in obtaining a "critical mass" of minority students and that its consideration of race in the admissions process was narrowly tailored to achieve that interest.[81] The Supreme Court similarly upheld the University of Texas at Austin's race-sensitive admissions policy in 2016 by a 4–3 vote.[82] But with President Trump's appointments, the Supreme Court may now be poised to reverse course. A case in the lower court challenging Harvard University's affirmative action will likely provide that opportunity, if the Court wishes to take it.[83]

## APOLOGIES AND REPARATIONS

The U.S. House and Senate (but not the U.S. president) have formally apologized for slavery; President Obama signed a law in 2009 that included an apology to Native Americans; President Reagan signed a law apologizing to Japanese Americans for their internment during World War II; and in 2012, the House passed a resolution apologizing for the Chinese Exclusion Act.

Some argue that apologies are not enough and that more tangible action needs to be taken to atone for past discrimination, such as reparations paid to Japanese Americans who had been placed in relocation camps during World War II. In that case, money was paid only to those who had been sent to the relocation camps, not to their descendants. Why has the government paid reparations to Japanese Americans and not to former slaves or Native Americans?

Various arguments have been made in support of reparations. The most obvious is atonement for past injustices. For example, thousands of slaves were subjected to forced, unpaid labor in the years before the Civil War, and some argue that their descendants should be compensated for that. Others see reparations as a way to redistribute wealth and political power that continue to be held disproportionately by whites as a lasting legacy of past discrimination. Still others see reparations as primarily a symbolic gesture—even a teaching moment.[84] Various arguments have also been made against reparations. One argument raised by opponents of reparations is that those who would pay for reparations had nothing to do with the injustices that took place. Another argument is that reparations have already been effectively paid through affirmative action and other social services programs. Yet another is that administering reparations programs would be impracticable, divisive, and hugely expensive.[85] How would you deal with this issue?

## CONSEQUENCES FOR DEMOCRACY

Despite the Founders' assertions of liberty and equality, large segments of our population have found both to be elusive during much of our history. During that time, the government often played an active role in restricting civil rights, or at least in condoning such restrictions.

However, in the last half century in particular, the government has taken actions to advance civil rights and correct past discrimination through legislation, court cases, affirmative action policies, and other measures.

Citizen mobilization did much to spur these advances. Boycotts, nonviolent resistance, public gatherings, and dynamic leaders have all been integral parts of a wide variety of civil rights movements. From the Seneca Falls Convention in 1848 to the 1963 March on Washington and Martin Luther King, Jr.'s galvanizing "I Have a Dream" speech to more recent gay pride parades and marches for immigrant rights, citizen mobilization draws publicity and can be used to exert political pressure to secure legislative victories such as the Civil Rights Act of 1964, the Voting Rights Act of 1965, Title IX, and the Lilly Ledbetter Fair Pay Act. Notwithstanding the significance of those victories, many advances in civil rights have been brought about by federal courts. Judicial independence has allowed judges to take actions that legislators could not or would not dare to take. Interest groups such as the NAACP, NARF, and MALDEF have played an important role in bringing litigation to spur judicial action. But the resulting judicial decrees have led to some degree of controversy, since some people feel that policy decisions are best made by legislators rather than judges.

The changes brought about by legislation, court cases, and executive action have meant greater access to the democratic process (through the expansion of the right to vote). In turn, these expanded rights and the policies that flow from them directly affect you. You are, for example, protected from many forms of discrimination that were routine for previous generations of Americans. You are not compelled to attend segregated schools or sit at the back of the bus because you are black; denied the right to vote because you are a woman; kept off a jury because you are Hispanic; precluded from serving in the military because you are gay; or unable to access public facilities because you are handicapped.

Nonetheless, past discrimination continues to affect our national identity, citizen discourse, and the way Americans view each other today. Opposition to social welfare programs often has racial overtones, as do views about immigration. And social and religious values weigh heavily in debates about controversial civil rights issues such as same-sex marriage and the right of transgendered individuals to serve in the military. Indeed, one dilemma for democracy is how to balance competing rights and liberties. At what point, for example, does protecting the rights of same-sex couples interfere with religious liberties discussed in Chapter 4? Or, to look at it from the opposite perspective, at what point do laws enacted to protect religious liberty sanction discrimination?

Such dilemmas have contributed to the "culture war" in America and sharpened the edge of polarized politics. Think about the issues discussed in this chapter: immigration, the rights of transgender people, the #MeToo Movement, Confederate monuments, #BlackLivesMatter, and voter ID laws. These are not issues on which people readily agree. A consequence for democracy is an ongoing struggle to resolve these issues and gain consensus.

## Critical Thinking Questions

1. What types of discrimination have African Americans faced? How and to what extent have they overcome this discrimination?

2. How have women in the United States earned rights in the workplace? Where do women still face challenges?

3. How should the United States deal with the issue of illegal immigration? Do state laws that restrict the rights of illegal immigrants raise civil rights issues?

4. Should transgender people be allowed to serve in the military? How should transgender students be treated in public schools? How should the issue of bathrooms and locker rooms be handled?

## Key Terms

Visit edge.sagepub.com/maltese to help you accomplish your coursework goals in an easy-to-use learning environment.

AAron Ontiveroz / Denver Post / Getty Images

# 6
# PUBLIC OPINION AND POLITICAL SOCIALIZATION

## After reading this chapter, you should be able to do the following:

- Describe American political culture and explain how it has evolved over time.

- Understand political socialization and the sources through which Americans learn their values.

- Identify the ways in which different groups affect public opinion and politics in general.

- Evaluate the factors that bring about changes in public opinion.

- Explain how ideologies acquire their structure.

- Explore the different methods by which public opinion can be measured.

## Perspective: What Difference Does Public Opinion Make?

The United States spends less than most prosperous countries to provide for the basic welfare of its people. In 2016, the government spent less than one-fourth of our gross domestic product (GDP) on housing, health, recreation, education, and social programs. (GDP is the total amount spent in a country in a year on all goods and services.) In that same year, the Netherlands spent 30 percent of its GDP on such programs.[1] The Netherlands is considered a "welfare state" whose government spends a great deal to meet basic human needs. It provides several hundred dollars a month of basic support to all families with children, full health care for everyone in the country, and heavily subsidized university education for all.

We might expect from this that the Dutch are especially supportive of government programs to provide for people. But ironically, when Americans and the Dutch are asked whether their government should ensure that everyone is provided for or whether people should take more responsibility to provide for themselves, only 37 percent of the Dutch thought their government should provide for people. Americans actually supported welfare state programs somewhat more than the Dutch, with 41 percent in favor.[2]

Why is it that these countries' policies do not match the wishes of their citizens more closely? How is it that the Dutch, who believe a bit less in government intervention than Americans, spend more on government support for their citizens than we do? What role does public opinion play in determining a country's policies? What factors limit its influence? **«**

## PUBLIC OPINION AND POLITICAL CULTURE

**Public opinion** consists of the combined voices of all the people in a society on political issues. Today, to measure public opinion, we usually ask people in a poll or survey how they feel about an issue and then tally up their answers; we treat this as public opinion on the issue. However, public opinion as it actually enters political decision making is not a simple sum of everyone's opinions on an issue. Some people are heard more in politics than others. Bloggers, newspaper columnists, citizens who write or e-mail their representatives in Congress, those who are active in electoral campaigns—all of these individuals add more than other people to public opinion as it is actually heard by government officials. Think of a choir in which some people have especially strong voices. What decision makers hear is determined more by the strong voices than by other members of the choir. It is very difficult to come up with a full picture of public opinion in this sense, because it would mean taking into account thousands of variations in how much impact different individuals have. As a general rule, political scientists look at the simpler version of public opinion as the sum of all individual opinions, and that is how we will discuss it in this chapter, but you should always remember that what politicians actually hear is the richer, more variegated public opinion. If you want to affect what goes on in the world, you should try to be one of the strong voices rather than one of the weak ones.

In a sense, public opinion was born at the founding of the republic. Although some of his colleagues—including Alexander Hamilton—were less enthusiastic about its role in the new country, James Madison argued for a strong role for public opinion. Along with Thomas Jefferson, he argued that the social and intellectual elites could not be assumed to have a monopoly on truth, and he encouraged the growth of newspapers to facilitate a "general intercourse of sentiments."[3] Ever since that time, public opinion has been recognized as an important factor in American democracy.

Until the 1940s, public opinion was thought of solely as the more complex entity composed of writers, lecturers, party activists, and others whose voices were heard publicly. After polling and survey analysis were invented in the 1940s, however, it became possible to measure how all people in the country felt about an issue, and from then on, *public opinion* more and more began to mean the average of all individual opinions.

Public opinion is, in part, a product of a country's political culture. The **political culture** of a country consists of the political attitudes and beliefs held broadly among its citizens, which form the basis for their political behavior. These attitudes are not so much about specific policy issues as about the basic underlying political system.

Political culture varies a good deal from one country to another, and it is often responsible for major differences in how politics is conducted. We can sometimes detect differences in culture by looking at popular behaviors and sayings. For instance, the Japanese tend to emphasize consensus and dislike conflict to a greater extent than Americans, as illustrated by two popular sayings:

- The nail that sticks out gets hammered down. (Japan)
- The squeaky wheel gets the grease. (United States)

The basic differences reflected in these two sayings surely have something to do with the fact that political decisions are more likely in Japan than in the United States to be made on the basis of

**public opinion**
The collective opinion of citizens on a policy issue or a principle of politics.

**political culture**
A people's attitudes, beliefs, and factual assumptions about the basic nature of society and basic principles of politics.

*Apic / Getty Images*

**American political culture emphasizes individuality and freedom—a frontier mentality epitomized by the cowboys of the Old West.**

unanimous consent rather than by a vote in which one side wins and the other side loses. Individualistic assertion and challenges are highly valued in the United States, but less so in Japan.

Political culture usually changes slowly. French political thinker Alexis de Tocqueville visited the United States in the early nineteenth century to examine the workings of U.S. democracy. In his seminal work, *Democracy in America*,[4] he outlined the American approach to politics—its emphasis on individuality and freedom, its reliance on local politics and voluntary organizations, its restlessness and desire for progress. These attitudes still guide American politics today. That is stunning when we consider the fact that the America he saw was an almost totally agricultural society, without modern means of communication or a preeminent role in world politics. Since that time, American society has absorbed many waves of immigrants who initially came to the United States with very different cultures. Our country and society have changed immensely since de Tocqueville wrote his book, yet the underlying political culture has remained almost unchanged.

The basic American values of fairness, individualism, religion, and the rule of law that we introduced in Chapter 1 are an important part of America's political culture. In addition, four other aspects of any political culture are especially important if democracy is to work well:

- *Tolerance of those advocating unpopular ideas.* If those who dissent are not allowed to present their positions publicly, there will be no opportunities to debate new ideas and no possibility for change.
- *Trust in the system of government.* Although citizens in a democracy must be willing to criticize individual officeholders, they need to trust that the overall system will be fair.
- *Political efficacy.* People must believe that what they do can make a difference in government policies.
- *Political knowledge and attention to policies.* People must know enough about politicians and their policy positions to choose between them.

Let us see how well Americans' attitudes fit with these four cornerstones of democracy.

## POLITICAL TOLERANCE

In 2014, 32 percent of Americans thought that someone who is against churches and religion should be barred from teaching in a college, and 20 percent thought that such a person should not be allowed to give a public speech. Similarly, 38 percent thought that speeches offensive to

FIGURE 6.1

## *Is Intolerance Decreasing in America?*

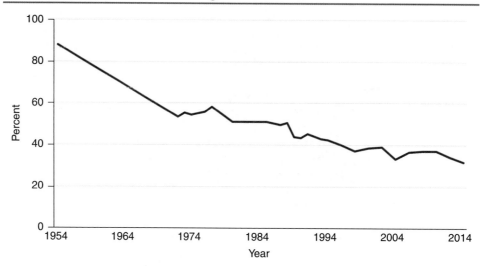

*Shown here is the percentage of Americans who believe that a person who is against churches and religion should be barred from teaching in college. What may have brought about the decrease in such intolerance since the 1950s?*

Source: Samuel Stouffer, Communism, Conformity, and Civil Liberties *(Garden City, NY: Doubleday, 1955);* "General Social Survey Final Report: Trends in Public Attitudes About Civil Liberties, 1972-2014," *National Opinion Research Center, April 2015, http://www.norc.org/PDFs/GSS%20Reports/GSS_CivLib15_final_formatted.pdf*

ethnic groups should not be allowed.[5] Intolerance of this sort is not uncommon in democracies around the world. Levels of tolerance in Israel, Great Britain, and New Zealand are fairly similar to those in the United States.[6]

Americans' level of tolerance for dissent may seem disappointingly low, but over the last few decades, Americans appear to have become increasingly tolerant of dissent. In 1954, as seen in Figure 6.1, a surprising 88 percent of Americans thought that someone opposed to religion should not be allowed to teach in a college, but the proportion of people who hold this viewpoint has declined steadily since then.[7] There have been similar declines in intolerance for other forms of dissenting speech and action.

## TRUST IN GOVERNMENT

Democracy requires that citizens must be skeptical about individual officeholders and be prepared to vote them out of office. However, citizens also need to have a general, overall sense of trust that the system is fair. A general distrust of the government breeds corrosive cynicism and apathy.

As Figure 6.2 shows, trust in government has fluctuated widely over the last several decades. Overall, the level of trust has dropped significantly since the 1950s and early 1960s, although the movement has not been continuously downward. Trust seemed to reach a nadir in the early 1990s. It recovered somewhat after that but dropped sharply again after 2002.

To some extent, trust in government responds to events. Trust dropped sharply following the divisive Vietnam War in the mid-1960s. Patriotism surged following the destruction of the World Trade Center in 2001, and the level of trust in government increased along with it. However, the general drop in trust that has occurred since the late 1950s and early 1960s goes beyond any particular set of events, and opinion cannot seem to bounce back to its pre-1968 levels. What happened? It might be argued, of course, that the events associated with the Vietnam War from 1963 to 1975 seared the American psyche so deeply that we have never recovered from them. But over half of the American electorate in 2019 were small children, or not yet born, when the war ended in 1975. So, our low levels of trust today must be a result of more than the initial drop in trust that was apparently caused by Vietnam.

# FIGURE 6.2

## *Trust in Government*

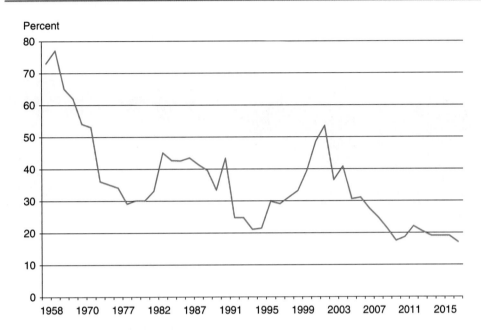

Percent

*Shown here is the percentage of Americans who trust government "all or most of the time," measured at two-year intervals. What might explain the rise and fall of people's trust in the government?*
*Source: "Public Trust in Government: 1958-2019," Pew Research Center, April 11, 2019, https://www.people-press.org/2019/04/11/public-trust-in-government-1958-2019/*
*The Pew report gathers results from several sources, often with multiple studies in a single year; we have averaged all of their reports for any single year, and this figure charts those averages year to year.*

Another possibility is that the way the media reports on government officials changed in the early 1970s when reporters learned during the Watergate affair in 1974 that investigating unpleasant stories about officials could be a virtuous act that served democracy. In the past, the press had been deferential to officials, collaborating to mask unpleasant facts about them. President John F. Kennedy, for example, was often unfaithful to his wife, but there was no mention of that character flaw in the press during the 1960s. But by the late 1990s, the press feasted on the story of President Bill Clinton's sexual relationship with Monica Lewinsky, and the U.S. House of Representatives impeached the president for obstructing justice when they claimed that he had lied about this relationship. The presidency of Donald Trump has made investigative reporting and the debunking of false statements a major industry.

We do not want to overemphasize the role of the media as an explanation for declining trust in government, however. The truth is that nobody really knows for certain why trust has declined. Furthermore, the decline of trust may not be an entirely bad thing. Too much trust can leave officials unchallenged, and a deferential press may allow corruption to flourish. On the other hand, too little trust can lead to ineffective cynicism and an urge to throw out all politicians, good or bad. *Some* level of popular trust in government is needed for democracy, but there is no magic number that is the right amount of trust. Are current levels of trust too low? About right? How would one find the answer to this question?

After the terrorist attacks of September 11, 2001, patriotism surged around the country. In New York City, street vendors filled their racks with flag-themed clothing and memorabilia.

President Kennedy's extramarital affairs, including a rumored relationship with Marilyn Monroe, went entirely unreported during his presidency, despite the fact that they were two of the most famous people in the world at the time. President Clinton's affair with a previously unknown White House intern consumed the news media—and Congress—for months.

## POLITICAL EFFICACY

Similar to trust in government, Americans' sense of *political efficacy*—the belief that they can affect what the government does—has declined over the last several decades. In 1960, only 27 percent of Americans believed that people have no say in what the government does, but by 2016, this figure had risen to 50 percent.[8] This change is probably related to the decline in trust, but it also reflects what citizens think is possible for them in the American democracy.

Although this sense of efficacy has declined somewhat over the years, United States citizens generally rank highly on this factor in comparison with citizens of other countries. In one study comparing 38 different countries, the United States ranked first in the number of its citizens who believed that if the government passed an unjust law, they would be able to do something to get the law changed.[9]

## POLITICAL KNOWLEDGE AND ATTENTION TO ISSUES

How well do Americans follow politics and how much do they know about political issues? Americans are uncomfortable with politics, especially if it involves conflict. We love "leaders," for instance, but dislike "politicians." Sometimes to devalue a proposal, Americans will say, "Oh, that's just politics." This attitude goes back a long way. In 1863, Henry David Thoreau called politics "the gizzard of society."[10]

Americans do not like political conflict. They regularly tell interviewers that they wish the political parties would not spend so much time quarreling but would just sit down and work out good policies everyone could agree on. (Whether this kind of solution is actually possible on most issues is, of course, another question.) In fact, it appears that most Americans are more concerned about the style of politics than about which policies are put in place. Their main concern is that the process should be civil and fair.[11]

With their relative interest in style over the substance of policies, Americans are often not well informed about policy and political issues. A study conducted after the 2016 election showed that only 71 percent knew that Republicans had controlled the House of Representatives in the run-up to the election.[12] And more importantly for voters choosing between candidates, a study in 2008 showed that although abortion has long been an important issue in American politics, only 52 percent knew that Barack Obama was pro-choice; 10 percent thought he was pro-life, while 38

# As a Young Person in China

As a young person who was born and raised in China, what was your political socialization like? Probably the two strongest agents of socialization in your life were your family and the schools you attended. Both emphasized values from a political culture (going back thousands of years) that places a high premium on political stability and fears chaos. The old Confucian culture of China viewed all parts of the universe, right down to the family, as being in harmony under the strong leadership of a benign head (the emperor, the father, and so on) who was expected to work selflessly for the general good. Any threat to this authority ran the risk of chaos; the frequent chaotic periods in the history of China show that this risk was very real. After the communist revolution in 1949, the communist government, fearing challenges to its authority, adapted the old Confucian values to meet its own needs.

Your parents and teachers have instilled in you the view that challenges to authority invite social breakdown. Note, by the way, that the schools have been so effective because they reinforced rather than challenged what you learned in your family. In school, your teachers have also emphasized in two semester-long courses that Britain, France, Germany, Japan, Russia, and the United States have repeatedly humiliated and exploited China. By the time you reached the university, you and your friends had become strongly nationalistic, and you regard foreign criticism of China as a continuation of this humiliation. You are not challenged by great diversity in society; 92 percent of Chinese people belong to a single ethnic group, the Han, and most non-Han are concentrated in Tibet and southwestern China.*

You and your friends are very optimistic. After all, China's economy has grown by 10 percent nearly every year for the last quarter century. You live in a way your parents only dreamed of. Because of China's rule of one child per family, which was enforced strictly for many years, you are probably an only child and are perhaps a bit spoiled.

You and your friends are also very idealistic. You want to change the world for the better and are not at all cynical about this ambition. Again, this quality fits with long-established Confucian values, which have a strongly positive view of human possibilities. In the Chinese tradition, both people and nature are seen as innately good, a view that contrasts sharply with the Western tradition, which considers people to be innately sinful and in need of divine forgiveness and perceives nature as an adversary and a danger. This ancient view of people is alive and present in your perception of what you should do in the world, leading you to expect the best of yourself and of others.

Now you find yourself in a time of turmoil brought on by the very economic progress that makes you proud of your country. The growth of the economy, fueled by entrepreneurs willing to make huge speculative bets, has upended the Chinese ideal of harmony in the world. Some people have become fabulously rich without respecting the old rules for how people deal with each other, while peasants remain poor and are often exploited by the new rich. All of these changes have left you about two parts optimistic and one part confused.

## Questions to Consider

1. What is the value of dissent? The political culture of the United States, emphasizing individualism and freedom from control, does not stress the dangers of social breakdown as much as Chinese political culture. Could that be a danger for the United States? Or is the Chinese emphasis on the dangers of breakdown a problem for them because it stultifies dissent?
2. When a culture is confronted with rapid economic change, as in China, how can it adapt? Has the political culture of the United States changed as a result of the economic turmoil of the period since 2001?

* "The World Factbook," Central Intelligence Agency, accessed July 21, 2019, https://www.cia.gov/library/publications/the-world-factbook/

percent did not know one way or another. Similarly, only 45 percent knew that John McCain, the Republican candidate, was pro-life; 17 percent thought he was pro-choice.[13]

# POLITICAL SOCIALIZATION

Individuals form political beliefs through **political socialization**, the learning of political values and factual assumptions about politics. In principle, this process can occur at any age and under any circumstances, but it tends to be concentrated at certain points in our lives.

> **political socialization**
> The process of learning political values and factual assumptions about politics.

As with most learning, political socialization occurs most readily in childhood and diminishes as people grow older. From their families, children learn many basic social attitudes, such as trust in people and attitudes toward authority, which will be important in shaping their later response to politics. But most children acquire only rather primitive ideas about what government is and how politics works ("the president runs things," for instance). It is only later, in adolescence and early adulthood, that people form more concrete ideas about politics (for instance, it makes a difference whether the president is a Democrat or a Republican). They can also continue to learn and change throughout their adult lives, especially if they are exposed to extraordinary events.

The basic attitudes about politics that constitute political culture (trust, efficacy, tolerance, etc.) are a large part of what is passed on to new generations through political socialization. But people also learn the **political identities** that will form the basis of their political lives: their religion (to the extent that it has political content) and their identification with a political party. Initially, most Americans identify with their parents' religion, although new experiences later in their lives may cause their beliefs to evolve. Similarly, many Americans identify in a fairly basic way with one of the two major political parties ("I'm a Democrat" or "I'm a Republican"). We call this **party identification**, and it can color and shape the way we approach politics. We will examine party identification in detail in Chapter 9.

A variety of sources influence the political learning process. These sources are called **agents of political socialization**. In order to have a strong impact on socialization, an agent must meet two conditions:

- The agent must be *credible*.
- The agent must be seen as *relevant* to politics.

As we will see, some potential agents meet only one of these conditions and therefore fall short of the influence they otherwise would wield. Important agents include families, peer groups (friends), schools, college, the media, and political events.

## FAMILIES

Families are the most important agents of socialization. Parents have great *credibility* with their children, especially when children are young. They are not specifically *relevant* to politics, but since they are relevant to just about everything, politics is included. Parents instill basic underlying values in young children, such as respect (or disrespect) for authority, definitions of fairness, and obligations to others, that provide much of the basis for their later political beliefs. In adolescence and young adulthood, children often adopt their parents' specific beliefs or views, though they are apt to challenge and question their parents' views on everything from proper dress to politics as they establish an independent identity in adolescence. Studies find that parents' attitudes still play a significant role at this age in areas such as party identification, beliefs about how the economy should function, and understandings of how foreign relations work. For example, one study that followed children as they grew to adulthood found that the children of Democratic parents were three times more likely to identify themselves as Democrats than as Republicans by their mid-30s, while children of Republican parents were more than twice as likely to be Republicans as Democrats.[14] Parents also influence how their children view specific policy issues, although not as strongly as they influence party identification.[15]

## PEER GROUPS

Young people find peer groups—friends, acquaintances, and others in the same social circumstances—highly *credible*. However, friends often have little *relevance* to politics. They may strongly influence your choice in clothes, your economic habits, and your understanding of sexual morality, but unless they themselves are interested in and informed about politics (which many are not), they will have little influence on your political views. The exception to this rule, of course, would be groups of friends who form precisely because the members are interested in politics. A group of friends who met at a Bernie Sanders rally are going to be very strong agents in molding one another's views on politics.

**political identities**
The images of who you are, to the extent that your identity carries political content, such as your religion or your membership in a political party.

**party identification**
A sense of belonging to one or another of the political parties.

**agents of political socialization**
The people and institutions from whom we learn about politics.

## SCHOOLS

Schools are the one place where the government can deliberately try to reshape a country's political culture by controlling part of the political socialization process. Revolutionary governments that wish to remake their population—governments such as those of Nazi Germany, the Soviet Union, or North Korea—have devoted extensive resources to political socialization in their schools. But all countries attempt to socialize children to some extent. Schools in the United States try to develop patriotic, informed citizens both directly through such devices as a reciting the Pledge of Allegiance each day and indirectly through instruction in courses such as civics or government. Projects such as Kids Voting USA, which holds mock elections in schools on the same day as official elections, encourage civic participation.

Students from around the country take part in Model United Nations events, often through their schools. Model United Nations and similar activities reinforce values of cooperation and diplomacy.

In general, the impact of schools on political socialization appears to be limited. Schools meet the *relevance* test—they obviously are relevant to politics when they teach politics. But unless what they are teaching is consistent with what parents and friends are already saying, their *credibility* on the subject is weak. The Nazis in Germany, for instance, replaced large numbers of teachers in German schools in an attempt to create the "new German man," and many feared that after World War II, a horrid generation of young adults would have emerged from those schools. It never happened; surveys of political attitudes after the War showed that young adults' attitudes were similar to other Germans. Parents—not the Nazis' educational programs—had shaped students' views about politics.

## COLLEGE

Attending college appears to be a stronger formative influence than elementary and secondary schools. When students attend college, they are often living apart from their parents for the first time. Furthermore, American college instruction generally encourages students to question accepted truths and think critically about issues.

We might expect from this openness to new thinking that college students would often be in the forefront in new directions in politics. A survey of students across the country in 1976—a fairly liberal period in American history during the aftermath of the Vietnam War—showed that at that time, many more students were liberal than conservative. But when the same survey was repeated in 1984 at the height of Reagan's new conservative era, a majority were conservatives.[16] Students often gravitate to new movements. In 2008, students were one of the major sources of support for Barack Obama's "change" candidacy, and in 2016, they were key in Bernie Sanders's antiestablishment campaign for the presidency.

These surveys and examples do not suggest that students gravitate ideologically toward one extreme or the other. The research simply suggests that college students are more willing than most citizens to adopt new ideas. One common misconception is that colleges make students more politically liberal. A nationwide study that followed incoming freshmen through graduation found that they did become slightly more liberal over their time in college, but the shift was not large. Twenty-five percent were liberal when they entered college; 33 percent were liberal when they graduated. And by the time they graduated, they were no more liberal than the population of 18- to 24-year-olds generally.[17] Probably the greatest impact of a college education is an increase in political interest and the ability to comprehend information about politics. Colleges have considerable *credibility* about politics and other matters. It appears that they are not *relevant* to political choices per se but rather provide students the tools for thinking about politics.

## MEDIA

As we will see in Chapter 10, the media functions as a source of political information for the public as well as a filter that identifies which political issues are important enough to cover, investigate, or debate. Mass media is becoming increasingly important as an agent of socialization. Up until the 1990s, the media consisted of newspapers, magazines, network television, and radio. None of these sources of information had great credibility with citizens when they dealt with politics, because people thought the media should be neutral politically and resisted any overt attempts at persuasion.

In recent decades, with the advent of the Internet and the rising popularity of talk radio, people have increasingly turned to new media sources that are accepted as more partisan. Talk radio personalities such as Rush Limbaugh, TV figures such as Rachel Maddow, and bloggers of all persuasions are viewed as appropriately political because they make no claims to neutrality or objectivity. Oddly enough, TV comedians such as Jimmy Kimmel or Trevor Noah are trusted precisely because they do not *look* as though they are about politics; their primary job is to get laughs, not to drive a political agenda.

How much impact does the media have as a provider of information? A study of beliefs about the Iraq War found that of those who relied mainly on print media for their news, about 17 percent believed (incorrectly) that weapons of mass destruction (WMDs) had been found in Iraq after American forces deposed Saddam Hussein's government in 2003. Of those who relied primarily on CNN or the established national television networks—NBC, ABC, and CBS—about 20 percent believed WMDs had been found. Of those who relied primarily on Fox network for their news, about 33 percent shared this belief.[18] More recently, a study found that using conservative media led viewers to be skeptical of global warming—probably not surprising, but the more interesting finding of the study was that this effect was, in part, indirect. Their consumption of conservative media also reduced viewers' trust in scientists, which led to an additional increase in their skepticism.[19] Clearly, media can make a difference in what you believe, if it is viewed as both *credible* and *relevant*.

## WORLD AND POLITICAL EVENTS

Not only can people and institutions serve as agents of socialization, but major life-changing events can as well. Events such as the Vietnam War or the terrorist attacks of 9/11 can affect the political perspectives of an entire generation, in a process often called the generational effect. Even the decisions of politicians themselves can have profound effects. For example, Democratic President Lyndon Johnson spearheaded the passage of the Civil Rights Act of 1964, which outlawed racial segregation of restaurants and other facilities. During the presidential campaign that year, Republican presidential candidate Barry Goldwater argued against the bill. The conflict permanently shifted the party loyalties of both African Americans and Southern whites. From 1952 through 1962, 58 percent of African Americans had identified as Democrats; in 1964, this figure jumped to 80 percent and has remained at that level ever since. In the decades following 1964, white Southerners, who largely opposed the civil rights legislation, gradually migrated to the Republican Party.

Figure 6.3 provides a dramatic illustration of another event that had clear socializing effects on a generation of young people: the Great Depression of the 1930s and Democratic President Franklin D. Roosevelt's New Deal. The figure shows the partisan direction for different age groups 50 years later. The oldest age group, those 82 years old and older at the time of the study, had come of age before the Depression hit in 1930. As befit the Republican era of Calvin Coolidge (1923–1929) and Herbert Hoover (1929–1933), the members of this group were distinctly Republican in their sympathies. But young people, whose political views are less firmly fixed than older people's, always react more to events and are shaped more by them. Starting with the group who were 16 to 19 years old in 1932, the year Americans elected Roosevelt, a strongly Democratic generation emerged.[20]

## AMERICAN EXCEPTIONALISM

The end result of political socialization is, of course, a *political culture*—a particular constellation of political values. Americans have often defined themselves by their values, and indeed, the

**generational effect**
A change in a whole generation's political viewpoint brought about by an event.

## FIGURE 6.3

## *Emergence of the New Deal Generation*

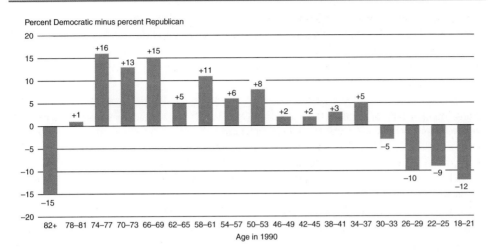

The partisan direction for age groups is calculated here by subtracting the percentage who identified with the Republican Party in 1990 from the percentage who identified with the Democratic Party. Which group appears to have been most affected by the Great Depression and the New Deal?
Source: Robert S. Erikson and Kent L. Tedin, American Public Opinion, updated 7th ed. (New York, NY: Taylor & Francis).

United States is one of the few countries in the world that originated not in a race or language group but in a set of values. How special is the American political culture?

Some speak of **American exceptionalism**, the idea that the United States is different from the rest of the world and, therefore, is very special. In general, this idea stems from the history of the United States as a revolutionary country, the first modern democracy. The phrase *American exceptionalism* actually is used in a number of different ways:

- to some, it refers to a uniquely American ideology, based on freedom, equality, and individualism (see Chapter 1);
- to some, it has to do with our immigrant history (more than most countries, we are a nation of immigrants and our society is a multicultural blend of cultures, sending a message of openness and tolerance);
- to some, it embodies the idea that America is a shining city on the hill, an example and promoter of democracy around the world;
- and often, the concept is merely used to convey a sense that Americans are different from the rest of the world and that the United States is better than other countries.

One setting in which American exceptionalism has been cited in recent years is the Mideast, where Americans led in opposing Islamic fundamentalism after the attacks of September 11, 2001. The United States began occupying Afghanistan in 2002 in an attempt to establish a democratic government there, then invaded Iraq in 2003 to depose dictator Saddam Hussein and establish democracy. In these efforts, there was a strong sense of fulfilling a mission to bring democracy to the Mideast, but there was also a concern that America's democratic values might be perceived as too alien to be assimilated by Islamic political culture. Many Americans have expressed the view that American democratic values are antithetical to fundamentalist Islam. In 2001, President George W. Bush said of the 9/11 Islamic terrorists, "They hate our freedoms—our freedom of religion, our freedom of speech, our freedom to vote and assemble and disagree with each other."[21]

The Mideast, then, may provide a good test of whether American values are truly exceptional. After all, the United States has been in conflict with various Islamic entities, including ISIS (Islamic State of Iraq and Syria), the Taliban, and Iran, and Islamic terrorists have attacked U.S. citizens in the past. If any part of the world were to exhibit different values from ours, it would seem to be the Mideast.

**American exceptionalism**
The idea that the political culture of the United States is distinctive in the world and that the United States has a special role to build democracy in the world.

**TABLE 6.1**

## Values of Americans and Iranians

|  | USA | Iran |
|---|---|---|
| Attitudes on Democracy |  |  |
| Agree: It is important to live in a democracy. | 85% | 81% |
| Agree: Religious leaders should not influence how people vote. | 60% | 60% |
| Social Values |  |  |
| Agree: Homosexuality is never justified. | 32% | 82% |
| Agree: Abortion is never justified. | 26% | 61% |
| Agree: University is more important for a boy than for a girl. | 8% | 56% |

*Source: Inglehart, R., C. Haerpfer, A. Moreno, C. Welzel, K. Kizilova, J. Diez-Medrano, M. Lagos, P. Norris, E. Ponarin, & B. Puranen et al. (eds.). 2014. World Values Survey: Round Five—Country-Pooled Datafile Version: www.worldvaluessurvey.org/WVSDocumentationWV5.jsp. Madrid: JD Systems Institute.*

*World Values Survey, 2005-2008 Wave.*

But does American exceptionalism truly set the United States apart from the Islamic world? Table 6.1 compares the values of Americans and citizens of Iran. On social issues such as homosexuality, abortion, and equal treatment of women and men, there are indeed significant differences between the two cultures. But on basic ideas about how politics should operate, the two are very close. Support for democracy is about the same, and Iranians are about as likely as Americans to believe that religious leaders should not be involved in politics. These results do not indicate basic cultural differences on the question of democracy.

## GROUP DIFFERENCES IN THE UNITED STATES

Demographic, social, economic, and religious groups in American politics often share common political values, views, and experiences. As members of a group interact, they may share information or misinformation about events or candidates. They often tend to respond similarly to particular candidates or issues. Politics often consists of marshalling a coalition of groups in the population either to win an election or to build support for a particular policy, so groups' opinions may serve as important building blocks for politics.

### AGE

We might expect that younger and older Americans would differ on issues that affect their self-interest. For example, we might expect older Americans to want higher Social Security retirement benefits and younger Americans to be more concerned about help for first-time home buyers. Surprisingly, however, there is little evidence that these sorts of issues divide younger and older Americans. In a survey, 88 percent of Americans over 58 years old supported raising taxes to avoid having to cut Social Security—but 79 percent of those under 34 years old also felt the same way.[22]

Differences between younger and older Americans do show up, however, when views on an issue are changing, such as same-sex marriage or marijuana legalization. In these circumstances, older generations often hold on to the accepted view on the emerging issue while younger generations are more willing to embrace the newer view. Younger voters are also more likely to support new faces in elections. For example, during the Democratic presidential primary race in 2016, young voters flocked to Bernie Sanders, an insurgent face in national politics, while older voters were more likely to support Hillary Clinton, who had been a national figure since the 1990s. In the New Hampshire primary, 83 percent of voters under 29 supported Sanders but only 16 percent supported Clinton; of voters over 65, 45 percent supported Sanders, but 54 percent supported Clinton.[23]

This is not a peculiarly American phenomenon. In the 2017 German parliamentary elections, for instance, 13 percent of voters under 25 voted for the new-ish Green Party, which was supported by only 4 percent of voters over 70.[24] When Mao Zedong led an insurgent revitalization of China's Communist Party in the Cultural Revolution, almost all of the activists involved were young people.

## RACE AND ETHNICITY

America is becoming increasingly diverse in its racial and ethnic makeup; projections indicate that by 2055, only half of the population will consist of non-Hispanic whites. Most of the increase in population is among Hispanics and Asian Americans. The percentage of African Americans has remained steady and is projected to remain so, while the percentage of non-Hispanic whites has declined sharply and is projected to decline more. Figure 6.4 shows these shifts in the major ethnic groups. As we will see in Chapter 9, these shifts are likely to have important effects on American politics.

Differences in opinion between racial and ethnic groups are due partly to economic disparities between the groups. African Americans, for example, have lower average incomes than whites and, not surprisingly, are much more in favor of government programs for the poor than are whites. In a survey, 42 percent of African Americans thought that the government should see to it that every person has a job and a good standard of living, but only 25 percent of whites agreed; 44 percent of African Americans (but only 27 percent of whites) thought that the government should provide more services, even if that means an increase in government spending.[25]

Although differences such as these between the races are due partly to the fact that whites' average incomes are higher than those of other groups, there is something more at work as well. In a survey comparing whites and non-whites, nonwhites were distinctly more likely than whites to favor governmental action to make incomes more equal, even taking into account differences in the groups' income levels.[26]

Racial and ethnic groups often have strong feelings on specific issues that affect them directly. For example, African Americans support affirmative action more strongly than other groups, while Hispanics favor pro-immigrant policies such as bilingual education in public schools and amnesty for undocumented immigrants. Some issues can be so important that they determine long-term partisan loyalties. In 2018, half a century after the Civil Rights Acts, 90 percent of African Americans still voted for Democratic candidates in House races.[27]

Common experience and frequent interaction within ethnic and racial groups can also shape more general political attitudes. For instance, trust in government is lower among African Americans than among other groups—an attitude that may be reinforced by a general sense among African Americans that the police single them out for stops and searches and for prosecution. When African American athlete O. J. Simpson was tried for murdering his wife in a

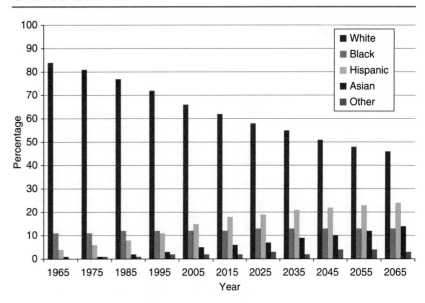

China's young people were a key force supporting the Cultural Revolution in China in the 1960s. Are there any political issues on which you and your peers seem to differ from your parents or grandparents?

**FIGURE 6.4**

## The Changing Racial Makeup of the United States

*Source: Pew Research Center 2015 report, "Modern Immigration Wave Brings 59 Million to US, Driving Population Growth and Change Through 2065", https://www.pewhispanic .org/2015/09/28/modern-immigration-wave-brings-59-million-to-u-s-driving-population-growth-and-change-through-2065/*

*Note: Whites, blacks and Asians include only single-race non-Hispanics; Asians include Pacific Islanders. Hispanics can be of any race.*

FIGURE 6.5

## *Importance of Religion in America*

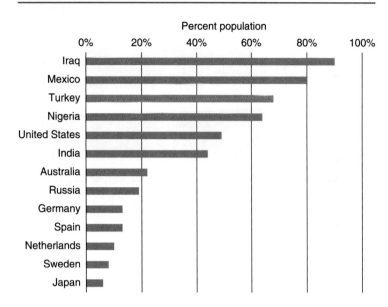

Percent population

*This figure shows the percent of the population for whom God is very important in their lives. In general, religion is more important in poorer countries. Why might this be? Why might religion be more important in the United States than in other rich countries?*

*Source: Inglehart, R., C. Haerpfer, A. Moreno, C. Welzel, K. Kizilova, J. Diez-Medrano, M. Lagos, P. Norris, E. Ponarin & B. Puranen et al. (eds.). 2014. World Values Survey: Round Six—Country-Pooled Datafile Version: www.worldvaluessurvey.org/WVSDocumentationWV6.jsp. Madrid: JD Systems Institute.*

widely watched televised trial in the early 1990s, whites generally believed he was guilty but African Americans generally believed that the Los Angeles police had planted fake evidence to falsely convict him. In a survey taken at the time, 72 percent of white respondents thought Simpson was guilty, while 71 percent of African Americans thought he was innocent.[28]

Voting patterns have historically been more evenly divided among Hispanics than among African Americans. On the one hand, Hispanics tend to back Democratic economic policies. On the other hand, as a group with many devout Catholics, Hispanics tend to identify with Republicans' socially conservative values. However, the current debate over immigration policies may have the potential to move Hispanics solidly into the Democratic camp, since on the whole Republican members of Congress have taken a much harder line than Democrats. In 2018, 69 percent of Hispanics voted for Democratic candidates in House races.[29]

## RELIGION

As shown in Figure 6.5, Americans are more religious than citizens of other economically well-off countries. Only the populations of less-developed countries are more religious than Americans.

Religion is an important determinant of voting behavior. Shared values can lead a religious group toward or away from a political party. Catholics were a core part of Roosevelt's New Deal coalition in the 1930s and continued to be a solid part of the Democratic Party until the 1970s, held largely by economic issues and general party loyalty. The rise to prominence of the abortion issue, however, led to a gradual movement of Catholics away from the Democratic Party as Catholic doctrine conflicted with what became the Democratic position favoring freedom of choice. Today, as evidenced by the 2018 election (see Figure 6.6), Catholic voters are almost evenly divided between the two parties.

Protestants are divided between "mainline" denominations and Evangelicals. About 40 percent of white Protestants are members of mainline denominations such as Presbyterian, Episcopal, Methodist, and the United Church of Christ. As we see in Figure 6.6, members of these denominations tend to be split fairly evenly between the parties, although there is a slight tilt toward the Democrats. Evangelicals, who make up about 60 percent of white Protestants, are growing in number. Evangelicals hold conservative moral values that are central to their politics, and thus, they have become a mainstay of the Republican Party, which tends to voice their views in such matters as abortion and gay rights. As indicated in the figure, this group voted strongly Republican in 2018.

The "Other" category in the figure encompasses Orthodox Christians, Jews (about 2 percent of the U.S. population), Muslims (1.1 percent), smaller numbers of Buddhists, Hindus, Sikhs, and other sects, and those with no specific religion. Of these, Jews tend to be liberal on most economic and social issues. Much more than any of the major Christian groups, they support higher taxes, governmental help for the poor and minorities, international engagement by the United States, freedom of choice on abortion, and legalization of same-sex marriage. Of Jews in the United States, 68 percent identify themselves as Democrats and only 21 percent as Republican.[30] On average, Jews are relatively well-off economically and might be expected therefore to be conservative at least on economic issues. However, their shared historical experience as an oppressed minority appears to have led most Jews to hold a solidly liberal position on political issues across the board.

Muslims are a small but growing minority in the American religious landscape. They identify as strongly with the Democratic Party as Jews do, possibly because of the Iraq War and their personal experiences during the War on Terror, which has often caused them to encounter a fairly generalized suspicion of all Muslims.[31] Their incomes tend to be a bit above the average for the overall population. However, they strongly favor generous government services for the poor. Their position on this issue may reflect Islam's strong emphasis on caring for the needy. At the same time, they are conservative on moral issues: 61 percent think homosexuality should be discouraged, and 59 percent think the government should do more to protect morality. These positions, too, are consistent with general Islamic principles. Overall, America's Muslims tend to be economically liberal but socially conservative.[32] Notably, 82 percent of American Muslims state that they are concerned about the rise of Islamic extremism around the world.[33]

## SOCIAL CLASS

Income differences in America are greater than they are in most of the world and, as shown in Figure 6.7, the disparity has been increasing over time. In 2018, the United States ranked 115th worldwide among 154 countries in the gap between the incomes of the richest 20 percent of the population and the poorest 20 percent. (Ranking number 1 meant a country had the smallest gap between rich and poor; ranking 154 meant it had the largest gap.) And among prosperous, fully developed economies, the United States ranked right at the bottom.[34]

Social class became a dividing line in American politics starting with Roosevelt's New Deal in the 1930s, which transformed the Democratic Party into a liberal party committed to policies that benefit the poor.[35] Low-income Americans continue to be strong supporters of economic programs similar to those of the New Deal that promote economic equality and opportunities for the poor, but, as shown in Figure 6.8, they are more conservative when it comes to the social and religious positions that also characterize liberalism today.[36] Thus, low-income Americans are torn. Economic issues pull them toward the Democratic Party, while social and religious issues pull them toward the Republican Party. Overall, they tend to be Democrats.

High-income Americans include business executives as well as professionals such as lawyers and doctors. Those associated with business strongly favor the Republican Party, as they have since the 1930s. But the growing population of well-paid professionals tend to side with the liberals on social issues.

### FIGURE 6.6

## 2018 Congressional Vote by Religious Group

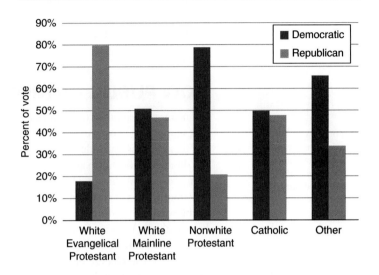

Source: Calculated from Fox News exit polls.

### FIGURE 6.7

## Widening Income Differences

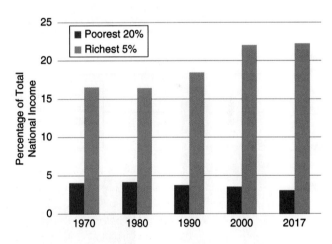

*From 1970 to 2008, the share of all income going to the richest 5 percent of Americans increased, while the share going to the poorest 20 percent declined. What are the likely political effects of this trend?*

Source: United Nations, Human Development Report 2010, 2010, http://hdr.undp.org/sites/default/files/reports/270/hdr_2010_en_complete_reprint.pdf; "Historical Income Tables: Households," United States Census, accessed August 12, 2019, https://www.census.gov/data/tables/time-series/demo/income-poverty/historical-income-households.html

## GENDER

Before the 1980s, men and women voted alike and held similar views on political issues. Over the last few decades, however, a gender gap has opened up in which women usually vote in greater numbers for Democratic candidates than men do (or men vote in greater numbers for Republican candidates than women do—you can describe the gender gap either way). In 2018, the gap was 12 percentage points.

Surprisingly, however, men and women do not differ greatly on political issues. In 2016, for instance, men and women both supported government-provided health insurance equally.[37] And while 13 percent of men thought abortion should never be permitted under any circumstances, so did 15 percent of women. The difference between how men and women vote, given this lack of differences on issues, is perplexing.

## HOW PUBLIC OPINION CHANGES

On many issues, public opinion remains fairly stable over time. Figure 6.9, for example, shows that support for a government-provided health insurance program has been rather stable over the last four decades. Attitudes on many other social programs such as aid to children or support for the disabled have shown similar patterns. However, over the same period the United States has seen great social change. Different groups in society relate to one another differently from the way they did in the past, and attitudes toward these groups have changed. In the last few decades of the twentieth century, for example, many women moved into the workforce instead of being homemakers. As shown in Figure 6.9, attitudes on whether women should have an "equal role with men in running business, industry, and government" have shown steady, evolutionary change.

Opinion can change in the population in two main ways. First, political events or leaders may actively work to shift people's opinions. In 1992, there was an upward jog in the otherwise rather stable support for government health care, as shown in Figure 6.9, after Bill Clinton campaigned for this policy during the presidential election. In 2012, the figure dropped after Republicans mobilized opposition to the Affordable Care Act.

The terrorist attacks on 9/11 brought about a swift transformation of public opinion. In a survey administered just before the attacks, 53 percent thought that "the world is more dangerous now compared to ten years ago." When the same survey was repeated two years later in 2003, 73 percent had this opinion.[38] Similarly, in the wake of the botched relief effort after Hurricane Katrina struck New Orleans in 2005, a decade of gradual decline in the number of people who thought that the government "is almost always wasteful and inefficient" was suddenly reversed, with a jump from 47 percent agreeing with the statement before the storm to 56 percent after.[39]

### GENERATIONAL REPLACEMENT

In contrast to quick changes such as these, steady changes in public opinion usually come about by a different process: generational replacement. The change in opinions about the role of women shown in Figure 6.9 is an example of this phenomenon. Sometimes a change in the overall attitude of Americans occurs not because everyone's opinions change at the same time but because younger Americans take a new position, while older Americans do not change or, at least, do not change as much as the younger ones do. As time passes and the oldest Americans gradually die off and are replaced by younger ones, the overall state of American opinion on the issue transforms gradually and steadily. It takes about 30 to 50 years for generational replacement to happen.

Generational replacement was a major factor in Americans' gradual acceptance of an equal role for women in business and government, a change that occurred approximately from 1975 to 2005.[40] In 1972, the electorate consisted wholly of people born before 1958, and only 47

**gender gap** The difference between the percent of women and the percent of men voting for a candidate, which has been significant since about 1980.

**generational replacement** Change in overall attitudes caused by differences of opinion between young and old that gradually lead to a shift in overall opinion as older citizens pass from the scene.

## FIGURE 6.8

### *Attitude Differences by Social Class*

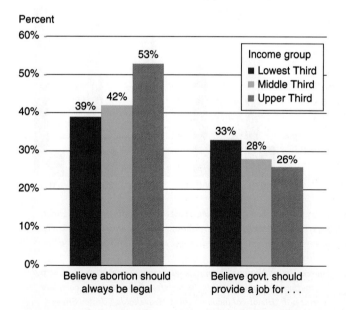

Percent

Income group
- ■ Lowest Third
- ■ Middle Third
- ■ Upper Third

Believe abortion should always be legal: 39%, 42%, 53%

Believe govt. should provide a job for . . . : 33%, 28%, 26%

*The less well-off favor government creation of jobs but oppose abortion. Is politics made more complicated because the social classes break down differently with regard to social and economic issues, or does this serve to make politics more moderate?*
*Source: "The ANES Guide to Public Opinion and Electoral Behavior," ANES, 2017, https://electionstudies.org/resources/anes-guide/*

FIGURE 6.9

## Evolution of Opinion on Two Issues

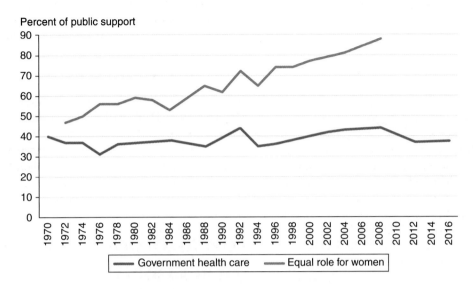

See the changes over time in support for an equal role for women and a government health insurance plan for everyone. What are the implications for politics of these two patterns of change?

Source: "The ANES Guide to Public Opinion and Electoral Behavior," ANES, 2017, https://electionstudies.org/resources/anes-guide/

percent of those voters supported an equal role for women. As time passed, many of this group died and were replaced by younger voters, who were more supportive of women's rights. By 2008, almost all voters were born after 1958; the small sliver of older voters still alive had only moved a little bit in the direction of equal rights for women, but they were overwhelmed by the new generation, about 80 percent of whom supported those rights.

## CHANGES IN PARTY IDENTIFICATION

Over the last few decades, a particularly important change in public opinion in the United States has been a slow decline in party identification. Party identification is a fairly stable attitude. It can shift in response to events, as shown in Figure 6.10, where Democratic identification increased in 2008 in response to the unpopular presidency of George W. Bush; Republican identification grew from 1980 to 1988 in response to the popular presidency of Ronald Reagan.[41] Such shifts are usually fairly small, but the figure has examples of two large shifts in the 1960s. In 1964, Democratic identification jumped and Republican identification dropped in response to the unpopular candidacy of Republican Barry Goldwater. Then, in 1968 and 1972, Democratic identification dropped sharply because of the Vietnam War and the general social unrest associated with the war. However, the Republicans did not benefit from these drops. The biggest "winner" was a general discouragement with both parties, leading to a lasting increase in the number of independents.

A long-term evolution of party identifications has occurred over the past 50 years, however. First, the gap between the number of Democrats and Republicans created by the New Deal has narrowed, probably by a process of generational replacement as the New Deal generation dies. Secondly, the number of independents—voters who do not identify with either party—has increased. This figure grew from 23 percent in 1952 to 37 percent in 2016, with most of the growth occurring in the 1960s and early 1970s. That timing might suggest that the decline resulted from disenchantment with political parties after the Vietnam War. But if that was the cause, why has the number of independents remained high, even as the Vietnam era fades ever further in our rearview mirror?

FIGURE 6.10

## Changes in Party Identification

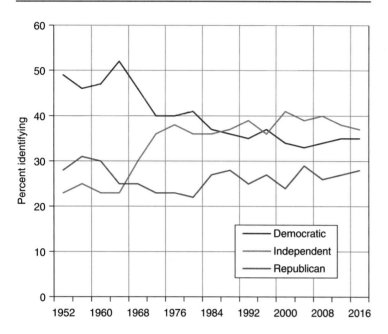

See the change in the percentage of those identifying as Democrats, Republicans, and Independents from 1953 to 2016. Which has been more important—the narrowing of the Democratic advantage over Republicans or the increase in the percentage identifying as Independents?

Source:"The ANES Guide to Public Opinion and Electoral Behavior," ANES, 2017, https://electionstudies.org/resources/anes-guide/

A key to understanding the trend may lie in the fact that similar increases in the numbers of independents have occurred in most industrialized democracies, even those that were not involved in Vietnam. Is this growth in political independence caused by increased levels of education, which might make citizens less dependent on the parties for leadership and guidance on policies? Or could the increasingly aggressive investigative press, by criticizing politicians and revealing scandals, have led to a diminished faith in all political institutions, including the parties? Or could the increase in the number of independents be related to the overall decrease in trust in government? Political scientists do not have a clear, agreed-upon explanation for this rise of independents.

# HOW IDEOLOGIES GAIN THEIR STRUCTURE

We introduced and described American ideologies in Chapter 1. *Ideologies* are clusters of ideas that relate to each other and bolster each other. No belief or value you hold exists in isolation from your other beliefs and values. Here's a simple example: If you believe that individuals should make their own choices and not have their decisions made for them by government, it is likely that you oppose tight regulation of guns. Our ideas are interconnected and bolster each other, although the connections are not always as obvious as this one.

Ideologies help structure public opinion. But how do ideologies develop? How does a particular cluster of ideas form into an ideology, and why does that set of ideas, rather than another, cohere?

Every ideology has a structuring principle that causes its parts to relate to each other. Most European ideologies, such as socialism or Christian democracy, are structured around a central, organizing idea. In the United States, libertarianism is similarly organized around a central idea: that government should intervene as little as possible in people's lives in order to maximize individuals' freedom to make their own decisions. From this one idea, positions follow on a wide range of policies: opposition to using taxes to make people more equal, opposition to gun control, legalization of recreational drugs, and freedom of choice on abortion. Libertarianism, because it is organized strictly around the core idea of maximizing individual freedom, holds together tightly. Each position its adherents take can be deduced logically from this central core principle.

However, ideologies can be structured in other ways as well. Liberalism and conservatism have central ideas that help to determine their structure, but to some extent, their structure also comes from the long-running competition between the Democratic and Republican parties. Liberals share a central goal of caring for the weaker members of society and accordingly welcome an active role for government in the economy. Conservatives share two central goals: maintaining traditional values and societal structures and minimizing governmental intervention in the economy. These general goals help to determine liberals' and conservatives' positions on many issues of the day. But unlike libertarianism, liberalism and conservatism have also been strongly influenced by the evolution of the Democratic and Republican parties.

How have the parties shaped liberalism and conservatism? Abortion policy provides an example. Today, opposition to abortion is an important belief of conservatives, and liberals support freedom of choice on abortion. However, at the time of the 1973 *Roe v. Wade* Supreme Court decision that kicked off the modern conflict over abortion, many liberals opposed abortion. By accidents of immigration history, large numbers of Italians, Poles, and other Catholic immigrant groups were part of the Democratic Party's liberal coalition at that time, and most members of these groups opposed abortion because of their Catholic faith. However, another important part of the liberal coalition in the Democratic Party—the feminist movement—insisted on a woman's right to choose an abortion, a position known as pro-choice. Over the 1970s and 1980s, bitter fights took place within the Democratic Party between pro-life forces and pro-choice feminists. As the pro-life side gradually lost these intraparty debates, some of its adherents moved over to the Republican Party and became conservative, but others shifted their position to blend feminism with the other facets of their liberalism. A striking example is the evolution of Senator Ted Kennedy of Massachusetts, a leader of liberals nationally until his death in 2009. In 1971, two years before the Supreme Court decision, Kennedy said in a speech that the Democratic Party would always defend the rights of the unborn; by the mid-1970s, he was a leading pro-choice figure.[42] It was not that Kennedy had shifted from being conservative on abortion to being liberal on abortion. Rather, his liberalism was consistent with opposing abortion in 1971, but by the mid-1970s, freedom of choice had become part of liberalism.[43]

This outcome was not inevitable. If the pro-life wing had won the debate in the Democratic Party, the freedom-of-choice position might have become part of conservatism, with its general opposition to government regulation. And opposition to abortion (remember liberalism's central concern of caring for the weak) could have been a part of liberalism. This alternative path only seems strange to us because events worked out the other way historically, and we are used to what we have today.[44]

## HOW PUBLIC OPINION IS MEASURED

To get a sense of how public opinion may be shifting, researchers need to be able to measure it accurately. The most frequently used tool to measure public opinion is the poll, a set of questions asked of a carefully drawn sampling of some population (for instance, the population of a state, a city, or the whole country), selected in such a way that the respondents are likely to mirror the total population fairly accurately. The best way to construct this sample—and polling today always involves some variation of this method—is to draw a random sample of the population. A random sample is a sample drawn from the full population so that every member of the population has an equal probability of being picked to be in the sample. One way of thinking about it is to imagine that everyone in the country has their name written on a slip of paper and put in a hat and that a certain number of them are then drawn from the hat to make up the sample. This is, in fact, approximately how a random sample is drawn, except that the selection is done by computer instead of from a hat.

Polling organizations draw a sample for the obvious reason that for a large population, it would be too expensive and time-consuming to ask everybody in the population to answer a question. If a sample is random and includes a large enough number of people, it will provide an accurate estimate and will not be biased toward one viewpoint or another. Any single person would of course be an inaccurate predictor of the views of the whole population, but as you add another person and then another and another, people whose opinions differ greatly will tend to cancel each other out so that the average of all of the people you have drawn will come to be fairly close to the average of the whole population.

A simple test can help show how this system works. If you choose one member of your class randomly by drawing names from a hat, and you measure her height, that result will obviously not be an accurate measure of the average height of members of your class. But if you now add nine more class members, similarly pulled from the hat at random, the average of their heights will probably be fairly close to that of the class as a whole.

It turns out, somewhat surprisingly, that a random sample of a few thousand Americans is large enough to provide a

> **poll** A set of questions asked of a carefully constructed sampling of a population, selected in such a way that the people in the sample are likely to mirror the total population fairly accurately.
>
> **random sample** A sample drawn from the full population in such a way that every member of the population has an equal probability of belonging to the sample.

Major polling organizations (such as Gallup) have hundreds of employees based in call centers to contact the thousands of people who make up the samples for their polls.

fairly accurate estimate of anything you wish to measure for the full population—anything from their average height to their opinion of the president's performance. The estimate is not perfect, of course; the only way to get a perfect measure would be to ask everyone. Polling agencies accordingly measure, and report, their **margin of error** in the estimate. The margin of error is a measure of how close the sample estimate is likely to be to the true value, based on statistical theory and given the size of the sample. A poll result showing that 55 percent of a state's likely voters support candidate X, for example, with a margin of error of plus or minus 3 percent means that 95 percent of the time, the actual support for candidate X should be somewhere between 52 and 58 percent. A margin of error of plus or minus 3 percentage points is usually considered satisfactory for public opinion estimates.

## POLLING TECHNIQUES

However, no one uses a classic random sample of the entire population because it simply costs too much. Picking one person in Twin Falls, Idaho, and sending an interviewer to ask her questions, then picking another person on a remote farm in Arkansas, and so on, would be impossibly expensive. Some sort of compromise is necessary.

**CLUSTER SAMPLING** In **cluster sampling**, a random selection of perhaps a hundred locations in the country is made, an interviewer is sent to each, and a small random sample of perhaps 20 or 30 people are interviewed at each site. When the interviews from all the sites are added together, they approximate a true random sample.

**RANDOM DIGIT DIALING** Even easier to administer than cluster sampling is a **random digit dialing (RDD)** telephone poll. In this method, telephone numbers are dialed randomly, drawing something like a true random sample. This system is faster and cheaper than sending interviewers out to cluster sample localities, but it has some serious drawbacks. Since about 95 percent of American homes have telephones, randomly selecting numbers from the phone book would seem to be a good way to approximate a true random sample. Unfortunately, though, different sorts of people have very different patterns of phone access. People working two jobs are rarely at home to answer the phone. And some people whose phones are equipped with caller identification will simply never answer the phone unless they know the caller. Nonetheless, this method of sampling is used a great deal because of its convenience. For instance, if a campaign or news organization wants to ascertain overnight what the effect of a presidential debate has been, there is no other way to reach a roughly random sample as quickly.

**INTERNET POLLING** A recently developed alternative is **Internet polling**, in which a genuinely random sample of Americans agree to fill out a certain number of survey questionnaires online. In order to avoid the problem that not everyone has a computer, those who have been picked for the sample but do not have computers are often given a free one. Because all people in the sample can be reached and they can respond to the questionnaires at a time that fits their own inclinations and convenience, Internet polling approximates a random sample better than RDD sampling and gives more accurate results. Because of its accuracy and flexibility, Internet polling is becoming very popular in social scientific research. It is important to distinguish scientific Internet polls of this sort from the many "straw polls" on the Internet or television that people voluntarily respond to; those straw polls are utterly unreliable. In true Internet polling, the investigators pick their sample of people so that it will be random; people cannot simply volunteer to participate.

## POLLS IN POLITICAL CAMPAIGNS

As political campaigns, and the media coverage of them, have become more sophisticated, various polls have developed to serve special purposes for either the media or candidates in an election campaign. Some examples follow.

**TRACKING POLLS** Candidates use **tracking polls** throughout their campaigns. These are short, simple polls—often the pollster asks whom the respondent will vote for or how he or she

---

**margin of error**
Statistical measure of how much the sample estimate from a poll is likely to deviate from the true amount in the full population.

**cluster sampling**
An approximation of a true random sample in which a sample of localities is randomly drawn and then a small random sample of individuals are interviewed in each locality.

**random digit dialing (RDD)** Drawing a roughly random sample by randomly dialing telephone numbers.

**internet polling**
Drawing a truly random sample and getting the people in the sample to agree (in return for an incentive) to take part in surveys administered online.

**tracking polls**
Short, simple polls that are repeated day after day to allow a candidate to track exactly how a campaign is going on a daily basis.

responds on a particular issue. These polls are repeated day after day to allow a candidate to track exactly how the campaign is going on a daily basis. These polls are always done by phone to provide instant turnaround.

**EXIT POLLS** News networks use **exit polls** to enable them to call the results of an election as quickly as possible after the polling stations close. News networks also use these results to provide some simple analysis for their viewers, such as how women voted, how many people were concerned about the economy, and so on. They poll people throughout Election Day by stopping them as they leave the voting place and asking them for information about how they voted and how they feel about various issues. Because they have drawn a random sample of voting places and a random sample of people at each voting place, their poll is based on a cluster sample that approximates a true random sample. And because it occurs during the voting, it provides an instantaneous read on what was moving the voters that day.

**PUSH POLLS** These are not true polls at all, but a perversion of polling. A **push poll** consists of questions posed to voters in such a way that they present negative information about a candidate. The purpose of a push poll is not to find out what the voter thinks but to communicate a negative message by taking advantage of the trust people feel for pollsters. Push poll questions are not used by pollsters, but by political campaigns masquerading as pollsters in order to hurt their opponent. The purported pollster does not even bother to write down the answer. A famous example was the question asked of many thousands of South Carolina voters before the 2000 Republican presidential primary: "Would you be more likely or less likely to vote for John McCain for President if you knew he had fathered an illegitimate black child?" McCain and his wife had in fact adopted a girl from Bangladesh.[45]

## LIMITATIONS OF POLLS

Polls are not a perfect measure of public opinion. They have several limitations. First of all, as we have noted, a poll result is an approximation based on a sample of the overall population. There is some margin of error around any poll result.

A more serious problem, however, is that how a question is phrased can change the outcome of the poll. When a survey asked people in 2011 whether global warming is real, 44 percent of Republicans and 87 percent of Democrats said yes. But when it asked whether climate change is real, the number of Republican saying yes climbed to 60 percent while Democrats stayed the same, at 87 percent.[46] Republicans responded differently to the two terms, so depending on how the question was worded, you would find either a deep divide between the parties or a less striking difference.

Another difficulty with polls is that asking the public about policy questions puts them in an artificial situation; responding to hypothetical questions cannot substitute for actual law making. For instance, each of the following three statements would probably attract a solid majority of support in a poll: "Taxes should be lowered." "Government services should be increased." "The budget should be balanced." But it is impossible to achieve all three simultaneously. Respondents in a survey have the luxury of saying yes to all three at once, but the government is limited to doing what is actually possible. Obviously, this particular problem with polls limits the extent to which they should serve as a mandate for policy makers.

These limitations do not mean that polls are useless. They merely mean that pollsters must be skillful and must operate

> **exit polls** Polls conducted on Election Day at the voting places to provide television news stations with instantaneous analysis of what was moving the voters on that day.
>
> **push poll** A set of questions used by political campaigns to present negative information about an opposing candidate by taking advantage of the trust people feel for pollsters.

Bettmann / Getty Images

On Election Night in 1948, the *Chicago Daily Tribune* declared that Thomas E. Dewey had defeated incumbent Harry S. Truman in the race for the presidency. Though voting was still open when the paper went to press, polls showed Dewey to be the clear favorite. The next day, having defied the polls and coasted to an easy victory, a jubilant Truman held the *Tribune* aloft.

with care, both in constructing their surveys and in interpreting the results for candidates, officials, and the media. And they mean that you should read poll results with care.

When you see results from a poll, you should first note how large the sample size is and how large a range of error the pollster reports. A sample of a couple of thousand people is usually adequate nationally, and this would yield a range of error of something like plus or minus 3 percent. Then, you should note how people were contacted—if it was a telephone poll, for example, you should bear in mind that the pollsters will have missed people who are less accessible by phone, though the pollsters have techniques by which they can approximately correct for such errors. And finally, you should read the question that people were asked, and see whether it looks to you as though the question was subject to misunderstanding or seemed intended to yield a biased result. With these precautions, you can become a good critic of polling data.

## CONSEQUENCES FOR DEMOCRACY

How much difference does public opinion make? We began this chapter with a puzzle: Americans are roughly as likely as the citizens of the Netherlands and many other prosperous democracies to believe that people should provide for themselves as opposed to the government providing for people's welfare. But there is a big difference between how much the United States government does for people's welfare and how much the Dutch government and the governments of other countries do. This incongruity raises a very basic question: How much difference does public opinion make to what the U.S. government does? If opinion is about the same in the Netherlands and the United States, why is it that the Dutch government does so much more in providing for people's welfare than the government of the United States?

The answer, obviously, must be that public opinion is only part of what goes into governmental policy making. The public does not make laws; government makes laws. And as we will see in succeeding chapters, this process involves interest groups, political parties, courts, and a variety of elected entities. We probably should not expect a one-to-one relationship between opinions and policy. But on the other hand, in a democracy, there should be some sort of relationship.

Clearly, something else about American politics limits governmental involvement in social programs, keeping it below what public opinion seemingly would support, as indicated by the comparison with the Netherlands. We can also point to other areas in which policy departs fairly markedly from public opinion. For instance, with few exceptions over the last 25 years, a majority of Americans have said they favor stricter gun control laws; in 2018, 67 percent of the public supported such laws.[47] And yet, there is little national regulation of gun ownership; and outside of large cities, advocating gun control is a stand candidates believe will hurt them in elections.

We should not conclude, though, that public opinion has no impact on policy. Public opinion certainly does not always determine public policy; we have shown examples in which it does not, and more are available. But in both direct and indirect ways, public opinion often does affect policy.

For example, public opinion did contribute in various ways to the massive increase in defense spending under President Ronald Reagan after 1980.[48] Starting in 1978, Congressional Republicans led a strong campaign charging that under Democratic President Jimmy Carter, the United States was falling behind the Soviet Union in military power. At the time, public opinion was very responsive to this charge; in 1978, for the first time in a decade, more Americans thought defense spending should be increased than thought it should be reduced. Over the next two years, support for defense spending surged, so that by 1980, about 45 percent more Americans thought defense spending should be increased than thought it should be reduced. The new president, Ronald Reagan, came into office in 1980 on a wave of support for increased defense spending, and he promptly proposed a large military buildup. Social scientists have estimated that the issue of defense spending contributed about 8 percentage points to Reagan's share of the vote in 1980, providing most of the margin by which he won.[49]

Thus, public opinion on defense spending helped put in place a president who had pledged to increase spending. At the level of individual congressional districts as well, variations in opinion from one district to another led to marked differences in how much spending members of Congress voted for in 1981.[50] Members from districts where opinion most strongly favored the buildup voted on average for about $45 billion more in defense spending than members from districts where the public was least supportive of the buildup. Both at the overall national level and at the level of individual congressional districts, public opinion played a significant role in the decision to increase defense spending.

The Reagan defense buildup is a single example of the effect of public opinion on policy. But a broader study of almost 2,000 policy proposals, drawn from across all areas of policy for the period from 1981 to 2002, showed the following:

- If only 20 percent of the public supported a change, the change occurred an estimated 19 percent of the time.
- If public support for a change reached 80 percent, the change occurred an estimated 43 percent of the time.[51]

The study shows both the substantial impact of public opinion and its limitations. Proposals with broad public support were more likely to be enacted than those the public opposed. But even when the public overwhelmingly supported a proposed change, it only happened about half the time. And when the public was wholeheartedly against a proposed change, 19 percent of the time, the change occurred anyway.

How does public opinion exercise its influence? Public opinion can operate by so many paths that it is difficult to pin down its effects on any given policy very precisely. It may work through electoral change, as voters put in place officials whose views are closer to theirs. We saw this in the case of Ronald Reagan's 1980 election bid.

It may work via the media, as opinions from the public work their way into the pronouncements of the elite and from there into policy making. For example, popular concerns about free trade worked in this way across the last two decades to gradually reduce many officeholders' commitment to expand free trade.

It may work by strengthening the hand of a president, who can point to public opinion favoring a policy in getting Congress to act. In 2011, for instance, President Obama campaigned for an extension of payroll tax reductions, using public opinion polls that showed strong support for the extension. Or it may not work at all, as in the question of gun control.

In short, public opinion has a significant, but not determinative, role in the making of policy.

## Critical Thinking Questions

1. In an election environment dominated by 30-second television commercials, how much confidence can we have in the people's ability to make wise decisions about candidates' fitness for office?
2. How much impact do you think parents have on Americans' approaches to politics? What attitudes do you think parents help to shape in their children? What has your own experience been?
3. We saw that poorer Americans are more liberal on economic issues than better-off Americans, but the differences are not huge. Is it surprising that social class differences in attitudes are no larger than this, given the high degree of economic inequality in America? What might lead to such small differences across social classes?
4. Americans generally value independence and appear to shun strict partisanship. Yet, party identification is an important determinant of how they vote, and it adds stability and predictability to U.S. politics. Do you think, on balance, that the impact of strong party identifications on American politics is a good thing or a bad thing? Why?

## Key Terms

Visit edge.sagepub.com/maltese to help you accomplish your coursework goals in an easy-to-use learning environment.

# 7
# POLITICAL PARTIES AND INTEREST GROUPS

## After reading this chapter, you should be able to do the following:

- Define *political party* and identify key players, how they function in the party, and how a political party is distinct from an interest group.

- Examine the history of political party development in the United States and explore the two waves of political reform that weakened party organization.

- Describe how American parties are organized and the impact of party structure on political processes in the United States.

- Understand the causes and effects of a two-party system.

- Define responsible party government and explain why parties in the United States have been successful or unsuccessful in fulfilling this governing doctrine.

- Define *interest groups* and understand the role each type of group plays in American politics.

- Describe the issues that affect how accurately and equally interest groups represent the concerns of all segments of American society.

## Perspective: How Centralized Can Political Parties Be?

The American humorist Will Rogers once quipped, "I am not a member of an organized party. I am a Democrat." Democratic and Republican Parties in the United States are loosely organized, evolving political groups that have no formal enrollment or membership process; those who wish to work for the party can just show up. Most importantly, no one person or office controls the entire organization. Chuck Schumer is the leader of Democrats in the United States

Senate and Nancy Pelosi leads Democrats in the House of Representatives, but neither leads the Democratic Party as a whole. In fact, they cannot even tell their own senators or representatives what to do but must negotiate—and sometimes even plead—with them and with state party leaders as well.

In contrast, Mao Zedong, the former chairman of China's Communist Party, rejected all forms of negotiation and pleading. On May 16, 1966, he unleashed the "Cultural Revolution," a decade of upheaval and violence within the party that he hoped would bring it back to its original revolutionary roots. Mao had headed the Communist Party since it began as a revolutionary movement in prewar China, and he had led it to national victory in 1949. Since then, the party had ruled China as a one-party state, allowing no political opposition. By the 1960s, though, Mao thought that many newer members of the party, those who had not shared in the long revolutionary struggle before 1949, were simply opportunists who saw that the only route to a good government job was through the party. Many were well-educated children of the middle class.

In an effort to bring the party back to its working-class roots, Mao's Cultural Revolution mobilized large groups of young Chinese called "Red Guards" to terrorize landowners, intellectuals, and established leaders such as teachers, university presidents, and government officials. Hundreds of thousands were killed or committed suicide.

After Mao's death in 1976, the Cultural Revolution ended and new leadership in the Party reversed many of Mao's actions. The Party today still rules the state, allowing no organized political opposition, but it presides over a partially free-market economy that bears little resemblance to Mao's socialist vision. It continues to be a tightly controlled, centralized organization, however. The Party is huge, with 90 million enrolled members as of the last National Party Congress.[1] Becoming a member is not easy. Aspirants must first be recommended by an existing Party member and then pass a one-year probationary period; many who apply to join the Party are rejected.

No one person or group could direct an American political party as Mao did or as his successors have done. It is impossible to imagine an event such as the Cultural Revolution—organized violence orchestrated for the purpose of reshaping a party's membership or ideology—taking place in the United States. **«**

# DEFINING POLITICAL PARTIES AND INTEREST GROUPS

Political parties are found in almost all countries, democracies and non-democracies alike, although they may fulfill varying purposes, depending on the country. As we saw in this chapter's "Perspective," the Democratic and Republican parties of the United States and the Communist Party of China are very different organizations, but all three are political parties. A **political party** is an organization comprising officeholders or would-be officeholders and activist supporters spread throughout the population, whose primary purpose is to put its members into government office. It can accomplish this purpose either by competing with other parties for government office in democratic elections (as in the United States) or by banning all other parties and appointing its own leaders to office (as in a non-democracy such as China). Political parties should not be confused with interest groups.

An **interest group**, similar to a party, is a group of people with shared policy goals; but while the primary purpose of a party is to help determine who holds political office, the primary goal of an interest group is to influence what policy choices those officeholders make. There are several distinct types of interest groups in the United States, and they fill an essential role in American politics. We will discuss these in more detail later in the chapter.

Political parties were invented for a specific purpose by politicians in the United States and (a little later) in the United Kingdom. Before democracy was developed in these two countries during the late eighteenth and early nineteenth centuries, there were many ways

**political party** An organization combining activists and potential officeholders, whose purpose is to determine who will hold office.

**interest group** A group of people organized to influence government policies.

to attain office, but none involved appealing simultaneously to large numbers of people. You might be born into a hereditary office, you might be appointed, or you might actually buy the office. Once Britain and the United States became democracies, however, these positions were filled by election; this system required prospective officials to seek the votes of a thousand or more people. Politicians soon realized that organizing voters into a single, nationwide club—that is, a party—would help to mobilize them to support the party's candidates. It could also help to retain voters for the party, even as they moved from one place to another. A popular official could travel from place to place, helping to convince voters to choose other candidates from the same party, and eventually raise enough money to hire professional staff who could help with the job of organizing thousands of voters. And so, the political party was created.

But what kind of an organization is a political party? In many countries, political parties are formal organizations that people apply to join; if they are accepted, they pay dues to the party. Parties in many democracies are organized in this way. For example, the Conservative Party of Great Britain has 150,000 enrolled members, and unless you pay your dues, you cannot consider yourself a member—though you may, of course, vote for the party's candidates.[2] (To get a sense of what being a member is like, see the "Picture Yourself" section in this chapter.)

In the United States, political parties are constructed more loosely. There is no single list of all the people who are members of either of the two main parties; in fact, it is hard to state exactly what set of people makes up the Democratic Party or the Republican Party. Does the Republican Party consist of all those in the United States who voted for the Republican presidential candidate in the last election? Or does it consist of all those who have registered to vote as Republicans? (A registration list might answer our question, except that almost half the states do not require a voter to designate a party when registering to vote.) Does the party consist only of Republican officeholders? What about the office that calls itself the *Republican National Committee*? There is no clear boundary to indicate which people belong to the party and which ones do not.

With loosely organized parties, politics plays out differently in the United States than in most other democracies. A tight, formal party organization can exert much more control over what its officials do than can the loosely organized American parties. In Argentina, for instance, party officials control who can be on the ballot for a congressional election, and they use this power to punish any members of Congress who vote differently from their party's position. Members who do this regularly are usually expelled from the party and taken off the ballot. As a result, members of Argentina's Congress are very obedient to party leaders.[3]

In the United States, candidates essentially make their own way to Congress. They get on the ballot by their own efforts, usually through a primary election, and although they then receive some help from their party in getting elected, they are in Congress primarily because of their own initiative and funds they have raised for themselves. As a result, party leaders in Congress have only limited power over what members do and they sometimes vote differently from how their leaders have asked them to vote.

## PURPOSES OF A POLITICAL PARTY

One of the wonders of modern politics is that the political party, originally devised in order to help some officeholders attain and keep their jobs, has proved to be useful for many other purposes as well. Because it is an organization that uniquely combines government officials and a network of activists around the country, the political party has become the central organizing force linking the government to the people in almost all countries of the world—democracies and non-democracies alike. It has performed a variety of functions beyond its original role as a campaign machine, including campaigning, mobilization, recruitment and socialization of leaders, providing identity, and providing a channel for control. Through these functions, political parties have become the glue that holds modern politics together.

ANWAR AMRO / Getty Images

Hezbollah in 2005 showed its influence in Lebanon when it was able to mobilize half a million people to attend a pro-Syria demonstration in Beirut.

The Washington Post / Getty Images

The Young Republicans gives interested youth a way to learn more about the party, connect with others, and meet Republican activists and lawmakers, such as Virginia state delegate Tom Rust (left). Have you ever attended an event hosted by a political party?

**mobilization** The energizing of large numbers of people to act together.

**CAMPAIGNING** Obviously, parties are useful for their original purpose: to campaign and build support for the candidates of the party. They help to identify candidates, raise money to support their campaigns, share expertise on election law, provide policy research and advice on presenting issues, and conduct get-out-the-vote drives to bring their supporters to the polls.

**MOBILIZATION** Because they join together leaders and a geographically dispersed membership, parties are an ideal tool for mobilization. Mobilization involves systematically energizing large numbers of people to act together in a demonstration, an election, or any other combined action. For example, when Syria came under intense international pressure in 2005 to withdraw its troops from the neighboring state of Lebanon, its allies in the Lebanese Hezbollah Party mobilized a demonstration of 500,000 supporters (out of the total Lebanese population of 3.7 million people!) to support Syria's role there. This example reveals the potential of parties to mobilize populations at critical moments in a nation's history.

American political parties are less united on political issues than many parties in other countries, so they do not often sponsor large, issue-oriented demonstrations. But they do mobilize their supporters at each election to get them to the polls.

**RECRUITMENT AND SOCIALIZATION OF LEADERS** Recruitment—identifying promising young people and bringing them into positions of public leadership—is vital for any country. Once recruited, leaders and officials also need to be socialized into their political roles. Socialization is the process, discussed in Chapter 6, by which people learn political values and factual assumptions about politics. In addition to what most people learn, newly recruited future leaders need to acquire an additional body of lore, responsibilities, and leadership skills in order to perform well. Because a political party brings together within its organization both seasoned political leaders and young activists, it is well placed to seek out promising young people, give them experience at relatively small jobs, and gradually move those who do well to more important jobs, while imbuing them with the values that the political leadership wishes to encourage.

**PROVIDING IDENTITY** For active members, the political party can become a vital, central part of their identity. Party identification (which we examined in Chapter 6 and will discuss later under "Party in the Electorate") can be a strong feeling. As a source of identity, parties provide continuity and a political community in a political world that is otherwise quite fluid. If party connections are passed on from parents to children or if local party organizations continue their activity across generations, political continuity can extend even beyond a single lifetime.

The three maps of Tennessee in Figure 7.1 exemplify this tendency. At the time of the Civil War, the state was divided over the issue of secession. The shaded counties in Map A were most strongly opposed to secession, as indicated by the vote for the Constitutional Union candidate in 1860. Two areas of opposition stand out: eastern Tennessee, and a small pocket in the west. After the War, opposition to secession translated into support for the Republican Party, which had held the Union together. This made sense at the time, but the pattern continued to hold in election after election, long after the issues of the Civil War had receded into the depths of history. In Map B, we see that the areas in which Republican Richard Nixon ran most strongly in 1960 are approximately the same areas that opposed secession in 1860. And in Map C, we continue to see the same two main areas of strength in the vote for Republican Donald Trump in 2016, even though Trump was a very different kind of candidate than Republican candidates who had gone before him.

**PROVIDING A CHANNEL FOR CONTROL**  Sam Rayburn, who was for many years the leader of the Democratic Party in the U.S. House of Representatives, used to caution new members, "To get along, go along." In other words, to advance within the House hierarchy, obey orders.

Rayburn's advice points to another characteristic of a party: It brings together a group of officeholders in an overarching organization, providing a means by which some of the officeholders can control what others do. In other words, the party does not exercise control directly but provides a channel within which control can be exercised. This function helps to make governmental decision making possible. The leaders of a party have many rewards and punishments at their disposal: nominations for various offices, support in passing favored legislation, and so on—or the withholding of such support. Leaders use these inducements to encourage obedience among lesser party figures in legislative votes and in campaign activity.

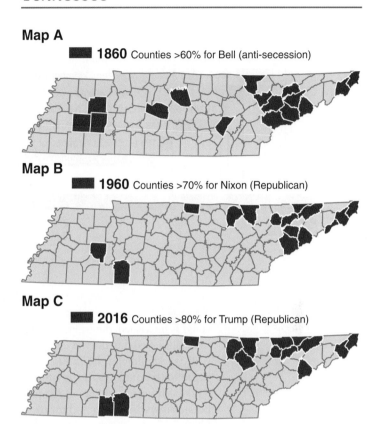

**FIGURE 7.1**

*Continuity of Republican Strength in Tennessee*

**Map A**

1860 Counties >60% for Bell (anti-secession)

**Map B**

1960 Counties >70% for Nixon (Republican)

**Map C**

2016 Counties >80% for Trump (Republican)

*Source: W. Phillips Shively,* Power and Choice, *15th ed. (Lanham, MD, Rowman & Littlefield, 2019). Used by permission.*

# THE DEVELOPMENT OF AMERICAN POLITICAL PARTIES

As we have seen, the United States, as the first electoral democracy in the world, invented political parties. The process took only a few decades (see Figure 7.2), and by the late 1820s, these parties were well organized. The Democratic Party, which can trace its roots back to that time, is the oldest political party in the world.

## EARLY PARTY FORMATION

The Founders did not envision political parties contesting elections. Indeed, they designed a system in which the president and senators would not be elected directly at all. An Electoral College of distinguished citizens selected by the states would choose the president, and each state's legislature would appoint its senators. Although elections were to be held for members of the House of Representatives, the Founders expected that men of local standing and reputation would be elevated to the House of Representatives in a quiet, dignified fashion and not in hotly contested campaigns. George Washington, for instance, was unopposed in the presidential elections of 1789 and 1792.

However, after a few years, serious conflicts began to develop in the House. A Federalist group centering on Treasury Secretary Alexander Hamilton favored the creation of a centralized national bank to control the economy and was suspicious of extending the control of government to voters. A loosely knit group dubbed the "Anti-Federalists" crystallized around

FIGURE 7.2

# Timeline of Party Development in the United States

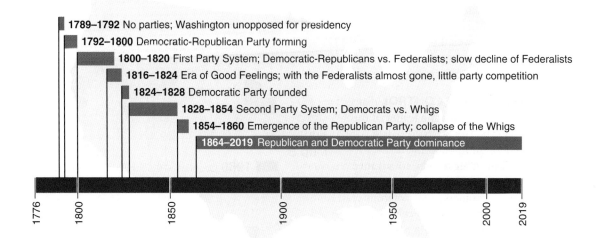

1789–1792 No parties; Washington unopposed for presidency

1792–1800 Democratic-Republican Party forming

1800–1820 First Party System; Democratic-Republicans vs. Federalists; slow decline of Federalists

1816–1824 Era of Good Feelings; with the Federalists almost gone, little party competition

1824–1828 Democratic Party founded

1828–1854 Second Party System; Democrats vs. Whigs

1854–1860 Emergence of the Republican Party; collapse of the Whigs

1864–2019 Republican and Democratic Party dominance

1776    1800    1850    1900    1950    2000  2019

Thomas Jefferson in opposition to Hamilton's proposals. While Hamilton's supporters often voted as he wished, they opposed him some of the time as well, and the same was true of Jefferson's allies. Stability did not characterize either the Federalists or their opposition.

By the middle of the 1790s, the Anti-Federalists were losing steadily in Congress. They began to try to change the situation by getting more of their own sympathizers into Congress. Thomas Jefferson and James Madison vacationed in New York in 1791, ostensibly to conduct botanical studies. In fact, they are thought to have met with New Yorkers Aaron Burr and George Clinton to arrange an alliance in the Congress between opponents of Hamilton in the North and the planters of Virginia and others in the South.

Eventually, this alliance took the name Democratic-Republican Party. At about the same time, activist clubs supporting democratic policies began to form around the country, with the first two Democratic clubs forming in Philadelphia in 1793. Eventually, 40 to 50 Democratic clubs developed, an impressive number considering that only 65 congressional districts existed nationwide at the time.[4] Between politicians seeking alliances and active citizens in the electorate, the first American political party was born.

**THE FIRST PARTY SYSTEM, 1800–1820** The new party proved immediately successful, winning a majority of the seats in the House of Representatives in the election of 1800. The period between 1800 and 1820, marked by conflict between the Democratic-Republicans and the Federalists, is called the **First Party System**. Federalist power gradually declined, and it did not even offer a presidential candidate in the election of 1820. That election marked the start of the "**Era of Good Feelings**." With the Federalists on the verge of disappearing, there was no opposition to the Democratic-Republican Party and thus no partisan conflict.

The Era of Good Feelings could not last, however. In a large society, there are simply too many sources of conflict to allow government to proceed for long without organized political conflict. In 1824, Senator Martin Van Buren of New York launched an ultimately successful effort to elect Andrew Jackson in the 1828 presidential election. To do this, Van Buren invented a new kind of party, focused on attracting and mobilizing mass support among voters. This was the Democratic Party, the oldest political party in the world today.

The rise of the Democratic party was made possible by a change in the way presidential electors were selected. Until 1820, electors were chosen by the legislature in about half the states, without the involvement of voters.

By 1828, this had shifted markedly, with voters choosing electors in almost all states (see Figure 7.3). Van Buren realized that a coordinated nationwide campaign could be very effective under

**First Party System**
The period from 1800 to 1820, which was marked by the appearance of the new Democratic-Republican Party and the gradual decline of their opponents, the Federalists.

**Era of Good Feelings**
A brief period centering on the election of 1820 when the Federalists were in sharp decline and there was no organized opposition to the dominant Democratic-Republican Party.

these circumstances. The new Democratic Party (actually a revamping of the old Democratic-Republican Party) raised money and established a network of newspapers around the country. It held campaign rallies and parades and introduced campaign paraphernalia—including hickory sticks, to play off of Jackson's nickname, "Old Hickory." Jackson won with 56 percent of the vote, gaining 178 of the 261 Electoral College votes.

**THE SECOND PARTY SYSTEM, 1828–1854** Over the next decade, the Democratic Party expanded its reach. At the same time, the remnants of the old Federalist Party joined with Democratic-Republicans who opposed Jackson's policies to form a rival party, the **Whig Party**. Thus was born the **Second Party System**, a system of party alliances and conflicts that characterized American politics from the early 1830s until just before the Civil War. The Whigs differed from the Democrats mainly in opposing extensions of the president's authority and in pushing for policies to build up the nation's infrastructure and support the development of manufacturing.

The Second Party System was also marked by an abundance of smaller parties, many of which were active for only a few elections. Americans experimented with a variety of policy-based parties, including the Anti-Masonic Party and the American Party (also known as the "Know-Nothing Party"), which opposed immigration. Many of these, including the Liberty Party and the Free Soil Party, represented early manifestations of the growing debate over slavery that would eventually tear the Second Party System apart.

## FIGURE 7.3

## *Percentage of States Selecting Presidential Electors in the State Legislature*

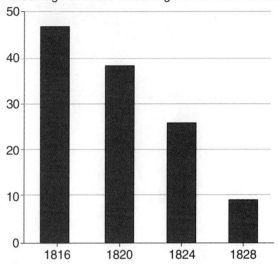

Percentage of states where legislators chose electors

*By 1828, almost all states held elections at which the voters (rather than the state legislature) chose the state's presidential electors. How did this affect the development of political parties?*

## 150 YEARS OF DEMOCRATS AND REPUBLICANS

In 1854, a new anti-slavery party was formed: the Republican Party. It rapidly replaced the Whig Party as the main opposition to the Democratic Party, gaining power for the first time in 1860 with the election of Abraham Lincoln. This election ignited the Civil War. After the Civil War, the American party system settled into two main parties: the Democratic Party and the Republican Party. This two-party system continues today, although the parties have changed dramatically over the intervening century and a half.

**THE GOLDEN AGE OF PARTIES, 1860–1900** Two characteristics defined the political period between 1860 and 1900: (1) a fairly close division between the Democratic and Republican parties and (2) intensely partisan voters lined up in well-organized, strong parties. It is for the latter of these characteristics that the period is often dubbed the "Golden Age" of parties.

The election of 1860, and the ensuing Civil War, resulted in a Republican North arrayed against a Democratic South. For about 40 years, voters primarily replayed the Civil War with each election. After the Civil War, or at least after the end of the Reconstruction period during which southern African Americans had been able to vote, the Democrats dominated the South and Republicans held a similar lock on the North. The Golden Age represented a period of intense partisanship and high voter turnout—perhaps a reflection of the passion of the Civil War. Between 1876 and 1892, although Republicans won most national elections, the parties were actually fairly evenly matched. During this period, the largest margin by which any presidential candidate won was only three percentage points.

At this time, local parties were well organized and active, and local party "bosses" with **political machines** wielded great power. In both rural areas and cities, local organizations of both parties established networks of supporters whom they rewarded with **patronage**—jobs on the public payroll given in return for their loyalty to the party. In large cities especially, party bosses took advantage of the immigrants arriving from Europe. These new Americans needed help getting along after they arrived. Parties helped immigrants get city jobs, gave them food when

**Whig Party** A party active from 1830 to the verge of the Civil War; it opposed the extension of presidential power and supported development of transportation and infrastructure.

**Second Party System** The period from the early 1830s until just before the Civil War, which was marked by rivalry between the Democratic Party and the Whigs.

**political machines** Party organizations providing their supporters with benefits such as city jobs and other favors and, in return, controlling them politically.

**patronage** Financial rewards (especially public jobs) given to people in return for their political support.

The legendary Democratic party "boss" William Tweed was so powerful that this 1872 cartoon wondered if "the law"—personified by a miniature police officer—could even reach him.

times were especially hard, and provided other favors; in return, the party machine expected the new arrivals to vote for its candidates and organize their friends to vote for them.

**REPUBLICAN DOMINANCE AND PROGRESSIVE REFORM, 1900–1932** Two characteristics defined the political period between 1900 and 1932. After the election of 1896, the Republican Party enjoyed a long era of electoral dominance. They had held a slight edge in the close contests of the Golden Age, but from 1896 to 1928, the average margin of victory for Republicans in presidential elections rose to 15 percent. The only Democrat elected president during this period was Woodrow Wilson (1913–1921), whose victory in 1912 was made possible because the Republicans temporarily split into two parties. During this period, people's economic status had little to do with whether they voted for the Republicans or the Democrats; instead, voters' support for one party or the other was determined primarily by the region in which they lived.[5] The Republican Party dominated all states in the Northeast and Midwest; it faced a Democratic Party with primarily rural roots, considerable support in the West, and a strong base among white Southerners.

Another important development of this period was the rise of the **Progressive movement**, a loose collection of reformers who brought to an end the Golden Age. The Progressives' goals were to make politics more open and issue-oriented by eliminating many of the ways that party machines had been able to reward their supporters.[6] The rising middle class did not need help from the parties as poor immigrants had. They resented the domination of machines and thought (often with reason) that they were corrupt—that they used government money and public jobs to enrich themselves and get people to vote for them. Reform candidates challenged the older politicians, and machines gradually lost influence in American politics.[7]

Progressives also worked to change the political rules that had allowed bosses to rule. Under Progressive influence, many states took the power to nominate candidates for office away from party officials and gave it to voters by adopting **direct primaries**—preliminary elections in which voters choose each party's candidates for the general election. The Progressives also made it more difficult for machines to provide public jobs to their workers through new civil service laws, which required job-seekers to pass competitive examinations. (The civil service system is analyzed in detail in Chapter 13.) In the end, the party bosses did not have enough power over elections or enough rewards to offer their troops to maintain their dominance. As an indirect result of the reforms, not only the city bosses, but *all* party organizations became looser and more decentralized because they had fewer tools with which to reward or punish their members.

**THE NEW DEAL AND DEMOCRATIC DOMINANCE, 1932–1964** Throughout the period from 1900 to 1932, various smaller parties had tried to raise issues related to the problems of the poor, such as the right of workers to form unions and strike and income redistribution through taxation. None, however, were able to shake up the basic regional alignment of the two major parties or unseat the Republicans from power.

Then the disastrous Depression hit in 1929, with massive unemployment and bankruptcies across the country. Franklin Roosevelt and the Democrats swept the Republicans away and initiated a new era of Democratic dominance based on a new set of political alignments. With Roosevelt's election in 1932, the parties reshaped themselves quickly into a business-oriented Republican Party with strong support from the upper middle class and lingering regional support in rural areas of the Northeast and Midwest and a labor-oriented Democratic Party that drew support from unions, liberals, and northern African Americans while maintaining a stronghold in the white South.

**Progressive movement** A movement of mostly middle-class reformers in the early twentieth century who worked to eliminate machine politics.

**direct primaries** Elections to determine a party's nominee for a general election.

The new orientation of the two parties ushered in a period of Democratic dominance. Democratic candidates won six of the eight next presidential elections with an average margin of 5 percentage points. The transformation of the Democrats nationally into a liberal party during the New Deal created a basic tension within the organization. While the party increasingly emphasized extending rights to members of labor unions and other disadvantaged groups, its southern branch continued to defend a harsh system of segregation that denied rights to African Americans. For many years, the party existed as an uneasy coalition between these two very different impulses.

**REPUBLICAN RECOVERY, 1964–PRESENT** With the rise of the civil rights movement in the 1960s, it became impossible to hold the two incompatible parts of the Democratic Party together. Things came to a head when Democratic presidents John F. Kennedy (1961–1963) and Lyndon Johnson (1963–1968) developed laws in 1964 and 1965 to end racial segregation. With the signing of these laws, the South began a shift from the Democrats to the Republicans that reshaped electoral politics. Johnson is said to have told an aide, as he signed the 1964 bill, "We have lost the South for a generation." He was right. From 1880 to 1960, the Democratic candidate for president had carried the South in every single election; from 1964 to the present, the Democratic candidate

The signing of the Civil Rights Act of 1964 by President Lyndon Johnson, after which he gave the pen he had used to Martin Luther King, Jr., precipitated a shift that reshaped electoral politics and put the South squarely in Republican hands.

has lost the South in every election except when Southerner Jimmy Carter of Georgia ran in 1976. The Civil Rights Act of 1964 marks a rare moment when a single act changed the shape of the political landscape.

Absorbing the South brought more conservative voters into the Republican Party and pulled the party to the right. As a result, the party lost strength in many areas where its members had traditionally been more liberal, such as the Northeast and West Coast. The Democrats picked up the slack. In 1960, 57 Republicans and 55 Democrats were elected to the House of Representatives from the Northeast and the West Coast; by 2018, only 17 Republicans were elected, compared with 99 Democrats. In nationwide elections, however, these gains did not make up for the Democrats' loss of their Southern bastion. From 1932 to 1960, Democrats had won 6 of 8 presidential elections. From 1964 to 2018, they won only 6 of 14.

**REFORMS WEAKEN THE PARTIES: ROUND TWO** We described earlier how the reforms of the Progressive movement ended the Golden Age of strong party organizations. In the 1970s, a second wave of reform further weakened party organizations. Prior to these reforms, only 14 states and the District of Columbia held primaries to select parties' delegates to the national conventions. Those delegates would attend the convention with the intention of casting their ballots for the candidate they had supported in the primary campaign (see Chapter 8). In the other 36 states, delegates were chosen by the state party organizations. A broad movement in opposition to the Vietnam War had appealed to the Democratic Party to nominate Eugene McCarthy at its 1968 convention. McCarthy and Robert Kennedy (who was assassinated during the campaign) had energized large numbers of supporters in the primaries. McCarthy, however, lost to Hubert Humphrey, who had not run in a single primary that year. Humphrey was able to garner a majority of delegates, drawn from the states without primaries, on the strength of his connection to party officials.

In reaction to public outcry about this "back-room deal," the Democratic Party set up the McGovern-Fraser Commission to recommend reform. The commission proposed rules that would lead to the selection of a broader and more diverse range of delegates, with a better representation of women, different age groups, and racial and ethnic minorities. Most states saw primary elections as the easiest way to comply with the new rules and moved quickly to adopt them, thereby taking away one of the remaining powers of many state party organizations.

At about the same time, Congress enacted the Federal Election Campaign Act of 1971, a reform that regulated party expenditures and limited state party activities in federal elections. The act caused state parties to concentrate more on state elections and to be less active in congressional and presidential elections. It also led to a proliferation of political action committees (PACs), which contribute funds to candidates independently of the parties, further lessening the parties' influence over candidates. We discuss this act in more detail in Chapter 8.

Along with these reforms, technological changes during this period hurt the parties by making it possible for candidates to campaign more independently. In the Golden Age, candidates depended on their parties for large numbers of foot soldiers to distribute campaign literature, gather names of supporters, and get voters to the polls on Election Day. With new technologies, candidates could raise contributions and conduct their campaigns mainly through television advertisements and direct mailings, without depending on the party apparatus.

As party organizations became less important, candidates became more central to the campaigns, with their own personal campaign groups, their own money, and their own television advertisements and campaign flyers urging a vote for them specifically rather than for the party generally. With this increased emphasis on the characteristics of individual candidates, **split-ticket voting**, in which voters cast their ballot for a mix of Democratic and Republican candidates rather than voting for the candidates of only one party, increased markedly during the early 1970s (see Figure 8.6). None of this means that parties disappeared, but the cumulative effect of all of these changes was that state and city party organizations became less important in national politics than they had once been and that candidates at all levels did not need to depend as much on party organizations as they once had done.

> **split-ticket voting** When several candidates for different offices appear on a ballot, the practice of voting for a candidate of one party for one office and a candidate of another party for another office.

## THE PARTIES TODAY

What do the parties look like today? The answer to that question has two components: their core beliefs and their bases of support in the population. We can get a sense of their beliefs by examining the parties' platforms during the 2016 election (see Table 7.1). In every presidential election year, each party holds a national convention at which it nominates candidates and

**TABLE 7.1**

## *Items From the Democratic and Republican Platforms in 2016*

|  | Democratic Platform | Republican Platform |
|---|---|---|
| *Taxes* | Eliminate special tax breaks for large corporations. Add a special additional income tax on multimillionaires. | Reduce corporate taxes to make corporations more competitive internationally. In general, reduce all taxes to increase investment. |
| *Abortion* | Ensure access to safe and legal abortion. | Guarantee that "the unborn child has a fundamental right to life which cannot be infringed [upon]." |
| *Same-sex marriage* | Go beyond legalizing same-sex marriage to provide further legal protections for lesbian, gay, bisexual, and transgender (LGBT) Americans. | Seek to change the Supreme Court's decisions legalizing same-sex marriage, either by amending the Constitution or changing the makeup of the Court. |
| *Health care* | Build on the Affordable Care Act by extending Medicare to those over 55 years old. Expand Medicaid in all states. | Repeal the Affordable Care Act. Let states regulate insurance markets. Reduce costs of health care by limiting how much patients may sue doctors for. |
| *Immigration* | Pass comprehensive immigration reform and the DREAM Act, which would allow young undocumented immigrants to stay in the country for college or military service. Protect families from threat of deportation. | Do not provide any form of amnesty for undocumented immigrants. Highest priority is to secure our borders and enforce immigration laws. |
| *Energy* | Build a clean energy economy to fight climate change and provide jobs. | Climate change is far from the nation's most pressing national security issue. Oppose any carbon tax. Coal is "an abundant, clean, affordable and reliable domestic energy resource." |

writes a platform laying out its positions on political issues. The platforms are long and comprehensive (the Democrats' platform in 2016 was 45 pages long; the Republicans' was 54 pages). In general, they show a Republican party that is supportive of business as a driver of the economy, favors conservative positions on social issues such as abortion and same-sex marriage, and is very concerned about immigration. They show a Democratic party that is concerned especially with economic equality and social services, favors promoting and defending social diversity, and is concerned with protecting the environment.

The parties' members are deeply connected to their positions. Table 7.2 shows how different parts of the population voted in elections for the House of Representatives in 2018. The base support for the Republican Party includes men, whites, born-again Evangelical Christians, those with higher incomes, and the South and the Midwest. The Democrats' base of support is the opposite.

**TABLE 7.2**

## *Party Support by Different Groups, 2018*

| | Percent Voted Democratic | Percent Voted Republican |
|---|---|---|
| *Gender* | | |
| Men | 47 | 51 |
| Women | 59 | 40 |
| *Ethnicity* | | |
| White | 44 | 54 |
| African American | 90 | 9 |
| Hispanic/Latino | 69 | 29 |
| Asian | 77 | 23 |
| *Family income* | | |
| Less than $30,000 | 63 | 34 |
| $30,000–$49,999 | 57 | 41 |
| $50,000–$99,999 | 52 | 47 |
| $100,000–$199,999 | 47 | 51 |
| $200,000 or more | 47 | 52 |
| *Religious right* | | |
| White Evangelical/Born-again Christians | 22 | 75 |
| All others | 66 | 32 |
| *Region* | | |
| East | 61 | 37 |
| West | 60 | 38 |
| Midwest | 48 | 50 |
| South | 47 | 52 |

*Source: Data compiled from CBS exit polls.*

Another important difference between the parties is that Republicans are more strictly ideological than Democrats, perhaps because of the importance of religion to party members and the party's emphasis on adherence to central principles. In a 2011 poll, 68 percent of Republicans said that they would rather have a representative in Congress who stuck to his or her principles, no matter what; only 32 percent wanted a representative who compromised to get things done; the numbers were exactly reversed for Democrats. In a 2018 poll, 54 percent of Democrats wanted their party to be more moderate, while 41 percent wanted it to be more liberal; the numbers were reversed for Republicans, with only 37 percent wanting their party to be more moderate and 57 percent wanting it to be more conservative.[8]

**ELECTORAL REALIGNMENTS AND PARTISAN CHANGE** We have reviewed in the preceding sections how parties have changed and developed in the United States since the founding of the country. Up to 1860, change often occurred by old parties dying out and new parties being founded. But since 1860, no new party has succeeded in displacing the Democratic and Republican parties. How, then, has change occurred? It has been made possible by the ability of the two parties to evolve and change internally over time. This capacity for change is one advantage of the loose organizational connection between the party organization and its members that we described earlier. A tightly organized party with close control by its leaders and a large, entrenched central staff might find it more difficult to absorb new policy directions and to respond to new sources of conflict.

An election that causes the parties to change significantly in response to new issues is called a **critical election**. As we saw in Figure 7.1, party support in different segments of the population and different parts of the country, such as in Tennessee, usually remains stable over time. American electoral politics since 1860 has been marked by long periods of such stability. After a long period of stability, however, a critical election may occur, during which major parts of the population switch their party support and a new period of stability ensues. The lasting change produced by a critical election is called an **electoral realignment**. We have described three such realignments: one that began with the election of 1896, ushering in decades of Republican dominance; the New Deal realignment of 1932 and 1936; and the realignment of the 1960s and 1970s, in which the South shifted to the Republicans and the Democrats strengthened their position in the Northeast.

It is a little misleading to call the changes that bring about realignment "critical elections," because change has usually extended over more than one election. Critical elections have often been preceded by a series of abortive attempts at change by new third parties who have raised issues that eventually help to bring about the critical change. Also, the critical change itself may take more than a single election to occur. For instance, the shift of the South to the Republicans, which started in 1964, was only completed at the presidential level in the 1980s. And in the House of Representatives, where seats are slower to change because of personal and local ties, it was only in 1994 that the Republicans gained a majority of House seats in the South. The basic outline of this process is clear, however: Republican and Democratic support remains stable over a long period of time, even as new issues arise that are not consistent with the orientation of the two parties and pressure builds up for a change; finally, an election or series of elections occurs in which the two main parties reorient themselves along the new issue lines.

# THE STRUCTURE OF AMERICAN PARTIES

Since American parties are not formal organizations with clearly drawn boundaries, we usually analyze them by looking at three broad groups of people who are loosely joined by their shared ideology and goals: the party in the electorate, the party organization, and the party in government. The **party in the electorate** consists of all citizens who have a tie to the party and participate in elections. To a large extent, these are simply citizens who identify with the party and vote for it, but the party in the electorate also includes activists who work to elect the party's candidates. A party also needs a **party organization**, a formal structure of party officers and committees to conduct conventions, handle the legal paperwork of campaign laws, raise money, and perform other necessary functions. Finally, the **party in government** consists of a party's elected officials

**critical election** An election that causes the bases of support for the two main parties to change fairly suddenly.

**electoral realignment** A new and lasting rearrangement of the geographic and social bases of support for the parties, ushered in by a critical election.

**party in the electorate** The party's supporters in the electorate, including those who identify with the party and vote for it and activists who campaign for it.

**party organization** A formal structure that conducts managerial and legal tasks for the party.

**party in government** The elected officials of a party, who organize themselves along party lines.

in Congress, state legislatures, and executive offices such as governors or the president; these officials share common party ties and organize themselves along party lines.

These three parts exist independently of each other in the sense that they are not combined within a single organizational structure. Each part supports and influences the other two, however. The members of the party in government are only in government because the party in the electorate voted for them; and the party organization supports the party's elected officials and new candidates in elections.

Some other democracies such as Brazil have loosely organized parties, but most countries' parties are clearly defined organizations, with formal membership, as we noted above. Compared with these other countries, the loose organization of American parties may have some advantages in that it allows them to be flexible and adapt to changing times and circumstances.

The three components of parties (party in the electorate, party organization, and party in government) are found in all countries that have political parties. Even if, as in most countries, membership in a party requires formal enrollment, the "party in the electorate" encompasses much more than the formal members. The United Kingdom's Conservative Party receives millions of votes at each election, so its 160,000 enrolled members are only part of that electoral support. How the three components relate to each other varies widely. In China, for instance, where the Communist Party is the sole legal party, the "party in the electorate" is, in effect, a device to ensure support for the Communist regime; elections function not to choose between candidates, since there is only a single slate on the ballot, but rather as devices to stimulate praise and allegiance to the government. As for the other two components, in China, the party organization dominates the party in government. Under Mao Zedong in the 1960s and 1970s, the government did not even pass many laws; all policies of the state were simply enunciated by leaders in the party organization. Today, laws are indeed enacted by the party in government, but the driving force in shaping them is still the party organization.

In the United States, the three components are in a loose arrangement of mutual influence, with no one part dominating the others.

Although China holds elections to select delegates to its National People's Congress, which conducts business in the enormous Great Hall of the People in Beijing, the vast majority of candidates are selected by and are members of the Community Party.

## THE PARTY IN THE ELECTORATE

As Chapter 6 explained, most Americans identify with one of the two major parties, and this party identification is not casual. Once a person decides that he or she is a Democrat or a Republican, it is unusual for that identity to change. Party identification strongly affects which candidate people will vote for, and it colors how they view political issues.

As the parties became less influential in the 1960s and 1970s, the party in the electorate also decreased in size. The number of Americans identifying with one of the parties dropped steadily during that period, and the percentage of independents increased from about 20 percent in the early 1960s to about 40 percent in the mid-1970s.[9] The number of party identifiers has remained stable at roughly 60 percent since then, however.

Another way to look at the party in the electorate is to note those who vote Democratic and those who vote Republican, as we did in Table 7.2. These are not exactly the same people as the Democratic and Republican party identifiers, since independents vote and identifiers may vote a split ticket or even desert their preferred party entirely in a given election. As we noted at the beginning of this chapter, the outlines of an American party are fairly blurred. We can think of the party in the electorate as either the party's voters, its party identifiers, or some blend of the two.

Party identifiers and voters form the broad base of each party. As we see in Figure 7.4, for decades, there has almost always been a larger number of Democratic identifiers than Republican identifiers in the population. However, the Republicans generally turn out in larger numbers to vote, which may help to even out the electoral strength of the two parties.

## FIGURE 7.4
*Party Identification and Turnout*

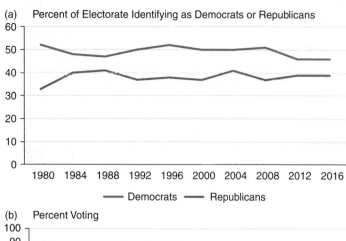

(a) Percent of Electorate Identifying as Democrats or Republicans

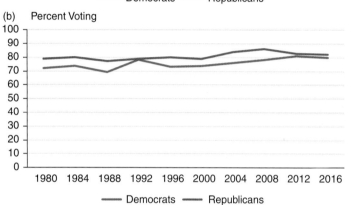

(b) Percent Voting

*Identifiers for each party include independents who "lean" to that party.*
Source: "The ANES Guide to Public Opinion and Political Behavior," ANES, accessed July 23, 2019, https://electionstudies.org/resources/anes-guide/

Some party supporters do more for their party than vote. They contribute money to candidates, work in campaigns, wear campaign buttons, or put bumper stickers on their cars in an effort to convince their friends, neighbors, and family to vote for their favored candidate. They provide a significant source of campaign funds and do much of the campaign work. These activists' opinions have a greater impact on the party's leaders than those of supporters who merely vote for them. This is partly because activists are more likely to involve themselves in the nomination process by voting in primary elections or attending party nominating conventions—so politicians need to pay attention to them to get their support for nomination—and partly because the party needs activists to work enthusiastically during campaigns.

In any church, club, or other type of organization, those who are most active tend to believe most strongly in the group's goals. This general rule holds true for political parties as well and has been observed to be true in many democracies around the world: Those who are most active in a political party usually adhere more strongly to its ideology than those who are less active. This means that most parties are controlled by members who are more unified ideologically than the general membership. American parties are no exception to this rule. For instance, a study in Utah of delegates to the state's 2016 party conventions found that the delegates for the two parties were more divided ideologically than their parties' voters in the state. Seventy-five percent of Democratic delegates (compared with 55 percent of Democratic voters) were strongly liberal, while 46 percent of Republican delegates (compared with 27 percent of Republican voters) were strongly conservative.[10]

## THE PARTY ORGANIZATION

To mobilize the party's supporters and to coordinate the efforts of activists, a party needs something beyond the personal commitment of its activists. It also needs a permanent organization. Today, each party is organized into three types of structures that—as befits our loosely organized parties—operate independently of each other: state and local party organizations, a national committee, and congressional campaign committees.

**STATE AND LOCAL PARTY ORGANIZATIONS** Parties have an organization in each state, with a state party chairperson and a central committee that concerns itself primarily with helping candidates in statewide and state legislative races. Each state organization, in turn, is based on numerous local party organizations. Although their role varies from state to state, these state and local organizations are not like the machines of the old days. They generally do not try to determine who will be nominated for office but rather operate as a support structure for those who achieve nomination through their own efforts in primary elections or at state conventions. The work of state and local parties primarily involves fundraising, conducting issue research and polls for candidates, and organizing state nominating conventions in those states that use a convention. State and local organizations also provide the troops for grassroots campaigning in elections.

**NATIONAL COMMITTEES**  Each party has a national committee that oversees the day-to-day business of the party, raises money to support candidates and to assist state party organizations, and organizes the national presidential nominating convention every four years. Organizing the convention is one of the most important things a national committee does. The national nominating convention is attended by several hundred delegates from around the country who have either been elected in their state's primary election or chosen at a state convention. These delegates choose the party's presidential and vice presidential candidate for that year and write a party platform that lays out the party's principles and positions. The platform reflects the judgment of the convention's delegates and is usually influenced strongly by the likely nominee. In keeping with the decentralized nature of American parties, however, it is not binding on any of the party's candidates; many candidates will ignore important points of the platform if they disagree with them or think they would not work well politically in their races.

Each party organizes a national nominating convention to formally select a presidential candidate. In 2016, the Republicans met in Cleveland to nominate Donald Trump.

The Democratic National Committee, which has about 500 members in all, includes all state party chairs and vice-chairs, plus two hundred additional members who are either elected in primary elections or at state conventions and a variety of members representing affiliated groups. The Republican National Committee is smaller, with about 150 members. It is made up of two members—one man and one woman—from each state and territory, plus the state chair of any state that the Republicans carried in the preceding presidential election or that has a significant Republican presence in other ways. Both committees also employ staff to help in accomplishing the committees' goals.

**CONGRESSIONAL CAMPAIGN COMMITTEES**  Each party has a committee in the Senate and a committee in the House of Representatives whose purpose is to raise money for candidates for Senate or House seats and to recruit able candidates. These four congressional campaign committees consist of House members or senators, plus large staffs, but are not official committees of Congress (see Chapter 11). They raise money (the Democratic Congressional Campaign Committee in the House raised over $100 million in 2018) and maintain field operations to help their parties' candidates. They usually focus their support on candidates who have a chance to win and thereby increase the size of their party's delegation in the Senate or House.

**THE RESURGENCE OF NATIONAL PARTY ORGANIZATIONS**  Although the three national organizations for each party—the national committee and the two congressional campaign committees—operate independently of each other, all have thrived in recent years. State party organizations declined beginning in the 1960s as technological changes such as television advertising, polling, direct marketing, and Internet campaigning made candidates less dependent on them. But ironically, those same technological changes meant that national organizations were increasingly important to candidates. Candidates today need large sums of money as well as support and tutoring in the technical aspects of campaigning. The national organizations help to provide these. Figure 7.5 shows how the amount of money raised by national party committees has grown as the committees have become more central to campaigns.

Over the last 30 years, as shown in Figure 7.5, the six national committees have grown enormously, with combined budgets in 2016 of well over a billion dollars. During this period, they grew from small operations with a few staff members who worked out of rented offices to organizations with several hundred employees housed in their own dedicated buildings near the Capitol. In an earlier era, the state party organizations sent money to the national organizations to help keep them going, but now the flow has reversed, with the two parties' national committees helping to subsidize the operations of the state party organizations.

**national committee**  A committee that oversees the day-to-day business of the political parties at the national level.

**national nominating convention**  A national gathering of delegates to choose a political party's presidential nominee, write a platform of policy positions, and transact other national party business.

**party platform**  A set of policy positions adopted by a party at its national nominating convention.

**congressional campaign committees**  Four committees, one for each party in both the Senate and the House of Representatives, that recruit able candidates for Senate or House seats and raise money for congressional campaigns.

FIGURE 7.5

## Money Raised by National Party Contributions (in millions of dollars)

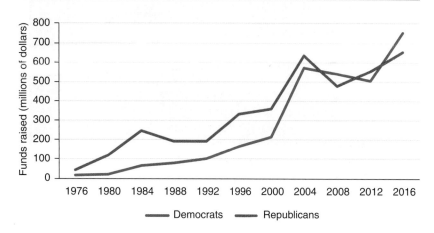

*Source: Data compiled from Paul S. Herrnson, "National Party Organizations at the Dawn of the Twenty-First Century," in* The Parties Respond, *4th ed., ed. L. Sandy Maisel (Cambridge, MA: Westview Press, 2002), 55; Federal Election Commission press releases.*

## THE PARTY IN GOVERNMENT

As noted earlier in the chapter, parties provide leading government officials with a means of influencing, and often controlling, what other officials of their party do. The party in government provides the structure through which officials exercise this control. All of a party's elected officials share a common partisan identity, and they are tied together organizationally as well; to some extent at least, all of them rely on the party organization for help with their campaigns. They also share a common ideology. The party's structure enables them to work together and also allows their leaders to guide them in this collective effort. The party in government most clearly provides structure and coherence to policy making within each of the houses of Congress and in the relations of Congress with the president.

In most countries of the world, political parties operate even more strongly than in the United States to help government leaders control fellow officeholders of their party. In many authoritarian states such as China, of course, the party is essentially the same thing as the government, and promotion to higher office is simply controlled by the party's leaders. But even in most democracies, since parties are more tightly structured, the party is a more potent channel for control than in the United States.

**PARTIES IN CONGRESS** Members of both houses of Congress are organized by party and do much of their most important business through their party organizations. House members actually spend a considerable amount of their time working only with other members of their own party. Republicans are members of the House Republican Conference, and Democrats are members of the House Democratic Caucus. During meetings of these two groups, which happen at least once a week, party leaders communicate the party's positions on issues as well as the party's legislative strategy—and the rank-and-file members raise issues and push back if they disagree with their leaders.

The two parties in the Senate are organized into a Senate Republican Conference and a Senate Democratic Conference, with an internal structure similar to the Conference and Caucus in the House. In contrast with the House, however, individual senators have traditionally been more powerful in their own right than House members have been. If nothing else, each senator is one of 100, while each House member is one of 435. Party leaders in the Senate have to tolerate more defections from their ranks than leaders in the House do, and they also have to negotiate more often with members of the opposite party to get bills passed.

This stands in stark contrast to other countries. In Germany, for instance, individual members of the parliament can do little without the support of the party's leaders. They cannot introduce bills in the parliament, they cannot introduce amendments, and they cannot pose questions to the government except through their party. And when bills are voted on, they must almost always vote with their party. In fact, on many bills the members do not vote at all, but the party leader simply announces that the party's votes are cast for (or against) the bill. Such party discipline sounds strange to individualistic American ears, but it allows effective, focused decision making by the parties in the parliament.

**PRESIDENTS AND PARTIES** Presidents are recognized as the leader of their party nationally. A sitting president is the public face of his or her party, and the party's fortunes rise or fall with the popularity of the president. The president appoints the chair of the party's national committee and is invaluable to the party as a fundraiser. (For the party that does not hold the presidency, the national committee elects its chair.) In addition, presidents use their importance to their party to help them govern. Party ties are especially important in the president's relations with Congress. President Donald Trump was able to use the Republican party structure to great advantage in his relations with Congress after he was elected in 2016. He was very popular with Republican party identifiers (the party in the electorate), so even though arguably most Republican members of Congress were opposed to large parts of his program, he was able to force them to support him. They feared that Republican voters would replace them if they did not do so.

**PARTIES IN STATE GOVERNMENT**  Governmental structures in the states are similar to those of the national government—with a governor and a legislature rather than a president and Congress—but parties generally affect decision making even more strongly at the state level than they do nationally. In many states, the division of powers between the governor and the legislature is less strict than it is at the national level, so a governor can work more directly with the legislators of his or her party. For instance, governors in some states help to name the party leaders in the legislature and join in the regular meetings of their party's legislators.

## THE TWO-PARTY SYSTEM

Since 1864, the Democratic and Republican parties have had a virtual monopoly on elected office in the United States. In that period, every president has been either a Democrat or a Republican, and 99 percent of all members of the House of Representatives have belonged to one of these two parties. Many other parties have tried to enter government, but no other party has been able to establish itself as a serious contender for power on a continuing basis. The Greenback Party, Populists, Prohibition Party, Socialists, Progressives, and others, as well as independent candidates such as Ross Perot (who ran for president in 1992) have all tried, but none have been able to break the hold of the Republicans and Democrats.

The United States, in other words, has a **two-party system** in which two—and only two— parties are regular contenders for governmental office. Some countries are one-party systems where only a single party is allowed to nominate candidates for office. (China, whose politics we examined at the opening of this chapter, is an example of a one-party system.) Most other countries have **multiparty systems** in which three or more parties regularly contend for office

**two-party system**  A party system with two— and only two—parties that regularly nominate candidates with a serious chance of winning office.

**multiparty systems**  Party systems in which three or more parties regularly have a significant chance of gaining office.

### FIGURE 7.6
## *Party Systems of the World's Democracies*

Party Systems of the World's Democracies
- ■ Two-party system
- ■ Multiparty system
- ■ Not an electoral democracy

*Source: Data compiled from the CIA World Factbook.*

*Note: A cutoff point always has to be set between two-party systems and multiparty systems. In this case, we have defined two-party systems to be electoral democracies in which the two largest parties hold at least 85 percent of the seats in the lower house of the congress or parliament.*

with a significant chance of success (see Figure 7.6). Brazil, for instance, has seven major parties and many smaller parties that regularly win some seats in Congress. Twenty-seven different parties hold at least one seat in Brazil's Congress.

Having a two-party system affects United States politics in at least two important ways. For one, compared with most multiparty countries, the range of policy options offered by parties in the United States is narrower. Neither of the two major parties in the United States has argued that the government should nationalize major industries, for instance, or that it should establish a national religion. Individuals *within* one of the parties may have argued for these or other radical proposals, but because each party must appeal to a broad range of people in order to be large enough to win in a two-party system, it cannot adopt a distinctively radical position and still gain the 50 percent of the votes it needs to win an election. In contrast, Norway, with its multiparty system, has a moderately socialist Labor Party; a more socialist Left Socialist Party; an environmentalist Green Party; an anti-immigrant, anti-tax Progress party; a free-enterprise Conservative Party; a Christian Party; and more—all with representation in the Norwegian parliament.

Secondly, the fact that each party in a two-party system must be large enough to include a range of differing opinions is probably one reason for the loose organization of American political parties. If a party is a "big tent," it is harder for it to enforce uniform political views on its members or its candidates.

## THE U.S. ELECTORAL SYSTEM AND THE TWO-PARTY SYSTEM

Why does the United States have a two-party system when most democracies in the world are multiparty systems? A diverse country such as the United States certainly would have a wide enough range of opinions to sustain a variety of parties, so there must be something that regularly forces American politics to fit into only two parties. That "something" is our winner-take-all system of elections, in which candidates run in a district (or a state, or the country as a whole), and the one candidate who does best in the district takes office.

We will look at the U.S. electoral system in detail in Chapter 8 and will also see that elections can be organized in other ways. For our purposes in this chapter, the important thing is to realize that winner-take-all systems, such as those in the United States, generally help large parties and hurt small ones, and for this reason, they have a strong tendency over time to produce two-party systems. To see why this would be so, consider congressional elections. Congressional elections pose a steep challenge for a small party, such as the Green Party. With the support (let us say) of no more than a tenth of the population, spread fairly evenly across the country, it is difficult for the Greens to win congressional seats. In a three-way race, even if the Democratic and Republican candidates were tied, the Green candidate would have to get over 33 percent of the vote to win, which would be more than three times its national average. An even higher percentage would be necessary if the two major parties were not tied.

In a presidential race, the odds are even starker. It's possible to imagine the Greens building a few local pockets of strength in which they could get three, four, or five times their national average and win a few congressional districts. But in the national vote for president, winning with 10 percent would be impossible. The Greens would have to get at least 34 percent of the entire national vote, and even that number would work only if the Democratic and Republican candidates split the rest of the vote evenly. In this way, our winner-take-all electoral system punishes small parties and rewards large parties. As a result, over time, small parties disappear and a two-party system emerges.

## THIRD PARTIES IN THE TWO-PARTY SYSTEM

Even with our basic two-party system, there have always been additional, smaller parties such as the Libertarian Party in American politics. They are commonly called **third parties**, even though they might more properly be called *minor parties*, since there are often four, five, or more parties running candidates in an election. In the 2016 presidential election, there were actually 29 candidates for president on the ballot in at least some states: Democrat Hillary Clinton and Republican Donald Trump, of course, but also candidates of significant parties such as Gary Johnson of the Libertarian Party (on the ballot in 48 states) and less significant ones such as Rod Silva of the

**third parties**
Small political parties that are so greatly handicapped by the single-member, plurality electoral system in the United States and other obstacles that they have a low probability of winning office.

Nutrition Party (on the ballot in only 1 state). None of the other 27 candidates had much chance to win.

Not only are third parties handicapped by the winner-take-all electoral system, but they also face other barriers. Most states have special rules designed to limit "nuisance" candidacies; these rules generally require candidates of any party but the two major ones to gather large numbers of signatures before they can appear on the ballot. Also, public funding of campaigns, where it is available, is usually based on the size of the vote a party gained in the preceding election. Because their share of the vote is generally slight, third parties get only a small subsidy (if any) for their campaign, which hinders their ability to gain more votes—and more funds for the next cycle.

Despite all of these handicaps, however, third parties have been active throughout American history and have sometimes had a significant impact. Third parties come in many varieties, including three major types: offshoots from a major party, ideological or single-issue parties, and vehicles for independent candidates.

The Libertarian Party regularly fields candidates but has not found success at the national level. Gary Johnson, the party's 2016 nominee for president, won only three percent of the popular vote.

Some third parties arise when there is a split in a major party. Party splits can occur for a variety of reasons. In 1912, for instance, followers of Theodore Roosevelt left the Republican Party to form the Progressive Party, with Roosevelt as its presidential candidate. Roosevelt broke from the Republicans for personal reasons and also to pursue the goals of the Progressive movement. In 1948, southerners bolted from the Democratic Party and formed the States' Rights Democratic Party, with Strom Thurmond as their candidate. Their break from the Democrats was made in an effort to try to maintain racial segregation in the South.

Some long-term third parties promote a single issue or a broad ideology. Especially in the nineteenth and early twentieth centuries, ideological parties such as the Populist Party and the Socialist Party ran candidates in a number of elections and enjoyed some success, at least at the congressional level. And single-issue parties such as the Free Silver party and the Prohibition Party likewise were stable fixtures for at least a period of time, with some successes. Enduring parties of this sort in contemporary politics include the Green Party and the Libertarian Party. The Green Party supports sustainable environmental policies, local involvement in politics and the economy, and social justice. The Libertarian Party supports limited government and individual freedom.

Since the middle of the twentieth century, the most prominent third parties have formed to serve the needs of independent candidates, who used them to get access to the national stage. In 1992, Ross Perot, a wealthy businessman, financed his own campaign and ran as an independent but with a national organization of supporters he called United We Stand America. With a platform that emphasized balancing the budget, he received 19 percent of the vote.

## THIRD PARTIES CAN MAKE A DIFFERENCE

Can third parties accomplish anything politically, beyond giving their candidates the thrill of the campaign? One effect of third parties, for which they draw criticism, is that they sometimes act as "spoilers," drawing most of their supporters from one of the two major parties and causing that party to lose the election. In 1912, Theodore Roosevelt's Progressive Party drew its voters mainly from the Republican Party and ensured the election of Democrat Woodrow Wilson (1913–1921). In the very close election of 2000, it is likely that Democrat Al Gore would have won instead of Republican George W. Bush (2001–2009) if Ralph Nader had not run as the Green Party's candidate. Bush carried Florida by only 307 votes, while Nader got 97,488 votes in that state. Since Nader's Green Party supporters were more likely to have voted Democratic than Republican were he not in the race, Gore would probably have carried Florida if Nader had not been on the ballot. And if Gore had carried Florida, he would have won the election.

More importantly, however, third parties have often been able to bring issues to national attention and force the two major parties to deal with them. Several times in American history, third parties have successfully promoted an issue or an ideology, even if they themselves have not been able to gain office to implement their ideas. The Democratic and Republican parties are constantly evolving in their ideologies and policy positions, and third-party campaigns have often influenced that evolution.

The Populist Party, for instance, which received 9 percent of the national vote and carried five states in 1892 with its "free silver" program of inflationary policies to help farmers and debtors, succeeded in taking over the Democratic Party in 1896, and William Jennings Bryan, a Populist figure, was nominated for president by the Democrats. The Prohibition Party never achieved more than local success in electing candidates, but it did succeed in its goal of national prohibition when the Eighteenth Amendment to the Constitution, outlawing the sale and consumption of alcoholic beverages in the United States, was passed in 1919. (The policy proved unpopular, however, and was reversed by the Twenty-First Amendment in 1933.)

The Green Party today has seen its environmental concerns incorporated into many public policies, and the Libertarian Party's concern for limited government has been adopted strongly by the Republican Party. Third-party efforts, then, are not necessarily in vain. They can lead to policy successes even if the third party rarely wins an election.

## RESPONSIBLE PARTY GOVERNMENT

As we have seen, parties are formed with the purpose of helping to determine who holds office. There are two general views on how American parties might do this.[11] One view is that because our two major parties are necessarily large, they therefore need to be broad and inclusive. The fact that a party, if it is to succeed in the United States, must win the support of at least half the population means that each will probably be a coalition of various interests. From this perspective, parties bring together diverse groups of interests and shape them into an organization capable of acting in government. Parties, in this view, are holding companies for evolving, changing groups of interests. To the extent that they have programs, the programs are a blend of the various interests that make up the party. A party that attains office should run the government by making compromises and putting together policies based on its supporters' interests and the needs of the nation. In other words, parties should reflect and coordinate public opinion.

An alternative view is that a party should articulate a clear program, offer it to the electorate, and if it wins an election, put that program into effect. If it is out of office, it should offer an alternative program that it would put into effect if it could displace the governing party. In other words, parties should lead public opinion and offer the public distinct choices. This is the doctrine of **responsible party government**, under which parties should

1. present policies to the electorate,
2. carry them out if elected,
3. develop alternatives to the government's policies when out of office, and
4. differ sufficiently between each other to offer voters a choice.[12]

Though this doctrine necessarily entails distinctive parties in conflict with each other and the possibility of heightened tensions between the contending parties, it also can be attractive because it provides clear accountability. Before an election, voters consider parties offering two alternative programs. They choose one of the parties (with its program), and once in office, the party implements that program. If voters are pleased with the result, they keep the party in office. If not, they vote in the alternative party to implement its program.

In the United States, for many years, parties were more of the "holding companies" sort, but over the last few decades, as party unity has increased and the division between the Democrats and Republicans has widened, American parties appear to have evolved to become more similar to responsible parties. Although the parties are still rather broad and diverse, each party has developed a unified core of ideas that makes it distinguishable on the political party landscape. Each party in Congress is increasingly unified and more distinct from the other party in its voting on bills. The Contract with America, developed by House Republicans under the leadership of Newt Gingrich in the 1994 election, is an example of a strong attempt at making a party "responsible" in the sense used here. This Contract laid out a set

**responsible party government** Doctrine stating that parties should present clear alternative programs and enact them faithfully once in office.

# As a Member of Great Britain's Conservative Party

You have been interested in politics for a long time, favoring the Conservative Party. You had always hesitated about joining the party because it seemed stodgy and stuck in the past. Now, though, the United Kingdom faces a political crisis over "Brexit"—the question of whether and how to leave the European Union (EU). The Conservative Party is in power and will be able to determine the answer to Brexit, and you would like to have a voice in the decision. Its new leader, Boris Johnson, is a flamboyant, controversial figure who is adamantly committed to leaving the EU. He has a very casual approach to true facts, and you are not really sure about him, but you joined the party, paying the annual dues (about $40 U.S. a year, but $8 a year if you are under 23). By joining, you became one of about 150,000 members of the party, half of whom are over 55. (The predominance of older members was one of the reasons the party had always seemed to you to be covered in cobwebs.) It is a party that has traditionally favored free enterprise but was socially moderate, with policy positions ranging from keeping taxes low to combating global warming to saving local British pubs. At the moment, though, it is consumed by the fight over Brexit.

Unlike a political party in the United States, the Conservative Party in Great Britain has a single, unified organizational structure. The key position is the leader of the party, a member of the House of Commons who leads the party both in the House and in the country. Boris Johnson became the party leader in 2019. Theresa May had been ousted at that time because of her failure to negotiate an agreement with the EU that could satisfy the members of the House of Commons. Johnson was chosen as the new leader through a two-step process in which his fellow Conservative members of the House first narrowed the choice to two candidates (both members of the House), and then the party's 150,000 dues-paying members around the country voted to choose one of the two. (As a member, you were able to vote in this process, which is one of the reasons you chose to join.)

All other parts of the party serve as a supporting structure for Johnson and the party's elected members in the House of Commons. As leader, Johnson dominates the party. Ordinarily, he controls the other members of his party in the House because the only way to advance to positions of greater power is through appointment by the leader. Members of the House rarely vote against proposals from the leader. Johnson controls a large national staff that hires regional and local party agents, conducts research on policy, and publishes propaganda. He also appoints a majority of the members of a Management Committee that oversees the party's day-to-day operations. Ordinary party members are organized in constituency associations, one for each parliamentary district in the country. Each association chooses the party's candidate for its district, but the associations have little influence otherwise in national party policies. This is a very centralized party.

Because you are fascinated by politics and are ambitious, you may well try to stand as a candidate for the House of Commons yourself at some point within the next several years. To do this, you will need to convince a selection committee in one of the constituency associations to nominate you for that district, and then you will, of course, need to win the election. But you have high hopes.

## Questions to Consider

1. What are some disadvantages of a tightly organized party? What are its advantages?
2. Why do you think British citizens pay money to join a party and work actively in it, when members of the House of Commons control most of what happens in the party and, therefore, ordinary members have little say over its decisions?
3. What sorts of incentives might draw people into joining a party such as this?

of 10 bills that Republicans promised to bring to a vote if they acquired a majority of the House in the election. They did win the election and did introduce the bills they had promised, though their bills largely failed in the Senate and did not become law. The Republicans controlled the Senate as well as the House, but they were not able to get all of their members to vote for the Contract bills.

Even though the parties have become more distinct from each other, however, it is not clear that the accountability that should in theory go with responsible parties has materialized. The parties do

The Contract with America, promoted by Speaker of the House Newt Gingrich, was an attempt to implement responsible party government in the United States. The bicameral structure of the legislature proved its undoing, however, when Gingrich's Republican colleagues in the Senate were not supportive.

present competing programs, but our presidential system of government, with its divided powers and numerous checks and balances, makes it difficult for a victorious party to put its program into place after it has been elected. Parliamentary systems, which will be discussed in Chapter 12, do not have divided powers and checks and balances, so they can theoretically implement their campaign promises with little problem. If parties in such a system are responsible, they seem to work better and accomplish their function of accountability better than in presidential systems. This may be why parties in the United Kingdom, which has a parliamentary system, have long been responsible parties.

Another reason for the inability of parties in the United States to function well as responsible parties is that they are so decentralized that they do not offer a good vehicle for disciplining officials and making them unite behind the party's policies. In 2017, the victorious Republicans—who in 2016 had achieved the presidency and control of both the House of Representatives and the Senate—endured a year of frustration as major parts of their program failed in Congress. President Trump's two key campaign planks—repealing Obamacare and building a wall along the southern border—both failed to pass. The repeal of Obamacare failed when some Republican senators broke with the party leadership to vote against it. Similarly, in 2008 with Democratic control of both the House and Senate, Democratic President Barack Obama was unable to enact either immigration reform or a carbon tax to reduce global warming. With the parties in their current form, we may have gained the less pleasant part of responsible party government—heightened conflict and tension between the parties—without reaping the benefit of increased accountability.

## INTEREST GROUPS IN AMERICAN POLITICS

An *interest group* is a group of people who put forth a coordinated effort to influence the government's policies. This purpose distinguishes it from a political party, which aims primarily to determine who will hold office in government. Although political parties often promote policies in order to get their candidates into office and interest groups often work to elect representatives who are sympathetic to their policy proposals, the difference is one of emphasis. Parties' central concern is getting their candidates elected, while interest groups' central concern is achieving their policy objectives. This difference in emphasis leads to differences in what they do politically. Interest groups emphasize two broad activities: organizing and mobilizing supporters and lobbying to persuade officials to enact a policy.

Organized interest groups are necessary for politics. Without them, the government might ignore the needs of many people. In the South Asian country of Bangladesh, for instance, citizens typically rely on a patron, who provides them with emergency help when needed and helps to intercede with the government on their behalf. In return, they offer their patron loyalty and support. The population consists of innumerable networks of this sort, which function in much the same way that big-city party machines did in the United States in the late nineteenth and early twentieth centuries. Bangladeshis' reliance on these local networks makes it difficult to form national interest groups centered around a shared idea or occupation. As a result, interest groups are found almost solely among the one-quarter of the Bangladeshi population that live in large cities. These interest groups comprise mostly the urban elites who agitate to protect their own interests in government, leaving many other possible interests unrepresented. For instance, there is not a well-organized interest group for agriculture, even though Bangladesh is a predominantly agricultural country. As a result, the political elite live in a world of their own, where the problems of the country's people rarely intrude. For instance, when a hurricane struck southwestern Bangladesh in June 2009, killing 200 people and leaving hundreds of thousands homeless, the prime minister never visited the site nor did the government do much to help those who were affected. With no political organizations representing the rural populations of southwestern Bangladesh, the government felt free to ignore the problem.

While interest groups perform a vital function, however, Americans have long been ambivalent about them. In 1787, James Madison wrote in *The Federalist No. 10* that the ability of interests to organize is the essence of freedom—but he also complained of the "mischief of factions." Today, people often refer to interest groups as *pressure groups* or *special interests*, reflecting the prevailing view that they are often too strident and that they pursue their own interests at the expense of the common good. Nonetheless, interest groups are a powerful force in the United States. They fall into one of several distinct types.

## CITIZEN GROUPS

Citizen groups are membership organizations open to all who agree with the policy goals of the organization. Since members are brought together by a shared idea rather than by a material interest, citizen groups tend to be ideological and idealistic. Examples include the environmental group Clean Water Action, which works to keep water in drinking supplies and in the environment clean and safe; National Right to Life, which works to limit or eliminate abortion; UnidosUS, which works to further the interests of Hispanic Americans; and the National Rifle Association (NRA), which works to ensure that Americans may own guns with minimal restrictions.

## CORPORATIONS

Corporations often operate directly in the political arena to help shape policy that will enhance their profits. Most large corporations have an official with a title such as "Vice President for Public Affairs," who is responsible for coordinating the corporation's relations with government and trying to influence how laws and regulations are written. Over 750 corporations maintain special offices in Washington, DC, to manage their relations with the government. Microsoft, for instance, has four vice presidents or assistant vice presidents in its home office who deal with government relations and a staff of 24 in a special office in Washington, DC.[13] In 2018, it spent $7,180,000 on its lobbying efforts.[14]

## LABOR UNIONS

Most unions are active in elections and maintain political staff in Washington to represent them. Their goals are often broader than the goals of a corporation, embracing many issues such as health care, workplace safety, or tax policies that affect their members. Unions also lobby to protect and expand their ability to bargain collectively with employers. Over the last decade, unions around the country have been forced into great activity to defend themselves as Republican governors and legislatures have tried to pass a number of laws making it more difficult to unionize workers. In Missouri, for instance, unions organized a massive petition in 2018 to put a measure on the ballot overturning a "right to work" law that would have made it easier for workers to avoid joining a union. The law had been passed by the legislature and signed by the governor, but when the unions campaigned heavily against it in the election, voters defeated it by a 2 to 1 margin.

**citizen groups**
Membership organizations based on a shared set of policy goals; a group is open to all who agree with the policy goals of the organization.

**trade associations**
Organizations of businesses who share the same trade.

## TRADE, PROFESSIONAL, AND AGRICULTURAL ASSOCIATIONS

Many organizations represent companies or individuals who provide a product or service. Trade associations are organizations of businesses who share the same trade, such as the Printing Industries of America or the National Automobile Dealers Association. There are also broader organizations that represent larger groups of businesses, such as the National Association of Manufacturers, which represents all manufacturing businesses, and the U.S. Chamber of Commerce, which represents all businesses of any sort. Where individual corporations generally work to influence narrow regulatory or tax issues that will make a specific difference to them, trade associations lobby on broader issues such as general tax policies or trade policies that affect all their members.

Missouri labor unions organized demonstrations, including at the inauguration of the state's new governor, to protest a "right to work" law passed in the state. They were ultimately successful in overturning the law via referendum.

**Professional associations** are organizations of members of a profession, such as the American Medical Association (AMA) or the National Society of Accountants. They may lobby for benefits for their members or on issues in which their members are experts by virtue of their profession. For instance, the AMA lobbies to increase Medicare reimbursements to doctors but also lobbies to influence how the government responds to epidemics. Even lobbyists are represented by a professional association, the National Institute for Lobbying and Ethics!

**Agricultural associations** are organizations either of farmers in general or of particular kinds of farmers, such as the Southern Peanut Growers. They tend to focus fairly narrowly on issues important to their members' farming activities, such as trade policy, environmental regulations, and price supports.

## OTHER GROUPS THAT LOBBY OFFICIALS

Some groups that do not represent a broad-based membership nonetheless maintain an active lobbying presence in Washington. Governmental and nonprofit institutions such as the armed forces, the Red Cross, and many universities maintain a lobbying presence to advance the interests of their offices. Also, foreign governments often hire Washington lobbying and public relations firms to represent their interests, set up contacts with members of Congress and the executive branch, and advise them on how to relate to the broad public.

## SOCIAL MOVEMENTS

We have included social movements with interest groups here, but they are really a separate type of group, alongside parties and traditional interest groups. **Social movements** are informally organized, often temporary groups that spring up around an issue or an event. They have minimal structure and deal with politics outside of normal governmental decision making, usually emphasizing demonstrations rather than formal lobbying. Take a look at Figure 7.7 for one way to understand what a social movement is and how it compares to a political party or a traditional interest group. What defines social movements is not their goal, which is what distinguishes parties from interest groups, but their extremely loose organization.

Examples include the many groups in the civil rights movement of the 1960s, the Tea Party movement, Black Lives Matter, and local groups opposed to the construction of an airport or highway. A social movement is more a network of activists than an organization. Typically, it consists of a number of people who engage in political activities such as demonstrations more or less spontaneously, and it has a number of competing leaders rather than a single structure with one leader.

**MOVEMENTS THAT HAVE MADE A MAJOR IMPACT** Social movements have often had a major impact on politics. The most famous example is the success of the civil rights movement in the 1960s in desegregating public facilities and gaining the right to vote for African Americans. Another important social movement in American politics is Gay Pride. Gay Pride parades started in commemoration of the Stonewall Riots in New York City in 1969 but have developed into an annual event in many cities around the country, raising the visibility of the gay community and promoting the cause of gay rights.

The feminist movement of the 1960s was another successful social movement. Many groups of women joined together to discuss common problems and define those problems as political (involving government policies or general practices in society) rather than as the personal fault of women. From these groups sprung a general, loosely coordinated campaign for changes in reproductive policy, workplace practices, and government regulations based on gender.

**professional associations**
Organizations of members of a profession.

**agricultural associations**
Organizations either of farmers in general or of a particular kind of farmer.

**social movements**
Informally organized, often temporary groups that spring up around an issue or an event to advance a specific point of view.

## FIGURE 7.7

*Parties, Traditional Interest Groups, and Social Movements*

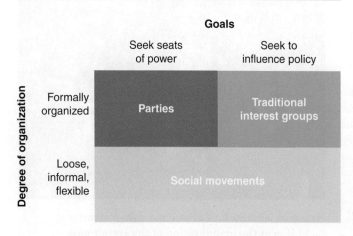

*Source: W. Phillips Shively,* Power and Choice: An Introduction to Political Science, *12th ed. (New York, NY: McGraw-Hill Education).*

More recent is the Tea Party movement, which started in 2009 as a series of protests against taxes and the Obama administration's health care bill. The Tea Party is not a party and, in fact, has no unified central leadership, but the core beliefs of its members suggest a distrust of elected officials and government. It is a strongly anti-elite movement of people who have historically felt scorned by what they view as the political and media elites.

The Black Lives Matter movement originated in 2013 with the hashtag #BlackLivesMatter after Trayvon Martin, a black teenager, was shot by a white neighbor who considered him suspicious. It is a loose movement of local groups of (mostly young) African Americans who speak out against violence and racism toward black people.

All of these movements have in common the fact that they were based on under-represented groups in society that did not have many political resources: African Americans, gays and lesbians, women in the 1960s, and nonpolitical, anti-elite members of the middle class. U.S. social movements typically are a last resort for the under-represented, but in poor countries such as Bangladesh or in non-democracies that do not have regular avenues for participation, they may be the main or only outlet available for most citizens. In 2011, for instance, after 23 years of dictatorial rule in Tunisia, a social movement arose that toppled the government and led to a new, democratic regime; from there, social movements spread to Egypt and the rest of the Middle East, though they found less success. In China, where organized opposition is illegal, thousands of loosely organized social movements arise to protest local issues each year. In Bangladesh, which as we have noted has few interest groups, the only recourse for students concerned about traffic safety in 2018 was to take to the streets in spontaneous demonstrations.

Black Lives Matter was born after Trayvon Martin was shot and killed by a white neighbor who thought he seemed suspicious. It has since grown into an international movement that seeks to end violence and systemic racism against black people.

## INTEREST GROUP REPRESENTATION AND THE ORGANIZATION OF PUBLIC OPINION

Interest groups are the part of the political system that can best represent public opinion and bring it to bear in an organized way on governmental authorities. Political parties cannot do this very well, because they are involved in trying to acquire governmental power for themselves. This quest for power—and the need to compete in a two-party system—compels parties to incorporate many compromises in their programs to appeal to the broadest spectrum of support. A party seeks to merge differences, but an interest group seeks to represent its members' wishes clearly and precisely.

This works well if all parts of society are represented by well-organized groups, but the United States is something of a half-filled glass in this regard. Despite its well-developed interest group system, it does not always reflect American society accurately. The parts of society that are well represented by organized interest groups diverge from the overall society in various ways. First, interest groups tend to represent those who are financially well-off more than those who are not so well-off. Secondly, producer interests—those involved in making a product—are easier to organize than consumer interests—those who purchase the product. Accordingly, producers are more thoroughly organized than consumers. Finally, some groups enjoy other special advantages that make it easier for them to organize themselves and influence officials.

### ORGANIZATION OF THE WELL-OFF

In general, interest groups tend to represent the concerns of those who are relatively well-off. Two-thirds of registered lobbyists represent either corporations or trade and professional groups, but even citizen groups have a tendency to overrepresent the well-off.

Because joining a citizen group is a voluntary act that is not based primarily on economic incentives, the sorts of people who tend to join citizen groups are the same as those who tend to volunteer or turn out to vote in elections: older, better-educated, more economically prosperous Americans. As a result, citizen groups tend to organize around issues that reflect the interests of such segments of society—issues such as the protection of historic buildings, the environment, and animals' rights.

Another reason why the well-off are more strongly represented in the interest group universe is that those who enjoy greater financial comfort are likely to have acquired, either from their education or from their jobs, the sorts of organizational and technical skills that interest groups need. As a result, groups representing the well-off are more likely than others to be effectively organized. For all of these reasons, those in the society who are well-off are better represented than those who are not. There are relatively few interest groups seeking to help poor, rural Americans or other disadvantaged groups.

## PRODUCER INTERESTS AND CONSUMER INTERESTS

Another distortion in the interest group universe is caused by the difference between *producer interests* and *consumer interests*. A **producer interest** is any group of people involved in making a product. Any product may involve a number of producer interests: a corporation, a trade union, and one or more professional organizations. Examples of producer interests are Microsoft Corporation, the United Auto Workers union, the AMA, and the National Farmers' Union—any economic entity made up of those who produce something. A **consumer interest** is any group of people who use or purchase the producers' goods or services. Most groups of consumers are not formally organized, but some examples include the American Automobile Association (AAA), the Center for Science in the Public Interest, and the Consumer Federation of America.

Note that the producer/consumer distinction differs from the well-off/less well-off distinction. Groups of consumers may be relatively well-off—those who buy cruise vacations, for instance, or upscale clothing—or they may be less well-off. And producer groups, while they include corporations and well-paid professionals, also include trade unions representing workers who are not so well-off.

Producer interests are always easier than consumer interests to organize due to the higher concentration of producer interests. To take one example, every family in the United States pays about $40 more for food each year because of import restrictions on sugar, which the powerful American Sugar Alliance of sugar growers defends.[15] The higher cost of sugar shows up not only in candies and soft drinks but also influences the cost of many other food items containing sugar, such as mayonnaise and bread. Although the added expense for families is significant, it is not large enough that they will give up evenings and weekends to organize for a change in the restrictions. The nationwide total, however, comes to $1.9 billion—all of which goes to sugar cane and beet growers and sugar-processing plants. This is enough money to make a difference of 10 or 20 percent in the profits of the companies and the earnings of their workers, and that is something for which people will give up their evenings and weekends. Washington is saturated with letters, campaign contributions, and lobbying visits from the affected companies and their workers—but Washington hears almost nothing from the people who bear the extra costs. The producers' strong organization supports the restrictions and faces very little organized opposition.

The bias of interest group activity toward producer groups pervades a wide range of policies—from regulations on telecommunications, finance, and other areas to product safety and the prices paid by consumers. This difference between producers and consumers is found in all countries, not only the United States. In a survey of German interest groups, for example, 61 percent of all interest groups consisted of corporate groups, unions, or professional associations. Only 3 percent represented other economic groups, mostly consumer groups.[16]

## SPECIAL CIRCUMSTANCES AFFECTING GROUP ORGANIZATION

A variety of special circumstances also make it easier to organize some groups than others, either by virtue of their location or personal characteristics.

**CONTIGUOUS RESIDENCE** It is easier to organize a group of people if they live close together and communicate with each other frequently than if they are spread throughout society and have only sporadic contact with each other. In the early days of the labor movement, the first groups to organize were groups such as lumberjacks (who lived together in lumber camps in the forest)

**producer interest**
A group of people involved in producing a product.

**consumer interest**
A group of people consuming a product.

and miners (who lived together in company towns built near the mine). It was harder at that time to organize live-in servants, who by definition, lived separately from each other in the houses that they served. Today, contiguity continues to have its advantages: Church groups are relatively easy to organize, for instance, because they congregate once a week for worship services.

**AGE**  Just as citizens under 30 tend not to vote as regularly as older citizens, they are also more difficult to organize in interest groups. This is due in part to the same reasons that make them less likely to vote. Younger citizens are often not as fully engaged with their role as citizens as they will be when they are older. Young people also typically do not have the same resources as older generations, either in terms of money or time. They may be transient, serving in the military or studying in a state or city that they do not regard as their long-term residence and thus are less likely to commit time and money to improving the local situation. As a result of all these factors, many students and other young people are not active in interest groups, and their needs tend to receive relatively little attention in public policies involving health care, transportation, and housing.[17]

**STRATEGIC LOCATION**  Some groups are strategically located and thus important to elected officials. For instance, while there are only about 1.25 million Cuban Americans in the United States, most of them are concentrated in Florida. With Florida wielding 27 electoral votes and evenly divided politically, it is very difficult for a presidential candidate to win there without the Cuban American vote. So, Cuban Americans in the state get close attention from presidential candidates. This has helped Cuban American interest groups, such as the Cuban American National Foundation, to exert a strong influence on American policy toward Cuba.

# CONSEQUENCES FOR DEMOCRACY

Parties matter to us because they are the most effective device available to bring together policy makers and politically concerned citizens throughout the country. If we want to address problems through government policy, political parties are indispensable to the effort.

Having only two parties seems to work satisfactorily for this purpose because our parties have proved themselves able to evolve in response to changing policy needs, especially with help from the periodic rise of third parties that push them to evolve.

The loose and decentralized structure of our parties, however, is another story. In combination with the division of our government into competing units that check and balance each other, the loose organization of our parties makes it difficult to address national policy issues. As Madison foresaw, compromise is required to bridge the divisions of government. But in an increasingly ideological, polarized party system, *compromise* has become a dirty word.

The parties' contribution to policy making is therefore mixed. Compromise across the two parties is difficult because the parties are so polarized ideologically, but because of their loose internal structure and the division of powers in government, it is also difficult for either party acting alone to drive its proposals to become actual policy. Often, the end result is paralysis.

With our weak, stymied political parties, interest groups take on added importance in policy making. If political parties find it difficult to drive clear policy agendas, then government policy making comes to be influenced more by the push and pull of interest groups than it would be if there were clear party leadership. But as we have seen, the well-off get stronger and better representation from interest groups than the poor.

This combination of interest groups that represent the well-off, together with weak parties, leads to government policies that are biased in favor of the well-off. A study examining 2,000 policy proposals compared how responsive the government is to the poorest tenth of Americans and to the most well-off tenth. When the poorest and the most well-off diverge in their views on a policy, the government adopts the views of the well-off approximately half the time; it adopts the views of the poor only 2 percent of the time. The researchers found a similar result when comparing the well-off to those in the middle tenth of the population.[18] It is hard to escape the conclusion that at least some of this disparity is due to the bias of the interest group universe toward those who are well off and the inability of parties to counterbalance this bias.

# Critical Thinking Questions

1. Should American parties be more like coalitions of interests or should they act like responsible parties? Why?

2. What do you think American politics would be like if political parties were eliminated? (For example, a few cities in the United States have nonpartisan elections in which the candidates' political party affiliations are not listed on the ballot.) Would elected officials view their responsibilities in the same way if we had no political parties? How might campaigns and elections change without political parties? Do you think the influence of special interests would decrease or increase? Explain your answer.

3. As illustrated in Figure 7.1, political parties provide structure and continuity to elections by establishing long-lasting identities among voters. Is the sort of continuity illustrated in the figure a good thing? Why or why not? What are its benefits and its drawbacks?

4. Given the increasing ideological unity of the two parties, could the two parties become so far apart ideologically that there would be an opening for a new, more moderate party that was situated somewhere between the other two? Consider the difficulties of breaking into the two-party system of the United States. What would need to happen to allow a new party to establish itself and become permanently competitive?

5. How could the universe of interest groups in the United States be made to represent the full population better than they now do?

# Key Terms

agricultural associations, 184
citizen groups, 183
congressional campaign committees, 175
consumer interest, 186
critical election, 172
direct primaries, 168
electoral realignment, 172
Era of Good Feelings, 166
First Party System, 166
interest group, 162
mobilization, 164

multiparty systems, 177
national committee, 175
national nominating convention, 175
party in government, 172
party in the electorate, 172
party organization, 172
party platform, 175
patronage, 167
political machines, 167
political party, 162
producer interest, 186

professional associations, 184
Progressive movement, 168
responsible party government, 180
Second Party System, 167
social movements, 184
split-ticket voting, 170
third parties, 178
trade associations, 183
two-party system, 177
Whig Party, 167

Visit edge.sagepub.com/maltese to help you accomplish your coursework goals in an easy-to-use learning environment.

# 8
# NOMINATIONS AND ELECTIONS

## *After reading this chapter, you should be able to do the following:*

- Analyze the factors that contributed to the development of U.S. elections.

- Describe each phase of the presidential campaign and the strategies that determine candidates' success.

- Examine the congressional election process and understand what makes it so difficult to unseat incumbent members.

- Describe the different types of electoral systems and their impact, including that of the Electoral College.

- Analyze how the U.S. electoral system affects the representation of women and minorities in government.

- Understand why it is difficult to regulate campaign expenditures.

## *Perspective: How Long Should Election Campaigns Last?*

The 2016 presidential campaign in the United States lasted either 596 days (counting from the date Senator Ted Cruz opened the campaign by announcing he was running) or 281 days (counting from the first caucus, held in Iowa). Either way, the United States has long and elaborate campaigns by international standards. After the Iowa caucus on February 1, 2016, primary elections or caucuses were held in other states every few weeks until mid-June. Then, in the second half of July, the parties held their nominating conventions, each a four-day spectacle of speeches and entertainment during which they formally selected Donald J. Trump and Hillary Clinton as their candidates. After the conventions, a strenuous three-month campaign culminated in the election on November 8. Along the way, the candidates engaged in many debates vying for their party's nomination (44 in all!), plus three debates between Trump and Clinton after the conventions.

Instead of letting the campaign begin whenever candidates choose, the Canadian prime minister has the right to choose the date for the next election. The campaign starts when he announces the date for voting, so his announcement determines the length of the campaign. The average campaign is only 37 days long, but in 2015, Prime Minister Stephen Harper set the longest campaign in a century, at 78 days—still much shorter than a campaign in the United States. He apparently chose to do this because his Conservative Party had more money than its rival, the Liberal Party, and he thought it could better handle the longer campaign. His ploy did not work, though. The Liberals raised as much money as the Conservatives, won the election, and made their leader, Justin Trudeau, the new prime minister.

Not that the amounts of money involved were very large by United States standards. In 2016, elections in the United States, taking into account both presidential and congressional races, cost $6.5 billion. The Canadian campaign of 2015, counting all parties' expenditures, cost only $99 million. This was partly because Canada limits campaign spending, but it was also because of the short campaign.

Which kind of campaign is better? One disadvantage of a long campaign is that it requires candidates to spend more money than a short campaign, increasing the role of big money in politics. On the other hand, a longer campaign might be expected to give voters more information on which to base their vote. It might also get voters more engaged in the election and in politics—or it could exhaust them. Which is it? Apparently, neither. Turnout in the 2016 United States election was 60 percent, and in the 2015 Canadian election, it was 69 percent. When asked, "How important is politics in my life?" approximately half of the citizens in each country responded that it was important.1 It appears that Canadian and United States citizens are similar in their engagement with elections and politics. The longer campaigns in the United States seem neither to especially engage voters nor to turn them off. **‹‹**

## THE DEVELOPMENT OF ELECTIONS IN THE UNITED STATES

The history of the United States has seen a long march toward (usually) broader and more inclusive elections and (usually) more fair and secret elections. The Founders were not initially eager to establish direct democratic control of the government by citizens. Only the House of Representatives was to be directly elected, and because most states required voters to meet property requirements, participation was severely restricted. Over time, however, selection of the president came to be closely tied to the votes of citizens in the states; the Senate became directly elected (1913); and voting rights were extended to former male slaves (1870), women (1920), and 18- to 20-year-olds (1971). In 1965 the Voting Rights Act effectively ended widespread practices that disenfranchised African Americans in the South. As a result of these changes, national elections today include a far larger proportion of the population than they once did.

Historically, the United States has generally been a leader, rather than a follower, in extending voting rights to its citizens. The United States was one of the first democracies in the world, at least in the sense of establishing general manhood suffrage (suffrage not limited by property ownership or education requirements) by the middle of the nineteenth century. And it was the fourteenth country in the world to extend suffrage fully to women (see Figure 8.1).[2] In this regard, it compares favorably with other countries of the time, such as the United Kingdom or France, which granted women the right to vote on the same terms as men in 1928 and 1944, respectively.

The march toward universal suffrage has not necessarily ended, however. Not all adult Americans can vote, even today. The most notable exclusion is of felons—people who have been convicted of crimes ranging in seriousness from shoplifting to murder. Today, 48 states bar incarcerated prisoners from voting (Maine and Vermont are the exceptions). But 12 states deny

## FIGURE 8.1
## *Women's Suffrage Around the World*

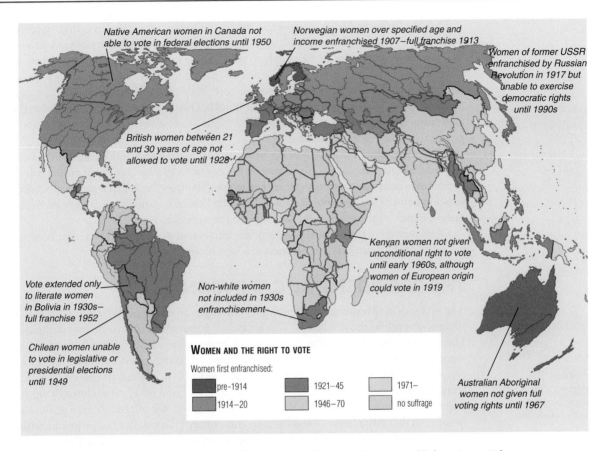

Native American women in Canada not able to vote in federal elections until 1950

Norwegian women over specified age and income enfranchised 1907—full franchise 1913

Women of former USSR enfranchised by Russian Revolution in 1917 but unable to exercise democratic rights until 1990s

British women between 21 and 30 years of age not allowed to vote until 1928

Kenyan women not given unconditional right to vote until early 1960s, although women of European origin could vote in 1919

Vote extended only to literate women in Bolivia in 1930s— full franchise 1952

Non-white women not included in 1930s enfranchisement

Chilean women unable to vote in legislative or presidential elections until 1949

**WOMEN AND THE RIGHT TO VOTE**

Women first enfranchised:

| | |
|---|---|
| ■ pre-1914 | ■ 1921–45 | □ 1971– |
| ■ 1914–20 | □ 1946–70 | □ no suffrage |

Australian Aboriginal women not given full voting rights until 1967

Source: From Philip's Atlas of World History. Copyright © Philip's, a division of Octopus Publishing Group Ltd.

the vote—in some cases, permanently—even to ex-felons who have done their time. This especially disenfranchises minorities and lower-income citizens, who are more likely to have run afoul of the criminal justice system.

Elections also have evolved over time. In the 1880s and 1890s, as we saw in Chapter 7, major reforms introduced several procedures we now take for granted:

- The government, not the political parties, prints the official ballots.
- Ballots include the names of all candidates who have been certified for the election.
- Ballots are distributed only by election officials.
- Ballots are cast secretly, not openly, in order to shield voters from outside pressures.

Together, these provisions are referred to as the **Australian ballot** because they were first adopted in Australia. They are intended to ensure that elections are fair and secret.

This evolution continues today. After the extremely close 2000 election, which was only decided after painstaking examination of ballots in various counties of Florida, many people realized for the first time that voting procedures vary greatly from one state to another and even from one county to another within the same state. This awareness encouraged politicians to develop clearer rules regarding voter registration and to instill in the people greater confidence

**Australian ballot** A set of reforms introduced in the 1880s and 1890s to make elections more fair and secret.

that a vote cast will be a vote counted, regardless of the type of voting machine being used. Accordingly, Congress adopted the Help America Vote Act in 2002,[3] which provided money to update voting machines; it also established a national commission to help the states administer elections fairly.

Over the last several years, however, a somewhat different set of initiatives to change election procedures has emerged. Since 2010, legislators in 25 states, primarily Republicans, have passed bills to make it more difficult for people to vote.[4] These involve a mix of requirements, including photo identification at the polls, a shortened period for early voting, and longer periods of residence in the district before registering to vote. Proponents of the bills argue that they will eliminate fraud, while opponents argue that fraud has not been a real problem and that the real motivation is to make voting more difficult for ethnic minorities, the elderly, students, and other groups that often vote Democratic.

At the same time, a smaller number of states, both Republican and Democratic, have taken steps to make it easier for people to vote. Measures to do this include using mailed ballots and registering voters automatically rather than making them go through a separate process of registration before they can vote. Relatedly, Florida, Louisiana, and Virginia have taken steps to make it easier for those who have served prison sentences to vote.

Obviously, there are various and conflicting currents at work here. On balance, however, the net effect of all of these moves has been to lessen voters' access.

## THE PRESIDENTIAL CAMPAIGN

The first step in determining who will hold any office, from the presidency on down, is determining who will be the candidates. This process of **nomination** is a critical part of the election. Voters in the United States can exercise much more influence by helping to nominate candidates than by merely choosing between the nominated candidates on Election Day, since there is typically greater scope for choice in the primaries. In 2016, Democrats chose Hillary Clinton from among a field of six, while Donald Trump was one of 17 candidates vying for the Republican nomination. It is true that the general election still offered voters a genuine choice in the final two candidates, Donald Trump and Hillary Clinton. But the primaries, with their wider range of alternatives, offered voters greater influence on the outcome than the choice in the **general election** between only two candidates.

Narrowing the list of hopefuls down to one candidate from each party is a long, grueling, exciting, and expensive process. Parties nominate their presidential candidates at national conventions, where the convention delegates—individuals from around the country—vote to choose the party's candidate. The trick for a candidate is to have won enough delegates by the time of the convention to ensure receiving a majority of the votes. The delegates are the key. How, then, are they selected?

> **nomination** The designation of candidates among whom voters will choose in an election.
>
> **general election** A regularly scheduled election at which voters make their final choices of public officials.

Ten of the 17 Republican presidential hopefuls participated in a debate in Boulder, Colorado, in October 2015. The primary process eventually winnowed the field to one: Donald Trump.

## SELECTING THE DELEGATES

Most delegates are chosen in the states, with the national parties designating how many delegates each state will be allocated.[5] For the two main parties, the number of delegates per state is based not only on the state's population but also on how much support the voters of that state have historically given to the party's candidates. Therefore, the geographic makeup of the two conventions will differ. Republicans have relatively more delegates from the South and from mountain states, because historically, these have been strong areas for the party; Democrats have relatively more delegates from the two coasts for the same reason.

Each state government decides by law how the delegates for that state will be chosen. Two main devices are used to choose delegates: caucuses followed by state conventions, and primary elections. The overwhelming majority of delegates for both parties are chosen through one of these two devices. In addition, each party also has a small but significant number of delegates who are called **superdelegates** in the Democratic Party and **unpledged delegates** in the Republican Party. These are elected officials and members of the parties' National Committees who get automatic seats at the conventions based on their roles in the parties. They are not chosen by the voters, and their votes at the convention are not determined through their states' primaries or caucuses. The Democrats' superdelegates do not vote on the first round of voting, but they do vote in later rounds if no one has won on the first round; the Republicans' unpledged delegates vote on all rounds.

## PRIMARIES AND CAUCUSES

Since 1972, most states have used primary elections to choose the parties' convention delegates. In 2016, for instance, 38 states held presidential primary elections for the Republican nomination, and 37 states held primary elections for the Democratic nomination. In a presidential primary, all who aspire to be the party's candidate submit to the voters lists of delegates who support them. Voters in the 2016 Republican primaries may have seen a list of candidates on their ballots, but they were really choosing among a Trump list of delegates, a Jeb Bush list, a Ted Cruz list, and so on.

States and localities use primary elections not only to choose delegates to the parties' presidential nominating conventions but also to determine who the candidates will be in many other political races—for instance, congressional elections and elections for local offices such as mayor. The two main types of primary election are the closed primary and the open primary: In a **closed primary**, only voters who choose to be affiliated with a party when they register may vote in that party's primary; independents do not vote. In an **open primary**, all voters including independents may choose one party primary in which to vote, regardless of how they are registered.[6]

Open primaries have two key effects. First, voters who support one party may choose to vote in the other party's primary. Often, this happens because there is a more important choice in the other party's primary than in their own. (In 2012, for instance, with President Obama unopposed in the Democratic primaries, some Democratic voters probably decided to vote in the Republican primary—where there was some choice—rather than in their own where there was no choice.) This is called **crossover voting**. There has always been some worry about crossover voting because of another possibility—that a party's supporters might cross over in an attempt to hurt the other party by getting a weak candidate nominated. There is little evidence that this has ever happened in a meaningful way; voters do not usually respond in large numbers when candidates or others try to organize a mischievous crossover of this sort.

A second, more important effect of open primaries is that "independents"—those who have registered to vote but have not declared for either party—can vote in the primary. Independents often play a major role in these contests. In the 2016 Democratic primary in Michigan, for instance, 58 percent of registered Democrats who voted chose Hillary Clinton, while 41 percent selected Bernie Sanders. Clinton lost the primary, however, because independents who voted in the Democratic primary went strongly for Sanders.

Instead of primaries, some states—including Iowa, Minnesota, and Nevada—use party **caucuses** and state conventions to select convention delegates. Legislatures of caucus states set a date on which state party organizations hold their caucuses (meetings). First, each party organizes precinct caucuses—neighborhood meetings of party supporters. Anyone living in the neighborhood, including independents, can attend, whether or not they are active in politics. At the meeting, which usually takes a few hours, those who attend vote to send some of their fellow attendees on as delegates to the next round of the party's caucuses. In the next round, held a few weeks later, these delegates attend a convention covering a larger geographic

**superdelegates** Delegates to the Democratic Party's national nominating convention who are not selected through a primary or caucus procedure but go to the convention because of the office they hold in the party or the government.

**unpledged delegates** Delegates to the Republican Party's national nominating convention who are not selected through a primary or caucus procedure but go to the convention by right of the office they hold in the party or the government.

**closed primary** A primary election in which only those who have registered with a party designation may vote; they may vote only in that party's primary.

**open primary** A primary election in which all voters may participate and may choose which party's primary they wish to vote in.

**crossover voting** Voting in a primary election for a party other than the one with which you are registered.

**caucuses** Gatherings of party supporters at the neighborhood level who select delegates to a state nominating convention, which in turn selects delegates to the national nominating convention.

area—usually a county or congressional district—to choose delegates to the party's state convention. The state convention then selects the state's delegates to the party's national convention. At every level, candidates' advocates compete to send delegates who support their candidate to the next level.

Primary elections involve more formal campaigning and advertising than caucuses, while caucuses entail more of grassroots conversations among neighbors and active party supporters. Another difference between the two is that more people usually participate in a primary election than in caucuses, since showing up to vote in a primary takes less time than attending a caucus meeting. In 2016, for instance, 16 percent of those eligible to vote in Iowa attended a party caucus, but 52 percent of those eligible to vote in New Hampshire voted in that state's presidential primary.[7]

**HOW REPRESENTATIVE ARE PRIMARIES AND CAUCUSES?**  In both primaries and caucuses, participation is low compared with the general election. As we noted above, in 2016 only 16 percent of eligible voters attended Iowa's caucus and 52 percent voted in New Hampshire's primary, but general election turnout in those states was 69 percent and 73 percent, respectively, which was higher than participation in either the caucus or the primary. We saw in Chapter 7 that activists usually hold stronger, more ideological views than the general electorate, and we might expect from this that those who make the extra effort to vote in primaries or attend caucuses would be more extreme in their views than the average voters of their parties. Many commentators and political scientists argue that if this is the case, then our system of primaries and caucuses might be an important source of the current polarization of American politics, since candidates would have to appeal to ideologues to get the nomination.

Apparently, however, it does not work that way. Even though primaries and caucuses draw less broadly from among the party's supporters than the general election does, they draw broadly enough that those who participate in them are not very different from the full base of party supporters. We see in Figure 8.2 that in 2008, Iowans who planned to attend their parties' caucuses were more polarized than registered voters of the two parties, but only by a little bit. When asked whether immigration was an important issue, the difference in answers between those planning to attend the two caucuses was only slightly greater than the difference between registered Democrats and Republicans as a whole. On other issues as well (not shown in the figure), caucus attendees were only slightly more polarized than their parties' registered voters.[8]

We find the same thing in primary elections. Two studies, one by Alan Abramowitz and another by John Sides, Chris Tausanovitch, Lynn Vavreck, and Christopher Warshaw, have found that Democratic primary voters are similar to Democrats voting in the general election, and Republican primary voters are similar to Republicans voting in the general election.[9] The fact that caucus attendees and primary voters are reasonably representative of their parties' voters is reassuring.

But even if primaries and caucuses are fairly representative of each party's voters, they are not representative of the full electorate. And that sometimes causes a problem for the parties, when the partisans who vote in the primaries or go to caucuses produce candidates who are so ideologically oriented that they do not do well in the general election (where more moderate independents often determine the outcome).

This has not proved to be a problem in recent presidential nominations, but it does happen from time to time in nominations for Congress or for state offices. For instance, in the Republican primary election for governor in Kansas in 2018, Kris Kobach—a very anti-immigrant, pro-Trump candidate—defeated the sitting Republican governor and became his party's candidate. Even though Kansas is a generally

## FIGURE 8.2

### *Caucus Attenders Versus Registered Voters*

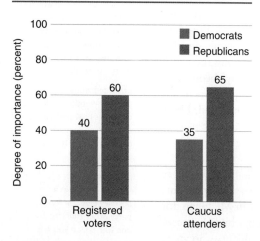

*This graph shows how important the immigration issue was to registered voters and caucus attenders in Iowa. How much more polarized are those who went to the caucuses, compared with the electorate as a whole? What does this indicate about how well the caucuses represented the parties' voters in general? Source: Data from David P. Redlawsk, Caroline J. Tolbert, and Todd Donovan, Why Iowa? (Chicago: University of Chicago Press, 2011), p. 131.*

Republican state, Kobach proved to be too far to the right for its voters and lost to a Democrat in the general election.

## THE ROAD TO NOMINATION

For the presidential candidates, the hectic schedule of primaries and caucuses determines a great deal of their strategy. Typically, a large number of candidates jockey for a party's nomination, unless a sitting president or vice president is running (which usually results in no opposition for that party's nomination). In order to win in the many state primaries and caucuses, candidates must make themselves known to the voters. Five factors can help with this:

- prior fame (In 2016, for instance, Donald Trump was already well-known in part because he had starred in the TV show *The Apprentice*.)
- media coverage
- volunteers
- money for advertising
- an appealing message

Candidates cannot do much about the first factor—they are either well-known at the start or they are not. What they can control, at least to an extent, is how much media attention they get, how effective their campaign organization is, how clearly they present their message, and how much money they raise. Success in early contests can help both with media attention and fundraising, so candidates focus a great deal of their effort on those contests.

**THE EARLY CONTESTS: THE IMPORTANCE OF TIMING** Traditionally, the Iowa caucuses open the nomination contest for both parties and are followed by the primary election in New Hampshire. In 2008, two other contests were added: the Nevada caucuses and the South Carolina primary. These four states now are always the first nomination contests. Candidates have learned to invest a huge effort in these early contests because success at this stage convinces pundits and activists that the candidate has a genuine chance to win the nomination. More extensive attention in the media, and increased cash contributions, follow.

In 2016, for instance, the Republicans entered the year with nine main candidates. The Iowa caucuses narrowed things sharply when only three candidates scored in the double digits. Ted Cruz won Iowa with 28 percent of the caucus attenders, but Donald Trump (with 24 percent) and Marco Rubio (with 23 percent) were very close. John Kasich, the moderate governor of Ohio, had stayed out of the Iowa contest because he did not think he could do well among the conservative delegates there; he concentrated on the next contest, in New Hampshire. In New Hampshire, however, Trump scored a big win with 35 percent of the vote. Kasich was second with 16 percent, and Cruz followed with 12 percent. By the time of the Arizona primary in mid-March, only Trump, Cruz, and Kasich were left of the original nine candidates, and by early May, only Trump was left standing. This result is typical. Since 1976, no candidate of either party who lost both in Iowa and New Hampshire has received the party's nomination.[10] Candidates who have won only one of the two contests have received their party's

The Washington Post / Getty Images

The Iowa caucuses, as the first nominating contest of the presidential campaign, take on extra importance. Candidates may start holding events there more than a year before the caucus. Elizabeth Warren visited the state frequently after declaring her candidacy, including during this event in May 2019.

nomination half the time. And every candidate who has won in both states has gone on to get the party's nomination. These two small states have a disproportionate influence on national nominations, simply by virtue of holding their contests first.

**FRONTLOADING AND THE SCHEDULE OF CONTESTS** States know that candidates pay attention to the early contests. An early date pays off for a state financially because candidates spend a great deal of money on these crucial early races, and it also means that candidates emphasize political issues that matter to the state. Primary and caucus dates are set by the states' legislatures, and many states try to push their primaries and caucuses forward as much as they can to take advantage of this candidate attention. In the run-up to the 2016 conventions, states engaged in a scramble to frontload their delegate selection, getting it as close to the front of the lineup as possible. In an attempt to limit this contest among the states, both parties set strict rules that no states could hold caucuses or primaries before the end of January and that only the four approved early states (Iowa, New Hampshire, South Carolina, and Nevada) could hold them in February. As a result of these rules, there was a traffic jam in early March, with many states scheduling their primaries or caucuses as early as permitted under party rules. On March 1, twelve states held primaries or caucuses for one or both parties. Other states followed closely behind them, and by March 15, about half of the delegates for each national convention had already been selected. The remaining primaries and caucuses were spread out through early June.

Given these schedules, candidates could rely on highly personal appeals ("retail" politics) with small groups of people in the four early states but had to shift sharply to televised ads, social media, and mass rallies ("wholesale" politics) as they campaigned across a dozen states at a time in early March.

Once all delegates have been chosen, they come together in each party's national convention. At the convention, the delegates formally choose the party's candidates for president and vice president and write the party's platform.

**THE NATIONAL CONVENTION** The role of the national convention has changed dramatically over the last 50 years. Before 1972, only a few states relied on presidential primaries or used caucus/convention systems to choose their delegates. Most states' delegations were appointed by the state's party leaders and included mostly hard-boiled political pros. When these delegations got together for bargaining and horse-trading, the conventions were filled with suspense and drama. Often, balloting would run through the night—sometimes even longer. The 1924 Democratic convention, for instance, required 103 ballots over a period of 17 days to produce a nominee.

All of this changed in 1972. As we saw in Chapter 7, the troubled 1968 Democratic convention led to a series of rule changes that caused states to move to primary elections and more open caucuses for their delegate selection. Since 1972, with all but a few delegates chosen through primaries or caucuses, it has almost always been the case that one candidate shows up with enough delegates to win the nomination outright on the first ballot.

Actually, this shift to primaries and caucuses after the 1972 reforms would not have been enough in itself to turn the nominating conventions into foregone conclusions. With many candidates vying for the nomination in dozens of primaries and state conventions, in theory, four or five candidates could each do well in different states, and no one candidate would arrive at the convention with a majority of the delegates. Balloting could still run through the night. The crucial added ingredient, as we have seen, is that the initial primaries in states such as Iowa and New Hampshire winnow the field by concentrating resources and media attention on one or two early winners. The extended wave of contests in other states takes it from there, almost always leaving one clear winner by the eve of the convention.

Thus, no major party convention has opened with any doubt about who was going to be nominated since 1976. Today, conventions are managed affairs, with music and entertainment, videos about the soon-to-be-candidate's life, testimonials from ordinary citizens, funny hats, and anything else that will hold viewers' attention. The expected nominee oversees the writing of the party platform to ensure that the it will be consistent with his or her policy positions. Usually, some minor but heated conflict about the platform takes place, and television

**frontload** To move a state's primary or caucuses to the earliest date that the party's rules will permit.

commentators try to use such disputes to keep viewers interested, though media coverage has declined sharply from the days when conventions received gavel to gavel exposure. The party also helps to stimulate interest about the convention with suspense about the candidate-to-be's choice for a vice presidential running mate—a decision usually made a few days before the convention opens. In effect, though, the convention serves as a weeklong infomercial for the candidate-to-be.

## CANDIDATE SELECTION COMPARED WITH OTHER COUNTRIES

The U.S. system of nominations is more spontaneous and unpredictable than systems in other parts of the world. This can be both good and bad. Political parties in most other democracies are more tightly organized than ours, and they control their nominations carefully, not involving the broad population as much as is done in the United States. This usually means that candidates are nominated by people who have worked with them personally or know them well in other ways. The Labor Party candidate for prime minister in Australia, for instance, is always a member of the House of Representatives, elected by the other Labor members of the House. The current prime minister, Scott Morrison, was chosen to lead the party in 2018 by a vote just of the 98 Liberal members of the House of Representatives. No one else participated in the choice (though, of course, Morrison was first elected to the House by his district). This example is typical of parliamentary systems, which we will look at in Chapter 13; about half of the world's democracies are parliamentary systems.

Note that this selection was made by fellow Liberal members of the House who had worked with Morrison on a daily basis and knew his strengths and weaknesses well. While systems like this have the obvious advantage that those choosing the nominee know what they are doing, it also means that nominees tend to be of a predictable type—

The nominating conventions' organizers look for any way to make the events compelling for television viewers at home, with elaborate video packages and A-list celebrities. This even extends to the delegates, who are encouraged to show their enthusiasm in both attitude and apparel.

experienced, not a maverick in the House of Representatives, able to get along within the organization. That profile sounds good, but perhaps Australians might yearn sometimes for someone a little less predictable.

The looser selection system in the United States provides a wider range of candidates, which can have both disadvantages and advantages. Primary voters, who have little direct knowledge of any of the candidates, may respond to fame, name recognition, or unusual approaches to the issues. In the 2008, 2012, and 2016 elections, serious presidential candidates in the United States included a charismatic lawyer and community organizer who had served part of a term in the Senate (Barack Obama); a lawyer and wife of a former president, who had served as a senator and as secretary of state (Hillary Clinton); a former CEO of Godfather's Pizza and syndicated columnist (Herman Cain); the former governor of Florida and brother and son of two past presidents (Jeb Bush); a neurosurgeon and inspirational speaker (Ben Carson); a real estate developer and television personality (Donald Trump); and several other governors and senators. Although some candidates similar to these have been criticized for lacking experience, the more spontaneous U.S. system has also helped to bring forward unusual talents such as Harry S. Truman, a clothing store owner and senator, and Ronald Reagan, a former actor and governor of California.

As a result of America's unusual system of nominations, American leaders are different from leaders of most other democracies.[11] They have more varied backgrounds than other leaders and are sometimes less experienced, so there is often more change when a new person takes office than is seen in other countries. And America's leaders more often bring unusual backgrounds or perspectives to their office.

## PICTURE YOURSELF · · ·
# As an Engaged Voter

How do you become an engaged voter? First of all, you vote—but the United States, unlike many other countries in the world, requires you also to register in order to vote, and registering might take some effort on your part, depending on where you live. (The one exception to this requirement is North Dakota.) Every state has different rules for this, which you can find on the website of your state's secretary of state. Some states require you to register weeks or maybe a month before the election, while others allow you to register on election day when you show up to vote. Whatever the procedure, you will probably need identification. That could well be true on Election Day as well, even if you have long been registered or even if you have voted before at the same place. And not all kinds of ID may be accepted. In many states, this is not a problem, but some states have made registering and voting difficult in order to make it more likely that some groups, including students, will not vote. Stick with it!

If you are an engaged voter, you will want to help select the nominees that will appear on the ballot. This means voting in the primary election or attending the caucus. You can exercise greater influence by helping choose among the many candidates vying for the nomination and not simply choosing between two candidates that others have preselected for you.

What's needed to make a good choice among candidates? Voters have the burden of finding out on their own what the parties and candidates stand for. Coverage in the media often concentrates on the process—who raised money, who won a debate, who is using attack ads—rather than the substance of each candidate's policies. To be thorough, you need to do a bit of research. You can go to candidates' websites, which often include position papers on issues. Independent websites might prove helpful; http://votesmart.org, for instance, provides a wealth of information.

There are ways you can exert even more influence than only by voting, important as that is. You could work with an organization—a local political party or a campus organization—to help others get registered and vote, for instance. Many of these groups are fueled by young voters. As one example, two young people formed Lancaster Stand Up in the small city of Lancaster, Pennsylvania, shortly after the 2016 election to register new, young voters opposed to President Trump. In its first year, it grew to 800 members. Or, on the Republican side, local chapters of the Young Republicans exist all over the country.[a]

Or you may volunteer for a candidate's campaign. This will probably involve a good deal of grunt work, but you may also get an inside look at what's happening. Depending on the size of the district, you may meet the candidate and the candidate's family (more likely in a small state or a town than in New York or California). You may also learn about some of the strategic decisions taken by the candidate and his or her circle of closest advisers as well as the disappointments of efforts gone awry. And the surge of adrenalin on election night—especially if your candidate wins—is incredible.

The United States is unusual in how complex we make the acts of registering and voting. But the United States is also unusual in how open it is to citizen involvement. Being an engaged voter—doing what a citizen should do—takes some work, and not everyone will do all of the things we have described above, but you can do a lot of them. You are likely to discover that these activities are both gratifying and fun.

### Questions for Reflection

1. What effect do you think the difficulty of voting in the United States has on what sorts of citizens become engaged voters?
2. Who will have more effect on the outcome of an election—someone who only votes in the election or someone who only votes in a primary election?

[a] Dan Levin, "They're Young. They Want Change. And Now They Can Vote," *The New York Times*, August 26, 2018, 13.

## THE GENERAL ELECTION

Presidential campaigns for the general election start when it becomes clear who the Democratic and Republican nominees will be. To get the nomination, the candidates had to engage in highly partisan rhetoric to appeal to the partisans who voted in primaries or attended caucuses. But in the general election, they must typically move more to the political center, where the majority of the votes lie.

The conventions, and then the candidate debates, provide noteworthy points in the campaign that can shift candidates' chances. Though today, conventions do not attract the television audience they had when they were wide-open contests, they still command a large audience. As a result, conventions always provide a favorable bump in the polls for their candidate. Immediately after the 2016 Republican convention, the percentage of likely voters who told pollsters they planned to vote for Trump rose by 4.6 percentage points relative to Hillary Clinton. Clinton got an even better bump from the Democratic convention, raising her standing by 7.5 percentage points.[12]

Debates are major events for the campaign because they allow the candidates to argue their positions and share their platforms with an engaged audience. They usually do not shift campaigns greatly, however, and 2016 was no exception. The first two debates each lifted Clinton by about 1.5 percentage points in the polls, while the third lifted Trump by a fraction of a point. The debates were dramatic, and much commented on, but none of them changed things much.[13]

# CONGRESSIONAL ELECTIONS

Congressional elections determine who will sit in the Senate and the House of Representatives. In presidential election years, the party that wins the presidency usually gains seats in the Senate and House as well, although the president still may face a Congress with one or more of the houses controlled by the opposite party. In midterm elections—conducted two years later, when the president is not on the ballot—congressional races offer the electorate a chance to react to the president's program two years into his or her term in office. Midterm elections almost always result in the president's party losing seats, but they often bring only minor changes in the Congress. Sometimes, however, they can change politics dramatically—as happened in 2018. Republicans lost 40 seats in a Democratic landslide that left President Trump facing a House of Representatives newly controlled by the Democrats.

Congressional elections play out much like presidential elections, with one important difference: Presidential elections are always competitive, with two or more candidates vying in closely fought general election contests. But in congressional races, most incumbents (those who already hold a seat) face easy contests. It is usually so difficult to oust members of Congress when they run for reelection that most are either unopposed or face weak, underfunded opponents who know they have little chance of winning. (See Figure 8.3.)

The basic nomination process for congressional candidates is similar to that for presidents. All states rely on primaries for congressional nominations, but some state parties employ caucuses or conventions to give favored candidates an endorsement before the primary.

One unusual twist in congressional primaries is the so-called **top-two primary**, sometimes called a "jungle primary," which is used in Louisiana's, California's, and Washington State's primaries for congressional and statewide offices and in Nebraska for state legislative seats. In a top-two primary, all candidates are listed on the same primary ballot, and the two candidates with the most votes go on to the general election. One possible outcome of this is that two members of the same party might win the primary and run against each other in the general election. The advantage of the top-two primary is that, unlike a normal primary in which candidates must appeal to their base to win their party's primary, in the top-two primary they must appeal to the whole electorate to be nominated. The hope is that this should produce more moderate candidates, who will be more willing to compromise with the other party. There is a drawback to top-two primaries, however. If one party has only two possible nominees running while the other party has a dozen or so, the many candidates of the one party may split that party's voters among them, allowing the two candidates from the other party to win the primary and go on to the

> **top-two primary** All candidates are listed on the same primary ballot, and the two candidates with the most votes go on to the general election.

FIGURE 8.3

## House Incumbent Success, 2000–2018

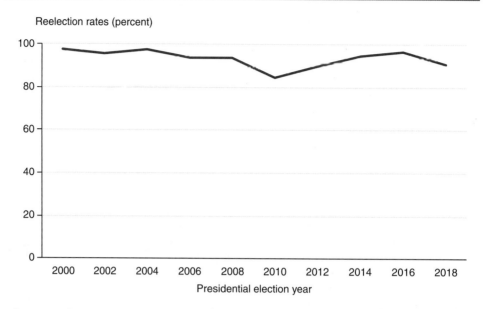

*Why are people so reluctant to challenge an incumbent? Being an incumbent brings real advantages, and the overwhelming majority of House incumbents seeking reelection over the past four decades have been successful.*

Source: Data from Center for Responsive Politics, https://www.opensecrets.org/overview/reelect.php

In 1812, Governor Elbridge Gerry created an ungainly district in northeastern Massachusetts, designed to help an incumbent of his Democratic-Republican party. Elkanah Tisdale drew this cartoon for *The Boston Gazette* depicting the district as a reptilian monster. It looked to some like a salamander, so an editor said, "Let's call it a Gerry-mander." And so the word was born.

general election. This could produce the perverse result, for instance, of a predominantly Republican district being forced to choose one of two Democrats in the general election.

Usually few or no candidates from either party challenge a sitting member of Congress because incumbent members hold many advantages in elections and are difficult to dislodge. Since no one of real substance steps up to challenge the incumbent often, it is unusual to have a real contest. Rising stars in a party do not want to risk an ugly defeat, so a party may consider itself lucky if it has even one serious candidate to run against an incumbent of the other party. In many districts, party leaders have to work hard to convince any promising person to run. In 2018, for instance, of the 387 members of the House of Representatives who ran for reelection, 43 ran unopposed by the other party.

The big exception to this situation occurs when there is an **open seat**, which happens when a sitting member retires, runs for some other office, or dies. When a seat opens up, both parties engage in spirited contests, because they see their best chance. In 2018, there were 70 open House seats (about 16 percent of all seats).

How big an advantage do incumbents enjoy? For many years, incumbents received a bonus of 8 percent or more of the vote in their districts over what candidates of their party should have been expected to get. This advantage has declined over time, however. In 2000, it stood at 6 percentage points, but a good estimate is that in 2018, their advantage was 3 percentage points.[14] This still gives an extra cushion of votes to candidates who had already been good enough to win at their first election, before they became incumbents. The cushion makes them difficult to beat.

## MANIPULATION OF DISTRICT BOUNDARIES

One source of incumbents' advantage, at least for House members, is that their district boundaries are sometimes manipulated to help them gain reelection. This cannot happen for senators, since they are elected from states, whose boundaries are fixed. But every 10 years, after the national census is held, House district boundaries undergo **redistricting**.[15] Some areas lose population and others grow, so district boundaries need to be redrawn in order to keep the geographic size of the districts approximately equal, as required by rulings of the Supreme Court.[16]

State governments are responsible for setting the boundaries of congressional districts. Some states, including California (since 2008), have given bipartisan commissions responsibility for doing this, and there is increasing interest in taking redistricting out of legislators' hands. In 2018, voters in Missouri, Utah, Colorado, Michigan, and Ohio passed measures restricting legislators' ability to draw district lines for partisan advantage. But in most states, governors and state legislatures are still in charge. And as might be expected, district boundaries are often manipulated to benefit powerful individual politicians or a political party. Setting boundaries in this way is called gerrymandering, a term coined when Governor Elbridge Gerry signed a law setting up a distorted district in Massachusetts in 1812 intended to help his own party.

Gerrymandering relies on making your opponents waste votes. It works like this: Suppose you are in a state that is split roughly 50–50 in party allegiance and has four House seats. A fair election would generally result in two seats for each party. If you can control how the boundaries for the four districts are drawn, however, you can construct one district that is made up of places where the opposing party is traditionally strong and can expect to get about 80 percent of the vote. (You may have to pull together some areas that aren't right next to each other, which is why Governor Gerry's "Gerry-mander" stretches out in ungainly ways.) Since you have shoehorned so many of your opponent's supporters into this single vote-heavy district, the rest of the state now has more of your voters than of your opponent's. If you spread these remaining voters evenly across the other three districts, all three should be safe for your party. As a result, your gerrymandering has transformed a state that is evenly divided into one with a 3 to 1 advantage in congressional representation for your party. This process is illustrated in Figure 8.4, where each D stands for 10,000 voters for Party D, each R stands for 10,000 voters for Party R. In Figure 8.4.a, for example, boundaries have been drawn within the square to divide it into four districts with equal populations, but only one representative from Party R.

The redistricting of North Carolina in 2011 is a good example of gerrymandering in action. After Republicans gained control of both the state legislature and the governor's office in 2010, they redrew the boundaries of the state's congressional districts. With the new boundaries, the North Carolina congressional delegation shifted from 7 Democrats and

> **gerrymandering**
> Drawing the boundaries of congressional or legislative districts with the deliberate intent to affect the outcomes of elections.

## FIGURE 8.4

### *How Each Party Could Turn 50 Percent of the Vote Into 75 Percent of Seats*

#### a) A Gerrymander to favor the D's

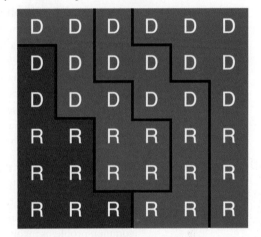

#### b) A Gerrymander to favor the R's

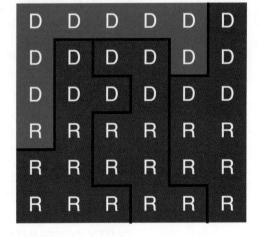

*It would also be possible to create two 65 percent R seats and two 65 percent D seats, thus creating four very safe seats for incumbents. Do you see what you would need to do to accomplish this?*

6 Republicans in 2010 to 4 Democrats and 9 Republicans in 2012, a net gain for the Republicans of 3 seats—even though the Democrats received 51 percent of votes cast in the state in 2012.

A variant of gerrymandering can occur if neither party fully controls the state government. In that case, the two parties sometimes cooperate to rig the boundaries so that the incumbent members of Congress or the legislature from both parties get safe seats. This compromise makes both parties happy because their members are less vulnerable. Only the public loses: An incumbent gerrymander does not distort party strengths the way a party-line gerrymander does, but it does reduce competition by creating a large number of safely Republican and safely Democratic seats.

The United States is one of only a few countries where gerrymandering is common. Malaysia also gerrymanders districts regularly, and the practice existed until a few decades ago in Ireland and France. But most countries that base their elections on districts—the United Kingdom, Australia, and Canada, for instance—use nonpartisan commissions to draw district boundaries.

## INCUMBENTS' OTHER ADVANTAGES

Although gerrymandering contributes to the lack of competition in congressional elections, so do a variety of other advantages that incumbents enjoy after they have first been elected, namely control of the news, staff to support constituents, easier access to campaign contributions, and experience.

**CONTROL OF THE NEWS**  In general, the news media does not follow closely what any individual member of the House of Representatives does. It does not even follow closely what senators do, except for a few with star appeal, such as Elizabeth Warren (D-MA) or Lindsey Graham (R-SC). This leaves members of Congress free to fill the void by providing their own news about what they have been doing, putting all of their activities in a positive light. They send glowing newsletters to their constituents (they receive free postage, called *franking*, for the newsletters). And they send press releases about their activities to newspapers and television stations; since the media generally do not have reporters shadowing a member, the member gets to be his or her own reporter.

**STAFF TO SUPPORT CONSTITUENTS**  Citizens have long been encouraged to "call your member of Congress" when they run into trouble with government procedures. Members maintain skilled staffs to help their constituents make their way through the federal bureaucracy. One member's staff, for instance, reported assisting more than 700 constituents in a year; the most common problems involved Social Security, Medicare, and the Veterans Administration.[17]

**EASIER ACCESS TO CAMPAIGN CONTRIBUTIONS**  Congressional and senatorial campaigns are expensive, and all candidates have to raise money to pay for them. This is easier for incumbents than for challengers, because lobbyists, businesses, and political groups are eager to get access to sitting members and will contribute as a way to get in to talk to a member of Congress. In 2018, for instance, incumbent House members were able to raise an average of $1,865,735 for their campaigns, compared with an average of $439,499 raised by their challengers.[18] (See Figure 8.5.)

**EXPERIENCE**  Not all of the advantages enjoyed by incumbents are bad. Incumbents have gained experience in office, after all, and have learned how to do their jobs. They have mastered policy issues. They have learned a lot about the district they represent. In short, to some extent, their service in Congress has made them better prepared to serve again. This advantage shows up in head-to-head debates with challengers, where the incumbent often seems more articulate and better informed. It is likely that some portion of the 3 percent advantage incumbents enjoy simply consists of true value added.

## PARTY ACCOUNTABILITY

Because of gerrymandering and the special advantages described in the previous section, voters have a difficult time holding individual members accountable for what they do in office. It almost seems to take a well-publicized scandal to make an incumbent vulnerable enough to be ousted. As an alternative to holding individual members accountable, however, voters can

## FIGURE 8.5

## *Campaign Contributions to House Incumbents and Their Challengers*

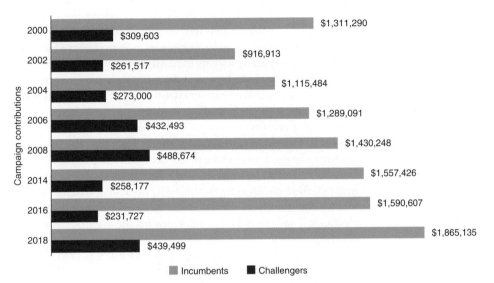

Average contributions to incumbents and those challenging them. Is the gap between incumbents and their challengers narrowing or stable?

Source: opensecrets.org

instead use elections to hold the two parties accountable as governing teams. Since the parties are covered by the news media much more than individual members are, it is easier for voters to assess the parties and hold them accountable than to do this for individual members. This would fit with the idea of responsible party government that we introduced in Chapter 7. To hold parties accountable as teams, voters who do not like the policies that have been passed by a party can punish the party by voting against its candidates at the next election.

Congressional elections in recent years have, in fact, begun to hinge more on support for the two parties than for individual candidates, though it is also true that voters still vote to a significant extent for the individual member, regardless of party. This trend toward voting by party has happened partly because the anomaly of a conservative but Democratic South, which endured from the Civil War into the 1970s, has gradually been replaced by the more natural conservative Republican South. It has also occurred because activists of both parties have become more polarized. Since the parties now offer the voters a clearer choice than they have in the past, voters have responded by using party affiliation as a stronger basis for deciding how they will vote in a given election.

Clear evidence for a closer coupling of incumbents' races to their parties is seen in the decline of split-ticket voting (Figure 8.6), in which people vote for a candidate of one party in one race while simultaneously voting for a candidate of the other party in another race. The percentage of voters voting for a member of Congress of a different party from their presidential choice has declined fairly steadily from 28 percent in 1980 to 15 percent in 2016. Today, the fate of members of Congress is more closely tied to their party than it used to be.

## FIGURE 8.6

## *Percent of Voters Splitting Their Ticket, 1980–2016*

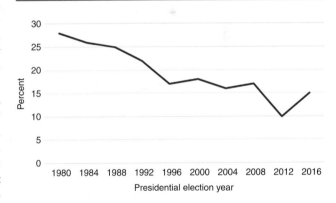

How steady has the decline in split-ticket voting been over this period? Does this indicate anything about the rise in party-based voting?

Source: Data from National Election Studies. ANES Guide to Public Opinion and Voting Behavior.

**accountability** The capacity to impose consequences on officials for their actions, including removal from office.

FIGURE 8.7

## Elections That Change Congress

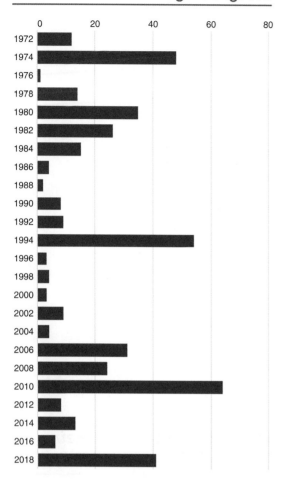

The figure shows the number of seats gained by the winning party at each election to the House of Representatives since 1972. Note the infrequent, large "wave" elections of 1974, 1994, 2010, and 2018.

Source: "Party Divisions of the House of Representatives, 1789 to Present," United States House of Representatives, 2019, https://history.house.gov/Institution/Party-Divisions/Party-Divisions/

Elections that change Congress significantly, such as we might expect to see with party **accountability**, have increased since the 1970s. As shown in Figure 8.7, since 1972, only eight congressional elections led to a net shift of 20 or more seats, but half of these have occurred since 2006. As you will see in Chapter 11, members of Congress now vote more uniformly along party lines than they used to, presenting two clear alternative policy visions to the voters. And, as we would expect, voters are responding by using elections as tools to choose which party will govern. Party accountability is increasing.

So, taken as a whole, how well does our system of congressional elections work to make representatives accountable and responsive to the people, given its mix of a certain amount of sheltered incumbency and a certain amount of party accountability? One way to answer this question is to compare the U.S. system with one where gerrymandering does not take place (because a nonpolitical commission draws district boundaries) and where incumbents do not enjoy many individual advantages. This can provide a baseline of how much we might expect accountability to be a factor in congressional elections. The United Kingdom, which fits these criteria, provides a good comparison.

Even in the United Kingdom, we should still expect to see some districts that are safe for one party or another. Just as in the United States, British people tend to live in areas with others who agree with them politically, so many districts naturally will be heavily Conservative or heavily Labour. But that is the only thing that should give incumbents any safety—members of the United Kingdom's parliament do not have large staffs to help with the press or constituent service, and the amount candidates may spend in a campaign is limited to $44,000, which does not give incumbents much chance to establish an advantage over challengers. Under these circumstances, how much incumbent turnover is there in British elections? The answer: In elections from 2010 to 2017, 13 percent of incumbents who stood for election each year were defeated.[19]

This is much more turnover than is typical in the United States, where an average of only 8 percent of incumbents were defeated at each election from 2010 to 2018—a period comparable to the years we looked at for Britain. This provides a rough estimate that gerrymandering and incumbents' other advantages reduce turnover by a third to a half in the United States.

## ELECTORAL SYSTEMS AND THEIR EFFECTS

**electoral system** A set of rules to determine, based on the outcome of an election, which individuals will hold office.

**single-member-district, plurality (SMDP) system** An electoral system in which the country is divided into districts, each of which elects a single member to the Congress or parliament. The candidate receiving a plurality of votes wins the seat.

An **electoral system** is a set of rules that determine, from the votes cast in an election, which individuals will hold power in the government. We shall look here at the two major types of electoral systems, starting with the system used in the United States.

### THE UNITED STATES: WINNER-TAKE-ALL

The United States uses the **single-member-district, plurality (SMDP) system** for its congressional elections and also for its presidential elections (except for the intervening step of the Electoral College). In an SMDP system, a country is divided into districts, usually with roughly equal populations.[20] Each district elects a single official—a member of Congress, for instance. Parties nominate candidates to run in the district, and the candidate who wins a plurality of the votes—the largest number of votes, though not necessarily a majority—wins the seat. For obvious reasons, SMDP systems are often called "winner-take-all."

For a presidential election, the whole country makes up one big single "district," with the candidate who gets a plurality of the votes usually winning the election. As noted, the Electoral

College complicates this situation, but it only rarely changes the outcome of the election from what the simple SMDP result would be.

The use of the SMDP system has affected politics in the United States profoundly because of one very important side effect: SMDP systems generally help large parties and hurt small ones, and for this reason, they tend to produce two-party systems. It is very difficult for a third party to start up in an SMDP system (see Chapter 7).

To see why SMDP has this effect, think of the challenge congressional elections would represent under our system for a hypothetical small party, the Revolutionary Inaction Party (RIP). With the support (let us say) of about a tenth of the population, spread fairly evenly across the country, it would be difficult for the RIP to win many seats; in fact, the RIP likely would win none at all. In a three-way race, even if the Democratic and Republican candidates were exactly tied, the RIP candidate would have to get over 33 percent of the vote to win, which would be more than three times its national average. An even higher percentage would be necessary if the two major parties were not tied.

In a presidential race, the odds are even starker. At least the RIP might have local pockets of strength in which it could get three, four, or five times its national average and thus win a few congressional districts. But in the national vote for president, winning with 10 percent would be impossible.[21] The RIP would have to get at least 34 percent of the entire national vote, and even that number would work only if the Democratic and Republican candidates split the rest of the vote evenly. In this way, SMDP electoral systems punish small parties and reward large parties. As a result, over time, small parties disappear or are short-lived, and a two-party system emerges and endures.

It is almost certainly true that the United States has a two-party system because we have an SMDP electoral system, including an elected president.

## PROPORTIONAL REPRESENTATION

Many other democracies around the world use a different electoral system—**proportional representation (PR)**. Most European and Latin American countries use PR, as do many other democracies, including Israel, South Africa, and Indonesia. Though there are a number of variants of PR, at its heart, it is simple: Each party registers a ranked list of candidates with a commission prior to the election; the people vote, and the commission calculates the percentage of the vote each party received; the commission then allots to each party that percentage of seats in the parliament, counting down from the top of the ranked list.

For example, there are 435 members of the House of Representatives in the United States. If the United States had a PR system, our hypothetical RIP would submit in advance a list of candidates ranked in order by how much the party wants them to be in Congress. The names at the top of the list would be party leaders, promising young figures would come a bit further down, and willing drudges would appear near the bottom. After the election, if the RIP candidates received 10 percent of the vote, the electoral commission would assign them 10 percent of the House seats (43 or 44, depending on rounding); the commission would count down from the top of the list, and the first 43 or 44 names would become members of the House. The RIP, who got practically no seats under the SMDP system, would get their proportional share under PR.

Since PR systems do not hurt small parties as SMDP does, countries using PR systems tend to have multiple parties involved in their politics. Norway has 9 parties sitting in its parliament; Germany has 6, Israel has 11, and Brazil has 16. As Table 8.1 shows, the great majority of countries with SMDP systems have only two major parties, while very few countries with PR systems are limited to two.[22] The map in Figure 8.8 shows the countries around the world that use winner-take-all systems or PR. A number of countries are marked as neither, because they use a blend of the two.

Given the many diverse interests in American politics, if the United States had PR in its congressional elections and did not have an elected president, we would almost certainly have more than two major parties engaged in our government. At the very least, there would probably be a labor party, a party representing middle-class and business interests, an African American party, a conservative religious party, a farmers' party, and an environmentalist party. Under PR, the nature of American politics would be markedly different.

**proportional representation (PR) electoral system** An electoral system in which seats are allocated to parties in proportion to their shares of the vote.

## TABLE 8.1

## *The Prevalence of Two-Party Systems in SMDP Electoral Systems*

Most countries using proportional representation (PR) have multiparty systems, and most countries using SMDP systems have two-party systems. Of the 71 PR countries in the table, only 9 have two-party systems, while of the 14 SMDP countries, all but 3 have two-party systems.

|  | PR | SMDP |
|---|---|---|
| Two-party systems | 9 | 11 |
| Multiparty systems | 62 | 3 |

*Source: Data from International IDEA Table of Electoral Systems Worldwide (www.idea.int); Election Worldwide Project.*

## FIGURE 8.8

## *Electoral Systems Around the World*

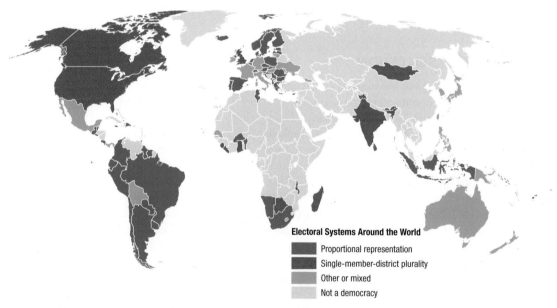

**Electoral Systems Around the World**

- Proportional representation
- Single-member-district plurality
- Other or mixed
- Not a democracy

*Source: International IDEA, Electoral System Design Database, https://www.idea.int/data-tools/question-view/130357*

## THE ELECTORAL COLLEGE AND PRESIDENTIAL ELECTIONS

We have written so far as if Americans simply vote for a presidential candidate, and the candidate with the most votes (a plurality) wins. This is almost true, but the **Electoral College** provides a twist that occasionally changes the outcome from what a simple plurality vote would give. It also modifies candidates' strategies in the campaign. Given how infrequently it actually changes the outcome of an election, the way it modifies candidates' strategies may actually be its most significant effect.

The writers of the Constitution devised the Electoral College because they did not want a direct electoral connection between citizens and the president. They decided instead to base the selection of a president on the states. Each state was to select a group of electors, equal to the number of representatives and senators the state had in Congress. These electors would

**Electoral College** The system by which presidents are elected in the United States. Voters vote for a set of electors, and the set that wins casts its vote for the candidate to which it is pledged.

then meet to cast votes to determine who would be president.

The Constitution did not specify how the electors were to be chosen, and indeed, until 1816, most states' electors were appointed by the states' legislatures. But during the early nineteenth century, with the development of national political parties and the growing popularity of electoral democracy, the system as we see it today took shape. The parties' presidential nominees conduct a national campaign, and each party in each state names a set of electors pledged to vote for its candidate. On Election Day, when you step inside the voting booth and choose your candidate, you are not in fact choosing that candidate directly. Instead, you are choosing the slate of electors that represent him or her. Although you see your candidates' names on the ballot, Candidate A or Candidate B, when you cast your vote, you're choosing the electors on behalf of A or the electors on behalf of B.

In most states, the slate that gets the plurality of votes wins, so in effect, each state is

After the popular vote totals are tallied, the chosen electors gather in each state to cast their votes in the Electoral College. Massachusetts's eleven electors formally voted for Hillary Clinton on December 9, 2016, after which their ballots were delivered to Congress.

"winner-take-all." The two exceptions are Maine and Nebraska, which have decided to choose their electors partly by congressional district and partly statewide, so that it is possible for some of the state's electors to be for one candidate, others for another candidate. (In 2016, for instance, Maine split its electoral votes, with one going to Donald Trump and three to Hillary Clinton; all five of Nebraska's votes went to Trump.) Each state's electors gather in the state capital to cast their votes for president and vice president. Thus, the Electoral College never actually meets as a body but consists of the sum of 51 separate meetings in the states and the District of Columbia.

The use of the Electoral College, rather than a simple majority vote, affects the presidential election in six ways:

- A candidate with the most popular votes will not necessarily win the election.
- Candidates' campaign strategies are affected.
- Citizens living in strongly one-party states are discouraged from voting, and United States citizens living outside the fifty states and the District of Columbia may not participate.
- States with small populations have a slightly exaggerated impact on the outcome.
- Many states do not legally require electors to vote as they had originally pledged to do before the election.

**POPULAR VERSUS ELECTORAL VOTES** The most obvious effect of the Electoral College—and the one that draws people's attention to it—is the possibility that the candidate with the higher total popular vote can lose if the opposing candidate comes out ahead in electoral votes. This outcome is most likely to happen if one candidate's support is concentrated geographically so that the candidate rolls up huge majorities in the relatively small number of states he or she does win. If one of the candidates has won in a number of such states, that candidate might have received more votes in the end than the opposing candidate while still failing to win in enough states to get a plurality of electors in the Electoral College. This scenario has happened in the United States in only four presidential elections—1876, 1888, 2000, and 2016.[23] Even though the situation is uncommon, when it does happen, it feels very wrong to many people.

**STRATEGIC CAMPAIGNING** A second significant impact of the Electoral College, and one that probably matters more year in and year out than the occasional overturning of popular majorities, is its effect on candidates' strategies. Since all states except Maine and Nebraska vote as unitary blocs, with all of a state's electoral votes going to the candidate who wins a plurality in that state, it makes sense for candidates to pay little attention to states where they already know they are very strong (that is, states they will win even if they don't show up often during the campaign—say, Utah for a Republican or Massachusetts for a Democrat) or very weak (where they could show up every day and still never carry the state—Utah for a Democrat or Massachusetts for a Republican). Instead, candidates spend a lot of time and money on closely contested states, and they also focus their campaign messages on those states.

In 2016, only 11 states were considered "not safe" for one party or the other, and so the candidates focused almost solely on those battleground states: Colorado, Florida, Iowa, Michigan, Nevada, New Hampshire, North Carolina, Ohio, Pennsylvania, Virginia, and Wisconsin. In the 2016 campaign, Hillary Clinton held 5 campaign events in Wisconsin and Donald Trump held 9 events there. But Massachusetts, with slightly more electoral votes than Wisconsin, never saw either candidate.[24] Voters in Ohio probably became sick of political ads on TV, while viewers in Utah may have considered them occasional, almost refreshing, breaks in the routine. This discrepancy happens only because the Electoral College system packages voters into states, some of which are worth competing for and some of which are not. If the elections were a straight popular plurality vote, candidates would work as hard for additional votes in Massachusetts or Utah as in Ohio. Any vote, anywhere, would count equally.

**ANTI-PARTICIPATION EFFECTS**  A third effect is that for the many citizens who live in states where the winner is predictable, there is little incentive to participate since the result is virtually known (as we have noted, Republicans in Massachusetts or Democrats in Utah). The winner-take-all system makes it seem as though many citizens' votes do not count. In addition, approximately 4 million US citizens live in territories outside the 50 states and DC. These include Puerto Rico, the American Virgin Islands, American Samoa, and Guam. Only residents of the fifty states and DC help choose presidential electors, although there are provisions for US servicemen and those traveling abroad to cast their ballots from a distance.

**SMALL-POPULATION VERSUS LARGE-POPULATION STATES**  A fourth effect of the Electoral College, less important than the first three, is that states with small populations have a slightly exaggerated impact on the election. House seats are divided proportionally according to a state's population, but each state also gets two senators, no matter what its population is. As a result, for instance, although Colorado has nine times as many people as its neighbor Wyoming, it has only three times as many electoral votes as Wyoming. Wyoming has three electoral votes (based on one House seat plus two senators); Colorado has nine (based on seven House seats plus two senators).

**CASTING PLEDGED VOTES**  A final quirk of the Electoral College is that many states do not have any legal provision requiring electors to vote in the end as they had originally pledged to do before the election. This type of incident is rare and has never changed the outcome of an election. Usually it occurs by accident or is done to make a point. In 2016, however, there were seven faithless electors. In Texas, one elector voted for Ron Paul instead of Donald Trump and another Trump elector voted for John Kasich. In Hawaii, one Clinton elector voted for Bernie Sanders. And in Washington, three Clinton electors voted for Colin Powell while a fourth voted for Faith Spotted Eagle.

**POSITIVE EFFECTS**  There are also several possible advantages to having an Electoral College. The system emphasizes the federal nature of the country, based as it is on states. It also forces a candidate to have a reasonably broad appeal across the different regions of the country, since under the Electoral College, one cannot win with 90 or 100 percent of the vote in one region but little or no support elsewhere. And finally, minorities may benefit from the Electoral College since they are often concentrated in battleground states such as Ohio, Florida, and Pennsylvania.

## PROPOSALS FOR CHANGING THE ELECTORAL COLLEGE

Many changes have been suggested for the Electoral College, mainly because of the possibility that the winner of the popular vote could lose in electoral votes but also, to some extent, because of the Electoral College's exaggeration of the effects of battleground states and its overrepresentation of small states.

The three main proposals are

- replace the Electoral College with a simple popular vote,
- retain the Electoral College structure but have each state allot its electors by congressional district, as is done in Maine and Nebraska, or
- have most or all states pledge to cast their electoral votes for whichever candidate wins the national popular vote, regardless of the winner in their own state.

The first proposal would be hard to accomplish since it would involve a constitutional amendment, which requires the consent of three-fourths of the states, and many small states would be reluctant to give up the minor advantage they enjoy under the current system.

The second proposal would not eliminate the advantage enjoyed by small states, but it would reduce the emphasis on battleground states, since states would not vote as units. And because the outcome would be based on a larger number of smaller units, it would probably make it less likely that the winner of the popular vote could lose the election in the Electoral College. One drawback to this proposal is that electoral votes would be based on congressional districts, which are often gerrymandered. Gerrymandering, which is already a problem in congressional elections, would now be a problem in presidential elections as well; states that were gerrymandered would inflate the electoral votes for the candidate whose party had done the gerrymandering. There have been recent attempts to introduce the method in California, North Carolina, Wisconsin, and Pennsylvania, but all four proposals failed.

The third proposal is intriguing. Without amending the constitution at all, states could achieve the same effect as if the Electoral College had been abolished. The winner of the national popular vote would always get a majority of electoral votes no matter where those votes had been cast. Fourteen states and the District of Columbia representing 189 electoral votes have pledged to take this step if enough other states will adopt a similar rule.[25]

## ELECTIONS AND THE REPRESENTATION OF WOMEN AND MINORITIES

Women and members of minority groups have unique experiences, and if these are not fully represented in the government, officials will be limited in the ways they understand and respond to issues. As shown in Figure 8.9, however, women and minority groups are represented in Congress at less than their proportion in the population. And they are even more underrepresented in the presidency. Until Barack Obama, there had never been a president who was anything other than white and male.

Even with a surge in women members after the 2018 election, only 24 percent of the members of the U.S. House of Representatives are women. Women are underrepresented in almost all democracies. Their average representation in parliaments worldwide is 24 percent; Bolivia and the central African country of Rwanda are the champions of women's representation with 61 percent of the seats in Rwanda's lower house and 53 percent of the seats in Bolivia's lower house held by women.[26]

A country's electoral system affects how easily the country can accomplish more equal representation of women and minorities. In a PR system where each party submits a ranked list of candidates to the electoral commission in advance of the election, it is fairly easy to require that the lists be balanced by gender and ethnicity. By law, for instance, 50 percent of the candidates on party lists in Italy must be women, and 30 percent in Argentina.[27]

FIGURE 8.9

*Representation of Women and Minorities in the House of Representatives*

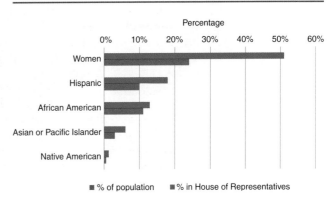

*Which groups are closest to having representation equal to their share of the population? Why do you think that might be so?*
*Source: U.S. Census, 2018 estimates; Grace Panetta and Samantha Lee, "This One Graphic Shows How Much More Diverse the House of Representatives Will Become in January," businessinsider.com, December 16, 2018.*

SMDP systems, such as the one used in the United States, offer fewer ways to encourage female or minority representation. Because only one party nominee can run for office in each district, parties cannot ensure a balanced mix of candidates in any single district. In addition, because the United States uses primary elections, parties have little control over who is nominated in a district, since this decision is up to the primary voters in each district.

A special device has been developed to help ensure minority representation in some House districts. The Supreme Court, which otherwise tries to minimize extreme gerrymandering, has allowed states to create very strange-looking gerrymandered districts in several cases—**majority-minority districts**, in which a majority of the district's voters belong to an ethnic minority. This makes it likely that the district will elect a minority member.[28] Figure 8.10 shows Illinois's 4th Congressional District, which was specially tailored to produce a Hispanic majority.

Majority-minority districts usually succeed in their goal of assuring added minority representation. A good example is the 6th District of South Carolina, which was created in 1992 to ensure an African American representative for parts of Charleston and Columbia. James Clyburn won the seat and has held it ever since, going on to become a member of the Democratic Party leadership in the House of Representatives.

Majority-minority districts have a serious drawback, however. By concentrating minority voters in one district, they make it possible for the party that is less supported by minority voters to do well in a number of other districts. African Americans tend strongly to vote Democratic, for instance, so a majority-minority African American district would do exactly what a Republican gerrymander might aim for—concentrate a large number of Democratic voters in one district. In fact, the 6th District of South Carolina was originally created by a coalition of African American legislators (who wanted to be sure of electing an African American member of Congress) and

> **majority-minority districts** Congressional districts in which a majority of the electorate are of an ethnic minority. Sometimes these are deliberately created through gerrymandering.

## FIGURE 8.10
### *Illinois's 4th Congressional District*

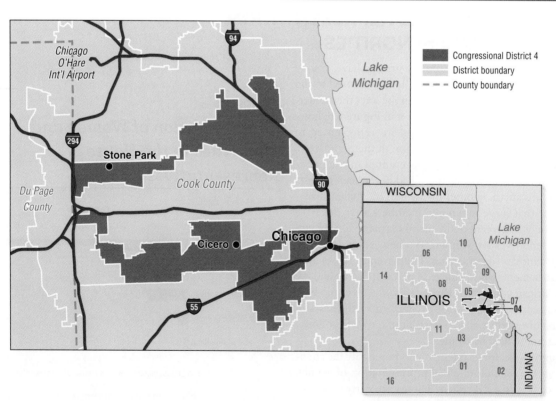

This majority-minority district was constructed to produce a Hispanic majority. Would a member of Congress find it difficult to represent such a strung-out district?

Source: "Illinois' 4th Congressional District," The Encyclopedia of American Politics, accessed July 26, 2019, https://ballotpedia.org/Illinois%27_4th_Congressional_District

Republican legislators (who wanted to gerrymander the district to help Republican candidates in all of the surrounding districts). Creating a special district to help an ethnic minority may end up simultaneously hurting the minority's partisan interests elsewhere.

# CAMPAIGN FINANCE

American political campaigns are expensive affairs. In the United States in 2016, candidates for the presidency, for seats in the Senate and the House of Representatives, and for state and local offices—along with advocacy groups working from outside the candidates' campaigns—spent about $6.5 billion on the campaigns.[29] To truly appreciate how much money this is, consider the amount of money spent during the United Kingdom's 2017 national election, where candidates and parties spent a total of only $52 million on their campaigns.[30]

The United States is not the only country in the world with expensive campaigns. In Japan in 2000, parties reported expenditures of $3.1 billion.[31] But there are only a few countries with campaigns as expensive as those in the United States.

Obviously, nothing is free in this world, and assembling effective campaigns to challenge incumbent officials can require a great deal of time and money. Expensive campaigns have two negative side effects, however. First, officials must spend a great deal of time soliciting contributions. In what has come to be called the "permanent campaign," elected officials have to start calling potential donors for their next campaign almost immediately after they take office. On average, United States senators must collect $9,000 every single day they are in office, including weekends and holidays, to prepare for the next election.[32]

Second, elected officials' need for large amounts of money exposes them to groups such as automobile dealers, trial lawyers, investment bankers, and labor unions who may contribute hundreds of thousands of dollars to their campaigns, hoping to gain influence with them once they are elected.

## THE DILEMMA OF LIMITING CAMPAIGN SPENDING

Numerous efforts have been made to limit the role of money in electoral politics. Attempts to put caps on campaign spending raise a basic dilemma, however, since the First Amendment of the Constitution guarantees freedom of speech, and the Supreme Court has ruled that to limit campaign expenditures is to limit free speech.[33] Accordingly, past laws that attempted to limit the role of money in politics by capping candidates' expenditures have been struck down by the Court. Reformers have sought other ways to accomplish the same goal, but these attempts have never been fully successful. No matter how Congress tries to regulate campaign finance, concerns about free speech have always forced reformers to leave open some avenues for finance and expression, which then become loopholes through which campaigns can draw funds indirectly. Today, there are regulations attempting to limit large contributions to candidates, to require that contributions be reported, and to regulate the format of campaign advertisements. But there is no limit on what candidates or other groups may spend on campaigns.

## REGULATING CAMPAIGN FINANCE FOR PARTIES AND CANDIDATES

Over the years, Congress has passed several laws to regulate campaign finance, most recently the Bipartisan Campaign Reform Act of 2002, better known as the McCain-Feingold Act. As a result of these laws, and modifications made in them by Supreme Court decisions, campaign finance is now regulated in the following ways:

- Compliance and disclosure
- Limits to contributions
- Public financing for presidential candidates
- "Stand by your ad"

**COMPLIANCE AND DISCLOSURE** The Federal Election Commission (FEC) was created in 1974 to oversee compliance with election laws and publish information on candidates' spending. Candidates are required to report to the FEC who contributed to the campaign and how the campaign's funds were spent.

**LIMITS TO CONTRIBUTIONS**  Individuals' contributions to candidates and parties are limited. In 2018, these limits were $2,700 to any candidate, $5,000 to any political action committee, $10,000 to any local party committee, and $33,900 to national party committees.

Groups such as the National Association of Realtors, the Sierra Club, and the Pro-Life Campaign Committee can form **political action committees (PACs)** to gather and coordinate their members' contributions. PACs are special organizations set up by groups to make contributions to candidates. They are allowed to contribute up to $5,000 per candidate. There are now about 4,000 PACs, so they make up a significant part of the political landscape.

**PUBLIC FINANCING FOR PRESIDENTIAL CANDIDATES**  In an attempt to persuade presidential candidates to voluntarily accept limits on their expenditure, the government provides public financing for presidential candidates, both for primary elections and for the general election—but with a significant string attached. Any candidate who accepts the subsidy must also voluntarily agree to a limit on expenditures. In 2016, the limits if a candidate accepted the public funding were approximately $48 million for the primary season and $96 million for the general election.

This subsidy succeeded for a quarter century in limiting candidates' direct spending in presidential elections. But in 2008, Barack Obama became the first presidential candidate ever to refuse the subsidy and limits for the general election campaign. Obama gambled that with his sophisticated Internet operation, he could raise enough in individual contributions to justify turning down the public subsidy. His gamble was spectacularly successful, as he raised $657 million in individual contributions.[34] It may be that the ease of raising money over the Internet is making the carrot of public subsidies less effective as a way to regulate spending. In fact, some have called 2008 the "death knell" of public financing. Since 2008, only minor candidates have accepted public funding during the primary stage, and no major party candidate has accepted public funding for the general election.

**"STAND BY YOUR AD"**  The McCain-Feingold Act added a new provision, presumably to improve the tone of campaigning, that requires candidates to take public responsibility for their advertisements. Every ad in a campaign has to include a statement by the candidate: "I'm Representative Dottard, and I approve this ad."

## INDEPENDENT EXPENDITURES BY OTHERS

All of the provisions we have reviewed here apply to political parties and candidates for office. However, a huge loophole in the regulation of campaign finance arose in the 2004 election in the form of **527 committees** (named after the provision of the tax law that applies to them)—nonprofit political organizations that are formally independent from the parties or any candidate's campaign. Because 527 committees are not formally part of any campaign, they do not fall under the regulation of the FEC. They can even run very nasty television ads attacking a candidate, as long as they are formally set up as issue advocacy ads rather than as campaign ads. An ad might conclude with the line "So, please call Representative Dottard and ask him to stop supporting international terrorism" instead of "So, please vote against Representative Dottard." This makes the 527 committee technically not part of a campaign.

Since they are not subject to the FEC's regulation, 527 committees may accept contributions of any size and do not need to disclose their sources. In the first presidential election under the new rules, "independent" groups spent about one-third of the total amount spent on the campaign that year from all sources.

In 2010, the Supreme Court expanded the possibilities of independent expenditure when they decided the case *Citizens United v. Federal Election Commission*.[35] Citizens United is a nonprofit organization that "seeks to reassert the traditional American values of limited government, freedom of enterprise, strong families, and national sovereignty." It released a film in 2008, *Hillary: The Movie*, which painted a very unflattering portrait of Democratic candidate Hillary Clinton. A lower court ruled that the movie could not be aired on television within 30 days of a primary because the McCain-Feingold Act prohibited all organizations from broadcasting "electioneering communications" close to elections. The Supreme Court decided that this provision of the Act violated the First Amendment and ruled therefore that corporations and unions could not be limited in their funding of independent political broadcasts during elections.

**political action committees (PACs)** Organizations that donate money to political candidates and officeholders.

**527 committees** Advocacy groups that are allowed to advertise on political issues and are not subject to regulation by the Federal Election Commission.

In light of the *Citizens United* decision and a related appeals court decision, the FEC established an additional type of independent campaign organization, the **Super PAC**.[36] A Super PAC may raise unlimited amounts of money from corporations, unions, and individuals. And, unlike 527 committees, Super PACs may spend money on overt attacks or support for candidates. However, they must report their donors' contributions to the FEC, which 527 committees do not need to do. Similar to 527 committees, they may not donate money to candidates, and they may not coordinate their activities with the campaign.[37]

The advent of 527 committees and Super PACs is rapidly changing the political terrain. In 2016, a single Super PAC, Priorities USA Action, a group supporting Hillary Clinton, spent $133 million—and of course, this was only one of the largest among many Super PACs.

Three aspects of Super PACs are especially notable:

Super PACs are typically dominated by wealthy individuals. Sheldon Adelson, the billionaire casino owner, typically gives millions to Republican PACs each election cycle.

- Flexibility. Thanks to their flexibility, Super PACs dominate advertising. In the run-up to **Super Tuesday** in 2012, for instance, Mitt Romney's campaign spent $1.2 million on advertising, while his associated Super PAC, "Restore Our Future," spent $7 million.[38]
- Degree of dependence. Super PACs are usually not truly independent of the candidate's campaign, although the two must stay technically unconnected. In 2012, the Romney national campaign office and the Restore Our Future Super PAC were located in the same suite of offices, and they shared many consultants; many officers of Restore Our Future were former Romney campaign aides.[39]
- Large donors. Since there are no limits on individual contributions, Super PACs are usually dominated by large donors. In 2016, thirty individuals contributed $3 million or more to Democratic candidates and committees, while 43 individuals contributed $3 million or more to Republican candidates and committees. Top donors Thomas Steyer and his wife contributed $91 million to Democrats and liberals, while Sheldon Adelson and his wife contributed $83 million to Republicans and conservatives. Twenty others contributed at least $10 million.[40]

527 committees and Super PACs have at least two probably negative side effects on elections. First, because their contributors tend to be ideological, they often take stances on the far left or far right, increasing the polarization of politics. Second, candidates lose some control over their own campaigns, since the rhetoric of "independent" ads is outside their direct control. The ads may be largely welcome to the campaign, but they also carry a risk of backfiring.

## FOREIGN INTERFERENCE IN CAMPAIGNS AND ELECTIONS

It is illegal for foreign governments to help a political campaign in the United States by contributing cash or anything else of value to the campaign. And it is also illegal for a campaign to accept such help.[41] In the past, violations of these laws have been minor and foreign interference has not been a major factor in campaigns. Today, however, the efficiency of the Internet makes it possible for governments to interfere substantially in campaigns at little cost.

In the 2016 election, Russian intelligence agencies took advantage of these efficiencies to mount an ambitious program of electoral interference. They hacked e-mails and files from Hillary Clinton's campaign and the Democratic National Committee, releasing embarrassing bits in a strategic way that was timed to help Donald Trump's campaign. Using fictional American personas, they made thousands of posts on Facebook and other social media platforms, some to confuse Democratic voters about where and how to vote, some to divert Clinton voters

**Super PAC** An independent campaign organization that may raise unlimited funds and spend them on overt attacks or support for candidates; it may not directly coordinate its strategy with campaigns.

**Super Tuesday** The first Tuesday in a primary season on which parties allow states (except for early contests such as New Hampshire or Iowa) to schedule primaries or caucuses; large numbers of states usually schedule their contests for this day, which makes it "super."

to vote for minor parties, and some to heighten racial tensions and anti-immigrant feelings. They tried unsuccessfully to hack states' systems of voting machines.[42]

It is difficult to defend against such interference by foreign governments. Americans cooperating with foreign interference can be prosecuted, but the governments themselves are outside U.S. law. One possible defense is to make social media responsible for the truth of what is posted on their platforms, but that involves extremely thorny issues of free speech. Facebook is currently trying to find ways to do this that will single out foreign counterfeits, but the problems are obvious. Do any of us really want Facebook to decide whether what we post is worthy of being seen by others?

One precaution that could readily be taken is for states to make their systems of voting more secure, but so far, little has been done in this area. In general, large-scale foreign interference in U.S. elections is such a new phenomenon that the government has not yet developed coherent ways to react to it.

## HOW OTHER COUNTRIES REGULATE CAMPAIGN FINANCE

Many countries regulate campaign finance more strictly than the United States, which may be one reason why our campaigns are as expensive as they are. Almost half of the world's democracies, including Canada, France, Great Britain, India, Japan, and Mexico, put strict limits on what candidates may spend in their campaigns.[43] In the United States, the courts have ruled that such limits violate the First Amendment right of free speech.

As an example of how things are done in one other country, consider Great Britain: The British government puts very few restrictions on how much donors can give to parties or candidates, but limits how much candidates and parties can spend on a campaign and how they spend it. Parties are limited to spending approximately $43,000 for each seat in which they run a candidate, and candidates are limited to spending an additional $44,000 for their race. Paid television and radio advertisements are banned, but the government provides all parties a certain amount of free radio and television time on the national networks. Crucially, independent expenditures by others are also strictly limited. Outside groups are limited to spending approximately $642,000 over the year leading up to an election.[44]

Britain's decision to restrict spending rather than donations allows it to control the cost of elections more efficiently than the United States. And, because it does not allow candidates to spend much on their campaigns, it largely frees them from the distraction of fundraising and from obligations to donors. Of course, the question of whether limitations on spending infringe on free speech remains a serious one to consider.

# CONSEQUENCES FOR DEMOCRACY

Americans exercise a wider range of electoral choices than citizens of many other countries—not only in general elections but also in primary elections. Our campaigns are long, complex, and expensive, involving many offices over a long campaign season. We use an SMDP electoral system to elect members of Congress and an Electoral College to elect presidents. And while citizens exercise limited accountability through elections, especially elections to Congress, the level of accountability for parties appears to be increasing. These ways in which we conduct elections have consequences that go beyond the winners in each race.

First, we can judge elections partly by how well they produce accountability. It is not entirely clear whether America's long and complex campaigns strengthen citizen control or weaken it. On the one hand, voters' participation in the nomination process through primaries or caucuses gives them greater influence than simply voting in elections. But on the other hand, weakening the parties by giving voters this power makes it less easy for parties to operate in a unified way and present themselves as teams for party accountability. We have seen that the key to accountability in congressional elections may be for parties to be accountable as teams. So it may be that providing more voter impact on the choice of individual candidates, at the expense of parties' organizational strength, actually lessens overall accountability.

We can also judge elections by their effect on public policies we care about. Many aspects of our elections—our system of nominating presidents (especially the emphasis on early primaries and caucuses), the SMDP system, and the Electoral College—lead politicians to emphasize the needs of pivotal states or districts and distract them from broader social needs. Just as one example, presidential candidates generally feel a need to support subsidies for corn ethan`ol because of the many corn growers in Iowa, which is a pivotal state for nomination.

Officials can also be distracted from general needs by the huge cost of our elections. The importance of money in our elections makes candidates dependent on large donors, and this often competes with the wishes of the voters as a whole.

All of these aspects of our electoral system—the Electoral College, the SMDP system, the long series of primaries and caucuses, and the importance of campaign funds—lead politicians away from attending to the broader needs of the population, motivating them to focus instead on narrow geographic or economic interests.

Looking at electoral systems, this may be why countries with PR tend to spend more on broad social security, health, and similar policies (by about 8 percent of their gross domestic product) than countries with SMDP systems do. It is important to keep in mind, however, that the direction of causation is not entirely clear on this. It is at least possible that the difference comes about not because PR leads to more social spending, but because countries where social spending is popular (Sweden, for instance) have been more likely to adopt PR in the first place.

Accountability and politicians' focus in making policies provide two very strong reasons why elections matter.

## Critical Thinking Questions

1. Should the Electoral College be changed, and if so, in what way? How would you accomplish the changes you suggest, and what would be their effects?
2. How could American elections be changed to reduce the effect of large campaign contributions on officeholders' decisions? (Remember that any changes must be consistent with the Constitution's guarantees of free speech.)
3. It has been suggested that all states should hold their presidential primaries on the same day rather than

stretching out the nomination process over many months. How would this affect U.S. politics? Consider all of the varied effects of our current system—the nature of campaigning in early states, the effect on campaign costs, and so on.
4. Do you think individual accountability or party accountability is a better way for voters to hold Congress accountable? Why?
5. Are majority-minority districts a good thing for politics? Why or why not?

## Key Terms

accountability, 204
Australian ballot, 191
caucuses, 193
closed primary, 193
527 committee, 212
crossover voting, 193
Electoral College, 206
electoral system, 204
frontload, 196

general election, 192
gerrymandering, 201
majority-minority districts, 210
nomination, 192
open primary, 193
open seat, 200
political action committees (PACs), 212
proportional representation (PR)
    electoral system, 205

redistricting, 201
single-member-district, plurality (SMDP)
    system, 204
Super PAC, 213
Super Tuesday, 213
superdelegates, 193
top-two primary, 199
unpledged delegates, 193

Visit edge.sagepub.com/maltese to help you accomplish your coursework goals in an easy-to-use learning environment.

# 9

# PARTICIPATION, VOTING BEHAVIOR, AND CAMPAIGNS

## After reading this chapter, you should be able to do the following:

- Define the different ways in which citizens can participate in the political process.
- Analyze the dynamics of voter turnout and explore its impact on the party system and political decision making.
- Summarize the key factors that influence people's voting decisions.
- Understand how campaigns influence citizens' choices and examine the strategic decisions campaigns face.
- Evaluate the causes of party polarization and its impact on U.S. politics.

## Perspective: Why Is Voter Turnout Lower in the United States Than in Many Countries?

The day after the 2016 presidential election, Americans celebrated the fact that the 61 percent turnout for the election was one of the highest in 40 years. By contrast, after their 2017 parliamentary election, Norwegians expressed deep concern that their turnout had been only 78 percent, down from their usual levels. Norwegians are used to a higher level of voter turnout than Americans are (see Figure 9.1), and they are not alone in this. In the second half of the twentieth century, more than 100 countries experienced a higher average turnout in elections than did the United States.[1]

Turnout matters. The flip side of the relatively high turnout for the U.S. election in 2016 is that while 61 percent voted, fully 39 percent of Americans who were eligible to vote neglected to do so. And as we will see later in this chapter, that figure has real consequences for U.S. politics.

Figure 9.1 traces voter turnout for the United States and Norway over more than a century. As you can see, the low turnout rate in the United States is not a simple story. From the 1870s to 1900, turnout in the United States was in the 70 to 80 percent range, but then it dropped sharply over the next 20 years, settling in at a range of about 55 to 65 percent. Norway's path was the opposite. Starting from Norway's first election in 1900, turnout grew steadily over about 40 years and settled into a range of 75 to 85 percent.

It is not that Americans are less interested in politics than Norwegians are. In surveys, Americans are a bit more likely than Norwegians to report that politics is important in their lives (55 percent in the United States, 52 percent in Norway).[2] People in the two countries appear to be fairly evenly matched when it comes to political interest.

Instead, the discrepancy in voter turnout between the United States and Norway suggests a more complex story. What caused turnout in the United States to drop as turnout was rising in Norway? Since general interest in politics is comparable in the two countries, we must look to other factors to explain this puzzle. **«**

**FIGURE 9.1**

## *Voter Turnout in the United States and Norway, 1860–2017*

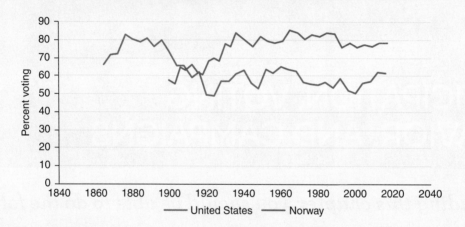

*Sources:* Historical Statistics of the United States, *millennial ed., ed. Susan B. Carter (New York, NY: Cambridge University Press, 2006); US Census, Statistical Abstract of the United States 2012; US Census, biennial "Voting and Registration Reports" for 2012, 2014, 2016, and 2018; International IDEA, Voter Turnout Base, https://www.idea.int;data-tools/data/voiter-turnout; Statistiske Centralbureau (Norway), various annual editions of Statistisches Aarbok for Kongeriket Norge, 1906-1939.*

> **political participation** All of the various actions that citizens can take to influence the government.
>
> **unconventional participation** Behavior that challenges the normal workings of government by disrupting it or by making people uncomfortable.

# POLITICAL PARTICIPATION

Voting is the most basic way citizens participate in democracies, but it is not the only way. We call citizens' varied political actions—all of the various ways that citizens attempt to exert influence on the government—**political participation**. It may be either *unconventional* or *conventional*.

## UNCONVENTIONAL PARTICIPATION

People engage in **unconventional participation** when they seek to publicize a cause through dramatically confrontational behavior, often making other citizens uncomfortable in the process, or by disrupting the normal workings of government. Unconventional participation includes such acts as joining boycotts, attending demonstrations and sit-ins, and occupying government offices. In the twentieth century, Mahatma Gandhi popularized the use of civil disobedience in his campaign to rid India of its colonial rule. Gandhi's movement shamed Britain, advertising to the world India's desire for independence. In the 1960s, Dr. Martin Luther King, Jr., adopted these same techniques as a leader of the civil rights movement in the United States. Citizens resort to unconventional participation for two reasons: because normal democratic participation is closed to them or because they believe unconventional tactics will be more effective than conventional ones.

### UNCONVENTIONAL PARTICIPATION AS A NECESSITY
In many nondemocratic countries, citizens participate unconventionally because such means are the only avenue open to them. For instance, after an earthquake in 2019 in the Sichuan province of China, where there had been widespread fracking for oil, thousands of marchers converged on the main county government building, carrying banners calling for an end to fracking. The government got them to disperse by announcing a suspension of fracking activity.[3]

In one of his signature acts of civil disobedience, Gandhi led a march of tens of thousands of people across hundreds of miles to the sea, where he collected salt in defiance of British law, which required Indians to buy salt from the British and pay a hefty tax. His action inspired millions across the country to follow suit.

In 2011, large demonstrations occurred in many countries across the Mideast and North Africa, as citizens tried to overturn nondemocratic regimes. The demonstrators prevailed in Egypt and Tunisia, but in other countries, they were put down by brutal retaliation.

Sometimes, even in what are nominally democracies, large groups of people are shut off from the workings of the democratic process, and they may then turn to unconventional participation to make their voices heard. In the 1960s in the United States, African Americans were effectively barred from voting throughout most of the South, and the civil rights movement used unconventional participation—boycotts, demonstrations, and sit-ins—to build sympathy and force change.

### UNCONVENTIONAL PARTICIPATION AS A TACTIC
In a democracy such as the United States, even if a group in the population has full access to the normal processes of democratic government, it may decide that it cannot marshal enough influence through those processes to win the change it is seeking. Groups with few financial resources or without an established organization may choose unconventional participation to publicize their cause in a way that does not require either. The demonstrations in the late 1960s against the Vietnam War, which contributed to the United States' withdrawal from that country in 1975, are an example of how unconventional participation can succeed in effecting policy change.

But unconventional participation has limitations. Unless a group can build sympathy by appealing to a basic value such as fairness or equality, it may simply generate a backlash by those who are made uncomfortable by the confrontation. Pro-life groups picketing Planned Parenthood clinics have not appeared to generate broader support for their position, for example. Angry faces berating young women entering the clinics have probably generated more negative backlash than positive responses from the general public.

Unconventional participation is nothing new in the American experience. The famous Boston Tea Party, which helped to initiate the American Revolution, was an exercise in unconventional participation. During that incident, Bostonians threw crates of British tea into the harbor waters to protest favorable treatment for the British East India Company, which was undercutting colonial merchants. In 1863, during the Civil War, protests against the military draft by New Yorkers—mostly poor Irish immigrants—developed into six days of general riots that left more than 100 dead.

Americans have been at least as active in unconventional participation as citizens of other countries. In a study of 55 countries, Americans ranked third in frequency of joining boycotts and ranked near the middle (22nd) in their participation in peaceful demonstrations.[4]

## CONVENTIONAL PARTICIPATION

Most participation in democracies is conventional. **Conventional participation** is routine behavior that occurs within the regularly instituted processes of democracy. People engage in conventional participation by voting in elections, working for a candidate or party, joining an interest group, contributing to a campaign or a political cause, displaying a bumper sticker on their cars, signing a petition, writing a letter to a member of Congress, or pursuing a constitutional case in the courts. Conventional participation is necessary for the proper functioning of a democracy, providing ordinary citizens with a voice in government. Table 9.1 shows how often Americans participated politically in various ways during the 2016 election.[5] Some people simply voted and did not participate in any other way, but many others went beyond that to try other ways of influencing the outcome of the election.

Some of those who pursue conventional participation do so via canvassing: knocking on doors of likely supporters and encouraging them to vote.

Compared with other countries, conventional forms of participation (other than voting) are relatively common in the United States. For instance, in the study of 55 countries that we referred to earlier, Americans ranked third in how often they signed petitions.[6] The big puzzle about Americans is their low voting turnout relative to other countries, given how active they are in other ways. Why do Americans, who established the first modern democracy, choose to exercise their voting rights less frequently than citizens of other countries? What factors affect voting decisions? It is to these issues that we now turn.

## VOTER TURNOUT

Americans vote in smaller numbers than the citizens of many other countries. Political scientists have no single explanation for why voter turnout is low in the United

**conventional participation** Routine behavior that occurs within the formal governmental process of a democracy, such as voting in elections, working for a candidate or party, putting a bumper sticker on your car, or contacting a member of Congress.

TABLE 9.1

## Conventional Participation in the 2016 Election

| Percent of eligible voters who . . . | |
| --- | --- |
| Voted in the 2016 election | 61% |
| Tried to influence votes of others by talking to them | 49% |
| Displayed a button or bumper sticker | 13% |
| Contributed money | 12% |
| Attended a meeting, rally, speech, etc. | 7% |
| Worked for a party or candidate | 3% |

Source: 8. "The ANES Guide to Public Opinion and Electoral Behavior," ANES, 2017, https://electionstudies.org/resources/anes-guide

States, but they believe a variety of factors may play a role. Part of the explanation may be found in the factors that caused voter turnout to drop so sharply in the early twentieth century. But part of the explanation also must be sought in conditions today that affect how likely citizens are to vote.

## THE DECLINE OF VOTER TURNOUT IN THE TWENTIETH CENTURY

The right to vote was progressively extended to almost all adults during the nineteenth and twentieth centuries, but actual voter turnout declined significantly in the early twentieth century. As is often the case with groups that have recently received the right to vote, women did not fully exercise this right immediately after they won it in 1920. As late as the 1950s, women turned out to vote at rates that were about 10 percentage points behind those of men, and it was not until 1984 that women matched men's voting turnout.

This was probably one cause of the general decline of voter turnout in the twentieth century, but that decline was not only a matter of women having been added to the mix. The decline in turnout had actually started well before 1920.

A second partial cause for the general decline was the adoption of a number of devices by Southern states starting in the 1890s to discourage voting—among others, a poll tax that had to be paid in order to vote, primary elections that were restricted to whites, and special barriers to registration such as literacy tests. These devices were put in place to prevent African American citizens from voting, but they also tended to discourage voting by everyone. However, these special policies in the South are not a complete explanation for the general drop in turnout, because the 1890 turnout also dropped outside the South, in states that had not implemented any of these devices to discourage voting. It did not drop as much elsewhere as it did in the South, but clearly, something else was happening at the same time that led to decreased turnout.

Finally, the introduction of the Australian ballot in the late nineteenth century may have played a role. (See Chapter 8 for an explanation of the Australian ballot.) The ballot was now secret, and parties could not oversee how their supporters voted. This may have led them to pay less attention to getting their voters to the polls, thus contributing to the drop in turnout.[7]

All of these were probably part of the cause, but political scientists still have not fully explained the early drop in voting turnout. We also wonder why turnout never recovered fully after its decline, continuing today at levels lower than in the nineteenth century and at levels lower than in many other countries. There are many puzzling aspects of voter turnout today.

For instance, as Figure 9.2 shows, the percentage of the population that is high school and college educated grew steadily after the Second World War, but this increase in education levels had no impact on turnout.[8] We would have expected it to raise turnout, because in general, the more highly educated people are, the more likely they are to vote. (In the 2018 congressional election, 63 percent of college graduates voted, 42 percent of high school graduates did so, and only 20 percent of those with less

FIGURE 9.2

## *Turnout and the Rise of Education*

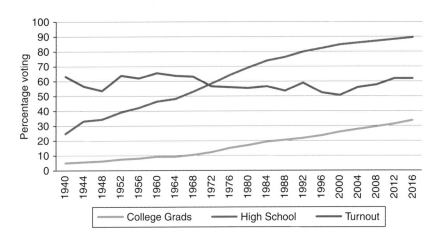

*As Americans became more highly educated, they did not participate at higher levels. How might you explain the fact that participation did not rise with increased education?*

*Source: US Census, "Educational Attainment in the United States 2018," CPS Historical Time Series Tables, https://www.census.gov/data/tables/time-series/demo/educational-attainment/cps-historical-time-series.html; for turnout, same US sources as for Figure 9.1*

than a high school education went to the polls.)[9] This puzzle is only one of many posed by the decline of voter turnout in the twentieth century.

The decline of voter turnout over the early twentieth century helps us to some extent to understand the current level of turnout, but it also leaves us with additional questions. What other factors affect voter turnout today?

## FACTORS AFFECTING TURNOUT

Why don't more people who are eligible to vote do so? Why is turnout lower in the United States than in countries such as Indonesia and Israel, where more than 80 percent of eligible voters go to the polls? What brings people to the polls or encourages them to stay home?

**CONVENIENCE** One obstacle to voting is that it may simply be difficult to do so. As you no doubt realize if you have voted, almost all states in the United States require prior **registration** by voters before they can vote, which is not the case in most countries. In most states, this procedure must have been completed at least a few weeks before the election itself.[10] Thus not one, but two, actions are required to vote. In a study comparing the United States with 20 other democracies, all but a few of the other countries entered citizens automatically on the voting rolls, without requiring any extra action by the individual, in a process known as **automatic registration**. The study estimated that if the United States used automatic registration, it would have raised voting participation by about 14 percentage points.[11] This difference alone would have been enough to close much of the gap between the United States and Norway shown in Figure 9.1. On the other hand, in the nineteenth century, the United States had Norway-like levels of voting turnout without automatic registration. So clearly, other factors must be at work as well.

An additional complication arises in the 35 states that have passed laws either requiring or requesting that voters show a picture ID when they come to the polls. If nothing else, this can slow down the process of voting and can create long lines that deter voters from staying to cast their ballot. And in some states, the form of ID required can also be restrictive. For instance, seven states will accept other forms of picture ID but do not allow the use of student identification cards.[12]

Another, probably more minor, inconvenience for American voters is that Election Day always falls on a Tuesday, which means that many people who work during the day must either vote during their lunch break or before or after work. Most other countries hold their elections on a Sunday or declare Election Day a national holiday so it is more convenient for working people to go to the polls. In recent years, a number of state governments have enacted early voting reforms that minimize the inconvenience of voting on a workday by allowing registered voters to cast their ballots at any time they wish during the weeks leading up to the election or to vote by mail. In 1992, only 7 percent of all votes were cast before Election Day, but this figure increased to 20 percent in 2004 and 34 percent in 2016.[13] The growth of early voting almost surely will help to raise levels of participation.

The complexity of the ballot creates an additional obstacle for American voters to overcome. We saw in Chapter 8 that United States elections are typified by the "long ballot" with many offices open to election. In 2016, for instance, voters in Braxton County, West Virginia, had to choose whom to vote for in each of the following offices: president, member of the United States House of Representatives, governor, secretary of state (of West Virginia), auditor, treasurer, commissioner of agriculture, county clerk, county commissioner, sheriff, prosecuting attorney, assessor, surveyor, circuit clerk, and member of the board of education. In the United Kingdom, by contrast, in a national election, voters face a ballot with only one office: member of the House of Commons. There is no other office elected in the United Kingdom, except for separate town and city elections for mayor and city council. The amount of information American voters must seek out and digest in order to make an educated choice during an election is undoubtedly a further deterrent to turnout.

**registration** A requirement by almost all states that citizens who wish to vote enroll prior to the election.

**automatic registration** Enrollment of voters done by the government automatically, without requiring the individual to take any particular action to be eligible to vote.

**MOTIVATION** Aside from the question of whether voting is easy or difficult to do, people must want to vote in the first place. A famous paradox in political science, the **paradox of voting**, suggests that it should actually make no sense to vote. The argument goes like this: If a person is seeking to accomplish a policy goal by voting in a national election, the probability that his or her single vote will change the outcome of that election is so low as to be effectively zero. In order for the person to change policy by his or her vote, the election would have to be decided by a single vote—but in an election in which 100,000,000 votes are cast, the probability is near zero that the result will be exactly a tie except for that one vote. As psychologist B. F. Skinner once wrote, "The chance that one man's vote will decide the issue in a national election is less than the chance that he will be killed on his way to the polls. We pay no attention to chances of that magnitude in our daily affairs. We should call a man a fool who bought a sweepstakes ticket with similar odds against him."[14] This argument ultimately does not make sense, of course, since if everybody else followed the advice not to vote, the one person left voting would control everything. But it does leave open the reasonable question, why *do* people want to vote?

A few people only get out and vote if they think an election will be close. Studies of voters have fairly consistently shown that those who think an election will be close vote more than other voters by a few percentage points.[15] This is why turnout in presidential elections is usually higher in close "battleground states" than in states that are safely in one candidate's column. In 2016, across the battleground states of Colorado, Florida, Iowa, Michigan, Nevada, New Hampshire, North Carolina, Ohio, Pennsylvania, Virginia, and Wisconsin, 65 percent of eligible citizens voted; in the rest of the states, 57 percent voted.[16] This is not a large difference, however, and some of it is probably due to parties having spent more and made more of an effort in battleground states. The real question is, why do so many people vote even when the election is not close and their vote cannot be the determining one? There must be something else that leads them to vote.

A much more important motivating factor is an individual's sense that voting is part of his or her role and duty as a citizen. It is this sense of civic responsibility that resolves the paradox of voting by suggesting that voters do not vote to benefit themselves as individuals, but because of a sense of obligation as a citizen and a member of the community to participate in elections. People feel fulfilled when they vote, similar to how they feel when they volunteer in their communities. In fact, as we see in Figure 9.3, states that have high levels of volunteering have high voter turnout and vice versa.[17]

Each dot in the figure represents a state of the United States. Its vertical height in the chart indicates the percent of its population voting in the 2018 congressional election, while the dot's distance from the left indicates the percent of its population that volunteered in community organizations in that year.[18] For instance, Kansas, with a volunteer rate of 36.5 percent and voting turnout in the congressional election of 53.6 percent, is located 36.5 units across the graph from left to right, and up 53.6 units from the bottom. Its dot is circled on the graph. Most states whose citizens volunteered at high rates also had a high turnout in the election.

> **paradox of voting** The fact that one person's vote is highly unlikely to change the outcome of an election, so there is no concrete benefit for an individual who chooses to vote.

**FIGURE 9.3**

## Volunteering and Turnout in States

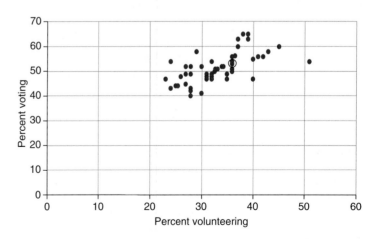

*States (the blue dots in the figure) with high levels of volunteering also have high voter turnout.*

Source: Data from U.S. Census Bureau, (http://www.census.gov/hhes/www/socdemo/voting/publications/p20/2010/tables.htm)

## WHO VOTES?

Different groups in the population are affected differently by the factors that make people more or less likely to vote. In this section, we look specifically at the relationship between voting and age, voting and ethnic identification, and voting and socioeconomic status.

# As A Voter In Israel

Israel has had full electoral democracy since its founding in 1948. Its proportional election system can accommodate small political parties, and it does. In the 2019 election, for example, you could choose among 40 different parties, of which 11 garnered enough votes to win seats in the Knesset (the parliament of Israel). As an Israeli citizen, you probably voted. Israel generally has a high turnout; its turnout was 68 percent in 2019. Turnout among the Arab minority, who have become increasingly discouraged with Israel's government and policies, was much lower at 49 percent.[a]

Because Israel has a proportional representation electoral system, when you walked into the voting booth, you did not vote for a particular candidate. Instead, you simply voted for one of the parties. The more people who voted for a party, the more members that party would have in the Knesset. A party that received ten percent of the vote would be awarded ten percent of the seats in the legislature.

Your choice of which party to vote for was largely determined by security issues and your ethnic group. The dominant issue in Israeli politics is security—how to relate to your country's Arab neighbors. Voters in Israel are so absorbed by questions of whether (and how) to pursue peace initiatives with their neighbors, what to do about Israeli outposts in neighboring Palestinian areas, and how to ensure that their armed forces are strong that economic and social issues tend to play a less important role than they do in other countries.

Beyond that one big issue, politics is also occupied by sparring between different linguistic and ethnic groups within the population. Arabs, who compose 20 percent of Israel's population and who divide themselves further as either Bedouin or Druze Arabs, vote primarily for a few Arab parties. As for the Jewish population, some parties appeal especially to the large population of Russian immigrants and those descended from them, some appeal especially to North African immigrants, and some appeal especially to the older immigrant population from Europe.

Of course, other issues do also play a role. Some parties appeal to strictly religious Jews and others to secular Jews. These groups conflict on social issues such as what public services should operate on the Sabbath. And to some extent economic issues also influence your party choice. In 2019, in particular, much of the campaign centered on allegations of gross corruption by the prime minister Benjamin Netanyahu. But at the end of the day, as usual, the security issue and ethnic divisions dominated the vote in 2019.

More than in most established democracies, the parties remain very fluid, and voting does not appear to be strongly anchored by party identification. For instance, the party that got one of the biggest shares of the vote in the 2019 election was Blue and White, a new centrist party that did not even exist two elections ago.

## Questions to Consider

1. What would it be like to choose among so many different parties, if our electoral system were like Israel's and we had perhaps a dozen significant parties vying for congressional seats?
2. What do you think electoral politics would be like in the United States if our elections were as dominated by security issues as they are in Israel? Since the terrorist attack on September 11, 2001, have elections in the United States had some of this character?

[a] Omar H. Rahman, "Why Did Arab Voter Turnout for Israel's Election Plunge?" Brookings Institution, April 16, 2019. https://www.brookings.edu/blog/order-from-chaos/2019/04/16/why-did-arab-voter-turnout-for-israels-election-plunge/

**AGE** Young voters participate less in American elections than older voters (see Figure 9.4). Voting participation only reaches its full stride when Americans are in their fifties or sixties. After that age, it grows slowly until advanced old age, when it declines because of general frailty and increased difficulty in getting to the polls. Lower participation by younger citizens has been fairly constant over the period in which polling allows us to examine it. In 1948, the youngest group of potential voters was a full 20 percentage points behind the next age group, and similar differences have held in almost every election since then.[19] In almost every democracy in the world, young people participate less than older people. The United States is not alone in this.

A likely explanation for the lower participation of younger people is that they do not appear to engage fully in their role as citizens until they are older. In 2018, different age groups were asked whether they were very much interested in the election campaign.[20] The percent interested increased sharply with age. Only 25 percent of those 18 to 26 years old were interested, but that increased to 37 percent of those 27 to 43 years old, 56 percent of those 44 to 59 years old, and 64 percent of those who were 60 to 75 years old.

**ETHNICITY** Asians, Hispanics, and African Americans do not vote as regularly as non-Hispanic whites (see Figure 9.4). The reasons for this pattern are unclear. Their lower participation may result from the difficulty of voting in minority neighborhoods, lower income levels, or the absence of specific organizations to mobilize them politically. African Americans have the highest turnout of the minority ethnic groups; in the 2008 election, in fact, they turned out to vote at higher levels even than whites, as Barack Obama's candidacy meant that in that election, there was a mobilizing organization with a special appeal to African American voters. Their participation fell back somewhat after Obama left the presidency but remained higher than it had been before 2008.

**FIGURE 9.4**

## Voter Turnout by Age, Ethnicity, and Income, 2018

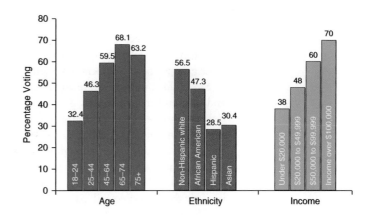

Source: "Voting and Registration in the Election of November 2018," United States Census Bureau, April 2019, https://www.census.gov/data/tables/time-series/demo/voting-and-registration/p20-583.html

**INCOME** People of different income levels also vary markedly in their propensity to vote. The higher an individual's income, the more likely he or she is to vote, as Figure 9.4 indicates. As was true of age and ethnicity, differences such as these have held consistently for as long as they have been measured.

In many countries of the world, there is not as great a difference between how much people of different income levels vote as there is in the United States. As we see in Table 9.2, the differences are much smaller in France, Italy, and India.[21]

In these three countries, there is at least one political party that represents the interests of the poor more explicitly than either party does in the United States, making special efforts to mobilize them and get them to the polls.[22] This shows up in a much lower difference between turnout of the well-off and the poor in these countries than in the United States. Additionally, voting is compulsory in Italy, which further helps to decrease differences in turnout between different groups.[23] These countries show that it is possible to reduce the gap between high- and low-income groups.

**TABLE 9.2**

## Differences in Income and Voting Turnout

|  | Percent Voting of the Poorest 20% of the Population | Percent Voting of the Richest 20% of the Population | Difference |
|---|---|---|---|
| France | 73 | 84 | 11 |
| Italy | 86 | 92 | 6 |
| India | 57 | 47 | − 10 |
| United States | 55 | 83 | 28 |

## WHAT DIFFERENCE DOES IT MAKE WHO VOTES?

One reason nonvoting is a serious problem for democracy is that when different groups participate at different rates, the outcome of the election no longer mirrors the overall population's interests accurately. Although an individual voter is very unlikely to change the outcome of an election, when a *group* of people with shared interests do not vote as much as other groups, the impact of their individual decisions not to vote is multiplied by the size of the group. Group differences in participation can change the election outcome, and as a result, political officials will probably not consider all groups in the population equally when they craft policies. They are more likely to pay attention to those groups whose members vote regularly—those on whom their jobs depend.

Since older, well-off white citizens are more likely to vote than those who are young, poor, and/or members of minority groups, most public officials who wish to be reelected are especially attentive to their needs. It is surely no coincidence that Social Security is one of the hardest programs to change in American politics. In 2018, citizens over 65 made up 27 percent of those who actually voted, though they made up only 22 percent of eligible voters.[24] Similarly, the fact that those with incomes under $20,000 a year in 2018 made up only 4 percent of those who voted, although they were 6 percent of those eligible to vote, probably makes it more unlikely that Congress will pass legislation that helps poor people.

The group differences we have seen here pose a recurring problem for the Democratic Party. Because Democratic supporters tend to be poorer and members of ethnic minorities, in general, they are less likely to vote than supporters of the Republican Party. In the 2016 election, 82 percent of those who said they identified with the Republican Party reported voting, while 80 percent of those who said they identified with the Democratic Party did so.[25] These differences in turnout by their supporters make it harder for Democratic Party candidates to win elections.

## TURNOUT IN CONGRESSIONAL ELECTIONS

Because presidential elections involve longer and more intense campaigns and the single most powerful governmental office in the United States, there is almost always higher turnout for presidential elections than for so-called midterm elections. Presidents are elected every four years, but members of the House of Representatives are elected every two years. Senators serve six-year terms on an overlapping basis, so every two years, one-third of Senate seats are up for election. In between presidential elections, therefore, there is always a midterm election at which voters choose members of the House of Representatives, a third of the senators, and a number of state officials.

Without the greater visibility of presidential candidates on the ballot, turnout drops in midterm elections as compared with presidential elections. Over time, this produces a "sawtooth" pattern in turnout, as shown in Figure 9.5.

Because many presidential-year voters drop out two years later, those who vote in the off-year are different from those who vote in the presidential election. First of all, any groups that are underrepresented among those who vote become even more underrepresented in the less-exciting midterm elections. For instance, those who were under 45 years old made up 38 percent of all voters in 2016 but dropped to 35 percent of all voters in 2018.[26]

Also, voters in the midterm election are less likely to be supporters of the president's party than those who voted in the presidential election. In the 2012 presidential election, for instance, turnout was swollen by voters who were drawn to the winner, Barack Obama. This surge of support for the winner's party is true of any presidential election; with that candidate off the ballot two years later, the president's supporters lose their special motivation to vote and the president's party almost always loses some seats in the off-year election. (We have a less clear case in 2016 because Donald Trump won the Electoral College but actually got fewer votes than Hillary Clinton. See Chapter 8 for more on the Electoral College.)

## VOTING IN REFERENDUMS

Up to this point, we have looked at elections in which voters choose among candidates to decide who should hold office. As we saw in Chapter 7, however, during the Progressive era, a number of states established provisions for citizens to vote directly on policies rather than only elect represen-

**midterm elections**
Elections held two years after a presidential election, in which all members of the House of Representatives and one-third of senators are elected and many states hold elections for governor and other state offices.

## FIGURE 9.5

## *Voter Turnout in Presidential and Midterm Elections*

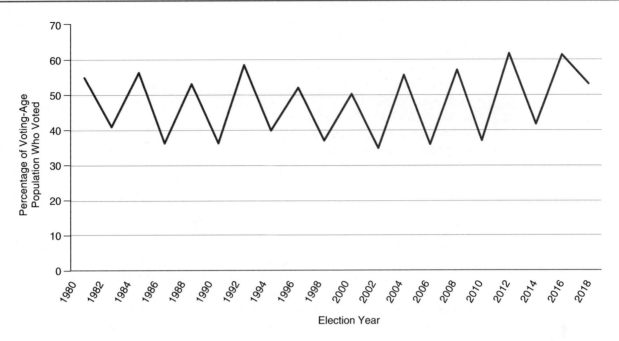

The graph shows turnout in elections since 1980. With such lower turnout in off-year elections, do these elections mean something different from presidential elections?

Sources: Historical Statistics of the United States, *millennial ed., ed. Susan B. Carter (New York, NY: Cambridge University Press, 2006); US Census, Statistical Abstract of the United States 2012; US Census, biennial "Voting and Registration Reports" for 2012, 2014, 2016, and 2018.*

tatives to decide on policy. A **referendum** puts on the ballot a proposed policy or an amendment to the state's constitution. Voters vote "yes" or "no" on whether the proposal should become law. The **initiative** is a related reform. It allows a sufficient number of voters, by petition, to require that a proposal be voted on by the legislature or submitted to voters as a referendum in a future election.

A referendum places a large burden on the voter. As we will see in the next section, most Americans have limited information even about the positions candidates have taken on major issues in well-publicized presidential campaigns. A referendum demands even more effort on the part of the voter. Before each election, for instance, California's secretary of state mails every voter a book listing the various propositions, analyzing them and giving pro and con arguments. How likely is it that voters who have demonstrated an inability to seek out and absorb presidential candidates' positions on issues will study this book well enough to be informed about the propositions they are voting on? In most election years, one or two propositions get a great deal of publicity and are probably well understood by most voters. In 2018, for example, electorates in three states voted on proposals to eliminate gerrymandering, and in seven states, they voted on referendums to legalize either medical or recreational marijuana. But most propositions involve narrow, sometimes technical questions that do not attract a great deal of news coverage or advertising.

Turnout in referendums is surprisingly high, considering the challenge they pose to voters. Of course, the voters are usually in the voting booth anyway to vote for candidates, but most of them also cast votes on all of the propositions on the ballot rather than skipping those questions. In 2018, for instance, the lowest total vote for any proposition on the North Carolina ballot (on a proposition regarding legislative appointments to the Elections Board) was fully 95 percent of those who showed up at the polls.[27]

Most states in the United States use referendums from time to time, but only a few, such as California, make them a regular and prominent procedure for law making. Internationally, only Switzerland and a few other countries use the referendum routinely for law making, but many countries use it occasionally on matters of great importance. In these cases, the question of whether or not voters are informed does not really arise because the issues are so

**referendum** A provision of elections allowing citizens to vote directly on constitutional amendments or changes in law.

**initiative** A procedure by which a sufficient number of voters, by petition, can place a proposition on the ballot to be decided in a referendum.

The United States has no provision for national referendums, unlike the United Kingdom, where citizens voted in 2016 to decide whether to leave the European Union or remain part of the bloc. The "leave" supporters carried the day, but British leaders struggled over the next three years to develop a satisfactory plan for "Brexit."

important and widely publicized that all voters are probably very familiar with them. Spain, for instance, has used the referendum three times: in 1976 to approve the new constitution establishing Spain as a democracy; in 1986 on the question of whether to join the NATO (North Atlantic Treaty Organization) military alliance with the United States; and in 2005 to approve the new constitution for the European Union. And in 2016, the United Kingdom voted in a referendum for "Brexit," a proposal to leave the European Union. The United States has no provision for national referendums, however, so this kind of referendum, on a dramatic national issue, has never happened.

# HOW PEOPLE MAKE VOTING DECISIONS

So far, we have looked at how citizens participate in politics in the United States and what factors affect whether they turn out to vote in elections. But how do they decide whom to vote for when they do vote? This is, after all, the determining event in democratic politics: Citizens control policies and candidates through their use of the vote. Four factors shape voters' decisions when they vote: what they think personally of the candidates, how they view the state of the nation and the economy, the candidates' party, and policy issues. How they evaluate these things, however, is conditioned by their generally rather low level of knowledge about the candidates and issues.

## LOW LEVELS OF INFORMATION

Voters obviously cannot spend their entire lives gathering facts on which to make an intelligent choice, so we would expect them to base their decisions on information that is somewhat limited. However, by any standard, voters in the United States are underinformed—though voters in most other democracies are no better. A study conducted after the 2016 election showed that only 71 percent knew that Republicans controlled the House of Representatives in the run-up to the election.[28] And more importantly for voters choosing between candidates, a study in 2008 showed that although abortion has long been an important issue in American politics, only 52 percent knew that Barack Obama was pro-choice; 10 percent thought he was pro-life, while 38 percent did not know one way or another. Similarly, only 45 percent knew that John McCain, the Republican candidate, was pro-life; 17 percent thought he was pro-choice.[29]

Some voters are well informed, of course, but many are not. As a result, as we will see in the following sections, they must often make their decisions based on limited evidence.

## THE CANDIDATES

Voters look for two main qualities when they choose a candidate for office. First, they consider how well the candidate can perform the job. Second, they seek a candidate who is honest.[30]

Voters judge competence from a candidate's track record when holding other positions and also from how intelligent and well-informed the candidate appears to be in debates and interviews. Before a Republican presidential primary debate in 2011, Governor Rick Perry of Texas had been surging in the polls and looked like a strong contender to win the nomination. But he sunk his chances when in the debate he stated that he would eliminate three departments of the government if he were elected but could only name two. He tried agonizingly to remember the third but concluded with a plaintive "oops." He firmly set in the public's mind that he was not up to the task, and his campaign collapsed.

Honesty is not as easy to assess as performance, except in rare and dramatic instances where officials are caught committing illegal acts, as in the case of Representative William J. Jefferson (D-LA). Jefferson was indicted in 2007 on charges of receiving bribes. Included in the evidence was a film showing him receiving a briefcase containing a $100,000 bribe, along with $90,000 that investigators found in his freezer. The indictment and the scandal led to his defeat in the next election.

Such cases are rare, however, and therefore, voters need to assess a more normal version of honesty: not whether an official is corrupt and will take a bribe, but whether his or her word can be trusted. Such judgments can be difficult to make because there is usually not much evidence to go on, so voters look for indirect indicators of honesty. Designers of attack ads seek out inconsistencies in the candidate's past behavior or statements, which may suggest a lack of integrity to voters.

Other characteristics that can attract voters are a lively speaking style, a voice that carries well on radio and television, and the ability to connect with listeners and to project a feeling of empathy. In 2012, Mitt Romney, who had made a fortune in the private sector before becoming Massachusetts governor, made several gaffes suggesting he was out of touch with ordinary people, including offering in a debate to bet Rick Perry $10,000 in a disagreement about health insurance and telling a group of unemployed workers "I'm unemployed, too."

In presidential elections, although we can point to occasional gaffes such as these, the two candidates are usually quite well matched. The grueling series of primary elections that candidates must survive mean that the eventual nominee almost has to be a superior candidate. How else would he or she have won dozens of primary races? It is precisely because the two candidates are usually evenly matched that small lapses can make a difference.

In races for House or Senate seats, or state and local government positions, the candidates often differ more noticeably in their appeal. One reason that many House members coast to reelection is that it is difficult for the challenging party to find a candidate with broad experience and proven performance to run successfully against the incumbent. Often, a member of Congress is opposed by someone with only a limited background in public service—not enough to demonstrate competence to the voters.

## THE STATE OF THE NATION AND THE ECONOMY

If voters are satisfied with the state of the nation and believe the economy is doing well, they tend to reelect a sitting president or to vote for the nominee of a retiring president's party. Conversely, if they feel things are going badly, they punish the incumbent party by voting against the sitting president or the president's designated successor. The punishment or reward is most dramatic in the presidential race because voters view presidents more than any other elected official as responsible for the overall state of the nation and economy. Nevertheless, voter satisfaction influences their views of all candidates, including those running for state and local offices.

Two especially notable examples of economic voting were the elections of 2008 and 2010. In 2008, an unpopular war in Iraq, a severe economic downturn, and some instances of poor performance by the national government, such as lingering memories of the failure to bring relief to the victims of Hurricane Katrina in 2005, led to a wave of Democratic successes at all levels. Republicans lost the presidential race, 10 percent of their seats in the House of Representatives, and 14 percent of their Senate seats. They lost seats in 33 state legislatures while gaining seats in only eight.

By 2010, the parties' positions had reversed. The Great Recession that started in 2007 had barely ended, and unemployment was still high. Since the Democrats controlled the White House and both houses of Congress, it was now their turn to be punished for bad economic times. They lost 25 percent of their House seats and 10 percent of their Senate seats; in the states, they lost seats in 44 legislatures while gaining seats in only two.

Economic well-being influences voters' choices more than any other issue except war. Political scientist Robert Erikson has estimated that an annual average change of 1 percent in people's disposable income over a president's four years results in an expected change in his party's vote at the next presidential election of 2.8 percentage points, a powerful effect.[31] A compilation of studies found similar effects from economic well-being in the United Kingdom, the Czech Republic, Portugal, Germany, Italy, Spain, Sweden, Taiwan, Venezuela, and a large number of developing countries.[32]

Beyond the state of the economy, changes in any aspect of the quality of people's lives can help or hurt candidates. In fact, political scientists Christopher H. Achen and Larry M. Bartels have shown that voters punish incumbents if bad things happen, even if the government could not have done anything about them.[33] Achen and Bartels have investigated droughts and other such adverse events, including voter reaction to a rash of deadly shark attacks on the southern New Jersey coast in July 1916. In the presidential election that November, support for President Woodrow Wilson, who was running for reelection, dropped by about 3 percentage points in the coastal counties. The president could not have prevented the shark attacks, but he was nonetheless punished at the polls for them.

Voting behavior like this is called **retrospective voting**. Voters look back at the years an official has been in office and vote to reelect the official if their lives and the lives of those around them have gone well over those years. While voters may sometimes be moved by odd issues such as shark attacks, by far the most important retrospective voting occurs when voters respond to national conditions such as wars or the state of the economy.

Retrospective voting helps to overcome one challenge democracies face. In a democracy, voters are supposed to choose candidates whose actions and policies will best meet their needs. But we have seen that many voters are uninformed or wrongly informed about public issues and candidates' specific policy positions. Retrospective voting may allow voters who are not familiar with public policy debates to select candidates who serve them well. They may not know the candidates' economic proposals in detail, but they know how well-off they have been for the past four years. Retrospective voting may allow even the most uninformed citizens to hold their government accountable to some extent, but it is a blunt instrument. Officials may be ousted because of occurrences that were beyond their control, be they shark attacks or a worldwide recession.

## PARTY IDENTIFICATION

As we saw in Chapter 6, many voters develop *party identification*, a sense of belonging to one of the political parties: "I am a Democrat" or "I am a Republican" or for those who are not attached to a party, "I am an independent." Unlike candidate characteristics and the state of the nation, party identification does not vary greatly from election to election. Hence, it has a stabilizing impact on voter choice.

It is true that party identification can change in response to events. Many African Americans changed their identification from Republican ("the party of Lincoln") to Democrat in the 1960s when the Democratic Party pushed through desegregation measures under Presidents Kennedy and Johnson. Identification can also shift by small amounts in response to less monumental events.

Overall, however, party identification tends to be stable. A person who is a Republican at age 30 is likely to be a Republican at age 50. Once people develop an identification with the Democratic or Republican Party, they begin to interpret events and evaluate candidates in a way that is consistent with that identity. For instance, Republicans had generally been suspicious of Russia for many decades leading up to 2016. But after Republican Donald Trump became president and began espousing friendly relations with Russia, support for Russia among Republicans doubled in only four years.[34] Similarly, in December of 2016, after Donald Trump had won the election but before he had been inaugurated as president, 46 percent of Democrats believed the economy was in good or excellent shape, but only 14 percent of Republicans thought that. Once Trump was in the White House, these positions reversed. By March of 2018, 74 percent of Republicans thought the economy was in good or excellent shape, but only 37 percent of Democrats thought that.[35] Voters' party identification strongly colored what they thought was happening in the economy. Party identification is thus self-reinforcing. Attachment to the party leads a voter to adopt attitudes on issues and candidates that in turn further strengthen the voter's attachment to the party.

**retrospective voting** Voting to reelect an official if your life and the lives of those around you have gone well over the years that the person has been in office; if not, voting to oust the official.

FIGURE 9.6

## *Age and Strength of Party Identification*

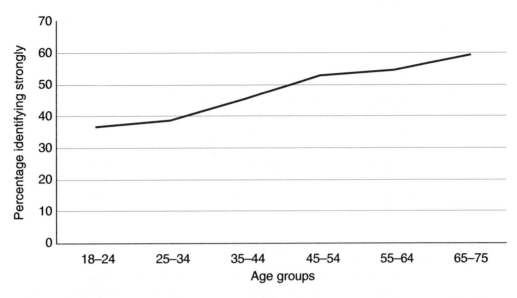

*The graph shows percentages of party identifiers of various ages who identify "strongly." What factors might lead partisans to strengthen their identification as they get older?*

Source: Michael S. Lewis-Beck, William G. Jacoby, Helmut Norpoth, and Herbert F. Weisberg, The American Voter Revisited *(Ann Arbor: University of Michigan Press, 2008), Table 7.6.*

Partly as a result of this process of continual reinforcement, voters generally become stronger partisans as they grow older. We see in Figure 9.6 that as they get older, party identifiers steadily become more likely to describe themselves as identifying "strongly" with the party rather than identifying "weakly" with it.[36]

Party identification strongly determines how people vote. Look at how party identifiers and non-identifiers voted in 2016:

- 9 percent of Democratic identifiers voted for Donald Trump
- 48 percent of independents voted for Donald Trump
- 90 percent of Republican identifiers voted for Donald Trump

The stability of voters' party identifications affects campaign strategies. Consider, for example, that early in the 2016 campaign, media pundits and the nominees' strategists were clearly able to identify "battleground states" such as Ohio and Nevada where the race would be close. They could also predict that other states such as Utah and Massachusetts would vote so one-sidedly for one party or the other that they could be safely ignored. The only reason they could make such predictions about the states was the voters' party identifications. Donald Trump was new to the scene, never having been nominated for any office before, and the state of the nation had changed in important ways since 2012. But because everyone knew that a state whose voters had voted heavily Democratic or Republican in 2012 was likely to vote that way again in 2016, analysts could confidently predict which states would be close in 2016 and which would not.

Party identification adds structure to elections in another way that has profound effects on government. Because Republican identifiers are likely to vote for the Republican candidate for president, for Congress, for governor, and for local offices, the outcome of one race becomes closely tied to the outcomes of the others. As a result, all sorts of officeholders find that they have a stake in the success or failure of other officials from their party. As we saw in Chapter 7, these relationships provide a central party structure that strongly affects how the different parts of the government work with each other.

## POLICY ISSUES

To a lesser extent than candidates' qualifications or party connections, particular policy issues such as lowering or raising taxes, abortion rights, gun control, or health care play some role in voters' decisions. It is true that voters' answers when they were asked about abortion or gun control affected their choices in the election (see Table 9.3).[37] Most who favored abortion or controls on guns voted for a Democratic candidate. Most who opposed abortion or controls on guns voted for a Republican candidate. However, plenty of voters chose a candidate who did not fit with their own preference on these issues.

The issue positions expressed by voters in Table 9.3 may be partly a reflection of their party identification, as voters adopt the issue positions of their party. So, issues probably have less direct effect on voters' choices than the table would suggest. In some ways, the limited impact of issues on voting should not be a great surprise. We have seen that many voters are simply unaware of candidates' positions on issues. Further, one issue may cancel out another one. For instance, what is a voter to do if she favors restricting abortion (a Republican position) but also favors national health care (a Democratic position)? Unavoidably, she will have to vote for a candidate who disagrees with her on one of these two issues.

## WHO VOTES FOR WHOM?

What do all of the factors involved in people's voting choice mean for different groups in the population? We know that because of their historical experiences, some groups have very distinctive party identifications. African Americans overwhelmingly identify themselves as Democrats, and Hispanics are also strongly pulled in that direction.

Also, candidates often have personal attributes that allow them to appeal to specific groups in the population. George W. Bush, a born-again Christian, had a special appeal for born-again Christians in 2000 and 2004. Barack Obama won a larger number of votes from African Americans in 2008 and 2012 than most Democratic candidates would usually have received, while receiving fewer votes than usual from Southern whites.

In 2016, major sources of Trump's victory were whites, older voters, voters with higher incomes, and of course, Republican party identifiers (see Figure 9.7). Two important contributing factors were the gender gap, with 53 percent of men voting for Trump compared with 42 percent of women, and the fact that independents split evenly between Clinton and Trump, with 48 percent for each candidate.

Except for the differences between age groups, which have varied over the years, these group loyalties to the two parties are generally stable across elections. Gender, race, and income have shown the relationship seen in Figure 9.7 for decades. Education, too, had had a constant relationship to vote choice over earlier elections. From the 1980s to 2016, voters who were less educated favored Democrats in every election, and Republican support

TABLE 9.3

## *Issues and Voting in 2018*

### (a) Keep abortion legal

|  | Favored | Opposed |
|---|---|---|
| Percentage Voted for a Democratic Candidate | 69 | 21 |
| Percentage Voted for a Republican Candidate | 30 | 79 |

### (b) Make gun controls stricter

|  | Favored | Opposed |
|---|---|---|
| Percentage Voted for a Democratic Candidate | 76 | 22 |
| Percentage Voted for a Republican Candidate | 22 | 76 |

FIGURE 9.7

## Support for Donald Trump in 2016

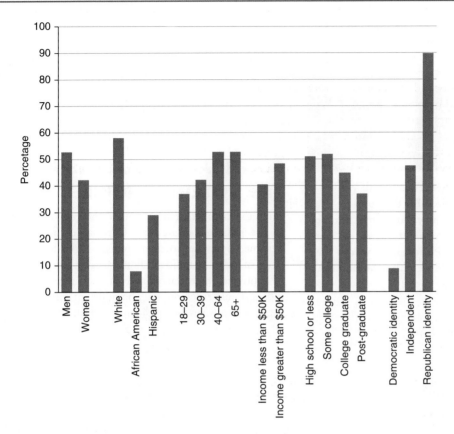

*The bars show the share of each group that voted for the Republican candidate, Donald Trump. Which groups differed most sharply from each other?*

*Source: Exit Polls.*

increased with each higher level of education, except for a flip back toward the Democrats among those with post-graduate degrees. In 2016, however, Donald Trump accomplished the very difficult task of shifting this stable relationship. As we see in Figure 9.7, he turned the relationship around, getting his greatest support from voters without a college degree. Whether this was a fluke of his unusual candidacy or a shift that will prove enduring remains to be seen.

The groups in the population among whom Democratic candidates have done well in recent years are mostly those whose numbers are increasing: racial and ethnic minorities and college-educated whites. The electorate is changing so quickly in this regard that, if these groups had been present among voters in 2016 in the same proportions they were in 2008 (the year that Barack Obama was first elected president), Donald Trump would have done much better than he did. Though Trump received more electoral college votes than Hillary Clinton in 2016, he actually lost the popular vote by several million votes; if the population of voters in 2016 had looked like that in 2008, however, he would have instead *won* the popular vote by some millions of votes.[38] In eight short years, demographic change had transformed the political landscape. That the Democrats' demographic bases of support are all growing poses a potential problem for the Republican Party. Whites with less than a college degree, the mainstay of Republican strength, shrank from 39 percent of voters in 2008 to 34 percent in 2016, and this trend is projected to continue into the future.

Does this situation mean that the Republican Party is doomed? Hardly. The American two-party system has a way of keeping itself competitive. Over the last 150 years, neither the Democratic Party nor the Republican Party has ever received more than two-thirds of

The Asahi Shimbun / Getty Images

Modern campaigns are carefully orchestrated. Joe Biden's campaign kickoff event for the 2020 presidential race was held in Pennsylvania—the state of his birth and a swing state with 20 electoral votes. The campaign selected a location in Philadelphia where the city's picturesque city hall would be visible behind the candidate in photographs.

the two-party vote in a presidential election, and over that period, the longest string of successive wins by one party in presidential elections has been five in a row.[39] Apparently, when one party becomes disadvantaged, either it tries harder or the party that is on top becomes complacent, and the tables turn. If history is a guide, it is likely that the demographic shifts of coming decades will not result in Democratic Party hegemony. But one way or another, the Republican Party will need to increase its support from among minorities and/or college-educated whites.

## POLITICAL CAMPAIGNS AND THE VOTERS' CHOICES

All of the factors that affect voters' choices come together in the **political campaign**. Campaigns are carefully designed by professional strategists, right down to what color of jacket a candidate should wear, what states should be contested or written off, and what social groups the candidate should reach out to. The **political consultant** is an expert who advises the candidate on all such matters. There are about 7,000 professional political consultants in the United States, and they sometimes acquire star power in their own right.[40]

### TECHNOLOGY AND THE TOOLS OF THE CAMPAIGN

The technology available to consultants—and their candidates—has exploded in recent years. Tools available to campaigns include polls, focus groups, television advertisements, free media, websites and social networking sites, and targeted marketing.

**POLLS** Presidential candidates get daily tracking polls to follow every up-tick and down-tick of the campaign so that they can adjust quickly to shifts. (See the discussion of polling and public opinion surveys in Chapter 6.)

**FOCUS GROUPS** A **focus group** is a small group of 10 or 20 people, usually people who are likely to vote, who discuss issues and the candidate in a meeting led and monitored by a professional from the campaign. They may be shown trial advertisements, for instance, to see how they react to them. Or the leader may ask the participants what they like or dislike about the candidates. A focus group offers a nuanced and in-depth look at what voters think, what they are feeling, and what appeals to them.

**TELEVISION ADVERTISEMENTS** These are a basic workhorse for candidates and are also, because they cost so much, one of the great money-soaks of campaigns. Early in campaigns, candidates tend to use feel-good **"introduce" ads**, which attempt to familiarize voters with the candidate, who is often pictured surrounded by children and puppies, or—with sleeves carefully rolled up above the elbow—talking with voters.

Later in the campaign, candidates often spar back and forth with **attack ads** that try to portray their opponent in a bad light. These include more content on issues than the earlier ads, since in attack ads the candidates—and "independent" groups that back them—try to paint their opponents as supporting unpopular issue positions: "Representative Rascal *says* she will not raise your taxes, but she voted 20 times over the last 16 years to raise taxes." Attack ads are unpopular, probably because of the sarcastic tone they often adopt and their use of unfair, unflattering photographs of the opponent. In fact, however, they deal much more with political issues than other advertisements do.[41]

**political campaign** The period during which candidates try to convince voters to support them.

**political consultant** Professional political strategist who advises candidates on broad strategy as well as specific logistics.

**focus group** A small group of people who meet with campaign workers to discuss issues and a candidate.

**"introduce" ads** Upbeat television ads, usually appearing early in a campaign, that are designed to create a positive first impression of a candidate.

**attack ads** Television ads criticizing the opponent, usually in terms of the opponent's positions on issues and his or her record in office.

**FREE MEDIA** Specialized media consultants have developed many ways to get the news media to spread the word about a candidate, saving the candidate precious advertising dollars and possibly also adding credibility to the candidate's message. For instance, if an ad is controversial or clever, the ad itself may become a news story and be broadcast over and over for free, or it may go viral on YouTube. The famous "Swift-boat" ads of the 2004 presidential campaign falsely accusing Democratic presidential candidate John Kerry of lying about his military record were shown more often for free than as paid ads because of the controversy they generated. In 2016, Donald Trump skillfully used his knowledge of television and entertainment to create newsworthy events and rallies that garnered him an estimated $5.6 billion worth of free media.[42]

**WEBSITES AND SOCIAL NETWORKING SITES** All campaigns now build and maintain elaborate websites. A website provides an incredibly efficient way to reach millions of people at once with a political message or fundraising pitch. Barack Obama's 2008 campaign took the use of technology to a new level with a website that was compared favorably to Apple's slick and highly functional site.[43] Websites are an excellent vehicle for raising money. They also may include message boards where supporters can compare notes and encourage one another, a sign-up page to recruit volunteers, daily blogs from campaign staff, and other features. And following those who click on the site automatically gives the campaign a list of possible donors and volunteers.

Social networking has also opened up new ways of reaching out to potential voters for campaigns. As they did with websites, the Obama campaign advanced the use of Facebook and Twitter in elections in 2008, but the Trump campaign in 2016 showed the full possibilities of social media. Trump has 55 million Twitter followers, whom he entertains with frequently outrageous messages. Twitter allows him to reach voters directly, not filtered by the news media.

Focus groups provide in-depth insight into what people think but are necessarily limited to a small group. Here, participants answer questions posed by the moderator while the session is recorded through a one-way mirror.

After Hillary Clinton appeared to nearly collapse after a campaign event in October 2016—her campaign said she had pneumonia—Trump attacked her repeatedly, implying that she wasn't physically up to the job of being president. The ads were covered by the media, including CNN, providing free additional exposure.

The advent of the Internet and multiple forms of social media has significantly altered the way candidates run their campaigns. Because it allows for anonymity, community, and immediacy, the Internet has introduced a new kind of energy and creativity to campaigns. The Internet has changed the overall nature of campaign discussion and expanded the mix of people involved. In addition to the regular media, an informal and mostly amateur universe of political blogs now keeps a running commentary on the campaign. Every statement a candidate makes is immediately fact-checked and analyzed by hundreds of political junkies. Before the days of YouTube, a candidate could misspeak or trip over a chair in Dallas without the incident having any impact beyond Dallas, but now that image will spread over the Internet and land on Facebook walls, in Twitter posts, or in text messages in a matter of seconds.

**TARGETED MARKETING** Since the mid-1990s, businesses have used a technique known as **targeted marketing**. In 2004, Republicans introduced it into politics. The process works like this:

1. Analyze public opinion surveys to compare people's patterns of consumption and voting (research the model of car they own, the magazines they subscribe to, whether they

> **targeted marketing** Using consumer research to divide voters into tiny segments based on a wide variety of indicators so that different messages can be sent to various groups of voters.

have cable TV, and so on and then see if people who, say, subscribe to *The New Yorker* are more likely to vote for Democrats).

2. Gather voluminous, publicly available information about individuals in the electorate—the model of their car, their income, their magazine subscriptions, their street address, and so on.

3. Put the two together to predict how each citizen will vote. In 2008, the Republican Party had such a list, which included almost all households in the United States; with this list, they could identify individually every voter who was likely to support a Republican candidate. By 2012, both parties were using the technique.

Before the advent of targeted marketing, a party that wanted to get its supporters out to vote would target precincts where, because of past election returns, it knew it had a lot of supporters. But this strategy meant that the party would accidentally approach many of its opponents (who lived in neighborhoods that in general supported the party) and would miss many of its supporters (who lived in neighborhoods with lots of its opponents). Targeted marketing allows a party to go into all neighborhoods, even those where its opponents are strong, and target only its supporters in each location. Working from its list of potential supporters, a campaign can contact them to encourage them to vote.

## THE FLOW OF FACTORS IN THE CAMPAIGN

The four factors that affect voters' choices—the candidates, the state of the nation and the economy, voters' party identification, and specific issues—play out somewhat differently over the course of the campaign.

**THE CANDIDATES** Except for well-known incumbents, candidates are often unknown. A predictable rhythm of campaigning derives from that weakness. To raise their profile, candidates tend to start their campaigns with "introduce" ads, so at this stage, issues do not figure prominently in the campaign. Most of the attention that issues do receive comes in lengthy and little-read **position papers** in which candidates detail their positions on various sets of issues. Later in the campaign, attack ads predominate and, therefore, candidates' positions on issues come under more scrutiny.

**STATE OF THE NATION AND THE ECONOMY** The basic context for the campaign is often set by what is going on in the country and economy, potentially posing problems for an incumbent and opportunities for a challenger throughout the campaign. Both candidates are likely to expend some effort in trying to shape or reshape people's impression of how things are going with the economy, but there are limits to what candidates can do to spin the voter's perception of economic conditions.

**PARTY IDENTIFICATION** Similarly, there is not much candidates can do to affect voters' party identification. However, party identification helps to determine campaign strategies. A candidate in a district where most voters identify with the other party is likely to minimize his association with the party. His lawn signs, for instance, may not have any indication of party affiliation: "Representative Piffle—Fighting for You!" His opponent is likely to feature her party affiliation prominently: "Reelect Representative Whiffle to Ensure a Republican Majority!"

The outcome of a campaign often will hinge on the ebb and flow of these factors that shape voter choice, due at least in part to how successful the candidates have been in manipulating them. In 2016, for instance, party identification shaped the election strongly in that both Hillary Clinton and Donald Trump were controversial within their parties, and large numbers in each party felt betrayed by the fact that Clinton or Trump was its nominee. Nonetheless, by the end of the campaign, party identification had exerted its usual strong pull on each party's adherents—about 90 percent of Democratic identifiers voted for Clinton, while about 90 percent of Republicans voted for Trump.

The state of the economy did not play a strong role in 2016. There was not an incumbent president to be attacked or praised for the state of the economy. And even if there had

**position papers** Documents prepared by candidates describing their stances on various issues in detail.

been, the overall effect of the economy was close to neutral. After the disastrous recession of 2007–2008, the economy had been steadily recovering but was not yet something to feel jubilant about.

## ELECTORAL MOBILIZATION VERSUS CHANGING MINDS

We have dealt with two aspects of voting in this chapter—voter turnout (whether potential voters get to the polls at all) and the choices voters make once they are ready to cast their vote. These provide two broad strategies for a campaign: try to change the minds of those who support the other candidate and/or rely on **electoral mobilization** of its own supporters—making sure they actually get out and vote.

Some campaign tools are more useful for one of these strategies than for the other. For instance, television ads and political debates are effective for changing people's minds because an ad or a candidate's arguments in the debate can be persuasive. They are poor devices for mobilizing a candidate's supporters, however, because the entire television audience sees the ad or debate; a candidate's supporters see it and are presumably motivated to vote, but so are the opponent's supporters.

By contrast, targeted marketing is a great tool for mobilization but not a tool for changing minds; its whole point is to focus on a candidate's supporters. Similarly, the Internet allows the campaign to mobilize its supporters by writing, cheaply and instantaneously, to a list of e-mail addresses consisting only of supporters or likely supporters, and Google can allow a candidate's ad to follow a voter from site to site, based on the voter's searches.

Over the years, the relative weight that campaigns have placed on mobilization versus changing voters' minds has changed more than once. Before the 1950s, most elections were determined not by voters shifting from one party to another but by one party being more successful than the other at getting its supporters out to vote. From the 1950s until around 2000, most elections were determined primarily by voters switching their support between one election and the next.[44] But in the last twenty years, the tide seems to have turned, with parties' success at mobilization once again becoming part of a winning strategy.

It is likely that changing technology has had much to do with these changes. The emphasis on changing voters' minds from the 1950s to the 1990s was probably due to the arrival of television, which first began to figure in presidential elections in the 1950s, and to presidential debates, which were first held in 1960. Both of these were better suited to changing minds than to mobilizing supporters. In the 1990s, however, cable television arrived with its more specialized channels, which allowed a party to target particular kinds of voters by airing its ads on particular channels. This, plus the advent of the Internet and, later, targeted marketing, shifted campaign strategy back toward mobilization.

Whatever its cause, the shift to a greater reliance on mobilization in the twenty-first century is significant because these two strategies correspond to differing approaches to politics. When candidates are trying to change voters' minds, they focus on the voters who are in the middle and are uncertain which of the two candidates to support; these are the easiest voters to sway to one side. This means that the candidate must aim for the moderate center of public opinion. However, when the strategy is to get your supporters out to vote, the candidate must excite supporters. This strategy requires a partisan—not a moderate—approach. So, the renewed emphasis on mobilization has probably helped to encourage a more partisan, less centrist form of politics. This may be one contributing factor in the heightened partisan tone of politics that we examine in the next section.

## PARTY POLARIZATION AMONG VOTERS

Starting roughly in the late 1970s, American voters have become increasingly divided by **party polarization**.[45] That is, those who identify with each party have felt more strongly that their party is right and the other is wrong, and those party identifiers have voted increasingly along straight party lines. As you see in Figure 9.8, the average percentage of Democrats or Republicans willing to vote for the other party's presidential candidate has decreased gradually from 19 percent in 1964 to 8.5 percent in 2016.

**electoral mobilization** An election strategy that relies on getting a candidate's supporters to the polls.

**party polarization** Increased feelings among partisans that their party is right and the other is wrong.

## FIGURE 9.8

### Voting for the Other Party

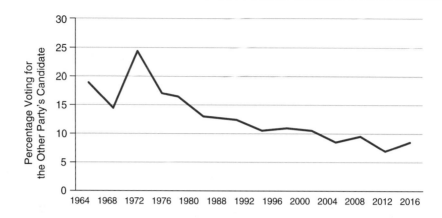

*Fewer voters select the other party's candidate today than in the past. What might be the effect on politics of this decline?*

Source: Data from National Election Studies, Guide to the Public Opinion (http://www.electionstudies.org/nesguide/nesguide.htm).

Democrats and Republicans have also become more ideologically distinct over this period, with Democrats more consistently liberal and Republicans more consistently conservative. Republicans are increasingly likely to describe themselves as conservative and Democrats increasingly unlikely to do so, as shown in Figure 9.9.

Party polarization promotes bad feelings about partisans and candidates of the other side. There has been a dramatic increase in such feelings over the last several decades. In 1960, for instance, a survey showed that 5 percent of Republicans and 4 percent of Democrats would feel displeased if their child married someone from the opposite party. By 2010, partisan prejudice had jumped so that 49 percent of Republicans and 33 percent of Democrats said they would be unhappy if their child married outside their party.[46] In a similar trend, from 1994 to 2016, the percentage of Democrats viewing the Republican Party "very unfavorably" rose steadily from 17 percent to 55 percent, while the percentage of Republicans viewing Democrats very unfavorably rose from 21 percent to 58 percent.[47]

Polarization makes it very difficult for people to take the arguments of the opposing party seriously, and it arouses dangerous levels of contempt and fear of members of the other party. In 2016, nearly half of Republicans thought that Democrats were immoral, dishonest, and lazy, while more than a third of Democrats thought Republicans were immoral, dishonest, and unintelligent.[48] Perhaps most importantly, party polarization makes it very difficult for officials to compromise with each other.

On the other hand, strong partisan feelings do appear to energize the electorate and engage them more in politics. We see in Figure 9.10 a sharp increase from 1976 to 2016 in the percentage of voters who say they care a lot about who wins the presidential election. This increase closely follows the growth of party polarization. The increase in voting turnout that we saw for the United States after 2004 in Figure 9.1 may have resulted partly from the passions aroused by party polarization.

What has caused the increased polarization along party lines in the United States over the last few decades? This is not the first time in American history that voters have been sharply polarized along party lines. From the Civil War until the 1930s, Americans were deeply divided by party. With the exception of occasional distractions such as Teddy Roosevelt's third-party candidacy in the 1912 election, the country was deeply divided into "red" states (most of the Northeast and Midwest) and "blue" states (the South)—even more than it is today. In essence, voters refought the Civil War at every election. The South and several regions within northern states that had been sympathetic to the Confederacy (such as southern Indiana and parts of

## FIGURE 9.9
### *Party and Ideology*

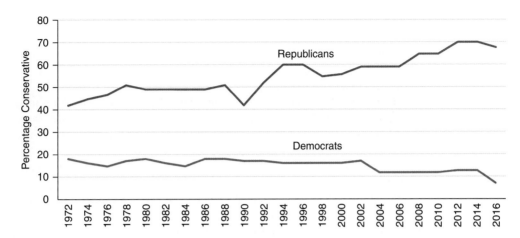

Democrats and Republicans have been drawing away from each other ideologically since 1970. Which party has shifted the most in ideology over this period?

Source: Data from National Election Studies, Guide to the Public Opinion (http://www.electionstudies.org/nesguide/nesguide.htm).

## FIGURE 9.10
### *Increasingly, Voters Care Who Wins*

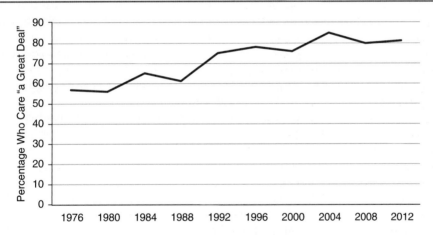

The flip side of polarization is that Americans are more engaged in elections. Is our greater engagement worth the polarization that seems to have caused it?

Source: Data from National Election Studies, Guide to the Public Opinion (http://www.electionstudies.org/nesguide/nesguide.htm).

northeastern Pennsylvania) voted for the Democrats, while the rest of the country mostly voted for the Republicans.

As we saw in Chapter 7, however, this clear geographic division by party was shaken up by Roosevelt's New Deal realignment, which created an uneasy alliance of conservative white segregationist Democrats from the South, liberal northern Democrats, and African Americans—opposed by a basically northern and western Republican Party that was predominantly conservative but itself had a liberal minority. As a result of these alliances, the voters of the two major parties did not line up cleanly on opposite sides of important issues. Conservative southern Democrats actually agreed more with Republicans on issues than with their northern cousins, but they remained Democrats. And liberal Republicans often found that they shared many interests with Democrats, although they belonged to opposing parties. Consequently, the hostility between the parties diminished.

Party differences remained muted until the 1960s. When the Democratic Party began to advocate racial desegregation in the South, white Southerners began to move in large numbers from the Democratic to the Republican Party. At the same time, as conservatives began to dominate the Republican Party, many liberal northern Republicans left their party. These shifts, which eliminated much of the ideological overlap between the parties, sharpened party polarization.

In addition to the reduction in ideological overlap, new patterns of residential migration seem also to have reinforced party polarization over the last several decades. Increasingly, when Americans move, they relocate to communities where people share their lifestyle and their broad beliefs about politics and society. Hip young people move to Seattle or to Cambridge, Massachusetts. Well-off retirees move to golf resorts. Others move to communities where they will find people who share their religious beliefs.

Communities have always been politically distinctive, but it appears that the increasing mobility of Americans has resulted in a population that is increasingly segregated in terms of values. In the very close presidential race in 1976, for instance, only 27 percent of Americans lived in "landslide" counties that Jimmy Carter either won or lost by more than 20 percentage points. But by 2000, in a similarly close presidential election, 43 percent lived in landslide counties.[49] In 2016, 78 percent lived in landslide counties.[50]

To some extent, then, the rise of party polarization in recent decades is a return to a state of affairs that was interrupted for 60 years or so by the unstable, moderating coalitions that followed the New Deal. But the recent sharp increases in animosity, especially those seen since the 2016 election, surely go beyond what we would expect merely from people sorting themselves by party. It is true that voters live in more homogeneous geographical areas, but the growth of social media and partisan news sources on television and the Internet has also made it possible for voters to live in homogeneous *informational* environments, where they choose to hear only from those who reinforce their own ideas. This adds further to polarization.

The growth of negative advertising over the last few decades, including negative advertising from foreign actors such as Russia, has also heightened polarization. It has been found, for instance, that states in which large numbers of negative ads are run in a campaign exhibit greater polarization than those with fewer negative ads.[51]

One final contributing factor to polarization is probably the worldwide economic decline that started with the Great Recession of 2008. Voters who are distressed economically are probably on edge about all other aspects of their lives, including politics. One reason for thinking that the economic decline helped to intensify polarization in the United States is that political polarization has increased since 2008 in most countries of the world. Many countries, such as India, Venezuela, Italy, and France, have seen the rise of aggressively right-wing or left-wing parties that appeal to people's economic unease. An important difference between polarization in the United States and polarization in these countries is that, probably due to our two-party system, polarization in the United States results in a deeper division between the two parties, with hostility and distrust that did not exist before. Polarization in countries with multiparty systems results instead in the emergence of a greater range of parties, with more extreme ideologies.

## CONSEQUENCES FOR DEMOCRACY

Elections are essential in order to hold officials accountable for their actions, so how voters exercise their right to vote is a critical part of democracy. Voting certainly maintains much accountability in the United States. Officials are far more accountable to the citizenry than is the case, for instance, in an authoritarian non-democracy such as Saudi Arabia. Still, there are flaws in Americans' voting that weaken accountability.

First, participation in voting is skewed toward those who are better off. As we saw in Chapter 7, government policies tend to follow the preferences of those who are well-off more than they do those of the poor. One likely reason for this is that, as we have seen in this chapter, those who are not well-off turn out to vote at lower rates than those who are well-off. And politicians are

Cable television allowed for the proliferation of channels, including news channels tailored to viewers' political preferences. Democrats can now choose to watch exclusively left-leaning news programs, such as the one hosted by Rachel Maddow on MSNBC, and Republicans can tune in to Tucker Carlson on Fox News.

naturally likely to listen more attentively to those who vote. One reason for lower participation among the poor may be that there is not a party in the United States that distinctly serves the interests of the poor and tries to mobilize them for elections. Another explanation, however, is that all of the difficulties of voting that explain low turnout in general have an even greater effect on the poor. Complex elections that force the voter to gather information about many candidates are especially difficult for those with less education. And inconvenient elections, with requirements for prior registration and voting on a workday, are more difficult for those working two jobs than for those who are retired or working one job. Simply eliminating separate registration might do away with a large part of the difference in turnout between the poor and the well-off.

Another flaw in Americans' voting is that many American voters pay little attention to politics and have little information on which to base their choice among candidates. This is of course true in almost all democracies but is nonetheless a problem for American democracy. Retrospective voting, as we have seen, is a blunt tool that offers only a weak substitute for well-informed voting.

A third problem with voting in the United States is the cynical view of many voters that all politicians are untrustworthy and/or incompetent. Voters are often drawn to a candidate who has never held office before and therefore has no past record of actions to be attacked. In no other job search would "no experience" be a strong plus, but that is how many voters approach selecting presidents, members of Congress, and other officials.

Voters' party identification, which usually leads them to vote for their party's nominee, has the potential to offer a stabilizing influence to counter at least the second and third of these problems. If parties can vet candidates through the nominating process, then voters' low levels of information and their tendency to turn to fresh faces whether or not they are qualified can be mitigated by the fact that all candidates are first preselected for quality. This has often worked well in American elections, but unfortunately, as we saw in Chapter 7, American parties are weak and are not able to strongly control the selection of their own candidates. It is possible for a flashy but poorly qualified candidate to short-circuit the process.

The truth is, there is no perfect system for selecting officials. American democracy is not an exception to this universal truth.

# Critical Thinking Questions

1. What roles do conventional participation and unconventional participation play in a democratic society?

2. A number of countries make voting mandatory. For instance, a number of years ago, Australia made nonvoting a misdemeanor, issuing a ticket comparable to that for a traffic violation for failing to vote. Generally, mandatory voting increases turnout sharply—in Australia, turnout rose immediately from under 60 percent to 91 percent. Would mandatory voting be a good solution for the low turnout in American elections? What would be its possible drawbacks?

3. How does party polarization benefit and harm American politics?

4. Does retrospective voting provide a good corrective to the problem of ill-informed voters? Explain your answer.

# Key Terms

attack ads, 234
automatic registration, 222
conventional participation, 220
electoral mobilization, 237
focus group, 234
initiative, 227
"introduce" ads, 234

midterm elections, 226
paradox of voting, 223
party polarization, 237
political campaign, 234
political consultant, 234
political participation, 218
position papers, 236

referendum, 227
registration, 222
retrospective voting, 230
targeted marketing, 235
unconventional
    participation, 218

Visit edge.sagepub.com/maltese to help you accomplish your coursework goals in an easy-to-use learning environment.

Mark Wilson / Getty Images

# 10
# MEDIA AND POLITICS

## After reading this chapter, you should be able to do the following:

- Discuss the role and responsibility of the media in a democratic system.

- Examine new advances in media dissemination and explore their influence on the democratic process in the United States.

- Explain why the federal government has more power to regulate broadcast media than print media.

- Analyze the relationship between the government and media reporters.

- Assess the way the media reports the news and consider how such reporting can lead to certain types of media bias and formulaic news coverage.

## Perspective: How Have the Internet and Social Media Affected Politics?

Mohamed Bouazizi, similar to many people in Tunisia, could not find a job. He was 26 years old and had a university degree in computer science, but he was a victim of his country's soaring unemployment. In desperation, he began to sell fruit from a cart in his rural hometown of Sidi Bouzid to support himself and his family. However, he did so without a license, and on December 17, 2010, a government official ordered him to stop. She confiscated the scale he used to weigh his fruit, an expensive item for him. This had happened before, and he knew he would have to pay a bribe to get his scale back. He complained, but the official merely slapped him in the face. When Bouazizi went to the government office to retrieve his scale, officials would not let him in. Outraged, Bouazizi doused himself with gasoline in the middle of the street outside the government office. Shouting, "How do you expect me to make a living?" he lit himself on fire. He initially survived, but finally died on January 4, 2011.[1] This extraordinary act of defiance sparked a revolution in Tunisia that soon spread to other countries in the Middle East.

Not long before Bouazizi's defiant act, Tunisia's state-controlled media could have suppressed news coverage of it. But word of his act spread among Tunisian citizens by way of Twitter and other social media. The news led to a mass uprising that was, in turn, publicized on blogs, social networking sites, and YouTube. With his security forces unable to put down the uprising, the authoritarian President Zine El Abidine Ben Ali fled the country. The result was dubbed a "Twitter Revolution." Pundits had similarly dubbed earlier uprisings in Iran and Moldavia as *Twitter revolts*, and unrest in Tunisia soon spread to Egypt and beyond, with transformative results.

In the United States, the Internet and social media have helped to fuel different kinds of revolutions: from the Tea Party movement that began in 2009 to the more recent #MeToo and #BlackLivesMatter movements. All three brought together like-minded individuals to promote events and sponsor protests. None of the three had a single leader; instead, their grassroots activists used social media to organize, mobilize, and promote their message to others. Millions of Americans took notice and joined all three movements with great fervor. Just as the Tea Party movement led to political victories in the 2010 midterm elections, the #MeToo movement contributed to the mobilization of women that produced many female candidates and winners in the 2018 midterm elections.

Throughout the world, social media is influencing politics and altering the way news is consumed and reported. Mainstream media is no longer the sole, or even the primary, source of news access and delivery. Smartphones allow anyone to become a news producer and to share photos and videos with an increasingly global audience. **«**

News of the self-immolation of Mohamed Bouazizi spread across Tunisia via social media and led to widespread protests and the ousting of the president in January 2011.

# THE FUNCTIONS OF THE MEDIA

Throughout history, the media has played a central role in providing information to the people. Elements of the **mass media**—the wide array of organizations and outlets that collect and distribute that information—has changed considerably over time, but its basic functions have remained largely the same. These functions include reporting and interpreting the news, helping to set the public agenda, serving as agents of socialization, providing a public forum, and of course, providing entertainment. In this section, we analyze these functions to assess the significant impact of the mass media on our political system.

## REPORTING AND INTERPRETING THE NEWS

An informed citizenry is an essential part of democracy: Voting, taking stances on issues of public policy, and ensuring governmental accountability all depend upon it. As a result, one of the

**mass media** The wide array of organizations and outlets that collect and distribute information to the people.

most important functions of the media is to convey information, *to report the news*. Media outlets from local newspapers to network news broadcasts and political blogs provide vital information on public policy and government performance that citizens in a democracy need. Reporters evaluate how the government responds to natural disasters and notify the public of legislative initiatives. They inform their audience of crime and poverty rates, of the environmental and economic consequences of new industries in local areas, and of the deeds and misdeeds of public officials. In a democracy, we use all of this information to guide our decisions as we participate in public affairs—whether through posting a comment about an article, sharing the article on social media, or casting a vote based on the information it contains.

## HELPING TO SET THE PUBLIC AGENDA

The media confronts important decisions when reporting the news. First, it must decide what, exactly, constitutes "news." Much more happens every day than we learn about through the news. Reporters must decide which events and issues to cover. This decision about what to cover and what not to cover is known as filtering. As we shall see later, factors ranging from the routines of reporters to profit motives influence such decisions.

Deciding *what* to cover is only the first step. Next, reporters must decide *how to interpret* what they report. The way that the media interprets a story—how they present it—is often referred to as framing. News stories provide us with a window on reality, but what we see depends upon on how the window is framed. *Framing* involves choosing certain organizing themes that highlight particular aspects of a story at the expense of others. That frame, intentional or not, promotes a particular perspective.[2]

By choosing what to report and how to report it, the media play an important role in setting the public agenda. Coverage of a particular issue may, for example, influence whether or not legislation is enacted and how public figures react to particular issues. For example, articles by Samuel Hopkins Adams were published in *Collier's Weekly* in 1905, highlighting the false claims of and dangers posed by "patent medicines" (liniments, tonics, and pills peddled to consumers as a cure for everything from venereal disease to cancer), creating a public furor that led Congress to pass the Pure Food and Drug Act in 1906. More recently, on *The Daily Show*, Jon Stewart urged Congress to enact a victim compensation fund for first responders to the September 11, 2001, terrorist attacks; his advocacy raised public awareness of the issue and has been credited as an important factor that convinced Congress to create such a fund in December 2010, made permanent in 2019.[3]

For many years, a Gallup poll has asked, "What is the most important issue facing the country?" Studies suggest that on some issues, such as crime, the level of concern expressed by respondents has more to do with the amount of media coverage the issue has received than with objective standards such as the crime rate.[4] It goes without saying that the public will not consider an issue to be important if they have never heard about it.

The way the media frames a story can also have long-term implications. In the 1980s, for example, the media brought American attention to the famine in Ethiopia, but an international media watchdog group criticized that coverage: It noted that international media first ignored the famine; then, when they focused attention on it, they promoted short-term humanitarian relief rather than publicizing structural solutions that might have prevented another famine from occurring in the future.[5] Media attention prompted Michael Jackson and Lionel Richie to write the song "We Are the World." Together with fellow musicians (including a legendary appearance by Freddie Mercury and the band Queen), they raised more than $150 million through a globally televised Live Aid concert in 1985 to benefit victims of the famine, but the absence of structural reform has made Ethiopia increasingly dependent on food aid from other countries.[6] Thus, the media helped to set the agenda by publicizing the situation in Ethiopia, but its decision to frame the famine as a humanitarian relief story rather than a structural reform story meant that the activism of the 1980s did not prevent the recurrence of famine, which erupted again in Ethiopia in 1999.

## SERVING AS AGENTS OF SOCIALIZATION

The media serves as important agents of political socialization. As discussed in Chapter 6, *socialization* refers to the process by which people form beliefs: the shaping of norms, customs,

filtering The process by which the media decides what constitutes "news"— what to cover and what not to cover.

framing The way the media interprets or presents the news that it has decided to cover.

The series of Live Aid concerts in 1985 raised more than $150 million for famine relief in Ethiopia. The concerts drew massive public attention to the immediate crisis of the famine but largely ignored the underlying issues at its root.

values, traditions, and social roles. The media socializes audiences not only through news reporting but also through entertainment programming. Thus, television dramas and comedy shows teach viewers about the values and standards that Americans apply to life, about the roles played by various groups in society (such as minorities, immigrants, women, and the lesbian, gay, bisexual, and transgender [LGBT] community), and about government institutions (such as the criminal justice system). Even sporting events reinforce political values: competition (a hallmark of our capitalist system), the importance of rules, the regulation of behavior by authorities such as referees and umpires, and—through international events such as the Olympics—nationalism. Studies have suggested that young people who watch sports on television have higher levels of national loyalty and are more likely than their peers to view authority figures as legitimate.[7]

## SERVING AS A PUBLIC FORUM

The media provides an opportunity for the exchange of views on political issues. Candidates and public figures use the media to publicize their differing views on public policy and to promote their agendas. The media has long given citizens an opportunity to express their views through letters to the editor in newspapers and call-in shows on radio and television. The rise of the Internet and social media has exponentially increased such opportunities. Blogs, YouTube, Facebook, Twitter, and other social media make it possible for anyone to share his or her views. As a result, the line between news consumer and news producer has blurred.

This democratization of the news is both good and bad. On the positive side, the amount of information available to us from many different points of view has vastly increased. But this availability has undermined the **gatekeeping** role that mainstream media used to play. Professional reporters are supposed to vet the information they write, verifying facts and sources before publication. As gatekeepers, they are expected to avoid publishing rumors and outright falsehoods. Now that anyone can post a story, those safeguards have been undermined, as was vividly illustrated by the efforts of Russia's Internet Research Agency (IRA) to disrupt the 2016 presidential election through activity on Facebook, YouTube, Twitter, and other forms of social media. According to the report on the investigation into Russian interference in the 2016 presidential election by special counsel Robert Mueller, Facebook "identified 470 IRA-controlled Facebook accounts that collectively made 80,000 posts between January 2015 and August 2017. Facebook estimated the IRA reached as many as 126 million people through its Facebook accounts."[8] There were also over 3,800 Twitter accounts controlled by the Russians that, according to Twitter, posted almost 176,000 tweets in the ten weeks leading up to the 2016 election.[9] Many people considered these and other fly-by-night blogs and social media posts to have the same legitimacy as *The Wall Street Journal* or *The New York Times*.

In addition to using technology to express one's views, smartphones have allowed individuals to provide coverage of breaking news. Thus, even when the mainstream media are not present, officials now run the risk of having any action or statement recorded and uploaded for worldwide consumption. Professional "trackers" even follow candidates at all levels and constantly record their statements, hoping to capture viral videos that can be used to embarrass or even derail opponents. As a result, some candidates and officials avoid events where they might face tough questions.[10] Others in authority, such as police officers, are also subject to such videos. Two videos in 2014—one of New York City police officers applying a chokehold that led to the death of 43-year-old Eric Garner in July and another a month later showing the fatal shooting of 18-year-old Michael Brown, Jr., by a Ferguson,

**gatekeeping** The role played by reporters in vetting and verifying information and news sources in order to prevent publication of inaccurate information.

Missouri, police officer—galvanized the #BlackLivesMatter movement (see Chapter 5). In response, some jurisdictions, such as New York City, now require police officers to wear body cameras of their own.[11]

Videos, of course, can be doctored and manipulated, and some individuals and groups have attempted to exploit them for more nefarious purposes. For example, conservative activist James O'Keefe—a self-described **citizen journalist** (a nonprofessional who nonetheless sets out to report news via alternative outlets)—used undercover videos to embarrass a variety of organizations, including the community action group ACORN (the Association of Community Organizations for Reform Now). In 2009, he and a sidekick posed as a pimp and a prostitute and secretly recorded the conversations they shared with low-level workers from ACORN. Selectively edited videos of the pair seeking advice for how to secure a low-interest federal loan to buy a house were uploaded to the Internet and then eventually leaked to the mainstream media. The pair indicated the house would be used as a brothel populated by underage Salvadoran girls. The videos portrayed ACORN employees as apparently condoning illegal activity (prostitution) and offering advice for how to evade federal tax laws.[12] The videos were widely criticized for being purposely misleading, and in 2013, O'Keefe agreed to pay a $100,000 settlement to a former ACORN employee for misrepresentation in the undercover videos, but by then, negative publicity from the videos had already put ACORN out of business.[13]

The arrest of Julian Assange in April 2019 and his indictment under the U.S. Espionage Act renewed concerns about free speech and whether Assange should be treated as a journalist or a criminal hacker.

The Internet has also made it easier to expose government secrets. In 2010, WikiLeaks—a nonprofit website launched in 2006 as a whistle-blowing site to bring "important news and information to the public"—published more than 250,000 leaked U.S. diplomatic cables, some of which were classified.[14] *The New York Times* and other news organizations subsequently published excerpts from those cables.[15] That monumental leak led to denunciations by government officials and to debates about whether WikiLeaks' editor-in-chief, Julian Assange, should be treated as a journalist or be forced to reveal his sources. Unlike conventional media, Assange's organization was not transparent. Except for Assange, the names of WikiLeaks personnel were mostly not known to the public nor was there any way for the public to know how WikiLeaks chose what to leak or if that selection was designed to promote a particular agenda. In 2012—faced with extradition to Sweden to face sexual assault allegations and concerned about potential espionage charges from the U.S. government for his leak of classified information—Assange sought asylum in Ecuador's embassy in London. Then, in the midst of the 2016 presidential campaign, WikiLeaks (with Assange still holed up at the embassy) released thousands of hacked e-mails from the Democratic National Committee and Hillary Clinton's campaign chairman, John Podesta. The e-mails embarrassed the Clinton campaign and arguably helped Trump win the election. After seven years of asylum in the Ecuadorean Embassy, Assange was arrested in April 2019 and the U.S. indicted him on 17 counts for violating the Espionage Act for hacking a Pentagon computer and releasing classified documents in 2010.[16]

## PROVIDING ENTERTAINMENT

Of course, another important function of the media is entertainment. Not surprisingly, even news programs and talk shows are designed, in part, to entertain their audiences. Media outlets pick stories and decide how much coverage to allot to specific issues with this goal in mind. In the United States, most media outlets are for-profit corporations that are motivated to increase the size of their audience in order to make more money. Making news entertaining furthers this goal. The profit motive leads to the reduction of complex issues to simple

**citizen journalist** A nonprofessional who reports news via alternative outlets such as the Internet or other social media.

Immensely popular crime dramas such as *CSI* have given the public an unrealistic sense of what forensic investigations can determine and how often various techniques are used, which has been a challenge for prosecutors facing juries who expect cases to mirror what they've seen on television.

narratives with an emphasis on drama, conflict, personalities, and brevity. Crime, scandal, partisan battles, unsolved mysteries, the rise and fall of celebrities, and titillation attract audiences. Elite media outlets such as *The New York Times* and *Wall Street Journal* may provide more in-depth coverage in a less flamboyant style than, say, the *New York Daily News*, but profit is as much of a motive for them.

Unlike the media in many countries, media in the United States are mostly privately owned and operated enterprises that exist to make money (as opposed to state-run operations designed to promote the regime). Thus, much of what appears in American media is pure entertainment. Indeed, news constitutes a small fraction of the schedule on network television. Even the Public Broadcasting Service (PBS) is part of the Corporation for Public Broadcasting, a private nonprofit organization, and is dependent upon financial contributions from viewers and other forms of private financial support. Unlike, say, the British Broadcasting Corporation (BBC), which is a quasi-governmental institution supported by U.K. taxpayers, less than 14 percent of the budget for PBS comes from the U.S. government (and President Trump suggested abolishing all federal funding for PBS).

Newspapers also devote a great deal of space to entertainment: style, food, sports, music, and movie reviews. On television, entertainment programming can actually sometimes inform viewers about government and current events. People, for example, learn about the criminal justice system from crime dramas and about current events from *Saturday Night Live* and *The Daily Show*. On the one hand, these entertainment programs can raise public awareness of important issues, as we saw with *The Daily Show* and public health care for first responders. On the other hand, these programs can create misconceptions among the public. Do police regularly use brutality to elicit confessions from persons accused of crimes? Is blood splatter analysis or DNA evidence as reliable as dramatic depictions would have you believe? In recent years, legal analysts and law journals have noted a tendency among juries to acquit a suspect when they believe prosecutors did not produce sufficient forensic evidence, which they have termed the *CSI* effect, after the long-running CBS drama. Jurors ask questions about "mitochondrial DNA" or "latent prints" when no such terms had been introduced during the court case.[17] The Ohio State Bar Association has even crafted instructions that can be issued to juries warning of the *CSI* effect, and individual judges have done the same.

## TRACING THE DEVELOPMENT OF MEDIA IN THE UNITED STATES

The mass media in America began with the opening of the first commercial press in 1638. By the 1800s, improvements in the printing press and the manufacture of paper made it quicker and easier to print newspapers. In 1837, Samuel Morse patented the telegraph, which allowed information to be transmitted long distances using Morse code. Several newspapers created the New York Associated Press in 1848 to share the cost of transmitting news via telegraph.[18] By 1861, telegraph cables linked the east and west coasts of North America, and by 1866, a successful trans-Atlantic cable—an amazing feat at the time—facilitated continuous communication among continents.[19]

The twentieth century saw the advent of radio and television, and the twenty-first century experienced the rise of social media. Each of these developments has radically altered the way news is delivered while giving public figures new ways to communicate with the people.

## BEGINNINGS

When the first commercial press opened in Cambridge, Massachusetts, in 1638, it churned out almanacs, sermons, and religious tracts as well as books for the fledgling Harvard College, but newspapers did not become a fixture until the 1700s. The first colonial newspaper, *Publick Occurrences Both Forreign and Domestick*, published its one and only monthly edition in Boston in 1690. The paper was full of sensational stories and salacious rumors (including a report that the King of France had slept with his son's wife). The entertainment value of these stories intrigued readers but shocked Boston's Puritan clergy. Royal authorities banned further publication.[20] Fourteen years passed before another colonial newspaper, the Boston *News-Letter*, appeared. By 1765, there were newspapers in all but two of the colonies.[21] Then, concurrent with the American Revolution and its aftermath, came an information explosion: 100 newspapers by 1790, a number that doubled in the next decade alone.[22]

The media played an important role in the period leading up to the American Revolution. Although newspapers fanned the flames of revolution, the real catalyst proved to be the pamphlet *Common Sense*, anonymously published by Thomas Paine in January 1776. This pamphlet became a runaway bestseller and a potent rallying cry for revolution (see Chapter 2). American patriots recognized the power of the printed word to further their cause, and by the time the colonies declared independence, newspapers were passed from household to household and read aloud at meetings in coffee houses and inns. The press thus gained a prestige that made it an important player in the creation of the United States.[23]

## THE PARTISAN PRESS

Newspapers became an important venue for debating the merits of the proposed U.S. Constitution during the ratification debates of 1787–1788. These debates helped to set the stage for the era of the partisan press that emerged when the new federal government created by the Constitution began to operate in New York, the nation's first capital. Political leaders sought to use newspapers to mold public opinion in support of their positions. Alexander Hamilton created the *Gazette of the United States* in 1789 to serve as the official mouthpiece of the incumbent Federalists.[24] In return, the Federalist-controlled government awarded the paper patronage. Hamilton, who was secretary of the treasury, arranged for printing orders from the Treasury Department to go its way and also anonymously wrote many *Gazette* articles. For a time, the paper also printed the nation's laws, and its masthead carried the words "By Authority," thereby indicating its status with the government.[25]

When the nation's capital moved to Philadelphia in 1791, Secretary of State Thomas Jefferson created an opposition newspaper, the *National Gazette*, to criticize Federalist policy. These rival newspapers reflected the breach between Hamilton and Jefferson and helped to foster the development of political parties in the United States. The rival newspapers' polarized positions on matters of public policy, coupled with their frequent editorial attacks on each other, drew attention from around the nation. As a result, other newspapers followed their lead, aligning themselves with one party or the other.[26]

## THE PENNY PRESS AND YELLOW JOURNALISM

Technological developments transformed newspapers in the 1800s. Instead of making paper by hand, as had been done for eighteenth-century newspapers, newly developed machines made paper quickly and easily. Before these developments, a printer could only produce about a thousand copies of a newspaper per day.[27] Further advances in printing presses allowed publishers to print newspapers cheaply and rapidly, leading to the emergence in 1830 of the penny press—newspapers that literally sold for a penny (rather than the six cents that was typical at that time). The sharp reduction in price made newspapers accessible to people of every economic class and led to a dramatic increase in sales. Economic incentives spurred newspapers to focus on issues other than politics, such as style and entertainment. As a result, the era of the partisan press came to an end. By the 1850s, members of Congress were using their *franking* privilege (their

**partisan press** A type of journalism associated with the late 1700s through the early 1800s when newspapers were affiliated with and controlled by a particular political party or emerging political party.

**penny press** Newspapers that emerged in 1830 and that, due to technological advances, sold for one penny—a sixth of what papers had previously sold for. This development made newspapers accessible to a wide array of people from all economic classes.

ability to send mail to constituents free of charge) as a means to bypass the press and communicate directly with the people.

The large daily circulation of the penny press spurred advertising—another important source of revenue for newspapers. More money allowed newspapers to hire more reporters, and the telegraph allowed reporters around the nation to transmit information quickly to newspapers. This helped give rise to Washington correspondents who covered political news in the nation's capital.

Competition for readership—epitomized by the heated rivalry between publishing giants William Randolph Hearst and Joseph Pulitzer—led to the rise of yellow journalism in the late 1800s. The phrase was inspired by a popular comic strip featuring a goofy-looking "Yellow Kid" that appeared in Pulitzer's *New York World* and later Hearst's rival *New York Journal*. Critics began to derisively refer to these newspapers, which were known for scandalmongering and sensationalism, as the "yellow press," and the term *yellow journalism* became a pejorative term denoting poorly researched and exaggerated reporting. Whatever its faults, yellow journalism led to soaring circulation. By 1898, the *New York Journal*'s Sunday edition had reached more than 600,000 readers.[28]

## THE RISE OF OBJECTIVE JOURNALISM AND THE FOURTH ESTATE

A backlash against yellow journalism led to the rise of objective journalism, the idea that newspapers should report facts in a fair and neutral manner that was devoid of partisanship and sensationalism. Arthur Ochs, who bought *The New York Times* in 1896, embraced this view, and the *Times*—in contrast with the *Journal* and *World*—tried to exemplify this new approach.

Objective journalism is the antithesis of the partisan press, and it was promoted by another early twentieth century development: journalism schools. Joseph Pulitzer served as the catalyst for this development. The University of Missouri opened the first journalism school at his urging in 1908, and when Pulitzer died in 1911, he left two million dollars to Columbia University. As a result of this bequest, Columbia opened a School of Journalism in 1912 and created the Pulitzer Prizes, which included awards for outstanding journalism. Thus, many people today associate Pulitzer with journalistic excellence rather than yellow journalism.

The rise of objective journalism helped to make newspapers watchdogs for government accountability. The term Fourth Estate is often used to describe the press as a force independent of government. During the Progressive Era of the 1890s through the 1920s, reporters and other authors began to write about corruption in government and business and on social issues such as child labor and working conditions. This early investigative reporting came to be known as muckraking and it often prompted governmental action, such as the enactment of the Pure Food and Drug Act discussed earlier.

The term *muckraking* is associated with early twentieth century reporting, but investigative journalism and book-length exposés continued beyond that point. Ralph Nader's 1965 book *Unsafe at Any Speed* exposed the dangers of automobiles, prompted the passage of legislation to promote auto safety—including seat belt laws—and fostered a consumer rights movement in the United States. The reporting of Carl Bernstein and Bob Woodward for *The Washington Post* in the 1970s helped to expose the Watergate scandal that led to the resignation of President Richard Nixon in 1974.

**yellow journalism** A type of journalism that emerged in the late 1800s, characterized by scandalmongering and sensationalistic reporting.

**objective journalism** A type of journalism that embraces the idea that newspapers should report news in a fair and neutral manner, devoid of partisanship and sensationalism (as opposed to yellow journalism).

**Fourth Estate** A term used to describe the press as a social and political force independent of government.

**muckraking** A type of journalism prevalent in the early part of the twentieth century that exposed corruption in business and government in order to promote reform.

Buyenlarge / Getty Images

Around the turn of the twentieth century, investigative journalism began to develop. A common target was child labor and poor working conditions in the nation's factories and mills, like this cotton mill in North Carolina. Vivid descriptions by reporters helped motivate the Progressive movement behind the country's first labor laws.

## RADIO

Wireless communication of telegraph signals began in the late 1890s, and experiments in transmitting the human voice soon followed. Commercial radio emerged in the 1920s, with the number of licensed radio stations in the United States rising from 30 in January 1922 to almost 500 a year later.[29] With the development of commercial broadcasting came expanded coverage of news and politics. Print media allowed for the widespread distribution of news, but the development of radio in the twentieth century provided an intimacy and immediacy that the print media could never have achieved. Edward R. Murrow's reports on the German bombing of London in 1940 transmitted the sounds of war to a spellbound radio audience in the United States.

Although politicians had long communicated with their constituents using printed material, radio provided a more potent opportunity for them to bypass the critical filter of reporters and bring their messages, in their own voices, directly into the living rooms of Americans. Starting on March 12, 1933—just days after his inauguration—President Franklin D. Roosevelt gave the first of 31 radio speeches called "Fireside Chats." His relaxed tone and friendly voice calmed an anxious nation in the grips of the Great Depression and, later, World War II. He used simple language, stories, and analogies to justify his policies, and he addressed his audience as *you* and *we*—thereby forging an intimate bond with the people and building a sense of shared purpose. Millions wrote to the president to express their appreciation.

Radio continues to play an important role in politics today. This is largely because of **talk radio**, a media forum that opens the lines to listeners to discuss various topics of interest; talk radio became a major political force in the 1990s. Americans who felt that mainstream television and newspaper media outlets articulated liberal viewpoints found an outlet in these talk shows. Hosts with a clear-cut conservative viewpoint, such as Rush Limbaugh, Laura Ingraham, and Sean Hannity, not only voiced their own opinions but interacted with callers on the air. This allowed for a direct (and sometimes emotional) form of public discourse. By 1997, news/talk had become the most popular radio format in America.[30] As of 2018, talk radio remained the most popular radio format among all listeners, but for listeners ages 18 to 34, talk radio tied for fifth place behind different types of music.[31] Efforts by liberals to break into the talk radio market have had only limited success. Air America, a network designed to promote talk show programming with a liberal viewpoint, lasted only six years—from 2004 to 2010.

## TELEVISION

Bell Laboratories first demonstrated television in the United States in 1927, telecasting the image and voice of Commerce Secretary Herbert Hoover (elected President of the United States the next year) from Washington, DC, to New York City, but commercial broadcasting did not begin until the late 1940s. Like radio before it, television exploded onto the national scene, as Figure 10.1 depicts, bringing an even greater immediacy than radio, for the obvious reason that it allowed people to watch as well as listen to events.[32]

By 1982, a government report concluded that more Americans owned televisions than refrigerators or indoor plumbing.[33] Since viewing was then primarily limited to the three broadcast networks (ABC, CBS, and NBC), Americans watched events together. The assassination of President John F. Kennedy on November 22, 1963, demonstrated the power of the new medium. Over the next three days, Americans were glued to their television screens as they watched, live, the shooting of the alleged assassin Lee Harvey Oswald by Jack Ruby, the return of the president's body to Washington, and the state funeral. NBC alone aired over 71 hours of coverage. Some 166 million Americans in more than 51 million homes watched the events unfold, often for hours on end, with an average of 93 percent of all households with a television set tuned in.[34] Television thus created a national community with shared political experiences.

By the 1960s, the nightly newscasts of the three major television networks became a staple of American television. Newspapers had been Americans' primary source of news through the early 1960s, but by 1967, Americans cited television as their primary source of news. Walter Cronkite, the anchorman of the *CBS Nightly News* and a major on-screen presence during the Kennedy assassination, earned the moniker "the most trusted man in America."[35] Television strongly influenced public perceptions. For example, many argue that the daily television images of the war in Vietnam helped to turn public sentiment against the war. When Cronkite concluded in a 1968 televised report that the war was likely to end in stalemate, it sent "shock waves" through the White House.[36] Later, during the 1970s, dramatic televised hearings by congressional committees investigating the Watergate affair helped to convince the nation that President Nixon should resign or be impeached.

**talk radio** A radio forum that opens the lines to listeners to discuss various topics of interest.

## FIGURE 10.1

### The Explosion of Television Onto the National Scene

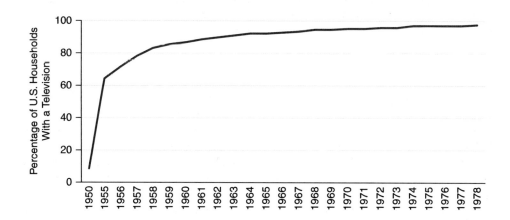

Only about 9 percent of U.S. households had television in 1950, but in only 30 years, that figure rose to almost 100 percent.

Source: Data from Steve M. Barkin, American Television News: The Media Marketplace and the Public Interest (Armonk, NY: M. E. Sharpe, 2003), p. 37.

Such changes in public opinion based on the influence of news sources are referred to as **media effects.** These changes can lead to volatility in everything from policy stances to voting preferences. Those without strong preexisting views on a particular topic are most susceptible to media effects. Stories about events in faraway countries may have greater media effects because such stories often involve topics far removed from our ordinary experiences and about which we have few established opinions.

Television was transformed by the development of satellite technology and cable television in the 1970s and '80s. Satellites allowed for the instant transmission of video images around the world, including those of President Nixon's pathbreaking visit to China in 1972. The technology allowed Americans to watch in real time as Nixon met with Chinese leaders and visited historic sites such as the Great Wall. Satellite technology also spurred the proliferation of cable television networks, which gave television viewers a huge array of programming to choose from. Cable television had long existed to provide access to the broadcast networks in remote areas but only became a venue for separate cable networks in the 1970s. By 1980, there were 28 cable television networks, but only a little over 10 percent of American households had cable service. By the end of the decade, there were 79 cable networks and more than half the homes in the United States were connected.[37]

The creation of the 24-hour Cable News Network (CNN) in 1980 fundamentally altered the nature of television news by helping to create a never-ending news cycle. Fox News and MSNBC joined the fray in 1996. Political scientists and other analysts have studied the impact of these 24-hour news channels on politics, sometimes referred to as the *CNN effect*. Cable news created an even greater immediacy to the news, focusing public attention on crises as soon as they occurred. Instantaneous reporting forced politicians and public officials to respond publicly to crises more quickly than they used to, giving them less time to reflect on their decisions. In addition, cable news relied heavily on talk shows because they were cheap, easy to produce, and appealed to viewers. However, the heated rhetoric of such shows sometimes blurs the line between news and entertainment.

Prior to cable and satellite television, ABC, CBS, and NBC had truly been *broadcast* networks—each appealing to as wide an audience as possible. The proliferation of channels provided by cable and satellite services led to **narrowcasting**, which is designed to target a particular niche in the market. This has led to channels that focus on specialized programming

**media effects** Changes in public opinion based on the influence of the media.

**narrowcasting** Programming designed to appeal to a particular segment of the population (as opposed to broadcasting, which is designed to appeal to as many people as possible).

dealing with everything from sports to food; target a particular demographic group such as Spanish-speaking viewers (Telemundo), African Americans (Black Entertainment Television), or young people (MTV); or appeal to people with particular ideological views. Fox News, for instance, appeals to more conservative viewers, while MSNBC appeals to more liberal viewers. Narrowcasting thus polarizes the American public along both demographic and partisan lines rather than uniting them as the three networks used to do.

## SOCIAL MEDIA AND THE INTERNET

The media were transformed yet again by a series of technological developments in the late twentieth and early twenty-first centuries. Satellite technology and cable were early examples of the so-called new media. They paved the way for the Internet and smartphones, which created unparalleled opportunities for direct communication with the American people. At the same time, social media outlets such as blogs, Twitter, YouTube, Instagram, and Facebook not only democratized the process by giving ordinary citizens an easy opportunity to express and share their views but also became themselves sources of news.

In 2018, a poll conducted by the Pew Research Center found that television remained the preferred source for news by Americans as a whole (44%), followed by online (34%), radio (14%), and print (7%).[38] Those numbers, however, were skewed by older Americans, suggesting that the trends will change (see Figure 10.2). While 81 percent of Americans 65 years of age and older relied on television for news, only 16 percent of 18- to 29-year-olds did (for them social media—at 38 percent—was identified as their main source of news). Thirty-nine percent of those 65 and over still read print newspapers, compared with only 2 percent of those 18 to 29.[39] In comparison, Pew found in January 1999 that over 80 percent of Americans relied on television news and that over 40 percent still read newspapers.[40] By 2018, about two-thirds of adults in America (68 percent) claimed to get their news from social media at least occasionally. Twenty percent relied on social media "often" as a news source, and 43 percent said they got news on Facebook. Forty-two percent considered news on social media to be "largely accurate."[41] Yet we all know that social media is rife with disinformation and outright fabrications—fake news in the truest sense of the word.[42]

> **new media** Media, such as cable television and the Internet, that led to a vast increase in the amount of information available to the people and allowed targeting of particular segments of the population via specialized channels and websites.
>
> **social media** Technologies such as blogs, texting, video file sharing, and other Internet resources that enable people to exchange information. These technologies have helped to blur the line between news consumer and news producer.

## FIGURE 10.2
### Americans' News Sources by Age

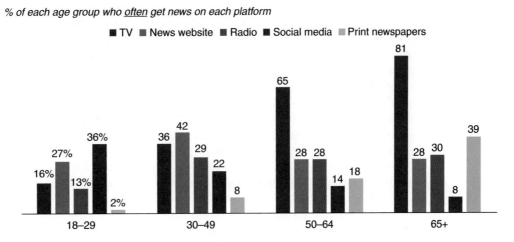

*% of each age group who <u>often</u> get news on each platform*

■ TV  ■ News website  ■ Radio  ■ Social media  ■ Print newspapers

| | 18–29 | 30–49 | 50–64 | 65+ |
|---|---|---|---|---|
| TV | 16% | 36 | 65 | 81 |
| News website | 27% | 42 | 28 | 28 |
| Radio | 13% | 29 | 28 | 30 |
| Social media | 36% | 22 | 14 | 8 |
| Print newspapers | 2% | 8 | 18 | 39 |

*Television news dominates as a news source for older Americans. What impact might that have? How might this trend change politics as the oldest generation of Americans dies?*

Source: "Social Media Outpaces Print Newspapers in the U.S. as a News Source," Pew Research Center, December 10, 2018, https://www.pewresearch.org/fact-tank/2018/12/10/social-media-outpaces-print-newspapers-in-the-u-s-as-a-news-source/

FIGURE 10.3

## Party Identifiers' Trust in Media

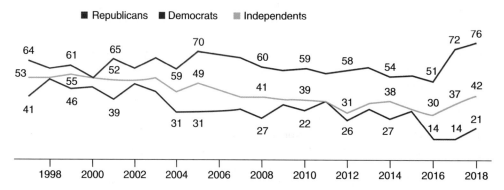

% Great deal/Fair amount of trust and confidence

■ Republicans    ■ Democrats    ■ Independents

*Republicans' trust in the mass media has been lower than Democrats' for decades. Trust in general has rebounded from an all-time low in 2016. What do you think accounts for these two facts?*

*Source: Jeffrey M. Jones, "U.S. Media Trust Continues to Recover From 2016 Low, Gallup, October 12, 2018, https://news.gallup.com/poll/243665/media-trust-continues-recover-2016-low.aspx*

This became a problem in the 2016 presidential election when made-up stories began to proliferate on Facebook—many of them orchestrated by Russia to disrupt the election. Even as the election was under way, Buzzfeed's media editor identified at least 140 fake news websites that generated a great deal of Facebook traffic (as noted earlier, the Mueller Report eventually identified some 470 Facebook accounts operated by Russia's IRA to generate false information). After she lost, Hillary Clinton made a speech condemning "the epidemic of malicious fake news and false propaganda that flooded social media over the last year." Starting in January 2017, Donald Trump appropriated the term *fake news,* but used it to discredit critical coverage by reputable news sources (as opposed to the completely made-up stories that Clinton complained of).[43]

Meanwhile, public trust in the news media as a whole eroded. A 2018 Gallup poll found that 69 percent of all respondents claimed that their trust in the news media had dropped over the past decade, but responses varied according to partisanship. Ninety-four percent of Republicans reported less trust, compared with only 42 percent of Democrats.[44] The Pew Research Center found a similar partisan gap, with 86 percent of Republicans believing that the news media tend to favor one side compared with only 52 percent of Democrats. When asked about the news media's watchdog role, 82 percent of Democrats agreed with the statement, "Media criticism of political leaders keeps them from doing things they shouldn't" compared with only 38 percent of Republicans.[45] Another Pew survey found that while only 47 percent felt the news media reported political issues "fairly," 56 percent nonetheless believed the news was "accurate." This is behind countries such as Canada (where 73 percent felt the media covered issues fairly, and 78 percent felt they covered issues accurately), Germany (72 and 75 percent), India (65 and 80), Japan (55 and 65), and even Russia (55 and 60).

Social media and the Internet have arguably contributed to the partisan divide in America. Websites, blogs, and social media are, after all, an ideal venue for narrowcasting. Conservatives turn to blogs and other social media sites that reinforce their views, while liberals turn to ones that reinforce *their* views. By allowing consumers to rely on news sources that merely reinforce their preexisting views, narrowcasting may increase partisanship, polarize public opinion, and make political compromise by policy makers more difficult.

# GOVERNMENT REGULATION OF THE MEDIA

In many other countries, state-run media is common. Even in some democracies, such as Great Britain, radio and television have been run as a public corporation, with government subsidizing the cost of technological development and news gathering. The BBC, which began radio transmissions in 1922 and television transmissions in 1936, is an example of a public service broadcaster. In other words, it was designed to provide high-quality, balanced coverage without the economic pressures associated with private ownership. However, state-run media in many other countries—ranging from China to Iran—is a far cry from the BBC. There, state-run media is used to tout the party line and squelch news that might put the government in an unfavorable light. Indeed, much of the world enjoys little freedom of the press (see Figure 10.4).

By contrast, the media in the United States are mostly privately owned and operated for profit. Moreover, the First Amendment of the Constitution guarantees extraordinary freedom of the press. Nonetheless, some government regulation of the media does exist in the United States. This is especially true of broadcast media (radio and television) for the simple reason that airwaves are limited. When commercial radio stations began to proliferate in the 1920s, their signals often interfered with each other. As more and more stations went on the air, more and more chaos ensued. As a result, the radio industry sought government regulation to allocate the scarce airwaves.

## REGULATING THE AIRWAVES

The Communications Act of 1934 created the Federal Communications Commission (FCC) to issue broadcast licenses (which could be revoked for failure to abide by FCC rules), allocate broadcast frequencies (which are treated as public property to be leased by the government), and regulate broadcasters to ensure that their use of scarce airwaves is in the public interest.[46] The FCC's power extends over radio, television, wire, and cable communications.

The FCC has considerable power to determine who can broadcast (send radio and television signals over the airwaves, which are limited, as opposed to sending them via cable or satellite, which do not face the same constraints). It has the authority to issue, revoke, or deny renewal

> **Federal Communications Commission (FCC)** An independent U.S. government agency created by the Communications Act of 1934 to oversee and regulate the broadcast industry.

**FIGURE 10.4**

*Press Freedom Around the World, 2019*

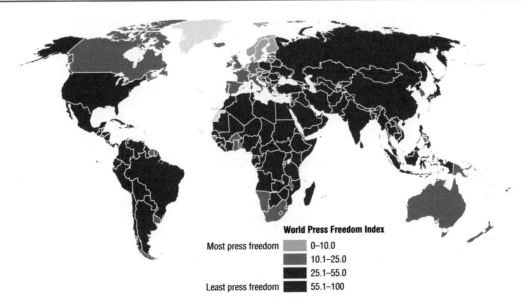

**World Press Freedom Index**

Most press freedom — 0–10.0
10.1–25.0
25.1–55.0
Least press freedom — 55.1–100

*Source: Data from Reporters Without Borders. https://rsf.org/en/ranking*

of broadcast licenses to radio and television stations. The FCC also has the ability to regulate private ownership of the broadcast media by limiting the number of broadcast stations a single entity can own. Regulation of ownership was originally designed to prevent a monopoly of scarce airwaves by a small number of broadcasters. The emergence of cable and satellite technologies diminished the scarcity argument and led Congress to pass the Telecommunications Act of 1996, which abolished many of the cross-market barriers that had previously prevented companies from simultaneously offering telephone, cable, and broadcast services.[47]

This deregulation allowed single companies to offer a wide array of services, such as telephone, cable, satellite, and Internet. Critics have complained that this has led to too much concentration of ownership in a few large corporations such as Comcast and Time Warner. The Telecommunications Act still barred a single entity from owning stations with an aggregate national audience of more than 35 percent, but the FCC—which reviews ownership rules every four years—subsequently took steps to allow greater concentration of ownership. In 2003, it proposed increasing the aggregate national audience cap from 35 to 45 percent. The proposal generated strong opposition, but Congress agreed to increase the cap from 35 to 39 percent. Then, in November 2017, the FCC voted 3–2 along partisan lines to abandon its remaining rules limiting cross-ownership. In announcing the decision, FCC Chairman Ajit Pai (appointed by President Trump) said that "the media ownership regulations of 2017 should match the media marketplace of 2017." In a dissenting opinion, FCC Commissioner Mignon Clyburn (appointed by President Obama) contended that "today will go down in history as the day when the FCC abdicated its responsibility to uphold the core values of localism and diversity in broadcasting."[48]

In another controversial decision, the FCC under Chairman Pai abandoned so-called net neutrality—the unhindered flow of information over the Internet without interference by those that run or own the service providers. In other words, Internet service providers (ISPs) cannot charge consumers for tiers of service or penalize or prioritize traffic from a particular domain, service, or publisher. Under net neutrality, for example, an ISP could not block or slow down content from a rival video streaming site. Proponents say that this promotes freedom of expression by giving everyone equal access to the Internet and also promotes innovation and competition by giving startups the same access and speed as large, established companies. ISPs, however, could maximize profits and upgrade their networks if they could charge more for bandwidth-heavy services like video streaming services such as Netflix.[49] After Congress failed to pass legislation protecting net neutrality, the FCC issued rules in 2015 protecting net neutrality. The DC Court of Appeals subsequently upheld the rules, and the Supreme Court refused to take up the case.[50] But then, in December 2017, the FCC voted 3–2, again along partisan lines, to repeal the regulations and block states from imposing their own rules to guarantee an open Internet. That, in turn, faced a legal challenge from a group of 22 state attorneys general and the District of Columbia.[51]

Prior to 2015, Europe maintained a largely hands-off approach to the issue, with mobile providers having considerable discretion to manage and prioritize data. It was common, for example, to block the use of Skype because it would undercut the revenue that could be generated by an operator's own calling services. However, the European Parliament passed regulations to protect net neutrality in 2015.[52]

## REGULATING BROADCAST CONTENT

The FCC's interest in assuring that scarce airwaves are used in the public interest has led to content regulation of the broadcast media. From early in its history, the FCC sought to assure that broadcasters offer fair, balanced coverage of public issues and political campaigns.

One example of content regulation is the equal time rule. If broadcast stations sell airtime for a political advertisement for one candidate, they must provide equal time to any other candidate who wishes to purchase it. From 1949 to 1987, the FCC also tried to promote balanced coverage of public issues more generally through the so-called Fairness Doctrine. As described by the FCC, the Fairness Doctrine required licensees to

> devote a reasonable percentage of their broadcasting time to the discussion of public issues of interest to the community served by their stations and [to ensure] that such

**net neutrality** The unhindered flow of information over the Internet without interference by those who run or own the service providers.

**equal time rule** An FCC regulation that requires a broadcast outlet that sells airtime for a political advertisement for one candidate to provide equal time for any other candidate who wishes to purchase it.

**Fairness Doctrine** An FCC regulation in place from 1949 to 1987 that required broadcast licensees to devote a reasonable percentage of their broadcast time to conveying a balanced discussion of public issues of interest and importance to the community.

programs be designed so that the public has a reasonable opportunity to hear different opposing positions on the public issues of interest and importance to the community.[53]

The wording of the Fairness Doctrine was vague. What exactly is a *reasonable percentage* of broadcasting time? How does one determine which issues are *of interest and importance to the community*? Nonetheless, the FCC continued to enforce the doctrine, and the U.S. Supreme Court unanimously upheld its constitutionality in 1969.[54] Some, however, believed that the Fairness Doctrine actually inhibited the discussion of competing viewpoints rather than promoting it because stations found it easier to avoid discussing certain topics altogether than to broadcast competing viewpoints. In addition, cable and satellite technology undermined the scarcity argument that had been used to justify the Fairness Doctrine.

The FCC stopped enforcing the Fairness Doctrine in 1987. This had an unexpected consequence: It led to the emergence of political talk radio. Rush Limbaugh began his nationally syndicated radio talk show in 1988. When the Fairness Doctrine was enforced, a radio station airing a conservative talk show also had to air a liberal talk show or otherwise provide balanced coverage of issues in a single show. This mostly prevented stations from airing political talk radio. Without the Fairness Doctrine, political talk radio—often vitriolic in tone—exploded onto the scene and has expanded to cable television.

In the wake of the bombing of the Alfred P. Murrah Federal Building in Oklahoma City in 1995, President Bill Clinton denounced "promoters of paranoia" who spread hatred on the public airwaves, noting that "bitter words can have consequences."[55] Clinton claimed that he was not targeting conservative talk radio with that comment, but such programs dominated the airwaves. In 2009, Clinton, though no longer president, suggested reinstating the Fairness Doctrine to provide public exposure for countervailing points of view and ensure a more balanced coverage of issues on the air, and he is not alone in making this suggestion.[56]

In its effort to promote "the public interest," the FCC also has the power to issue fines to stations that broadcast indecent or obscene material, and to revoke or deny renewal of such a station's license. As discussed in Chapter 4, obscene material is not protected by the First Amendment. "Indecent" material that would otherwise pass constitutional muster may still draw punishment if broadcast. The FCC has cited the following reasons for this lower threshold for punishing indecent broadcast material: access to broadcasts by unsupervised children, the need to protect nonconsenting adults who may inadvertently tune in to offensive broadcasts, protection of the privacy of households that broadcast signals invade, and the scarcity of spectrum argument that allows government to regulate airwaves in the public interest.[57]

The Supreme Court ruled in favor of the FCC position in a landmark 1978 case involving a New York radio station that aired comedian George Carlin's "Seven Dirty Words" monologue.[58] More recently, the FCC fined CBS for broadcasting the infamous "wardrobe malfunction" that occurred during the halftime of the 2004 Super Bowl when Justin Timberlake tore off part of Janet Jackson's costume, briefly exposing her breast on national television, although a federal court later voided the fine. The Supreme Court heard another challenge to FCC regulation of the airwaves in 2012, but ultimately declined to rule on whether FCC regulations violate the First Amendment.[59]

Cable and satellite transmissions are not subject to the same restrictions as the traditional broadcast media (since the scarce spectrum argument does not apply and people pay to receive these transmissions). Thus, shock jock Howard Stern abandoned FM radio as the broadcast medium for his sexually provocative show and moved to satellite radio in 2006 in order to avoid FCC regulations.

## REGULATING THE INTERNET

Congress has made several attempts to regulate the Internet. Many of these efforts have been designed to protect children from access to sexually oriented material. In 1996, Congress passed the Communications Decency Act (CDA), which criminalized the posting of indecent or obscene material on the Internet. The Supreme Court struck down the law in 1997 on the grounds that it was overly broad.[60] By criminalizing not only "obscene" material but also

# As a Journalist in Saudi Arabia

Sandwiched between the Red Sea and the Persian Gulf, northeast of Africa and south of Iraq and Iran, oil rich Saudi Arabia—a Muslim country that is often described as the birthplace of Islam—enforces Sharia law and has an absolute monarchy which, according to the independent watchdog organization Freedom House, "restricts almost all political rights and civil liberties."[a] Reporters Without Borders ranked Saudi Arabia among the worst countries in the world for press freedom in its 2019 World Press Freedom Index (172 out of 180 countries).[b] Although most newspapers in Saudi Arabia are privately owned, they are subsidized and regulated by the government, which is known for its censorship of all types of media.

As a journalist in Saudi Arabia, you must be very careful. Reporters Without Borders has noted an increased crackdown on reporters since the appointment of Mohammad bin Salman as crown prince in 2017. Within 16 months of his appointment, the number of journalists and bloggers imprisoned had doubled to at least 28. For example, the journalist Saleh al Shehi was arrested and ultimately sentenced to five years in prison for "insulting the royal court" when he said in a televised interview that the royal family in Saudi Arabia tolerated corruption and nepotism.[c] Other forms of free speech also suffered. Although Saudi Arabia lifted its long-standing ban on women drivers in May 2018, a crackdown on women's rights activists began a month later, with at least nine jailed (some facing up to 20 years in prison) for undermining the "security and stability" of the government. International human rights organizations reported that at least four of the imprisoned activists had been tortured with electric shocks and had been whipped on their thighs.[d]

You know, of course, that journalists were certainly not free before the prince came to power. Take, for example, the Saudi blogger Raif Badawi, who argued for secularism, democracy, and human rights on his blog, only to be arrested for insulting Islam and sentenced to 10 years in prison and 1,000 lashes—for all practical purposes, a sentence to death by torture. He received 50 lashes in a public flogging in January 2015 that attracted hundreds of spectators, and the government said that it would continue with 50 lashes a week for 20 weeks. But Badawi almost died from the first 50 lashes, and Saudi Arabia backed down from further lashes after widespread international criticism. Badawi, though, remained in prison.[e]

Most disconcerting was the October 2018 murder and dismemberment of *Washington Post* reporter Jamal Khashoggi in the Saudi consulate in Istanbul, Turkey. Khashoggi had been the general manager and editor-in-chief of the Al-Arab News Channel, which the Saudi government shut down because of its criticism of the regime, including the crown prince. After the shutdown, Khashoggi fled Saudi Arabia but had visited the consulate in Istanbul to obtain documents for his impending marriage. Evidence indicated that the crown prince had ordered his killing. U.S. Senator Bob Corker (R-SC), chairman of the Foreign Relations Committee, said after being presented with the evidence, "We know he ordered it. We know he monitored it."[f] In a rare bipartisan move, the Senate then voted unanimously in December 2018 to condemn the prince for the killing.[g]

President Trump, whose first foreign trip after taking office had been to Saudi Arabia and who did not want to endanger a multibillion-dollar sale of weapons to the Saudis by the U.S. government, dismissed the assessment of his own Central Intelligence Agency that the Saudi crown prince ordered the killing and called Saudi Arabia "a very good ally."[h] When Congress tried to block the $8.1 billion sale of weapons to Saudi Arabia in response to the killing, Trump used his emergency power to allow the sale to continue without legislative oversight.[i] As he put it shortly after the killing, stopping the arms sale would cost U.S. jobs: "Do people really want me to give up hundreds of thousands of jobs—and frankly, if we went by this standard, we wouldn't have anybody as an ally."[j]

*Time* magazine subsequently named Khashoggi "Person of the Year" along with a group of other journalists for being "guardians of the truth." Khashoggi was also posthumously awarded the Amnesty International USA Press Freedom Award in February 2019 and the Golden Pen of Freedom from the World Association of Newspapers and News Publishers in June 2019. Meanwhile, you forge on as a journalist in Saudi Arabia.

## Questions to Consider

1. How should the U.S. respond to egregious violations of press freedom, such as the murder of Jamal Khashoggi? Compare the responses of President Trump and the Republican-controlled U.S. Senate.
2. The 2019 World Press Freedom Index that ranked Saudi Arabia 172 out of 180 countries, ranked the

United States 48th. That is lower than you might expect. What factors might have led to concerns about freedom of the press in the United States in 2019?

3. Would you consider being a journalist in Saudi Arabia? Can the press still serve as a watchdog there?

a "Freedom in the World 2019: Saudi Arabia," *Freedom House,* accessed July 29, 2019, https://freedomhouse.org/report/freedom-world/2019/saudi-arabia.

b "2019 World Press Freedom Index," *Reporters Without Borders,* accessed July 29, 2019, https://rsf.org/en/ranking/

c "RSF Issues Warning About Saudi Arabia's Press Freedom Index Ranking," *Reporters Without Borders,* October 22, 2018, https://rsf.org/en/news/rsf-issues-warning-about-saudi-arabias-press-freedom-index-ranking

d "Saudi Arabia: Events of 2018," *Human Rights Watch,* accessed July 29, 2019, https://www.hrw.org/world-report/2019/country-chapters/saudi-arabia

e Andrew Brown, "Ten Years in Jail and 1,000 Lashes: Why We Must Defend Saudi Blogger Raif Badawi," *The Guardian,* June 18, 2017, https://www.theguardian.com/commentisfree/2017/jun/18/raif-badawi-saudi-arabia-blogger; Khaleda Rahman, "Saudi Blogger Sentenced to 1,000 Lashes Is 'Very Depressed' and Seriously Ill Says His Wife on Fourth Anniversary of His Flogging," *Daily Mail,* January 7, 2019, https://www.dailymail.co.uk/news/article-6566155/Saudi-blogger-sentenced-1-000-lashes-depressed-seriously-ill-says-wife.html.

f Stephen Dinan, "Sen. Lindsey Graham: Smoking Saw' Ties Saudi Crown Prince to Khashoggi Killing," *The Washington Post,* December 4, 2018, https://www.washingtontimes.com/news/2018/dec/4/lindsey-graham-sees-smoking-saw-khashoggi-killing/

g Karoun Damirjian, "Senate Votes to Condemn Saudi Crown Prince for Khashoggi Killing, End Support for Yemen War," *The Washington Post,* December 13, 2018, https://www.washingtonpost.com/powerpost/senate-prepares-vote-to-curtail-us-support-for-saudi-led-military-effort-in-yemen/2018/12/13/cf934a96-fed7-11e8-862a-b6a6f3ce8199_story.html?utm_term=.30d7e402bee4

h Steve Holland and Roberta Rampton, "Exclusive: Trump Says Standing by Saudi Crown Prince Despite Pleas From Senate," *Reuters,* December 11, 2018, https://www.reuters.com/article/us-usa-trump-saudi-exclusive/exclusive-trump-says-standing-by-saudi-crown-prince-despite-pleas-from-senate-idUSKBN1OB01C

i David Brown, "Weapons Worth $8B Headed to Middle East Over Congress' Objections," *Politico,* May 24, 2019, https://www.politico.com/story/2019/05/24/8-billion-weapons-middle-east-3323593

j Kathryn Watson, "Trump Defends Saudis, Says 'Maybe the World' Should Be Held Accountable for Khashoggi's Murder," CBS News, November 22, 2018, https://www.cbsnews.com/news/trump-on-thanksgiving-defends-saudi-crown-prince-after-khashoggi-muder-2018-11/

"indecent" and "patently offensive" material, the act could have held someone criminally liable for posting material that otherwise had First Amendment protection, such as novels that contained adult themes (for example, J. D. Salinger's *The Catcher in the Rye* and James Joyce's *Ulysses*).

The next year, Congress passed the Child Online Protection Act (COPA). Unlike the CDA, which criminalized postings by anyone (including participants in chat groups), COPA targeted commercial distributors. It imposed a $50,000 fine and six months in prison for any commercial distributor who knowingly posted "material harmful to minors" without restricting their site to those who could prove that they were adults. Federal courts again struck down the law on the grounds that it was too broad.[61] For example, the law considered any nudity, whether or not it met the legal definition of obscenity, to constitute "material harmful to minors."

Then, in 2000, Congress passed the Children's Internet Protection Act (CIPA). CIPA requires schools and libraries whose computers and Internet access are subsidized by the government to install filters to block images that are pornographic or harmful to minors. The library may temporarily disable filters for adults who need access to such sites for "bona fide research or other lawful purposes." This time, the Supreme Court upheld the law.[62]

More recently, countries around the world have—in the wake of disinformation campaigns on the Internet—debated whether or not greater regulation is needed. Outrage in Australia and New Zealand after a white nationalist livestreamed part of his mass shootings at two mosques in Christchurch, New Zealand, in March 2019, similarly led to proposals to make social media more responsible for the content they host.[63] But how does one compare such calls for regulation by democratic regimes with attempts by authoritarian regimes, such as the one in Venezuela, to crack down on social media? Are regulations to protect against disinformation and other harmful content, maintain election integrity, and ensure privacy a good thing? Should the U.S. consider such regulation of social media sites, such as Facebook? Or does the danger of squelching freedom of expression outweigh the benefits of such regulation?[64]

## GOVERNMENT AND THE MEDIA

Most of what we know about government and current events comes from the news media. Yet, as political scientist W. Lance Bennett once pointed out, "the typical news fare covers only a narrow range of issues, from the viewpoints of an even narrower range of sources, with emphasis placed

The White House press corps is traditionally briefed each day by the press secretary, which can result in stories that largely parrot the administration's official line on a topic. Starting with Press Secretary Sarah Huckabee Sanders, however, these briefings became much rarer and, under her successor Stephanie Grisham, virtually non-existent.

*Chip Somodevilla / Getty Images*

on drama over depth, human interest over social significance, and formula reporting over perceptive analysis."[65]

Not surprisingly, government officials try to influence what the media will and will not report. They also try to influence—or spin—how that news will be reported. As a result, government officials have established public relations infrastructures through which they provide information and access to reporters. Such infrastructures organize and provide routine channels of information for the media. These include things such as press briefings, press releases, and access to official proceedings (such as congressional hearings and court trials) and other non-spontaneous events (such as speeches and staged ceremonies).[66]

Large groups of reporters, often referred to as "packs," are assigned to cover these routine channels. A good example is the White House press corps, which gathers much of its information from the White House Press Office and its briefings. This so-called pack journalism has consequences. Studies have found that a substantial majority of news stories are based on these routine channels. Stories based on enterprise (independent research by reporters, including interviews conducted at the reporter's own initiative) are less common because they require more work. In a landmark study, Leon V. Sigal studied a sample of stories printed in *The New York Times* and *The Washington Post* between 1949 and 1969. He found that 58.2 percent of those stories were based on routine channels and only 25.8 percent were based on enterprise.[67]

## PRESIDENTS AND THE PRESS

Public support is a president's most visible source of political power. In addition to relying on the press to convey news, presidents and their surrogates routinely take messages directly to the people in an effort to mold mandates for policy initiatives. This process of going public was largely a twentieth-century phenomenon, aided in the twenty-first century by Twitter and other forms of social media.[68] Nineteenth-century presidents made few public speeches.[69] They also had limited interactions with the press.

Theodore Roosevelt (1901–1909) began the practice of meeting regularly with reporters (often during his late-afternoon shave), and he was the first president to provide a room for them in the White House.[70] Woodrow Wilson (1913–1921) was the first president to hold regularly scheduled press conferences. He was also the first president since John Adams (1797–1801) to deliver the State of the Union address orally (instead of sending a written message to Congress), thus establishing a tradition that continues to this day. Not until 1933 did Franklin Roosevelt create the White House Press Office, a quintessential public relations infrastructure. Similarly, a Downing Street press secretary emerged in the United Kingdom in 1945 to perform for the British prime minister the tasks that a White House press secretary already performed for the U.S. president.

The Press Office is the most visible White House staff unit that deals with the media. The Press Office, under the direction of the White House Press Secretary, has long distributed the news of the day and responded to questions from the White House press corps. But, under Press Secretary Sarah Huckabee Sanders, the Trump administration cut back sharply on press briefings. In 2019, Sanders went a record six weeks without holding one—and, at least initially, her successor, Stephanie Grisham, was dubbed "the president's silent spokeswoman."[71] By September 11, 2019, the White House had gone a full six months without a traditional briefing.[72] Sanders's credibility was also called into question by the Mueller Report, which concluded that Sanders had lied to the press corps (she characterized it as a "slip of the tongue").[73] President Trump has also confronted credibility issues. By April 29, 2019, *The Washington Post*'s Fact Checker database pointed to over 10,000 false or misleading claims Trump had made as president.[74]

**spin** Attempts by government officials to influence how the media will report an event by suggesting how a story should be framed.

**pack journalism** A type of journalism conducted by groups (or "packs") of reporters who are assigned to cover the same institution and characterized by uniform coverage of issues, reliance on official channels of information, and lack of original research.

**going public** A presidential strategy designed to influence Congress by appealing directly to the public, asking them to pressure legislators for passage of the president's proposals.

In 1969, Richard Nixon created an additional White House Office of Communications to target the presidential messages to local media, coordinate the flow of information from the entire executive branch, and plot long-term communications strategy. In subsequent administrations, some of these functions have been carried out by other staff units, but all three functions are now commonplace.[75] Similarly, a Downing Street Director of Communications emerged in the United Kingdom in 2000 to plot a long-range communication strategy for the British prime minister.

Radio and television gave presidents the opportunity to communicate directly with the American people, often in very personal terms. Since the three major networks dominated television until the advent of cable television in the 1980s, and since those networks typically cancelled regularly scheduled programming for newsworthy events such as a presidential speech or news conference, presidents could command a huge audience that had nowhere else on television to turn.

President John F. Kennedy (1961–1963) mastered the art of the televised press conference. Witty, quick, and telegenic, he turned press conferences into an opportunity for the president to speak to the people as well as the press. With more and more Americans getting their news from television, presidents also became adept at creating **photo opportunities** to reinforce themes they were trying to convey. The Reagan White House (1980–1989) perfected the art of staging events so as to guarantee compelling images for use on the evening newscasts of the three major networks.

The explosion in the number of channels on cable and satellite television in the 1980s and 1990s diminished the ability of presidents to monopolize the airwaves when they gave a speech or news conference. Nonetheless, these channels opened up other opportunities for politicians to transmit direct, targeted messages to particular constituencies. Presidential candidate Bill Clinton used MTV in 1992 to target young voters, a then-novel practice that soon became commonplace. As president, Barack Obama appeared on everything from ESPN, where he filled out his brackets for the NCAA Men's Basketball Championship, to a music awards show on the Spanish-language channel Univision. Social media has made it even easier for the president to target messages, as evidenced by President Trump's steady stream of tweets. By 2019, he had some 60 million followers.

## CONGRESS AND THE PRESS

The sheer size of Congress and the diversity of its membership make it much more difficult for the media to cover Congress as an institution than to cover the president. At the national level, the media tends to focus on congressional leaders and key committee chairs. Congressional hearings are also ideally suited for media coverage, especially those covering dramatic issues. The same obstacles make coverage of other large legislative bodies, such as Parliament in England, difficult.

Congress built press galleries in the 1850s for the emerging Washington press corps (England's Parliament had a designated press gallery starting in 1803). Even more reporters came to Washington, DC, during the Civil War (1861–1865). Competition among newspapers also led them to send high-profile individual correspondents to Washington to report for their paper with a distinctive voice, rather than relying on pool reporting via wire services as they might from more remote locales.[76] By the 1870s, such correspondents were a fixture in Washington.

In the twentieth century, efforts to broadcast public sessions of the House and Senate faced stiff resistance in Congress. The first bill to allow radio coverage of the House of Representatives was introduced in 1922 but failed. Finally, in 1947, Congress allowed various committee hearings from both houses to be televised. Television coverage of two Senate hearings in the 1950s created a sensation—one investigating organized crime and another (chaired by Senator Joseph McCarthy) investigating alleged communist infiltration of the U.S. military. Later, in 1973, televised hearings of a Senate committee investigating Watergate also created a sensation. Nonetheless, the House did not allow regular television coverage of its proceedings until 1979 (experimental broadcasts had taken place in 1977). The Senate did not allow television coverage until 1986. Today, C-SPAN provides gavel-to-gavel coverage of both, along with many committee hearings. In England, televising the proceedings of the House of Lords began in 1985,

**photo opportunity** A time period reserved for the media to photograph a public official, usually staged to reinforce a particular frame or theme that the official wishes to convey to the public.

followed by the proceedings of the House of Commons in 1989. Such broadcasts have spread to many other legislative bodies around the world. C-SPAN now provides access to broadcasts of many countries' legislative debates.

The media is especially important to individual members of Congress as a way to communicate with their constituents. In his landmark 1974 study, political scientist David Mayhew argued that members of Congress engage in three primary activities: advertising, credit claiming, and position taking.[77] The media immeasurably aids all three. In this age of polarized politics, the media aids another activity, as noted by political scientist Gary King: taunting opponents. King found that between 2005 and 2007, about 27 percent of congressional press releases were devoted to taunting.[78]

Twitter began in 2006 and became, along with other social media outlets, an important tool in the 2008 presidential election. Members of Congress took note and, in 2009, began to use social media themselves to share information with constituents. Initially, Republicans were more active than Democrats. For example, the House Republican caucus established a team in 2009 to respond almost immediately on Twitter to announcements or comments from the White House or from Democrats on the floors of Congress. A staff member for House Speaker John Boehner (R-OH) sat at a desk with several television sets showing different stations as well as action on the floor of the House and Senate. When a Democrat made a comment meriting a response, he did some rapid research, often including a check with Republican officials to make sure that the response would be consistent with party policy, and replied within minutes. Thus, the response did not miss the news cycle in which the original statement appeared and addressed a wide audience through Twitter.[79] By 2018, a social media presence was essential for politicians, with every member of Congress maintaining a Twitter account (see Figure 10.5). The Parliament in England lagged slightly behind. As of May 2019, 89 percent (576 out of 650 Members of Parliament) had a Twitter account.[80]

**FIGURE 10.5**

## *Social Media Use by Members of Congress*

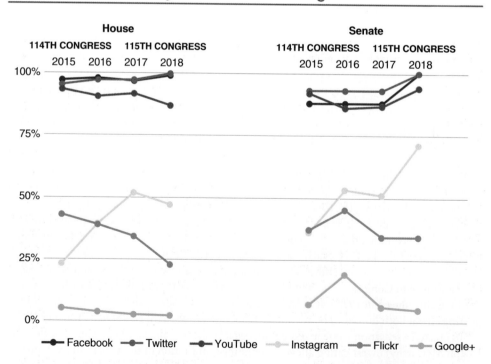

Sources: *LBJ School of Public Affairs and CRS data analysis.*

Note: *Percentages represent a snapshot of platform adoption at the time of collection during the Congress mentioned.*

## THE SUPREME COURT AND THE PRESS

The Supreme Court is covered far less by the media than Congress or the president. This is largely because of the nature of the institution. Supreme Court justices are appointed for life and perform most of their duties behind closed doors. The expectation that they remain objective precludes public scrutiny. And even though oral arguments are open to the public and audio recordings are available, the Court does not allow them to be televised. In contrast, proceedings of the Canadian Supreme Court have been televised since the mid-1990s.[81] Brazil goes even further: Since 2002, it has broadcast actual deliberations (the meetings where justices decide how to vote on cases) as well as the proceedings before the court.[82] In so doing, it has become one of the most transparent high courts in the world.[83]

When U.S. Supreme Court decisions are handed down, they are often lengthy and complicated. Thus, expert analysts help to interpret decisions for broadcast and online media outlets. And yet, justices need the press to convey their decisions to the public. Moreover, they need *positive* coverage to help maintain their legitimacy.[84] Thus, savvy justices sometimes craft opinions for public consumption—as Chief Justice Earl Warren did in *Brown v. Board of Education* (see Chapter 5).

The Supreme Court does have a public information office that distributes copies of decisions when they are handed down and provides reporters with access to oral arguments, but there are no press briefings—nor does the Supreme Court have an official Twitter account (although SCOTUSblog's Twitter account is sometimes mistaken for one). The rare press releases that are issued are usually confined to bland announcements related to personnel. Media coverage is limited mainly to coverage of decisions in highly charged cases. Lack of coverage of the many other cases before the Court is sometimes coupled with misrepresentation of what the Court does. For example, the media frequently misinterpret the Court's refusal to review an action by a lower court (which simply means that the Court has chosen not to intervene and will let the lower court ruling stand) as a decision on the merits of the case (as if the Court were actually embracing the ruling of the lower court that they have left untouched).[85]

## ELECTIONS

The media plays an important role in elections. Television, in particular, affected the way political candidates campaign for public office. Style, image, and the ability to communicate well in front of television cameras all became more important. News values also influence campaigns. Television news, which usually devotes, at most, two or three minutes to any given story, thrives on drama and conflict. It tends to treat politics like a sporting event. Strategy, momentum, competition, and error often receive more coverage than a candidate's stance on policy, which may be complicated and difficult to explain accurately in a short news report.

Candidates, of course, try to get their messages to the voters through a combination of free media coverage and paid political advertising. Sometimes the two converge. For example, a controversial television advertisement may be released online and then shared on social media and aired free of charge on news shows that are reporting about it. Indeed, social media is transforming the way candidates communicate, with viral videos substituting for more expensive traditional ads.[86] Campaign speeches, photo opportunities, media interviews, and debates are other vehicles for free media exposure, although the traditional news media have a considerable amount of control over what they present and how they present it. For example, television news programs may air snippets from a speech, but reporters choose which snippets to air and also add their interpretation. Such news reports of candidate activities are sometimes referred to as *mostly mediated* messages because candidates do not appear to exercise much control over them. However, precisely because they appear to be out of the candidate's control, such coverage can have the most influence over the public.[87]

*Partially mediated* messages include things such as television interviews, debates, and press conferences where candidates have considerable leeway to say what they want. Nonetheless, they are partially mediated because members of the media are asking questions. Such questions act as a constraint on what the candidate can talk about, and reporters can also challenge what the candidates say. Candidates who respond well to tough questioning can win over swing

Debates are a form of partially mediated messaging. While candidates can say what they like, they are constrained by the moderators, who ask questions and may cut off a candidate who strays from the topic at hand.

voters.[88] Live coverage of presidential nominating conventions is another example of a partially mediated event.

Paid advertising—including on television, radio, and social media—is another way that candidates communicate their messages. Such communications are called *unmediated* messages because the media are mere conduits for their distribution. Although candidates control the content of advertising, the public know that they are meant to be self-serving and may be more apt to discount them than other types of messages.[89] Negative advertising has emerged as an especially common form of campaign advertising. The public claims to dislike such ads, but when they strike a chord with what voters already think or crystallize a perception, they can be very effective.

## ASSESSING THE MEDIA

Building upon what we have learned in the rest of this chapter, we now turn to an assessment of the media. In particular, we examine media bias and explore how journalistic norms structure the news and influence what we know (and don't know) about politics. Many factors can potentially create bias—including the personal political views of reporters, ownership patterns, and even the norms, values, and routines involved in the gathering and delivering of the news.

### BIASED NEWS

As we have already seen, the media engage in filtering and framing whenever they report the news. A frame may be consciously chosen to promote a particular agenda (such as an ideological bias). But the choice of a frame is sometimes merely a reflection of shared journalistic norms and conventions. For example, norms of objective journalism often lead to stories depicting two sides of an issue when, in reality, there may be *many* sides to that issue. And what if the sides (whether they are two or more) do not merit equal coverage? Should the media still give equal time to all of them? Quite simply, the frame can distort or oversimplify the issue, providing a false sense of "either–or." Attempts to create balanced coverage may also give a false impression that both sides of an issue are equally valid.

Consider a story on gun control. One possibility would be to frame it as a constitutional issue: Does gun control legislation violate your Second Amendment rights? Another would be to frame it as an issue of public safety: Does gun control legislation protect your children? Yet another might be to focus on the impact of gun control legislation on free enterprise. How might it affect jobs created by gun manufacturers? Such choices are inevitable. It is impossible to report the news or write anything—even this book—without framing the issues that are discussed. But the choice of a frame may alter the way the public interprets the issue. This leads to a persistent question: Is the media biased? And, if so, *how* is it biased? Is it an ideological bias? A corporate bias? Or is it a structural bias—one influenced by journalistic values and norms?

The media is often accused of ideological bias. President Nixon, for example, accused the media of a liberal bias, and President Trump has gone even further in his allegations of fake news and the charge that major media outlets are the "enemy of the American people." A 2018 Pew poll found that 68 percent of those surveyed believed that news organizations had a partisan bias (up from 45 percent in 1985). But that figure varies with party identification. Sixty-eight percent of Republicans but only 52 percent of Democrats believed that news organizations had a partisan bias.[90]

Some observers say that ideology is less important in influencing news stories than the corporate interests of those who own the media and that concentration of media ownership may make this corporate bias even worse. For example, reporters for daily newspapers may tend to be liberal, but those who own the newspapers tend to be conservative. How does this affect media coverage? Political scientist Michael Parenti is a proponent of the view that owners, often out of the fear of offending corporate advertisers, dictate what can and (probably more importantly) what *cannot* be covered. Thus, Parenti points to efforts to squelch stories that would harm corporate interests. For example, *The New York Times* publisher Arthur Sulzberger urged editors in the 1970s not to write stories about automobile safety and pollution that might offend the auto industry, which happened to be one of the paper's biggest advertisers.[91]

In short, private ownership of the media creates a commercial bias. The media is in business to make money and that purpose influences the way they market themselves. In addition to avoiding stories that may offend corporate sponsors, they may frame stories in such a way as to generate the largest possible audience. Concentration of media ownership fuels this concern. Six corporate conglomerates now dominate the industry.

## FORMULAIC NEWS

While some critics point to ideological or corporate bias in the news, others—such as political scientist Lance Bennett—have argued that journalistic values, norms, and routines may be more influential in structuring what the media reports and how it reports it. This structural bias results in the use of news formulas that shape the information we receive but which may not advance the cause of democracy. These formulas include personalization, dramatization, fragmentation, and what Bennett calls the "authority-disorder bias."[92]

*Personalization* refers to "the overwhelming tendency to downplay the big social, economic, or political picture in favor of the human trials, tragedies, and triumphs that sit at the surface of events." An emphasis on *dramatization* means that issues are presented as simple narratives that "emphasize crisis over continuity, the present over the past or future, and the personalities at their center."[93]

Personalization and dramatization work hand in hand to squelch in-depth analysis of complex policy issues such as health care reform. Instead, the media tend to offer dramatic narratives that emphasize conflicts between sharply drawn characters at the center of policy debates. Thus, instead of educating the public so that they can become informed, active participants in the political process, the media tend to treat politics as a spectator sport to be watched from the sidelines.

The emphasis on individual actors over the broader political context and on self-contained dramatic narratives at the expense of in-depth analysis promotes fragmentation. Stories are isolated from each other and from a broader context that would explain the issue or problem. Rather, they are presented as "dramatic capsules that make it difficult to see the causes of problems, their significance, or the connections across issues."[94] Stories of the famine in Ethiopia, discussed earlier in this chapter, suffered from the problem of fragmentation. Moreover, an issue that receives a great deal of attention one day may be displaced by another issue the next, making it difficult to trace the development of policy over time.

Finally, the so-called *authority-disorder bias* refers to the tendency of the news media to be preoccupied with stories about disorder—occasions when the normal world is called into question—framed by the questions of how, when, and whether authorities can establish or restore order. Natural disasters, economic crises, terrorist attacks, killers on the loose, and scandals perpetrated by supposedly trustworthy officials all inflict disorder in various ways. Bennett notes that the generic plot device of authorities attempting to restore order "can be combined endlessly within personalized, dramatized, and fragmented news episodes."[95] Thus, stories about the BP oil leak in the Gulf of Mexico were less likely to focus on the broader policy issues associated with offshore drilling and its safety and more likely to focus on the short-term success or failure of BP executives and government officials to stop the leak. The story largely went away when the oil leak was plugged, even though the policy issues involved were as important as ever.

# CONSEQUENCES FOR DEMOCRACY

Clearly, the media plays a very important role in a democracy: It provides information about government and politics to the people. Our system of government depends upon free and open lines of communication. How well the media actually performs this function has been affected by technological changes, government regulation, and the relationship between reporters and public officials.

Radio, television, satellites, cable television, the Internet, and social media have all expanded the range of information we receive and the immediacy with which we receive it. What are the consequences of that for democracy? On the one hand, greater information should allow Americans to hold political representatives more fully accountable. On the other hand, disinformation spread through social media and other new technologies can be used to undermine our democratic system. For better or worse, the way news is conveyed affects the body politic. Media helped to foment the American Revolution in the 1700s, just as it helped to unite a nation against foreign enemies during World War II. Today, narrowcasting, social media, cable news rants, and anonymous blogs exacerbate polarized politics even as they offer us unprecedented amounts of information and an unprecedented ability to share our views. Is this flood of information a good thing?

Government regulation of the media is also a double-edged sword. It can be used to protect against disinformation on social media, the concentration of media ownership (thereby promoting localism and the diversity of news sources), and offensive broadcasts of indecent material. But at what point does such regulation violate the First Amendment, interfere with free enterprise, or even violate privacy rights? Is democracy better or worse served by regulation?

Finally, the relationship between reporters and officials has consequences for democracy. Reporters act as gatekeepers of information—filtering and framing the news—and pack journalism can promote uniform coverage spoon-fed to reporters by government officials (as opposed to independent analysis and hard-hitting reports). But what are the alternatives? Could we survive without the White House press corps or other packs that cover candidates and institutions? Do we really want news with no professional gatekeeping? That is what has happened on social media. Without gatekeepers to filter the accuracy and importance of news, it is difficult for news consumers to assess the significance and accuracy of the information they receive.

All of this ought to matter to you. First and foremost, your ability to influence government decisions is diminished if you do not understand the basis of those decisions, the consequences of those decisions, and how to affect those decisions. Knowledge is power—power that allows you to make political decisions that are in your best interest. The media provide access to that knowledge and venues to express your opinions. Many people in many parts of the world lack that opportunity. In such places, state-run media, censorship, and harsh government crackdowns stifle freedom of the press and the ability of the citizenry to express their views.

## Critical Thinking Questions

1. As you read the news and watch reports on television, can you identify examples of personalization, dramatization, and fragmentation in the news? Can you find examples of authority-disorder bias? Are these a problem?

2. Is it bad that so many media reports come from routine channels of information? Is it practical to move away from such dependence?

3. Does the media do a good job of socializing our young people?

4. Is the new media good or bad for democracy? Why?

## Key Terms

citizen journalist, 247

equal time rule, 256

Fairness Doctrine, 256

Federal Communications Commission (FCC), 255

filtering, 245

Fourth Estate, 250

framing, 245

gatekeeping, 246

going public, 260

mass media, 244

media effects, 252

muckraking, 250

narrowcasting, 252

net neutrality, 256

new media, 253

objective journalism, 250

pack journalism, 260

partisan press, 249

penny press, 249

photo opportunity, 261

social media, 253

spin, 260

talk radio, 251

yellow journalism, 250

Visit edge.sagepub.com/maltese to help you accomplish your coursework goals in an easy-to-use learning environment.

# 11
# CONGRESS

## After reading this chapter, you should be able to do the following:

- Explain the responsibilities of Congress to the American people and its relationship with the other institutions of government.

- Describe the powers granted to Congress by the Constitution, how Congress uses these powers, and the situations in which Congress would carry out or extend these powers.

- Explain how the historical context that produced the current congressional structure creates a complex lawmaking process.

- Identify the key players and the critical building blocks that allow Congress to function effectively.

- Understand how Congress builds enough agreement among members to ensure coherent action.

- Explain the idealized version of how a bill becomes a law and how Congress adopts an annual budget.

## Perspective: Can Legislatures Exercise Effective Control Over the Use of Force?

Representative Barbara Lee (D-CA) stood alone on September 14, 2001. When the House considered the authorization to use military force (AUMF) in response to the terrorist attacks carried out by al-Qaeda in New York City and Washington, DC, she cast the sole negative vote in either house of Congress. The congressional resolution authorized the president

> to use all necessary and appropriate force against those nations, organizations, or persons he determines planned, authorized, committed, or aided the terrorist attacks that occurred on September 11, 2001, or harbored such organizations or persons, in order to prevent any future acts of international terrorism against the United States by such nations, organizations or persons.[1]

That day, the Senate adopted the resolution by a vote of 98–0 with two senators absent, and the House approved the resolution 420–1 with 10 absences. Rep. Lee explained that she feared the authorization was too open-ended, included neither an exit strategy nor a clear target, and reminded her of the Gulf of Tonkin Resolution, a 1964 authorization to use force that had served as the foundation for a dramatic expansion of U.S. involvement in Vietnam.[2] In the following days, she became the target of hate mail and received police protection, but the vote did not damage her career, as she continued to be elected from her San Francisco Bay-area district by overwhelming margins.

No decision of government is more significant than deciding to use military force, a life-and-death commitment of a nation's people. Under the Constitution of the United States, Congress is given the exclusive power to declare war, as it has done five times, but Congress has authorized presidents to use force 30 additional times in American history.[3] Following the AUMF, the Bush administration began bombing Taliban targets and terrorist training camps in Afghanistan in early October, then sent combat forces to pursue the responsible terrorists, but became bogged down in a long-running civil war. In 2003, Congress again authorized using military forces in the Middle East when the Bush administration sought and received congressional approval to invade Iraq.

The U.S. now finds itself at war with terrorist groups around the globe, an effort that the Bush, Obama, and Trump administrations justified by stretching the original purpose of the 2001 AUMF, something that Congress never intended. Tom Daschle (D-SD), the Senate Majority Leader in 2001, rejected more open-ended language sought by the administration—to "deter and pre-empt any future acts of terrorism or aggression against the United States"[4]— precisely to avoid uncontrolled expansion of a military commitment. During floor debate on the resolution, several senators made this intent quite clear. Today's global war on terror is unlimited by geography, time, or tactics. Members of terrorist groups that did not exist in 2001 and could have had no connection to al-Qaeda are the targets of U.S. kidnapping, assassination, and drone attacks. At the outset of 2019, U.S. military forces engaged terrorist splinter groups on six continents in 80 nations. Housed on 40 military bases, U.S. troops conducted 65 counterterrorism training programs, engaged in combat in 14 nations, and targeted air and drone strikes in 7 nations.[5]

Rep. Lee still speaks out against the original AUMF and is no longer alone. After losing repeated efforts to repeal the 2001 resolution, she convinced a bipartisan majority on the House Appropriations Committee in June 2017 to support her amendment to the Department of Defense appropriation bill to end the AUMF eight months after Congress voted to do so, allowing time for Congress to create a new AUMF that covered the dramatically different situation sixteen years later. Despite winning the committee's support, the Speaker of the House of Representatives had the Rules Committee strip Lee's amendment from the bill that was considered on the floor of the House.[6] Thus, the 2001 authorization continues in force.

While Congress has struggled to reassert control over the use of military force, the British Parliament has been more successful in establishing a new claim to exercise that power. Sixty-seven citizens of the United Kingdom died in the attacks on September 11, the largest loss of life by any nation other than the United States. Reflecting that shared loss and the long tradition of a close U.S.–United Kingdom (UK) alliance, when President Bush spoke with Prime Minister Tony Blair early on September 12, the British PM pledged his government's support. British air and ground forces joined the U.S. in Afghanistan until they were withdrawn in 2014. Although the British Parliament met three times in the wake of 9/11, including the day after the U.S. and UK bombing campaign began, Parliament adopted no AUMF comparable to that in the U.S., as it has no formal authority to participate in decisions to use force. Without a constitutional role in decision making, war has always been regarded as a royal prerogative with the prime minister acting in the sovereign's stead. The British government has the authority to use force without involving Parliament.[7]

As a way to defend himself against mounting criticism within his own Labour Party, however, Tony Blair decided to break with tradition and asked Parliament to support sending military forces to join U.S. troops in Iraq in 2003.[8] Parliament voted yes, though much controversy later arose around whether Blair had told the truth about the threat posed by Iraq's dictator. Since then there has been a flourishing debate about whether Parliament should expect to play such a role in the future for "significant non-routine" deployments. There was a watershed in 2013: Parliament rejected the government's proposed use of force in response to Syria's use of chemical weapons against its citizens. Parliament has since twice voted in favor of using force against Islamic State of Iraq and Syria (ISIS), an especially brutal terrorist group, in Iraq in 2014 and again in Syria in 2015. But the UK government, without consulting Parliament, ordered air power to join the U.S. and France in punishing the Syrian government for attacking its civilians in 2018.

Rather than being formally authorized by a constitution or law, Parliament's role is considered a "convention," a widely accepted understanding about the role Parliament should play. If public and elite opinion insist that the use of military force is only legitimate if the prime minister secures prior approval from Parliament, then members of Parliament may now exercise greater power over these critical life-and-death decisions than members of Congress who have enjoyed that constitutional power for more than two centuries. **«**

# THE FUNCTIONS OF CONGRESS

Congress is the branch of government charged with making laws and representing the people. In this section, we will first consider how citizens can use Congress to guide government. Then we will look closely at services provided to constituents and mechanisms for overseeing the executive branch.

## LEGITIMACY AND REPRESENTATION

Legislatures arose in history as a way for monarchs to meet their subjects' demand to participate in governing and to voice their views on public affairs. In this way, legislatures provide government with **popular legitimacy**, the sense that because citizens help shape the government's decisions, these decisions will be accepted by the people. Legislatures help constituents navigate the bureaucracy and, at the same time, represent local interests. This is true even in nations where legislatures are overshadowed by powerful executives.[9]

Congress was intended by the framers of the Constitution to be "the people's branch" and the principal means for the people to control the government. From the outset, voters directly elected members of the House of Representatives. Senators were originally chosen by state legislatures, but the nation established popular election of senators in 1917 when states ratified the Seventeenth Amendment.[10] Because legislators expect to be held accountable by voters in their states or districts, members of Congress are likely to translate the people's will into programs and policies.

There is a strong tradition in the United States for legislators to represent the local interests of their constituents, which are not always in line with those of the nation as a whole. Local representation was paramount under the Articles of Confederation when members of Congress represented the interests of their states. Under the Constitution, members of the House link the national government to even smaller areas within states, and representatives are attentive to the particular needs of their districts' residents. Instead of readily articulating a single vision, it is therefore the job of Congress to construct a common vision out of the 435 House and 100 Senate views of what the nation's interest really is.

U.S. election rules heighten this constituency-first perspective. By using single-member districts (as discussed in Chapter 8—one representative chosen for a smaller area rather than several from a large district), it is virtually certain that members of Congress working in Washington will be attentive to the top priorities of the folks who elected them back home. Voting systems make a big difference in this regard. Many parliamentary democracies use proportional voting systems that de-emphasize ties to a local constituency and instead produce a more general party perspective. Germany tries to produce a legislature with both a local and a larger perspective; each voter casts two ballots for members of the lower house of parliament, one vote for a

> **popular legitimacy:** The belief among the citizens of a political system that the government's actions deserve to be obeyed because they reflect the will of the people.

legislator chosen from a geographic constituency and the other for a party. Party votes determine how many candidates on a party list obtain seats based on the party's share of the vote in each land (state).[11]

**MODELS OF REPRESENTATION**  Members of Congress are generally expected to represent their constituencies' interests and ideals. But do they? Do they vote in line with what their constituents want? Or do they rise above these localized needs to serve what they see as the greater interests of the nation? Congress sometimes chooses a course contrary to public opinion. To explain this behavior, political scientists have identified three different models of representation: the trustee model, the delegate model, and the politico model.

The **trustee model** of representation conflicts with widely held beliefs in the United States. In this view, elected representatives should draw on their own competence and follow their own convictions in making decisions on behalf of their constituents; constituents chose them and expect them to use their judgment in making decisions; elections will later determine whether they continue to enjoy voters' confidence. Under this model, legislators are elected for their skills, good character, and judgment. Once in office, they are not obliged to respond to the preferences of their constituents, which are seldom clear enough to use as a guide in making decisions. Edmund Burke, an eighteenth-century Irish philosopher who was a longtime member of the British Parliament, is credited with articulating this view of the relationship with his constituents.

The contrary position, the **delegate model** of representation, contends that representatives should consult their constituents on pending issues and follow the views of their district's voters, even if doing so goes against their own personal preferences or best judgment. Voters can be more confident this will happen if they elect a representative who shares their policy preferences. Many legislators now use district polls—mail or phone—to determine their constituents' views on pending policy issues. Visits back home allow legislators to hear constituents' views in person, and town hall meetings are one way to ensure that those views reflect a cross-section rather than only the legislator's closest supporters.

It is unlikely that any one legislator is always a trustee or always a delegate. Instead, a legislator's approach to representation is likely to be located along a sliding scale with trustee and delegate at opposite poles. The **politico model** of representation recognizes that legislators are likely to respond to their constituents' views differently at different times. Politicos will be sensitive to the needs of their constituents some of the time but will also follow their own judgment at others.[12] In fact, adept politicians will strike a balance between relying on their own judgment and following the apparent wishes of their constituency, particularly when these are strongly expressed. However, it would be difficult to determine constituents' wishes on every issue, and we know that public opinion often shifts. At a minimum, legislators will not want to follow every whim of constituency opinion, but they also realize they must have an explanation for going against strongly held views on important issues.

To make sure legislators are representing their values and interests, citizens can scrutinize the activities of their representatives. Since 1979, the House has televised its proceedings on the floor; the Senate began to televise its proceedings in 1986. Even more complete is the *Congressional Record*, a nearly verbatim account of the events on the House and Senate floors, corrected for grammatical errors and with extended comments supplied by the members, that has been published overnight since 1873. The *Congressional Record* includes a digest of congressional activities for that day—bills introduced, votes taken, and committee meetings held—and full versions of amendments and bills. The Library of Congress maintains a computerized database of these materials dubbed *THOMAS* in honor of Thomas Jefferson. Gavel-to-gavel coverage of House and Senate proceedings is available on C-SPAN (the Cable-Satellite Public Affairs Network), as are many committee hearings. Transparency can be found in other nations as well. The British House of Lords began televising its proceedings in 1985 and the House of Commons followed in 1989. Online coverage includes up to 18 channels of committee and floor proceedings.[13] Germany began televising the work of its lower house in 1999; other parliaments and public service broadcasters around the world

**trustee model:**  A form of representation in which legislators are not required to reflect the preferences and opinions of their constituents because voters expect them to use their own knowledge and good judgment.

**delegate model:**  A form of representation in which legislators closely reflect the preferences and opinions of constituents in discharging their representative responsibilities—for example, voting the way constituents prefer on an issue.

**politico model:**  A form of representation in which legislators play different roles depending on whether constituents have strong views on an issue and the nature of that issue.

have discussed how to provide greater public access to the work of national legislatures.[14]

**PORK BARREL PROJECTS AND EARMARKS** Legislators are not only sensitive to their constituency's political interests but have also historically served local economic needs. Until late in the nineteenth century, serving in Congress was largely a part-time job while farming, operating a business, or practicing law was a full-time job back home. Having a part-time legislature ensured that representatives would remain closely tied to their constituents' lives. Local representatives traveled to Washington, DC, to encourage support for westward expansion and economic growth by allocating public money for the construction of roads, canals, and railroads as well as jobs and contracts for services and supplies. By the last half of the nineteenth century, it was widely expected that legislators would deliver a share of this public **pork barrel**, the benefits funded by the national treasury and distributed throughout the nation to their districts' residents. Today, federal dollars for weapons systems, highway construction, government research, and education can sometimes be pieces of pork that legislators are expected to deliver back home. When serving in Congress became a full-time job, legislators spent most of their time in Washington, DC, rather than in their districts. Pork barrel spending grew, especially in the 1990s, as it became a way for members hoping to secure reelection to show what they had done for their districts. There is also enormous temptation for legislators to help campaign donors or benefit themselves.

The proposed Gravina Island Bridge in Ketchikan, Alaska, would have connected the mainland to an island with 50 residents at a cost of nearly $400 million. It was strongly supported by the Alaska congressional delegation but, after critics dubbed it "the Bridge to Nowhere," it became a symbol of wasteful earmark spending.

Pressures to meet the needs of local constituents are by no means limited to the United States. One study found that the election rules used to select members of the German parliament influenced how responsive they were to meeting constituency needs. Remember, Germany follows a two-tiered system described earlier. Members of parliament chosen by constituency-based votes (single-member districts) are more likely to serve on legislative committees that benefit their local voters, while legislators chosen by party-list votes (proportional representation) serve on committees likely to benefit their parties.[15] In Australia, parties find ways to funnel benefits to those areas of the country where their candidates have been less successful as a way to improve their electoral chances.[16] Brazil was long believed to be a classic example of how legislators pursue pork to help themselves get reelected, but closer research found that the real goal of sending benefits back home was not so much to win votes as to obtain campaign funds from wealthy interests benefiting from the distribution of public programs.[17] Thus, we find legislators in many parts of the world behaving in similar though not identical ways.

With the U.S. federal budget deficit ballooning in the new century, there was growing pressure to reduce the amount of federal pork returned to constituents. Controversy especially focused on **earmarks**, spending on projects authorized by Congress without undergoing the usual process of review. These projects are typically relatively small, such as a park, an arts center, a road or bridge, a summer camp, or jobs in a local factory. Each earmark may be modest, but the cumulative effect is significant. As documented by Citizens Against Government Waste, an advocacy group opposed to wasteful spending, the number of earmarks peaked at 14,000 in 2005 (see Figure 11.1) and their dollar value at $29 billion in 2006.

While it is easy to denounce earmarks as examples of wasteful spending and invitations to corruption, they also reflect legislators' response to local needs by committing a small percentage of the federal budget (one-third of one percent in 2018). Some students of Congress defend earmarks as part of the legislature's legitimate constitutional role; others condemn them. Under pressure from Tea Party members, House Republicans adopted a two-year ban on earmarks in

**pork barrel:** The traditional way to preserve pork for gradual consumption; it refers more recently to public money used to meet local needs that lack a sound public purpose.

**earmarks:** Provisions in a bill that provide a benefit to a specific organization or for a specific project either through direct spending or a tax break.

## FIGURE 11.1

## *Earmark Spending, 1991 to 2018*

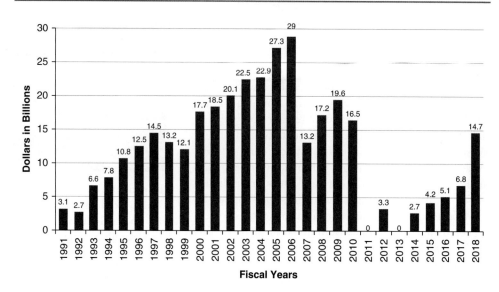

Source: *Citizens Against Government Waste*, 2018 Congressional Pig Book, *https://www.cagw.org/reporting/pig-book*

2010. Both Senate Democrats and Republicans did the same for 2011, and the practice declined dramatically. But Congress devised other, less obvious ways to direct funds to local projects, and in 2019, House Democrats began discussing how to establish a reformed earmarking system.[18]

## DEMOGRAPHIC REPRESENTATION

Although members of Congress are expected to represent the people who elected them to office, they do not reflect the demographic composition of the larger population. In other words, Congress is not a microcosm of American society (see Table 11.1). Consistently, the proportion of women in Congress is lower than in the general population, and the same is true for African Americans and Hispanics. In fact, most members in both chambers are older, white men. Likewise, they are far better educated and drawn from a rather narrow range of professional fields.

Although minority representation remains disproportionately low, there has been a gradual increase in the number of women and persons of color in Congress over the past 30 years. There were fewer than 20 women in Congress in 1977. After a record number of women ran for Congress in the 2018 midterms, there were 132 women members, 25 in the Senate and 107 in the House. In both chambers, female Democrats outnumbered female Republicans by a substantial margin, 17–6 in the Senate and 91–16 in the House.[19] The number of African Americans has also grown: There were about 20 African American members of Congress in 1977 and 56 in 2019. All told, 116 nonwhite lawmakers were serving in Congress in January 2019, a dramatic 84 percent increase from the total of 63 in 2001. African American representation in Congress is close to their proportion of the national population (13 percent), and representation for Native Americans is equal at one percent. Hispanic representation (8 percent) is half their share of the general population (18 percent), and Asians make up 3 percent of the House and 6 percent of the general population.[20]

**TABLE 11.1**

*Selected Comparisons of the 116th Congress and the U.S. National Population*

| Characteristic | 116th Congress | National Population |
|---|---|---|
| Average age | 47 years (House) 65 years (Senate) | 38 |
| Completed associate's, bachelor's, or higher degree | 96% (House) 100% (Senate) | 30.9% completed BA |
| Law degree | 33% (House) 47% (Senate) | 0.41% (registered attorneys) |
| Women | 24.5% | 50.8% |
| African American | 10.1% | 13.4% |
| Hispanic | 7.8% | 18.1% |

*Sources: Statistical data on the composition of the national population is gathered from government sources including the U.S. Census and National Center for Education Statistics. Data on 116th Congress from CQ Magazine (November 12, 2018) and Pew Research Center.*

Moreover, African Americans and women have become more influential in Congress. Nancy Pelosi's service as Speaker of the House from January 2007 to January 2011 and again in January 2019 demonstrates how women have become part of the congressional power structure. For the session that began in 2019, 10 of the 21 standing House committees were chaired by an African American, Latino, Asian, or female member. (See Figure 11.2.) Despite long-term improvements, however, the United States still trails many other nations in terms of the percentage of women in the lower house of the legislature, ranking 76th in a 2018 report examining 187 nations.[21]

If you believe that only someone with your own demographic characteristics can accurately reflect your views, a position known as **descriptive representation,** Congress will inevitably perform its representation function poorly for most of us. The other possibility is **substantive representation,** in which a legislator advocates for a group's interests even without sharing that group's demographic characteristics. This view shifts the emphasis from who representatives *are* to what they *do*. John, Teddy, and Robert Kennedy provide classic examples of politicians who came from a wealthy Massachusetts family but championed the interests of minorities and the poor. Lawyers—of whom there are many in Congress—are trained to represent clients' interests regardless of their background, perhaps helping them to understand as well as represent the needs of people unlike themselves.

## CONSTITUENCY SERVICE

Many scholars argue that above all else, modern legislators who make a career of public service are concerned with reelection.[22] To ensure reelection, they must go beyond the responsibilities of legislating in DC to serve their constituents. Through their offices at home and on Capitol Hill, representatives and senators have staffs to provide **constituency service** to residents of their districts—to offer information about federal programs, intercede on the citizens' behalf in their dealings with government bureaucrats, and assist in applying for benefits or federal jobs. District-based staffs help constituents with numerous concerns such as contacting federal agencies to resolve problems, assisting with passports, dealing with Social Security and veterans' benefits, obtaining federal grants, flying flags over the Capitol that can be presented as keepsakes, and arranging tours of the U.S.

**descriptive representation:** The belief that the extent to which a legislature reflects the demographic composition of the larger population is vitally important in determining the legislature's responsiveness to group needs.

**substantive representation:** The capacity of a legislator or a legislature to represent the interests of groups despite not sharing the demographic characteristics of that group.

**constituency service:** Assistance provided by representatives and senators to help residents of their districts or states resolve problems involving government programs and agencies.

FIGURE 11.2

## *Growing Racial and Ethnic Diversity in Congress, 2001–2019*

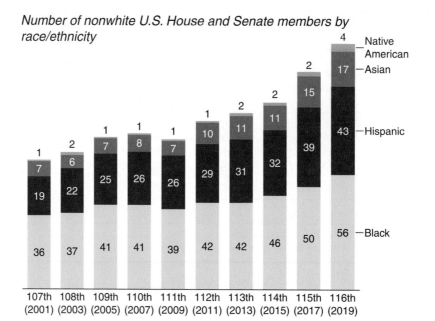

Number of nonwhite U.S. House and Senate members by race/ethnicity

*Note: Nonvoting delegates and commissioners excluded. Figures represent makeup of Congress on the first day of each session. Only first year of each Congress is labeled. Asian includes Pacific Islanders. Members who have more than one racial or ethnic identity are counted in each applicable group.*

*Source: Kristen Bialik, "For the Fifth Time in a Row, the New Congress Is the Most Racially and Ethnically Diverse Ever," Pew Research Center, February 8, 2019, http://www.pewresearch.org/fact-tank/2019/02/08/for-the-fifth-time-in-a-row-the-new-congress-is-the-most-racially-and-ethnically-diverse-ever/*

**Although Congress remains predominantly white and male, it is becoming more representative of the population at large. The 116th Congress includes more women than ever before, including the 89 Democratic members of the House seen here.**

Capitol. A list of services offered by a given representative can be found on his or her website, usually under a paragraph explaining how important constituency service is to the legislator.

Legislators meet regularly with constituents in Washington, DC, and back in their home districts. Members of Congress have meals at their neighborhood restaurants and attend Rotary Club meetings, religious gatherings, and other community events; all of these activities provide opportunities to connect with constituents and make their presence known in the community.[23] In Chapter 8, we discussed the advantages incumbents have over challengers. Research has shown that representatives serving their first terms (freshmen) are most vulnerable to being defeated for reelection and are therefore more likely to make more frequent home visits than colleagues with greater seniority. This reinforces the notion that home service is particularly valuable for those seeking reelection.

## LAWMAKING

Lawmaking is perhaps the most important activity of Congress, and the process is always complex and often unappealing. Otto von Bismarck, a nineteenth-century German leader, supposedly remarked, "Laws are like sausages; it is better not to see them being made." Regardless whether this statement is real or apocryphal, its meaning is clear—the process is not pretty.

Nonetheless, as Figure 11.3 shows, Congress devotes tremendous amounts of time and attention to lawmaking—the process of considering and passing bills. A **bill** is a proposal for a government program or action, originating in either the House or Senate, that applies to the entire nation. Over a period of 15 Congresses—each Congress consists of the two-year period between national elections—one sees variation in the number of public laws approved through the legislative process. Not all are significant—fully 30 percent of the laws passed in 2017–2019 were not.[24] Far more proposals were introduced during those two years—a staggering 13,556—than passed.[25] Winnowing down the volume of proposed bills usually falls to congressional committees who ignore some requests, combine others, or simply cannot muster sufficient support to act on still others. In other words, the steep drop-off between bills introduced and enacted could well reflect a great deal of work, not always a failure to act.

## EXECUTIVE OVERSIGHT

Under the U.S. system of separate institutions sharing powers, Congress checks the actions of the executive branch, including both presidents and bureaucrats. Congress investigates actions of the president and the bureaucracy in multiple ways. Individual members of Congress can write letters to federal officials inquiring into problems encountered by constituents. Such efforts are likely to bear greater fruit if a committee or subcommittee initiates the investigation by holding formal hearings where agency officials and nongovernmental experts provide testimony on key questions. Committee staff might also conduct extensive research or ask a research arm of Congress—the Congressional Research Service or the Government Accountability Office—to conduct an evaluation. Executive officials, of course, frequently view such oversight efforts as intrusive, interfering with the discharge of their duties.

One of the more delicate areas of Congressional oversight is the collection of national intelligence and the activities of U.S. spy agencies. A Senate investigation conducted in the 1970s revealed that the Central Intelligence Agency (CIA) had conducted surveillance on U.S. citizens who opposed the Vietnam War. The agency had also plotted to assassinate at least five foreign leaders (although officials reported never having been successful) and had overthrown several constitutionally elected governments (Guatemala and Iran, 1954; Greece, 1967; and Chile, 1973) regarded as too radical for the safety of American interests. Congress replaced the weak and informal oversight that it had exercised over intelligence activities for decades with new and permanent intelligence committees.

Concern about overseeing spy agencies is not limited to the United States. The UK Parliament's Intelligence and Security Committee (ISC) now has power to oversee the operations of Britain's intelligence agencies—MI5 (comparable to the Federal

### FIGURE 11.3

## Three Decades of Legislative Productivity in U.S. Congress

*Number of public laws enacted by each Congress, by type*

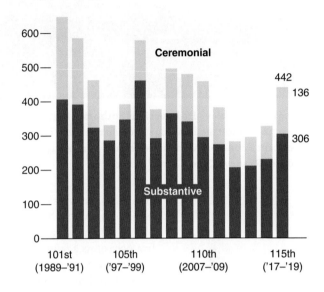

*Note: "Substantive" laws include any passed legislation that makes a change in federal law or authorizes the spending of taxpayer dollars. "Ceremonial" laws include those that rename buildings, award medals, designate special days, authorize commemorative coins, or otherwise memorialize historic events.*

*Source: Drew Desilver, "A Productivity Scorecard for the 115th Congress: More Laws Than Before, but Not More Substance," Pew Research Center, January 25, 2019, http://www.pewresearch.org/fact-tank/2019/01/25/a-productivity-scorecard-for-115th-congress/*

> **bill:** A proposal for government action that is introduced in either the House or Senate and may result in a law.

Congress exercises its oversight authority in part through committee hearings such as this one, in which the Joint Economic Committee heard testimony from Federal Reserve Chair Janet Yellen.

Bureau of Investigation), MI6 (comparable to the CIA), and Government Communications Headquarters (GCHQ, comparable to the National Security Agency). For years, the committee could only oversee policy, organization, and budget questions and could not require the agencies to share classified material. This changed in 2013, and the ISC has investigated several alleged intelligence failures or misdeeds.[26] Such investigations are unusual in a parliamentary system where ministers in the government also hold seats in parliament, the government's actions are aligned with the parliament's preferences, and parliament is not constitutionally independent.[27]

## SHAPING FOREIGN POLICY

Congress sometimes flexes its muscles in foreign policy—that is, asserts its institutional prerogatives. Declaring war is one of the constitutional powers the framers granted to Congress, an open acknowledgement of the Founders' concern that monarchs (and executives) are less reluctant to engage in war than the people's representatives assembled in Congress. In U.S. history, Congress and the president have agreed to wage war on five occasions against 11 foreign nations. In addition, several extended military engagements have occurred that critics have called *undeclared wars*—conflicts for which the government did not formally declare war. In these instances, Congress provided necessary funding and sometimes explicitly approved the use of force through means other than a formal declaration of war, most recently the Iraq War (2003–2011). Further, there have been hundreds of other instances in which U.S. forces have been deployed at the president's direction and without explicit congressional approval.[28]

Following the withdrawal of U.S. combat forces from Vietnam, Congress sought to avoid a repeat of a war that critics widely regarded as a "presidential war." Over President Nixon's veto, Congress passed the War Powers Resolution, a statute that legislators hoped would guarantee that Congress would be fully consulted before presidents made military commitments and would give Congress the option of forcing future presidents to withdraw the military from combat operations. This resolution has done little to restrain presidential action, however, and Congress continues to feel bypassed by presidents who use military forces when they deem it necessary to do so (see Chapter 12). This was true in 2011, when President Barack Obama used American forces to support the military operations of NATO (North Atlantic Treaty Organization) allies against Libya, and twice when President Trump ordered limited U.S. air strikes on Syrian targets in retaliation for that government's use of chemical weapons on civilians. Congress was not consulted beforehand in either instance—something that members of the opposition party decried.

The Senate is charged with providing "advice and consent" on treaties (Article II, Section 2 of the Constitution). Treaties require a two-thirds vote for approval. Few have been rejected outright (only 22 of several thousand submitted), but some have been withdrawn by the president in the face of certain defeat (at least 85) or been amended by a simple majority vote before being approved.[29] Presidents may object to the changes in an already negotiated treaty that the Senate insists upon including in the final product. Most famously, Senate critics presented President Woodrow Wilson with a list of 14 conditions if he wanted their approval of the Treaty of Versailles that ended World War I and established the League of Nations. Wilson angrily rejected the conditions and directed his Senate allies to vote against it. Consequently, the United States never approved the treaty nor did it join the League. Other treaties have died in committee when senators opposed to the agreement refuse to take action.

An example of this sort of delay is the Convention on the Elimination of All Forms of Discrimination Against Women (CEDAW), what is commonly described as a universal bill of rights for women. The United States is one of only seven nations in the world that have not yet ratified this treaty signed in July 1980. The Senate Foreign Relations Committee recommended the treaty in 1994, 2002, and 2010, but opponents have blocked action on the floor. Opponents claim to be concerned about workplace rights such as mandatory paid maternity leave and equal pay for work of equal value, abortion rights, and military service.[30]

There are no provisions in the Constitution for terminating treaties, so it is unclear whether presidents can do so on their own or whether presidents require the Senate's advice and consent. President Carter unilaterally terminated a U.S. defense treaty with Taiwan in 1978 as a prelude to establishing diplomatic relations with China, setting off a controversy, but his action prevailed. In the post–World War II period, presidents have turned increasingly to the use of executive agreements rather than treaties as a way to conduct foreign relations. Executive agreements do not require Senate approval. (See the discussion in Chapter 12.)

# CONSTITUTIONAL POWERS

In Chapter 2, we learned that Congress exercises both *enumerated* and *implied powers* (see Table 11.2). In this section, we explore some of these powers in greater depth.

## NECESSARY AND PROPER CLAUSE

Congress has used its final power, found in the necessary and proper clause, to expand its influence beyond the enumerated powers. Because of its catch-all character, the necessary and proper clause provides Congress with enormous flexibility, giving it another name—the elastic clause—because it has allowed Congress to stretch its institutional power to include responsibilities the Founders did not originally describe. The clause has given rise to countless actions by Congress that have expanded its reach. For example, while federal criminal laws probably numbered about 100 in 1900, they now are estimated at more than 3,000, some dealing with areas of law traditionally reserved for the states. As we have seen, the boundary between state and federal powers is not clearly drawn and is sometimes a matter of dispute. In a June 2011 Supreme Court case, Carol Bond of Pennsylvania appealed a six-year sentence

**TABLE 11.2**

## Abridged Version of the Enumerated Powers of Congress, Found in Article I, Section 8 of the Constitution

- Provide for national revenues—taxes, import and export duties, and special fees—as long as they apply equally across the nation.
- Borrow money to meet national expenses.
- Regulate international as well as interstate trade.
- Regulate bankruptcies, establishing laws that apply across the nation.
- Coin money and regulate its value relative to foreign currencies.
- Establish a uniform system of weights and measures.
- Establish and enforce laws against counterfeiting.
- Establish a system of post offices and highways.
- Oversee copyrights and patents for new inventions.
- Establish uniform rules about becoming a citizen.
- Create a system of federal courts below the Supreme Court.
- Define and punish piracy and violations of international law.
- Declare war as well as establish, maintain, and govern land and naval forces.
- Organize, arm, oversee, and call out the national guard ("the militia") to enforce national law, suppress rebellions, and repel invasions.
- Make all laws that are necessary and proper to carry out these and its other powers.

for violating a federal chemical weapons law when she spread chemicals on the car, front-door handle, and mailbox of a woman having an affair with her husband. The Court ruled unanimously that she could challenge the federal law as impinging on state jurisdiction, where she would have received a much lighter sentence.[31]

## IMPEACHMENT

Although the two congressional chambers must exercise many powers jointly, the Constitution also enumerates a few powers specific to each chamber. The House is authorized to initiate all revenue bills (Article I, Section 7), for instance, and to initiate impeachment of government officials, including the president (Article I, Section 2).

Since 1789, the House has initiated impeachment proceedings 17 times, twice against a president—Andrew Johnson in 1868 and Bill Clinton in 1998. (The House came close to taking action against John Tyler in 1842, and in 1974, the House Judiciary Committee approved charges against Richard Nixon, but the president resigned before the entire House voted on articles of impeachment.) The other cases involved the impeachment of federal judges. In these proceedings, which are often likened to a trial, the House serves as prosecutor and the Senate fills the role of judge and jury (the Chief Justice of the Supreme Court presides in cases against presidents), voting on the charges, with a two-thirds majority required for removal. The Senate has removed eight federal judges from office, acquitted six judges, halted action after one judge resigned, and acquitted the two presidents. Most recently, G. Thomas Porteous, Jr., of the U.S. District Court for the Eastern District of Louisiana, was impeached by the U.S. House of Representatives on charges of accepting bribes and making false statements under penalty of perjury. He was convicted by the U.S. Senate and removed from office on December 8, 2010.[32]

## APPOINTMENTS

Article II, Section 2 requires the Senate to give its advice and consent on many presidential nominations. Given the large number of appointments subject to Senate approval, the chamber seldom rejects nominees. According to an official estimate, roughly 4,000 civilian and 65,000 military nominations are submitted to the Senate during each two-year session of Congress.[33] Most appointees subject to Senate confirmation leave office when the president departs, but federal judges hold office for life (unless they are removed for misbehavior), giving the Senate considerable influence over the judiciary. Throughout its entire history, the Senate has voted down only nine presidential nominees for cabinet positions (most recently in 1989), though additional nominees have withdrawn during the process. For example, Andrew Puzder, a former fast food chain executive nominated by President Trump to serve as secretary of labor, withdrew from consideration the day before he was to have a committee confirmation hearing in 2017 amidst allegations of domestic abuse and sexual harassment.[34] The Senate has also rejected 12 nominees for Supreme Court vacancies; another 12 withdrew their nominations, and the Senate took no action on 10 more.[35] (See Chapters 12 and 14.)

## THE STRUCTURE OF CONGRESS

Globally, legislatures arose in different historical contexts and developed differently. Although Canada and the United States share a common history as colonies of Great Britain, Canada remained a colony longer, did not rebel against the monarchy, and adopted British practices drawn from a later period in British constitutional development. Hence, Canada's prime minister heads a government supported by a majority in the House of Commons and leads a cabinet with collective responsibility for executive policies. Both of these were developments in British politics that followed American independence. (See Chapter 12 for more on the parliamentary model.) In the same way, many African and Asian nations adopted legislative systems closely resembling those of their colonizers; often, those systems were established by the colonizing countries prior to withdrawing from the nation.

## BICAMERALISM

As we discussed in Chapter 2, congressional representation was a major issue at the constitutional convention in 1787 and ultimately resulted in a **bicameral legislature**, meaning that Congress is composed of two parts, with proportional representation in the House and equal representation of states in the Senate. The House of Representatives, with directly elected representatives, was intended to be more responsive to the wishes of the people and face reelection—and evaluation by the public—every two years. Senators, originally chosen by the state legislatures and serving for longer terms, were expected to be less responsive to the opinions of the day and serve six-year terms, with one-third standing for election each two-year cycle.

Worldwide, about 40 percent of national legislatures have some degree of bicameralism,[36] and 49 of the 50 U.S. states have legislatures with two chambers—Nebraska alone has a unicameral legislature. Most legislative bodies in the world are unicameral or function as though they are unicameral because one branch is substantially stronger than the other. For example, the British House of Lords can delay action on legislation, but the House of Commons may take action without the Lords' approval. Having a second chamber is more common in federal systems where states/provinces/länder/cantons exercise substantial public powers. Sometimes the two chambers of a legislature reflect different interests in society, while at other times, they are largely redundant, representing the same social interests as in today's U.S. House and Senate. Germany's upper chamber represents the interests of the nation's states even more strongly than is the case in the U.S. Senate; its members are, quite literally, elected officials from the state governments. Representation in that chamber varies from 3 to 6, depending on the state's population, unlike the U.S. Senate, where California has the same weight as Delaware.

Having two constitutionally equal chambers, as the United States does, makes policy making more complex and often more time-consuming. Even members of the same party may find themselves feuding because the dynamics within the two houses are different and the party structures separate. For example, although the Republicans controlled both chambers of Congress from 2003 to 2007 and again from 2013 to 2019, House Republicans were more conservative than Senate Republicans, who were more likely to compromise with their Democratic colleagues. The result was a family feud—Republicans from the two chambers sometimes openly criticized each other. Loyalty to a chamber can also get in the way of legislative work; House members will seek to defend their turf from encroachment by senators and vice versa.

The effects of bicameralism are wide-ranging and pervasive, adding a level of complexity absent in many other political systems. Bicameralism increases the number of politically important figures in the decision-making process. American legislators first must find enough votes to pass proposals inside their own chamber and then must resolve differences with the second chamber. Negotiations and bargaining are also important in unicameral legislatures, but decision making is more streamlined.

> **bicameral legislature:** A legislature that has two chambers, with each chamber typically reflecting a different part of society or political grouping.

*China News Service / Getty Images*

**The House of Representatives and the Senate usually operate separately. However, on occasion, they come together for a joint session. This is most often for the president's annual State of the Union address, but joint sessions are also held to mark important anniversaries or to hear from visiting dignitaries, such as President Emmanuel Macron of France, seen here.**

## DISTINCTIVE HOUSE AND SENATE RULES

Life in the Senate and House is very different. Not only are senators under less immediate pressure to defend their jobs in reelection campaigns, but many also aspire to move to the White House. As the saying goes, each morning, senators see a future president in the mirror. Senators represent larger and more diverse statewide constituencies and receive more media attention than members of the House; the media cover Senate floor debates more widely, and the additional visibility fuels personal ambition. Debates in the House are rarely covered because discussion must be more structured and is subject to many more rules and constraints.

In fact, because of its larger size, the House generally follows more structured procedures than the Senate. To get anything accomplished, the House cannot allow all 435 members to have their say on a bill. In contrast, the tradition in the Senate is to allow any senator to speak for as long as the member deems necessary on any issue, allowing unlimited discussion that might last for days or even weeks. The classic example is the filibuster, a delay tactic developed in the Senate during the mid-nineteenth century. In the event of a filibuster, one senator or a group of senators may talk for an unlimited amount of time, monopolizing the floor and preventing a vote on an issue. This tradition gives minorities in the chamber enormous power to frustrate a majority. Although no limits originally existed on senators' use of the filibuster, these days, a vote by 60 senators can limit additional debate to no more than 30 hours. The use of a filibuster or even the threat of one is often enough to deter a bill from ever reaching the floor for a vote because a filibuster would hold up all the other business before the Senate, as discussed later in this chapter. Minority parties or even individual senators use the threat of a filibuster as a strategy to force concessions from the majority leader.

Committees are more important in the operations of the House than the Senate, again due to differences in the chambers' size. Although the House has more committees, those in the Senate typically have more members. The Senate completes more work in full committee than in subcommittees and spends more time working with legislation as a committee of the whole. As a result, an individual senator is probably more consequential in the lawmaking process than a rank-and-file representative.[37]

Political parties are also more prominent in the House, providing a critical structure to organize the work of the body. The majority party in the House determines the rules under which a bill may be debated and voted upon by the full membership on the floor. Historically senators operated in a "clubby" atmosphere, where cross-party friendships and bipartisan coalitions were more readily formed than in the House, although the rise of partisan conflict and the accompanying emphasis on party unity now threatens that tradition. The Senate's majority and minority party leaders normally negotiate about the scheduling of bills and operate, of course, within the tradition of full debate. House party leaders are forced to exercise greater control in order to get work accomplished.

## CONGRESSIONAL SESSIONS

Each session of Congress is numbered according to the election cycle of House members. Thus, the 116th Congress runs from January 2019 to January 2021, when a new class of members—435 representatives and one-third of the Senate—will be sworn in for the 117th Congress. The 89 new members of the House sworn in on January 3, 2019, included a large number of freshman Democrats who had promised to exercise a check on President Trump, lower middle-class taxes rather than those of the wealthy, and protect the environment. They entered the House with the least political experience in history (only 41 percent brought prior political experience), but they were the best educated (72 percent had completed a graduate degree).[38] This experience and education could help them shape new solutions to national problems. No legislation under consideration during one Congress carries over to the next. The legislative process must begin anew, a reasonable rule since members of the new Congress may disagree with the thinking of their predecessors. Similar to the bicameral nature of Congress, this practice makes the legislative process more complex than in most parliamentary systems.

filibuster: A delay tactic used in the Senate that rests on members' right to speak as long as they desire on a topic, thereby preventing a vote from being taken.

## COMMITTEES AND SUBCOMMITTEES

Congressional committees are not expressly mentioned in the Constitution, yet they are structures that are vital for the legislature's daily operations. When legislative bodies deal with public problems, they seldom work effectively as a **committee of the whole**, the entire group meeting together to gather information, discuss possible solutions, and craft legislative language. Instead, Congress creates subgroups to develop recommendations for the larger body to consider. As legislators become knowledgeable about specific areas of public policy, the collective ability of Congress to make better policies grows. Nonetheless, this specialization becomes a source of internal division and differential influence.

Early in their history, both the House and Senate began to rely on committees to help complete their work. These early committees were *ad hoc* or **select committees**; that is, they were temporary groups appointed to work on specific problems. After hearing a debate on the floor of the House, committees would assemble to draft legislation. The House, however, moved quickly toward adopting more permanent committee structures, or **standing committees**, whose members continued working throughout a full session of Congress and even across sessions on the same policy problems, their **committee jurisdictions**. One of the most influential House committees, Ways and Means, which is responsible for overseeing the government's sources of revenue, was created as a select committee in 1789 and became a standing committee

**TABLE 11.3**

## *Standing Committees in the 116th Congress*

| House Committees | Senate Committees |
| --- | --- |
| Agriculture | Agriculture, Nutrition, and Forestry |
| Appropriations | Appropriations |
| Armed Services | Armed Services |
| Budget | Banking, Housing, and Urban Affairs |
| Education and Workforce | Budget |
| Energy and Commerce | Commerce, Science, and Transportation |
| Ethics | Energy and Natural Resources |
| Financial Services | Environment and Public Works |
| Foreign Affairs | Finance |
| Homeland Security | Foreign Relations |
| House Administration | Health, Education, Labor, and Pensions |
| Judiciary | Homeland Security and Governmental Affairs |
| Natural Resources | Judiciary |
| Oversight and Government Reform | Rules and Administration |
| Rules | Small Business |
| Science, Space, and Technology | Veterans' Affairs |
| Small Business | |
| Transportation and Infrastructure | |
| Veterans' Affairs | |
| Ways and Means | |

*Source: http://www.house.gov/committees/; https://www.senate.gov/committees/index.htm*

**committee of the whole:** A situation in which the whole House or whole Senate considers business rather than delegating work to committees.

**select committees:** Congressional committees formed for a specific purpose and limited period of time.

**standing committees:** Permanent committees in the House or Senate whose responsibilities carry over from one Congress to the next, as does much of its membership.

**committee jurisdictions:** Defined areas of standing committee responsibilities, comprising the policy areas, programs, and agencies that each committee oversees.

in 1795. It remains one of the most powerful committees in the House but was even more influential until 1865, when the House created a separate Appropriations Committee and shifted responsibility for government spending away from Ways and Means. The Senate did not create committees until 1816, when it created 11 standing committees. Table 11.3 lists the House and Senate standing committees of the 116th Congress.

Today, there are 16 standing Senate committees and four special or select committees. In the House, there are 20 standing committees and three select committees. There are also four joint committees with members from both the House and Senate. Most committees also maintain subcommittees that focus members' efforts on an even narrower range of policies.

# HOW CONGRESS OPERATES

Congress employs thousands of people in addition to its elected members. To understand how this complex institution functions, we start by examining its critical building blocks and then ask whether Congress can act in a coherent manner.

## INFLUENCE IN CONGRESS

We can think of Congress as having multiple centers of power and decision making. Jockeying for power are the rank-and-file members, the party leaders, and the committee chairs. Assisting these legislators in their efforts to influence decisions are the legislative, committee, and professional staffs.

**RANK-AND-FILE MEMBERS** The 535 members of Congress are constitutional equals. Each has an independent claim to a role established by the Constitution to represent the interests of the people who elected him or her. Members of Congress often coordinate their efforts with those of other members. Representatives from the same state will work together on projects that produce common benefits. Members work with legislators in other states who hail from districts with similar economic interests. They form groups based on shared interests, known as *congressional member organizations*, which meet regularly to share information and coordinate strategy so they can act as a bloc of votes. There were 854 such informal organizations in 2017–2018 with House members, on average, belonging to 34 and senators to 16.[39] For example, members from districts with steel factories comprise a steel caucus, those concerned about specific diseases caucus together, and members especially interested in particular parts of the world coordinate discussion and action. Sometimes ideology or identity forms the basis of shared interests. About three dozen conservative and libertarian Republican members of the House coordinated strategy as the House Freedom Caucus during the 115th Congress. The Congressional Black Caucus, a group of 55 African American members in the 116th Congress (most serving in the House), promotes legislation favorable to African Americans and has grown in importance as their membership has expanded.

Members of the Congressional Black Caucus, Congressional Hispanic Caucus, and Congressional Asian Pacific American Caucus held a joint news conference to address protests against police brutality by professional athletes. These informal groupings allow rank-and-file members to amplify their messages and coordinate action.

AP Photo / Andrew Harnik

Almost all rank-and-file members have a party affiliation, which influences how they behave and how they vote. (There are two independents in the 116th Senate who typically vote and caucus with the Democrats, and one Republican House member changed his affiliation to independent during 2019.) At times, party leaders are able to pressure rank-and-file members to consistently vote together, but most of the time, leaders appeal to loyalty and emphasize how standing together will help them get reelected. The influence of party on rank-and-file members waxes and wanes, as we discuss below.

Inside Congress, party has also become more important, as shown by how often voting follows party lines.

For decades, *Congressional Quarterly* has tracked **party unity**, a measure of how often a majority of Democrats are aligned against a majority of Republicans on votes with recorded positions, so-called roll call votes. The pattern is clear: Around 1970, party members voted with the majority of their party only 50 to 60 percent of the time; substantial cross-party voting happened on 40 to 50 percent of all votes. By the 1990s, members went with party majorities 85 to 90 percent of the time in both the House and the Senate. In 2017, party unity hit an all-time high (see Figure 11.4), though it declined in both houses in 2018.

Today, members who abandon party loyalty stand out like sore thumbs and there is less tolerance for rank-and-file members who vote their conscience or support bipartisan solutions. Susan Collins (R-ME) and Lisa Murkowski (R-AK) came under enormous pressure from fellow Republicans in the 115th Congress (Trump's first) because of their willingness to occasionally cast votes against their party's majority and against the president. They both voted against the bill that would have repealed the Affordable Care Act (often called Obamacare—see Chapter 15) and against the president's nominee for secretary of education, Betsy DeVos, who was nonetheless confirmed. Murkowski also voted against the high-profile nomination of Brett Kavanaugh for the Supreme Court, though his nomination also was approved.[40]

In some respects, the influence of parties in the U.S. Congress is becoming more similar to that found in parliamentary systems. For decades, we could say that rank-and-file members were largely unmoved by pressure from party leaders in Congress because they had been chosen by voters in primaries whereas parliamentary leaders could deny renomination to disloyal members. Party endorsements mean everything in parliamentary systems; parties select the nominees and provide the message as well as the campaign organization required for success. In the U.S., candidates decide whether to run, put together the appeals needed to attract support, raise money needed for the campaign, and assemble the group of loyalists and hired assistants critical to the effort. U.S. parties can be helpful, but they do not control the process. The eventual winner owes less to the party than to his or her own efforts to secure nomination and election. (See Chapter 8.)

But more recently, other factors have gained influence. Ideological subgroups within the parties have been purging incumbents who do not meet their litmus test of policy positions.

## FIGURE 11.4

### *Party Unity in House and Senate, 1956–2017*

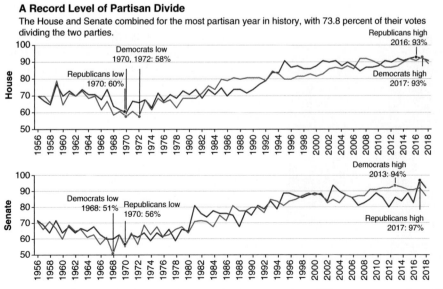

**A Record Level of Partisan Divide**

The House and Senate combined for the most partisan year in history, with 73.8 percent of their votes dividing the two parties.

*Source: "CQ Vote Studies: Party Unity," CQ Magazine, February 12, 2018, https://library.cqpress.com/cqweekly/index.php?issue=20180212*

**party unity:** A measure of how often a majority of Republican legislators vote against a majority of Democratic legislators.

In 2010, for example, the Tea Party Movement within the Republican Party prompted primary challenges to a number of incumbents who were criticized for being RINOs (Republicans In Name Only) because their voting records were not conservative enough. Similarly, challengers from the progressive wing of the Democratic party challenged incumbents not considered liberal enough for some nominations in 2018; most notably, Alexandria Ocasio-Cortez defeated the fourth-ranking Democrat in the House, making her the youngest woman elected to the U.S. Congress in history.[41] Presidents can also get into the act. In 2018, after Rep. Mark Sanford (R-SC) criticized President Trump, the president endorsed Sanford's primary challenger, Katie Arrington, who went on to win the nomination. Although Arrington lost the seat to the Democrat in the race, Trump claimed after the general election that those Republicans who had embraced his policies had been successful at the polls and those who had avoided him suffered defeat.[42]

**PARTY LEADERS** Despite sharing an equal constitutional status, not all members of Congress have equal influence. Among the most influential are party leaders. Congress has four separate party organizations: Democrats and Republicans in the House and in the Senate. When the party's members meet together, they constitute a **party conference** (Republicans) or **party caucus** (Democrats). Each of the four party groups follows different rules in selecting its leadership, in creating specific party committees that develop policy positions, and in appointing members to committees. The leader of the majority party becomes the leading figure in the chamber: The **Speaker of the House** is a position established in the Constitution, while the **Senate Majority Leader,** with far fewer powers, has emerged as the leading figure in the Senate.

Today's House Speaker wields wide-ranging powers over the legislative process, determining when legislation comes up for a vote, who can speak on the floor, which amendments will be considered (as we saw with Barbara Lee's proposal that opened this chapter), and how votes are taken. The Speaker is also a strategist who seeks to keep the majority party in power by articulating an agenda, working toward its achievement, and coordinating election strategy. By comparison, the Senate Majority Leader has far fewer powers over the rules but is still responsible for scheduling the work of the Senate. Most of the Majority Leader's influence resides in convincing others to cooperate, a task likened to herding cats because of senators' deep independence.

The vice president presides over floor sessions of the Senate (recognizes members to speak, enforces rules of debate) when he can attend and can cast a vote in the event of a tie. When the vice president is absent, the chair is taken by the *president pro tempore*, the senior member of the majority party and a position specified in the Constitution, but junior members of the majority party often fill the chair, a largely powerless position. The Speaker of the House presides over House sessions only on the most important occasions, typically asking another member of the majority party to preside the rest of the time. Unlike the United States, many other nations do not rely on a partisan figure to control legislative debate. In Britain, Canada, India, and Israel, for example, the presiding officer of the lower house (or only house, in the case of Israel) is a nonpartisan, impartial figure who organizes debate and maintains order. His or her rulings are intentionally devoid of partisanship, favoring neither the majority party nor whatever minority parties might be represented. Seldom does the speaker participate in debate or vote, though there are sometimes exceptions—for example, in the event of ties.[43] In all of these nations, except Israel, the speaker has no role in succession, that is, in filling a vacancy in the office of prime minister. In the U.S., the vice president, the Speaker of the House, and the *president pro tempore* are the next three persons in the line of succession should there be a vacancy in the presidency.

Nancy Pelosi was selected as Speaker of the House for the 116th Congress by the new Democratic majority. Republican members chose Kevin McCarthy as the minority leader.

There are also subordinate party leadership positions, members who are principally responsible for ensuring that their colleagues work together when necessary. Because they enforce party discipline, they are known as whips, a British term derived from fox hunting when one member of the hunting group was responsible for keeping the dogs from straying, an apt image for the party whip's job.[44] Party whips inform members of the work schedule, party strategies, and party-preferred positions on issues, and they make sure members are present for important votes. They also seek to determine members' intentions so they know how each vote is likely to turn out. Even with the efforts of the whips and other leaders, party discipline is difficult to enforce in the U.S. Congress.

Political parties and their leaders play a fundamental role in organizing Congress. Not only do they organize the proposed legislation that comes to the floor for the entire chamber to consider, but they also exercise pervasive influence through the committees. The chair of every standing committee and subcommittee in both the House and Senate is a member of the majority party in that chamber—in essence, party leaders shaping the work of those committees. And the majority party in the chamber also has a majority of members on every committee. That means that in the 116th Congress, Democrats chaired and held a majority on every House committee and Republicans chaired and held a majority on every Senate committee. In the 115th Congress, Republicans held majorities in both chambers and on every committee. As shown in Figure 11.5, Democrats controlled both the House and Senate from 1955 to 1981; even more impressively, Democrats held an uninterrupted majority in the House from 1955 to 1995.

Parties help members make decisions on pending policy issues, both in the committees and on the floor of the chambers. Similar to the voting cues that citizens receive from party identification (see Chapter 9), legislators' party identification guides them in making voting decisions. On issues that are particularly complex or outside of the legislator's area of expertise, the member is likely to defer to the party's position or that of a trusted colleague to make the required decision.

Legislators weigh the benefits and drawbacks when deciding whether to vote for or against the party's position. Party leaders consider a member's party loyalty when placing bills on the legislative calendar, distributing valued legislative benefits (such as committee assignments), and determining which members' bills may be considered on the floor. Along with ways to reward loyalty inside the chamber, party leaders can help loyal members by providing campaign help.[45]

Thus, members can benefit from party loyalty or be punished for too much independence. Tom DeLay (R-TX), who served House Republicans as Majority Whip for eight years and then as Majority Leader for two and a half, earned the nickname "The Hammer" for his tough enforcement of party loyalty. He proudly displayed a long leather bullwhip in his office to symbolize this reputation. One example of DeLay's toughness involved Connecticut Republican Christopher Shays, who defied the party's leadership and forced action on a campaign finance reform bill that the Republican leaders opposed. In the next Congress, when Shays sought to become chair of the Government Reform Committee, party leaders punished him by refusing to give him the job, a position he was next in line to hold.[46] The message was clear to fellow Republicans: If you oppose the leadership, there will be consequences. Democrats can also play rough: Nancy Pelosi refused to appoint the senior Democrat, Jane Harman (D-CA), as chair of the House Intelligence Committee in 2007, possibly because Harman had supported the U.S. invasion of Iraq while Pelosi and most other Democrats had opposed it. Pelosi stressed to the press that Harman had already served two terms as committee chair, but gaining the reputation of enforcing party loyalty certainly did not hurt.[47]

**COMMITTEE AND SUBCOMMITTEE CHAIRS** The chairs of committees and subcommittees wield great power, including the ability to move a bill forward in the lawmaking process or let it die in committee. Thus, members seek to serve on committees dealing with issues that have a direct bearing on their constituencies or with policies of personal interest. Committees are often described as the "workhorses" of Congress, and without them, Congress would face an even greater challenge: Every legislator would have to gain the knowledge and specialization needed to decide on the thousands of pieces of legislation introduced every year.

whips: The members of the party leadership team charged with keeping the members in line—that is, getting them to cast votes in the way the party leaders would like.

**FIGURE 11.5**

## Party Control of Congress, 1949–2019

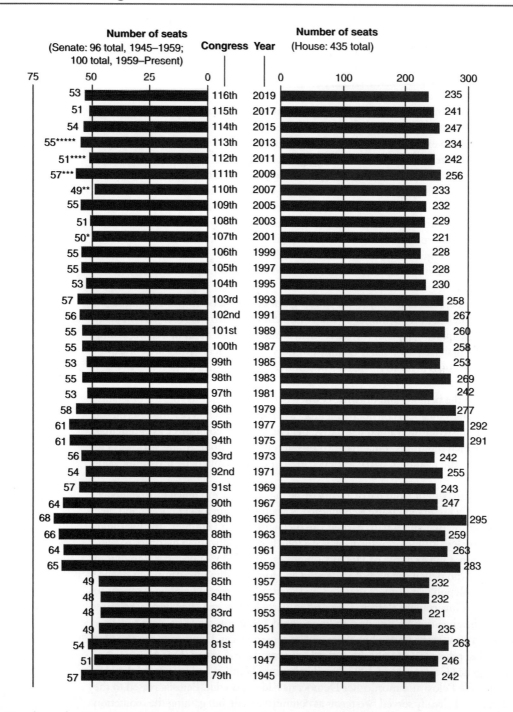

| Number of seats (Senate: 96 total, 1945–1959; 100 total, 1959–Present) | Congress | Year | Number of seats (House: 435 total) |
|---|---|---|---|
| 53 | 116th | 2019 | 235 |
| 51 | 115th | 2017 | 241 |
| 54 | 114th | 2015 | 247 |
| 55***** | 113th | 2013 | 234 |
| 51**** | 112th | 2011 | 242 |
| 57*** | 111th | 2009 | 256 |
| 49** | 110th | 2007 | 233 |
| 55 | 109th | 2005 | 232 |
| 51 | 108th | 2003 | 229 |
| 50* | 107th | 2001 | 221 |
| 55 | 106th | 1999 | 228 |
| 55 | 105th | 1997 | 228 |
| 53 | 104th | 1995 | 230 |
| 57 | 103rd | 1993 | 258 |
| 56 | 102nd | 1991 | 267 |
| 55 | 101st | 1989 | 260 |
| 55 | 100th | 1987 | 258 |
| 53 | 99th | 1985 | 253 |
| 55 | 98th | 1983 | 269 |
| 53 | 97th | 1981 | 242 |
| 58 | 96th | 1979 | 277 |
| 61 | 95th | 1977 | 292 |
| 61 | 94th | 1975 | 291 |
| 56 | 93rd | 1973 | 242 |
| 54 | 92nd | 1971 | 255 |
| 57 | 91st | 1969 | 243 |
| 64 | 90th | 1967 | 247 |
| 68 | 89th | 1965 | 295 |
| 66 | 88th | 1963 | 259 |
| 64 | 87th | 1961 | 263 |
| 65 | 86th | 1959 | 283 |
| 49 | 85th | 1957 | 232 |
| 48 | 84th | 1955 | 232 |
| 48 | 83rd | 1953 | 221 |
| 49 | 82nd | 1951 | 235 |
| 54 | 81st | 1949 | 263 |
| 51 | 80th | 1947 | 246 |
| 57 | 79th | 1945 | 242 |

*Based on what you know about parties and elections, how do you explain the long period of Democratic domination in the House and the more recent party control changes in both the House and Senate?*

\* *There were 50 Ds and 50 Rs until May 24, 2001, when Sen. James Jeffords {R-VT) switched to Independent status, effective June 6, 2001; he announced that he would caucus with the Democrats, giving the Democrats a one-seat advantage.*

\*\* *Independent Sen. Bernard Sanders (VT) and Independent Democrat Sen. Joseph Lieberman (CT) gave the Democrats a one-seat majority.*

\*\*\* *Senators Sanders and Lieberman voted with the Democrats. Republican Senator Arlen Specter (PA) became a Democrat in April 2009.*

\*\*\*\*\**Senators Sanders and Lieberman voted with the Democrats.*

\*\*\*\*\**Senators Sanders and Angus King (ME) voted with the Democrats.*

*Source: http://artandhistory.house.gov/house_history/partyDiv.aspx; http://www.senate.gov/pagelayout/history/one_item_and_teasers/partydiv.htm*

Richard Fenno, an expert on Congress, identified three goals of every member of Congress: reelection, power within the chamber, and good public policy.[48] The committee system advances all three goals. By serving on committees with a direct bearing on their constituency, legislators increase the likelihood of benefiting their district and thereby increasing their chances of reelection. For example, virtually all the members of the House Committee on Agriculture come from districts with major farming interests, including California, Florida, Georgia, Illinois, and Minnesota. Committees also provide the best opportunity to shape public policy, as committees consider proposed legislation and often redraft the original language, as explained below.[49]

Not all committees are created equal. Those considered more prestigious deal with important areas of government action such as taxes, spending, business and banking policies, and foreign intelligence and defense policies. First-year members of Congress tend to start their service on committees with lower prestige (though there are notable exceptions), and then need to decide whether to build their seniority on these committees or try to move to more prestigious committees in a future Congress. Party leaders balance seniority, party loyalty, and geographic representation in making committee appointments.

In a system of government that relies on a strong legislature to check the power of the executive, such as that found in the United States, it makes sense that committees have powerful roles. In contrast, parliamentary systems have different needs. Although there are some differences found around the world, parliamentary committees exercise limited powers and are less involved in policy making than their U.S. counterparts. Instead, policy making is ordinarily centered in the hands of the majority party, led by the cabinet. In Italy, for example, parliamentary committees can exercise discretion over minor legislation, but they have little power to shape significant legislation, which is dominated by the government ministers and their parliamentary majority.

There is little reason for parliaments to develop strong centers of policy specialization. Department ministers, who are also members of parliament (MPs), function as the legislature's policy experts, making it unnecessary for MPs to develop broad and comparable expertise, either individually or in committees. The cabinet—acting individually as ministers and collectively as the government—performs many of the same functions as American legislative committees, shaping policy that reflects the views of the larger legislature. Ministers, appointed by the prime minister to oversee a part of the government, in turn rely on career government officials to provide them with expert guidance. Thus, under the U.S. Constitution, a strong committee system, coupled with the independent professional staffs created by Congress, creates a legislature capable of overseeing the bureaucracy and challenging the executive.[50]

**CONGRESSIONAL STAFF** Members of Congress rely heavily on the efforts of personal and committee staff members, whose positions were created to help them discharge their many responsibilities and to achieve Fenno's three goals. They have become so integral to the operation of Congress that they wield influence of their own. Many congressional aides, particularly those working back home in the district or state, are engaged primarily in constituency service. Committee staffers tend to be policy specialists who assist with lawmaking and oversight. Each House member is allowed to employ no more than 18 full-time staff members and four part-time assistants or paid interns; there is no limit on the number of aides a senator may employ, although there is a budget limit.[51] Members of Congress can decide how to distribute their staff between their Washington, DC, and district offices.

Both the majority and minority members of committees and subcommittees receive support from committee staff; the majority staff is always larger. These aides work to draft legislation, write committee reports, and oversee executive agencies within the committee's jurisdiction.

The thousands of congressional staff members are essential to the smooth operation of Congress, from performing constituent services to drafting legislation and writing committee reports to maintaining schedules and responding to public inquiries.

They also maintain committee records, manage funds, maintain schedules, and respond to public inquiries about committee activities.

Party leaders are allotted additional staff members to help steer the caucus or conference's activities. And there are staffers who work for the entire House and Senate to keep the chambers operating efficiently. In 2016, there were over 15,000 legislative staff members—most working for members rather than committees—and additional thousands of aides working in three nonpartisan professional support agencies.[52]

**CONGRESSIONAL SUPPORT AGENCIES** Early in the twentieth century, Congress recognized that to make well-informed policies, it required far more extensive information than its members and personal and committee staffs could provide. As a result, it created several research agencies to assist in its policy making. The Congressional Research Service (1914) examines historical and legal foundations of programs and legislation as well as alternative options to grapple with issues as requested by members of the House and Senate. The Government Accountability Office (1921), better known for most of its history as the Government Accounting Office, specializes in monitoring how federal money is spent, the efficiency and effectiveness of government programs, and how to improve program management. The Congressional Budget Office (1974), created to provide a counterbalance to the president's advantages in expert economic information, analyzes the annual executive budget submitted by the president (see the discussion below) and its likely impact on the economy. As we will see in Chapter 12, presidents have created a range of specialized staffs to advise them on policy issues, and Congress has done the same.

PICTURE YOURSELF · · ·

# Visiting the Parliament House in New Delhi, India

Standing in front of the Parliament House, you can't help but be impressed. The circular building, completed in 1927, is ringed by 144 columns and known commonly as *Sansad Bhawan*. You hear the sound of fountains as you gaze at the extensive lawns and ponds that dot the surrounding estate. And all this is within a city of nearly 12 million residents. Inside Parliament House are the 555 members of the Lok Sabha, the directly elected representatives of India's 1.34 billion citizens, and the members of the Rajya Sabha, not to exceed 250, who are chosen by the legislatures of India's 29 states and seven union territories.

As India approached the general elections of 2019, there were nearly 900 million registered voters eligible to choose among the candidates of close to 2,000 parties running in 543 single-member districts. You know from past experience that Indian elections are complex, colorful, and seldom pretty, almost always beset with serious questions about the accuracy of results. With a history of alleged election fraud, India introduced electronic voting machines in 2000 and planned to deploy 1.6 million in 2019. (By comparison, the United States uses about 35,000.)[a] Though messy, India's

experiment in democracy has been unusually successful. Most stable democracies are prosperous, industrialized countries. Today, after more than a decade of rapid economic growth, incomes have been rising, though there are still crushing levels of poverty, especially in the countryside. Even more of a problem than economic inequality are the many religious, ethnic, linguistic, caste, and nationalist loyalties that make Indian politics a swirl of competing identities. Despite these challenges, India has sustained a democratic government since gaining its independence from Britain in 1947.

Getting inside the Sansad Bhawan is not easy. Similar to many other nations, India must deal with terrorists targeting major national symbols, in this case, activity by separatist groups from several regions of the country. Five terrorists died during a suicide attack on the parliament in December 2001; the exchange of fire killed seven guards and injured 22 bystanders. Once you are past security and able to observe parliament's operations, you see a curious combination of practices derived from both Britain, India's longtime colonial ruler, and the United States. As in Britain, the Indian prime minister and members of the Council of

Ministers (the cabinet) are members of and accountable to the lower, elected house of parliament and subject to close interrogation during Question Hour—the regular opportunity for members of the legislature to pose direct questions to the prime minister and members of the cabinet. Reformers of the American system of government often advocate introducing this practice in the United States.

Behind the scenes, though, you find several practices that are more similar to the U.S. Congress than to the British Parliament. Foremost among these is the system of relatively powerful standing committees, 24 groups that correspond to the principal departments of the government. Through these committees, the Indian parliament exercises oversight of the government's administration—ministers are not eligible to serve on the committees, which means that their investigations are likely to be more searching and critical, with a level of scrutiny that is more typical of the United States than Britain.

You would also notice the great diversity among delegates to India's parliament; 84 seats are reserved for "scheduled castes" (members of the economically depressed "untouchable" class) and 47 seats for "scheduled tribes" (historically disadvantaged indigenous peoples). Delegates also come from speakers of India's 30 main languages and members of six major religions. As one might expect, India's political parties are diverse as well—thirty-five parties had representatives in the parliament elected in 2014, though there were two principal alliances that organized the activities of twenty.

## Questions to Consider

1. Should members of the United States Congress have the opportunity to question the president in public as members of the Indian parliament can quiz their prime minister?
2. Should the Indian parliament become more like the U.S. government and exclude government ministers not only from the work of standing committees but from all parliamentary activities?
3. In what ways does heightened security as a protection against terrorism affect the operations of legislatures?

ᵃ Soutik Biswas, "India Election 2019: Are Fears of a Mass Hack Credible?" BBC News, January 25, 2019, https://www.bbc.com/news/world-asia-india-46987319

# ASSEMBLING COALITIONS MAKES ACTION POSSIBLE

As a multimember body with many centers of decision making, Congress faces an especially daunting challenge: how to build enough agreement among members to act on pressing public problems. Countervailing forces are at work in Congress: Powerful decentralizing forces pull members in different directions while centralizing forces, mainly party leaders, attempt to pull together enough support to coordinate action. Over time, Congress has sometimes strengthened party leaders' ability to provide central coordination but later reacted against an excessive consolidation of power. These pushes and pulls are a permanent feature of congressional life.

## DECENTRALIZING FORCES

Imagine yourself as a member of Congress. As a constitutional equal to 534 others, you have no reason to defer to other members' ideas or preferences, and there are many incentives to prefer your own views. In your desire to be reelected, you seek greater visibility. Voters back home will want to know how you helped them during the previous two or six years. Serving your personal interests and those of the constituency easily take priority over serving the common interests of the party. And only in extraordinary circumstances, such as the terrorist attacks of September 11, 2001, will the residents of diverse districts scattered across the nation demand the same action from government as we saw in the opening of this chapter.

Legislative committees divide a chamber's collective labor into specialized groups, making it possible for the House and Senate to consider more problems and to examine them in greater detail than could be accomplished by the committee of the whole, but committees also divide the chamber. Each standing committee has a jurisdiction—perhaps 10 to 15 areas of government policy and programs over which it exercises authority. Sometimes bills that fit in several jurisdictions are referred to more than one committee as a way to avoid arguments between committees with different ideas of how to proceed or those determined to defend their turf.[53] But committees and subcommittees exercise considerable autonomy as they make policy decisions, and this can fragment efforts to coordinate action. Homeland Security, for example, is the concern of more than two dozen separate committees in Congress, with each having the potential to provide different program guidance.

Interest groups have a potentially decentralizing impact on Congress, which is beset by thousands of lobbyists who visit and phone Congress every day. Collectively, members of Congress represent a highly diverse nation, but lobbyists make some of those diverse interests more prominent than others. According to the Center for Responsive Politics, a nonpartisan public watchdog group in Washington, more than 11,000 people registered to lobby Congress during 2017 and 2018. This total includes hundreds of former members of the House and Senate (425 in 2019) who assumed lucrative lobbying jobs after they retired or were defeated, a career path called the "revolving door."[54] It is good to have an accessible legislature, but do the plethora of interests pull the elected representatives in so many directions that it makes unified action more difficult to achieve?

Lobbyists seek to sway legislative action so that it benefits the interest they represent. This means communicating favorable information to the legislators, sharing reports based on technical research, circulating surveys of their members' opinions, even drafting legislative language that can be introduced by members who share a group's views and try to lead on the issue.[55] Even working with congressional staffers who have their bosses' ear may have an important impact on legislative action.[56] And research shows that legislators give priority to issues that attract higher levels of campaign contributions (think legislation affecting insurance, investment and real estate interests, or abortion rights, gun rights, and environmental protection), dedicating more effort to mastering details of these policies.[57]

## CENTRALIZING FORCES

Parties have the greatest potential to mold the many pieces of Congress into a coherent whole. The same is true in parliaments around the world, where parties assume responsibility for amassing enough support behind policy initiatives to make action possible. In governments based on the British system, parties develop policy proposals before an election and campaign on those proposals. The winning party is considered to have received the public mandate to govern and implement its policies. Because members have campaigned on the same platform and were elected on that basis, they all made similar promises to their constituents. This aligns their priorities and serves as a strong centralizing force. In the alternative model—prominent on the European continent—parties compete in elections for shares of power in the legislature and develop policy understandings after the election to build a governing coalition, which again helps create unity among members. This system prevails in both Italy and Germany. Under both approaches, parties are more powerful than in the United States, although that may be changing as the influence of party grows in the U.S.

As we saw earlier, party unity has risen in Congress over the past four decades, but leaders must overcome resistant committee chairs, party factions, and individual members who choose not to support the party on votes that conflict with their district's or state's interests, threaten their chances for reelection, or violate a personal belief. We have a centuries-long history in Congress of strong party leaders establishing tight discipline over a balky membership who then rebel against leaders who are viewed as dictatorial. This pattern is most dramatic in the House of Representatives, where Speakers are more or less successful in coordinating action.

**FROM CZARS TO COMMITTEE GOVERNMENT TO PARTY DICTATORS**  A strong Speaker has provided the best opportunity for the House of Representatives to function effectively. Originally, the Speaker of the House resembled the Speaker in the House of Commons in England—a neutral moderator of debate expected to preside over the chamber impartially. Henry Clay, selected as Speaker in 1811 during his first term in the House (something that would never happen today), transformed the Speakership into a position that mobilizes the majority party. Clay participated in debates, insisted on exercising the right to vote—showing he was a partisan leader and not merely a neutral figurehead—and used his power to appoint committee members in a way to advantage his own party and enhance centralized control.[58] Subsequent Speakers have aspired to but not always achieved Clay's model, relying on a set of formal powers wielded more or less effectively with the potential to control their colleagues and the chamber.

Centralized control does not exist automatically. It waxes and wanes. At the end of the nineteenth century, Speaker Thomas B. Reed (R-ME) imposed order on a highly disorderly chamber when a new set of rules gave him control over the chamber's business and dramatically reduced the minority party's influence. Speaker Reed, called "czar" behind his back, and his successor Joseph G. Cannon punished party members who failed to follow their lead—denying them support for legislation that might help their constituency and help them get reelected. But rank-and-file members resented central control. In 1910, thirty rebellious progressive Republicans joined with Democrats to remove the Speaker as chair of the powerful Rules Committee, the key to the Speaker's power.

From 1925 to 1975, decision making in the House was dominated by the chairs of standing committees, creating the era of **committee government**, a period when power was distributed broadly and no one exercised effective control. Chairs gained power through their automatic selection according to the **seniority rule**—the member of the majority party with the longest continuous service on a committee served as its chair. The road to power was getting reelected year after year and decade after decade from **safe seats**, where they were unlikely to face serious challenges. Committee chairs ran their committees like little fiefdoms, deciding which pieces of legislation could move forward and resisting the preferences of presidents, party leaders, and the members of their own conference or caucus. Finally, in the mid-1970s, Democrats refused to reappoint three senior members who had expected to continue serving as committee chairs— the first violation of seniority in 50 years. Chairs no longer exercised a personal veto over legislation coming before their committees but had to acknowledge the views of their own party's majority expressed through the party leaders.

After this breakthrough, Congressional reformers in the last quarter of the twentieth century pushed changes that once again consolidated power into the hands of a party leader chosen by the full membership of the majority party. A classic example was Newt Gingrich (R-GA), an especially charismatic Republican who led his party to electoral victory in 1994, the first time they had won a House majority in four decades. Gingrich unified the party's candidates around ten proposals that he promised to act upon, the so-called Contract with America. After leading the party to its earth-shaking victory, he imposed new methods of control: He personally selected committee chairs while pointedly ignoring seniority, limited chairs to a maximum six-year term, eliminated three committees altogether, renamed others, and realigned committee jurisdictions. As he pushed for action on legislation, Gingrich sometimes bypassed committees altogether by using task forces to rewrite legislation the committees had produced. But Gingrich's impulsive, confrontational style increasingly upset his Republican colleagues and they pressured him to resign after Republicans lost seats in the 1996 and 1998 elections. (Gingrich also was charged with ethical misconduct.) After Gingrich, House Republicans chose consensus-building leaders, and subgroups within the party constantly challenged their leadership.[59]

When Democrats won a majority in 2006, Nancy Pelosi mobilized House Democrats into a coherent force, first to confront President George W. Bush on budget and foreign policy issues during his final two years in office and then to support President Obama's programs. Republicans criticized her tactics as dictatorial—the minority party had little opportunity to influence business and Democrats had to toe the leadership's line. Pelosi's return to the speakership in 2019 promised to bring more of the same, but Pelosi agreed to create a select committee charged with modernizing the chamber's operations and endorsed a set of rule changes designed to encourage bipartisan action as well as to reduce the ability of dissatisfied representatives to disrupt House business.[60] Other Democrats were unhappy with some of the changes, suggesting future divisions in the caucus.[61]

## PRESIDENTIAL INFLUENCE ON CONGRESSIONAL COALITIONS

Presidents can help or hinder efforts to assemble working coalitions. A president with strong public approval and a clear legislative agenda can assist party leaders in rallying members of the

**committee government:** The period during the mid-twentieth century when chairs of the standing committees were the most powerful figures in the Congress.

**seniority rule:** A long-running practice followed in Congress in which the member of the majority party with the longest continuous service on a standing committee automatically becomes its chair.

**safe seats:** Members of Congress who, election after election, win by large margins.

President Lyndon B. Johnson has been called the "Master of the Senate" for the years he spent in that chamber before he became vice president and then president. He put his skills to good use in persuading recalcitrant members of Congress to support his programs, including Senator Richard Russell, who led the opposition to the Civil Rights Act.

majority party. But as we have seen, presidents often come from the other party, and their public approval varies, as discussed in Chapter 12.

Although they cannot directly introduce legislation, presidents since Franklin D. Roosevelt have had a significant impact on the operation of Congress in the following ways:

- Presidents set the agenda of national issues. This happens especially through the annual State of the Union Address and the president's budget request to Congress. (See Chapter 12.)
- Presidents propose specific solutions to national problems. Rather than simply point to issues and wait for Congress to act, presidents craft recommendations that their party allies in Congress will push forward.
- Presidents actively lobby individual members of Congress for their support. In fact, the executive branch has many legislative liaisons who serve as lobbyists for agency and presidential proposals.
- Presidents ask the public to pressure Congress. When Congress is reluctant to follow the president's lead, the chief executive may enlist the public to urge their representatives to support a specific proposal.

Helping a president from their own party can help legislators get reelected if the president is popular in their state or district. But support is not automatic. Unlike a parliamentary system where a party loses control of the government if it loses party unity on a key vote, any single vote against the president's proposals is unlikely to affect the party's control of the presidency in the next election. Thus, support from members of the president's own party is not guaranteed, and members can easily desert their colleagues if they disagree on ideological grounds or because of how a program is likely to affect their constituency. And at times, presidents from the same party will pursue policies different from the ones preferred by members of their own party in Congress, notably evident for both Presidents Carter and Clinton.

To succeed, presidents sometimes need votes from members of the opposition party. This is especially true for presidents who do not enjoy a majority in Congress. Presidents can then try to break the unity of the opposition party by appealing to groups whose policy views are closer to the executive's than to those of their colleagues. Southern Democrats, for example, voted frequently with Republican presidents and Republican members of Congress to form the so-called conservative coalition from 1940 to 1964, even when the Democrats controlled both the White House and Congress. At other times, presidents seek support from individual members of the opposition party who share their views on a specific policy or who need something for their district—funding for a bridge, a water project, or a new building. In short, presidents sometimes construct shifting coalitions to help them achieve their goals.

## THE LEGISLATIVE PROCESS

How do all the pieces we have reviewed—inside and outside of Congress—come together? Lawmaking is one of the most complex processes in American government. In simple terms, legislators introduce a bill with the support of cosponsors; then Congress subjects it to a grueling review, potentially modifying it until the proposal can ultimately win support in both the House and Senate.

Despite this general model, there is no single path by which bills become laws. Procedures will vary from case to case, so much so that the official explanation in a congressional publication requires 55 pages.[62] Increasingly, Congress has turned to using *atypical procedures* that do not follow the generic process. Figure 11.6 shows the idealized process, but in reality, the passage of statutes is almost always different from the sterile diagram: full of bargaining, contending with the unexpected, overcoming opposition—the elements of politics.

FIGURE 11.6

## How a Bill Becomes a Law

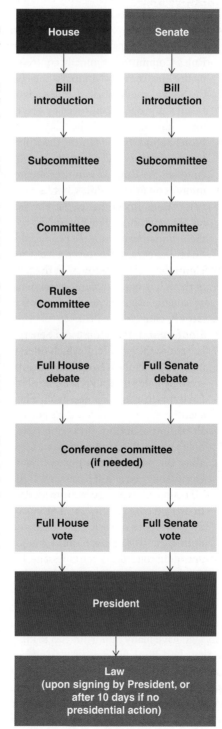

**Congress**
To become law, legislation must pass both the House and Senate in the same form.

**Bill introduction**
Bill is introduced by a member and assigned to a committee, which usually refers it to a subcommittee.

**Committee action**
Subcommittee conducts studies, holds hearings, and makes revisions. If approved, the bill goes to the full committee.

Full committee may amend or rewrite the bill, before deciding whether to send it to the floor, recommending its approval, or to kill it. If approved, the bill is reported to the full House or Senate and placed on the calendar.

House only: Rules Committee issues a rule governing the debate on the floor and sends the bill to the full House.

**Floor action**
Time for debate and opportunity to amend proposals are highly structured in the House. Senate procedures are more unstructured and allow for a filibuster.

**Conference action**
If necessary, a conference committee composed of members of both House and Senate meet to iron out the differences between the bills. The compromise bill is returned to both the House and Senate for a vote by the full chamber.

Each chamber votes on conference committee version. If it passes, the bill is sent to the president.

**Presidential decision**
President signs or vetoes the bill or takes no action. Congress may override a veto by a two-thirds vote in both the House and the Senate.

Diagram boxes:
House | Senate
Bill introduction | Bill introduction
Subcommittee | Subcommittee
Committee | Committee
Rules Committee |
Full House debate | Full Senate debate
Conference committee (if needed)
Full House vote | Full Senate vote
President
Law (upon signing by President, or after 10 days if no presidential action)

The idealized process includes the following steps:[63]

- **Introduction.** A proposal must be introduced by one or more representatives or senators—presidents cannot do so. Leaders then refer proposals to the committee or committees with jurisdiction.
- **Committee action.** Committee chairs, after consulting with party leaders, allow most bills to die rather than refer them to the subcommittee that might take action. If a subcommittee moves a proposal to the full committee, hearings might be held to collect additional information from interest groups or government officials. A proposal then undergoes markup, where it is read line-by-line while members consider changes, including amendments. Only after a committee majority votes to approve can a bill be considered by the full chamber.
- **Scheduling.** Party leaders decide when and if a proposal is considered on the floor of the House or Senate, which is another opportunity for delay or inaction. The House Rules Committee nominally controls this critical stage, but in reality, it is dominated by the Speaker who handpicks the chair and appoints the majority party's members. In the Senate, the Majority Leader negotiates the schedule of business with the Minority Leader. A proposal approved by one chamber may await action by the other chamber for months or indefinitely.
- **Floor action.** In the House, the Rules Committee proposes to the full chamber the length of debate and whether amendments will be considered. A floor vote usually endorses the Rules Committee recommendations. Debate is strictly limited—40 minutes on most business, but longer if the Speaker deems it necessary—and a **closed rule** forbids amendments, thereby ensuring that the committee's work will prevail or fail. An **open rule** allows members to amend the bill on the floor, usually indicating that the originating committee produced lower-quality legislation or could not resolve key disagreements. *Riders*, or unrelated amendments and provisions, are seldom attached to House bills but are allowed in the Senate, where debate is unlimited unless three-fifths of the full Senate invokes cloture, which limits further debate to 30 hours. Sponsors of Senate bills often need to fend off unwanted riders and deal with the potential for freewheeling debate.
- **Conference.** The House and Senate must adopt the same version of a bill before it can be sent to the president, which often requires that they form a **conference committee** including members from both chambers to resolve differences. Negotiators with strongly held views about the legislation may take months to iron out differences or fail to reach a compromise at all. The modified version must then be approved by both chambers.
- **Presidential action.** Presidents have ten days (excluding Sundays) to take action on bills sent for their consideration. The president may sign the bill into law, veto it, or allow the time limit to expire without taking action—in which case, the bill becomes law if Congress is still in session. If the president vetoes the bill, it is returned with his objections to the chamber in which it originated, where Congress has the opportunity to override the veto by a two-thirds vote in each chamber, thereby making it law over the president's opposition. This happens only rarely. If the president takes no action during the 10 days but Congress adjourns, thereby making it impossible for the president to return a veto message, he has exercised a "pocket veto" and the bill fails. Congress can avoid this possibility by not officially adjourning.

**closed rule:** Restrictive guidelines provided by the House Rules Committee that preclude amendments made from the floor during consideration of a bill.

**open rule:** Guidelines provided by the House Rules Committee that allow germane amendments to be made from the floor during consideration of a bill.

**conference committee:** A temporary committee consisting of both House and Senate members, formed to resolve differences in versions of a bill approved by both chambers before it can be sent to the president.

This summary, however, leaves out the real drama of lawmaking. Supporters devise strategies to win support from indifferent committee chairs or to counter the arguments of opponents who have many opportunities to kill proposals they do not want. Advocates may realize that their best hope for success is to add provisions to another bill more likely to pass. Proposals may also become part of an omnibus spending package—a single, massive piece of legislation funding many different government activities, in which many proposals can go unnoticed. Presidents and party leaders can also circumvent the time-consuming legislative process through fast-track legislation, sidestepping the standing committees and bringing legislation more directly to the House or Senate floor. Fast-track strategies come at the cost of deliberation and place greater control in the hands of party leaders.[64] Joint resolutions to authorize the use of military force, such as those highlighted in the chapter opening, have been handled this way.

Defenders of the laborious legislative process insist that thorough review of proposals results in better laws and ensures that they enjoy broad political support. Because the process provides many opportunities for opponents to block action, it also helps explain why negotiation and compromise are so essential in American politics.

## THE BUDGET PROCESS

Congress famously controls the "power of the purse." Congress has the principal say over how much money government spends and how it collects that money. As in the passage of legislation, the president must sign spending and tax bills before they go into law, but Congress largely controls the details.

Before 1921, each department and agency of the government sought its own separate budget from Congress, preventing the executive branch from having a coherent spending plan. With the aid of a staff unit created in 1921, the Bureau of the Budget (now renamed the Office of Management and Budget), presidents now present Congress with a set of proposals each February for how much should be spent on public programs, comparing those recommendations to past budgets and making projections for the next five to ten years. Congress—working in subcommittees, committees, and on the floor of the whole chamber—then has approximately eight months to make spending and tax decisions for the coming fiscal year. They may follow the president's recommendations or, more likely, follow their own inclinations.

The president's budget requests funding for **discretionary spending**—spending levels that must be reapproved by Congress each year—as well as **mandatory spending**—spending levels set by law. Discretionary spending includes funds for education, transportation, natural resources, environmental protection, foreign aid, homeland security, defense, science, space and technology, and the federal courts. Despite this long list, it makes up only about one-third of the budget. Mandatory spending funds entitlement programs such as Social Security, Medicare, and Medicaid, as well as smaller assistance programs such as unemployment compensation, food stamps, and child nutrition. In these cases, the government has made a standing commitment to provide benefits to those citizens who are entitled to the benefits under the law.

The budget-making process is so fragmented that it is amazing that a final product ever emerges. The goal is to complete the process by September 30 so that the full government knows its funding levels for the new **fiscal year** (financial year) that begins October 1. But disagreements within Congress as well as between Congress and the president often cause delays. This occurred in 1995, when President Clinton and the Republican-controlled Congress disagreed. Several continuing resolutions, which fund the government on a short-term basis, kept the government operating, but when the president objected to cuts made by Congress in these temporary funding arrangements, the government partially shut down. Nonessential personnel stayed home (technically, were *furloughed*) for one week in November 1995 and again for nearly three weeks over the holidays in 1995–1996. Much the same happened during the winter of 2018–2019, when nonessential personnel remained home for 35 days when Congress and the president could not agree on spending for constructing a wall along the border with Mexico.

Congress and the president may also make *supplemental appropriations*, spending decisions outside the regular

**discretionary spending:** One-third of the annual budget for which funding must be reapproved by Congress each year, which subjects programs using this funding to annual changes.

**mandatory spending:** Spending set by statute rather than an annual vote by Congress, sometimes called *entitlement spending* because recipients qualify for benefits according to qualifications established by law.

**fiscal year:** The period covered by the budget decisions made annually, running from October 1 to September 30 for the federal government and July 1 to June 30 for many state governments.

If Congress and the president are unable to agree on a budget, a government shutdown may occur, as happened in winter 2018–2019, resulting in the closure of many government offices and even national parks.

Joe Raedle / Getty Images

budget process. Congress funded the wars in Afghanistan and Iraq through such supplemental appropriations from 2001 to 2009. President Obama, however, included these costs as part of his annual budget.

## CONSEQUENCES FOR DEMOCRACY

Congress embodies the basic logic of the American Constitution: fragment power to prevent its abuse. Bicameralism divides Congress, and the many centers of congressional decision making and power within the chambers challenge the capacity of Congress to produce coherent policies. Although emergencies sometimes trigger a rapid institutional response, as with the decision to authorize the use of military force in 2001, assembling the support needed for action is almost always a tedious process and is sometimes impossible.

The U.S. election system helps explain much about Congress's difficulties in taking collective action. Members of Congress come from single-member districts and win primary and general elections largely because of their own efforts, not because they stand united with a party. Even presidents whose party controls a majority in both houses of Congress cannot be certain that legislators will support their initiatives. By contrast, members of the majority party in a parliamentary system risk losing their seats if they oppose their party's leader, the prime minister. In both presidential and parliamentary systems, parties provide a bridge to link executive and legislative action. In contrast with parliamentary systems, there is no guarantee in the United States that the same party will control Congress and the presidency, and party leaders have limited leverage over individual legislators.

Finding common ground between opposing positions in Congress entails working through an elaborate decision-making system. Committees, subcommittees, and their chairs play critical roles in the lawmaking process, far greater than one finds in parliamentary systems. Political parties, their leaders, and the subgroups that exist within them play important roles in the United States and in parliamentary systems, but party, despite its recent prominence in the United States, has historically been less important than elsewhere. Pulling all these pieces together into a unified whole almost never happens. Assembling enough pieces in order to take action is the more common goal. Congress has sometimes centralized power and, at other times, decentralized it. No strategy seems to work forever.

Ultimately, Congress has a separate constitutional responsibility to address national problems that is no less legitimate than the president's. And instead of working together, as happens in parliamentary systems most of the time, the U.S. executive and legislative branches often work at cross-purposes. Sometimes that independence is needed to check runaway presidents. There can also be runaway Congresses. Congress offers a deliberate approach to fashioning public policy, providing ample opportunity for multiple interests to be heard, for minorities to protect their interests, and for compromises to be negotiated. But this process can also produce flawed final products—slow responses (laden with deals needed to secure votes) more or less addressing the issues confronting the nation. If the public is primarily looking for quick responses and rapid solutions to major problems, Congress will almost always be a source of frustration. At least on the surface, presidential decisiveness trumps congressional deliberation in emergencies where quick action is required.

The public wants Congress to solve personal as well as national problems: provide affordable college loans, develop strategies to improve K–12 education, deliver new weapons systems for defense, ensure adequate Social Security benefits and health care, maintain a fair tax system for both individuals and corporations, and fund high-quality interstate highways. At the same time, Congress must respond to crises and check excessive executive power. Although there is a great deal of continuity in Congress's structures and ways of doing business, Congress is also a changing institution capable of adopting internal reforms intended to enhance its effectiveness. For example, at key points, it created the technical expertise needed to confront presidents and adopted reforms needed to reduce internal fragmentation. As the needs of the nation evolved, so did the legislative branch—without requiring changes in the Constitution. Such institutional change is both possible and likely. The most powerful force likely to motivate change is the public's demand that its legislators start doing business differently.

## Critical Thinking Questions

1. Many members of Congress relocate to Washington, weakening their ties to the constituents who elected them. Other candidates move to a district or state in order to run for office and start with weak ties to the area they represent. (This was the case when Hillary Clinton sought a Senate seat from New York.) Should Americans rethink the relationship between constituency and representation so that the quality of representation counts more than the strength of the representative's local roots?

2. Should members of Congress give greater priority to the demands of their constituency or the demands of their party? Placing emphasis on the constituency fulfills the legislator's representational function but sacrifices the lawmaking function, which requires that members work together in a coordinated way. Where should the balance lie?

3. Legislative committees perform valuable services for Congress as a whole, but they tend to be dominated by their leaders. How can Congress derive the maximum benefit from standing committees while avoiding the tendency for leaders to dictate their work? Is the reform introduced by Newt Gingrich of limiting committee chairs to six years of service the right answer?

4. Congressional staff members have become a powerful force on Capitol Hill. They are experts on politics and policy and are important advisers to the elected officials. How much assistance should U.S. legislators have? Are congressional aides the key to helping Congress play a coequal role to the executive or simply a way to help legislators get reelected?

## Key Terms

bicameral legislature, 281
bill, 277
closed rule, 296
committee government, 293
committee jurisdiction, 283
committee of the whole, 283
conference committee, 296
constituency service, 275
delegate model, 272
descriptive representation, 275
discretionary spending, 297

earmarks, 273
filibuster, 282
fiscal year, 297
mandatory spending, 297
open rule, 296
party caucus, 286
party conference, 286
party unity, 285
politico model, 272
popular legitimacy, 271
pork barrel, 273

safe seats, 293
select committees, 283
senate majority leader, 286
seniority rule, 293
Speaker of the House, 286
standing committee, 283
substantive representation, 275
trustee model, 272
whips, 287

Visit edge.sagepub.com/maltese to help you accomplish your coursework goals in an easy-to-use learning environment.

# 12

# THE PRESIDENCY

## After reading this chapter, you should be able to do the following:

- Explain the features that distinguish presidential from parliamentary systems.

- Describe the five principal roles of the president as laid out in the Constitution, new roles not found in the Constitution, and the reasons those roles have changed over time.

- Analyze the factors that affect a president's approval ratings.

- Describe the staff support that allows the president to manage and fulfill the responsibilities of his role.

- Understand the president's primary goals and the strategies the president employs to achieve these goals.

## Perspective: Why Have the Norms for Presidential Communication Changed?

In 1868, the House of Representatives impeached President Andrew Johnson, bringing eleven charges (articles of impeachment) to the Senate in an effort to secure votes from two-thirds of the senators to remove the president from office. This was the first time that a Congress had taken its unhappiness with the president so far in the constitutionally prescribed process, though it had come close on several other occasions.[1]

The tenth article of impeachment sounds strangely antiquated to our twenty-first century ears. It charged President Johnson with inappropriately seeking to generate popular support for his confrontations with Congress and, in doing so, publicly denouncing his opponents. He did attempt to bring into disgrace, ridicule, hatred, contempt and reproach, the Congress of the United States, and . . . to impair and destroy the regard and respect of all the good people of the United States for the Congress and legislative powers thereof, . . . and to excite the odium and resentment of all the good people of the United States against Congress and the laws . . . openly and publicly, and before divers assemblages of the citizens of the United States . . . make and deliver, with a loud voice, certain intemperate, inflammatory, and scandalous harangues, and did therein utter loud threats and bitter menaces . . . amid the cries, jeer, and laughter of the multitudes then assembled and in hearing.[2]

Obviously, what makes this charge seem odd is that we have become accustomed to presidents taking their case for one policy or another directly to the public. In the Trump era, this is a daily, sometimes hourly occurrence conveyed via Twitter. And President Trump's rallies, with ardent supporters wearing Make America Great Again (MAGA) hats and chanting approval, have become a staple of national politics. Nor does the president hesitate to denounce his critics in Congress and the media, eliciting "cries, jeer(s), and laughter" from the multitudes. How could such behavior be worthy of impeachment 150 years ago but be commonplace today?

In the eighteenth and nineteenth centuries, presidents seldom directly addressed the public. Most of the time, their rhetoric was written, not spoken, and was aimed at Congress, reaching the public only indirectly. Of course, they were not silent, but when called upon to speak to the public, presidents kept their comments formal, limited themselves to constitutional themes, and avoided discussing public policy issues.[3] Nor did presidents engage in active campaigning. While nineteenth-century election campaigns were notoriously rough-and-tumble affairs, presidents remained above the fray and let supporters do the talking.

Such restraint reflected a set of unwritten rules—norms—adopted by the nation's political class that arose from beliefs about how the leaders of a democracy should conduct themselves. The founding generation was concerned about potential excesses of democracy. The danger of majority tyranny—wherein the majority would run roughshod over the rights of minorities—was one. Another was the threat of demagoguery—that unscrupulous leaders would use fiery rhetoric to enflame the people's passions and lead them astray. Norms against politically charged public rhetoric protected the constitutional system from dangers posed by demagogues.

Over time, ideas about appropriate behavior have changed, particularly in the twentieth century. Teddy Roosevelt brought a new youth and vigor to the presidency when he assumed the job in 1901 after the assassination of William McKinley. Similarly, he reinterpreted the relationship between the president and the public, carving out a more energetic role that included actively advocating for policies that he felt the nation required. Roosevelt did this through speeches and newsworthy comments delivered to the public through expanding press coverage of national affairs.

Political scientist Jeffrey Tulis traces the development of this *rhetorical presidency* and argues that Roosevelt's expansion of the president's role—which he justified because of a crisis of economic inequality that he believed confronted the nation—became a permanent feature of the office under Woodrow Wilson (1913–1921). Wilson's belief that presidents should provide energy and direction for the nation thereafter became expected of all chief executives on an ongoing basis, not only when the nation faced an emergency. And Wilson built upon the president's unique advantage of speaking to the public as an individual, delivering clear messages and projecting a compelling image through the press. For example, Wilson dusted off a practice that Thomas Jefferson had discontinued—personally delivering the State of the Union address to Congress rather than providing a written document.

Franklin D. Roosevelt (FDR; 1933–1945), Teddy's cousin, made presidential communication even more personalized by using "fireside chats" to speak directly to the people using the new technology of radio. John F. Kennedy (JFK; 1961–1963) broadcast presidential news conferences live during prime time rather than via tape delay as Eisenhower had done. Television enabled JFK to project his more personal, youthful, and glamorously humorous presence into millions of households. By Kennedy's administration, norms had changed. It was expected that presidents *would* speak publicly about the problems of the day, respond to criticisms from their opponents, and campaign actively for their policy proposals. The nineteenth-century expectation of reticence and dignified behavior was long gone.

Donald Trump may have introduced a new era of presidential rhetoric. There seem to be no limits on how much communication originates from the White House—presidential tweets go to millions, starting early in the morning and flowing throughout the day, often determining the agenda for both Congress and the press. Similarly, there are few, if any, limits on the content of the communication—profanity, willful denial of facts, personalized insults, and blatant appeals for support fill the airwaves as well as presidential rallies. This is not only a break with the distant past but also a break with how immediate predecessors conducted themselves in office.[4] Benjamin Wittes, a much-respected commentator on legal matters, suggests in a podcast conversation with Tulis that Trump may have introduced a new era—the "entertainment presidency," where showmanship and entertaining outrageousness engage public attention for better or for worse. Trump has described his conduct of the presidency and use of social media as "modern day presidential."[5] Will Trump's approach prove to be the new normal for presidents moving forward? ««

# PRESIDENTIAL AND PARLIAMENTARY SYSTEMS

Democracies around the world can be considered to be presidential, parliamentary, or a hybrid of the two. All forms of democratic government perform legislative, executive, and judicial functions. The executive in a parliamentary system (the prime minister, chancellor, or premier) is a member of and is chosen by the legislature (parliament) so that the executive and legislative powers are fused rather than separate. Presidents are chosen independently from the legislature, most often through direct election or through an indirect system (such as the Electoral College used in the United States). Many parliamentary systems also have an elected president (Israel, Germany, Austria) whose functions are largely symbolic and ceremonial. France operates the best-known hybrid system where a powerful, separately elected president enjoys greater independence from parliament than is commonly the case.

U.S. presidents, of course, are elected to four-year terms and cannot be dismissed from office by the legislature except for extraordinary reasons. Impeachment, the constitutional process for removing a president from office before a term has expired, triggers such a major constitutional crisis that it has never been successfully used. Prime ministers, as elected members of parliament (MPs), serve as the leader of the legislative majority as long as they enjoy the support of their party colleagues—an uncertain length of time rather than a set term. For example, Tony Blair led his Labour party to victory in three general elections in the United Kingdom—1997, 2001, and 2005—but was forced by his Labour colleagues to step down as prime minister in 2007. His successor, Gordon Brown, served as prime minister for almost three years but failed to lead his party to a parliamentary majority in the 2010 general election and turned power over to the Tory party leader. Presidents direct the bureaucratic agencies of government (see Chapter 13), selecting members of the cabinet (principal heads of the departments, who must also be approved by the Senate) and enjoying exclusive power to fire them, though Congress can also impeach and remove them. U.S. cabinet members are subordinate to the president's greater authority. In parliamentary systems following the British tradition, the cabinet is a collective body of MPs who, at least in theory, stand or fall together and therefore reach decisions on policy with which they all agree. Prime ministers can dismiss cabinet members, but there is a less clearly defined hierarchy than in the American system.

The designers of the American Constitution invented the presidential system. Unhappy with the ineffective government that operated under the Articles of Confederation, they created a strong executive to provide energy for the central government. But they also did not want a king, an option that some members of the Constitutional Convention proposed. Although some analysts have suggested that the United States has an "elected king," that suggestion under-estimates the limits ordinarily placed on presidential power through the constitutional system of checks and balances.

Some other democracies have followed the American model. When Mexico and the South American countries won their independence from Spain and Portugal in the nineteenth

**impeachment** The power of Congress to remove a president from office before the elected term has expired. Technically, the House impeaches ("charges") a president with "high crimes and misdemeanors" and the Senate may find the president guilty or not guilty of the charges.

**prime minister** The executive officer in a parliamentary system who is supported in the legislature by a majority of his or her own party or a majority based on a coalition.

**presidential system** A political system distinguished by having an executive selected separately by the public rather than by the legislature; frequently characterized by fewer parties but higher levels of legislative–executive conflict.

century, they tended to set up presidential systems in imitation of the United States.[6] In the 1980s and 1990s, some aspiring democracies in Asia (South Korea, Philippines) and Eastern Europe also chose to establish presidential systems.[7] In other parts of the world, as nations gained independence in the period from 1945 to 1975, most emerging democracies adopted a **parliamentary system** along the lines of their colonial powers.[8]

Not all nations stick with their original design for executive power. Countries that have encountered problems with parliamentary government have sometimes adopted a presidential or a hybrid system that has both a directly elected president and a prime minister selected by the parliamentary majority. France set up its blend of parliamentary and presidential government in 1958, after a military mutiny and near–civil war had thrown the parliamentary government into chaos, giving rise to a new system with firmer leadership at the top. Nigeria established a presidential system in 1975 after an ineffective, squabbling parliamentary system had been succeeded by a series of military governments. Worldwide, presidential systems offer a clear focus for leadership—someone to hold accountable for the successes and failures of governments. Frequently, however, presidents have refused to give up power and have become dominant political leaders far beyond their original term of office (see the "Picture Yourself" feature in this chapter).

Prime ministers seldom have to deal with a divided government, a common problem in the United States where one party controls one or both houses of Congress while the president comes from the other party. Prime ministers and their cabinets usually remain in office only so long as they have the support of a majority in the lower house of parliament. A parliamentary majority may consist of a single party that controls a clear majority of seats or a coalition of parties that pool their votes in order to create a working majority. Many European nations (for example, the Netherlands, Belgium, and Italy) rely on coalition governments because seldom does one of the multiple competing parties enjoy majority support. When struggles among coalition partners produce internal divisions, coalition governments can resemble a divided U.S. government. Suddenly, prime ministers struggle to win legislative support, much as presidents eagerly try to persuade a Congress controlled by the opposition party.[9] Theresa May's struggles to find a successful path to exit the European Union in 2018–2019 ("Brexit") illustrates the point. May's working majority consisted of MPs from her own Tory party plus a small party in Northern Ireland. When a substantial number of her own party's MPs and those from Northern Ireland opposed her Brexit plan, the British Parliament floundered for months in 2019 trying to find a way forward, voting down one option after another as the exit deadline approached.

In a parliamentary system, majority parties will ordinarily replace prime ministers as soon as they lose the ability to command majority support in parliament, though that change might take some time to unfold in coalition governments. In this way, parliamentary systems largely avoid the problem of **lame ducks**, second-term presidents approaching the end of their service and unable to accomplish much because they will soon be gone. Either presidents or prime ministers can quickly become irrelevant if their public approval declines or their party loses important local or midterm elections.

The constitutional design of a government is a powerful influence on those holding official positions, but other factors also determine the role the president plays in our political system.

**parliamentary system** A political system in which the legislature (parliament) selects the executive either through a single party majority or a majority coalition, providing for closer institutional coordination.

**lame ducks** The description of presidents nearing the end of their fixed term in office who have little remaining leverage to accomplish their policy goals.

## THE EVOLVING JOB OF PRESIDENT

When the Founders invented this new job, what did they anticipate the president would do? Five core presidential responsibilities are suggested in the Constitution. Although the Constitution does little more than outline these responsibilities, they have been defined over the years as presidents interpreted their powers and took actions that then became

House of Commons - PA Images / Getty Images

**Despite the overall support of her party and coalition allies, British Prime Minister Theresa May was unable to secure enough votes in Parliament for her Brexit plan.**

precedents for their successors. Congress also helped shape the office by assigning new responsibilities for policy leadership to help the nation meet emerging national needs. As a result, today's presidency is far more robust and varied than the original outline of the job found in the Constitution.

## CONSTITUTIONAL ROLES

Foremost in the Constitution are the two roles played by presidents in international affairs: Presidents provide a unitary voice in dealing with security threats from abroad and in managing relations with the international community. These responsibilities were traditionally held by monarchs, and the writers of the Constitution placed them primarily, though not exclusively, in the president's hands. Congress jealously guards its prerogatives on the home front, however, and the president's domestic roles were relatively minor until the twentieth century, when they expanded rapidly.

**COMMANDER IN CHIEF OF THE ARMED FORCES**  Although Congress has the power to declare war (see Chapter 11), presidents order U.S. forces into action. In April 2017 and again in April 2018, President Donald Trump ordered American air strikes on military targets in Syria in response to the Syrian government's use of chemical weapons against civilians in the long-running civil war. The United Kingdom and France joined the United States in the second attack, punishing Syria for violating international laws against the use of chemical weapons. A few congressional voices criticized the attacks for failing to secure prior congressional authorization for the strategy or the attacks, though most responses, especially from Republicans, were supportive. Secretary of Defense James Mattis justified the attacks as consistent with Article II, Section 2 of the U.S. Constitution, which specifies that the president "shall be commander in chief of the Army and Navy of the United States, and of the militia of the several states, when called into the actual service of the United States."[10]

Congress and presidents have struck a working balance over the use of military force that clearly advantages the chief executive. In response to pirate attacks on American merchant vessels, Thomas Jefferson (1801–1809) built ships to provide coastal defense without obtaining prior congressional approval. Seeking to promote Western expansion, Andrew Jackson (1829–1837) used the military to forcibly drive Native Americans out of Mississippi, Florida, and Georgia despite widespread political opposition. In order to save the Union, Abraham Lincoln (1861–1865) took a series of steps—including calling the state militias into federal service without congressional authority or funding—at the outset of the Civil War that significantly stretched the boundaries of presidential powers. Teddy Roosevelt (1901–1909) famously deployed the navy on a round-the-world display of power that Congress had specifically prohibited, and Franklin Roosevelt (1933–1945) established new precedents for coordinating war policy in a global conflict.

> **War Powers Resolution**  Passed by Congress over Nixon's veto in 1973, this law establishes a framework for Congress to participate in presidential decisions to use force—short of a formal declaration of war—and to halt such a military deployment.

In a nuclear world where the United States confronted a hostile power, presidential actions took on enormous significance—wrong steps could trigger conflict with the Soviet Union, believed by Americans to be an implacable enemy. As a result, even greater latitude was given to presidents to deploy forces around the world to deal with regional problems in Korea, the Middle East, and Vietnam. Angered by President Richard Nixon's actions during the Vietnam War, however, Congress passed the **War Powers Resolution** in 1973. This resolution attempted to limit presidential commitments of troops, required the president to report promptly to Congress after ordering troops into combat, limited the involvement of U.S. forces to 60 days unless Congress approved the military action, and gave

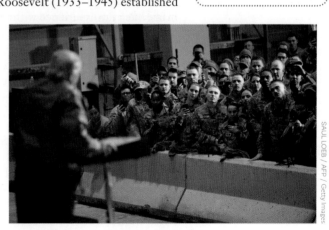

SAUL LOEB / AFP / Getty Images

**As part of their role as commander in chief, presidents often visit with U.S. troops stationed overseas, such as at this air base in Iraq.**

Congress the authority to terminate the commitment. Yet, the War Powers Resolution has failed to live up to expectations. Subsequent administrations have not done a better job of consulting with Congress before taking action. Presidents regard the War Powers Resolution as an infringement on their constitutional powers and adhere only to the letter of the law when meeting reporting requirements while denouncing its constitutionality. Congress continues to feel bypassed by presidents who use military forces when they deem it necessary to do so.

Congress now relies on authorizations to use military force (AUMF) rather than declarations of war to signal support for military actions. An AUMF was granted to the first Bush administration to pursue the Persian Gulf War (1990–1991) and to the second Bush administration in 2001 in response to the terrorist attacks on 9/11 (see Chapter 11). The George W. Bush, Obama, and Trump administrations have pointed to the 2001 AUMF as justification for American forces continuing counterterrorism operations around the world.

As the United States became ever more engaged with the world and war became a constant possibility, the need for decisiveness tilted the institutional balance toward presidents rather than Congress. Unlike the bicameral, multimember Congress, where power and influence are highly fragmented, presidents have the advantage of unity. Presidents can reach final decisions wholly on their own. Making a presidential decision is far easier than reaching one in Congress, where decisions require extensive coordination and consultation, as we saw in Chapter 11. With a single "decider," as George W. Bush once famously described himself, or a small circle of advisers, presidents also enjoy a level of secrecy that is unavailable to Congress, where leaks of important information are more likely. With these advantages, presidents can also act with dispatch—the ability to take action rapidly. Finally, presidents enjoy an advantage in the information that is available to them; it is the full-time job of the intelligence bureaucracy to gather and analyze information collected from satellites, electronic eavesdropping, spies, and public sources. Though it also relies on information from the same experts, Congress does not supervise or receive daily briefings and updates from all of these intelligence sources.

This gradual flow of power to the president sounds inevitable, but it is not. In the United Kingdom, even though a declaration of war is not required from Parliament, the prime minister's power is constrained by the need to maintain political support in the House of Commons (see Chapter 11). In France, where presidents have exercised considerable influence since Charles de Gaulle carved out a leading role in the 1950s, troops have been deployed without advance debate by the National Assembly, but that has depended on the balance of political power between the French president and the prime minister, who need not be from the same political party.

The German chancellor (head of the Bundesrat, the lower chamber of the parliament) clearly eclipses the German president's role in foreign affairs, but both the legislature and the courts have played important roles in issues surrounding the use of force. Postwar Germany, after the experience with the Nazis, is extremely sensitive about projecting German military power, and each instance of possible military involvement has given rise to extensive public discussion. Thus, while it might be true that the trend around the world has been for power to gravitate toward executives, no democracy has allowed that to happen without the exercise of checks on unilateral executive power. What sets the United States apart from these other democracies, however, is the nation's preeminent role in the world. The stakes are higher.

**CHIEF DIPLOMAT** In 2011, the Senate approved three trade agreements originally submitted by President Bush and supported by President Obama. These followed on the heels of eight free trade agreements negotiated by Bush and approved by the Senate during his two terms in office, including agreements with Australia, Chile, Singapore, and Ukraine. Unconvinced that these agreements were benefiting the United States, President Trump pursued a different strategy. He scuttled a trade agreement with eleven countries—the Trans-Pacific Partnership—that had been negotiated by Obama[11] and renegotiated both the free trade agreement with Korea and the North American Free Trade Agreement (NAFTA) that had been concluded by President Clinton in 1993 with Mexico and Canada. Only the altered NAFTA agreement required Congressional approval.

What if there were competing presidents, each supported by part of the nation and each recognized as legitimate by different segments of the international community? Venezuela confronted such a problem beginning in January 2019, when the National Assembly of Venezuela declared its president, Juan Guaidó, as acting president of the nation, an action supported by eleven members of the Organization of American States, including Brazil, Colombia, Canada, and the United States. The other claimant to the position was the incumbent, Nicolás Maduro, who had steadily expanded his powers since coming to office in 2013 after the death of his predecessor. Maduro's claim was supported by a collection of undemocratic regimes—Cuba, Russia, Iran, Turkey, and China. The immediate trigger to this standoff was the presidential election of May 2018, won by Maduro but considered illegitimate by his critics at home and abroad because the president had banned most opposition candidates, suppressed the media, rigged the election outcome, and pressured voters in the most heartless way—in the face of severe food shortages, he provided food to his supporters while denying it to those who voted for the opposition.[a]

This political crisis had developed over decades as the nation slipped deeper and deeper into economic and social turmoil. As recently as the 1970s, Venezuela had the highest per capita income in Latin America because of its extensive oil reserves. That wealth was never widely shared, however, and by 2014, a medical research group estimated that 85 percent of the population lived in poverty, including 60 percent in extreme poverty,[b] and an estimated 2.5 million citizens had fled the country, many to nearby Brazil and Colombia. Venezuelans suffered from chronic shortages of food, medicine, power, and water. Runaway inflation made it virtually impossible for most citizens to meet their daily human needs, with prices doubling every twenty-five days.[c] Malnutrition and violence were widespread.

How, you might ask, did once-wealthy Venezuela get to this point? In retrospect, it seems clear that Venezuela's problems stem from its extreme dependence on oil dollars. A small group of businessmen and politicians benefited from the high oil prices of the 1970s and 1980s. Those in powerful positions lined their pockets. Fewer efforts were made to encourage other industries or modernize the economy, and unless you were part of the favored few, you began to struggle for housing, health care, and even food. You had thought Hugo Chavez, a charismatic self-proclaimed socialist, would make everything better, and for a while, things improved—large estates were broken up and if you supported Chavez's party, your family got access to what they needed. But soon, Chavez and his own inner circle of associates were siphoning oil earnings into foreign bank accounts. At the same time, they mismanaged the nationalized oil company, driving out most of the engineers and longtime employees who kept the wells and refineries operating.

Things got worse as both annual oil production and the price for oil declined. Social unrest grew; after millions took to the streets, Maduro banned all protests.[d] While suppressing political opposition, President Maduro took direct aim at the remaining institutions of democracy: He appointed allies to the nation's highest court, undermined the National Assembly by creating a Constituent Assembly to rewrite the nation's constitution, and got the military and national militia on his side. There's a lesson here: As in other nations, electing a president with autocratic tendencies and no respect for the institutions of democracy became the springboard for a strong leader to assume dictatorial powers.

## Questions to Consider

1. If you had been put into a position similar to the Venezuelans, which would be more important to you, defending the traditions and forms of democracy or securing the necessities of food and housing for your family?
2. When do the citizens of a nation realize that their populist leader has changed and is determined to preserve personal power even if it undermines democracy? Is there a clear tipping point when democracy is lost?
3. What should U.S. policy have been toward the competing claims of Maduro and Guaidó?

[a] Nicholas Casey and Julie Hirschfeld Davis, "As Trump Adds Sanctions on Venezuela, Its Neighbors Reject Election Result," The New York Times, May 21, 2018, https://www.nytimes.com/2018/05/21/world/americas/venezuela-nicolas-maduro-sanctions.html; Ryan Dube, Kejal Vyas, and Anatoly Kurmanaev, "Venezuela's Maduro, Clinging to Power, Uses Hunger as an Election Weapon," The Wall Street Journal, March 22, 2018, https://www.wsj.com/articles/venezuelas-maduro-clinging-to-power-uses-hunger-as-an-electoral-weapon-152173462
[b] Dube, Vyas, Kurmanaev, "Venezuela's Maduro," The Wall Street Journal. Also see Rocio Cara Labrador, "Venezuela: The Rise and Fall of a Petrostate," Council on Foreign Relations, January 24, 2019, https://www.cfr.org/backgrounder/venezuela-crisis
[c] Moises Naim and Francisco Toro, "Venezuela's Suicide: Lessons from a Failed State," Foreign Affairs, November/December 2018, https://www.foreignaffairs.com/articles/south-america/2018-10-15/venezuelas-suicide
[d] Olga Onuch and Jeanmiguel Uva, "Venezuela's latest elections are likely to trigger a regional migration crisis," The Washington Post, October 19, 2017, https://www.washingtonpost.com/news/monkey-cage/wp/2017/10/19/venezuelas-latest-elections-are-likely-to-trigger-a-regional-migration-crisis/?utm_term=.89caccd0c548

Trump received both criticism and praise for his willingness, as part of his role as chief diplomat, to meet and negotiate with North Korea's leader, Kim Jong Un.

The president is required by the Constitution to report to Congress on the state of the union, but only since Woodrow Wilson has the report been given in person. It has become a chance for the president to set the national agenda and perform the role of chief legislator.

Under the U.S. Constitution, presidents can "make treaties, provided two thirds of the Senators present concur; . . . appoint ambassadors, other public ministers and consuls; [and] . . . receive ambassadors and other public ministers." In interpreting these powers, the Supreme Court has given the president wide powers to serve as the sole voice of the nation in international affairs, but still, the connections with Congress are blurred. Will the Senate approve treaties? Will the House, lacking a vote on the treaty itself, provide the money needed to implement the treaty agreements? Just how independently can Congress act in international relations?

Presidents have increasingly sought to be the sole voice of American foreign policy. In order to curtail the congressional role, administrations have shifted from using treaties to using executive agreements, commitments that are made by presidents alone but are as binding as treaties. A recent study found that 93 percent of international agreements concluded by presidents between 1990 and 2012 did not go through the process laid out in the Constitution requiring Senate approval by a two-thirds vote.[12] Presidents may also decide whether to receive ambassadors, thereby recognizing the legitimacy of other governments or refusing to do so. For example, unlike most other nations in the world, the United States refused to establish diplomatic relations with the communist government in China from 1949 until 1979, when Jimmy Carter extended official recognition. In 2018–2019, President Trump threw the weight of U.S. diplomatic recognition behind the challenger to the president of Venezuela, who had secured office through a corrupt election. Through the appointment of officials to conduct foreign and military policy (subject to Senate confirmation), presidents are also able to exercise considerable (though not total, as we will see in Chapter 13) control over the day-to-day operations of the departments of State and Defense.

**CHIEF LEGISLATOR** Article II of the Constitution suggests that the president "shall from time to time give to the Congress information of the state of the union and recommend to their consideration such measures as he shall judge necessary and expedient." This is the basis for modern presidents' role of providing leadership for Congress, demonstrated in the annual State of the Union Address, which has evolved into one of the central rituals of American government. In January of each year, presidents deliver a prime-time televised address to a joint session of Congress also attended by members of the cabinet (minus at least one member, who would be the sole survivor in the event of a mass catastrophe), the Supreme Court, the Joint Chiefs of Staff, and the ambassadorial corps. This setting is all the more dramatic for occurring so infrequently, unlike in Britain, where the prime minister appears in Parliament weekly to answer questions.

George Washington and his successor, John Adams, met with Congress personally to deliver this message, but Thomas Jefferson discontinued the personal presentation, thinking it resembled too closely the monarch's opening of parliament in Britain. A century later, President Woodrow Wilson (1913–1921) reestablished the practice. In his prepresidential writings, Wilson, considered one of the first political scientists, had developed a model of national leadership that emphasized an energetic, solution-generating president whose direct link with the people enabled him to give voice to their needs. By renewing the president's personal appearance before the joint session of Congress, Wilson embodied this new model of presidential leadership. Today, Americans expect presidents to direct the nation's attention to the agenda of issues and to provide policy answers.

> **State of the Union Address** The annual address delivered by the president in person to a joint session of Congress and other government leaders. Today, this address is broadcast to a prime-time television audience.

Presidents since Franklin Delano Roosevelt have set the national agenda not only through the annual State of the Union Address but also through the president's budget message and high-profile public appeals on specific issues. Presidents today also take agenda setting a step further by crafting legislative initiatives and by actively lobbying individual members of Congress to support these initiatives.

As you will see in Chapter 15, multiple presidents have proposed solutions to the nation's health care problems, starting with Teddy Roosevelt early in the twentieth century. Lyndon Johnson succeeded in establishing Medicare, a health care program for the elderly, but many other efforts failed. It was therefore historic when Congress narrowly approved the health care plan presented by President Obama in March 2010. After a long process, Obama was able to exercise the president's principal role in legislation—the prerogative to sign bills before they become law or veto them subject to an override by two-thirds of the members of both houses of Congress, found in Article I, Section 7.

**CHIEF ADMINISTRATOR** Remarkably, supervising the civilian federal bureaucracy, now totaling approximately 2 million employees, is barely suggested in the constitution's job description. As the central government assumed more power over time, the federal bureaucracy grew (see Chapter 13). Most of the federal establishment consists of career civil servants buffered from partisan interference, but presidents appoint senior officials to guide policy and program decisions. Through these appointments, presidents can impact policy.

In 1981, President Ronald Reagan nominated Anne Gorsuch Burford as head of the Environmental Protection Agency (EPA). Burford shared Reagan's view that federal environmental policies were too restrictive and should be regulated more by state than by federal governments. She therefore slashed the EPA's budget by 22 percent and stopped enforcing many EPA restrictions on polluters.[13] As a result, Reagan was able to curtail the implementation of environmental policies and reduce what he felt was their negative impact on the nation's economy. In a similar way, President Trump and his appointees in the EPA and the Departments of Agriculture and Interior have reversed many of the environmental regulations established during the Obama administration.[14]

**CHIEF MAGISTRATE** The Federal Bureau of Investigation (FBI) is charged with bringing violators of federal laws to court. The FBI investigates and apprehends suspects while the Department of Justice (DOJ) is responsible for prosecution, making the president the nation's chief law enforcer. In the four decades since the Nixon administration, a system of largely unwritten norms emerged that ensured that the laws would be enforced fairly and without regard to partisanship. But since the FBI's handling of investigations in 2016 into former Secretary of State Hillary Clinton's use of a private email server while in office, there have been growing concerns about the politicization of justice. The Trump administration challenged many of the accepted ways of ensuring that the White House would not interfere with FBI and DOJ affairs, further increasing fears of possible politicization.

The magistrate role is also associated with the president's responsibility to nominate federal judges. Because Americans rely heavily on the courts as a means to resolve disputes (not all political systems do so to the same degree), the selection of federal judges is particularly important and has become increasingly politicized over the past three decades at the federal level. Through the nomination of judges, presidents can exercise a major influence on the general direction of the federal judiciary, but there is no guarantee how many vacancies they will be able to fill during their service in office. Finally, the Constitution provides presidents with the exclusive power to issue pardons to violators of federal laws unchecked by Congress.

## EXTRA-CONSTITUTIONAL ROLES

Over time, Congress has passed laws that expand the president's job description. Congress delegates responsibility for overseeing specific policy areas to presidents and for issuing periodic reports, such as the President's Emergency Plan for AIDS Relief—a plan for helping people around the world suffering from HIV/AIDS.[15] Sometimes Congress arranges staff support to assist the president in meeting these requirements. In 1969, for example, in response to rising public awareness of environmental hazards, Congress created the Council on Environmental Quality as a presidential staff unit to coordinate federal environmental efforts.

Activist presidents might decide to initiate actions in areas not specifically forbidden in the Constitution or assigned elsewhere in the federal government. The 12 years of FDR's presidency (1933–1945) were a watershed for the office. Roosevelt confronted major crises at home and abroad—the Great Depression and World War II—and Congress came to depend upon the president to set its agenda. The media began to follow national politics by primarily reporting on the president, a practice encouraged by FDR giving frequent briefings to reporters. The president and a growing group of staff assistants made more systematic efforts to manage the burgeoning federal bureaucracy needed to implement a wide range of programs designed to combat unemployment, poverty, and business behaviors believed to have triggered the Depression, such as unfair trading practices in stocks and bonds. Both the size and nature of the federal government's activities expanded. FDR thus set the precedent for expanding the president's role as chief legislator and developing new roles. Taken as a whole, FDR's actions created the modern presidency, a combination of expanded activities, a larger staff to help discharge this growing job, and higher performance expectations than earlier presidents had faced.

**CHIEF BUDGETER**  During World War I, government officials recognized how inefficiently the normal budget process operated; as described in Chapter 11, each department and agency went directly to Congress with its requests for the next year while the president watched from the sidelines, even though he was nominally the chief administrator. Both Presidents William Howard Taft (1909–1913) and Wilson sought broader authority.

In 1921, Congress passed a law requiring the president to be the chief budgeter, assembling a single, unified budget that is presented to Congress each year. This action triggered the famous aphorism that "the president proposes and Congress disposes." Presidential budgets are never adopted unchanged, but all provide the starting point for the annual discussion about the budget for the next fiscal year. Subsequent presidents have introduced new budgeting techniques and expanded the policy and management roles of their budgeting aides. (See the discussions in Chapters 13 and 15.)

**CHIEF ECONOMIST**  After the Great Depression and World War II, as the nation returned to normal conditions, Congress charged the president with responsibility for maintaining full employment and a healthy economy. In essence, the country was affirming the expanded responsibilities that FDR had exercised at the height of the national crisis. The president performs the role of chief economist with the help of the Council of Economic Advisers (CEA), a group of professional economists, and the Federal Reserve Board and its chair, who is nominated by the president to an independent term. (See the discussion of fiscal and monetary policies in Chapter 15.)

**POLITICAL LEADER AND HEAD OF STATE**  Virtually all political systems find a way to fill two critical roles. A **political leader** is able to mobilize action directed at solving the nation's common problems, a position likely to trigger debate and conflict over both goals and the means to achieve them. At the same time, each system needs a **head of state** who symbolizes the unity of the nation, the sense of common identity and purpose that binds together its citizens. In many nations, these responsibilities are vested in different people. For example, the British prime minister is the political figure while the Queen is the symbolic unifier. In systems without a monarch, an elected president often functions as the head of state (as in Israel and Germany), operating largely outside the political realm while the prime minister or premier leads the government.

In the United States and a few other systems (see Table 12.1), the two roles are combined. Some presidents, such as Dwight D. Eisenhower,[16] may de-emphasize the more political aspects of the job, but all presidents must balance these two potentially conflicting roles. And not all presidents discharge both roles with the same effectiveness. For example, some commentators have suggested that President Trump is less effective in the unifying role of

**political leader**  The role played by the U.S. president and, in parliamentary systems, by the prime minister in mobilizing political support behind major policy initiatives, requiring that the leader engage in explicitly political efforts.

**head of state**  The role usually played by an elected president or a monarch who symbolizes the entire nation, is above politics, and, therefore, exercises very limited political powers, usually in only the most fundamental issues, such as forming a new cabinet.

WPA Pool / Getty Images

**The U.S. president serves as both head of state and political leader. Some countries separate these roles, like the United Kingdom, where the monarch is the head of state and the prime minister is political leader.**

soothing the nation's collective grief in the face of hurricanes, floods, and mass shootings than either of his immediate predecessors, one a Republican and one a Democrat.[17]

Heads of state usually serve as moral beacons for and representatives of the entire nation. Thus, when scandal rocks a monarchy, concerns arise about losing the image of rectitude that the royal family is expected to embody. Highly publicized scandals involving royal children have alarmed people in Britain, Spain, and Monaco over the past several decades. Similar concerns were raised about Bill Clinton's marital infidelity with White House intern Monica Lewinsky; George W. Bush not so subtly promised in 2000 to return trust and morality to the White House. More recently, even conservatives have questioned whether President Trump embodies the necessary "decency" to remain in office.[18]

Presidents face conflicting pressures: represent and advocate primarily for that portion of the nation who supported them or represent the needs and interests of the entire nation? When presidents appear to be appealing exclusively to their base of support, as in the case of Donald Trump, it is certain to trigger criticism that they are not fulfilling their responsibilities as leader of everyone.[19]

## THEORIES OF PRESIDENTIAL POWER

Not all presidents approach the job in the same way. Presidents vary in what they do depending on the situations they confront, and they have considerable flexibility in how they perform the job. Because the range of roles the president fulfills is so extensive, presidents must determine how to allocate their time and which roles to emphasize. Some responsibilities are probably inescapable. Defense, foreign, and economic policies seem to be permanent fixtures of the modern presidency, but even those areas can vary in importance from one president to another. In the post–Cold War world that Bill Clinton confronted in the 1990s, foreign and defense policy seemed substantially less important than the economy. After 9/11, however, Bush and Obama were forced to contend with security problems.

The Constitution's language is unclear: "The executive Power shall be vested in a President of the United States of America." What does that mean? Unlike the language found in the Constitution on Congress, there is no enumeration of presidential powers or limiting clauses. As a result, presidential power has been open to interpretation. Teddy Roosevelt and William Howard Taft engaged in the classic debate over the boundaries of presidential power. Although Taft had been Roosevelt's secretary of war and was his immediate successor (Taft also later became Chief Justice of the Supreme Court), he differed greatly in his interpretation of the president's role.

As noted earlier, Roosevelt helped to fashion a new definition of the president as the people's champion; he articulated what is now called the **stewardship theory** of presidential power. In Roosevelt's view, the only powers that are off-limits for presidents are those expressly forbidden by the Constitution (as we have seen, virtually none) or in congressional statutes. Taft, following on Roosevelt's heels, regarded the job in narrower terms, believing that Roosevelt had taken excessive freedoms in the position. Taft articulated the **constitutional theory** of presidential power, which denied that any president could call upon inherent powers (that is, powers that logically flow from the need to perform their responsibilities) to act in the interests of the people. Some take an even more expansive view; under the **prerogative theory** presidents can engage in even those activities that are expressly forbidden in the Constitution if they are in the national interest, such as Lincoln's suspension of the writ of habeas corpus during the Civil War. Over time, Americans have generally had a higher regard for presidents who approached the job aggressively—seizing opportunities and stretching powers to meet new challenges. Thus, Jackson, Lincoln, and the two Roosevelts get high marks from historians.

Aggressive interpretations are not always praised, however. Richard Nixon's assertion of presidential power at the time of Watergate in the 1970s produced widespread concern and a severe backlash from both Congress and the public. **Watergate** refers to a collection of political

**TABLE 12.1**

## Nations Combining and Separating Political Leader and Head of State Roles

| Combined | Separate |
|---|---|
| United States | United Kingdom (monarch) |
| Mexico | Israel (elected president) |
| Brazil | Germany (elected president) |
| Nigeria | France (elected president) |
| Philippines | Russia (elected president) |
| Kenya | South Africa (elected president) |

**stewardship theory** The view of the president's role as a "steward" of the people who serves their interests because of the president's unique role as the representative of the entire nation and who is therefore empowered to define the position as broadly as necessary.

**constitutional theory** The view of the president's powers, elaborated by William Howard Taft, as strictly limited to those enumerated in the Constitution or conferred by congressional statutes.

**prerogative theory** The view that justifies an executive using discretionary power to act in areas without congressional approval or even to violate the law if such action is for the public good and is consistent with the national interest.

**Watergate** The political scandals associated with Richard Nixon, triggered by the judicial, congressional, and media investigations into the illegal break-in at the Democratic National Committee's offices in the Watergate office complex in Washington, DC.

Wally McNamee / Corbis Historical / Getty Images

scandals that Congress revealed during the investigation into a break-in at the Democratic National Committee Headquarters at the Watergate complex in Washington, DC, on June 17, 1972. The probe uncovered political dirty tricks played on the Democrats, illegal campaign contributions made to Nixon's campaign, an "enemies list" of political critics maintained by the president, illegal wiretaps, and secret bombings in Laos and Cambodia.

In short, a host of embarrassments came to light that went well beyond a simple burglary. For Nixon, the problem grew when testimony revealed that the president was part of a conspiracy to cover up White House involvement in the break-in, all documented by a secret, voice-activated taping system in the Oval Office. This evidence led the House Judiciary Committee to approve three articles of impeachment for obstruction of justice, abuse of power, and contempt of Congress. Nixon resigned rather than face almost certain impeachment by the House of Representatives and then trial and conviction in the Senate. Throughout this prolonged political crisis, Nixon's legal claims were often seen as assertions that presidents are above the law rather than subject to it. As Nixon once told a television interviewer, "When the president does it, that means it is not illegal."[20]

**Nixon's assertion of additional presidential power and his apparent view of the president as above the law led to his eventual resignation after Congress had begun the impeachment process.**

The debate over the limits of presidential power is not purely historical. During George W. Bush's term, a major controversy arose in response to an aggressive assertion of presidential power—the unitary executive doctrine—advanced by Bush and Vice President Dick Cheney. After 9/11, Bush and Cheney tried to prevent another terrorist attack through the use of wiretaps without court warrants; harsh interrogations of terrorist suspects, regarded by human rights activists as torture; and holding terrorist detainees "without charge, without access to a lawyer and without regard to the laws of armed conflict."[21] The Bush administration also refused to share information with Congress and declined to obey specific provisions of laws the president disagreed with, even though he had signed them, through the use of so-called signing statements. Taken together, these actions suggested to some that the administration's true goal was aggressive expansion of presidential power.[22] This debate carried over to the next administrations when Obama and Trump continued to use signing statements, and Trump battled against investigations conducted by Special Counsel Robert Mueller III and Congress.

## PUBLIC APPROVAL OF PRESIDENTS

Presidents govern relatively alone, not as part of the political team one finds in parliamentary systems. It should not be surprising, then, that American history frequently portrays "great" presidents as wielding so much power that they can shape events and deliver both peace and prosperity to the nation. Washington, Lincoln, and Franklin Roosevelt often are portrayed in this way. Washington led American forces to victory in the Revolutionary War and later created a new government; Lincoln preserved the Union by defeating the Confederates; Franklin Roosevelt led the nation out of economic depression and to victory in World War II. These thumbnail descriptions simplify what really happened and give too much credit to the leaders. The opposite is also true. Those presidents who fall short of lofty expectations are largely ignored or considered failures. James Buchanan, depicted as ineffective on the eve of the Civil War, and Warren G. Harding, who brought a new low to White House morality, usually head this dubious list.

Americans also want to believe that the votes they cast in presidential elections have meaning. They expect winners to solve global warming, find a way to fund Social Security well into the future while keeping taxes low, and protect the nation from international terrorists and economic disruption. In truth, presidents confront severe limits to their power, even if the public's expectations seem unlimited.

As we noted in comparing parliamentary and presidential systems, political and economic power in the United States is fragmented. To be successful, presidents must find ways to convince those who control that power to work with them. This is the reality identified in 1960 by Richard Neustadt in his highly influential book, *Presidential Power*, where he famously argued that "Presidential power is the power to persuade."[23] In other words, although they may seem to command others, presidents are simply one among many influential figures in American political and economic life and must use bargaining and persuasion to achieve their goals. Subsequent studies have suggested that Neustadt understated the extent to which presidents truly can act without winning the support of others and that presidents also derive great influence from their ability to use modern means of communication.[24] But most scholars agree that U.S. presidents enjoy very constrained powers.

Congress, bureaucrats, judges, the public, the media, interest groups, state and local officials, business executives, and union officials all exercise a measure of political power. To succeed, presidents need to work with these other interests. Moreover, presidents do not have full freedom to choose which problems to address. The issues they confront are dictated by real or potential emergencies (terrorist attacks or climate change), the decisions of other nations (the pursuit of nuclear weapons by North Korea and Iran), or natural and man-made disasters (hurricanes, tornadoes, forest fires, and massive oil spills at home and the AIDS and Ebola epidemics in Africa). While presidents may enter the office with an agenda they want to address, their attention and energies are inevitably redirected toward unexpected problems.

After the terror attacks of September 11, 2001, public approval of George W. Bush soared to an all-time high. (See Figure 12.1.) Inevitably, Bush's approval rating declined from that unnaturally high level. But the figure also shows a striking pattern: Nearly all presidents leave the Oval Office with lower approval ratings than when they entered. Even when he was reelected, only about half of the public approved of George W. Bush's performance. After a controversial election in 2016, Donald Trump's initial public approval was 45 percent, the lowest of any president going back to Eisenhower. During his first two years in office, it ranged between a low of 35 and a high of 45 percent.[25]

## FIGURE 12.1

## *Presidential Approval Ratings Since Kennedy*

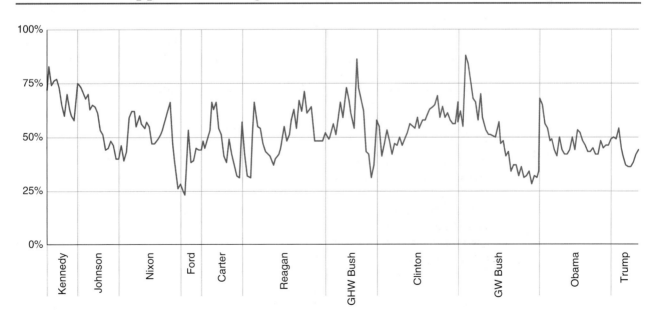

*Source: "Presidential Job Approval Center," Gallup, accessed August 2, 2019, https://news.gallup.com/interactives/185273/presidential-job-approval-center.aspx*

George W. Bush is the latest in a line of presidents who have been seen as failures when they left office—only Bill Clinton left the job with higher public approval than when he entered, partly because expectations were low at the outset of his service. (Note that Obama's approval ratings were on the rise as he left office but substantial numbers disapproved of him as well.) Given this historical record of declines in presidential support, some observers have wondered if the presidency is such an impossible job that no one is likely to succeed. It is reasonable to ask, *Does the job exceed the capacity of any individual?*

Comparing these U.S. patterns of public support with those for political leaders elsewhere can be tricky. In nations with multiple parties and a robust tradition of a free press, as found in the United States and Europe, citizens are more likely to openly criticize national leaders and their policies than in countries with less freedom of speech and the press.[26] And in parliamentary democracies, responsibility is not so clearly focused on the single figure of the prime minister or chancellor as it is on the U.S. president. Nonetheless, one study comparing the public support for President Reagan, Prime Minister Thatcher, and President Boris Yeltsin of Russia found striking similarities for the first two-and-one-half years of the leaders' terms, followed by a divergence as Reagan and Thatcher benefited from successful use of military force but a similar unsuccessful effort damaged Yeltsin's standing. Overall, the researchers found confirmation of an expected decay in public support for political leaders over time.[27]

# THE INSTITUTIONAL PRESIDENCY

The president's job is large—too large for one person—and still seems to be growing. Consequently, since the administration of FDR, presidents have received help from a staff of political and policy experts working in the White House and in the larger Executive Office of the President (EOP). Collectively, these staffs are referred to as the **institutional presidency**.

The institutional presidency protects presidents from the danger of overload. The president's time, energy, and knowledge are finite, but the demands of the job seem infinite, and the potential for exhaustion is high. Surrounding the president with policy experts and persons who can provide assistance is one way to avoid burnout and get the job done.

## THE EXECUTIVE OFFICE OF THE PRESIDENT

From a relatively small group that never exceeded 60 even at the height of World War II, the number of people working in the White House grew to more than 600 during the Nixon years and has leveled off at 400 to 500 in subsequent administrations. President Trump requested funding for 450 for 2018.[28] Some write speeches, some work with Congress, others give political advice or maintain the president's extensive schedule of meetings and public appearances. The White House staff is one component of the **Executive Office of the President (EOP)**, which includes an additional 1,400 policy experts. Some staff units are well known:

- Since 1947, presidents have assembled a group of senior cabinet advisers—the secretaries of state, defense, and the treasury as well as the vice president, chairman of the Joint Chiefs of Staff, and Central Intelligence Agency (CIA) director—to coordinate foreign policy advice through the **National Security Council (NSC)**. A group of policy specialists work for the NSC and provide the president with advice on the full range of international and security issues independent of the cabinet departments, who are sometimes suspected of having an organizational bias.
- The Office of Management and Budget (OMB; preceded from 1921 to 1971 by the Bureau of the Budget) assists the president in overseeing the annual budget process and managing the bureaucracy.

**institutional presidency** A term applied to the staff support enjoyed by modern presidents, especially those staff units with relatively continuous operation such as the Office of Management and Budget, the National Security Council, and the cabinet.

**Executive Office of the President (EOP)** A bureaucratic structure created in 1939 to house the personal staff and professional staff units created to help the president discharge a growing range of responsibilities.

**National Security Council (NSC)** A group created in 1947 to coordinate foreign, defense, financial, and intelligence policies for the president.

**Press Secretary Sarah Sanders and Director of the Office of Management and Budget Mick Mulvaney (who was also acting Chief of Staff) were two key members of the White House staff under President Trump.**

- The Council of Economic Advisers (CEA) helps the president develop policies to combat inflation and maintain full employment and a healthy economy.

Less well-known components of the EOP include the Office of National Drug Control Policy and the Office of Science and Technology Policy (see Table 12.2).

How do presidents use all this help? Staff members provide information for the president to use in making decisions and serve as the president's eyes and ears in Washington and throughout the world. As the public demands that the president address increasingly complex problems, the president requires additional staff to furnish expertise. Increasingly, fragmentation of political parties and Congress has also created a need for full-time liaisons who know the ins and outs of politics in different parts of the country and on Capitol Hill.[29]

The president's most senior advisers enjoy regular access to the Oval Office and become Washington power brokers operating in the shadow of the president. White House chiefs of staff are frequently the most powerful figures because they coordinate the president's schedule, control the flow of paper and people into the Oval Office, defend the president's interests in negotiations with Congress and the bureaucracy, and explain the administration's policies. The roster of advisers shifts with each administration and during the administration. Donald Trump is notorious for having the highest turnover in White House staff of any modern president,[30] including three chiefs of staff and five directors of communication in 25 months.

This "presidential bureaucracy" is not unique among western democracies. The United Kingdom's Cabinet Office employs more than 2,000 persons in support of the prime minister and the United Kingdom government more generally, exercising oversight of the civil service and coordinating government purchases of goods and services.[31] There is, however, a separate prime minister's office centered on 10 Downing Street, the official residence and workplace of British prime ministers, whose recent growth and activities resemble those of the White House staff. By 2008, there were 400 employees in the prime minister's office (down from a peak of more than 700). By contrast, in the mid-1960s, the prime minister received support from only 35 personal staff.[32] This striking growth was one of several developments that touched off a decades-old debate about whether the United Kingdom was experiencing a move toward presidentialism, with greater personal power concentrated in the hands of the prime minister rather than in the cabinet, the traditional collective decision-making body.[33] The German chancellor also has a support staff that works in the former palace that serves as a residence and official office, a practice that dates back to 1878 and Otto von Bismarck. After the reunification of East and West Germany, assistance grew so rapidly that a new building was required to house overflow for the staff of 750.[34] Japan has a Cabinet Office and a Cabinet Secretariat that oversee strategy, policy development, and public relations, as well as a specialized staff unit that oversees the reconstruction undertaken in the wake of the highly destructive 2011 earthquake (see Chapter 13).[35] In short, all executives need support, and the pattern has been for their centralized staffs to grow.

## THE VICE PRESIDENT

Jimmy Carter (1977–1981) elevated the vice presidency to a position of influence. Carter made Walter Mondale, his vice president (VP), a partner. Previously, vice presidents were the forgotten men of American government, occupying a job frequently derided even by its occupants. Under the Constitution, the VP's only regular responsibility is to preside over the Senate, voting only in the event of a tie. They also succeed to the presidency in the event of a vacancy resulting from death, resignation, disability, or removal through impeachment. Lyndon Johnson described this part of the job rather like being a vulture hovering in the wings of the White House and unlikely to endear himself to the president or his closest advisers. Most presidents since Carter have given vice presidents important tasks. Arguably, Dick Cheney, the VP for George W. Bush's two terms in office, and Joe Biden, the VP for Obama's two terms, became

**TABLE 12.2**

## Staff Units in the EOP and White House of President Trump

- Council of Economic Advisers
- Council on Environmental Quality
- National Security Council
- Office of Administration
- Office of Management and Budget
- Office of National Drug Control Policy
- Office of Science and Technology Policy
- Office of the United States Trade Representative
- National Space Council
- Office of the Vice President
- Executive Residence
- The White House

Bettmann / Getty Images

For much of the last century, presidential candidates chose their running mates to "balance" the ticket, as when the youthful New Englander John F. Kennedy selected Lyndon B. Johnson, a veteran senator from Texas.

the most powerful vice presidents in American history because of the responsibilities entrusted to them by their presidents.[36]

The original procedure for balloting in the Electoral College made the person receiving the second-highest number of electoral votes the VP—theoretically, the second most qualified person in the land to be president. But under this system, it was possible for presidents and vice presidents to be political enemies rather than allies. Thomas Jefferson, vice president to John Adams from 1797 to 1801, was regarded as Adams's principal political opponent and was not invited to cabinet meetings. (Can you even imagine President Trump serving with Vice President Hillary Clinton?) The Twelfth Amendment, adopted in 1804, partly solved this problem by establishing separate balloting for president and vice president in the Electoral College. With the growth of political parties during the early nineteenth century, presidents and vice presidents ran together, and VP nominees were selected to balance a party's national ticket—for example, Lyndon Johnson from Texas joined the Massachusetts-born John F. Kennedy on the Democrats' ticket in 1960. This meant that for much of American history, the office was filled by a parade of "also-rans" who gained their position because of the electoral votes they could deliver in the election.

## THE CABINET

For most of American history, presidents relied primarily on cabinet members to help them discharge their responsibilities. The president appoints the heads of the major departments of the federal government. There are currently 15 such positions: Secretaries of Agriculture, Commerce, Defense, Education, Energy, Health and Human Services, Homeland Security, Housing and Urban Development, Interior, Labor, State, Transportation, Treasury, Veterans Affairs, and the Attorney General (Justice). When most of these positions were created, there was no White House staff or EOP. Not all are equal in influence. Many analysts divide the cabinet into two groups, an inner and outer cabinet. The Secretaries of State, Treasury, and Defense and the Attorney General are usually close advisers to the president. Secretaries of the other departments—less critical areas of policy—usually have significantly less influence in the White House. However, most cabinet secretaries are overshadowed by personal advisers as presidents have increasingly centralized policy making in the White House. For example, the NSC rivals both the Department of Defense and the State Department for guiding foreign and national security policy.

In parliamentary systems, cabinet members share the political executive's burdens in a system of collective responsibility. The members of the cabinet reach decisions together and the government stands and falls as a group. But no such tradition exists in the United States, where the federal bureaucracy is created by and often heavily influenced by Congress as well as the clientele groups they serve (see Chapter 13). Whereas the cabinet may once have been an important instrument for developing and advancing policy ideas, it has never developed a tradition of collective responsibility in the United States.

Finding ways to lighten the president's burden has been an ongoing concern since FDR's administration. Ironically, this large collection of advisers poses its own challenges: Court politics[37] can become rampant with advisers maneuvering for influence; groupthink[38] poses the opposite danger if aides become more eager to agree with one another than to assess issues critically. Presidents might be isolated from reality and function in an echo chamber established by aides who tell them only what they believe the leader wants to hear. Or aides might use the reflected power from close proximity to the president for their own ends, leading to personal or political scandals that damage the administration. Staffing, then, is a two-edged sword, with the capacity to help or to damage a president.

cabinet A group of senior advisers to either a president or prime minister; these advisers each head a major department and meet collectively to discuss policy and political issues.

# PRESIDENTIAL GOALS AND KEYS TO SUCCESS

First-term presidents have three major goals: reelection, good public policy, and creating a legacy. Presidents ordinarily turn to the task of seeking reelection early in their third year, shortly after the congressional midterm elections. If they have not scored important policy accomplishments by the end of year two, they are unlikely to do so as the presidential election approaches. Criticism of the president's record rises as challengers compete for the opposition party's nomination, and challenges can be mounted within the president's party as well. From the perspective of the White House, then, good policy *is* good politics: Early policy success strengthens the president's chances for reelection.

Second-term presidents, no longer eligible for reelection, still push for policy success but largely as a way to fashion their legacies, hoping to make an even deeper mark on the nation's history. But second-term presidents face a briefer window of opportunity before they become lame ducks serving out the duration of a term. Franklin Roosevelt avoided lame duck status by winning four national elections in 1932, 1936, 1940, and 1944. By breaking the unwritten two-term limit, self-imposed by George Washington and then honored by his successors, Roosevelt ultimately triggered adoption of the Twenty-Second Amendment, which limits presidents to two terms and ensures that their final years in office will be less productive.

Ironically, presidents have the best chance of gaining congressional approval of their principal proposals when they first arrive in office, before they really know much about their new position or how to get things done. Later in the administration, political appointees are in place and able to formulate more thoughtful solutions to the nation's problems, but by then, the administration has usually experienced a decline in influence and is less able to get these proposals accepted.[39]

A "honeymoon period" follows the president's inauguration, when public approval is strong and disapproval normally low. Members of Congress are still evaluating the new leader in the White House and are eager to make a good first impression. Media discussions are largely positive. Unfortunately for the incumbent, the honeymoon cannot last forever. The president's party typically loses seats in the midterm elections, especially in the House, as happened in 2018. Media treatment becomes more critical. Public opinion shifts with events but generally moves in a negative direction, registering lower approval and greater disapproval of how the president is handling the job, as we saw in Figure 12.1. As a result, presidents are advised to hit the ground running by concentrating on a focused list of goals that will not overwhelm Congress and trying to achieve the greatest amount of change in the first year.

## PERSONAL ABILITY

Before reviewing the strategies presidents employ to achieve their goals, consider the personal qualities presidents need for success. According to presidential scholar Fred Greenstein, six personal traits matter most:[40]

- *Effectiveness as a public communicator.* With the rise of radio and television, presidents need to have oral communication skills that enable them to impress audiences in both formal speeches and extemporaneous settings.
- *Organizational capacity.* Presidents need to design an information processing and decision-making system that serves their needs. This skill has become critical with the rise of the institutionalized presidency.
- *Political skill.* Classically, presidents need to bargain with many skilled players, calculating their advantages, demonstrating their determination, and creating a record of rewarding friends and punishing opponents.
- *Vision.* Presidents need to inspire others—the general public as well as the fellow partisans and civil servants they lead. Insight into current problems and future challenges must then be translated into a compelling vision.
- *Cognitive style.* Presidents must cut to the heart of a problem, not become swamped in minutiae. Processing and analyzing large volumes of ideas and information is more important than mastery of specific knowledge.

- *Emotional intelligence. Character* is sometimes used as the shorthand term for a solid emotional foundation unlikely to fall victim to personal insecurity, suspicion, unwarranted anger, or irrational behavior.

Richard Neustadt argued that the best way for a presidential candidate to develop the job's necessary skills is to have had a career in political life, especially in Washington, DC. "Amateurs" in the ways of the capital, he predicted, were sure to fail. Nonetheless, Americans have seemed willing in the last quarter of the twentieth century and beginning of the twenty-first century to rely on "Washington outsiders" to serve as president. Presidents Carter, Reagan, Clinton, and George W. Bush came to Washington after serving as state governors. Barack Obama was still a first-term senator when he won the White House. And Donald Trump had no previous public experience in elected or appointed office, had not served in the military, and had no significant voluntary public service. With the exception of military heroes, most recently Eisenhower in 1952, very few presidential candidates who lacked experience in elected political office had even won a party's presidential nomination, let alone the general election.

Yet experience does not guarantee the psychological fitness or emotional intelligence needed for the presidency. Even with all the assistance they now receive, presidents must have the capacity to deal with severe on-the-job pressures, especially with the many defeats they will suffer in Washington's contentious political atmosphere. What kind of temperament should the president have? Ronald Reagan's sunny outlook seemed unshakeable even in the darkest moments of his presidency as he recovered from an attempted assassin's bullet in 1981, combated a severe economic recession in 1982, and suffered through a lingering foreign policy scandal that brought into question his own competence in 1986–1987. By contrast, Richard Nixon brooded in response to criticism and believed that he was the victim of a conspiracy triggered by the liberal media. Donald Trump's Twitter feed sometimes seemed to be a barometer of hurt feelings and resentment toward criticism.

Before entering the White House, Nixon had served in both houses of Congress and two terms as vice president. Upon assuming office, Nixon authorized a variety of tactics to silence his domestic critics: conducting government surveillance of student groups demonstrating against involvement in Vietnam; creating a special White House staff dubbed "the plumbers" who used illegal wiretaps and break-ins to plug leaks to the media; using Internal Revenue Service audits to harass critics; and undermining his opponents with dirty tricks during the 1972 presidential campaign. Personal insecurities seemed to lie at the heart of his problems. After Nixon tried to cover up his own involvement in the Watergate break-in, he became the first president to resign from office. Long service in government did not provide the kinds of coping mechanisms and temperamental resources needed for success.[41]

Few, if any, presidents will excel in all six of the traits we have identified. All will bring a mix of abilities in their efforts to achieve their goals of reelection, good policy, and a legacy for their successors. In general, presidents have pursued three strategies for success: legislative, administrative, and judicial.

## LEGISLATIVE STRATEGY

Most Americans think of presidents pursuing their policy goals by proposing legislation to Congress, similar to Franklin Roosevelt's New Deal or Lyndon Johnson's Great Society. Both Roosevelt and Johnson won congressional support for impressive lists of legislation that expanded the range of services that the government provides to citizens, including Social Security and Medicare, programs that changed the lives of millions of American seniors. (See the discussion in Chapter 15.) Most major initiatives require presidents to secure congressional agreement—that is, pursue a **legislative strategy**. This is particularly true if presidents want policies to endure beyond their own years in office. Broad, bipartisan support in Congress makes it less likely that the opposition party will reverse major policies as soon as it regains power on Capitol Hill or in the White House. Ideally, presidents would let members of Congress from both sides of the aisle shape major federal programs. When Republicans felt excluded from shaping the new national health care policy passed by Democrats in 2010, they quickly set about trying to dismantle "Obamacare," as they called it. *Newsweek* reported that

**legislative strategy** A presidential strategy to achieve goals based on proposals presented to Congress for statutory action.

after they gained control of Congress, Republicans tried at least seventy times to defund, modify, or scrap the law.[42] But bipartisan support is perhaps a dream in the polarized atmosphere that pervades Washington today and is one explanation for why presidents increasingly resort to the administrative strategy described below.

Cooperation between the president and Congress is not limited to major programs. In a system of "separated institutions sharing and competing for powers,"[43] government action on questions both large and small needs to be coordinated. In many situations—for example, the annual appropriations needed to pay for next year's programs, as described in Chapter 11—government can take action only through coordinated efforts. The alternative is paralysis, something we see more and more often.

**APPEALING TO PARTY** The president's party frequently serves as a bridge to build institutional cooperation. As we saw in Chapter 11, legislators do not always vote on the basis of party, but legislators' loyalty has been increasing. Party provides a set of beliefs that binds a president to many like-minded legislators, but presidents must activate those links by proposing initiatives based on those shared beliefs. President Trump, for example, enjoyed **unified government** during his first two years in office, conditions when actions by the president and Congress would ordinarily be aligned. But Republicans enjoyed only a very small majority in the Senate, and Trump's proposals often put moderates in a difficult position, asking them to be more conservative or more confrontational than they wanted—for example, by repealing Obamacare. Thus, a critical factor for presidents is how many members of their own party are serving in Congress. Presidents help members of their own party get elected in order to maximize the support they will have in Congress. George W. Bush, for example, campaigned aggressively for his party's candidates in 2002, traveling widely to generate publicity, raise campaign funds, and win voter support. The effort paid off when Republicans regained control of the Senate and expanded their majority in the House. Barack Obama tried the same approach in 2010 but without success; Democrats lost the majority in the House and saw their majority in the Senate shrink. In 2018, President Trump helped Republicans expand their seats in the Senate, but the party lost its House majority. **Divided government**, when presidents confront either one or two houses controlled by the opposite party, requires one of two strategies (see Figure 12.2). Presidents can compromise and bargain with the opposition in an effort to find common ground or engage in confrontation. In either case, if presidents lack the necessary skills, they need to tap the abilities of aides or rely on allies who possess them.

Working with members of the opposition party is a time-honored option. *Bipartisanship*—broad cooperation between members of both parties—was a staple of American foreign policy in the early post–World War II era but has declined in recent decades. Sometimes presidents find ways to work closely with congressional

**unified government** Distinct from divided government; a situation in which the presidency and the two houses of Congress are controlled by the same political party, providing the basis for joint action.

**divided government** When political systems elect the president and legislature independently, conflict can easily arise if Congress is controlled by a party other than that of the presidency.

**FIGURE 12.2**

## *Divided and Unified Control of Government, 1933–2019*

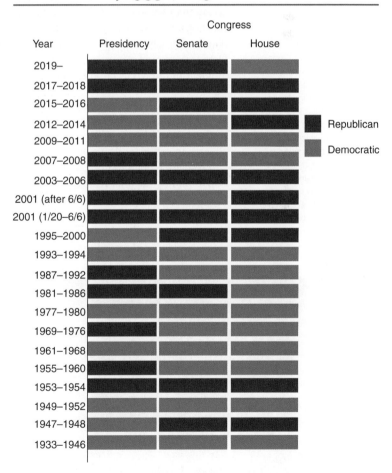

*As this table shows, periods of unified party control of Congress and the White House are not all that frequent. Since 1933, how many years has the United States had unified party control and how many years has there been divided party control?*

leaders of both parties (Eisenhower) and sometimes with a group of the opposite party's members (Nixon, Reagan). All presidents are happy to solicit support from individual legislators in the opposition party who are willing to break with their own party's majority based on principle or in exchange for presidential support on a goal important to the member, for example, a government project in the legislator's state or district. Many studies suggest that Capitol Hill itself has shifted dramatically. Partisan conflict has grown and cross-aisle friendships, let alone legislative partnerships between Democrats and Republicans, are less common than in the past. When Bill Clinton allied himself with Republicans and moderate Democrats to pass legislation such as NAFTA in 1993 and welfare reform in 1996, he outraged liberal Democrats who opposed both proposals. While President Trump enjoyed historically high levels of support among Republicans in the public during his first two years in office, he had great difficulty winning support from Democrats in either the House or Senate.[44]

**SETTING THE LEGISLATIVE AGENDA**   It is not unusual for presidential proposals and budgets to be declared "dead on arrival," without even a ghost of a chance at approval in Congress. This was frequently the case for Republican presidents such as Ronald Reagan, who annually proposed deep budget cuts in programs that the Democratic majority in Congress had created. Reagan had aggressively cut taxes but without corresponding spending cuts, the annual budget deficit grew rapidly. He had hoped to force Democrats to bargain and compromise, but they resisted. Alternatively, presidents can choose to make proposals that are intended to produce confrontation. Although it may sound strange, confrontation is sometimes preferred in order to dramatize programmatic and budgetary differences that will be highlighted in upcoming elections. In 1948, Harry Truman ran for president against what he termed the "do-nothing Congress" controlled by Republicans, and in 2019, Donald Trump continued to request that Congress approve funding to "build the wall" even though it was clear that House Democrats would refuse. In both cases, the president welcomed confrontation as a way to build momentum for a reelection campaign.

> **veto**  The constitutional power of a president to reject legislation passed by the legislature. In the United States, presidents have 10 days to act on legislation, which may be signed or returned with objections to the house in which it originated. Congress may override the veto and pass the bill by means of a two-thirds majority in both houses.

**ISSUING VETOES**   Presidential vetoes can be a powerful influence on policy, but it is a negative action, stopping undesirable things from happening. Sometimes the mere threat of a **veto** is sufficient to force legislative opponents to bargain and negotiate over matters of presidential concern in order to salvage other things the opponents want.

President Gerald R. Ford relied heavily on his veto power because of his weak political position. Fulfilling the final years of Nixon's second term, Ford was an unelected president (he was confirmed by Congress after Vice President Spiro Agnew was forced to resign even before President Nixon) and confronted an overwhelmingly Democratic Congress. Ford battled Democrats over economic and energy policies. His vetoes sometimes forced Democrats to negotiate. For example, after Ford vetoed a tax cut bill, Democrats agreed to adopt a dollar-for-dollar approach to tax cuts—each dollar of tax cuts had to be offset by a dollar in spending reductions.[45] Even though his vetoes were overridden more frequently than any other modern president, Ford prevailed on more than 80 percent of the vetoes he cast. Assembling the two-thirds majority required to override a veto in *both* houses of Congress is a difficult task.

Leaders in other presidential systems also exercise veto powers, but there is nothing similar in parliamentary systems, where the legislature's support is virtually automatic. Boris Yeltsin, Russia's first president after the fall of the Soviet Union, exercised his veto power 219 times in five years in a series of high-visibility showdowns with the Federal Assembly (the legislature), a rate so high that he was charged with abusing his powers and acting arbitrarily—he even vetoed one bill a second time, after it had been passed over his initial veto. Russia's Constitutional Court was called upon to mediate the conflict.[46] Some Latin American systems provide the president with an "amendatory" veto through which the executive can make

President Trump has continued to promote his plan to build a wall along the southern U.S. border, despite clear opposition from Congress, as it is popular with his supporters.

Joe Raedle / Getty Images

additions, deletions, and substitutions to bills. Only three Latin American countries (Honduras, Guatemala, and the Dominican Republic) empower their presidents to issue vetoes similar to those in the United States and fully reject a law passed by the legislature.

**GOING PUBLIC**  Not all presidents are willing to bargain and negotiate with Congress. Following the example of Teddy Roosevelt, some presidents prefer to appeal for public support over the heads of Congress; they do this by *going public*. Relying on techniques that resemble those used in campaigns, presidents who choose this route place pressure on legislators to support their initiatives or suffer the electoral consequences of blocking a popular president's proposals. Advisers to modern presidents devise photo opportunities—newsworthy activities to form the basis of reporters' stories—and draft speeches to help presidents make their case directly to the nation. Charles DeGaulle, France's World War II leader and president of the Fifth Republic from 1959 to 1969, brought major issues directly to the nation's citizens, relying heavily on his standing as a national hero to rally their support in plebiscites, direct votes of the public on important policy issues. But plebiscites or referenda do not always go the way the leader wishes, as demonstrated by the 2016 British referendum to leave the European Union—Brexit—which Prime Minister David Cameron opposed. When the public narrowly supported Brexit, Cameron resigned.

## ADMINISTRATIVE STRATEGY

When Congress resists presidents' appeals, chief executives sometimes use unilateral means to accomplish their goals. They can develop regulations or issue executive orders that advance the administration's goals. Such actions can be reversed by the next administration, but they have the force of law while in effect.

What happens when a chief executive of the national government gives an order? Harry Truman once predicted that Dwight Eisenhower, his successor, would be frustrated as president. As a longtime member of the military who served as Supreme Allied Commander during World War II, "poor Ike," in Truman's view, would expect obedience from the bureaucracy, but in Truman's experience, presidents seldom issue orders that others obey.

Truman, of course, was exaggerating, but only a little. Presidents do not *control* the executive branch. Congress determines the organization of the federal bureaucracy, ultimately establishes the budgets that support its operations, reserves to itself the right to control personnel, and is highly assertive in guiding federal programs and influencing agency decision making. For many reasons, presidents are said to "reign but do not rule"—that is, they are the head of the executive branch but do not exercise real control over it. Nonetheless, presidents can advance their programs using an **administrative strategy**. Presidents have a wide range of resources at their disposal to control the federal bureaucracy, including the oversight of personnel and budgets (reviewed in Chapter 13). Presidents also can develop regulations and issue unilateral edicts, discussed in the following section.

**REGULATIONS**  One of the oldest aphorisms in politics is that "the devil's in the details." Political parties, interest groups, and policy advocates can agree on general goals while disagreeing on how to achieve those goals. No political institution is more concerned with details than the bureaucracy, whose specialists thoroughly understand the ins and outs of policies and programs—their politics, histories, limitations, and funding. Such details lie at the heart of regulations that translate broad legislative goals into concrete programs of action, and bureaucrats play the central role in developing federal regulations.

For presidents, regulations provide an opportunity to shape programs while bypassing extensive bargaining with Congress. Anticipating that his party would lose the 2006 congressional elections, George W. Bush surveyed his cabinet for initiatives that could be accomplished through regulations.[47] The resulting list was long, including potential action in environmental, health, and labor policies. The administration even managed to use regulations to reduce health care spending—an area of rapid growth—in ways that Congress had already rejected.

By contrast, the Trump administration has pursued an aggressive *de*regulation strategy from the outset, particularly in areas such as the environment, land use, and consumer protections, where it believed regulations imposed undue burdens on businesses. Each government agency under Trump assigned officials to improve or rescind existing regulations, and the president established the

> **administrative strategy**  A strategy to achieve the administration's goals by using the president's budget, personnel, reorganization, and regulatory powers.

## TABLE 12.3

### *Average Executive Orders per Year*

| President |
| --- |
| Nixon 62 |
| Ford 69 |
| Carter 80 |
| Reagan 48 |
| George H. W. Bush 42 |
| Clinton 46 |
| George W. Bush 36 |
| Obama 35 |
| Trump 46 (first two years) |

Source: Gerhard Peters and John T. Woolley,—Executive Orders,|| The American Presidency Project, 2017, https://www.presidency .ucsb.edu/statistics/data/executive-orders

**Roosevelt's executive order during World War II authorized the detention of over 100,000 Americans of Japanese descent in camps such as this one.**

> **executive orders** Unilateral decrees issued by presidents to deal with policy or procedural matters that fall under their authority.

unprecedented guideline that for every new regulation added, two regulations were to be cut.[48] (See Chapter 15 for more on the regulatory process.)

**UNILATERAL EXECUTIVE ACTIONS** Legislation and vetoes often attract enormous media attention, but some presidential actions lie outside journalists' usual coverage. **Executive orders** and other actions initiated solely by presidents help chief executives accomplish goals unilaterally rather than through bargaining with Congress. Executive orders must be published in the Federal Register, a government publication in which all proposed and final regulations must appear, but memoranda are not subject to this requirement. Both are examples of the president's ability to govern by decree rather than by persuasion—to take direct, unilateral action in some aspect of government administration or public policy in order to modify laws or even take action in areas not covered by the Constitution or statute.[49] As shown in Table 12.3, some presidents rely more heavily on executive orders than others. Many executive orders have had important policy implications. For example, Franklin Roosevelt used an executive order in 1942 to authorize the forced relocation of Pacific Coast residents of Japanese heritage (including 70,000 American citizens) to internment camps during World War II. Harry S. Truman used an executive order to integrate America's armed forces in 1948. In the 1960s, Lyndon Johnson used an executive order to create the first government affirmative action program designed to open employment opportunities to minorities who formerly had been blocked from some professions.

During World Wars I and II, both Presidents Wilson and Roosevelt used executive orders to mobilize the nation for war, and FDR used them to take direct action to combat the Great Depression. But even under crisis conditions, executive orders can be challenged and reversed. Harry S. Truman issued an executive order authorizing the military to seize U.S. steel mills in the midst of the Korean War when a strike was about to close them. When mill owners went to the courts, the president was ordered to rescind his command. FDR's order to remove American citizens of Japanese descent from their homes in four western states and detain them in government camps to prevent sabotage was originally upheld by the courts and declared constitutional by the Supreme Court in the case *Korematsu v. United States* in December 1944. Recognizing the wrong that had been done, Congress later apologized and provided compensation for the victims in 1988. And the Supreme Court in 2018 explicitly disavowed the earlier decision when Chief Justice John Roberts wrote,

> The forcible relocation of U.S. citizens to concentration camps, solely and explicitly on the basis of race, is objectively unlawful and outside the scope of presidential authority.... *Korematsu* was gravely wrong the day it was decided, has been overruled in the court of history, and—to be clear—"has no place in law under the Constitution."[50]

Under President Obama, the DOJ further acknowledged that at the time of the internments, its leaders had suppressed important information that would have established the loyalty of the overwhelming majority of interned Japanese Americans.[51]

When presidents use regulations to pursue their goals, they must meet procedural requirements set forth in the Administrative Procedures Act. By contrast, there is no process for systematic review and comment before executive orders, presidential proclamations, and memoranda are issued.[52] But unilateral executive action comes at potential cost: Without full review, there is the risk of presidents making an error or triggering political controversy. Donald Trump's order that originally banned Muslims from entering the country faced widespread public outcry and court challenges, ultimately forcing him to make substantial modifications before it was upheld in the courts.

## JUDICIAL STRATEGY

Since the 1970s, presidents have pursued their policy goals using a **judicial strategy**, selecting like-minded nominees for the federal judiciary. Similarly, in guiding the enforcement activities of the DOJ, administrations make choices about priorities and areas to emphasize or de-emphasize.

**JUDICIAL SELECTION** Presidents since Ronald Reagan have made a conscious effort to select federal judges who share their political values and judicial philosophy. Although the media highlights battles over Supreme Court vacancies, far more vacancies arise on federal district and appeals courts, where more than 850 federal judges sit. Judges enjoy lifetime appointments unless they are impeached or leave office because of death or resignation. Thus, in selecting federal judges, the president can potentially have an impact on public policy for decades into the future.

Before the Reagan administration, judges were selected largely on the basis of their partisanship and professional qualifications—presidents overwhelmingly nominated judges from their own party whose qualifications had been evaluated favorably by a committee of the American Bar Association. Staff in Reagan's White House Counsel's office, however, began conducting extensive interviews with potential candidates for all vacancies, not only those for the Supreme Court. Staff members asked about policy views and judicial philosophy to ensure that a nominee's views were consistent with that of the administration.[53] Presidents since Reagan have followed similar procedures.

Depending on the number of vacancies that develop and whether Congress establishes new judgeships to deal with the growing caseload that burdens the federal courts, presidents have the potential to nominate a large number of judges. Reagan and Clinton, in particular, nominated large percentages of the total federal judiciary during their eight years in office. Not all nominees are confirmed. Moreover, the nomination process has become particularly contentious in recent decades. The average number of days required for the Senate to move from nomination to a confirmation vote was 78 days under Carter but 214 days during Obama's first two years.[54] As presidents have become more explicit about the policy goals they hope to achieve, the Senate has become more assertive in exercising its confirmation powers.

Not all presidents have the chance to name a Supreme Court Justice. Those who do invest enormous amounts of time and effort in selecting their nominees, but they do not always get what they had expected. President Eisenhower was surprised at the activism of Chief Justice Earl Warren and had strong reservations about the Warren Court's decision to integrate public schools (see Chapter 14).

**ENFORCEMENT** Presidents have the responsibility to enforce federal laws, which they delegate to the DOJ. Currently, the department's seven major enforcement divisions reflect the major categories of federal law that might be violated: criminal, civil, tax, antitrust, environment and natural resources, civil rights, and national security. Major operational subdivisions include the FBI; the Drug Enforcement Administration (DEA); the Bureau of Alcohol, Tobacco, Firearms & Explosives; and the U.S. Marshals Service.[55]

The DOJ can choose to be more or less aggressive in pursuing certain types of lawbreakers and launch special efforts in one or more areas. An administration might hire additional staff, appoint more aggressive leaders, increase budgets, and so on. These shifting priorities reflect administration priorities. For example, detecting and preventing the threat of terrorism stands as the number-one priority in the DOJ's strategic plan, along with securing the borders and enforcing immigration laws, reducing violent crime, and upholding the rule of law (including defending the rights to freedom of religion and speech). These priorities for Trump's DOJ differ from those under Obama, which included identifying and stopping computer crime (especially child pornography and intellectual property theft), stemming the flow of illegal drugs, penalizing corporate and civic corruption, and protecting civil rights and civil liberties.[56]

## CONSEQUENCES FOR DEMOCRACY

The contemporary presidency dramatically differs from the one invented in 1789. Congressional demands and activist presidents have fleshed out the original constitutional roles presidents were to play and created entirely new ones. More than ever, the nation relies on the ability of presidents

**judicial strategy** A presidential strategy designed to achieve the administration's goals through the appointment of like-minded judges to the federal judiciary and the establishment of clear priorities for federal law enforcement.

to act with secrecy, unity, and dispatch—institutional advantages that the Founders expected presidents to have over Congress—in addressing international and economic problems. Where once presidents were given expanded powers when the nation faced extraordinary problems (Lincoln and the Civil War, FDR and the Great Depression), presidents are now powerful even in ordinary times. Others in the government lean on them in dealing with even the most routine matters.

Today's world is far more complex than it was in the eighteenth century. Economic relationships, both domestic and international, are far more difficult to understand and control. Around the world, weapons are more dangerous, ideologies more threatening, and U.S. interests far more extensive. Most presidential elections find one or more candidates running televised ads that build on citizens' insecurities—impulsive opponents should not be trusted with nuclear weapons and those with limited experience are unprepared to deal with crises that arise in the middle of the night. As these issues became more prominent in the twentieth century, presidential power grew. Two world wars, a cold war, and a global depression led the nation to lean ever more heavily on presidents to define problems and solutions; presidents are also better able to coordinate complex government actions than Congress. Nor is this an exclusively U.S. phenomenon, as observers have noted the shift of influence toward executives around the world.

Nonetheless, American presidents are neither omnipotent nor omniscient. In fact, except in times of crisis, they spend much of their time assembling support for the policies they propose, whereas prime ministers can be assured of much more consistent cooperation. Why has the presidency evolved into the office it is today?

The challenges that presidents confront in doing their job are heavily determined by the basic constitutional design. Unlike a parliamentary system, in which the prime minister is also an elected member of the legislature and the leader of the majority party, presidential systems elect the executive separately from the legislature, which may be under the control of the opposite party. The Constitution's design also made the president's selection national in scope, giving individual presidents a claim to representing the interests of all the people. In a parliamentary system, the majority party makes a collective claim to hold a mandate from the public, but only so long as the party remains united. No comparable glue holds together the president's congressional supporters. National elections in a parliamentary system are called at the majority party's discretion, usually when their policies are popular; in a presidential system, elections are held at fixed intervals and can occur at a time when the president's popularity and that of the party are at low ebb. As a result, presidents always need to generate support.

Presidential systems also diffuse power—the responsibility for policy making is divided between legislative and executive branches. Presidents, then, are frequently isolated in their pursuit of legislative and bureaucratic support. By contrast, prime ministers can expect the legislature to support the government's policy goals. Cabinet members in a parliamentary system also serve as MPs, providing a direct link with the legislative majority, whereas cabinet members in a presidential system can come from a variety of careers in business and academia, and if they are drawn from the legislature, they must resign their positions (as was the case for Trump's first attorney general, Jeff Sessions, who had to resign his Senate seat).

Changes in political, social, and technological conditions have altered the presidency in important ways. The president's economic responsibilities—nowhere to be found in the Constitution—became a critical part of the job as thirteen very separate states evolved into an economically integrated nation. FDR's economic leadership at the time of the Great Depression made economic policies a permanent feature of the political system. New twentieth-century technologies made presidents the darlings of the mass media, encouraging journalists to provide personalized stories that capture the public's attention (whether delivered electronically or in print). And today's presidents are encouraged rather than discouraged, as they were in the past, to speak directly to the nation's citizens. President Trump can send messages to Americans or choose to communicate through television and radio. His tweets are seen by tens of millions. This accessibility makes modern presidents a real presence in the lives of Americans, heightening the personalized nature of the office.

Have presidents lived up to the tasks they are expected to perform? Some have, but many have not. And it may have become increasingly difficult for presidents to succeed, regardless of the help they receive and the strategies they pursue. Compared with executives in other political systems, presidents seem to confront higher expectations of individual performance while they are unable to command as much political support. Public expectations may have become so high that all presidents run a high risk of being perceived as failures.

Presidents have become more adept at mixing strategies—legislative, administrative, and judicial—to pursue the programmatic goals they set. And since the watershed administration of FDR, the nation has found new ways to help presidents succeed—providing them with more help and investing ever greater time and effort into finding a person with the right blend of skills and character. Nonetheless, pressure remains high to perform.

How powerful does the president need to be? This question was posed at the Constitutional Convention and has echoed throughout American history. Advocates for a more powerful president have argued that a highly decentralized nation—with power divided between federal and state governments as well as among separate branches within the federal government—needs a strong force at the center to pull the pieces together in times of national need, particularly in times of crisis. Thus, Congress and the courts have given presidents more power during wartime and during periods of economic crisis. And today, that power does not recede significantly during noncrisis periods. The opposite argument has also been consistent over time: Powerful executives pose a threat to citizens' rights and liberties; only by checking presidential power can the nation hope to preserve its hard-won rights. Can we afford a powerful presidency? Can we afford not to have a powerful president? Although questions still arise, the United States seems to have accepted a greatly expanded role for its chief executive.

## Critical Thinking Questions

1. In comparison with other presidents in U.S. history, how do you evaluate the performance of Barack Obama and Donald Trump as president? How might those evaluations be different in 20 years?

2. The argument is usually made that presidents are better able than Congress to respond rapidly to crises and to maintain secrecy in delicate situations. Do you agree? What advantages might Congress have over the presidency in such situations?

3. Are there ways to ensure that presidential candidates have the personal qualifications needed to be a successful president?

4. If you were president, how would you deal with the challenges posed by a divided government?

## Key Terms

administrative strategy, 321
cabinet, 316
constitutional theory, 311
divided government, 319
Executive Office of the President (EOP), 314
executive orders, 322
head of state, 310
impeachment, 303

institutional presidency, 314
judicial strategy, 323
lame ducks, 304
legislative strategy, 318
National Security Council (NSC), 314
parliamentary system, 304
political leader, 310
prerogative theory, 311
presidential system, 303

prime minister, 303
State of the Union Address, 308
stewardship theory, 311
unified government, 319
veto, 320
War Powers Resolution, 305
Watergate, 311

Visit edge.sagepub.com/maltese to help you accomplish your coursework goals in an easy-to-use learning environment.

Spencer Platt / Getty Images

# 13
# BUREAUCRACY

## *After reading this chapter, you should be able to do the following:*

- Explore the importance of bureaucracy in American government and understand the tensions between bureaucratic power and democratic ideals.

- Discuss how Weber's model reflects the development of modern bureaucracy and describe the features that distinguish the U.S. federal bureaucracy from other public bureaucracies around the world.

- Examine the growth of federal bureaucratic power in the United States.

- Identify the numerous organizational structures that make up the federal bureaucracy and describe the unique role that each one plays.

- Analyze the factors that determine the true size of the U.S. federal bureaucracy.

- Understand the means by which the public holds government administrators and their actions accountable.

## *Perspective: How Do Governments Respond During Natural Disasters?*

One of the worst natural disasters in American history occurred in August 2005, when Hurricane Katrina overwhelmed New Orleans, flooding sections of the city to depths of up to 15 feet, forcing hundreds of thousands of residents to flee their homes, and killing nearly 2,000 people. In the aftermath, public officials sought answers. How could this destruction have happened? Who failed to do his or her job? Why didn't the thousands of victims (most of them elderly or young and poor) who were jammed into the Louisiana Superdome or rescued from the rooftops of their houses receive help more quickly? Media and political attention immediately turned to FEMA, the Federal Emergency Management Agency, a part of the newly created Department of Homeland Security (DHS) and a small part of the federal bureaucracy.

President Jimmy Carter created FEMA in 1979, consolidating emergency relief programs scattered throughout the government. Under President Bill Clinton, FEMA made significant improvements. The agency positioned workers and supplies in anticipated disaster locations, worked closely with state and local officials to deal with displaced victims, and began to help communities repair problems that exposed them to floods. But FEMA dropped the ball in New Orleans. President George W. Bush had appointed administrators with more experience in politics than in emergency response, and when FEMA became part of the newly created DHS in 2003, it lost its direct line to the president.

The bottom-line judgment of FEMA's handling of Katrina was brutally simple: The agency was unprepared, disorganized, and poorly equipped.[1] Local authorities had tried to evacuate New Orleans, but thousands of residents had ignored a mandatory evacuation order and still others had no means by which to leave the city. Nearly 80 percent of the city was flooded, and emergency transportation was unable to reach many of those left stranded.

Poor response to disasters is by no means an exclusively American phenomenon. The earthquake and tsunami that struck Japan in 2011—devastating towns and triggering a crisis at a nuclear power facility—illustrate how even well-prepared nations can suffer devastating losses from natural disasters. Because of Japan's long history of tsunamis (the first one recorded in Japan was 1,300 years ago), the danger was well known, but no one had anticipated the speed and scale of the floodwaters. A wave more than thirty feet high arrived a half hour after a massive off-shore earthquake and reached more than five miles inland. Roads disappeared, communication collapsed, thousands died, and more than 500,000 people had to be evacuated and sheltered. Responders were overwhelmed, information was scarce, and transportation was difficult to impossible. Local and prefecture (state) governments were overwhelmed with fighting the 300 major fires that broke out, and the central government directed much of its attention toward resolving the looming crisis at the damaged nuclear reactor.[2]

Most governments around the world have programs in place to reduce the human costs of natural disasters. The United Nations Office for Disaster Risk Reduction conducts international conferences and shares best practices in the effort to build governments' capacities to meet these demands on their ability to help citizens.[3] Some nations have been more successful than others in coping with disasters. Cuba, for example, instituted widespread disaster planning after a 1963 hurricane killed 1,000 residents. When a Category 5 storm (the most severe level, with winds of 155+ mph) struck the island in 2004, it suffered no storm-related fatalities. By investing heavily in meteorological training and facilities, Cuba improved storm prediction and was able to alert residents at least three days in advance of a hurricane landing.

But Cuba takes other actions as well. Civil protection committees, organized down to the level of a city block, put plans into effect; public transportation supports mass evacuations, moving residents to higher ground. Students learn about hurricanes in school, and local authorities oversee emergency practice drills each year. Evacuees

Christopher Furlong / Getty Images

**The earthquake and resulting tsunami that hit Japan in 2011 caused significant damage to the Fukushima Daiichi nuclear power plant and left the government scrambling to contain the crisis.**

are expected to move to shelters or stay with relatives in safe areas; homes must be secured, windows covered, and debris removed from the streets. Public shelters are well stocked and supported by medical experts and social workers. Military deployments reassure evacuated residents that their personal possessions will be safe from looting. So effective are these plans that during Hurricane Ike in 2008, an estimated 2.6 million residents, nearly a quarter of Cuba's total population, evacuated their homes.[4]

What explains Cuba's effective emergency response? Part of the answer lies in the ruling Communist Party's power to coordinate action. It compels individual citizens to evacuate and commandeers the resources needed to accomplish the task. Cubans are not expected to fend for themselves by providing their own transportation, food, and medical care. When Katrina hit New Orleans, some segments of the city's population were unable to cope—the poor and needy (particularly those who were elderly and physically handicapped) suffered most. At worst, if citizens are forced to fend for themselves, economic differences will translate into unequal opportunities to survive.[5]

FEMA enjoys several assets in the United States—high levels of public literacy and a dense communication network that quickly spreads the word of impending danger. But FEMA must coordinate action across federal, state, and local government jurisdictions—governments that enjoy greater autonomy than those in Cuba. Moreover, Americans resent government intrusion in their lives and are confident that they can meet their own needs. **《**

# DEMOCRACY AND BUREAUCRACY IN THE UNITED STATES

Government does more than make laws, adjudicate disputes, and establish national priorities— the core activities of Congress, the courts, and the president. The government must build roads, deliver mail, patrol borders, inspect food, conduct medical research, protect the environment, collect taxes, protect citizens, and distribute Social Security payments, among many other things. Indeed, government bureaucracies provide many of the services essential to what we consider modern civilized life.[6] These tasks (and many more) fall to *bureaucrats*, a group of government employees who have been harshly criticized throughout American history. The federal **bureaucracy** is sometimes called the fourth branch of government, although the Constitution only hints of its existence. From a fledgling structure that was established under the Articles of Confederation, the administrative arm of the national government now sprawls throughout the country and around the world.

Growth of the government and expansion of its activities have been sources of concern for decades, and the terms *bureaucracy* and *bureaucrat* often imply ineffectiveness, red tape, and the unwelcome expansion of official activity into areas better left to the private sector. When Ronald Reagan was inaugurated as president in 1981, he identified bureaucracy as a particularly pressing problem in American life. As Reagan discussed the economic ills then facing the nation, he forcefully argued, "Government is not the solution to our problem; government *is* the problem."[7] This skepticism about government action was not exclusively a Republican attitude. Democrat Jimmy Carter had campaigned for the presidency in 1976 by railing against Washington and entered office promising to reorganize government and reduce the national budget, which he, like many of his successors, viewed as full of wasteful spending. And President Bill Clinton, addressing a joint session of Congress on January 23, 1996, delivered a similar message:

> We know big government does not have all the answers. We know there's not a program for every problem. We have worked to give the American people a smaller, less bureaucratic government in Washington. And we have to give the American people one that lives within its means. . . . The era of big government is over.[8]

**bureaucracy** A structure created to achieve complex goals through coordinated action undertaken either by governments (public bureaucracy) or corporations (private bureaucracy).

Politicians score political points by denouncing big government and chastising bureaucrats. Most recently, President Trump lumped bureaucrats into the Washington "swamp" that he had pledged to drain, and further called out the "deep state's" hostility to his election. In Trump's view, permanent government employees were not politically neutral, as they are supposed to be, and he regarded civil servants' commitments to ongoing programs and policies that he sought to dismantle as disloyal. Trump seemed unaware of the training and culture that shapes government bureaucrats.

But there is a larger underlying issue: Is democracy compatible with a powerful and influential government bureaucracy? This question arises more often in the United States than in other modern democracies because of our history and culture. Americans are suspicious that bureaucrats wield unchecked, concentrated, and ever-growing powers; multiplying government rules and regulations are unwarranted intrusions on their personal liberty. Yet unhappy citizens cannot vote bureaucrats out of office. In contrast, defenders of government action argue that bureaucrats enhance the liberty of Americans by providing necessary services and controlling the effects of otherwise unchecked private power. Protecting citizens from unsafe drugs, food, air, water, and myriad predatory financial practices makes liberty possible in a complex economic and social system. But the defense of bureaucrats largely falls on deaf ears. As one observer concludes, "The battle between bureaucracy and democracy is written into our history. So is the fact that democracy must win. All we have left to debate is the cost."[9]

# FEATURES OF A MODERN BUREAUCRACY

What do we mean by the term *bureaucracy?* What are the key elements that help us to recognize one when we see it? Is a bureaucracy hopelessly inefficient, as much of the public believes? In the next section, we look at the classic model of bureaucracy developed by sociologist Max Weber and see how his ideas have shaped our thinking about public bureaucracies.

## WEBER'S MODEL OF BUREAUCRACY

Many of our modern ideas about bureaucracies originate with the work of Max Weber, a German sociologist who wrote about the historical evolution of administrative systems at the turn of the twentieth century. Weber's bureaucracy accentuated certain features based on characteristics that were displayed by organizations in modern society but were unlikely to be found in reality—that is, an ideal type. Five basic qualities characterize Weber's model:

- *Hierarchy of authority.* The structure is usually represented as a pyramid, with an ultimate goal-setter at the apex and those higher up in the structure supervising those below.
- *System of rules.* Rules are typically extensive and used to guide decisions by organization members; they ensure that all citizens are treated impartially.
- *Division and specialization of labor.* Those with specific expertise will be responsible for the associated segment of an organization's work.
- *Written records.* Extensive recordkeeping guarantees that future decisions will be consistent with past practices and precedents.
- *Careers are based on merit.* Organization members obtain their positions and are promoted to higher positions based on personal ability rather than on political or family connections.

These key features can be found in both government and private-sector bureaucracies. In political systems, they are central to the ability to accomplish complex collective tasks, ranging from creating irrigation systems in ancient Egypt to providing for national defense in a nuclear age. Weber regarded the five characteristics as *functional features* of bureaucracy—that is, components that contribute to a positive result. Hierarchy creates obedience to direction from above, just as specialization allows the most knowledgeable employees to complete a task, and so on.

Weber and others also identified *dysfunctional features* of bureaucracies—components that might prevent positive results:

- *Understanding fades up the ladder.* Those at the top of the hierarchy know less about a problem than those who are closer to it, yet those higher up in the organization issue orders.
- *Bureaucrats make decisions based on rules.* People are treated as categories; impartial decisions, made by inflexibly following the rules, ignore the unique problems of individuals and make them feel depersonalized.
- *Specialization can blur the big picture.* Those lower in the hierarchy may be more committed to their immediate goals—obtaining the budget and materials required to complete their daily tasks—than to fulfilling the larger mission of the bureaucracy.
- *Written records delay responses to new developments.* This is especially true if the bureaucracy makes decisions based solely on precedents found in written records.
- *Career officials may value future benefits over current productivity.* Bureaucrats may be more interested in putting in their time until they reach retirement age than in doing the work expected of them.

In short, there are plenty of reasons to criticize bureaucracies as well as to appreciate the complex tasks they can accomplish. Inherently, bureaucracy is neither good nor bad, and while the term *bureaucrat* is often used in a derogatory way, the career employees working for the government fill many different types of jobs, all performing assignments that are designed to benefit citizens.

## DISTINCTIVE FEATURES OF U.S. BUREAUCRACY

Weber's concept of bureaucracy was intended to help scholars understand bureaucracies around the world and suggested that basic principles of modern organization transcend cultural differences; subsequent scholarship has both explored Weber's model and revealed how one nation's bureaucracies might vary from another's. Several factors have contributed to a distinctly American style of public bureaucracy, namely a cultural distrust of government power and capacity, a lack of constitutional standing, uncertain guidance, neutral agents forced to be political, and experimental structures.

### A CULTURAL DISTRUST OF GOVERNMENT POWER AND CAPACITY
Influential political scientist Harold Laski observed seven decades ago that "most Americans . . . tend to feel that what is done by a government institution is bound to be less well done than if it were undertaken by individuals, whether alone or in the form of private corporations."[10] Today, the situation is little changed. Gallup found that fewer than half of Americans trust the government's ability to handle either domestic or international problems, and while that figure has dropped notably under President Trump, barely half had confidence on domestic problems throughout the Obama era (see Figure 13.1). Americans frequently use *bureaucratic* as a synonym for slow and inefficient action. Individuals deeply believe that making separate decisions in a marketplace likely improves efficiency and that the government wastes money. By 2014, Americans believed that 51 cents of every tax dollar going to Washington, DC, was wasted.[11] Most European nations, on the other hand, have long histories of powerful central government structures (bureaucracies) that were essential to their emergence as nation-states. In some nations—France, for example—government administrators have a strong identity separate from politicians. In those nations, citizens have historically been more likely than Americans to respect and support actions taken by government administrators. However, this may be changing. The rise of populism throughout Europe means that more citizens express distrust of traditional institutions (with the exception of the military), and as trust in national government declines throughout Europe, the distinctive respect accorded administrators may erode.[12]

### LACK OF CONSTITUTIONAL STANDING
The federal bureaucracy is looked upon as an instrument that accomplishes the legislature's will and has no independent position in the system of checks and balances.[13] In truth, only Congress can create government agencies and departments, although these organizations largely fall within the executive branch. Thus, bureaucrats must pay attention to the guidance provided by both elective branches of government. Worse yet, bureaucrats seem to consolidate the legislative, judicial, and executive

## FIGURE 13.1

*Trust in Government to Handle Problems*

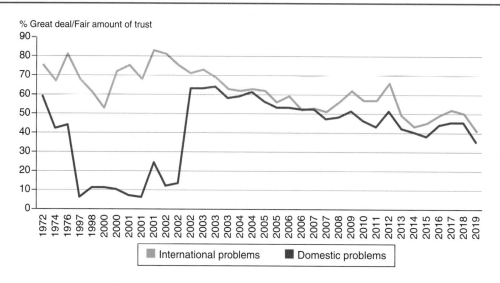

% Great deal/Fair amount of trust

Legend: International problems — Domestic problems

How much trust and confidence do you have in our federal government in Washington when it comes to handling (international/ domestic problems) — a great deal, a fair amount, not very much or none at all?

Source: Megan Brenan, "Americans' Trust in Government to Handle Problems at New Low," Gallup, January 31, 2019, https://news.gallup.com/ poll/246371/americans-trust-government-handle-problems-new-low.aspx

powers that the Constitution disperses to different branches: Drafting regulations is akin to legislative power; judging how rules apply in specific cases resembles judicial powers; managing the planning, staffing and budgeting of programs is executive power.

**UNCERTAIN GUIDANCE** If bureaucrats are to accomplish the people's will as expressed by the legislature but also be subject (in most cases) to direction by the executive, how do they know what to do when Congress and presidents disagree? Since the legislature is internally divided and the president separately elected, it is often difficult to determine the people's will and the public interest. As political scientist Norton Long posed in his classic question, "In case of conflict between any or all of these, who should be supreme as the authentic representative of what the people want?"[14] As we recall from Chapter 12, no such problem afflicts parliamentary systems around the world where legislative and executive powers are merged.

**NEUTRAL AGENTS ARE FORCED TO BE POLITICAL** Bureaucrats require political guidance and support in order to perform their public tasks. When they receive uncertain or conflicting guidance from above, they are forced to generate the political support they need on their own, turning to interest groups and beneficiaries in the public to lobby on behalf of larger budgets for their programs and expanded missions. As Long observed, "They must supplement the resources available through the hierarchy with those they can muster on their own, or accept the consequences in frustration."[15] Bureaucrats in most other nations need not engage in such openly political efforts to secure the support they need. In parliamentary systems such as India or England, legislative and executive authorities are almost always in agreement and bureaucrats do not need to find their own support.

**EXPERIMENTAL STRUCTURES** Rather than adopting a single set of organizational structures, the United States has willingly experimented with many different ones for public bureaucracies, crafting structures to suit particular circumstances in hopes of making them work. This has resulted in the dizzying array of arrangements discussed later in the chapter.

These features of American culture and government structure make the U.S. federal bureaucracy distinct from bureaucracies in other nations. Although career government officials operate in many of the same ways that officials in other countries do, the context differs and so do the challenges and constraints they face. In most respects, these factors—a distrustful public, a divided government, and the need to assemble their own supportive coalition in a highly fragmented political environment—make the lives of federal bureaucrats more difficult. Although bureaucrats are often portrayed as too powerful, most of these factors actually weaken the power they could potentially exercise.

# THE CHECKERED HISTORY OF BUREAUCRACY IN THE UNITED STATES

It should come as no surprise that a nation born with a strong sense of outrage at King George III's excessive exercise of power would distrust centralized government and the bureaucrats needed to implement its laws. The king's tax collectors and his army were the instruments of England's tyranny in the eighteenth century, violating basic rights itemized in the Declaration of Independence.[16] The colonists resisted creating a new central authority and distrusted its agents. During the Revolutionary War and immediately after independence, government was treated as a responsibility of the states.

The Constitutional Convention arose because the loose confederation of states, lacking an independent source of revenue and without authority over its citizens, was unable to provide for defense, maintain domestic order, or build a thriving economy. Faced with these same problems, European monarchs in the sixteenth and seventeenth centuries modernized their nations by establishing centralized administrations in France, England, Sweden, Russia, Prussia, Spain, and Portugal. In the case of the United States, constitutional reformers faced the challenge of convincing state leaders that an effective national government, complete with a permanent bureaucracy, would not endanger citizens' hard-won liberty. Under the Articles of Confederation, Congress created three departments of government staffed by permanent officials: Foreign Affairs, Treasury, and War. In addition, Benjamin Franklin, serving as the nation's first Postmaster General, organized a postal system.[17]

## HAMILTON VERSUS JEFFERSON

With the ratification of the Constitution and launch of the new government in 1789, George Washington and John Adams had to create new administrative structures. The Constitution was silent on what this new national bureaucracy would look like, leaving these critical decisions to the first cohort of national leaders.[18] Alexander Hamilton, the first secretary of the treasury (pictured on the $10 bill and subject of the hip-hop musical), became the driving force in creating the new agencies of government, providing answers that often provoked contrary responses from Thomas Jefferson, the first secretary of state. Treasury and State were two of four original government departments that also included War and the attorney general, the latter a lone legal adviser rather than the head of a large department, as is true today.

During the Constitutional Convention, Hamilton forcefully advocated for a strong, energetic central government. In the early years of the new republic, his ideas led to an effective central administration based on a sound financial foundation—predictable sources of revenue (tariffs on imports and excise taxes on whiskey), guaranteed repayment of public debts, a central bank, and a plan to help fledgling industries. Hamilton also made important contributions in foreign affairs, helped organize the military, and developed early policies affecting a small cadre of civil servants. In short, Hamilton sought to plan and direct the nation's emergence as a world power and endorsed a number of European administrative practices that he believed would further that goal.

Jefferson, in contrast, preferred to rely on the state governments, concerned that a strong central administration would pose a danger to liberty; he also distrusted the powers of both elected and appointed officials. Each leader was partly successful. Jefferson's vision of a weak central government with constrained powers and a small number of permanent officials prevailed throughout most of the nineteenth century. Most programs that touched citizens remained under the auspices of the states. In addition to defense, the national government expanded its territory and promoted economic development through internal improvements—roads, canals, railroads, river and harbor projects, and lighthouses.[19] In most communities, the clearest evidence of the federal government's

Through much of the nineteenth century, most Americans had little contact with the federal government. Post offices, such as this one in Ganado, Arizona, were one exception.

presence were "land offices, post offices and customhouses," providers of key services to an ever-growing population driven by the desire to make money.[20] Hamilton's vision of an active, directive central government came to fruition at the turn of the twentieth century, when the emergence of an interdependent, industrialized society triggered significant growth in the powers and reach of the U.S. government.[21]

Why did the federal bureaucracy in the United States develop more slowly than it did elsewhere? Beyond the culturally ingrained distrust of centralized power, most observers point to a *different sequence of political development* that unfolded in the United States. In the European nations, a powerful, central administration emerged prior to the establishment of institutions of democracy—elections, political parties, and widespread voting. In the United States, democracy came first and the demand for concentrated national power arose later, especially during the late nineteenth century, when millions of Americans moved from farms to the cities as industrialization spread. This change in the character of American life created new social and economic pressures just as the United States was emerging as a major world power in the Spanish–American War and World War I. In order to deal with these dramatic changes, the nation needed to provide the federal government with expanded powers and the administrative structures to exercise them.[22]

## NINETEENTH-CENTURY CHANGES

Although the Constitution called for separated powers and vested executive power in the hands of the president, it was Congress that stood at the center of national government for most of the nineteenth century. Heavily influenced by the powerful, locally based political parties that developed in the 1830s, members of Congress enthusiastically supported patronage—the promise of government jobs and contracts that would come with a presidential victory and one of the most powerful incentives available to the parties to win voters' support.

Andrew Jackson is credited with initiating the **spoils system**, the practice of appointing political supporters to government positions. After his victory in 1828, he established the practice of "rotation in office," replacing incumbent jobholders in the federal government with new appointees who supported the winner in the election. Jackson's supporters embraced the aggressively egalitarian view that all citizens were equally capable of doing the job, meaning that it made little difference precisely who held such positions.

Political scientist Matthew Crenson suggests that Jackson's rotation in office scheme created one condition for a modern bureaucracy: People in the organization's structure are interchangeable rather than irreplaceable. Jackson's administration also introduced several modern procedures for exercising control over the bureaucracy, including routine audits of spending, reorganizing government structures, explicitly stating an agency's mission, and specializing the jobs performed by employees.[23] These changes made the U.S. government more fully resemble the model of bureaucracy that Weber later articulated.

## THE CREATION OF THE U.S. CIVIL SERVICE

By the late nineteenth century, government reformers believed that only the most meritorious citizens should be chosen for government jobs, not simply those loyal to the party. Several nations—the United States among them—began to staff government agencies with better qualified professionals. Great Britain introduced competitive written examinations as a way to select government workers in 1870; those earning higher grades got the jobs. Canada adopted a similar system in 1882. Japan began using exams to determine promotions in 1887, and Prussia created a career system for its bureaucrats in 1873.[24] Other keys to the new systems included

**spoils system** A popular practice in the nineteenth century that allowed presidents to appoint party loyalists and campaign workers to government jobs as a reward for their support, establishing the adage of "to the victor belongs the spoils."

political neutrality and career security—that is, government workers could not be fired simply for disagreeing with the elected officials of the moment. Establishing a civil service system in the United States was part of an international trend.

Reform efforts in the U.S. started with President Ulysses S. Grant (1868–1876) and President Rutherford B. Hayes (1877–1881), but change came following a presidential assassination. James A. Garfield (1881) served as president for only 200 days. Shot in July 1881 by Charles J. Guiteau, a man usually described as a "disappointed office seeker" (actually an emotionally unstable campaign supporter of Garfield who was demanding a job), Garfield lingered until September. After Garfield's dramatic shooting and slow death, groups supporting civil service reform sprang up across the nation and coalesced into the National Civil Service Reform League, and journalists and political cartoonists in *Harper's Weekly* and *Puck*, two influential publications of the era, made the assassination into a *cause célèbre*, encouraging the nation to adopt reforms as a way to honor the fallen president. After two years of struggle, Congress adopted the Pendleton Civil Service Reform Act in January 1883. This bill mandated that only the best-qualified—not the best-connected—individuals would be selected for government jobs. All citizens would have an equal chance of competing for a government position, and the prestige of public jobs would grow.

Beginning in the late nineteenth century, civil service reforms began to favor job applicants who were best qualified rather than best connected. The Civil Service Commission held examinations, similar to this one in 1909, to find the best candidates for positions.

The Senate (38–5 and 33 not voting) and the House (155–47 and 85 not voting) reluctantly passed the civil service reform legislation. The high level of abstentions reflected the fact that the law would weaken legislators' ability to reward campaign supporters. Even after the passage of the Act in 1883, however, most federal jobs were still filled through the spoils system. Only 10 percent of federal jobs were covered by the new system. A provision in the Pendleton Act allowed future presidents to fold increasing numbers of positions into the system to expand its coverage; by 1904, that included 50 percent of federal positions, and by 1960, it had reached 85 percent.[25] From reform came a system that coordinated the way that government recruits, selects, trains, deploys, compensates, and retains employees. Although far from perfect, the new system was widely regarded as a marked improvement over the earlier patronage system, and most members of the civil service bring strong qualifications to the positions.

State, county, and municipal governments adopted central features of the federal system as well. Shifting government jobs from "who you know" (patronage) to "what you know" (competence) is a broadly embraced principle of good government, as is protecting government employees from undue partisan pressure. Extensive systems of rules and regulations grew up around testing, hiring, firing, transferring, assigning overtime, and so forth, all in the effort to guarantee observance of these principles and protections.

Each civil servant is assigned a position in a complex matrix that tries to establish consistency between a job's responsibilities and the occupant's pay—equal pay for equal work. Workers can earn more by increasing their responsibilities through promotion or transfer or remaining in a job and building seniority. Raises come regardless of performance. This pay structure was created in 1949 and remained in place for nearly half a century with workforce raises approved by Congress, but it came under heavy attack during the George W. Bush administration as being excessively inflexible.

Some high-level career bureaucrats are eligible for merit-pay bonuses, including members of the Senior Executive Service, who can be reassigned to new jobs more easily than the typical government employee. To have an elite group of administrators working in the space between political appointees and permanent bureaucrats is becoming more common worldwide. By 2009, only seven of the 30 nations in the Organization for Economic Cooperation and Development (OECD) did not maintain such an intermediary group of senior civil servants—Austria, Denmark, Germany, Ireland, Mexico, Sweden, and Switzerland.[26]

**Pendleton Civil Service Reform Act** Legislation approved in 1883 that created the U.S. civil service system, in which government employees are chosen based on expertise and experience rather than party loyalty.

# THE COMPLEX STRUCTURE OF THE FEDERAL BUREAUCRACY

People often think of the federal bureaucracy as a single structure with the president at the top of a pyramid issuing orders that subordinates must obey. In reality, it is a collection of separate bureaucracies, each one exhibiting some of the features that Weber described, but each also developing a distinctive culture and set of rules that guide its behavior. Some are under tight presidential control, but others have considerable autonomy, either wholly or in part. Some are larger and some are smaller, and they assume different forms. In this section, we discuss several of the organizational forms that make up the federal bureaucracy, and we note whether they are primarily managed by the president or by Congress or are independent.[27] Collectively, they are called the *federal bureaucracy*, and most organizations lie within the executive branch, but the president is decidedly not a single controlling figure as one would find in Weber's ideal type.

## DEPARTMENTS

The most significant building blocks of the federal bureaucracy are the executive departments, often referred to as the *cabinet departments* because their heads—secretaries—are members of the president's cabinet; these members form a line of succession in the event that the president, vice president, Speaker of the House, and Senate *president pro tempore* are unable to assume the tasks of president.[28] There are currently 15 cabinet-level departments, with the newest one, the DHS, created in 2002 (see the timeline in Figure 13.2).

Creating a new executive department is a big deal. Through this action, Congress and the president signal that the department's programs and policies reflect a major national commitment. This was true for transportation, urban planning, energy, and homeland security, for example, at the time those departments were created. Alternatively, the creation of a department signals that a segment of the population served by the programs is important—farmers, business, organized labor, veterans, and educators, for example, lobbied actively for creation of the departments that address their interests. In some instances, the president and Congress create a department to better address a set of public problems, often by consolidating related agencies under one roof. Consolidation was the principal reason for the creation of the Department of Defense in 1947, discussed later in this chapter. Similarly, President Eisenhower proposed creating the Department of Health, Education, and Welfare in 1954, later renamed Health and Human Services.[29]

Creating new departments is not easy, as the establishment of the DHS demonstrates. When it was created by Congress in 2002, it was given three primary missions:

- Prevent terrorist attacks within the United States.
- Reduce the vulnerability of the United States to terrorism.
- Minimize the damage caused by, and assist in the recovery from, terrorist attacks that occur within the United States.[30]

## FIGURE 13.2

## *Cabinet Departments of the U.S. Government*

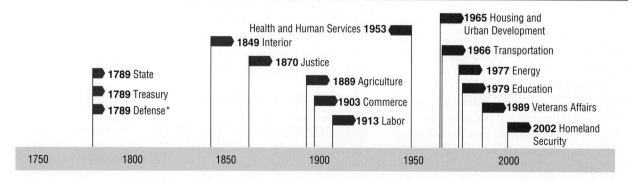

*Originally established as War and Navy.*

Such a structure would allow the DHS to better coordinate its activities, but to accomplish these goals, Congress needed to relocate 22 offices and agencies from other departments throughout the federal government and house them within a single organization.[31] Even the best-designed organizations evolve over time. Immigration services and border security, one of the department's lesser missions at the time of its creation, became one of its most controversial responsibilities during the Trump years.

This government-wide reshuffling of responsibilities triggered turf wars within both the bureaucracy and Congress. Departments did not want to lose units to the new DHS, and members of congressional committees with long-standing ties to these units wanted them to remain unchanged. The final grouping reflected many compromises and a number of missteps that later required correction.

## INDEPENDENT AGENCIES

In the twentieth century, Congress vastly expanded the number of federal agencies, many of which are not housed inside one of the principal executive departments. Each agency has a specific mission and often exercises authority delegated from Congress to make and enforce regulations. No single, comprehensive list of these independent agencies exists, but a partial catalog can be found at USA.gov.[32] Most independent agencies are part of the executive branch; familiar examples include the Central Intelligence Agency (CIA), the Environmental Protection Agency (EPA), and the National Aeronautics and Space Administration (NASA). A few agencies are part of the legislative branch, including the Government Accountability Office (GAO), the Library of Congress, and the Government Printing Office. Each agency has a list of responsibilities to fulfill, each operates under a separate budget, and each must have leaders to establish a set of relationships with the political masters it serves.

## INDEPENDENT REGULATORY COMMISSIONS

A special group of agencies, the so-called **independent regulatory commissions**, have an ambiguous status that makes them part of neither the executive nor the legislative branch. Congress created the Civil Service Commission (1883) and the Interstate Commerce Commission (ICC; 1887) as agencies that would be independent of the president's direct control. The goal was for these agencies to develop and enforce a set of regulations outside normal political channels. As noted earlier, government reformers were convinced that creating a professional civil service in place of patronage appointments would improve government performance and eliminate the corruption rampant in awarding government contracts. This new system was overseen by the Civil Service Commission. The ICC oversaw freight rates charged by railroads. The **Office of Personnel Management (OPM)** replaced the Civil Service Commission in 1978 and Congress abolished the ICC in 1995, when policy thinking shifted toward deregulating most transportation industries.

The creation of the Department of Homeland Security required congressional approval. The House National Security, Veterans Affairs, and International Relations Subcommittee held hearings on the plan, which combined 22 federal offices from across the government under the new department.

NASA is one of the best-known independent agencies. It was created in 1958 to research flight within and outside Earth's atmosphere. Its discoveries and innovations have fueled technological advances that have benefited the public in countless ways.

Numerous independent regulatory commissions arose in the twentieth century to oversee a segment of the economy or an area of public policy. A group of experts, appointed by the president and subject to Senate confirmation, exercise what are commonly called "quasi-legislative" and "quasi-judicial" powers delegated to them by Congress. In essence, each commission can develop and enforce regulations directly affecting businesses or individuals under its jurisdiction. Some of the commissions that are still operating are listed in Table 13.1.

The commissions are described as "independent" because they are not part of an executive department, and presidents can only remove commission members from office for specific reasons. They typically range in size from 3 to 11 members and are required to include members from both political parties who serve overlapping terms of office. Over time, presidents gained the power to appoint commission chairpersons, thereby giving them more influence over commission work but not full control. Most academic studies suggest that Congress and the interest groups directly affected by a commission's decisions influence commission members.[33]

For many years, the U.S. reliance on regulatory agencies was a unique approach to exercising government control over economic markets. However, other parts of the world have adopted the same strategy for regulating electricity, financial markets, and telecommunications; this is particularly true in Europe as nations increasingly adopt more market-driven policies. In this instance, the U.S. seems to have been the pace-setter for others.[34]

Ironically, as other nations began to emulate the U.S. approach to regulating parts of the economy, Washington changed its thinking. *Deregulation*—an approach that relies on market forces rather than government regulators to set prices and the conditions of competition—reigned supreme in the 1970s and 1980s. Congress eliminated several regulatory commissions (including the ICC) and encouraged competition to influence the price of airline, rail, bus, and truck services.

An especially dramatic example of deregulation involved the airline industry; the 1978 Airline Deregulation Act reduced the power of the Civil Aeronautics Board (CAB) to determine how many airlines served which cities at what prices, powers it had wielded since 1938 when Congress created it to guide development of the airline industry. The CAB was abolished altogether in 1985. Travelers immediately benefited from lower air fares driven by aggressive price competition launched by newly formed, low-cost airlines (such as Southwest Airlines), who also

**independent regulatory commissions** A type of federal government agency designed to allow experts, not politicians, to oversee and regulate a sector of the economy (for example, railroads) usually to protect consumers from unfair business practices but also to protect the businesses in that sector.

**Office of Personnel Management (OPM)** The agency created in 1978 as part of the Civil Service Reform Act to manage the civil service for presidents.

## TABLE 13.1
## *Notable Independent Regulatory Commissions*

| Commission | Year Established | Role |
|---|---|---|
| Federal Reserve Board of Governors | 1913 | The principal government body regulating banks in the United States; it seeks to fight inflation as a means to maintain economic growth by setting interest rates; it serves as the equivalent of a United States central bank. |
| Federal Trade Commission (FTC) | 1914 | Protects consumers from business practices that suppress competition and enforces antitrust laws, including reviewing proposed mergers between businesses |
| Federal Communications Commission (FCC) | 1934 | Regulates interstate and international communications by radio, television, wire, satellite, and cable |
| Securities and Exchange Commission (SEC) | 1934 | Regulates the stock markets and protects investors from unfair corporate practices |
| National Labor Relations Board (NLRB) | 1935 | Protects workers' right to organize, oversees union elections, and can intervene in unfair labor practices |
| Commodity Futures Trading Commission | 1974 | Originally created to protect against fraud and manipulation in the agricultural commodities and futures markets; it now shares responsibility with the SEC to police increasingly complex investment products. |
| Nuclear Regulatory Commission | 1974 | Succeeded the Atomic Energy Commission in overseeing the civilian nuclear energy industry in the United States, including safety, non-power use of nuclear materials, and managing nuclear waste |

added more flights to the most popular destinations. Before deregulation, the United States had 36 airlines, but that number grew to 123 by 1984. This proliferation triggered intense competition and forced established companies to go out of business or merge. It also dramatically reduced service to out-of-the-way destinations, reduced the number of nonstop flights, and adversely affected passenger services, including baggage charges and food service. But government did not totally abandon regulation of the industry. The Federal Aviation Administration (located in the Department of Transportation) continues to oversee the safety of aircraft, the professional training of pilots, and the air traffic control system.[35]

Amtrak was created in 1970 to shore up train service in the United States. Though it has never turned a profit as intended, ridership has continued to increase to more than 31 million in 2018.

## GOVERNMENT CORPORATIONS

The British and Dutch governments were the first to establish organizations that mixed public and private resources. The British East India Company, the Plymouth Company, and the Hudson Bay Company were seventeenth-century "corporations" that played a key role in establishing colonies around the globe. By the end of the twentieth century, there were somewhere between 25 and 50 U.S. federal **government corporations** (depending on how these are defined). Congress created them "to perform a public purpose, provide a market-oriented service and produce revenues to meet or approximate its expenditures."[36] The United States Postal Service, the Federal Deposit Insurance Corporation (FDIC), and Amtrak (the National Railroad Passenger Corporation) are among the better-known government corporations. Government corporations provide an advantage: They provide important services but with greater administrative flexibility because they lie outside of many federal regulations that apply to government agencies. For example, the customary budgetary process used in the federal system requires agencies to observe a host of federal guidelines, since they are fully funded by taxpayers.

Most government corporations have boards of directors that guide their operations. For example, Amtrak's 10-person board is appointed by the president and subject to Senate confirmation. When created in 1970, its mission was to salvage intercity passenger rail service, particularly between Washington and Boston, which was quickly disappearing in the 1970s. Although much of the system's operating expenses are covered by ticket income, the federal government provides subsidies to help cover the system's costs—about $1.5 billion in 2016–2017. Thus, while Amtrak is a for-profit undertaking, it has never actually made a profit.[37]

Although there are expectations that such entities will become self-sustaining and phase out their government subsidies, that hope has frequently fallen short, as in the case of Amtrak, triggering recurrent political crises about the government continuing to subsidize their budgets.

## HYBRID ORGANIZATIONS

**Quasi-governmental organizations ("quagos")** are sometimes described as *hybrid organizations* because they share some of the attributes of public- and private-sector bureaucracies.[38] Consider the Smithsonian Institution, for example, whose museums you almost certainly have visited if you have been to Washington, DC. It is owned and financially supported by the government and administered by employees working for the federal government, but it has many qualities of a private organization, with a governing board of regents, an endowment, and substantial profits from sales of magazines and gift shop items.

The quagos' counterparts in the private sector, the **quasi-nongovernmental organizations ("quangos")**, are essentially private-sector entities that exercise some public responsibilities, much as the American Red Cross does when it provides assistance to victims of disasters. They perform services frequently identical to those that government agencies provide, but not through the government. Students of public administration (the study of government management) have recently become more willing to blur the traditional distinctions between

**government corporations** Business enterprises wholly or partly owned by the government that Congress created to perform a public purpose or provide a market-oriented service but are designed to meet their costs by generating revenues through operations.

**quasi-governmental organizations ("quagos")** Hybrid organizations that share some characteristics of public agencies and some features of private corporations, such as the Smithsonian Institution.

**quasi-nongovernmental organizations ("quangos")** Private-sector organizations that fulfill some of the roles of government agencies, such as the disaster recovery activities of the American Red Cross.

public-sector and private-sector organizations. As such thinking changes, we are likely to see a proliferation of these hybrid examples in the future. Several that we discuss below have been much in the news.

**Government-sponsored enterprises (GSEs)** are financing agencies chartered by Congress to provide loans to help farmers, students, and homeowners.[39] In 2008, home loans became newsworthy when the two largest GSEs, Fannie Mae and Freddie Mac, required a $134 billion government bailout. Congress created Fannie Mae (the Federal National Mortgage Association) in 1938 to stabilize the mortgage market as the country was emerging from the Great Depression.[40] Later, in 1968, President Johnson convinced Congress to modify Fannie Mae's operations, making it a shareholder-owned business rather than a government agency as part of an effort to reduce the federal deficit. Freddie Mac (the Federal Home Loan Mortgage Corporation) was created as a GSE in 1970 to compete with Fannie Mae. These GSEs helped to stabilize the U.S. housing market by buying the mortgage loans issued by others and then issuing bonds that could be bought and sold on the open market. The bonds were a good investment because the federal government seemed to guarantee their value. In the process, they made fortunes for their shareholders—both businesses were enormously profitable with an implicit guarantee from the federal government that it would not let them fail—and advanced the public policy goal of helping citizens own their homes.

Fannie Mae and Freddie Mac helped provide U.S. homeowners with long-term, fixed-rate mortgages. Most frequently, the same interest rate was paid over the life of a typical 30-year mortgage. Few foreign nations have anything comparable, but that does not mean that the U.S. approach is better. Although Fannie, Freddie, and their congressional defenders argued that these policies produced a much higher percentage of U.S. citizens owning their own homes than anywhere else in the world, the data tell us otherwise. Several industrial nations had and continue to have home ownership rates higher than the United States. In most of these nations, homebuyers borrow money at interest rates that change frequently (often every 12 months in the United Kingdom, every five years in Canada), which makes buying a home much riskier—you cannot be sure what the monthly payment will be next year, let alone in 10 years. After the expensive government bailout of 2008, when the United States government acquired ownership of these two GSEs, the Obama administration proposed dismantling Fannie and Freddie and moving toward a system with features more similar to those of Denmark or Germany, where private lenders bear the risk of mortgage failures instead of placing the burden on the government, but that did not happen.

*Federally funded research and development centers* (FFRDCs) are government-owned, contractor-operated nonprofit corporations that perform work for the government. Their origins can be traced to World War II, when government-funded research efforts led to the development of radar and the atomic bomb.[41] Congress created many more FFRDCs during the 1950s and 1960s, especially to undertake military research. More recently, the Internal Revenue Service and the DHS created research centers to help them fulfill their responsibilities. There were 43 operating FFRDCs in 2018, and the National Science Foundation maintains an up-to-date listing.[42] Although there are complaints about the cozy relationship between agencies and the centers conducting research for them, FFRDCs are also praised for their ability to transfer new technologies developed by their research efforts into the private sector. However, the most spectacular example of technology transfer—the Internet—originated in the Defense Advanced Research and Projects Agency, a government agency, not an FFRDC.

# THE SIZE OF THE FEDERAL BUREAUCRACY

Most people in the United States consider the bureaucracy to be too big. Is this the case? To assess the size of the bureaucracy, we start with the number of federal employees. As we pointed out earlier, many people performing public services are *not* employed by the federal government. In fact, if we consider the number of civilian federal civil servants, the American government has been shrinking over the past two decades. In 2005, there were nearly half a million fewer federal employees than there were in 1990. But the calculation is more complicated than it might seem.

Paul Light, a specialist in the federal personnel system, has argued persuasively that in order to gauge the true size of government, we need to include other categories of workers. Two are

**government-sponsored enterprises (GSEs)** Financial services corporations created by Congress to provide credit to targeted areas of American life; for example, Fannie Mae and Freddie Mac specialize in home mortgages.

very obvious: active duty military personnel (another 1.33 million) and postal workers (about 510,000). But Light also argues that we should include the full range of people and organizations receiving government grants and contracts to get a full account of how many people are working to accomplish federal goals. Many government services are not performed by government employees but instead are handled by individuals and businesses who perform the work through government contracts. Together, grants and contracts employ another 5.3 million people. This group of workers has been expanding as direct federal employment declines, thereby constituting a "hidden workforce."[43] Light estimates that nearly 7.4 million Americans worked directly and indirectly for the federal government by the end of 2017, a modest *increase* over the total in 1990, though down 2 million from 2010.

Although politicians' rhetoric might make you think that the bureaucracy never stops growing, in fact, the number of federal employees intentionally declined during the 1990s. The Clinton administration launched an ambitious effort to "reinvent government" under the direction of Vice President Al Gore in 1993. Its proposals included a reduction in the size of the federal workforce, made possible by strategies to "work smarter," as the plan's architects liked to say. Although total federal employment fell by more than 365,000 from 1990 to 2005, the number of jobs supported by federal contracts over the same time period grew by more than 2.5 million and accelerated through the first years of the Obama administration. In short, government did not shrink; the workload merely shifted from federal employees to other workers paid by the federal government.

How do Light's findings compare with government size elsewhere? Comparisons are difficult. Most nations have arranged their public bureaucracies in ways that are as complex as those in the United States and some governments have additional responsibilities. For example, those with public-run health care systems include employees that the U.S. numbers do not. Using data collected by the OECD (similar to Light's but omitting contract workers), the OECD has calculated the percentage of the national labor force working for all levels of government and public corporations. As shown in Figure 13.3, the OECD ranks public sector employment in the United States well behind most Northern European nations and below the OECD average of 19 percent, about midway between Norway's 30 percent and Japan's 6 percent.

## FIGURE 13.3

### *Employment in General Government as a Percentage of Total Employment, 2015*

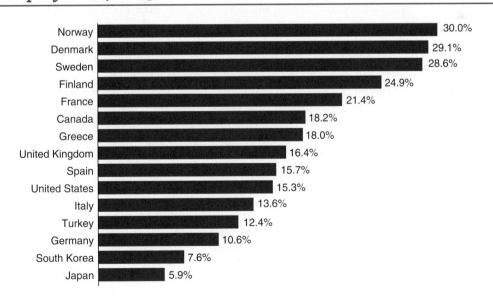

Source: Based on OECD data found in "Employment in the Public Sector," Government at a Glance 2015 (Paris, France: OECD Publishing, 2015). Figure from Niall McCarthy, "Scandinavia: First for Public Sector Employment," Statista, July 20, 2017, https://www.statista.com/chart/10346/scandinavia-first-for-public-sector-employment

These figures suggest that the public sector in the United States is not excessively large. State and local government employment is about seven times greater than federal. There has been growth in recent years, especially if we include the "hidden workforce" of people whose jobs depend on government grants or contracts, but relative to other nations, the size of the U.S. public sector seems a little smaller than average.

But is government larger than it *needs* to be? Given such an extensive enterprise, it seems almost inevitable that there will be some duplication of effort, redundancy of agency assignments, or overlapping of programs. Elected officials often cite waste, fraud, and abuse as the targets of their efforts to improve government performance. A 2011 report from the GAO provided insight into other structural problems, identifying the following overlapping efforts:

- 80 federal programs pursued economic development
- 100 federal programs dealt with surface transportation
- 54 federal programs addressed financial literacy
- 20 federal agencies managed government cars, trucks, and airplanes
- 15 federal agencies dealt with food safety[44]

Perhaps multiple public efforts are sometimes necessary, but as the report implied, a starting point for effective budget savings is to assess whether some of these efforts might be unnecessary. Beginning with this initial analysis, the GAO has reported to Congress annually on ways to reduce fragmentation, overlap, and duplication. By the 2018 annual report, the GAO reported that Congress had addressed 76 percent of its recommendations, resulting in savings of over $175 billion.[45] The conclusion: Watchdogs work.

## THE SEARCH FOR CONTROL

Who controls the bureaucrats? Because bureaucrats lie outside direct citizen control, the only way to make administrative actions accountable to the public is through indirect means—through actions taken by elected officials. Exercising control, however, has become a larger problem over time as the bureaucracy expanded and its powers grew. Congress gives government officials responsibility to develop and carry out the many plans required to accomplish its policy goals. Agencies create programs and adopt regulations under this **delegated authority** as a way to accomplish the general purposes stated by Congress. Rather than providing agency officials with highly detailed guidelines on how to proceed, Congress usually allows them considerable flexibility, termed **administrative discretion**, in determining how to achieve the general goals. Thus, agencies exercise considerable power over putting programs in place—**implementation** that translates the general goals of policy into concrete action.

With such an extensive structure making so many critical decisions about policies and programs, how is it possible to ensure that bureaucrats will not reinterpret the mandate they have been given? Where are the checks on bureaucratic power? How can the public hope to exercise control? In the traditional model for thinking about this issue, officials elected by the public must exercise control over the bureaucrats on behalf of the public. This indirect control can be exercised through many instruments, exercised in parallel by Congress and the president, as discussed below and summarized in Table 13.2.

### ANNUAL BUDGET REVIEWS

Few things are closer to bureaucrats' hearts than the budget resources they need to accomplish their mission. The budget determines the size of an agency's staff, its supplies and equipment, and the extent to which it can embark on new projects as well as complete those already underway. Both Congress and the president pose budget challenges to an agency. Until 1921, Congress dominated budget decisions. But the Budget and Accounting Act of 1921 required departments and agencies to submit their requests for next year's budget for presidential review before they went to Congress. Presidents now submit a single, unified executive budget assembled by the **Office of Management and Budget (OMB)**, known until 1970 as the Bureau of the Budget. At the same time, Congress created the General Accounting Office to give its members the capacity to track government spending. The General Accounting Office was renamed the Government Accountability Office in 2004.

**delegated authority** The power to make decisions enjoyed by an agency or department that was approved by Congress.

**administrative discretion** The opportunity granted to bureaucrats by Congress to use their judgment in making decisions between alternative courses of action.

**implementation** The process of carrying out the wishes of Congress as expressed in a policy through the creation and enforcement of programs and regulations by bureaucratic agencies.

**Office of Management and Budget (OMB)** The successor agency to the Bureau of the Budget, created in 1970 and designed to perform management oversight that went beyond the traditional budget and central clearance functions performed by the Bureau of the Budget.

**TABLE 13.2**

## *Techniques to Control Bureaucrats*

| President | Congress |
|---|---|
| **BUDGET**<br>• Office of Management and Budget (OMB)<br>• Annual budget | **BUDGET**<br>• Congressional Budget Office (CBO)<br>• Annual appropriations |
| **AUTHORIZATION**<br>• Legislative clearance | **AUTHORIZATION**<br>• Statutory review of programs |
| **OVERSIGHT**<br>• Monitoring<br>• Management systems | **OVERSIGHT**<br>• Committee hearings<br>• Investigations<br>• Case work |
| **NOMINATION**<br>• Select nominees | **CONFIRMATION**<br>• Review presidential nominees |
| **REORGANIZATION**<br>**PERSONNEL**<br>• Managed by OPM | **REORGANIZATION**<br>**PERSONNEL**<br>• Determined by civil service policies |

Assembling the president's budget takes nearly 18 months, starting with preliminary guidelines sent out to the government's many bureaucracies. As the deadline for submitting a budget to Congress approaches, OMB's officials review the projected budgets of all agencies and departments and make a final recommendation that agencies may appeal. Ultimately, an agency's budget becomes part of the president's annual recommended budget submitted to Congress for approval.

Then, as we saw in Chapter 11, Congress takes over. Members of the subcommittees within the House and Senate Appropriation Committees play the most important roles in the approval process. These senior legislators have experience in tracking presidential and agency budgets and receive expert assistance from the Congressional Budget Office (CBO). The full committees rely heavily on the expertise of their colleagues serving on the subcommittees, as they are the most familiar with the programs and services of the agencies they review. Congressional appropriations committees can agree with the president's request, increase it, or reduce it—hence their enormous power over the agencies subject to their review. Rather than review each budget from top to bottom, these committees focus particularly on the changes from the previous year's budget. By the end of September, Congress is supposed to have reviewed and approved the new budget for the fiscal year starting on October 1, but it often misses that deadline, triggering the kind of drama we witnessed in the winter of 2018 when the federal government shut down nonessential services until a new budget was in place.

**central clearance**
The central coordinating practice established in the 1930s to review all legislative proposals arising from executive branch agencies in light of the president's agenda to determine whether they were consistent or inconsistent with those goals.

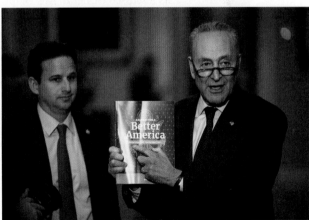

Each year, all the departments and agencies in the executive branch make budget requests of the White House, which considers them and creates the president's proposed budget, which is then printed and bound and submitted to Congress for consideration. Senate Minority Leader Chuck Schumer (D-NY) criticized President Trump's 2020 budget in a press conference shortly after its release.

## AUTHORIZATION OF PROGRAMS

As with the budget, presidents start the process of approving a new government activity (known as *program authorization*), but Congress has the last word. Presidents established a system of central clearance, essentially a review of agencies' program ideas and proposals performed by the OMB. Even before a proposal gets to the OMB, however, the department or agency's political appointees evaluate the proposal to determine whether it conforms to the president's goals. Once the proposal reaches the OMB, its staff determines whether the proposal is in accord with the president's agenda. At this point, bureaucratic advocates of the program might alert sympathetic interest groups and members of Congress, hoping that their support will help convince the president to support the program, or they might wait until later in the process to raise the idea again. Ultimately, Congress must approve (or authorize) all programs and they can only be continued if Congress reapproves (or reauthorizes) them.

Most congressional standing committees have permanent jurisdiction over a collection of government programs. Without a committee's approval (the original authorization), an agency cannot establish these programs. During program renewal (reauthorization), legislators assess whether the programs have achieved their stated goals and will make adjustments if needed. Reauthorization, then, marks a critical point in an agency's life as it determines whether existing programs will be renewed, discontinued, or modified.

## OVERSIGHT OF AGENCY PERFORMANCE

Both Congress and the president monitor agency and department performance at times other than during budget review and program reauthorization—this is only one of the many ways that Congress provides oversight, or routine review of program performance. In providing case work for their constituents, congressional staff members interact with bureaucrats as they try to determine why the folks back home are not getting the services or level of responsiveness they expect. Presidents, too, have staff members who perform this kind of work, but Congress collectively has larger staff resources. When interactions with the bureaucracy identify problems, they become the focus of further congressional study and are potentially the subject of a full-scale investigation.

Part of the job of presidential aides working in the Executive Office of the President (see Chapter 12) is to monitor the performance of agencies in their area of responsibility. The OMB has the broadest charge, and its employees maintain close oversight of the agencies in their portfolios. White House aides will also monitor what goes on in the bureaucracy, particularly on high-profile programs that are near and dear to the president's heart. The Obama White House staff, for example, closely monitored progress of implementing the health care reforms adopted in 2010. Trump's staff watched immigration like a hawk.

## NOMINATION AND CONFIRMATION OF POLITICAL APPOINTEES

As discussed earlier in this chapter, civil service reforms at the end of the nineteenth century removed a potentially powerful lever from the president's hands. Under the spoils system, presidents could choose loyalists to fill government positions, making it plain that appointees should follow his direction—or be replaced. Creating a politically neutral career civil service reduced the potential control presidents could exercise over the bureaucracy. Instead of having all federal jobs potentially under presidents' control, they suddenly controlled only a small number of positions that lay outside the civil service system. These still provide the president with political "plums" to distribute to loyal supporters.[46] They also include the most senior positions in departments and agencies, political appointees in policy-making positions, and appointments lower in the hierarchy. President Trump had approximately 3,700 positions that he could fill to help him manage the federal bureaucracy.[47] That may sound like a lot of help, but it is modest in relation to the 2 million bureaucrats they oversee.

Unlike political appointees in a parliamentary system, the president's political appointees cannot be members of Congress. Separation of powers requires the president to assemble his team rather than simply appoint members of the shadow government already serving in parliament to administrative posts (essentially a government in waiting assembled by the opposition party), as is done in the United Kingdom. For about 1,100 of these presidential nominations, the Senate has the power to advise and consent. (Congress determines which positions are subject to Senate review.) Since the mid-1800s, Senate committees have reviewed most of the nominated candidates' qualifications, and since the mid-twentieth century, the committees have customarily held public hearings to grill the candidates before reporting the nomination out to the larger Senate or refusing to do so.[48] On rare occasions, nominations can be reported out of committee to the

oversight Review and monitoring by Congress (particularly the relevant authorizing and appropriations committees) of executive branch activities to ensure that they are consistent with legislative intent.

full Senate without a positive committee vote. Most nominees are confirmed, reflecting the general belief that presidents should have the opportunity to assemble their own team.

Political appointees seldom stay in their positions for long; the average tenure of political appointees in federal agencies is two years, so their commitment to the agency's mission is shallower than that of the career bureaucrats with whom they work. Given the pattern of how often congressional incumbents win reelection and how committee leaders are chosen (see Chapter 11), bureaucrats can expect to be dealing with the same cast of congressional characters far longer than they will with the administration's appointees.

## REORGANIZATION OF THE BUREAUCRACY

Congress and executive branch officials care a great deal about how the government is structured because it will have a direct bearing on how programs are implemented. It also has a direct bearing on who has influence to shape what issues. Even if the quest for *power* lies at the heart of reorganization efforts, they are usually justified in public as desirable because such efforts will enhance efficiency, produce economies, or solve a pressing national problem.

For most of U.S. history, Congress and the president wrestled over the right to determine the structure of the federal bureaucracy, with Congress coming out on top. Ultimately, Congress must approve the creation of departments and agencies, and it jealously guards its right to manage government resources to achieve its ends. But is Congress or the president better able to determine how the government should be organized to accomplish its purposes? During the 1920s and 1930s, Congress and the president adopted many management reforms (for example, the centralized budgeting discussed earlier) designed to make presidents more effective at managing federal bureaucrats. In 1932, in the midst of an economic crisis, Congress allowed President Hoover to propose organizational changes that Congress promised they would act upon quickly to save money, but the Democrat-controlled Congress accepted none of the president's recommendations. Although Congress later provided greater flexibility to President Franklin D. Roosevelt, they were still unwilling to grant him a free hand to organize government as he wished.

Post-Depression and post–World War II, Congress gave presidents the power to propose changes in executive branch structures that would go into effect unless one or both houses of Congress used a legislative veto—that is, voted to reverse the proposal. Under the statutory authority, the president could transfer an agency from one location to another, consolidate functions from several agencies, abolish all or part of an agency or its functions, and delegate responsibilities. Executive departments, however, were off-limits; presidents could neither create nor abolish them. From 1949 to 1973, presidents submitted 85 proposals, and Congress accepted 65.[49]

But in the 1970s, Congress reasserted its constitutional powers in several areas, including reorganization. Following a series of showdowns with President Nixon over spending and war powers, Congress refused to renew the broad reorganization authority given to Nixon's predecessors. And in 1983, the Supreme Court declared the use of legislative vetoes unconstitutional because they violated the constitutional provisions that require a presidential signature for acts of Congress to go into effect. Once Congress lost the use of the procedure it had employed for decades to review and potentially reverse presidential reorganization proposals, it no longer even considered giving later presidents such broad authority. Now, Congress uses the normal legislative process when considering reorganization proposals as it did in the case of the DHS. Presidents want to reorganize, but Congress refuses to grant this power. Despite repeated efforts by President George W. Bush to restore greater presidential influence over reorganization, for instance, Congress rejected them all. President Obama requested similar powers in 2011, but Congress once again said no.

## DRAMATIC REORGANIZATIONS: THE NATIONAL SECURITY APPARATUS

Two events forced dramatic reshaping of how the federal government makes and implements national security policy: the Cold War and the terrorist attacks of 9/11. The growing post–World War II tensions with the Soviet Union prompted Congress to pass the National Security

Act of 1947, which formalized a number of policy-making arrangements that had been created on the fly during World War II.[50] The Act

- established the **Joint Chiefs of Staff**, a permanent structure to coordinate military action and strategy among the senior officers of the Army, Navy, Marines, and Air Force (1947) (a similar but temporary structure had existed during World War II);
- created the CIA, a permanent intelligence agency to replace the wartime Office of Strategic Services (1947);
- merged the departments of War and Navy (1947) into a single National Military Establishment, which was renamed the Department of Defense (DOD) two years later (1949); and
- created the National Security Council (NSC) to assist presidents in coordinating the activities of the many foreign policy advisers, including those from the Departments of State and Treasury (1947).

Other nations have comparable organizations; in fact, this new American structure was modeled after the United Kingdom system that U.S. officials had had the opportunity to observe during World War II. Harry Truman came to rely on the NSC as a policy-making forum during the Korean War. Truman's successor, President Dwight Eisenhower (1953–1961), created the position of National Security Advisor to oversee this new advisory system. Subsequent presidents have modified and refined these structures along the way (see Table 13.3).

Then, in 2001, the terrorist attacks of 9/11 produced a flurry of new organizational changes:

- President Bush created the Homeland Security Council, and Congress pushed for creation of the DHS, a step endorsed by President Bush and put in place (2002).
- Congress created a Director of National Intelligence (DNI) who has responsibility for coordinating the activities of the government's 16 intelligence agencies and for overcoming the divisions and traditional jealousies that arise among them (2005).[51]

Many other U.S. government agencies deal with aspects of foreign affairs. Predominantly domestic agencies such as Education, Agriculture, Commerce, Labor, Interior, and Health and

**TABLE 13.3**

## *Principal National Security Structures and Officials in U.S. Government, 2019*

| Agency | Year Created | Head as of 8/1/2019 |
| --- | --- | --- |
| Department of State | 1789 | Mike Pompeo |
| Department of Treasury | 1789 | Steven Mnuchin |
| Department of Defense | 1947 | Mark T. Esper |
| Central Intelligence Agency | 1947 | Gina Haspel |
| National Security Council | 1947 | John Bolton |
| Joint Chiefs of Staff (Chair) | 1947 | Gen. Joseph Dunford |
| U.S. Trade Representative | 1961 | Robert Lighthizer |
| Dept. of Homeland Security | 2002 | *Kevin McAleenan (Acting)* |
| Director of National Intelligence | 2005 | Dan Coats |

**Joint Chiefs of Staff** A structure created in 1947 to coordinate action among the separate military services and provide military advice to the president and the secretary of defense.

How can you wield influence on important issues of national policy? Almost all presidents realize that they need to hear from knowledgeable advisers before making foreign policy decisions. They seek advice from senior figures in the administration—the National Security adviser, the secretaries of State, Defense and Treasury, the directors of the CIA and National Intelligence. Each of these advisers heads a bureaucracy of experts that, in turn, provides them with information and analysis that informs their advice to the president. To become influential, you could aspire to become part of the president's inner circle or to occupy an influential position in one of the national security bureaucracies. Seldom does someone lower down in the hierarchy have a chance to shape policy, but it is not impossible.

When he was the number two official in the U.S. embassy in the Soviet Union, George F. Kennan seized upon a brief opportunity to help design American foreign policy at a critical point in the nation's history. He is acknowledged as the main architect of *containment*, America's principal policy to prevent the Soviet Union from expanding its influence during the Cold War (1947–1991). Kennan's experience illustrates how to become influential.

America was victorious in World War II, but its leaders were unsure of the nation's next steps. President Truman and his foreign policy advisers had to decide what to do with occupied Germany and Japan, how to deal with other members of the triumphant wartime alliance (the United Kingdom, the Soviet Union, France, and China), and how best to use its position as the world's economic powerhouse. Josef Stalin, leader of the Soviet Union, quickly became Truman's biggest headache. Soviet military forces occupied half of Germany and many neighboring nations that they had marched through at the end of the war. But Stalin was proving to be an uncooperative ally, leveling unreasonable charges at the U.S., resisting American efforts to rebuild Europe, and installing Communist governments in neighboring nations. Truman had little foreign policy experience, becoming president in April 1945 after the death of Franklin D. Roosevelt, who had been president since 1933.

Foreign service officers are members of a specialized civil service; members qualify through rigorous written and oral exams and undergo extensive training, and their superiors assign them as needed to postings around the world or in the department's Washington headquarters. After joining the foreign service in 1925, Kennan held posts in Geneva and Hamburg before deciding that his future lay in becoming an expert on the Soviet Union, a government that the United States still did not recognize as legitimate after it was formed in 1922 following a revolution and civil war.

Kennan spent three years studying Russian in Berlin, then held junior postings in several Baltic embassies where he could study the neighboring Soviet Union before finally being posted to Moscow for the first time in 1933. There, he had the opportunity to observe conditions firsthand. He was appalled by the widespread poverty and the intentional use of fear and brutality by Stalin's regime. After a sojourn in Washington, he was serving in Czechoslovakia when Nazi Germany occupied that nation in 1938 and was posted in Berlin when Germany declared war on the United States in December 1941. During the war, he served in Lisbon, Portugal (a neutral nation), and in London. He had not been in Moscow for seven years but was transferred there in 1944 as the war entered its final stages.

How did Kennan become an important adviser? He was not part of Washington's bureaucratic policy discussions. He did not know the president. He was not even the principal source of information and advice from Moscow, the role filled by the ambassador. But he had developed expertise in a specialized area. His opportunity arose in 1946 in response to a routine Treasury Department request for information about why the Soviets were resisting American efforts to create a World Bank that would provide loans for nations to rebuild and an International Monetary Fund that would help the world restore international trade. Kennan responded in February 1946 with "the long telegram," a nearly 6,000-word essay that urged U.S. decision makers to confront the Soviets diplomatically when they pushed for influence outside their own territory.* The telegram, which was widely circulated among senior government officials, provided coherent recommendations based on a sophisticated understanding of what motivated the Soviets and gave Kennan standing among policy makers. As he later wrote, "My official loneliness came to an end.... My reputation was made. My voice now carried."+

Kennan synthesized and elaborated many of the telegram's arguments into an influential article entitled "The Sources of Soviet Conduct," published in the elite

*(Continued)*

(Continued)

journal *Foreign Affairs* in July 1946.‡ Although the article's author was identified as "X," the true identity quickly became known. Kennan returned to Washington and was given a prestigious position—director of the newly created Policy Planning Staff in the Department of State. He was the right-hand adviser to Secretary George C. Marshall, probably the most respected of Truman's foreign policy advisers, and played a critical role in helping to shape America's postwar economic assistance to Europe as well as launch a strategy of covert actions against the Soviets undertaken by the CIA.** Kennan lost influence when Dean Acheson succeeded Marshall, leading to his departure from the foreign service, but his day in the sun made a real difference.

## Questions to Consider

1. What areas of government activity would you like to influence? How would you prepare yourself for such an opportunity?
2. Kennan nearly resigned from the foreign service when the U.S. wartime policy was to support the Soviet Union as an ally. How far would you go as an employee in objecting to a government policy with which you disagreed?
3. Was Kennan out of line in 1946 in lecturing decision makers back in Washington on how to combat the true nature of Soviet intentions?

* A complete copy of the "long telegram" can be found in George F. Kennan, *Memoirs: 1925–1950* (Boston, MA: Little, Brown and Co, 1967), 547–559.
† As quoted in *The New York Times* obituary of Mr. Kennan: Tim Weiner and Barbara Crossette, "George F. Kennan Dies at 101: Leading Strategist of Cold War," *The New York Times*, March 18, 2005, https://www.nytimes.com/2005/03/18/politics/george-f-kennan-dies-at-101-leading-strategist-of-cold-war.html.
‡ George F. Kennan, "The Sources of Soviet Conduct," *Foreign Affairs* 25 (July 1947).
** Walter L. Hixson, "Reassessing Kennan After the Fall of the Soviet Union: The Vindication of X?" *The Historian* 59, no. 4 (Summer 1997): 852; Richard H. Ullman, "Honoring George Kennan," *The Princeton University Library Chronicle* 66 (Winter 2005): 2.

The Washington Post / Getty Images

**Federal government agencies with seemingly domestic responsibilities do sometimes take on international roles. The U.S. Public Health Service responded to the Ebola outbreak in Liberia in 2014, sending medical staff to treat patients and help contain the disease.**

Human Services all have international components. Combating world health contagions (such as Ebola), food shortages, and refugee crises requires coordinated global action; education and cultural exchanges and financial transactions continue to expand. Other issues are inherently international; for example, many U.S. government agencies conduct research that has a bearing on global climate change. This reality inspired the creation in 1990 of the U.S. Global Change Research Program, which integrates findings generated through research sponsored by thirteen federal agencies, including the Agency for International Development, the EPA, and the National Science Foundation.[52]

The two reorganizations described above arose from jolts to the existing government apparatus, and it is reasonable to expect that future changes might similarly be designed to help the government better coordinate the response to new issues as they arise; for example, natural disasters occurring because of global warming.

## MANAGING PUBLIC EMPLOYEES

Congress establishes the broad outlines of personnel policies for government workers. Thus, the Civil Service Reform Act of 1978 replaced the Civil Service Commission and created new policies for the federal Civil Service. Presidents rely on the OPM to oversee that system. As the twenty-fifth anniversary of that statute approached, evaluations of what the last round had accomplished and proposals for additional reforms were in the air. Many discussions called for providing agency managers with greater flexibility in hiring workers, paying them at levels based on their job performance, and firing the lowest-producing employees. Civil service regulations—the product of decades of practice and precedent—restricted management discretion in all three areas. A behind-the-scenes battle raged during the George W. Bush years over which civil service protections would remain and which ones would disappear.

The terrorist attacks of 9/11 unexpectedly highlighted civil service practices. FEMA, for example, drew praise for its effectiveness; it was one of the few federal agencies to earn plaudits for its performance. Bush argued that unless the civil service personnel system was reformed, the nation could not win the war on terror.[53] As such, FEMA became part of the DHS, which Congress exempted from regulations in hiring (giving them more candidates to choose from), setting pay and job classifications (four or five broad salary ranges instead of 15 grades and raises based on performance), and dismissing employees. These modifications triggered a showdown between the administration and Senate Democrats in the fall of 2002. But when the midterm elections returned a supportive Republican majority to the Senate, Bush's proposed changes were adopted.

The exemptions given to the DHS were large in scope, applying to 170,000 employees; they could have paved the way for introducing a new *pay-for-performance* system throughout the government, compensating people based on their productivity rather than on the years served in their jobs. But Congress remained only partly convinced that modifications were needed.[54] Bush then sought to extend the new flexibility to the DOD civilian workforce of approximately 700,000. Federal employee unions challenged the changes in court, and after Democrats regained control of Congress in 2007, even the changes for DHS were reversed. Changes in the DOD survived into the second year of the Obama administration but then were cancelled.[55] A Republican president and a Republican-controlled Congress had been trying to give presidents additional management powers, but court action and a Democrat-controlled Congress halted the effort.

President Trump frequently butted heads with the bureaucracy, most obviously in his public battles with the intelligence community and his denunciations of the Justice Department, including the Federal Bureau of Investigation (FBI). He ignored their advice on high profile issues—Should he trust the word of Russian leader Putin or North Korea's Kim?—and openly questioned the impartiality of DOJ investigators. It is less clear that he followed a coherent management strategy, and once Republicans lost control of the House in 2019, there was no chance of pursuing major reforms.

Battles over the civil service are by no means limited to the United States. Margaret Thatcher's government in Great Britain (1979–1990) sought many of the same reforms in the British civil service system that George W. Bush sought in the United States—introducing performance-based pay systems, making it easier to dismiss low-performing civil servants, exercising greater political control over policy making by long-time civil servants, and attempting to increase government efficiency by contracting out government services to private firms—in essence, introducing competition with the private sector. Thatcher's successors continued many of these efforts.[56] Unlike the American system, the British parliament is relatively compliant in accepting administrative reforms and provides far less assistance to those who resist the changes.

State officials have also launched efforts to expand control over public workers. Three states—Georgia, Texas, and Florida—led the way in giving agency managers more control over whom they could hire and fire. Other states have followed the same path, including Wisconsin, where public employee bargaining rights became the center of a prolonged political drama during the winter of 2011. A new Republican governor had recently been elected, and the legislature adopted new work provisions that encountered strong opposition from unionized state employees. Days of public marches and vocal demonstrations in the Wisconsin state capitol building failed to derail the reforms that gave elected officials and their appointees much greater control over public workers.

## WHEN CONTROL PROVES ELUSIVE

Despite the many instruments of control at the disposal of the president and Congress, it remains unclear who *really* controls the bureaucracy. Exercising control requires effort, and both presidents and members of Congress have limited time, competing priorities, and finite knowledge. In addition, they disagree. Presidents insist they should be in control, but Congress jealously guards its prerogatives. With two masters, to whom should bureaucrats listen? Who speaks for the public in guiding the bureaucrats?

The separation of powers system makes it highly likely that differences will arise between the president and Congress as well as between the two houses of Congress. Consequently, an agency may find itself without clear policy guidance. In the absence of a consensus from above, bureaucrats—by necessity—must become politicians and construct the political support they require on their own. The resulting *bureaucratic politics* of budget and program battles have become the raw material of day-to-day life in the nation's capital, and bureaucrats are often the winners, bringing substantial resources to bear—longevity, expertise, and long-standing alliances.

It is not surprising, then, that bureaucrats form close alliances with the committee members and staffs with whom they work—alliances that also include the principal interest groups concerned with the agency's programs. Who will be more interested in the Department of Agriculture's policies on tobacco, pork, or milk production, for example, than the farmers and agricultural corporations who grow and market these products and the members of Congress who have secured seats on the authorizing committee that can help these farmers in their districts? Many government critics point to this so-called **iron triangle** of relationships comprising three parties—an agency, a congressional committee, and an interest group—who share a mutual interest to help each other shape policies that will benefit an identifiable group. Iron triangles exist for many, though not all, agencies and they are so strong that presidents find them difficult to break. The interest groups representing the program beneficiaries provide political support to members of Congress (votes, campaign contributions) and bureaucrats (political help) when needed. Both elected and career officials see it as their responsibility to maintain and expand existing programs; they are accustomed to working closely with each other in creating policies that meet their own needs, if not necessarily the public's.

If neither the Congress nor the president can establish a clear claim to interpreting the public's interest, perhaps bureaucrats can provide expert, neutral guidance for public policy on their own—that is, become an independent force. When the Senior Executive Service was created in 1978, one of the hopes was that career administrators would receive the respect they deserve for the professionalism and expertise they bring to their jobs. Such a tradition is well established in European systems and gives unelected officials independent standing—one of the aspects of British bureaucracy that Margaret Thatcher sought to reverse.

Europeans with a career in public administration have usually had training at some of the nation's most elite educational institutions and often enjoy more prestige than politicians. Thus, some students of public administration argue that bureaucrats provide government with an institutional memory of policy strategies tried and failed, and they serve as repositories of policy wisdom. If this is the case, should bureaucrats always be subordinate to elected officials? Wouldn't government that relies on expert guidance provide greater continuity and potentially better service to the public than government based on shifting political coalitions? In American political culture, though, it is assumed that if bureaucrats guide elected officials, turning the American model of administrative accountability upside down, they must represent unchecked administrative power and should be resisted. This traditional American view of democracy is likely to win out in the long run but might sacrifice the benefits to be gained were we to have more confidence in experts.

## CONSEQUENCES FOR DEMOCRACY

Government bureaucracy has grown in American life from a presence barely hinted at in the Constitution to a pervasive force in the twenty-first century. Contemporary politicians often describe bureaucratic power as dangerous, providing Americans with a new reminder of the hot-button issue of the Revolutionary War—government agents invading citizens' rights. But bureaucracy is not always bad; instead, the competent administration of public affairs promotes personal health, safety, and happiness. Admittedly, American bureaucracy is far from perfect,

**iron triangle** The close relationship established and maintained among a trio of actors: the beneficiaries of a government policy (interest groups), the agency responsible for the beneficial programs (bureaucracy), and the congressional committees responsible for authorizing and funding the programs.

and sometimes the failures can be spectacular, as in the case of FEMA and Hurricane Katrina. More often, successes go unnoticed.

Both the president and Congress seek to direct the activities of federal employees, and both use a wide array of mechanisms to assert control. Under Americans' theory of democracy, the people control bureaucrats through their elected representatives, but often, those elected officials disagree over what should be done and how it should be accomplished. Thus, the battle for control rages over the design of government-wide systems (such as the civil service) as well as how to implement very specific policies approved by both the legislative and executive branches (such as health care). One might think that such widespread struggles would limit the discretion of American bureaucrats. But in the midst of such conflict, they often find a way to steer a path toward the goal preferred by the professionals, arguably an even better outcome.

In other nations, bureaucrats are often more respected than they are in the United States. In the historical accounts that transmit political culture from one generation to the next, bureaucrats are credited with building and sustaining the modern nation, earning them greater cultural respect. And the permanent structure of government officials provides continuity in political systems where coalition governments come and go rapidly. In Italy, for example, where there have been nearly 60 governments since 1946, administrators provide some measure of stability. Facing a financial crisis in 2011, Italy turned to professionally trained "technocrats" to fill their cabinet positions—not politicians.

Donald Trump has disagreed with the intelligence and national security bureaucracy throughout his presidency; for instance, ignoring their warnings about the risks of trusting Russian president Vladimir Putin.

In other parliamentary systems, the boundary between the elected government and the bureaucracy is far less distinct than it is in the United States. In the United Kingdom, Canada, and Australia, members of parliament head the principal government agencies; they are political allies of the prime minister who hold legislative and executive positions at the same time. These members of the parliamentary team oversee the permanent bureaucracy, which must be able to serve either party effectively. In these British-patterned democracies, no constitutional divide is built into the relationship between civil servants and the executive branch as one finds in the United States. Thus, different histories and different constitutional structures produce distinctive roles for the government bureaucrats.

Government often appears very distant from us. It seems to be about current and potential military conflicts on the other side of the world or about abstract disagreements over economic policy. But unelected officials at federal, state, and local levels of government have an enormous impact on everyday life. From enforcing the speed limit to ensuring that the water is safe to drink to guaranteeing that there is enough electricity to cool our homes even in the hottest weather, government bureaucrats perform innumerable services that make modern life possible. They also make us angry—when April 15 rolls around each year and we have to pay our federal taxes; when our car fails to pass its safety inspection; when the student loan program that we depend on is changed and benefits are reduced. Numerous citizens feel that faceless bureaucrats are to blame for many of their ills: The government costs too much and taxes are too high; government officials are overpaid; rush hour traffic is ridiculously congested; there is no end in sight for the rising cost of gas. With growing government responsibilities have come growing public expectations of government performance.

Do bureaucrats pose a danger to the American way of life? Or do officials make that way of life possible? Politically, it has been easier to emphasize the threats posed by big government than the benefits that it might provide. Such attacks play to the nation's self-image—of rugged colonists overcoming hardships and frontiersmen winning the West, carving out a new life on their own with minimal government help or presence. Modern life is very different. It involves increased complexity and many interdependencies—of producers and consumers, suppliers and transporters, health care providers and the sick, banks and savers, emergency responders and potential victims of natural disasters. The list is endless, and government has a potential and often a real role to play in each area, making certain that competition is fair, patients receive safe services, and citizens are protected against catastrophic loss of savings, homes, or lives.

# Critical Thinking Questions

1. The research of Paul Light shows us that the federal government indirectly employs millions more workers than the usual estimate of 2 million. Does that tell us that government is too large? How do we determine what the right size is for the federal government?

2. The Trump administration has pursued an aggressive agenda to reduce the number of regulations imposed by the federal government. Regulatory commissions have regulation as their central mission. Is it time for the United States to get rid of regulatory commissions? What are the costs and benefits to U.S. citizens of relying on regulatory commissions? Are the unregulated operations of free markets always the better way to go?

3. When the United States created a federal civil service system in the last half of the nineteenth century, it was hailed as a major reform of U.S. government. Yet today, the protections provided by that system are often portrayed as preventing government from being more efficient and effective. Can the original benefits associated with civil service reform be retained in the twenty-first century, or do government workers need to work in a dramatically redesigned system? Justify your answer.

4. Would the United States be better served by a streamlined bureaucratic structure that answers wholly to the president and far less to Congress? Or does U.S. government work best when both the president and Congress share control?

5. Are bureaucracy and democracy basically incompatible?

# Key Terms

administrative discretion, 342

bureaucracy, 329

central clearance, 343

delegated authority, 342

government corporations, 339

government-sponsored enterprises (GSEs), 340

implementation, 342

independent regulatory commissions, 337

iron triangle, 350

Joint Chiefs of Staff, 346

Office of Management and Budget (OMB), 342

Office of Personnel Management (OPM), 337

oversight, 344

Pendleton Civil Service Reform Act, 335

quasi-governmental organizations ("quagos"), 339

quasi-nongovernmental organizations ("quangos"), 339

spoils system, 334

Visit edge.sagepub.com/maltese to help you accomplish your coursework goals in an easy-to-use learning environment.

# 14
## THE JUDICIARY

## After reading this chapter, you should be able to do the following:

- Explain judicial review, how it developed in the United States, how it is used to enforce the rule of law, and why judicial independence is vital.

- Describe the structure of the U.S. court system and identify the advantages and disadvantages of this type of system.

- Examine how a case reaches and gets decided by the Supreme Court.

- Understand the impact of judicial philosophy on how Supreme Court justices decide cases and craft legal opinions.

- Identify the range of limits placed on the Supreme Court to prevent it from overreaching or abusing its power.

- Compare and contrast the criteria used to select judges at the state and federal levels.

## Perspective: When Do Reactions to Unpopular Court Decisions Threaten Judicial Independence?

Judicial independence has long been a cornerstone of the American system of government. Specific court rulings and judges have sometimes prompted hostile reactions from politicians, interest groups, the media, and the public, but no matter how upset these opponents may be, official responses have been limited to employing legitimate checks on the court. For example, some critics were greatly angered by the Supreme Court's 1973 decision in *Roe v. Wade* that recognized a fundamental right of privacy that protects a pregnant woman's right to choose, with some restrictions, whether or not to have an abortion. But those critics—including several Republican presidents—worked within constitutional means to try to change the decision. They called for an amendment to the Constitution to overturn it and, as the composition of the Supreme Court moved in a more conservative direction, lobbied state legislatures to pass restrictive abortion laws in the hopes that they would be challenged in court and lead, on appeal, to overturning *Roe v. Wade*.

Donald Trump has sometimes been criticized for using abrasive rhetoric to criticize judges and specific court rulings. As noted in Chapter 5, he questioned during the 2016 presidential campaign whether an Indiana-born federal judge of Mexican descent could rule impartially because of his Mexican heritage. Once in office, Trump lashed out on Twitter at a federal judge in Washington State who temporarily blocked enforcement of his ban on travel from predominantly Muslim countries in February 2017, dismissing him as a "so-called judge" and calling the ruling "ridiculous."[1] "Just cannot believe a judge would put our country in such peril," he added in a tweet the next day. "If something happens blame him and [the] court system. People pouring in. Bad!"[2]

Several months later, President Trump again lashed out when a federal judge from the Ninth Circuit Court of Appeals blocked the enforcement of restrictions Trump had imposed on the rights of asylum-seekers crossing the U.S.–Mexico border. Trump called the ruling a "disgrace" and "not law," attacked Judge Jon Tigar who issued it as "an Obama judge," criticized the Ninth Circuit for consistently ruling against him, and threatened, "I'll tell you what, it's not going to happen like this anymore."[3] In response, Supreme Court Chief Justice John Roberts (appointed by Republican President George W. Bush) issued a statement saying,

> We do not have Obama judges or Trump judges, Bush judges or Clinton judges. What we have is an extraordinary group of dedicated judges doing their level best to do equal right to those appearing before them. That independent judiciary is something we should all be thankful for.

To this, the president retorted,

> Sorry Chief Justice John Roberts, but you do indeed have "Obama judges," and they have a much different point of view than the people who are charged with the safety of our country. . . . We need protection and security—these rulings are making our country unsafe! Very dangerous and unwise![4]

Some contend that such rhetoric threatens the independence of the American judiciary, even though Trump has so far allowed the judicial process to proceed unfettered. For example, the Brennan Center for Justice argues that Trump's attacks undermine "our entire system of government" because courts, as bulwarks of the law and our Constitution, "depend on the public to respect their judgments and on officials to obey and enforce their decisions." "Separation of powers," it added, "is not a threat to democracy; it is the essence of democracy."[5] Well before Trump became president, several U.S. Supreme Court justices, including Chief Justice John Roberts, publicly criticized what they perceived to be a rise in the number of threats to judicial independence.[6] Concerned about such threats, the American Judicature Society created a task force to monitor and respond to attacks on the judiciary. Likewise, the American Bar Association (ABA) has had a Standing Committee on Judicial Independence since 1997.

In many countries around the world, however, threats to judicial independence go far beyond rhetoric. In such places, the idea of judicial independence is often hard to fathom. Judges fear official reprisal for unpopular decisions—they might find themselves summarily fired, placed under arrest, or worse.

In 2019, for example, Nigeria's president, Muhammadu Buhari, unilaterally suspended that nation's chief justice, Walter Onnoghen, mere weeks before a general election. A United Nations–appointed independent rights expert condemned the suspension as an attack on judicial independence, saying that international human rights standards "provide that judges may be dismissed only on serious grounds of misconduct or incompetence" and that any decision "to suspend or remove a judge from office should be taken by an independent authority, such as a judicial council or a court."[7] Buhari claimed that he suspended the chief justice for an ethics violation, but critics pointed out that he suspended the chief justice without due process, and his rival presidential candidate decried the move as a "brazen dictatorial act."[8]

A few months earlier, in Poland, that country's Parliament approved and the country's president signed a measure to restructure Poland's Supreme Court. Under the guise of removing communists and obstructionists appointed under the previous regime, the law allowed for the removal of 27 judges of the Supreme Court, including the chief justice, to be replaced with judges loyal to the new ruling party.[9] After the European Union took steps to strip Poland of its voting rights in response, the government reversed course and the president signed legislation to reinstate the judges.[10] Still, many observers worry about ongoing threats to judicial independence not only in Poland but in other democracies, such as Hungary.

Could a law similar to the one passed in Poland to restructure its Supreme Court be passed in the United States? Could a popular president with strong support in Congress restructure our Supreme Court to minimize the power of "obstructionist judges" by adding new judges loyal to the new ruling party? That is actually not so different from what President Franklin D. Roosevelt suggested in 1937. Faced with a Supreme Court majority that consistently struck down major provisions of his "New Deal," President Roosevelt suggested that Congress take advantage of its power to change the size of the Supreme Court (see Chapter 3) and add one seat to the Supreme Court for every justice who was over the age of 70 years and six months, up to a maximum of six justices. That would have increased the size of the Supreme Court from nine to fifteen. No justices would have been fired—as they were in Poland—but Roosevelt would have nominated the new justices (presumably all of whom would be willing to uphold the New Deal) and his fellow Democrats in Congress would have confirmed them. Congress never enacted the legislation, but would there have been any recourse if it had? Can you imagine a similar proposal at some point in the future? Is judicial independence as strong a cornerstone in our system as we like to think it is? **«**

## AN INDEPENDENT JUDICIARY ENFORCING THE RULE OF LAW

Article III of the U.S. Constitution established the U.S. Supreme Court, gave Congress the power to create lower federal courts (state courts already existed), and established specific provisions to guarantee judicial independence. First, short of impeachment, federal judges have life tenure. They cannot, for example, be fired by the president, as in Nigeria. Second, the Constitution guarantees compensation to federal judges "which shall not be diminished during their continuance in office," thereby preventing Congress from using a pay cut to punish judges for their rulings. These constitutional guarantees reinforce the institutional independence of federal courts from the other branches and from threats of retaliation from the people.

An independent judiciary protects the rule of law, ensuring that all parts of government are subservient to the Constitution. As Thomas Paine famously put it, "A constitution is a thing *antecedent* to a government, and a government is only the creature of a constitution."[11] Not all countries that have a written constitution protect the rule of law. China has a written constitution, including guarantees of free speech and religious freedom, but its constitution is subservient to the Communist Party. Article 126 states that the courts shall "exercise judicial power independently and are not subject to interference by administrative organ, public organizations or individuals." Yet, involvement by the Chinese Communist Party leadership in court decisions is deemed "leadership" rather than "interference."[12] Moreover, China has neither separation of powers (which allows the judiciary to be independent of the other branches) nor judicial review (which allows the judiciary to enforce the Constitution). Both are key elements of judicial independence that are essential to the rule of law.

**Judicial review** is the power of courts to review acts of government and strike down those that violate the Constitution. In so doing, courts enforce the rule of law. Judicial review hinges upon both judicial independence and the separation of powers: The Court can strike down

> **judicial review** The power of courts, when confronted with a legitimate case, to review and strike down acts of government that violate the Constitution.

an act of Congress or declare other decisions by federal, state, and local governments unconstitutional.

## THE CREATION OF JUDICIAL REVIEW

The Constitution did not specifically enumerate the power of judicial review. Some of the framers, including Alexander Hamilton in *Federalist* 78, assumed that the power was implied, but the practice of judicial review was not firmly established until the 1803 Supreme Court case *Marbury v. Madison*.[13] However, precedents for judicial review had emerged long before the Constitution was written.

**PRECEDENTS FOR JUDICIAL REVIEW**  As early as 1610, a judge in England, Sir Edward Coke, suggested in *Dr. Bonham's Case* that "when an Act of Parliament is against common right and reason, or repugnant, or impossible to be performed, the common law will control it, and adjudge such Act to be void."[14] Coke's bold suggestion never took root in England. Some 150 years later, however, some American colonists—angered by actions of the British Parliament—embraced the concept of judicial review as a tool to check legislative abuse. Nonetheless, scholars are divided over not only how widely the doctrine of judicial review came to be accepted among the colonists but also over how frequently state courts actually exercised judicial review under the Articles of Confederation. Some claim that the practice of state courts using state constitutions to invalidate acts of state legislatures was widespread enough for the framers of the Constitution to simply assume the power without including any specific provision for it at the national level.[15] Others, however, disagree.[16]

**THE FRAMERS' INTENT**  Scholars also debate whether or not the framers intended for there to be judicial review, in part because notes recording what went on at the Constitutional Convention are sketchy and incomplete. The precise number of delegates who supported or rejected judicial review, and how strongly they held their views on that matter, may always remain unclear. Those who argue that the framers intended judicial review point to two clauses. The first is the "arising under" clause of Article III, Section 2, which states that "the judicial power shall extend to all cases, in law and equity, arising under this Constitution, the Laws of the United States, and Treaties." The other is the supremacy clause of Article VI, which says that "this Constitution, and the Laws of the United States which shall be made in pursuance thereof . . . shall be the supreme law of the Land." If federal courts have judicial power in all cases arising under the U.S. Constitution, and the U.S. Constitution is supreme, then surely the courts must enforce the Constitution against inferior laws that run contrary to it. But despite this logic, neither clause explicitly established judicial review, and both clauses could well have been passed without any expectation of judicial review.[17]

Those who argue that the framers assumed an inherent power of judicial review point to *Federalist* 78, where Alexander Hamilton wrote that courts are "the bulwarks of a limited Constitution against legislative encroachments"[18] and that no legislative act that is contrary to the Constitution can be valid. The Court, Hamilton concluded, is in the best position to enforce the Constitution and police the limits of legislative authority.

## *MARBURY V. MADISON*

Even if Hamilton's position enjoyed widespread support, the fact remains that the United States Supreme Court did not use the power of judicial review to invalidate an act of Congress for another 15 years.[19] This first use of judicial review came in *Marbury v. Madison*.

**THE CONTEXT OF *MARBURY V. MADISON***  *Marbury v. Madison* arose out of the great tensions that surrounded the elections of 1800, in which Federalists fared poorly at both the national and state level. They lost control of the White House and Congress to their rival Democratic-Republicans, and the elections turned out to be the beginning of the end of the Federalist Party. Thomas Jefferson's victory in the presidential election came only after high drama: A tie in the Electoral College threw the election to the Federalist-controlled House of Representatives.[20]

*Marbury v. Madison* The 1803 Supreme Court case that serves as a precedent for the use of judicial review.

In the midst of all the turmoil, the lame duck Federalists passed the Judiciary Act of 1801, creating 16 new federal judgeships with lifetime tenure. They also passed additional legislation that created 42 justices of the peace with fixed terms of office in the District of Columbia. All were to be nominated by the incumbent Federalist president, John Adams, and confirmed by the lame duck Federalist-controlled Senate. Federalists claimed the new judgeships were necessary, but the Democratic-Republicans cried foul, claiming they were a partisan ploy to pack the courts with loyal Federalists.

William Marbury was one of the 42 justices of the peace nominated by President Adams and confirmed by the Senate shortly before the Democratic-Republicans were due to take power. The last step in the appointment process was to deliver a commission: an official document signed by the president that conferred the post. The responsibility for delivering such commissions belonged to Adams's secretary of state, John Marshall, but Marbury's appointment had come so close to the end of the Adams administration that Marshall did not have time to deliver Marbury's commission. Thus, he left it for his successor to deliver. When President Jefferson took office, however, he forbade his secretary of state, James Madison, to deliver the commission. Marbury then sued, asking the Court to issue a writ of mandamus commanding Secretary of State Madison to perform his official duty of delivering the commission. Most cases before the Supreme Court are heard on appeal, having first been decided by lower courts, but Marbury brought his suit directly to the high court, under what is known as original jurisdiction.

John Marshall, who served as secretary of state under John Adams before being appointed Chief Justice of the Supreme Court, played a pivotal role in the establishment of judicial review, both by creating the conditions for the case *Marbury v. Madison* and by crafting the decision.

Marbury could not have chosen a more favorable court to hear his case. Not only were all six members of the Supreme Court loyal Federalists, but the man who was supposed to deliver the commission in the first place—John Marshall—was now chief justice (having been nominated by President Adams and confirmed by the Senate during the lame duck session controlled by the Federalists). Rather than recuse himself—that is, decline to participate in the case because of a conflict of interest—Marshall not only participated in the case but wrote the opinion for the Court.

The Court decided *Marbury v. Madison* in the midst of a major power struggle between the federal judiciary, controlled by Federalists, and the other two branches, controlled by the Democratic-Republicans. Convinced that the federal courts had been politicized, the Democratic-Republican Congress repealed the Judiciary Act of 1801, thereby abolishing the federal judgeships it had created, and considered impeaching Federalist judges. In a brazen threat to judicial independence, Congress even prevented the Supreme Court from holding its 1802 term. When the Court finally heard arguments in *Marbury v. Madison* in 1803, Madison sent no lawyer to argue his side. In not sending a lawyer, he seemed to be casting doubt on the Court's authority and was probably signaling that he would not comply if the Court ruled against him—another threat to judicial independence.

Chief Justice Marshall feared that any ruling in *Marbury v. Madison* could further undermine the power and legitimacy of the Supreme Court. If the Court issued the writ of mandamus but Secretary of State Madison ignored it, the weakness of the Court would be revealed. Madison's noncompliance would send a signal that others need not obey the Supreme Court either. On the other hand, if the Court did not issue the writ of mandamus, everyone would assume that it had simply caved in to pressure, so this decision, too, would seem to weaken the Court.

In the end, Marshall ingeniously crafted a decision in which the Court gave the Jefferson administration what it wanted (no writ of mandamus) but, in so doing, claimed for itself the power of judicial review. Rather than weakening the Court, the ruling in *Marbury v. Madison* actually increased its power—at least in the long run.

> **original jurisdiction**
> The authority of the Supreme Court to hear a case that originates before it (as opposed to an appeal from a lower court).

**THE DECISION IN *MARBURY V. MADISON*** In his opinion for the Court, Marshall conceded that Marbury had a right to his commission and that the Judiciary Act of 1789 offered a remedy in the form of a writ of mandamus. However, he concluded that the legislative provision in the Act that gave the Supreme Court the authority to issue such a writ was unconstitutional because it expanded the Court's original jurisdiction in violation of the Constitution. According to Marshall, the Court's original jurisdiction could only be expanded through constitutional amendment. Therefore, the Court lacked jurisdiction to issue the writ.[21]

In striking down this portion of the Judiciary Act, the Court exercised the power of judicial review. Although this power is not enumerated in the Constitution, Marshall insisted that it is essential to limited government. The Constitution, he argued, is "the fundamental and paramount law of the nation," and it is "emphatically, the province and duty" of the Court "to say what the law is." If two laws conflict, the Court must choose between them as part of its judicial function. And, if the Court regards the Constitution as "superior to any ordinary act of the legislature, the constitution, and not such ordinary act, must govern the case to which they both apply."[22]

Marshall's argument in support of judicial review is compelling, but it has not gone unchallenged. Critics have argued that it gives too much power to unelected judges and undermines the majoritarian process by eroding the power of duly elected representatives in Congress to legislate. Justice John Bannister Gibson, of the Pennsylvania Supreme Court, responded in 1825 with a classic retort to John Marshall. All branches of government are *equal*, Gibson argued, and the oath to support the Constitution is taken by all officers of government, not only judges. "For these reasons," he wrote, "I am of the opinion that it rests with the people, in whom full and absolute sovereign power resides, to correct abuses in legislation by instructing their representatives to repeal the obnoxious act."[23]

However, relying on the people to correct unconstitutional acts raises the threat of "tyranny of the majority." A majority can tyrannize as much as an authoritarian monarch. The majority might not take the necessary steps to reject an unconstitutional law, and it may even embrace such a law. Moreover, voters tend to have short memories and are motivated by many factors. By the time of the next election, the electorate might not remember their representative's support for an unconstitutional law, or they might cast their vote on the basis of other factors.

Gibson changed his mind 20 years later and came out in support of courts exercising the power of judicial review.[24] Today, the power of judicial review is so entrenched in the United States that doing away with it would probably require a constitutional amendment. But controversy regarding judicial review remains—not over *whether* courts have the power of judicial review, but over *when* and *how often* they should use it. We will return to this issue near the end of this chapter when we discuss judicial activism and judicial restraint.

## JUDICIAL REVIEW OF STATE ACTION

*Marbury v. Madison* established the Supreme Court's power to review actions of coequal branches of government, but the supremacy clause affirms the Supreme Court's right to review the constitutionality of state laws, which is arguably even more important. The United States probably could have survived—and survived quite well—without judicial review of coequal branches. The United Kingdom has. But if the Supreme Court did not have judicial review of state action, our nation's success would have been less certain, with conflicting state and federal laws pulling the nation apart and no central authority to rein in disobedience from the states. What if a state refused to follow a treaty or would not comply with a federal law such as the Clean Air Act? What if it enacted laws in violation of due process or equal protection? Without judicial review of state action, there would be no judicial enforcement of the supremacy clause and the weaknesses of the Articles of Confederation (see Chapter 2) would have continued under the new Constitution. As discussed in Chapter 4, the twentieth century saw the selective incorporation of the Bill of Rights. This process has left even less discretion to individual states and led to controversy because incorporation has expanded the opportunity for judicial review of state laws dealing with contentious topics such as abortion; lesbian, gay, bisexual, and transgender (LGBT) rights; school prayer; and obscenity.

## JUDICIAL REVIEW AROUND THE WORLD

The United States was the first country to embrace the use of judicial review, followed by a few countries (including Argentina and Canada) in the nineteenth century. After World War II, the defeated Axis powers—Italy, Japan, and West Germany—adopted judicial review as part of their

### PICTURE YOURSELF...
# As a U.S. Marshal Charged With Protecting Federal Judges

The U.S. Marshal Service is the oldest law enforcement agency in the United States, dating to 1789, and you are proud to work for it. You are one of 94 Marshals—one assigned to each judicial district in the country—with more than 3,750 Deputy Marshals and Criminal Investigators working under you and your fellow Marshals.

One of the most important parts of your job is to protect federal judges and others in the criminal justice system. In 2018, the number of threats and inappropriate communications against the judiciary rose to 4,542—up from 2,847 the year before, and up from 768 in 2014.[a] Should this make you nervous?

Most people probably assume that federal judges lead a comfortable life with interesting work, decent pay, and the respect of the community. They probably do not think of it as being particularly dangerous work. Nonetheless, three federal judges have been murdered in the United States since 1979. As a U.S. Marshal, it is your responsibility to prevent that from happening again, and you rightfully take pride in the job you and your fellow Marshals are doing. But you also know that the high degree of safety and security that U.S. judges enjoy does not exist everywhere around the world.

For example, being a judge in the South American country of Colombia was particularly dangerous in the 1980s. There, choosing to be a judge could easily have cost you your life. From 1978 to 1991, drug cartels murdered 278 judges in Colombia. Starting in 1991, the Colombian government instituted a system of protecting judges by holding hearings behind one-way mirrors and using voice-distortion equipment to prevent them from being recognized.[b] The identities of prosecutors and witnesses were also shielded.

Such danger was not unique to Colombia. Judges in Mexico also became targets of drug violence. In 2016,

Mexican federal judge Vicente Bermúdez Zacarias was assassinated while jogging. Zacarias had been assigned to preside over the trial of drug lord Joaquin "El Chapo" Guzman if U.S. authorities—who were then holding El Chapo—approved extradition of the kingpin to Mexico. (In fact, U.S. authorities continued to hold Guzman, who was found guilty by a U.S. court in February 2019 and given a life sentence in jail on July 17, 2019.) And in Iraq, where the United States helped to establish an independent judiciary after ousting Saddam Hussein, more than 30 judges were killed in the line of duty between 2003 and 2007.[c]

Violence against judges and other participants in the judicial system is a reality in some parts of the world, and it constitutes another threat to judicial independence. As a U.S. Marshal, how worried should you be about such violence in the United States?

### Questions to Consider

1. What is the best way to protect the safety of judges, prosecutors, and witnesses? Why do you think there has been an almost sixfold increase in the number of threats and inappropriate communications against the judiciary in the United States between 2014 and 2018?
2. Colombia chose to shield the identity of judges, prosecutors, and witnesses in order to protect them. Does such anonymity raise any due process concerns or other problems? For example, an anonymous judge in Colombia sentenced two leaders of a major drug cartel to very light sentences: only 10 and 12 years in prison.[d] Should the judge have been publicly accountable for the sentences by having his identity revealed?
3. What do you think is the greatest threat to judicial independence in the United States? Is the physical safety of judges high on that list of threats?

[a] "Judges Targeted Fast Facts," CNN, April 30, 2019, https://www.cnn.com/2013/11/04/us/judges-targeted-fast-facts/index.html
[b] Jeremy Schwartz, "Judges Latest Target in Mexico Drug War," Cox News, February 2, 2008.
[c] Robert H. Reid, "Wave of Attacks Threaten Iraqi Judges," Associated Press, June 30, 2008.
[d] David Aquila Lawrence, "'Faceless' Justice in Drug Wars Faces Scrutiny in Colombia," Las Vegas Sun, March 34, 1997, http://www.lasvegassun.com/news/1997/mar/24/faceless-justice-in-drug-war-faces-scrutiny-in-col/

new constitutions, and other countries, including Belgium and Spain, followed suit. Another wave came after the collapse of the Berlin Wall in 1989 and the disintegration of the Soviet Union. Eager to protect their newfound freedom, Eastern European countries that had been under the control of the Soviet Union embraced judicial review. By the start of the twenty-first century, some 70 countries had adopted some form of judicial review, including much of Latin America.[25]

The term *judicial review* means different things in different countries (and sometimes even within a country). In the United States, we usually associate judicial review with *constitutional review*, that is, with courts imposing constitutional limitations on government power. Some countries, such as England, do not give their courts this power, but do allow them to review administrative actions. This is also a type of judicial review used in the United States. For example, the Supreme Court may review a specific action of the Environmental Protection Agency to see if it complies with the Clean Air Act. If the Court were to strike down the regulation in such a case, it would be doing so because the regulation violated an act of Congress, not because it violated the Constitution. In such a case, Congress could overturn the Court's ruling through simple legislation, thereby maintaining legislative supremacy.

The United States Supreme Court does not issue *advisory opinions*—that is, rule on the constitutionality of a law before someone is directly and personally affected by it. Thus, a woman who is not pregnant cannot challenge an antiabortion law (even though she may eventually become pregnant) nor can a man because neither has a personal stake in the outcome of the case. Only a pregnant woman seeking an abortion can do so. Nor can Congress or a state legislature ask the Court to offer its judgment on the constitutionality of a law before it is enacted. By contrast, advisory opinions on the constitutionality of proposed legislation are the most common form of constitutional review in western European countries. German law, for example, requires constitutional courts to resolve constitutional questions whenever they are asked to do so by an elected official.

Another big difference is that constitutional courts in some countries, such as Italy, France, Germany, and Spain, can use their power of judicial review not only to strike down laws but also to compel legislative action by issuing directives to the legislature. Their constitutions not only place *limits* on what government can do but also impose *duties* by telling government what it *must* do.[26] For example, the German Federal Constitutional Court relied on the constitutional right of human dignity in Article One of the German constitution to declare that the government has a responsibility to rehabilitate criminals, and then the Court ordered legislation to accomplish that goal.[27]

## AN OVERVIEW OF THE U.S. COURT SYSTEM

Our system of federalism has led to a complicated network of both federal and state courts, a marked contrast to the court system in countries with a unitary system of government, such as France. The division in the United States between a system of federal courts and a system of state courts is sometimes referred to as a **dual court system**. But since each state creates its own system of courts, and since no two states have identical court systems, we really have 51 different court systems in the United States: one for each of the 50 states plus one at the federal level.

Cases typically originate in **trial courts**. Thousands of trial courts are spread out across the United States at both the state and federal levels. Different courts have jurisdiction to hear different types of cases. *Territorial jurisdiction* involves the power of a court to hear cases within a certain geographic boundary. *Subject matter jurisdiction* involves the ability of a particular court to hear particular types of cases. Thus, traffic courts do not have jurisdiction to try a murder case, nor does a court in Texas normally have the jurisdiction to hear a case involving a crime committed in Rhode Island.

The U.S. Supreme Court, by contrast, is primarily an **appellate court** (except in the very small number of cases that come to it under its original jurisdiction). Each state also has appellate courts, and there are lower appellate courts at the federal level, too. Appellate courts review actions of lower courts to make sure that there was no error in their judgments.

Both federal and state courts have the power to hear two basic types of disputes: civil cases and criminal cases. In civil cases, one party sues another. These involve legal disputes over such

**dual court system** The existence of separate national and local courts in a federal system.

**trial courts** Courts where cases originate and trials take place (as opposed to appellate courts).

**appellate court** A court that hears appeals from lower courts. Appeals involve questions of law rather than questions of fact.

matters as child custody, divorce, money, property, copyright infringement, personal injury, and failure to live up to a contractual obligation. Usually, the parties in civil cases are private individuals or businesses. Monetary damages are often involved. But the government, or a government official, can also be a party in a civil case. *Marbury v. Madison* is a good example. In that case, Marbury—a private citizen—was suing a government official to get what he thought was rightfully his: delivery of the commission that would allow him to become a justice of the peace. The party who brings a civil suit against another is called the *plaintiff*. The party being sued is called the *defendant*. Sometimes a group of individuals collectively bring a suit. In such a case, called a *class action*, each participant in the class has suffered the same injury.

Criminal cases are brought by the government against an individual or a business accused of breaking the law. Such cases can result in fines, jail sentences, and even the death penalty, depending upon the seriousness of the crime and the jurisdiction where it is committed.

Criminal justice in the United States is based on the **adversarial system,** which is also used in the United Kingdom. In this system, the defendant is presumed to be innocent, and guilt is determined through a process in which prosecutors face off against defense attorneys in a trial.

By contrast, the justice systems of many Latin American and European countries (such as France) are based on an **inquisitorial system.** The judge, in particular, plays a very different role in an inquisitorial system. Instead of presiding in a relatively passive fashion, as is the case in the adversarial system, the judge (or "magistrate") plays an active role in gathering evidence. It is the judge who decides if there is enough evidence to go to trial. If so, there is a presumption of guilt that the defendant must rebut. In the trial, the judge is primarily responsible for questioning witnesses. The attorneys in the case play a much more limited role than is the case in the adversarial system. The judge then decides the verdict and gives the sentence in the case. There is no jury. Rights of criminal defendants are more carefully protected in an adversarial system than they are in an inquisitorial system.

Since states are responsible for creating most criminal laws, most criminal trials take place in state court. But Congress also passes criminal laws, punishing such offenses as counterfeiting, tax evasion, and the murder of government officials. The amount of criminal legislation passed by Congress has increased in recent years and has included legislation in some areas traditionally thought to be the province of the states, such as gun control and labor laws. Congress has accomplished this by relying on broad interpretations of constitutional provisions, such as its power to regulate interstate commerce (see Chapter 3).

Sometimes a single action can result in both a criminal case and a civil case. For example, a barroom brawl could result in criminal charges, such as assault and battery, and a civil suit between the parties involved to recover monetary damages to pay for expenses such as medical treatment for injuries sustained. Thus, a jury famously found O. J. Simpson innocent in a state criminal trial for the murder of his ex-wife and her friend, but the jury in a subsequent civil case ordered Simpson to pay monetary damages to the families of the murder victims. The seemingly contradictory rulings are possible because the standard for guilt in a criminal case—guilty beyond all reasonable doubt—is higher than the standard in civil suits, where plaintiffs need only show that a preponderance of evidence supports their case.

Likewise, a single action can sometimes lead to separate cases in both state court and federal court. For example, officers from the Los Angeles Police Department were tried and acquitted in state court on multiple criminal charges—including assault, using excessive force, and filing a false police report—related to their conduct after stopping an African American man named Rodney King for speeding on the night of March 2, 1991. However, a bystander had videotaped the police kicking King and striking him more than 50 times with their batons while King, who appeared to pose no threat, struggled on the ground. Public airings of the videotape led many to conclude that the officers were guilty,

**adversarial system** The criminal justice system in which defendants are presumed innocent and guilt is determined when prosecutors face off against defense attorneys in a trial.

**inquisitorial system** The criminal justice system in which defendants are presumed guilty until proven innocent and guilt is determined by the judge (rather than a jury) who plays an active role in gathering evidence and questioning witnesses.

Douglas Burrows / Getty Images

The four white police officers charged after beating Rodney King, shown here, were acquitted of criminal charges under California law, but two were convicted of federal civil rights violations for the same actions.

and their acquittal, in 1992, triggered riots in Los Angeles. Separate charges were subsequently brought in federal court where the officers were tried for violating federal civil rights laws. This time, two of the officers were found guilty and sentenced to serve 30 months in prison. In addition to the state and federal criminal cases, King also filed a civil suit in Los Angeles court against the officers. He won, and the jury awarded him $3.8 million in damages.

## THE FEDERAL COURT SYSTEM

Only state courts existed under the Articles of Confederation, and those courts were free from control by the national government. Thus, courts in each state could interpret federal law differently. The resulting mayhem ensured a general agreement at the Constitutional Convention that there should be one national supreme court to hear appeals from state courts. But states' rights advocates were wary of a broader system of federal trial and appellate courts that they feared would undermine local control of justice and infringe upon the sovereignty of the states.[28]

The language of Article III of the Constitution was thus a compromise between those who wanted a powerful and extensive system of federal courts and those who remained fearful of such a system. Article III created one Supreme Court but postponed a decision about whether to create lower federal courts by leaving the decision to Congress. During the ratification debate, Anti-Federalists argued that even that compromise gave too much power to the national government.[29]

With the Judiciary Act of 1789, however, Congress quickly created a system of lower federal courts. Lower federal courts have been in place ever since, although Congress has changed the precise structure of those courts through legislation. The system comprises three levels of courts that form a sort of pyramid with the Supreme Court at the top (see Figure 14.1). The federal courts discussed below—district courts, courts of appeals, and the Supreme Court—all have general jurisdiction, or a broad power to hear a wide range of cases. These courts are categorized as *Article III courts*, and their judges, as mandated by the Constitution, have life tenure.

In addition to these courts of general jurisdiction, the federal judicial system also includes a number of more specialized courts. Some of these specialized courts are also Article III courts—for example, the U.S. Court of International Trade, which hears trade cases, such as customs and border protection disputes. Other specialized courts have been created by Congress. These

## FIGURE 14.1
## *The Structure of the Federal Court System*

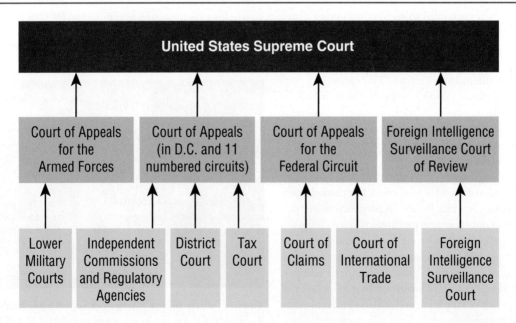

Source: *Adapted from* American Democracy Now, 2e Tx *Ed.*

are known as *Article I* courts. Their judges do not have life tenure. An example is the U.S. Tax Court, which has the authority to resolve disputes involving the Internal Revenue Service and federal income tax.

**U.S. DISTRICT COURTS** Courts designated as U.S. district courts are trial courts. Since this is where most federal cases originate, district courts hear more cases than any other type of court in the federal system. There are also more district courts than any other kind of federal court: currently 94 courts with 673 full-time judgeships.[30] District courts hear federal criminal cases as well as civil cases that meet one of these conditions:

- They are brought against the federal government.
- They involve a claim based on the U.S. Constitution, federal law, or a federal treaty.
- They involve a citizen of one state suing a citizen of another state when more than $75,000 is at issue.

Proceedings in district court are presided over by a single judge. Trials take place there, complete with jury, testimony by witnesses, cross examination, and the introduction of evidence. Each state has at least one district, and those with heavier caseloads have more than one (see Figure 14.2). No district extends beyond the boundary of a single state. In order to promote the legitimacy of its rulings, district courts are staffed with judges who are residents of the state that the district falls within. Like all federal judges, district court judges are nominated by the president and confirmed by the Senate.

**U.S. COURTS OF APPEALS** The middle tier of the federal court system consists of the U.S. courts of appeals. These were originally called *circuit courts* (the current name has been in effect since 1948) and each covers a geographic region that is still known as a circuit, with each circuit made up of several districts. Currently, there are 12 circuits: one for the District of Columbia and 11 others covering the remainder of the country. In addition, there is a U.S. Court of Appeals for the Federal Circuit, which has nationwide jurisdiction over a variety of specialized subject matters including international trade, government contracts, trademarks, and veterans' benefits. As shown in Figure 14.2, each of the numbered circuits has jurisdiction over several states, although the number of states varies from circuit to circuit. The number of judges also varies across circuits, from six for the First Circuit to 28 for the Ninth Circuit, for a current total of 167 full-time judgeships.

The courts of appeals have jurisdiction to hear appeals from the district courts that fall within their particular circuit. As appellate courts, they answer questions of *law* rather than questions of *fact*. In other words, they determine whether the lower court made an error in its application of the law. Appeals are usually heard by a panel of three judges. Since this is not a trial but an appeal, there are no witnesses, no testimony, and no jury. Instead, lawyers representing both sides present legal arguments in the form of written briefs.

In many appeals, attorneys also present oral arguments in front of the judges. A majority vote of the judges is needed to overturn a lower court ruling, and the court of appeals issues a written opinion explaining its ruling. One judge is responsible for writing that opinion. If all the judges agree, only one opinion is issued by the court. If, however, the court is divided, one judge is responsible for writing the majority opinion. A judge who disagrees with the ruling in the majority opinion explains why in a separate dissenting opinion. Even if the court is unanimous in arriving at a certain conclusion (say, overturning a conviction by a lower court), judges may disagree about some aspect of the reasoning used to arrive at that conclusion (such as the specific reason for overturning the conviction). If that is the case, a judge may write a separate concurring opinion to explain the alternate reasoning. All of these opinions are published, and the majority opinion serves as a precedent for rulings in subsequent cases decided in that circuit. Sometimes a precedent from one circuit conflicts with a precedent in another. Such disagreements can be resolved by appeal to the Supreme Court. If there is no appeal, or if the Supreme Court refuses to hear the appeal, such disagreements stand. Under such circumstances, a case might be resolved differently in one circuit from the way it would be resolved in another.

**U.S. district courts** Federal trial courts, where most federal cases are initiated.

**U.S. courts of appeals** An intermediate level of federal appellate courts.

**briefs** Written statements of legal arguments submitted by the parties in a case and sometimes by outside groups.

**oral arguments** The opportunity for lawyers on both sides of a case to appear before the appellate courts to give a verbal argument and respond to questions from the judges about why their side should prevail.

**majority opinion** A written opinion that expresses the legal reasoning used to justify an appellate court's ruling in a particular case.

**dissenting opinion** A written opinion by a judge who disagrees with the outcome of a case.

**concurring opinion** A written opinion by a judge who agrees with the outcome of a case but not with its legal reasoning.

**precedent** A previous court decision that is used to determine the outcome of subsequent cases involving a similar legal question.

FIGURE 14.2

# Geographical Boundaries of U.S. Judicial Circuits and U.S. Judicial Districts

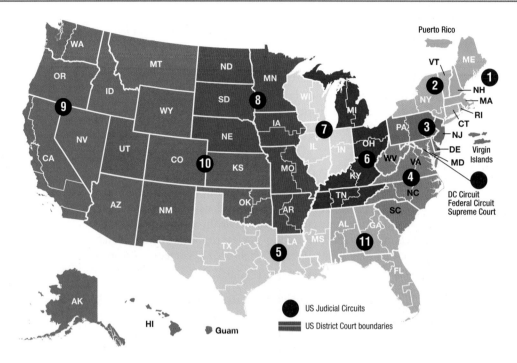

US Judicial Circuits

US District Court boundaries

Soruce: https://www.supremecourt.gov/about/Circuit%20Map.pdf

It is important to emphasize that reliance on past decisions is not rigidly mechanical. Precedents may be ignored in subsequent court decisions or—especially in the area of constitutional interpretation—they may be overruled by the Supreme Court. The doctrine of precedent, or *stare decisis* (Latin for "let the law stand"), has sometimes been compared with a coral reef. Both appear to be solid, permanent structures, but they do change, slowly, thereby offering continuity and predictability. Louis Brandeis, who served as a justice on the Supreme Court from 1916 to 1939, argued that the law is partly a matter of trial and error. Judges learn from their past mistakes and correct them. In such cases, he wrote, courts bow "to the lessons of experience and the force of better reasoning."[31] But precedents may also be jettisoned for more cynical reasons, such as a desire by judges to achieve a particular policy outcome in a case. After all, judges don't only discover the law; they also make it.

The members of the Supreme Court, as of the Fall 2019 term, were (left to right) Stephen Breyer, Neil Gorsuch, Clarence Thomas, Sonia Sotomayor, John Roberts, Elena Kagan, Ruth Bader Ginsberg, Brett Kavanaugh, and Samuel Alito.

**THE U.S. SUPREME COURT** The U.S. Supreme Court is the highest appellate court in the federal system. Its size is determined by Congress (another compromise at the Constitutional Convention). Originally set by the Judiciary Act of 1789 at six members, the Court fluctuated in size until after the Civil War, reaching a high of ten members in 1863 before being set at the current number of nine justices in 1869.[32] The nineteenth-century increases in size usually were intended to accommodate the increased caseload brought about by the addition of new states, especially since Supreme Court justices were then responsible for *circuit riding*—each justice was assigned a circuit in which he was required to hear cases (at that time, circuit courts did not have their own judges). Circuit riding was minimized by the creation of separate circuit court judges in the Judiciary Act of 1869 but not completely abolished until 1911.

The vast majority of the cases heard by the Supreme Court are appeals. Litigants can appeal a decision from the U.S. courts of appeals to the Supreme Court. Cases from the highest appellate court in a state can also be appealed to the Supreme Court as long as they involve a **federal question**—that is, a dispute over how to interpret the U.S. Constitution, federal law, or a federal treaty. Such cases would include, for example, appeals from criminal defendants convicted under state law who allege that their constitutional rights were violated by a coerced confession or the introduction of improperly obtained evidence.

## STATE COURT SYSTEMS

Most cases are not heard in federal court but in a state court system, where the vast majority of cases end. Since each state has its own distinct system of courts, a comprehensive overview is impossible. Some state court systems, such as New York's, are very complicated (see Figure 14.3), while others, such as Minnesota's, are much simpler (see Figure 14.4). Nonetheless, some generalizations about state courts can be made. Like federal courts, state courts are divided between trial courts and appellate courts, although the names of these courts differ from state to state.

In most states, trial courts, the point of entry into the state judicial system, are themselves subdivided. **Courts of limited jurisdiction** can hear only certain specialized types of cases. Divorce court, small claims court, and traffic court are all examples of courts of

**FIGURE 14.3**
## *State Court Structure of New York*

### Civil Court Structure

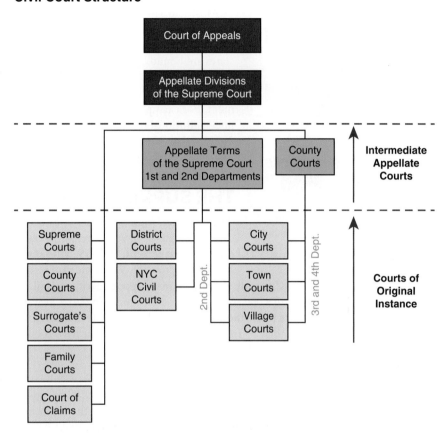

### Criminal Court Structure

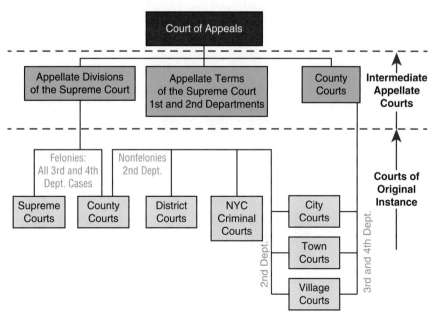

*Source: Office of Court Administration, New York State Unified Court System*

**FIGURE 14.4**

## State Court Structure of Minnesota

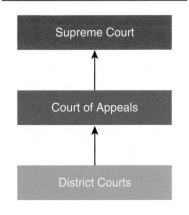

Source: From http://www.courtstatistics
.org/Other-Pages/State_Court_Structure_
Charts/Minnesota.aspx

---

**federal question** A dispute over how to interpret the U.S. Constitution, acts of Congress, or a federal treaty. Cases involving a federal question can move from state court to federal court.

---

limited jurisdiction. They hear cases that are less serious than those heard in courts of general jurisdiction. **Courts of general jurisdiction** have broad authority to hear a wide range of serious cases. These include civil suits involving large sums of money and criminal cases involving serious felonies. In contrast, most misdemeanors and minor civil disputes would be heard in courts of limited jurisdiction.

Most states have an intermediate level of appellate courts, which perform a function similar to the U.S. courts of appeals at the federal level. All states have an appellate court of last resort, which is usually called the state's "supreme court." Although states are bound by the Supremacy Clause to follow the U.S. Constitution, federal law, and federal treaties, it is possible—absent some explicit legal prohibition—for state constitutions and state courts to extend rights further than the federal government. For example, the Supreme Judicial Court of Massachusetts ruled that it was unconstitutional under the Massachusetts constitution to ban same-sex marriage in 2003, twelve years before the U.S. Supreme Court held that same-sex couples have a fundamental constitutional right to marry.[33]

## THE SUPREME COURT IN ACTION

The Supreme Court is obliged to hear those few cases that come before it under its original jurisdiction, which is spelled out in the Constitution and cannot be altered except by amendment. Since 1925, however, the Supreme Court, with rare exceptions, has had the power to decide which appeals it will accept, and today, it accepts very few. Currently, the U.S. courts of appeals decide roughly 50,000 cases each year, of which some 7,000 to 8,000 are appealed to the Supreme Court. On average, it accepts only about 80 for review.[34] As a result, the courts of appeals have the final word in over 99 percent of the cases that come before them.[35] To see the number of cases that have been decided by the Supreme Court from 1970 through 2015, see Figure 14.5.

## GETTING TO THE COURT

Since 1988, almost all appeals reach the Supreme Court by way of a **writ of certiorari**.[36] *Certiorari* is a Latin term that means "to make more certain." Litigants who petition the Court

**FIGURE 14.5**

## Number of Cases Decided by the U.S. Supreme Court, 1970–2015 Terms

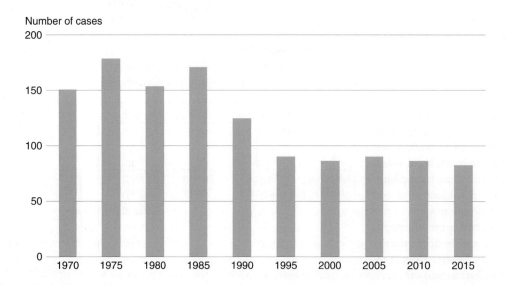

Source: "Federal Judicial Caseloads, 1789-2016," Federal Judicial Center, accessed August 12, 2019, https://www.fjc.gov/history/exhibits/graphs-and-maps/supreme-court-caseloads-1880-2015

for a writ of certiorari are asking it to review their case and make certain that it was decided correctly. Currently, it takes four of the nine justices on the Supreme Court to *grant cert*—that is, to accept the petition and agree to hear the case. This practice is known as the **rule of four**.

Law clerks—recent law school graduates who assist the individual justices—are responsible for the initial review of cert petitions. Currently, each justice can have up to four clerks. Almost all of the clerks have already held a similar position for a lower federal court judge.[37] One of the first tasks of the law clerks is to prepare "cert memos" for their justices, recommending whether cert should be granted in a case. Justices review these memos to help them decide how to vote. If the Supreme Court does not grant cert in a particular case, the lower court ruling is left undisturbed. The rejection of cert in a particular case is not an endorsement of the lower court ruling; it is simply a decision not to review that ruling.[38]

Cert is far more likely to be granted if the case is brought by the **solicitor general**, a senior member of the Justice Department, appointed by the president and confirmed by the Senate, who functions as the government's lawyer in cases before the Supreme Court. He or she plays an important role in setting the agenda for the courts of appeals and the Supreme Court by deciding which of the cases the government loses in lower federal courts will be appealed.[39]

The solicitor general also decides what position the government should take and argues the case before the Court. Such arguments stand a very good chance of being successful. Political scientist Kevin McGuire suggests that this high success rate is largely attributable to the solicitor general's extensive litigation experience before the Court.[40] Solicitors general and members of their staff argue far more cases before the Court than any other party (124 from 2013–2017; during that period, the most that any single private attorney argued was 15).[41] The solicitor general may also build up credit with the Court by minimizing the number of government appeals and thus helping the justices manage their caseload.

## HOW THE COURT DECIDES CASES

Once the Supreme Court grants cert, the case is added to the Court's **docket**, a list of cases that the Court will hear. Lawyers representing both sides of the case file written briefs with the Court containing detailed legal arguments. In addition, interest groups and other parties with a stake in the outcome of the case may, with the permission of the Court, file separate **amicus curiae briefs,** arguing in favor of a particular outcome. *Amicus briefs* are as close to lobbying the Court as interest groups get, and they are the most common type of interest group involvement in litigation.

After reviewing the written briefs, justices hear oral arguments. Early in our nation's history, there was no limit to how long oral arguments could last, and some went on for days. In 1848, the Court limited oral arguments in a single case to eight hours, with subsequent reductions in 1871 and 1911. Since 1925, each side has been allotted 30 minutes to argue its case, although more time is occasionally granted in exceptional cases.[42]

Justices frequently interrupt oral arguments with questions. Such questions are very important—not only as a way for the lawyers to respond to the justices, but as a way for the justices to communicate to each other which issues in the case they deem especially important. It is, after all, the first and only time that the justices gather as a group and concentrate on the single case before them until they meet at conference to vote. Oral arguments are the only public part of the Supreme Court's deliberation. Television cameras are not allowed, but oral arguments have been tape-recorded since 1955. In rare instances, such as *Bush v. Gore* in 2000, the Court released the audio immediately and allowed it to be broadcast. Since 2010, the Court has posted audio files of the oral arguments on its website (http://www.supremecourt.gov) the Friday of each week in

**Solicitor general is one of the many executive branch positions that must be confirmed by the Senate. Noel Francisco appeared before the Senate Judiciary Committee to testify before he was ultimately approved for the job.**

**courts of limited jurisdiction** Courts that hear a specialized type of case (such as traffic court).

**courts of general jurisdiction** Courts that have broad authority to hear a wide range of cases.

**writ of certiorari** An instruction to a lower court to send up the record in a particular case. This is the most common avenue for appeal to the U.S. Supreme Court.

**rule of four** The requirement that four of the nine justices on the Supreme Court vote to grant a writ of certiorari.

**solicitor general** A senior member of the Justice Department who is responsible for handling all appeals of cases in which the U.S. government is a party.

**docket** A list of cases that a court is scheduled to decide.

**amicus curiae briefs** "Friend of the court" briefs submitted by third parties who are not named in a case but who hope to influence the outcome of a particular case.

The Supreme Court does not allow video or still photography during oral arguments, so courtroom sketches are the only glimpse the public gets of the proceedings.

which arguments are heard. Transcripts are posted on the website the same day as the oral argument.

After oral arguments, the justices meet privately in their Friday **conference**, where they vote on how the case should be decided. The conference is highly structured. The justices usually come to it having already made up their minds about how to vote. The chief justice summarizes the case. Then each of the justices, starting with the chief and proceeding in order of seniority, announces his or her vote and summarizes the reasoning behind it. By the time the junior justices have their chance to speak, there is usually little left to say.[43] If the chief justice is in the majority, he chooses who will write the opinion. If he is not, the longest serving justice in the majority chooses. Any of the justices may write a separate dissenting or concurring opinion.

Law clerks often play an important role in drafting opinions. One law clerk estimated that "well over half of the text the Court now produces was generated by law clerks."[44] This has led some critics to argue that clerks have become too powerful, although others retort that clerks typically work under the close supervision of justices—writing what the justices want them to write—and that it is hard to imagine how justices could manage the workload without them.[45] Once written, all of the opinions are circulated among the justices, and revisions may ensue. Occasionally, justices will even change their vote. No opinion is considered final or binding until it is officially announced. As soon as the decision is announced in open court, the Supreme Court's public information office makes the full text of the opinions available to the public. They are posted online and also published by the government in volumes called *U.S. Reports*.

## THE ROLE OF JUDICIAL PHILOSOPHY IN DECISION MAKING

Scholars have identified three models to explain judicial decision making. The first, called the **legal model**, assumes that judges are impartial and that they simply apply the law by examining relevant legal texts. In other words, judging is a process of discovery. The emphasis is on a close reading of legal texts (sometimes called *strict construction*) and a strong reliance on precedent.

The second, called the **attitudinal model**, assumes that judges are policy makers and that they decide cases based on their personal policy preferences, or "attitudes." According to this approach, judging is a process of creation, with legal precedents being used to justify a particular outcome rather than to dictate that outcome. Thus, proponents of the attitudinal model use the ideology of individual judges, rather than an analysis of precedents and legal texts, to predict how they will vote.

The third, called the **strategic model**, also assumes that judges are policy makers but recognizes that judges operate under certain constraints. Blindly voting one's preference, as the attitudinal model predicts, may not make much sense if you are on the losing side. Instead, the strategic model assumes that judges are pragmatic, getting as close to their preferences as possible by building winning coalitions. This model explains why justices sometimes change their vote between the conference and the announcement of the court's decision.

Even if judges want to follow the legal model and discover the law, they face some major difficulties because the precise meaning of specific constitutional language and other legal texts is often elusive. The Fourth Amendment bans "unreasonable searches and seizures," but what exactly does that phrase mean? Judges disagree not only about what the word *unreasonable* means but also about what constitutes a *search* (for instance, is a wiretap a search? What about a DNA test?). The problem extends to many of the most important clauses of the Constitution. What exactly does *due process* mean? *Equal protection*? *Cruel and unusual punishment*? Even seemingly straightforward clauses, such as the First Amendment command that Congress shall make no law abridging freedom of speech, can lead to widely divergent interpretations because people can reasonably disagree about what constitutes *speech* (see Chapter 4). Hence, a judge's own value judgments and ideological predilections may influence how these questions are

**conference** A meeting of Supreme Court justices in which they discuss cases and vote on how those cases should be decided.

**legal model** A model of judicial decision making that assumes that judges will decide cases according to the law (as opposed to the attitudinal model).

**attitudinal model** A model of judicial decision making that assumes that judges will decide cases according to their ideological preferences (or attitudes).

**strategic model** A model of judicial decision making that assumes that judges are rational actors who will strategically try to get as close to their preferences as possible by building winning coalitions.

answered. To the extent that this happens, unelected judges expose themselves to charges that they are "legislating from the bench" and making policy. Concern about judicial policy making has led some to call for ways to limit the opportunity for judicial discretion.

## THE JURISPRUDENCE OF ORIGINAL INTENT

One suggestion for limiting judicial discretion is to try to minimize the ambiguity of constitutional language by determining the original intent of those who wrote it, but this approach is problematic. First, original intent may be impossible to discern. For one thing, the evidence may be lacking (notes from the Constitutional Convention are notoriously incomplete). For another, the Constitution was a jointly drafted document that required compromise. As a result, language was sometimes purposely ambiguous. Second, whose intent counts? Not only did members of the Constitutional Convention disagree, but so did those who voted on ratification of the Constitution. Third, even if the intent is clear, is it relevant for us today? Some argue that it is anachronistic to allow people who lived centuries before us in entirely different societal settings to dictate the current meaning of a phrase such as "cruel and unusual punishment." They argue that each generation must apply such language using contemporary standards. Nonetheless, proponents of the **jurisprudence of original intent** argue that the intent of the framers is as good as written into the Constitution if it can be determined.

## JUDICIAL RESTRAINT VERSUS JUDICIAL ACTIVISM

Some people suggest that another way to limit judicial discretion is for judges to minimize the opportunity for policy making by using self-restraint and employing judicial review very sparingly. According to this concept of **judicial restraint**, when a range of different interpretations are all plausible, judges should defer to the other branches and the will of the majority in choosing among the interpretations. To do otherwise would result in unelected judges substituting their policy preferences for the policy preferences of those who have been elected by the people.

Judges who use judicial restraint employ the *rational basis test* to assess laws whose constitutionality has been challenged. A judge who uses the rational basis test would start with the default position of deference to the other branches. For example, if an act of Congress is being challenged, the judge starts out with the assumption that it is constitutional. The burden of proof would then be on the party challenging the law to convince her otherwise. In other words, the judge must be convinced that the law lacks a rational basis—that it is arbitrary and unreasonable. This is difficult to do, so use of the rational basis test usually allows a law to stand.

Not everyone is content with so passive a use of judicial review. Those who favor a more aggressive use of judicial review—**judicial activism**—argue that whenever the Court reviews a case in which a law restricts a fundamental constitutional right, such as freedom of speech, the Court must subject the law to strict scrutiny. A judge who uses the *strict scrutiny test* starts with the assumption that any law that violates a fundamental right must initially be presumed to be unconstitutional. Therefore, the burden of proof shifts away from the party challenging the law to the government. In other words, the government must convince the Court that the law is, in fact, constitutional. To do this, the government must do more than merely show that there is a rational basis for the law. It must show that the government has a compelling interest that justifies restricting a fundamental right. The Court must also be convinced that the law is "narrowly tailored." When limiting speech, for example, strict scrutiny only allows government to restrict speech that poses a "clear and present danger." If a law is overbroad and limits other speech as well, the presumption of unconstitutionality would be maintained. Strict scrutiny is also triggered by laws that discriminate on the basis of race (see Chapter 5).

The problem, of course, is determining which constitutional rights are fundamental. Activists believe some constitutional rights are more important than others. These include, for example, freedom of speech and the press and religious freedoms. In contrast, restraintists insist that all constitutional rights should be treated equally.

Nothing compels a judge to use one test over another, so the decision of which test to use is his or her own choice. Decisions about these and other tests help to form a judge's "judicial philosophy"—an approach to how cases should be decided. But the choice of which test to use is often key

**jurisprudence of original intent** An approach to interpreting the Constitution that relies on the original intent of its framers to clarify the meaning of ambiguous clauses.

**judicial restraint** The idea that the Supreme Court should defer to the actions of other branches of government as long as they have a rational basis.

**judicial activism** The idea that the Supreme Court should strictly scrutinize actions of other branches of government that restrict fundamental rights, such as free speech.

to determining how a case will be resolved. That is why the judicial philosophy of a nominee for a federal judicial post, especially the Supreme Court, draws such close attention. Finally, it is essential to remember that the distinguishing characteristic that divides judicial activism from judicial restraint is the degree of deference to other parts of government and to the majoritarian process, *not ideology*. In certain time periods, ideology may be correlated with one or the other approach, but history clearly shows that such ideological links are not consistent over time.

# LIMITS ON THE SUPREME COURT

What recourse exists if the Supreme Court abuses its power of judicial review? The Constitution sanctions several limits on the Court's power. Beyond these is the potential for outright resistance to Court decisions through noncompliance.

## CONSTITUTIONAL CHECKS

The Constitution created several ways for Congress to limit the Supreme Court. These include constitutional amendments to overturn Court rulings, use of Congress's exceptions clause power to take away the Court's jurisdiction to hear certain types of appeals, impeachment of judges, and Congress's power to change the size of the Court (and thereby alter its composition).

Constitutional amendments are difficult to enact. Amendments have succeeded in overturning a Supreme Court decision only four times in U.S. history.[46] In 2012, President Obama called for a constitutional amendment to overturn the 2010 Supreme Court decision in *Citizens United v. Federal Elections Commission*, which held that the free speech clause of the First Amendment prohibits government from limiting corporate and union spending on electioneering communications.[47] In his 2010 State of the Union address, President Obama said, "With all due deference to separation of powers, last week the Supreme Court reversed a century of law that I believe will open the floodgates for special interests—including foreign corporations—to spend without limit in our elections."[48] Opposition to the ruling continues. In May 2019, Rep. Adam Schiff (D-CA) introduced a constitutional amendment to overturn *Citizens United*, saying, "Amending the Constitution is an extraordinary step, but it is the only way to safeguard our democratic process against the threat of unrestrained and anonymous spending by wealthy individuals and corporations."[49] If history is any indicator, the likelihood of its passage is slim.

Another potential check is the Constitution's exceptions clause, which gives Congress the power to exclude types of cases from the Supreme Court's constitutionally defined appellate jurisdiction. Use of this power to strip the Court of its ability to hear appeals in certain types of cases is extremely rare. It is also controversial because, if abused, it could possibly infringe on basic rights by closing off avenues of appeal. Since the exceptions clause contains no limit on the number of exceptions Congress can make, one can imagine a scenario in which so much appellate jurisdiction is withdrawn that the core function of the Supreme Court—its power to review actions of lower courts—is eviscerated. Would such an extreme use of the exceptions clause violate the separation of powers? Some legal scholars say yes. Luckily, we have never had to confront that issue. Most attempts to withdraw jurisdiction fail, but the Supreme Court did uphold the constitutionality of such withdrawals in an 1869 case in which Congress took away the Court's power to review habeas corpus appeals.[50]

Congress can also remove Supreme Court justices and other federal judges through impeachment, but impeachment is a difficult, time-consuming process that is seldom used. The only Supreme Court justice ever impeached by the House of Representatives (Samuel Chase in 1804) was acquitted by the Senate and remained on the bench. Only fourteen other federal judges have been impeached by the House in the entire history of the United States, and only seven have been removed after a Senate trial (four were acquitted and three resigned before the outcome of the trial).[51]

Finally, Congress can alter the size of the Supreme Court (thus providing the opportunity to pack it with a new majority of justices who could overturn earlier rulings). Congress has not changed the size of the Supreme Court since 1869. As we have seen, President Franklin

Roosevelt encouraged Congress to do so in 1937, but his suggestion was viewed as politically motivated and Congress did not comply.

Even though they are rarely carried out, the mere threat of these constitutional checks may be enough to influence the Court's decisions.

## NONCOMPLIANCE

It is also important to remember that the Supreme Court depends on other institutions to enforce its rulings. When the Court, in an opinion written by Chief Justice John Marshall, ruled that Cherokee Indians in Georgia had tribal sovereignty, President Andrew Jackson supposedly said, "John Marshall has made his decision; now let him enforce it."[52]

The Supreme Court hands down rulings, but the actual implementation of those rulings is left to others. The Court may rule, for example, that state-sponsored prayer in public schools violates the Constitution, but enforcement of that ruling depends upon the support of a wide array of players, including school administrators and teachers.

After Alabama Supreme Court Chief Justice Roy Moore installed a monument to the Ten Commandments in the courthouse, he was removed from office—and the monument was removed from the building.

Whether it be a public act of defiance—such as Roy Moore, the former Chief Justice of the Supreme Court of Alabama, defying an order by a federal court to remove a 5,280-pound granite monument to the Ten Commandments that he had installed in the rotunda of the state judicial building or Governor Orval Faubus of Arkansas standing in the schoolhouse door in Little Rock to block school desegregation ordered by the Supreme Court in *Brown v. Board of Education*—or a more subtle failure to implement some aspect of a judicial decision, noncompliance with Supreme Court rulings happens more often than one might think.[53] Noncompliance can be rectified (Moore was removed from office, and President Eisenhower called out the National Guard to enforce school desegregation), but not by the Supreme Court itself.

The Court's main source of power is its legitimacy. If it loses its legitimacy, compliance becomes much more difficult to achieve. As shown in Figure 14.6, the Supreme Court has maintained a relatively high level of public approval in recent years. A desire to maintain legitimacy is what motivates some to advocate judicial restraint and urge judges to defer to the will

**FIGURE 14.6**

## *Public Approval of the Supreme Court Compared With That of Congress*

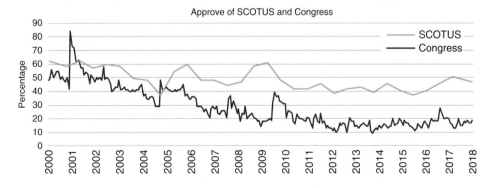

*How does public approval of the Supreme Court compare with public approval of Congress? Do you find it odd that approval is lower for an elected branch of government than it is for the unelected Court? What role might judicial independence play in the Court's approval ratings? Source: Data from Gallup.*

of the majority. And even though we sometimes focus on a few key cases in which the Supreme Court, rather than elected parts of government, spurred social change (such as *Brown v. Board of Education* and *Roe v. Wade*), the fact of the matter is that the Supreme Court seldom bucks public opinion for long. As political scientist Robert Dahl famously put it, "Except for short-lived transitional periods when the old alliance is disintegrating and the new one is struggling to take control of political institutions, the Supreme Court is inevitably a part of the dominant national alliance."[54] This is because the dominant national alliance ultimately chooses who sits on the Court.

# HOW JUDGES ARE SELECTED

The way judges are selected can have an important impact on just how independent judges really are. The framers designed the procedure for selecting federal judges to support judicial independence by preventing one part of government from dominating the selection process.

## THE SELECTION OF SUPREME COURT JUSTICES

Article II, Section 2 of the Constitution gives the president the power to nominate Supreme Court justices, but appointment comes only with the "advice and consent of the Senate." The Senate has the power to confirm or reject a president's nominee by a simple majority vote. The ability to filibuster a Supreme Court nominee—once an option available to senators—was eliminated by the Republican-controlled Senate in 2017. In 2013, Democrats had orchestrated a similar rule change regarding lower federal judicial nominees.

### CHOOSING SUPREME COURT NOMINEES
In contrast with its very specific requirements for presidents, senators, and representatives, the Constitution contains no specific requirements for Supreme Court justices—no minimum age requirement, no citizenship requirements, not even a requirement that justices be lawyers. While all Supreme Court justices have been lawyers, many were appointed without any prior experience as a judge. That lack of judicial experience did not seem to handicap justices such as John Marshall, Felix Frankfurter, Earl Warren, and William Rehnquist, none of whom had been a judge before serving on the Supreme Court. In stark contrast, many other nations, such as Japan and most European countries, have a cadre of professional judges. Similar to civil servants, they devote their careers to judging and are promoted through the judicial hierarchy.[55]

Lack of formal constitutional or statutory requirements does not mean that unofficial standards are not in place for screening prospective nominees. Since 1853, the Justice Department has identified and recommended potential nominees. Today, the Office of White House Counsel, created as part of the president's personal staff during the administration of Harry S. Truman (1946–1953), also plays an important role in the vetting process, and the Federal Bureau of Investigation (FBI) conducts background checks of all potential nominees.

In addition to the vetting process that goes on within the government, the ABA reviews the professional qualifications of all federal judicial nominees, including Supreme Court nominees, and rates each one. The ABA began this practice in 1946; in 1953, President Dwight D. Eisenhower established a formal relationship with the ABA, agreeing that the president would not nominate anyone without an ABA rating. At the time, the ABA was a conservative organization, but over the years, it has become more liberal. Conservatives have alleged that ABA ratings reflect the ideology of the nominee. At least one scholarly study reinforces this allegation.[56] This concern led George W. Bush to sever the White House relationship with the ABA in 2001. Barack Obama briefly reestablished it in 2009 before Trump again severed it. Under Trump, the ABA has only rated nominees after their names were publicly announced.[57]

High professional standards are a fundamental criterion for selecting Supreme Court nominees. That is not, however, the only criterion. Presidents take into account at least two other factors: representational and doctrinal considerations.

*Representational considerations* include the partisan affiliation of nominees, the geographic regions that they come from, and other factors such as their race, gender, religion, and ethnicity.

With rare exceptions, presidents appoint justices who share their political affiliation. Circuit riding made geographic representation a necessity in the early part of our history, but presidents still make an effort to have geographic diversity on the Court. Sometimes this is done for political reasons. Both Herbert Hoover and Richard Nixon nominated southerners to the Court as part of an effort to build electoral support in the South for their respective reelection bids.

For much of our history, the Court, like the nation's other political institutions, was overwhelmingly white, male, and Protestant. Lyndon Johnson appointed the first African American justice (Thurgood Marshall) to the Supreme Court in 1967, and Ronald Reagan appointed the first woman (Sandra Day O'Connor) in 1981. A "Catholic seat" on the Court existed by tradition starting in 1836, as did a "Jewish seat" since 1916 (except for 1969 to 1993). With George W. Bush's appointments of John G. Roberts, Jr., and Samuel A. Alito, Jr., in 2006, Catholics made up a majority of the Supreme Court for the first time, and with Barack Obama's appointments of Sonia Sotomayor and Elena Kagan, six Catholics and three Jews sat on the Court. It was the first time in history that no Protestants sat on the Court. Ethnic considerations are also a factor. Both Bill Clinton and George W. Bush seriously considered appointing a Hispanic justice to the Court, but the distinction went to Obama with his appointment of Sotomayor in 2009. In the U.S., we have never had more than three female justices serving on the Supreme Court at one time (one-third of the bench), but by 2016, women made up more than half of the constitutional court of last resort in Latvia and Slovenia, and Ghana and Portugal were close (both 46 percent female).[58]

President Obama's appointment of Sonia Sotomayor to the Court in 2009 put a Hispanic justice on the bench for the first time. What difference do you think it makes to have a diverse Court?

*Doctrinal considerations* center on a nominee's judicial philosophy and approach to public policy issues, with presidents seeking to choose individuals whose views are similar to their own. In theory, impartial judges who objectively apply the Constitution and other legal texts according to established standards of interpretation should all reach the same "correct" decision in cases that come before them. But, in practice, judges hold very different views about how to interpret such texts. After all, judges are human beings who are influenced, at least in part, by their backgrounds, political and religious beliefs, and personal predilections. Quite simply, different justices will often reach different conclusions when confronted with the same case. Thus, Donald Trump, similar to George W. Bush before him, relied on the conservative Federalist Society to help vet nominees.[59]

Doctrinal considerations are important because they can have an impact on how the Supreme Court will rule on important matters of public policy. Since federal judges have life tenure, presidents make appointments knowing that their choices can affect the outcome of cases for years to come. Presidents can never guarantee how their appointees will end up voting once they are on the bench, and the degree to which presidents now screen nominees for ideological purity varies from one administration to another. Still, doctrinal considerations continue to be an important factor in selecting judicial nominees.

**CONFIRMING SUPREME COURT NOMINEES**  Once nominated by the president, a candidate to the Supreme Court must be confirmed by the Senate. With senators no longer able to filibuster Supreme Court nominations, this now merely requires a simple majority vote. Some other countries, including Argentina, Latvia, and South Korea, have a system similar to ours in which the legislature confirms judicial nominees submitted by the executive. But in most countries, judges are appointed without legislative confirmation by some part of the executive branch, be it the monarch (as in Belgium, though from a list provided by Parliament), the president (as in India and Sri Lanka), or the prime minister (as in Canada, where the prime minister acts on the advice of the governor general).[60] Some other countries share the responsibility of appointing judges. For example, the Italian Supreme Constitutional Court consists of 15 judges. Five are appointed by the president, five are appointed by a joint session of the parliament, and five are chosen by judges from three Italian courts; none, however, are subject to a confirmation vote.[61]

Before the full U.S. Senate debates and votes on a nominee, the Senate Judiciary Committee holds hearings. Until the twentieth century, the deliberation of the Judiciary Committee was usually a very secretive process. Its hearings took place behind closed doors, as did Senate floor debate on judicial nominees, and there was often only a voice vote—not even a formal roll-call vote in which senators go on record as to how they voted. Nominees did not testify at the committee hearings, nor did they talk to the press. Presidents also remained publicly silent about their nominees.

The process changed over the course of the twentieth century. The ratification of the Seventeenth Amendment to the Constitution in 1913 led to the direct election of senators (thereby allowing the voting public to hold senators accountable for their votes), and Senate rule changes in 1929 opened floor debate on a regular basis (allowing interest groups and the public to see where senators stood). Shortly thereafter, the Senate Judiciary Committee opened its hearings to the public. Representatives of organized interest groups first testified at a Supreme Court confirmation hearing in 1930 and have testified at every confirmation hearing since 1971. Nominees have routinely testified at their confirmation hearings since 1955. Judiciary Committee hearings have been televised since 1981, and beginning with Ronald Reagan, presidents have customarily offered public support for their nominees during the confirmation process.[62]

Ronald Reagan's unsuccessful nomination of Robert Bork to the Supreme Court in 1987 is sometimes viewed as a watershed event in the modern Supreme Court confirmation process.[63] The Senate ultimately rejected Bork—not because of any lack of qualifications or because of unethical behavior, but simply because of how he would likely vote as a member of the Court. If confirmed, Bork would have become the decisive fifth vote necessary to overturn a variety of precedents, including *Roe v. Wade*, the landmark 1973 abortion rights case.

Interest groups mobilized in an unprecedented manner against the Bork nomination. They moved beyond simply testifying at confirmation hearings and mobilizing their own base to a full-fledged public relations offensive, including television, radio, and print ads; mass mailings; and the use of telephone banks to target the wider public. The Senate ended up rejecting Bork. Fifty-eight senators, including six Republicans, voted against confirmation.

The defeat of Bork's nomination was the culmination of a series of factors that came together to create an epic battle. It generated a new verb: to *bork*, which means to defeat a nominee by unleashing a lobbying and public relations campaign. It also hardened battle lines for future confirmations and helped to usher in what some have described as a "confirmation mess." But Bork was by no means the first Supreme Court nominee to be defeated nor was he even the first nominee to be "borked" (John Rutledge, nominated by George Washington in 1795, holds both of those distinctions).[64]

In fact, the failure rate of Supreme Court nominees is the highest for any appointive post requiring Senate confirmation.[65] If we exclude consecutive nominations of the same individual by the same president for the same seat on the Court, which has sometimes happened for technical reasons,

Donald Trump appeared with his Supreme Court nominee Brett Kavanaugh—and Kavanaugh's family—to announce his nomination to the public. They appeared together again after he was confirmed by the Senate.

Despite widespread protests against the nomination of Brett Kavanaugh to the Court, which exploded after Dr. Christine Blasey Ford alleged he had attempted to rape her as a teen, Kavanaugh was confirmed with the support of only one Democrat.

and Reagan's 1987 nomination of Douglas Ginsburg, which was announced but never formally submitted to the Senate, presidents submitted 154 Supreme Court nominations to the Senate as of May 2019. Out of these, seven individuals declined after being nominated, one died before taking office, one expected vacancy failed to materialize, and another for an associate justice seat was withdrawn before Senate action and resubmitted to fill the newly vacated chief justice seat. Of the remaining 144 nominations, 118 were confirmed by the Senate. The other 26 may be classified as "failed" nominations because Senate opposition blocked them.

The large number of failed Supreme Court nominees in recent years is partly a reflection of *divided government*, the situation in which different political parties control the White House and the Senate. The statistics regarding Supreme Court nominees are striking: Confirmation rates are close to 90 percent when the same party controls the White House and the Senate but are only about 55 percent when different parties are in control. From 1969 through 2019, the same party controlled the White House and the Senate for only 25 out of 51 years. In contrast, the same party controlled the White House and the Senate for 58 out of 68 years from 1901 through 1968.

Further compounding the problem was an increase in partisanship since 1969. With conservative southern Democrats being replaced by Republicans, and liberal Republicans being replaced by Democrats, the ideological gap between the parties widened. The result was a dramatic increase in partisan voting, even on Supreme Court nominees. In a particularly audacious move, the Republican-controlled Senate refused to even consider President Obama's March 16, 2016, nomination of Merrick Garland to fill the vacancy left by the unexpected death of Justice Antonin Scalia. The nomination expired at the end of the 114th Congress, on January 3, 2017, after languishing for 293 days. Donald Trump took office on January 20, 2017, and promptly nominated Neil Gorsuch to fill the vacancy; the Senate confirmed him 66 days later. Blocking the moderate Garland—a strictly partisan maneuver—allowed Trump to shift the Court in a decidedly more conservative direction.

The increase in partisanship is starkly illustrated in confirmation votes. With rare exceptions, Supreme Court nominees used to be confirmed by bipartisan majorities. For example, Antonin Scalia was confirmed by a vote of 98–0 in 1986 and Anthony Kennedy was confirmed by a vote of 97–0 in 1988. In contrast, George W. Bush's nominees, John Roberts and Samuel Alito, were confirmed by votes of 78–22 and 58–42 in 2005 and 2006; Obama's nominees, Sonia Sotomayor and Elena Kagan, were confirmed by votes of 68–31 and 63–37 in 2009 and 2010; and Trump's nominees, Neil Gorsuch and Brett Kavanaugh, were confirmed by votes of 54–45 and 50–48 in 2017 and 2019. Neither Gorsuch nor Kavanaugh would have likely been confirmed had the Republican Senate not eliminated the filibuster for Supreme Court nominees (ending a filibuster requires a three-fifths vote of the entire Senate: 60 votes).

The selection process for lower federal court judges, to which we now turn, is similar to that for Supreme Court justices. Not surprisingly, divided government and polarized politics have contributed to contentious confirmation battles for lower federal judicial nominees as well.

## THE SELECTION OF LOWER FEDERAL COURT JUDGES

Supreme Court appointments usually get more attention, but lower federal court appointments are also important, since over 99 percent of all federal cases end there. Indeed, the power to appoint the more than 800 judges who make up the lower federal judiciary is arguably one of the most important powers of the president. During his eight years in office, Barack Obama appointed 268 judges to the U.S. district courts and 48 judges to the U.S. courts of appeals (for a comparison with other presidents, see Table 14.1). By the end of his second year in office, Donald Trump had already appointed 53 judges to the U.S. district courts and 30 judges to the U.S. courts of appeals (more appeals court nominees than any president by that point in their term).[66] These lower federal court judges with life tenure have the power to affect the outcome of cases for years to come.

Many of the vacancies that Trump filled were the result of Republican obstruction. In addition to refusing to consider President Obama's nomination of Merrick Garland to fill a Supreme Court seat, Republicans confirmed only 18 of Obama's 62 district court nominees during

## TABLE 14.1

## Appointments to the U.S. District Courts and Courts of Appeals, by President

| President | Total Appointments | Male | Female | White | African American | Hispanic | Asian | Native American |
|---|---|---|---|---|---|---|---|---|
| Nixon (1969–1974) | 224 | 223 (99.6%) | 1 (0.4%) | 215 (96.0%) | 6 (2.6%) | 2 (0.9%) | 1 (0.4%) | 0 |
| Ford (1974–1977) | 64 | 63 (98.4%) | 1 (1.6%) | 58 (90.6%) | 3 (4.7%) | 1 (1.6%) | 2 (3.1%) | 0 |
| Carter (1977–1981) | 258 | 218 (84.5%) | 40 (15.5%) | 202 (78.3%) | 37 (14.3%) | 16 (6.2%) | 2 (0.8%) | 1 (0.4%) |
| Reagan (1981–1989) | 368 | 340 (92.4%) | 28 (7.6%) | 344 (93.5%) | 7 (1.9%) | 15 (4.1%) | 2 (0.5%) | 0 |
| George H. W. Bush (1989–1993) | 185 | 148 (80.0%) | 37 (20.0%) | 165 (89.2%) | 12 (6.5%) | 8 (4.3%) | 0 | 0 |
| Clinton (1993–2001) | 366 | 259 (70.8%) | 107 (29.2%) | 274 (74.9%) | 61 (16.7%) | 25 (6.8%) | 5 (1.4%) | 1 (0.3%) |
| George W. Bush (2001–2009) | 320 | 251 (78.4%) | 69 (21.6%) | 263 (82.2%) | 24 (7.5%) | 30 (9.4%) | 4 (1.3%) | 0 |
| Obama (2009–2017) | 316 | 184 (58.2%) | 132 (41.8%) | 202 (63.9%) | 60 (19%) | 34 (10.8%) | 19 (6.0%) | 1 (0.3%) |
| Trump (2017–2018) | 83 | 63 (75.9%) | 20 (24.1%) | 76 (91.6%) | 1 (1.2%) | 1 (1.2%) | 5 (6%) | 0 |

*Source: Drawn from Tables 2 and 4 in Sheldon Goldman, Elliot Slotnick, Gerard Gryski, and Sara Schiavoni, "Picking Judges in a Time of Turmoil: W. Bush's Judiciary During the 109th Congress," Judicature 90 (May–June 2007): 272, 282; and (for Ford and Nixon) from Table 6.1 in Sheldon Goldman, Picking Federal Judges: Lower Court Selection From Roosevelt Through Reagan (New Haven, CT: Yale University Press, 1997), 227–229. Figures for George W. Bush and Obama are drawn from Tables 6 and 7 of Elliot Slotnick, Sara Schiavoni, and Sheldon Goldman, "Obama's Judicial Legacy: The Final Chapter," Journal of Law and Courts (Fall 2017): 394–395, 400–401. Figures for Trump are drawn from "Judicial Nomination Statistics and Analysis: U.S. District and Circuit Courts, 1977–2018," Congressional Research Service, March 21, 2019, https://fas.org/sgp/crs/misc/R45622.pdf; and the list of Trump's judicial nominees at https://en.wikipedia.org/wiki/List_of_federal_judges_appointed_by_Donald_Trump*

Obama's last two years in office and only one of Obama's eight court of appeals court nominees—the lowest confirmation rate of the modern presidency.[67] The Senate refused to even consider 52 of Obama's nominations. Compare this with the final two years of other two-term presidents: The Senate confirmed 67 district court and 17 court of appeals judges nominated by Ronald Reagan, 58 district court and 15 court of appeals judges nominated by Bill Clinton, and 58 district court and 10 court of appeals judges nominated by George W. Bush. Thus, Trump entered office with the opportunity to fill a backlog of vacancies in addition to those that would arise during his tenure.

**SENATORIAL COURTESY VERSUS PRESIDENTIAL PREROGATIVE** Lower federal court appointments follow the same basic process as Supreme Court appointments: The president nominates and the Senate, after Judiciary Committee hearings, either confirms or rejects by majority vote. Historically, though, presidents have had less control over the selection of lower federal court judges than they do over the selection of Supreme Court justices because of **senatorial courtesy**, an informal rule that has existed since the presidency of George Washington. Traditionally, the Senate refused to confirm district court and court of appeals nominees who did not have the support of the senators from the state where the vacancy occurred.

Given the threat of senatorial courtesy, presidents traditionally turned to home-state senators for advice about whom to nominate. Senators began to treat lower court appointments as a form of patronage, even though the president technically made the nomination. In 1977,

**senatorial courtesy** An informal rule that senators will refuse to confirm nominees to the lower federal courts who do not have the support of the senators from the state where the vacancy occurs.

President Jimmy Carter tried to reform the system. He argued that judges should be selected based on merit. Therefore, he issued an executive order that created a Circuit Court Nominating Commission for each circuit to develop a short list of nominees for the courts of appeals based on merit. The president would then nominate someone from that list.[68] Carter also urged (but did not require) senators to create their own statewide nominating commissions to develop similar lists for district court vacancies. By 1979, senators from 31 states had complied with that request.[69]

When Ronald Reagan came to office in 1981, however, he abolished Carter's commission system. With Carter having wrested control of the initial screening process from home-state senators, Reagan was more readily able to centralize control of the process in the White House and to use that process to screen for ideology.[70] But while their power to tell the president whom to nominate was significantly diminished, home-state senators could still invoke senatorial courtesy to block nominees to both district courts and the courts of appeal. That power led to obstruction from both political parties. In 2019, Sen. Lindsey Graham (R-SC), the chair of the Senate Judiciary Committee, said that the so-called blue slip procedure (the mechanism used to enforce senatorial courtesy) would henceforth be honored only for district court nominees, not the more powerful court of appeals nominees.[71] Thus, the Senate confirmed Eric Miller by a vote of 53–46 to fill a seat on the 9th Circuit Court of Appeals without the support of either home-state senator on February 26, 2019. Senator Dianne Feinstein (D-CA), the ranking Democrat on the Judiciary Committee, issued an angry statement saying that before Miller, no nominee had been confirmed without the support of at least one home-state senator.[72]

**DIVERSIFYING THE BENCH**  The idea that federal courts should reflect the diversity of society at large is a recent one. For many years, courts and the legal profession remained the province of white males. Table 14.2 illustrates the early history of diversifying the bench. The first president to make a concerted effort to appoint women and minorities to the federal judiciary was Jimmy Carter (see Table 14.1). The task was not easy, as these groups were still vastly underrepresented in the legal profession. In fact, segregation had made legal training largely unavailable to African Americans until the 1950s. As late as 1970, African American, Hispanic, Native American, and Asian American lawyers combined made up only 2 percent of all lawyers in the United States, and women made up only 3 percent.[73]

During his four years as president (1977–1981), Carter appointed more women, African Americans, and Hispanics than had all of his predecessors combined. In his 258 appointments to the district courts and courts of appeals, Carter named 40 women, 37 African Americans, and 16 Hispanics as well as two Asian Americans and one Native American (see Table 14.1). Presidents from Franklin Roosevelt through Gerald Ford (1933–1977) combined appointed only 8 women, 22 African Americans, and 8 Hispanics to the district courts and courts of appeals.[74]

Republican presidents in the years following Carter (Reagan, George H. W. Bush, George W. Bush, and Trump) placed less emphasis on diversifying the bench. In contrast, Bill Clinton (1993–2001) appointed higher percentages of women and minorities than had Carter as well as far greater numbers because of his longer time in office (eight years rather than four). Diversity was also a major emphasis for President Obama, but 98.1 percent of Trump's appointments during his first two years were white, and 77.6 percent were male. Diversity is also becoming an issue in other countries. By 2018, only 29 percent of all court judges in England and Wales were women, and only 7 percent were Black, Asian, or another minority ethnicity.[75] There, a Judicial Diversity Committee of the Judges' Council has been created to encourage greater diversity on the bench.[76]

In 1981, Ronald Reagan appointed Sandra Day O'Connor to be the first female justice on the Supreme Court. She served alongside Thurgood Marshall, the first African American justice, until his retirement in 1991. The other seven members of the Court were all white men.

TABLE 14.2

# Diversifying the Bench—Significant Appointments

| President | Year | Appointment |
|-----------|------|-------------|
| Rutherford Hayes | 1873 | John A. Moss, an African American, appointed as a justice of the peace in the District of Columbia |
| Herbert Hoover | 1928 | Genevieve Cline, first woman appointed to a federal court (the U.S. Customs Court—now the U.S. Court of International Trade) |
| Franklin Roosevelt | 1934 | Florence Allen, first woman appointed to the U.S. Court of Appeals |
| Harry Truman | 1945 | Irvin C. Mollison, an African American, appointed to the U.S. Customs Court |
| Harry Truman | 1949 | Burnita Matthews, first woman appointed to a U.S. District Court |
| Harry Truman | 1950 | William H. Hastie, first African American appointed to the U.S. Court of Appeals |
| John F. Kennedy | 1961 | James B. Parsons, first African American appointed to a U.S. District Court |
| Lyndon Johnson | 1967 | Thurgood Marshall, first African American appointed to the Supreme Court |
| Ronald Reagan | 1981 | Sandra Day O'Connor, first woman appointed to the Supreme Court |

## JUDICIAL SELECTION IN THE STATES

The manner in which state court judges are selected varies not only from state to state but also within states according to the type of court, as do the requirements for becoming a judge. Nonetheless, a few generalizations can be made. Basically, there are five methods for choosing state court judges: (1) appointment by the governor, (2) election by the legislature, (3) partisan election, (4) nonpartisan election, and (5) the "merit plan" (sometimes referred to as the "Missouri Plan" after the state that first used it). State court judges usually serve a fixed term of office rather than having life tenure as federal judges do.[77]

The two oldest methods of judicial selection in the states are appointment by the governor and election by the legislature. All of the original 13 states selected judges by one of these two methods, but as of 2019, only seven of the 50 states use gubernatorial appointment for at least some of its judges (subject to approval by either the state senate or a governor's council, depending upon the state),[78] and only two still use legislative election for at least some of their judges.[79] Over the years, appointment was replaced by other methods as a result of several waves of reforms.

First, a wave of reform spurred by Jacksonian Democracy in the early 1800s led to the rise of partisan elections for judges. By the time of the Civil War, 24 of the 36 states had embraced the *partisan election* of judges, as did every new state until 1912.[80] As a result, judges became more accountable to the public but also less independent. Another wave of reform in the early twentieth century led to a push for the *nonpartisan election* of judges, in which judicial candidates ran without their party affiliation being listed next to their name. Reformers believed this would make judges more removed from political pressure.

The most recent wave of reform, starting in Missouri in 1940, resulted in judicial selection based on the *merit plan*. This method was designed to simultaneously minimize the role of politics in judicial selection, increase the emphasis on qualifications, and provide for accountability of judges. Under the merit plan, a commission is assigned the task of screening potential judges and providing a short list of names of the most qualified individuals. The governor then appoints one of those on the short list to serve a fixed term, after which the judge goes before the electorate in an uncontested retention election in which the voters decide whether the judge will stay in office. If the judge is voted out, the process starts all over again. The merit plan is currently the most popular form of judicial selection, with 34 states using it in some form.[81]

The only exception in our judicial system to the unwritten rule that judges be lawyers occurs at the lowest rung of some state court systems in certain types of courts of limited jurisdiction. These *lay judges* are often justices of the peace who preside over very minor types of civil and criminal cases. Such a post is usually not a full-time job nor is the salary very good. Lay judges often serve in rural areas where they are elected, and they seldom hear cases in formal court-rooms. They are trusted in their communities, though, and fill an important function in areas where it would be very expensive to maintain formal courthouses staffed by lawyer judges.[82] A quite accurate portrayal of a lay judge is provided by the character Andy Taylor on television's classic *Andy Griffith Show*. Wise and trusted, if not especially well educated, Sheriff Taylor turned his office in the Mayberry jail into a courtroom merely by turning the nameplate on his desk from "Sheriff" to "Justice of the Peace."

## CONSEQUENCES FOR DEMOCRACY

Although we have a rather complicated dual court system with overlapping jurisdiction in many areas of the law, our entire governmental system is based on the rule of law, and our system fosters judicial independence so that courts can issue decisions without fear of retribution. All of this is essential to our system of checks and balances. Judicial independence and adherence to the rule of law facilitate judicial review. This allows the Supreme Court and other parts of the American court system to protect civil rights and civil liberties, enforce federalism, and ensure that Congress and the president are not overstepping their constitutional bounds.

Unlike many other countries, we have a dual court system comprised of both state and federal courts. As we have seen, the precise structure of state courts varies from state to state, as do basic state laws. What is legal in one state (the use of medical marijuana, for example) is not necessarily legal in another, and some laws (such as those involving the sale of alcohol on Sundays) may vary from county to county within a state. Even judges are selected differently from state to state. This deference to local norms reflects the principle of local control of justice. So does the fact that not only state court judges, but also federal district court judges, are residents of the state in which the court operates. Such local control of justice helps to legitimize the authority of courts.

But the operation of a dual court system raises some of the same basic questions we faced in Chapter 3 about federalism: How should one balance local control of justice with federal oversight? As it stands, regional differences are reflected in our dual court system, with the assurance that—at least when there is a federal question involved—there is an opportunity for review by the U.S. Supreme Court. And, as we saw in Chapter 4, the opportunity for such review increased with the Supreme Court's incorporation of the Bill of Rights. How that balance is struck also has consequences.

Judges at all levels influence policy. Since the stakes are so high, it is important for you to be informed. In many states, you have the power to vote in judicial elections. Even at the federal level, where judges are nominated by the president and confirmed by the Senate, you can exercise at least some degree of power by lobbying your senator and exercising your right to vote. After all, judicial decisions help to determine how we live, how we work, how we vote, who we can marry, and even how we die.

## *Critical Thinking Questions*

1. Would the United States be better or worse off with a single-court system, as exists in Canada? How would it change the U.S. justice system? Why do you think such a system is not in place?

2. Would it be possible to enforce the rule of law without courts having the power of judicial review? Why or why not?

3. How concerned should we be about judicial independence in the United States? What are the greatest threats to that independence?

## Key Terms

adversarial system, 361

amicus curiae briefs, 367

appellate court, 360

attitudinal model, 368

briefs, 363

concurring opinion, 363

conference, 368

courts of general jurisdiction, 366

courts of limited jurisdiction, 365

dissenting opinion, 363

docket, 367

dual court system, 360

federal question, 365

inquisitorial system, 361

judicial activism, 369

judicial restraint, 369

judicial review, 355

jurisprudence of original intent, 369

legal model, 368

majority opinion, 363

*Marbury v. Madison*, 356

oral arguments, 363

original jurisdiction, 357

precedent, 363

rule of four, 367

senatorial courtesy, 376

solicitor general, 367

strategic model, 368

trial courts, 360

U.S. courts of appeals, 363

U.S. district courts, 363

writ of certiorari, 366

Visit edge.sagepub.com/maltese to help you accomplish your coursework goals in an easy-to-use learning environment.

# 15
# DOMESTIC AND ECONOMIC POLICY

## *After reading this chapter, you should be able to do the following:*

- Summarize the stages of making public policy and the impact of history and economic systems on that process.
- Understand the century-long debate surrounding the U.S. health care system and the current efforts to expand coverage.
- Explain how policy makers weigh benefits and revenues in making decisions about the long-term financial viability of Social Security.
- Compare and contrast U.S. policy goals of energy security and environmental protection.
- Analyze how the government influences U.S. economic policy and discuss the potential conflicts and concerns that can result.

## *Perspective: What Can the United States Learn From Canada's Legalization of Recreational Marijuana?*

Canada adopted a policy in 2018 that made the sale and consumption of marijuana legal across the nation.[1] The federal law establishes an overarching framework, and Canada's thirteen provinces and territories regulate the specific terms under which marijuana can be purchased and consumed. For example, at the outset, Ontario residents could only make purchases online through a government-run store (sales by private stores were planned for the future), whereas in Saskatchewan, more than fifty licensed retail stores could sell marijuana. In Quebec, British Columbia, Ontario, and Alberta, residents can smoke marijuana wherever tobacco can be used (though not in parks or on public beaches in British Columbia), and in Halifax, Nova Scotia, there are designated smoking zones (The New York Times dubbed them "toking zones").[2] But if you travel north, be aware—in the Yukon Territory, marijuana can only be used in private residences. Two provinces set the legal age at 18 and all the others set the legal age at 19.[3]

Canada's federal law permits but does not establish a right to use marijuana. Thus, employers can ban it from the workplace, apartment owners from their rental properties, and bars or restaurants from their customers. The federal government licenses and regulates growers, though individuals can grow up to four plants. THC, the active ingredient that provides a "high," must be at a lower concentration than what has been available illegally. Edible products were not immediately allowed but were planned for the future. Recreational users may not possess more than 30 grams without running afoul of the law. There is a stiff penalty of up to 14 years in prison for supplying anyone younger than 18. "Growing, importing, exporting or selling marijuana outside licensed channels will remain serious crimes."[4]

A national task force designed the law and explained that in drafting the statute, the nation was drawing on its experience in regulating the use of alcohol, tobacco, and medical marijuana. In fact, medical marijuana became legal throughout the nation in 1999, and the program expanded in 2001 after a federal court ordered broader access. Two of the government's main goals were to severely reduce illegal marijuana sales and to keep marijuana out of the hands of children and youth. The task force went to great lengths to emphasize ways to *discourage* rather than *encourage* marijuana's use (for example, sales must not be in the same location as cigarettes or alcohol), to carefully monitor the medical evidence about personal impairment and potential negative effects of usage, to aggressively prevent marketing to children, and to accommodate the nation's federal structure.[5]

What lessons might this experience hold for the United States? By the beginning of 2019, nine states had forged ahead, without a national framework, to legalize recreational use of marijuana: Alaska, California, Colorado, Maine, Massachusetts, Nevada, Oregon, Washington, Vermont, and Washington, DC. Even more states have legalized medicinal use of marijuana and decriminalized recreational use of small amounts. The next logical step would be to remove marijuana from the federal government's list of controlled substances and decriminalize it nationally. It seems that in the case of marijuana, policy is following public behavior: The National Academy of Medicine's exhaustive review of research on cannabis released in January 2017 noted that 22.2 million Americans age 12 and up reported using cannabis in the previous 30 days, and other surveys found that as many as 55 million persons had used it once or twice in the past year.[6] And while 31 percent of the American public supported legalization in 2000, support had risen to 62 percent in 2018.[7]

Canadians believe they know enough about the drug to put it into the same category as alcohol and tobacco—that is, substances whose use is allowed but discouraged. In the U.S., policies restrict the legal consumption of alcohol by anyone younger than 21, and sales are restricted in most states to licensed outlets. Tobacco products are more readily available but, again, are not to be sold to minors, and their use has been aggressively restricted in most states and cities to designated nonpublic areas. Alcohol and cigarettes are legal, even though we know much more about their negative health effects (impacts on mood, behavior, heart and liver for alcohol, lung cancer for smoking) than we do about cannabis and its active ingredient, TCH.

The National Academy report provided some strong cautions. Research on the health effects of marijuana use has been limited by its status as an illegal drug. There are indications that usage can have beneficial effects for those undergoing treatment of cancer (reductions in nausea and vomiting) but because it affects memory and attention, marijuana impairs driving and increases the likelihood of auto accidents. Use may also be associated with the onset of schizophrenia and other psychoses as well as the worsening of conditions for those suffering from bipolar disorder. There is moderate evidence that marijuana is an entry-level drug that makes users more susceptible to developing addictions to other, more serious drugs. (This has been one of the most common arguments against legalization in recent decades.) Part of the unknown about health effects arises from the new strands of marijuana that have been developed over time—far more potent than what your grandparents may have used in the 1960s. Researchers need to study how much of what types it is safe to consume over what periods of time.[8]

Canada's experiment—it has joined Uruguay as the two nations to legalize recreational use of marijuana[9]—provides the opportunity to answer many of the outstanding questions about both the public health effects of legalization and the political process one might follow to have a reasoned national debate. Peru, Spain, and South Africa have also moved in this direction, suggesting that the legalization of pot may be inevitable in the twenty-first century.[10] When, whether, and how that happens are big questions for U.S. policy makers. **«**

# MAKING PUBLIC POLICY

**Public policies** are government actions or inactions that affect the lives of citizens. Federal, state, and local governments provide services both explicitly and often implicitly called for in their constitutions and charters. Examples include providing "for the common defense," protecting the lives and property of law-abiding citizens, combatting the spread of diseases, allocating scarce natural and economic resources, and responding to citizens' many, many needs and demands for help in education, health, and business. In making their decisions, government officials in both elected and unelected positions respond to a variety of influences including elections, lobbying, and discussions in the media. All of this occurs within the context of historical and economic experiences that help shape decisions.

## AN IDEALIZED MODEL OF POLICY MAKING

How do officials create public policies? Students of American politics employ a model of policy making that includes four important stages: agenda setting, policy formulation, policy adoption, and policy implementation.

**AGENDA SETTING** Government officials engage in agenda setting when they identify the areas of public life that require action. Although officials make the final determination, many others help identify problems and propose alternatives about what to do.

During electoral campaigns, most candidates identify problems, propose possible solutions, and evaluate the progress made in addressing the problem since the last election. The media identify problems for action, as do interest groups. Farmers, business, and organized labor secured footholds in the federal government where they could press their demands on a continuing basis: Agriculture (1862), Commerce (1903), and Labor (1913). Veterans and educators accomplished the same goal in 1930 and 1979. Citizen activists use mass marches to highlight calls for equal treatment regardless of race, gender, age, disability, and sexual preference and to call for government action on issues of concern, such as gun control, abortion (for and against), or health care. Other groups carve out a special day each year, such as Earth Day, to highlight their concerns. Finally, events shape the public agenda. The largest wildfire in California history wiped a city of 26,000 off the map in 2018 and triggered a debate about how best to manage forests, protect lives and private property, and change the practices of utility companies.[11]

**POLICY FORMULATION** Both governmental and nongovernmental interests suggest solutions to identified problems during the policy formulation stage. Career bureaucrats draw on their expertise and institutional knowledge of programs, public needs, and past strategies, as do members of congressional staffs and

**public policies** Products of political pressures and governmental decision making that result in governmental action or inaction that affects the lives of citizens.

**agenda setting** The stage in the policy-making process where officials identify the problems that government needs to address.

**policy formulation** The stage in the policy-making process in which government officials and nongovernment activists identify solutions to address the nation's problems.

VCG / Getty Images

**Many environmental groups take advantage of Earth Day each year to draw attention to their cause with public protests and events similar to this one in China, where hundreds of children were invited to help paint an enormous picture of the earth.**

FIGURE 15.1

## *Think Tanks by Country, 2017*

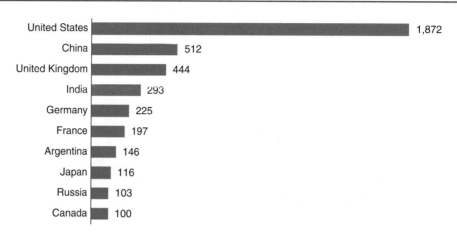

*Source: Niall McCarthy, "The Countries With the Most Think Tanks Worldwide," Forbes, August 13, 2018, https://www.forbes.com/sites/niallmccarthy/2018/08/13/the-countries-with-the-most-think-tanks-worldwide-infographic/#41c7fa319234*

specialized interest groups. Staffs in other government agencies play important roles, especially the Government Accountability Office (GAO) and the Office of Management and Budget (OMB), units discussed in Chapters 12 and 13. Think tanks (nonprofit research centers) with expertise in the budget, health care, education, the environment and other policy areas offer ideas as well (see Figure 15.1). In fact, the United States has the largest number of think tanks in the world—1,872, more than three times the total in China (512).[12] The United Kingdom, India, Germany, and France trail. Policy alternatives develop in a rich stew of ideas and proposals with groups releasing issue briefs (or *white papers*) that define problems and lay out alternative solutions. Task forces with representatives from inside and outside of the government study specific issues and formulate recommendations for action. For example, President Barack Obama organized task forces on climate change, gun control, childhood obesity, and police shootings of unarmed black men, seeking to craft a consensus on what should be done to address these highly visible public problems.

**POLICY ADOPTION** Ultimately, public officials decide whether action will be taken and what that action should be—the **policy adoption** stage. When action is taken through statutes, legislators share power with executives. The famous checks and balances swing into operation as negotiations unfold between the president and Congress, governors and state legislatures, mayors and city councils, or county executives and county councils. The U.S. separation of powers followed at multiple levels of government makes the process more complicated than it is in most other countries.

Americans expect that policies crafted by government officials will be reached through an open, accessible process that provides all affected parties with the opportunity to have their views heard and thereby participate in policy making. Frequently, however, negotiations occur behind the scenes. In legislatures, elected officials from the minority party complain that their views are ignored, and both the media and watchdog groups point out when the public's interests have not been fully considered. Those unhappy with the results often criticize the process. Most states have crafted *administrative procedure acts* that govern the process state agencies must follow in making rules. The guidelines require prior notification of meetings, publication of proposed rules, and opportunities for public comment. Transparency, consultation, and due process are broadly held principles in the U.S.

**policy adoption** The stage in the policy-making process in which officials decide whether action will be taken and what that action should be.

**POLICY IMPLEMENTATION** Governments take action by creating programs or drafting regulations designed to achieve the goals identified in statutes—that is, they engage in **policy implementation**. As we saw in Chapter 13, legislators often rely on career bureaucrats to fill in the details not specified in legislation, a practice called **delegation**. Who knows the best way to clean a river or bay and ensure safe drinking water, the generalist legislators or the specialists in the Office of Water in the Environmental Protection Agency (EPA)?[13] This practice is sometimes challenged as unconstitutional because it allows unelected officials to exercise considerable power as they use their discretion to translate broad legislative purposes into specific actions. At other times, critics fault Congress when it attempts to micromanage details of programs with which the members have only limited familiarity. Should elected officials make all the detailed decisions themselves, or are they justified in delegating the details to experts? There is no right answer to this question. And one finds that the distinction is almost uniquely American. When the British Parliament decides to take action, for example, the bureaucracy works in close partnership with the legislature because it is headed by Members of Parliament, not separately appointed agents of the executive branch.

**POLICY EVALUATION** After policies are implemented, someone needs to determine whether programs and regulations are achieving policy goals—that is, to engage in **policy evaluation**. How effective are the government's efforts? Do the programs need further modification?

Many officials and private citizens evaluate the effectiveness of a policy. Both the legislative and executive branches conduct systematic oversight of programs. In Congress, this occurs when committees reauthorize or renew programs, making adjustments, adopting new strategies, or discontinuing past efforts. The responsible career bureaucrats muster data to demonstrate how they are achieving the original goals or to prove that they need additional resources or different strategies to do so. Oversight also occurs when the appropriations committees in both the House and Senate determine the next year's budget. Presidents rely on the OMB to conduct evaluations of effectiveness during the annual budget process, and Congress can call for studies by research experts in the Congressional Research Service and the GAO.

Those affected by government programs seek opportunities to be heard. They lobby in Congress either for or against the programs in place and maintain close ties with the bureaucrats operating the programs, reflecting the tight relationships known as *iron triangles*, discussed in Chapter 13. If they are unable to convince Congress or the executive to adopt policies more to their liking, they can challenge programs in the courts. This process takes place within historical and economic contexts that are very influential.

## INFLUENCE OF HISTORICAL EXPERIENCE

Citizens vary in what they expect the government to do. This is true across time, across different regions of the country, and across nations. In the United States, there has been a long-standing presumption that citizens provide for themselves. This could be linked to Americans' distinctive historical experience. As settlers traveled westward, they moved into places where the government had little capacity to provide much help or assert much control. This frontier experience created a pervasive outlook that individuals and communities needed to provide for themselves and rely on a form of rugged individualism to meet their own needs. Later, with the establishment of territorial and eventually state governments, settlers surrendered some of this self-sufficiency in exchange for the benefits and obligations of belonging to a larger community.

Some parts of the country are more strongly influenced by the frontier experience than others. Think of Westerners who regard any government regulation of gun ownership as violating their constitutional right to bear arms. In this sense, many Americans have a *negative view of government*: To these people, when the government collects resources (taxes) from

**policy implementation** Programs or regulations designed to achieve the goals identified in legislative statutes.

**delegation** The reliance by elected officials on career bureaucrats to provide the details needed to translate broad policy goals into specific actions.

**policy evaluation** The final stage in the policy-making process in which officials determine whether the programs put into place are achieving the desired goals.

Building a log cabin

catalog #3185
Dewey 728.6

"WHEN MRS. OTWAY CAME OUT ON THAT DAY, SHE FOUND THE WALLS FULLY HALF UP."

Living on the western frontier of the United States required a great deal of self-sufficiency, often including the need to build one's own homestead, which contributed to the American values of individualism and freedom.

**laissez-faire** The view that originated with eighteenth-century French economists that government should play a minimal role in the economy.

**capitalism** An economic system distinguished by its reliance on the self-interested decisions of producers and consumers exchanging items of value in a market of supply and demand largely free of government direction.

**socialism** An economic system, developed in the nineteenth century as a way to correct the many excesses of capitalism, in which the government acts as both an owner of enterprises and a distributor of goods and services.

some citizens to meet the needs of others or regulates individual conduct, it is exceeding its legitimate powers. Citizens of other nations who experienced long periods of civil war that ended only after the creation of a strong central authority, as in France and the United Kingdom, are less likely to hold this kind of negative view of government. Those with a *positive view of government* hold that government action helps citizens meet their full potential, and government-run programs are the only way to accomplish some goals.

These opposing views of government coexist in U.S. politics today. While government was a more distant influence in the lives of nineteenth-century Americans, it became the indispensable means to combat international threats in World Wars I and II and to overcome unemployment and depression in the first half of the twentieth century. Radio, TV, and modern transportation also created a world far more connected than was true in the previous century. The positive view of government is more prevalent in Europe and Japan, where communal values are stronger than the individualistic orientation so prevalent in the United States. (See Chapter 6 for a more in-depth discussion of political culture.)

## INFLUENCE OF ECONOMIC SYSTEMS

Americans' economic experience also influences public policy. The famous Revolutionary War rallying cry of "no taxation without representation" expressed the colonists' frustration at having the mother country—Great Britain—impose taxes on them without giving them representatives in the British parliament. At issue was how much the colonists should share the costs for their own defense after the French and Indian Wars and their right to conduct business as they pleased. Under the dominant economic theory of the time, *mercantilism*, the British government sought to generate a trade surplus based on the colonies selling raw materials to Britain at low prices and buying British goods at inflated prices. Great Britain thus regulated the colonies' imports and exports.

Eighteenth-century reformers believed individual liberty lay at the heart of economic relations as well as political relations. Adam Smith's seminal work, *The Wealth of Nations*, published in 1776, called for a free-market system in which the government played a minimal role in the economy, a policy known as laissez-faire—French for "let them do [as they please]." Smith's ideas became a central component of capitalism, an economic system distinguished by its reliance on the self-interested decisions of producers and consumers exchanging items of value in a market of supply and demand largely free of government direction.

The proper degree of government involvement in the economy has been at the center of debates for the nearly two-and-a-half centuries since Smith's work. Socialism arose in the nineteenth century as the major economic system to challenge free-market capitalism. Rather than rely mainly on private ownership of production and on an unregulated market to allocate goods and services, a socialist system views government as both an owner of enterprises and a distributor of goods and services with the goal of maximizing the welfare of its citizens. In the first half of the twentieth century, France, England, and Germany nationalized whole industries, bringing them under public control. When the Labour Party came to power in Britain after World War II, they nationalized the steel and coal industries, most utilities, the railways, and the airlines but left most of the economy in the hands of private ownership. By the early 1950s, approximately 20 percent of the British economy was owned by the government, but

# Committed to Ending Slavery in 1843 America

You have just heard the most stirring speaker in your young life and can barely contain yourself. Frederick Douglass, a runaway slave in his early twenties, has just visited your town and presented a first-person account of life under the lash of slavery. In highly literate, very logical, sometimes emotional, and even comic terms, he pointed out the sanctimonious hypocrisy of his owners—leading church services for blacks and whites on Sundays, emphasizing bible passages of how slaves owe obedience to their masters, and even crying at how one should love thy neighbor, but never failing to revert to physical domination and brutal punishment on Mondays. Douglass called upon God-fearing Americans to rise up in moral indignation, not in physical or political rebellion, and denounce the institution of slavery as well as the God-fearing citizens who defend the constitution that enshrined human servitude. This action program was consistent with the one you found in each week's issue of *The Liberator*, abolitionist William Lloyd Garrison's newspaper. You had been moved to read several of the nearly one dozen newspapers calling on the nation to abandon slavery (but disagreeing over how that should happen).

But nothing moved you like Douglass's personal account. He mimicked characters from his slave life, recounted its trials and tribulations, and made you laugh, cry, and shiver over his dramatic escape from owners in Baltimore, MD. You were so moved that you traveled along with the group of speakers who had pledged to conduct "One Hundred Conventions" in 1843, moving by horse, stage coach, and even canal boat and railroad, wherever possible, across New York, Pennsylvania, Ohio, and Indiana, spreading the abolitionist word well beyond its heartland of support in Massachusetts, Rhode Island, New Hampshire, and Maine. Holding their meetings in lyceums in large towns, sympathetic churches in smaller ones, and even outside in fields or groves of trees, the group of speakers assembled sympathetic townsfolk and sometimes had to face down angry, drunken anti-abolitionist mobs determined to protect white and male dominance, as they were especially outraged by the presence of a woman, Abby Hutchinson, among the public speakers. Even in the North, Douglass constantly confronted racism—forced into separate seating on train cars and boats, refused service in restaurants, denied lodging in hotels.

Your commitment grew so strong that you attended the convention of the American Anti-Slavery Society (AASS) held annually in New York City. You agreed to become a representative of the AASS in your hometown, despite its unpopularity with many townspeople. You even began to distribute *The Liberator,* trying to expand its modest circulation and to raise money for the abolitionist cause. You later read about Douglass's triumphal tour of Ireland, Scotland, and England in 1845–1847 to encourage sales of his autobiography and spread support for American abolitionism internationally. You had to make a personal decision whether to support the Liberty Party's candidates. The AASS considered electoral politics a form of moral compromise, and you had to wrestle with your conscience as abolitionism entered more and more into mainstream political life, eventually producing an important strand in the Republican Party whose candidates you came to support. (Much like the evolution of your own views, Douglass gradually came to accept political abolitionism.)

In contrast to the decades-long abolitionist crusade, think how quickly the #MeToo movement spread in the United States when a hashtag went viral in 2017. Instead of building support through years of lecture tours, pamphlets, and newspapers denouncing a national disgrace, twenty-first century outrage could be triggered at lightning speed. But at the heart of both movements is a common theme—sparking outrage was the strategy to success. Finding ways to outrage the sensibility of everyday citizens and highlight the experiences of notable people—media celebrities today, a notorious runaway slave in the past—remains an effective way to grab public attention and stir empathy. Consequences can be far more rapid today, but winning the support of millions of citizens—one by one—to embrace a common cause is at the heart of both strategies.

## Questions to Consider

1. Is it more or less difficult today to become engaged in politics than it was in nineteenth-century America? What are the differences and similarities?
2. Is it more effective to carry a message of change through personal interaction or by using social media?
3. Is there a celebrity you follow on social media? Do the political views of that celebrity influence your own?

*Source: David W. Blight*, Frederick Douglass: Prophet of Freedom *(New York, NY: Simon & Schuster, 2018), 102–160.*

this was reversed in the 1980s, when the Conservative Party gained control of Parliament. Russia embraced an even more centrally controlled economic model under the leadership of the Communist Party, where the government controlled resources, production, and prices. After the disintegration of the Soviet Union, Russia unsuccessfully tried shifting to a market economy.

Most economies in the world are **mixed economies**. The government shares power with markets in influencing how resources are allocated in the economy. In Sweden, for example, policy makers use government power to exercise considerable control over the flow of resources, but they do so within a largely free-market system where 90 percent of industrial output comes from private firms.[14] In Australia, the government owns businesses that compete in communications, transportation, banking, and other sectors, but beginning in the mid-1980s, the government shifted many of those businesses from public to private ownership. In fact, countries around the world have moved toward the privatization of industry. Even China, still nominally a communist country, has moved in this direction as part of its economic modernization.

The United States strongly embraced the free-market system and has relied heavily on markets to make economic decisions, but the government has also played a substantial role in the American economy. The U.S. government has maintained a system of property rights that gives individuals an incentive to work hard in order to profit from their efforts, established a court system for resolving disputes in a fair and trustworthy way, and provided security from the physical destruction and disruption associated with war.[15] American governments also invested in internal improvements that make private economic activity more feasible. State governments led the way with heavy investments in roads and canals during the nation's first half century, which allowed both workers and goods to move more quickly and safely around the country. The national government then assumed the lead, encouraging expansion of the railroad, interstate highway, and airline systems. As cities grew, urban governments invested in schools, roads, water and sewage systems, and electrical infrastructure. In addition to providing these foundations, the federal government adopted policies to stabilize the economy, regulate corporate behavior, provide necessary services, and provide help to the needy. Despite this historically prominent role played by the public sector, proposals to expand programs for the poor, adopt more stringent regulations, or spread the tax burden by raising rates for the wealthy are often met with cries of "Socialism!" by their opponents.[16]

A strong commitment to capitalism also produces a preference in the United States for market-based solutions to public problems. We see this in public education, where many states have embraced charter schools—publicly funded, privately managed, and semiautonomous—as a way to encourage competition with traditional public schools serving K–12 students in an effort to improve student outcomes. In 43 states and Washington, DC, there is a competitive market in public education.[17]

Some people also believe that private business can perform traditional government functions better and more cheaply. As a result, cities and states have outsourced some public services (such as garbage collection and managing prisons) to private corporations. Finally, there's great interest in public–private partnerships as a wave of the future. Cash-strapped governments can turn over a share of toll income from roads or bridges to let a private company complete the project more rapidly and potentially maintain it more effectively than the government can alone. Roads, bridges, rapid rail systems, airport expansions, and sports stadiums can work this way.[18]

To illustrate policy making, we discuss three important areas of government action: health care, Social Security, and the energy/environment tradeoff. In each case, we organize the discussion into three parts: a background on the policy area; the problems and solutions identified by decision makers; and the politics of decision making. We then turn to an expanded discussion of economic policy in the United States.

> **mixed economy** An economic system in which government officials share power with markets in deciding or influencing how resources are allocated in the society.

# HEALTH CARE

In 2015, among the 36 member and partner nations monitored by the Organization for Economic Cooperation and Development (OECD), only Greece had a higher percentage of its population not covered by health care (14 percent) than the United States (9.1 percent).[19]

The OECD's members are commonly considered the world's most advanced industrial nations, and in most of them, coverage stood at 95 percent and higher. Moreover, U.S. health care spending was the highest among the members, and the quality of care trailed other member states in many areas. Why does the United States struggle in providing all its citizens with affordable, quality health care?

## BACKGROUND

European nations provide health insurance as one of several social insurance programs provided to everyone (health care, retirement, disability). Not all health insurance systems are the same. In Germany and Switzerland, for example, all citizens are required to participate but make payments to private insurance companies. By contrast, England smoothly transitioned from a wartime system of government-provided medical care to a publicly funded National Health Service in the years after World War II.[20] Nor was there one model of how the systems came into being: Conservative governments sometimes enacted these programs to stave off more radical political reforms—aristocrats in Prussia (the precursor to modern Germany) introduced health insurance in 1883 as a way to slow the growth of support for parties urging greater democracy—but in other nations, health care followed after a socialist or social democratic government came to power (France).

Since the beginning of the twentieth century, American politicians have debated about how to meet the nation's health care needs. At its founding convention in 1901, the Socialist Party of the United States endorsed government-provided health care insurance (along with accident, unemployment, and old age insurance) and the issue was later picked up by the mainstream political parties. Major proposals came from Teddy Roosevelt's Progressive Party in 1912, President Harry Truman in 1948, and President John F. Kennedy in 1960, but none of these proposals were adopted. For a brief time after 1915, the American Medical Association (AMA), the largest professional group representing physicians, supported a plan for compulsory health insurance, but it changed its position in 1918 and vigorously opposed subsequent proposals, labeling them "socialized medicine." As one might expect, labor unions have been staunch supporters of national health insurance.[21]

In the absence of public health insurance, the United States developed a system of private health insurance provided through employers. This benefit spread rapidly during World War II when employers, facing strict controls on wages (imposed to prevent inflation during a time of labor shortages), used health insurance and other benefits to attract workers.[22] Thus, the United States constructed a system in which employers and employees split the cost of premiums paid to insurance companies. As of 2017, just under half of the U.S. population was covered by employer-provided health care plans, a figure that varies from state to state but represents an overall decline of six percent in the past decade. Another seven percent of Americans purchase health care coverage for themselves and their families directly from an insurance company.[23]

The United States has devised ways to provide health care for some of those not covered by an employer plan. In 1965, pushed by President Lyndon Johnson (1963–1969), Congress approved government health care systems for elderly Americans (Medicare, now covering 14 percent) and for poor Americans (Medicaid, now covering 21 percent).[24] Medicare is health insurance—workers contribute a portion of their paychecks throughout their working lives to a fund that pays for the health care of retirees and then they become eligible to receive such coverage when they reach age 65. Most enrollees continue to pay monthly premiums even during retirement. Medicare is an example of an **entitlement program**—Congress establishes qualifications for participation, and each citizen who meets these qualifications is entitled to the benefits. Because the system is universal in the United States, those who contributed at some point in the past can expect to benefit later and, because contributions are a percentage of income, wealthier participants pay more.

By contrast, Medicaid is a **public assistance program**—only those Americans who meet a "means test" are eligible to receive benefits. Medicaid is designed to provide free or low-cost health care for families and children, pregnant women, the elderly, and people with disabilities (depending on income levels and family size).[25] Qualifying for Medicaid benefits depends on where you live; eligibility requirements vary from state to state and depend on whether you are pregnant, disabled, and married or single. (President Obama had tried to standardize

**entitlement program** A program, such as Medicare and Social Security, in which benefits are provided to all citizens who meet eligibility qualifications established by law.

**public assistance program** A policy that provides help to beneficiaries who meet a means test—that is, whose incomes are low enough for them to qualify to receive benefits from public sources.

The passage of Medicare was supported by various interest groups, including labor unions and many senior citizens.

requirements nationwide, but the Supreme Court struck down that provision.) For example, in California in 2018, a single person was eligible if he or she made $16,395; for a family of twelve, the income limit was $79,392. In most states, a family of four must have a total family income of less than $33,383 and few financial assets such as savings or a car.[26] The federal and state governments share the cost of Medicaid and use tax dollars to pay for these benefits. Thus, many who have contributed to Medicaid (by paying state and federal taxes) will never directly benefit from the program.

In addition to Medicare and Medicaid, the federal government maintains medical systems for military families and members of Native American tribes (combined about one percent of the total population), pays the employer's portion of health care insurance premiums for government employees, and allows employers and individuals to take tax deductions for insurance premiums and some out-of-pocket medical expenses. Depending on how all these expenditures and tax credits are calculated, experts estimate that the federal government covers from 40 to 60 percent of the total cost of U.S. health care. As shown in Figure 15.2, the United States spends a larger portion of the total value of all goods and services produced in its economy (gross domestic product) on health care than any of the other member states of the OECD (16.4 percent in 2015).[27]

## FIGURE 15.2

## Health Expenditures as a Share of GDP, OECD Countries, 2015

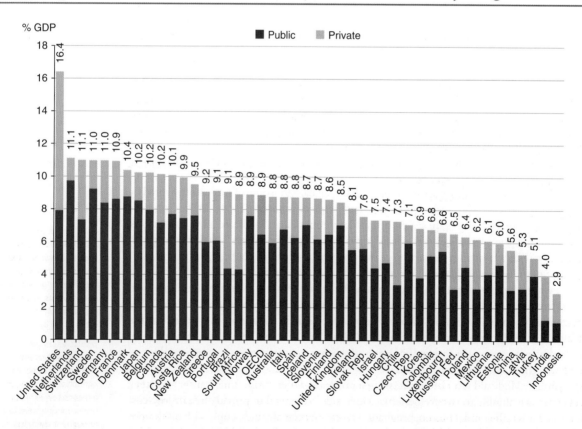

Source: "Health at a Glance 2015, How Does the United States Compare?" OECD, 2015, www.oecd.org/unitedstates/Health-at-a-Glance-2015-Key-Findings-UNITED-STATES.pdf

OECD member states have implemented two basic health care system models. Some established **single-payer systems** in which citizens' taxes pay for services from private or public providers (as in Canada) or from doctors and other professionals who are government employees (as in the United Kingdom, Denmark, and Sweden). Countries such as Germany, France, Japan, and the Netherlands created a **regulated multi-payer system** in which the government subsidizes insurance for some groups (for example, citizens with severe medical conditions) but a robust private health insurance industry, closely regulated by government, pays for patients' health services. Under either plan, all citizens are required to participate and therefore be covered. The United States system is best described as a private-employer–based and individual-based system that lacks automatic or compulsory enrollment.[28] As it has wrestled with the problem, Congress has considered these solutions and others, concentrating on three major problem areas—access, quality, and costs—that remain at the center of continued debate.

## PROBLEMS AND SOLUTIONS

Should health care solutions be national in scope or developed and implemented at the state level? A prevalent view on domestic policy in the United States is that "one size does not fit all." In other words, because problems vary across a nation as large and diverse as the United States, so must strategies and solutions. Furthermore, little progress was made at the national level during the 1970s and 1980s. President Bill Clinton (1993–2001) advanced a comprehensive health care proposal in 1993 that met with vigorous opposition and never came to a vote in Congress. George W. Bush (2001–2009) succeeded in convincing Congress to include prescription drug coverage through Medicare for the first time but went no further. So, when Washington decision makers failed to address important health problems such as reducing the number of uninsured and slowing the rise in health care costs, several states took on the problem themselves. Just two years after Massachusetts (in 2006) began requiring uninsured individuals to purchase insurance and subsidizing those who could not afford it, only 2.4 percent of the state's residents remained uninsured, the lowest percentage of any state in the country. Other states, including Vermont, Illinois, and Washington, pursued somewhat different strategies.

Thus, by 2009, the U.S. health care system reflected a strong preference for private solutions over public, had launched state rather than national solutions, had made purchase of insurance coverage voluntary rather than mandatory, and had private companies managing a majority of care, with government paying both directly and indirectly for a significant share. President Barack Obama (2009–2017) and his advisers sought comprehensive reform and partly based their plan on the successful Massachusetts program launched by a Republican governor. After much wrangling in Congress, Obama was able to gain passage of the Patient Protection and Affordable Care Act (ACA, also known as "Obamacare") in 2010. But Washington, DC, lacked the mutual trust between government and private interests found in other nations (such as the Netherlands) that have worked on health reform. Furthermore, though the plan introduced some of its changes gradually, when flaws emerged during implementation (for example, rising cost of premiums), critics labeled them *failures* rather than *problems* that required adjustments.

**ACCESS** In 2010, more than 15 percent of U.S. residents—an estimated 46.5 million—had no health insurance, making them unable to contend with major illnesses and unlikely to visit the doctor before becoming seriously ill. An equivalent number of citizens lost health coverage at some point each year because they changed jobs or worked for employers who had discontinued health insurance because of rapidly rising premiums. Among those frequently lacking health insurance were workers laid off from a job, college and graduate students, early retirees not yet covered by Medicare, workers in entry-level jobs in a service industry (for example, fast-food restaurants) or in a small business, and nonresidents. Young workers—ages 19 to 24—were especially unlikely to have health insurance in their part-time or beginning jobs; nearly a third of these young workers lacked insurance in 2004.[29] In addition, health insurance companies make money based on the difference between the amount of money they collect in premiums

**single-payer systems** Health care systems in which the government collects revenues and pays the providers for services delivered to citizens, as in Canada and the United Kingdom.

**regulated multi-payer system** A health care system in which the government regulates private health insurance companies that reimburse the government for medical services provided to its citizens.

and the amount they pay out to cover their customers' costs. Thus, companies have a simple incentive: "Seek out the healthy and avoid the sick."[30] Denying coverage to those who need it most—persons with previously existing health conditions—produces maximum profits.

The ACA increased access to health care. By 2017, the number of uninsured Americans had dropped to 9 percent, 27.4 million people.[31] One popular change was requiring that insurers continue to provide coverage for dependent children until age 26. Businesses that employed 50 persons or more had to provide health care for their employees or pay a penalty. Although the law required all states to expand Medicaid coverage, the Supreme Court made this provision voluntary and it was accepted in only 33 states and Washington, DC. Individuals were required to obtain health insurance (the so-called individual mandate) or pay a fine collected on their annual tax return ($695 per adult and up to $2,085 for a family) but the reform provided subsidies for middle-income Americans who did not qualify for Medicaid.[32] The requirement that all individuals participate would help hold down the cost of premiums by including more healthy citizens in the pool of those insured. New online health insurance marketplaces (also called *exchanges*) mirroring those in Massachusetts allowed consumers to comparison shop more easily among competing private plans that might offer more affordable coverage.

Taken together, the changes reduced the number of uninsured persons by nearly 20 million but still left millions uninsured. Even with the exchanges and associated subsidies, not all Americans can afford the insurance premiums, and comparing insurance options is so complex that many people require assistance.

**QUALITY AND COST**  Despite the large amount of money Americans pay for health care, quality is a major concern because it trails other comparable nations who are spending less. Americans receive excellent care for acute health problems such as heart attacks and strokes that require hospital care, but life expectancy in the U.S. today is two years less than the OECD average (it was a year longer as recently as 1970) and chronic diseases such as diabetes and asthma result in far higher rates of hospitalization than in other OECD nations. In the U.S., smoking rates are lower, but obesity rates are the highest in the OECD. Infant mortality rates (5.9 per 1,000 births) are only slightly better than those in Chile (6.9) and Costa Rica (8.5) and significantly lower than those in literally all European nations, led by Iceland at 0.7 deaths per 1,000 births.[33] The U.S. health system delivers less preventive and primary care to its citizens than other OECD nations, all while spending more per capita.

Health care spending as a portion of the nation's GDP has been rising since the middle of the twentieth century. Analysts have suggested many potential sources of high and rising costs: the high costs of developing new drugs and new medical technologies; heavy reliance on specialists to provide most medical care; the high costs of treating the uninsured, who tend to delay treatment until their medical conditions become serious and require hospital visits; health care providers' need for profits, contrasted with nonprofit service providers in other nations; and higher administrative costs because the U.S. system is highly decentralized, with individuals and businesses purchasing care separately.

A recent study of health care costs in eleven wealthy nations from 2013 to 2016 published in the influential *Journal of the American Medical Association* suggests a simpler answer: Costs are higher because U.S. providers charge considerably higher prices. Physician and hospital services, drugs, diagnostic tests, and administrative services were all priced at substantially higher levels than in comparable nations.[34] For example, the salaries of medical specialists and general practitioners in the United States were twice the average of those in the United Kingdom and Germany. The same study found that an MRI in the U.S. costs an average of $1,145 compared to $350 in Australia and $461 in the Netherlands. All those costs add up so that Americans pay about twice as much for their health care as citizens in the eleven other nations, but the quality of the overall results is lower.

## POLITICS

Advocates believed that the health care reform of 2010 addressed all three major issues: access, quality, and rising costs. However, Congress had adopted the reform with no Republican votes, laying the foundation for challenges to the new law in Congress, in the courts, and at the state level. The individual mandate became an immediate focus of challenge, as did the expansion of Medicaid. The Supreme Court in 2012 upheld the individual mandate, ruling 5–4 that it was constitutional to impose a financial penalty on citizens who failed to purchase health insurance, but the federal government could not compel the states to expand Medicaid. Some Republican governors therefore refused to accept the federal money allocated for that purpose.[35]

President Trump campaigned against Obamacare and repeatedly denounced it, but the administration was unable to kill it outright. Congressional Republicans sought to repeal the ACA but failed when three Republican senators voted against the effort, producing a dramatic 49–51 result. In part, it failed because there was never a clear plan for what would replace the ACA, and the consequences of simply eliminating the law convinced the small group of Republican senators to vote against repeal. Nonetheless, later in 2017, the Republican-controlled Congress eliminated the penalty for not having health insurance, essentially killing the individual mandate, effective January 1, 2019. This removed a key incentive for younger Americans, the healthiest group in the insurance pool, who had been reluctant to seek coverage and now would not be penalized for failing to do so.

The health care debate continues to be a vigorous one, with many on the left pushing for various plans that would ensure coverage for all Americans.

The Trump administration also took actions administratively. It changed a number of rules in ways that made insurance more expensive for some enrollees, weakened coverage for preexisting conditions, and dramatically reduced the government's outreach and public explanation programs.[36] Premiums had remained stable during the first three years of the ACA but rose dramatically for the seven million citizens who purchased coverage through the exchanges and were not covered by subsidies (nine million received subsidies).[37] Although the premium increases were Exhibit A for how the ACA was failing, the administration took several steps that arguably made the situation worse. It allowed some states to experiment with new policies that weakened protections for people with preexisting conditions. And, by reducing funding for advertising and counseling services, it became more difficult for people to purchase insurance on the health care exchanges.

Moving forward, it is abundantly clear that passage of the ACA did not resolve the health care debate. In fact, health care played a central role in the 2018 midterm elections and is likely to be highlighted in the 2020 presidential campaign as well. With the Democrats in control of the House of Representatives, one can expect more discussion of several alternatives introduced while they were still in the minority. The most ambitious of these is "Medicare for All," which would provide health care to all U.S. residents, automatically enrolling them at birth and paid for through federal taxes. Several public plan alternatives would allow individuals and businesses to purchase Medicare-like coverage through the ACA marketplace and buy-in options would allow individuals, regardless of age or income, to buy into Medicare or Medicaid through the marketplace.[38] Republicans have explored ways to modify the state-based exchanges, cut both Medicare and Medicaid coverages and budgets, and expand individual health savings plans, which allow people to set aside money for medical expenses that is exempt from federal income tax.[39]

If called upon to do so, comparing these and other alternatives will be a full-time job for voters, but fortunately (or perhaps unfortunately) we have lobbyists, congressional staffers, and think tanks to do that. The complex debate about access, cost, and quality will continue during the 2020 elections and, no doubt, beyond.

## SOCIAL SECURITY

Established in 1935, Social Security was a cornerstone of the New Deal, the collection of programs introduced by President Franklin D. Roosevelt (1933–1945) during the Great Depression in the 1930s. The legislation created a guaranteed income stream for retired persons who had previously had to rely on employer pensions (many of which vanished as companies went

Ida May Fuller, shown here holding one of her monthly Social Security checks, was the first person to receive benefits from the program. She received payments from the program's start in 1940 until her death in 1975.

bankrupt), their own savings, or the generosity of their families. This major entitlement program is now undergoing a stress test as millions of American baby boomers turn 65 and retire at the rate of 10,000 a day.

## BACKGROUND

The basic logic of the U.S. Social Security system is fairly simple: Current workers, through contributions made to a national fund, replace a portion of retired workers' income once they are no longer employed. By working and contributing to the Social Security trust fund for a minimum of 10 years, American workers can qualify for future benefits of their own. In this "pay as you go" system, current workers' contributions pay for the benefits of current retirees, and any surplus is set aside for future needs. Recipients qualify for Social Security benefits not because their low income makes them needy but because they contributed to the program in the past. Social Security, an entitlement program, is considered a **social insurance program** rather than a public assistance program. Unlike Medicaid, there is no means test.

When Social Security was created in 1935, millions of Americans lacked jobs, savings, or help from either family members or the government. Particularly vulnerable were the elderly, many of whom had lost their savings in bank failures and their pensions (if they had them) as former employers went out of business. Thirty-five million workers received Social Security cards during 1936 and began paying taxes into a fund from which the first monthly check was issued to Ida May Fuller of Vermont in 1940. Her benefits totaled more than $22,000 before she died at age 100 in 1975, far more than she had contributed during the three years before she retired. Since that modest beginning, the Social Security Administration has issued nearly 454 million cards.[40]

By 1950, Social Security covered about half of American workers, but the program gradually expanded coverage until it became nearly universal, with 174 million working Americans paying into the fund during 2018. Because of its complex financial structure and the need to project benefits payments decades into the future, the original law required policy makers to make 75-year plans for the Social Security program—far longer than virtually any other government program. From 1937 to 2009, Social Security had received nearly $14 trillion in revenue (tax payments and interest earned on securities bought with the surpluses) and paid out $11.3 trillion. During its long history, there have been only 11 years when Social Security's current tax receipts did not equal or exceed the benefits paid out, with most of these years falling in the mid- to late 1970s.[41] When current revenues do not equal current benefits, the program dips into the surplus revenues from the past to cover the difference.

Social Security affects a remarkably large number of citizens—one of every six Americans receives benefits through one of the Social Security programs. Monthly Social Security benefits are sent to more than 45 million former workers and spouses, and additional benefits go to more than 20 million others who are the surviving beneficiaries of former workers or unable to work because of a disability.

The program has kept many elderly Americans out of poverty. In 1959, nearly 39 percent of elderly Americans had incomes below the government-defined poverty level. By 2018, that figure had fallen to 9 percent, according to the Center on Budget and Policy Priorities, a highly respected nonpartisan source of information on policy, which also estimated that without Social Security, 20 to 30 percent of elderly Americans would be below the poverty line.[42] Women especially benefit from Social Security because they are less likely than men to have held jobs that

**social insurance program** A government program such as Social Security or Medicare that spreads the risk of income loss or illness across a broad population rather than requiring each individual to bear the risk alone.

provide a retirement pension, and women's pensions pay less than men's. Women are also likely to live longer, surviving husbands if they are married.

## PROBLEMS AND SOLUTIONS

As popular and effective as the Social Security program is, a problem is developing: The birth rate in the U.S. has been dropping, meaning there are fewer workers paying into the system compared to the number of retirees receiving payments. As a result, at some point in the future, the program will need to begin paying out more in benefits than it receives in revenue every year, eventually depleting its surplus. Virtually every member state in the OECD faces similar pressures on their old-age pension programs. And, as in the United States, these nations must weigh demographics, benefit levels, age requirements, and expectations about what is the appropriate retirement age even as life spans are lengthening. The search for solutions has focused on ways to reduce costs or enhance revenues.

**CHANGING DEMOGRAPHICS** Many members of the *baby boom generation*, those born between 1946 and 1964, are the children of families started after soldiers who had served in World War II returned home. Seventy-seven million children were born during this 18-year period as newly married couples or couples who had been separated during four years of war began to have children. The oldest members of that generation have begun to retire, and they are eligible for reduced Social Security benefits at 62 and for full benefits at 66. (For those born in 1960 and later, the age at which a worker can retire with full benefits is 67.) A structural problem has emerged: The ratio of contributing workers to beneficiaries has dropped from 16.5:1 in 1950 to 3.7:1 in 1970 to 2.8:1 in 2013 and is projected to be 2.2:1 by 2033.[43] Because of the projected number of baby boomer retirees, the financial drain on the Social Security trust fund will grow even as the number of contributors declines. And with the help of medical science, baby boomers are likely to live longer than previous generations, collecting benefits for many years after they retire. Your grandparents' longevity is a personal blessing but a policy problem.

As the baby boomers have aged, this large group has had ripple effects throughout society. Their numbers put pressure on school capacity in the 1950s and 1960s, and they will have a growing impact on the health care system as they age. During the period when baby boomers have been working, Social Security benefits could be set at relatively high levels because there were more workers per retiree. In 1990, the proportion of the U.S. population that was elderly was 11 percent. In 2020, this number is projected to be 16 percent. Many countries face similar problems caused by declining birthrates. By comparison, the percentage of Japan's population that is 65 and older is already at 27 percent and is projected to peak at 33 percent, but Japanese men remain in the work force longer (retiring at 70.2 years old versus 66.8 years old in the U.S.) and, even with a slightly longer projected life span, will spend fewer years in retirement (15.5 versus 17.2 for U.S. males).[44]

**CLOSING THE GAP BETWEEN BENEFITS AND REVENUE** Officials responsible for Social Security's ability to meet its financial obligations must ensure that contributions will cover future commitments. There is no "right" amount that should be paid to retirees as benefits. Social Security's architects aimed to replace about 40 percent of the income of an average American worker, now actually a bit lower at 38.3 percent. That is lower than found in many other nations; as reported by the OECD, the average replacement rate across OECD nations is 52.9 percent of the average wage earner's salary, although that varies from a low of 22.1 percent in the United Kingdom to 96.9 percent in the Netherlands.[45] (See Figure 15.3.) The expectation is that U.S. retirees will meet their remaining needs through personal savings, earnings from a part-time job, or from other sources, such as a pension provided by a former employer, though fewer than half of American workers have such pensions today. Many retired persons, however—nearly a third—depend almost entirely on their Social Security checks, and rising health care costs have severely pinched all retirees' budgets. Reducing the benefits of current recipients would be hard-hearted (who wants to make life worse for their grandparents, aunts, uncles, and parents?), not to mention politically unpopular.

## FIGURE 15.3

### *Average Public Retirement Benefit as a Percentage of Earnings, 2017*

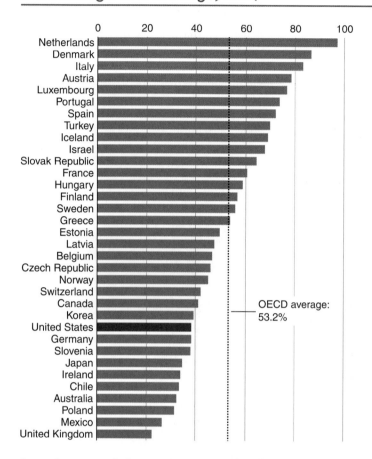

OECD average: 53.2%

*Source: Organization for Economic Cooperation and Development (OECD), Pensions at a Glance 2017: Retirement Income Systems in OECD Countries, https://doi .org/10.1787/pension_glance-2017-en; "Social Security Benefits Are Low Compared With Other Advanced Countries," Center on Budget and Policy Priorities, 2015, https://www.cbpp.org/social-security-benefits-are-low-compared-with-other- advanced-countries-3.*

REUTERS / ERIC THAYER

**Workers who postpone retirement into their seventies draw larger monthly Social Security benefits. How long should we, as a society, expect people to work?**

The focus, then, has been more on changing the promises made to future beneficiaries and the demands placed on current contributors. For example, by raising the retirement age, policy makers can delay the point at which the government must begin to pay benefits and reduce the number of years each person will draw benefits. By raising the tax paid by current workers, they can increase revenues. In the U.S., retirees with other sources of income (such as from personal retirement investments like 401(k)s) now pay federal taxes on part of their Social Security benefits, and that rate could be raised. Other OECD countries have adjusted tax rates and retirement ages over the past decade.

Increasingly, younger workers fear that they will never collect from the program they have been paying into, and the principal problem is the looming bill for benefits expected by the many Americans approaching retirement. Advanced industrial nations around the world struggle with this same problem. Fundamentally, to keep revenues higher than benefits, legislators face a simple yet difficult choice: either reduce benefits or raise revenues.

**POLICY ALTERNATIVES** Generally, Democrats prefer strategies that increase revenues without cutting benefits, and Republicans prefer the reverse. Since the program's creation in 1935, Congress has raised the Federal Insurance Contributions Act (FICA; the taxes used to pay for Social Security and Medicare) rates 20 times, so some ask, why not raise them again? Opponents of higher taxes recoil at the rate that would be needed to meet the program's full obligations over the next 75 years—around 18 percent rather than the current 12.4 percent (presently divided equally between employer and employee). An alternative would be to change current tax policy. At this point, only the first $127,000 in income a person earns is subject to FICA taxes, so lawmakers could raise that limit or make all income subject to FICA, which could mean a substantial tax increase for those most able to pay it—those earning higher incomes. On the flip side of the coin, paying Social Security benefits to millionaires or billionaires makes little sense, so some have suggested making Social Security means-tested, meaning that individuals exceeding a certain level of wealth would not receive benefits. Finally, policies could be structured to further encourage workers to delay retirement and stay in the workforce longer. In the U.S., workers who delay drawing Social Security until age 70 receive larger monthly payments than if they had retired earlier and can even continue to work afterward. Many nations have designed tax policy incentives that make it more favorable for those choosing to remain in the workforce longer. Most likely, lawmakers will consider some mix of these alternatives.

Without some changes to the program, Social Security will start to cause budget problems in 2034, when the trust fund reserves are expected to be depleted. At that point, current revenue from FICA contributions will cover about 79 percent of the promised benefits. The program will not be bankrupt (as some critics argue), but it will be stressed.[46]

## POLITICS

George W. Bush proposed a major restructuring of Social Security—he wanted to tie the program to the U.S. stock market on the theory that stocks would provide higher returns on the money paid into the trust fund. Bush's basic plan was to partially privatize the program by giving workers a few percentage points of their FICA taxes to invest in the stock market themselves. Assuming the stock market continued to rise, this would have provided a larger benefit for younger workers by the time they retired, but it did nothing to address the shortfall caused by the decline in birthrate after the baby boom generation. Bush's plan was his top domestic priority in his second term, and he campaigned hard for it during 2005. It failed miserably. The proposal never received a vote in Congress, even though his own party controlled both the House and Senate. Republican members of Congress were wary of any proposals to change Social Security because of the voter anger they feared would be directed their way. Unions and Democrats were adamantly opposed to privatization and the inherent riskiness of investing in the stock market.

Politicians are aware of the political muscle of the "gray lobby," the mobilized political power of retirees and near-retirees in American politics. Politicians realize that older people are far more likely to vote than younger ones, giving them extra power at the ballot box. In addition, the elderly have a powerful organization lobbying for their interests. The AARP (formerly the American Association of Retired Persons) boasts that it has more than 38 million members, making it the largest organization in U.S. politics, and it is able to mobilize its members into a political force aimed at protecting the interests of the elderly. This makes any attempt to reduce Social Security benefits or raise the retirement age a significant challenge.

The severe economic recession from 2007 to 2009 made changing Social Security more difficult than ever. When the stock markets crashed in September and October of 2008, millions of Americans saw large portions of their retirement savings evaporate. Social Security was a foundation that remained untouched even as 401(k)s shrank, and the lesson was obvious: Stock market returns might be greater during boom times, but those gains come with risk. After this experience, the public suddenly began to save more, reflecting a newfound awareness of the need to put aside resources rather than freely spend them.

President Obama proposed collecting FICA taxes on earnings over $250,000 a year as a way to generate additional revenue. But health care reform and the rising costs of Medicare took up more of Obama's attention than Social Security. President Trump promised during his 2016 campaign not to touch Social Security, and his administration's answer to the program's looming financial problem was to simply accelerate economic growth through lower taxes, better trade deals, and fewer regulations. The Congressional Budget Office has examined several ways to reduce costs. For example, calculating benefits on the basis of prices rather than wages would reduce payments $121 billion by 2028 (remember that small changes multiplied over many people and a decade or more adds up to real money).[47] Raising the full retirement age from 67 to 70 for those born after 1978 would save $28 billion through 2028. And the greatest savings would come from changing the way that cost of living adjustments (through which benefits go up as prices increase) are calculated—$203 billion in ten years if applied to all federal pension programs including veterans as well as Social Security. All of these, of course, mean reducing the benefits paid to retirees in one way or another. Any group attempting to solve the Social Security crisis will need to consider the possible budgetary savings for all the possible combinations we have reviewed.

Important questions linger: What obligation does the country have to Americans approaching retirement age? How much will the government require younger, working Americans to

Robert Alexander / Getty Images

**Wind provides an increasing share of the energy consumed in the U.S. as massive turbine farms, some with thousands of windmills, have sprung up around the country, particularly in the west.**

contribute to fulfill its promise to the baby boomers? These recurring questions will continue shaping the Social Security debate in the years to come.

# ENERGY AND THE ENVIRONMENT

During the second half of the twentieth century, scientists realized not only that technological and industrial development could have a negative impact on the environment but also that the world would eventually exhaust its supply of oil, natural gas, and other resources. To avert future disasters, presidents and Congress wrestled with how policy alternatives would affect the overall economy. They also considered the relative advantages of several options: developing new sources of power (hydrogen, nuclear, wind), redirecting the nation's economy and lifestyle away from fossil fuels (oil, natural gas, gasoline-powered automobiles), and finding new supplies of fossil fuels.

## BACKGROUND

We need energy to run our businesses, power the home appliances that free up time for work and leisure, maintain the suburb-centered lifestyle that developed after World War II, and support the United States' role in the world. National policy makers must ensure that energy is readily available, reasonably priced, and efficiently distributed. Consumers want cheap energy, while energy producers need profits to finance exploration, research, and development.

Today's U.S. energy needs are met primarily by carbon-based fossil fuels. These include coal, petroleum, and natural gas, each of which is the basis for a major industry whose growth and development in the late nineteenth and early twentieth centuries helped the United States become an industrial leader in the world. Coal surpassed wood as an energy source around 1885 and was subsequently surpassed by petroleum (1950) and natural gas (1960s). But the supply of carbon-based fuels is not inexhaustible—there are finite known oil and natural gas reserves. Coal is the most plentiful of the nonrenewable fuels in the United States, but its mining and burning have serious negative effects on the environment.

Plentiful natural resources drove rapid economic growth, but even in the nineteenth century, conservationists began to question whether all stands of timber should be cut, whether all mountains were fair game for mining operations, and whether all streams should be dammed for hydroelectric power. Yellowstone National Park became the world's first preserved nature area in 1872, but President Teddy Roosevelt (1901–1909) is often credited with crafting the first national policies on preserving forests and setting aside large areas of wilderness. Later in the century, public concern grew over a different set of problems: air pollution, water pollution, chemical dumps, and the harmful effects of pesticides. Important legislation adopted in the 1970s regulates pollution of air, water, and land and created the EPA to enforce the many new regulations affecting the production and consumption of energy. Industry, however, has consistently argued that the new regulations have harmful effects of their own—on the economy.

As the nation's demand for energy grew, the United States depleted its domestic supplies of petroleum. Oil companies tapped the readily accessible oil fields in the continental United States, in the Gulf of Mexico, and finally, Alaska. Annual petroleum production declined. U.S. companies aggressively sought to develop new deposits around the world. This supply, however, is subject to potential disruption by hostile nations and poses environmental risks of its own when transported. Producers have also pressed for the opportunity to develop new potential sources in U.S. territories that have been off-limits, such as the Arctic National Wildlife Refuge (ANWR) and off the Atlantic coast.

In the 1970s, two events heightened awareness of the nation's **energy security**, the ability of the United States to meet its energy needs. First, the Arab members of the Organization of Petroleum Exporting Countries (OPEC) refused to export oil to the United States in

**energy security** The ability of the United States to meet its own energy needs.

retaliation for U.S. support of Israel during the 1973 Arab–Israeli war. Gas shortages produced long lines and high prices, seriously disrupting everyday life. Then, in 1979, Iranian revolutionaries seized the American embassy in Tehran and took staff as hostages. The subsequent international tension severely disrupted global oil supplies, with prices again rising dramatically. Starting with President Ford (1974–1977), successive administrations have purchased and stored oil in the Strategic Petroleum Reserve as insurance against another supply disruption. At the rate of current consumption, however, the reserve can satisfy only about 50 days of the nation's needs.

In response to both disruptions, American officials sought to reduce oil imports by encouraging citizens to conserve energy, by mandating new standards of energy efficiency, and by encouraging the development of alternative sources of energy (including solar, geothermal, and wind), and by pursuing cleaner coal technology. The Carter administration (1977–1981) created the Department of Energy in 1977 to oversee these initiatives. The nation made modest progress in its efforts at conserving energy during the 1970s and 1980s, but new sources of oil that were developed in Alaska and the North Sea increased world supplies and lowered prices. With oil again cheap, the need to establish energy independence became less urgent. The Reagan administration (1981–1989) promoted two different strategies: developing clean coal technologies and expanding the use of nuclear power.

During the 1990s, concern shifted from adverse effects on the nation's environment to global climate change. Evidence mounted that the earth was undergoing a dramatic warming because of rising levels of atmospheric carbon dioxide, a by-product of the use of fossil fuels. Carbon dioxide is considered a **greenhouse gas** because it traps solar heat, preventing it from radiating back into space, which warms the earth. Industrial smokestacks, electric generating plants, home chimneys, and internal combustion engines have released carbon dioxide since the start of the Industrial Revolution in 1750. As more and more nations industrialize, the pace of climate change accelerates. To prevent future disasters, many countries have pursued international cooperation on this issue, and the American government at all levels has been developing policies to deal with the impact of climate change and to compensate for diminishing levels of resources. The Obama administration was especially committed to policies that would reduce U.S. contributions to global warming.

## PROBLEMS AND SOLUTIONS

There are no easy ways to satisfy the ever-growing demand for energy while also enacting more responsible environmental policies. Several problems seem paramount: the dependence on imported oil, global warming, potential problems with coal and nuclear power, an inefficient electrical system, and the public's reluctance to change.

**DECLINING DEPENDENCE ON IMPORTED OIL** In 2017, the United States relied on imported petroleum to meet about 19 percent of its petroleum needs, a dramatic *reduction* from 45 percent in 2011. Rather than the U.S. becoming even more dependent on imported oil, as experts had predicted, petroleum imports fell, due initially to the impact of the economic recession and later to improved auto fuel economy, changes in consumer habits, and expanded U.S. domestic production. New technologies now make it possible to tap deposits trapped in shale through a process known as *fracking*. Imports fill the declining gap between domestic production and consumption. Surprisingly, Canada is the largest supplier of imported petroleum to the United States, accounting for 40 percent of U.S. oil imports, followed by Saudi Arabia (9 percent), Mexico (9 percent), Venezuela (7 percent), and Iraq (6 percent). About 17 percent of the United States' imported petroleum still comes from the Persian Gulf, the site of supply disruptions in 1973 and 1979.

**CLIMATE CHANGE** Consuming energy, so essential to modern life, also has significant negative effects on the quality of air and water. Late in the twentieth century, scientists began reporting that global surface temperatures were rising. A worldwide consensus formed that this was the result of humans burning fossil fuels that release gases such as carbon dioxide into the earth's atmosphere. Sophisticated research identified numerous long-term adverse effects on

> **greenhouse gas** A gas emitted by human consumption of fuels that retains solar heat rather than allowing it to radiate back into space, therefore producing global warming.

plant, animal, and human habitats: diseases spreading into new areas; disrupted food supplies; melting polar ice caps and rising sea levels erasing entire island nations and flooding coastal cities; and new weather patterns producing floods, droughts, and more severe storms.

A scientific consensus did not produce a political consensus about how to respond to these environmental threats. Some conservatives believed that warnings of environmental threats were exaggerated, if not wholly untrue. And, if today's economy needed additional energy to fuel economic growth, adopting stricter regulations on fossil fuel consumption or trying to shift to a new paradigm of renewable energy (solar, wind, and thermal) would disrupt recovery from the 2008–2009 economic recession and put major industries at risk, including oil, natural gas, coal, and automobiles.

President Obama campaigned for election on the promise to pass legislation that would dramatically cap greenhouse gases. Democrats supported the effort, but Republicans opposed expanding government regulations. Instead of legislation, the administration adopted regulations that required better fuel economy for domestic automobiles and reductions on $CO_2$ emissions by power plants while also providing subsidies for renewable energy projects. Obama was also a leader in fashioning international agreements seeking a coordinated effort by the global community to reduce global warming.

In sharp contrast, the Trump administration regarded the Obama environmental agenda as anti-growth and used executive orders as well as its control of regulations to implement different policies. President Trump withdrew the United States from the Paris Climate Agreement, rewrote auto fuel economy standards by lowering the target from 54 miles per gallon to 34, rescinded the regulations that reduced carbon emissions from coal-burning electric generating plants, and reduced funding for research into the potential impacts of droughts, wildfires, and hurricanes.[48] In response, some Democrats have introduced a plan for a Green New Deal, a massive package addressing climate change and stimulating the economy over the next decade. Although several 2020 Democratic candidates for president endorsed the idea, gaining traction in Congress appears to be an uphill battle at best.

**CLEAN COAL**  Similar to oil, coal is a nonrenewable energy source that required millions of years to create, but it is more plentiful. The United States has the world's largest known reserves of coal, enough to last 225 years at current rates of consumption. About two-thirds of U.S. coal is excavated through surface mining in Western states and the remainder is available through underground mining, mainly in Appalachia. Coal-fired power plants generate 30 percent of the electricity in the United States, down sharply from 57 percent in the 1980s and about half in the 1990s.[49]

Despite its ready availability, coal has negative impacts on the environment. Surface mining leaves behind badly scarred landscapes that the EPA insists producers restore and polluted streams that the EPA seeks to prevent. Burning coal produces carbon dioxide, sulfur dioxide, coal ash, and other pollutants that contribute to global warming as well as acid rain. Mercury—another product of burning coal—has negative health effects on humans after it enters the food chain through fish.

Pressured by federal statutes mandating clean air, the electricity-generating industry has sought to develop chimney-scrubbing technology to reduce the most dangerous coal emissions, but critics argue that "clean coal" does not exist now and never will. The Department of Energy has run research and demonstration projects designed to assist the coal industry and proudly points to dramatic reductions of 88 percent in sulfur dioxide and 76 percent in nitrogen oxide emissions over twenty years.[50] But coal still accounts for nearly 70 percent of the $CO_2$ emissions from electricity generation, and that sector produces 34 percent of the nation's total $CO_2$ emissions.[51] To get clean, coal still has a long way to go. Even so, in an effort to reverse the decline of the coal industry and restore jobs to miners, the Trump administration loosened regulations on carbon and mercury emissions and sought to eliminate Obama-era requirements that new coal-fired electricity-generating plants install expensive technologies designed to reduce emissions.[52]

**NUCLEAR POWER**

Nuclear power is generated from the mineral uranium, an ore mined in the western United States and elsewhere around the world. Britain began operating the first nuclear-powered commercial electric-generating plant in 1956, and the United States followed in 1957 with the promise of clean, cheap, and plentiful power. Today, 65 nuclear power plants operate 104 reactors in 31 U.S. states. Nuclear power now accounts for about 20 percent of the electricity generated in the United States annually, constituting nearly one-third of all the nuclear energy generated in the world. Nuclear-generated power is usually cheaper than that provided by burning fossil fuels and produces no carbon dioxide or other gases associated with global warming.

Some nations have invested heavily in nuclear power and use it to meet a large share of their energy needs. In France, 72 percent of electrical power comes from 58 reactors. Responding to the oil shock of 1973, the French government increased its nuclear generating capacity, and the nation now exports large amounts of electricity to Italy, which has no nuclear reactors of its own. France is now an international leader in nuclear technology, enjoys the cheapest electricity prices in Europe, and is developing a fourth-generation reactor, but it has also decided to increase its use of wind and solar technologies.[53]

Fears about the Three Mile Island nuclear plant have lingered, even forty uneventful years after the accident that released radioactive coolant into the environment.

After rapid growth in the 1970s, the number of new U.S. nuclear power plants leveled off in 1980. Rising construction and maintenance costs prevented several decommissioned reactors from being replaced. Natural gas prices dropped so low that new nuclear plants became prohibitively expensive by comparison. In addition, safety became a major concern after an accident occurred in 1979 at Three Mile Island, a nuclear reactor near Harrisburg, Pennsylvania, resulting in the release of nuclear coolant into the environment. Although there was no official order to evacuate, more than 100,000 nearby residents left the area.

In 1986, a far more severe accident occurred at the Chernobyl reactor in what was then the Ukrainian Soviet Socialist Republic. The area within 30 miles of the plant is so radioactive, it is expected to be uninhabitable for thousands of years. And in March 2011, a 9.0 earthquake triggered a giant tsunami that knocked four reactors out of operation at Japan's Fukushima Daiichi power plant. Teams of workers frantically sought to control the threat of radiation being released from the melted cores either into the air or by the contaminated water used for cooling. In response to Chernobyl and prompted by the Green Party, Germany decided to decommission the nation's reactors after 2022 and shift to heavy reliance on wind energy. But a later German government reversed this decision because of the potential economic impacts. Then, in 2011, the government again announced that all nuclear reactors would be closed by 2022 in response to public concerns about the Japanese nuclear accident.[54] (The operator of Three Mile Island announced in May 2019 that it might close the final reactor, not because of safety concerns but because of operating costs.)

A persistent problem with nuclear power is the storage of nuclear waste. Plants must store high-level waste after it has been used to generate electricity—highly radioactive spent fuel rods from U.S. plants are maintained in temporary storage sites until the Department of Energy completes a permanent national repository to house waste materials that will be radioactive for millions of years. There are 80 temporary storage sites located in 35 states around the country. Until a permanent disposal plan is developed, the Department of Energy estimates that 161 million Americans will continue to live within 75 miles of nuclear storage facilities (see Figure 15.4). A California law adopted in 1976 prohibits the construction of any new nuclear plants in that state until the long-term waste problem is solved.[55]

**INEFFICIENT ELECTRICAL GRID** Together, coal and nuclear power generate 50 percent of U.S. electricity, which is consumed in almost equal shares by residential, industrial, and commercial users, with cooling accounting for the highest residential use. Electricity offers numerous advantages—it is clean (depending on how it is generated!), flexible, controllable, safe, effortless, and instantly available—but only about a third of the energy used to generate

## FIGURE 15.4

## Current Nuclear Waste Locations in the United States

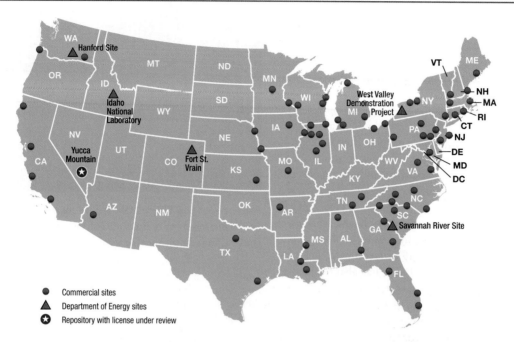

- Commercial sites
- ▲ Department of Energy sites
- ✪ Repository with license under review

Source: Government Accountability Office https://www.gao.gov/key_issues/disposal_of_highlevel_nuclear_waste/issue_summary

electricity is actually delivered to consumers in the form of usable current. Much energy is lost at the point of generation and then through the transmission process in the form of heat. The demand for electricity grows at an impressive rate, despite efforts to improve the efficiency of heating and cooling systems, household appliances, and lighting. Economic growth depends on continued expansion of the supply of electricity.

The U.S. electrical grid, the complex system of electrical transmission and delivery links that connect consumers with generating plants, uses technology developed in the first half of the twentieth century. This outdated infrastructure based on centralized generating stations contributes to power loss and prevents the use of new technologies projected to spread during the twenty-first century. Denmark, by contrast, has replaced a few massive generating plants with scores of generating points in a decentralized system based on wind and other renewable sources. The U.S. Department of Energy and major electricity companies have been working to design a "smart grid" that will meet the nation's needs moving into the future.[56]

**CONSUMER ATTITUDES** Americans consume an enormous amount of energy per capita compared with other nations. Americans constitute 5 percent of the world's population but account for 17 percent of its total energy usage.[57] Americans have become accustomed to cheap gas, cheap electricity, cool houses in the summer and warm houses in the winter, muscular cars capable of transporting large families and towing boats or campers, and homes far removed from their places of work. Many Americans are unconvinced that their behavior should change and that it has consequences for others. The Pew Charitable Trust found that strong majorities in seven African and six Latin American countries were convinced that "climate change is a very serious problem," but only 45 percent of Americans and 18 percent of Chinese citizens, two of the world's largest polluters, were as concerned (see Figure 15.5).[58] Yet as the growing scarcity of resources drives energy prices up and as Americans increasingly have to deal with the consequences of climate change, high-energy consumption habits need to change.

Moreover, American attitudes about the tradeoff between environmental protection and economic growth have varied over time. During the 1980s and 1990s, Gallup found that strong majorities preferred protection of the environment over economic growth (see Figure 15.6). But entering the new century, economic growth gained support and, during the economic recession, was considered more important than environmental protection. As the nation came out of the recession and growth resumed, so did support for the environment, but not as strongly as earlier.

## POLITICS

The Bush, Obama, and Trump administrations approached the energy/environment trade-off differently. Bush's energy task force recommended reducing regulations on oil and gas drilling, expanding the use of coal-fired plants with fewer demands for clean emissions, building more nuclear power plants, opening the untapped oil reserves in the ANWR, and making federal lands in the "lower 48" available for new oil and natural gas exploration. Congress approved expanded drilling offshore and on federal lands, but it rejected opening the ANWR.

Obama's economic stimulus package funded work on a smart grid similar to Denmark's, weatherizing the houses of low-income families, and renewable energy and energy efficiency at the state and local level. Renewable energy sources—air and solar—received strong encouragement so that by 2017, about 17 percent of electricity generation came from renewable sources—7.3 percent hydropower, 6.3 percent wind, and 1.3 percent solar. By comparison, in 2008, Bush's last year as president, electric generation was 6.0 percent hydropower, 2.3 percent wind, and 0.1 percent solar.[59] The Obama administration set strikingly ambitious goals for car and light truck fuel economy (54.5 miles per gallon by 2025) and for expanding the role of renewable sources, a goal of 25 percent of the nation's needs by 2025. Obama's EPA began to regulate carbon dioxide emissions, a major policy departure from the past that was upheld by the Supreme Court when challenged by the electric industry.

Under Trump, creating jobs and stimulating economic growth ranked above conserving energy, protecting the environment, and combating global climate change. The administration adopted a new brand for energy production—*energy dominance*, not merely *energy independence*, as in the past. This reflected policy shifts that encouraged full-bore production and exploration of fossil fuel energy sources in line with new opportunities to export liquefied natural gas and petroleum products.[60] Trump changed or altogether scrapped many Obama-era regulations issued by the EPA and the Interior Department. Administration policies and presidential executive orders encouraged growth of the coal industry, reduced controls on carbon dioxide emissions by power plants, expanded exploration for oil and natural gas into areas previously off-limits, sought to reduce the EPA budget, and initiated withdrawal from the Paris Climate Agreement.[61]

In 2018, the United Nations' Intergovernmental Panel on Climate Change issued a dire report. The world has ten years in which to dramatically change its fossil-fueled economies or face consequences far more serious and disruptive than had been previously forecast.[62] With a shorter time frame and necessarily more ambitious goals, but with some policy makers still believing that global warming is a hoax, we can expect the

**FIGURE 15.5**

## Public Opinion About Climate Change in Selected Nations, 2015

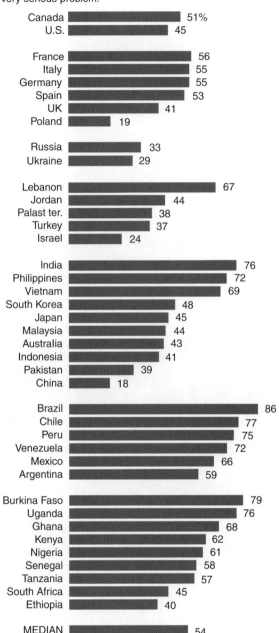

Percentage saying global climate change is a very serious problem:

Source: Pew Research Center Spring 2015 Global Attitudes Survey http://www.pewglobal.org/2015/11/05/1-concern-about-climate-change-and-its-consequences/

FIGURE 15.6

# *Environmental Protection Versus Economic Growth*

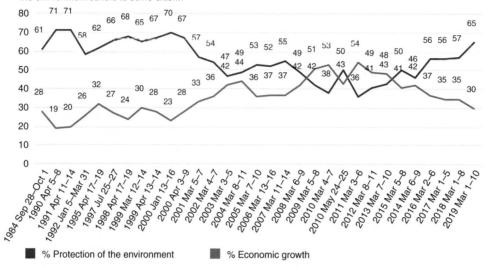

With which one of these statements do you most agree – protection of the environment should be given priority even at the risk of curbing economic growth (or) economic growth should be given priority even if the environment suffers to some extent?

■ % Protection of the environment    ■ % Economic growth

Source: "Environment," Gallup, 2019, https://news.gallup.com/poll/1615/environment.aspx

**Despite evidence of accelerating climate change, including the receding of the Rhone Glacier in Switzerland, seen here in 2015 (top) and 2018, current U.S. policy prioritizes the economy over the environment.**

debate to continue between environmental protection versus economic growth fueled by expanded energy production and use. If one believes the threat of climate catastrophe is real, ample evidence indicates the U.S. is moving in the wrong direction.[63]

## ECONOMIC POLICY

As we have seen, public policies in the United States are shaped by and have an impact on the nation's economy. But the economy is a highly complex policy area in itself. Many different public and private decision makers set economic policies in the United States. Consumers and producers—the key participants in a market economy—make the bulk of economic decisions. Government rules and tax policies influence those market decisions and shape the contexts within which the markets operate. For example, when government actions intentionally increase interest rates, both consumers and businesses are less likely to borrow money to pay for new property, new vehicles, additional education, or new manufacturing equipment. Likewise, if the government reduces taxes so that both consumers and businesses have more money to spend, then property sales, vehicle sales, and investments are likely to get a boost. By changing these policies, government can influence economic decisions made in the marketplace. Economists divide government economic policy into two broad categories: fiscal policy and monetary policy.

## FISCAL POLICY

The federal government enacts **fiscal policy** when the people's elected representatives intentionally adjust taxes, government spending, and government borrowing to stimulate or slow the economy. Although the federal government's fiscal policies have the greatest influence on the overall economy, state and local governments also make tax and spending decisions. Unlike the federal government, however, state and local governments must balance their revenues and expenditures annually. The federal government, by contrast, can run a **budget deficit**, spending more in any given year than it receives in revenues and making up the difference by borrowing money from citizens and noncitizens.

Despite concerns about the size of the national debt, there are economic justifications for running a deficit. Since the 1930s, government has intervened when the nation's economic activity has slowed down and the value of all goods and services, the **gross domestic product (GDP)**, has fallen. Economists call this a *recession* if it persists for at least six months or a *depression* when it becomes so severe that the GDP declines 10 percent or greater. During these downturns, workers typically see their earnings shrink or, worse yet, disappear altogether when they lose their jobs as employers reduce production and employment because of declining sales. With fewer workers earning less money, government revenues from income taxes also decline. To maintain a balanced budget during a recession or depression, the government needs to cut back its spending, as many states and cities were forced to do between 2008 and 2012. But such actions worsen the economic conditions. Some government workers lose their jobs; government programs to assist the unemployed or to retrain workers are reduced when citizens need them most; and the government's overall impact on the economy as a consumer of goods and services drops.

Since the 1930s, most economists have supported the view that government should play a countercyclical role in the economy in order to stabilize conditions. In their view, the government should increase its spending during economic downturns to help stimulate economic activity and combat unemployment. Today, specialists in the federal government closely monitor the levels of unemployment nationally, regionally, and in different sectors of the economy. They also follow the direction in which prices are moving, carefully monitoring the price of specific products that are important to economic growth, such as the costs of food, oil, iron ore, and other raw materials used in manufacturing. When these multiple indicators show a slowdown in the economy, federal policies are typically put in place to offset this trend.

**Keynesian economics**, a set of policy actions proposed by British economist John Maynard Keynes at the time of the Great Depression, endorses this countercyclical role of government. According to this approach, government policy during economic declines should stimulate the economy through increased spending, reduced taxes, or both. These actions are likely to produce an even greater deficit that the government must meet by borrowing money through the sale of bonds to investors at home and abroad. This is exactly what happened in the United States in response to the most recent recession that ran from 2007–2009, leading to a ballooning deficit. The opposite policy also holds true: During times when the economy is expanding at too rapid a pace, when rising wages trigger increased prices for goods and services—*inflationary conditions*—the government can reduce spending, increase taxes, or both. The resulting surplus can be used to reduce the national debt, but as we have seen, this rarely occurs because the public dislikes higher taxes and often votes against elected officials who adopt them. The public strongly desires the many services and programs provided by government, but it is reluctant to pay for them.

There are alternative strategies of government intervention. The most notable has been *supply-side economics*, in which the government stimulates the economy by providing incentives to produce goods and services. Lowering income tax rates and reducing regulation, say supply-siders, encourages people to

**fiscal policy** Efforts made by Congress and the president to stabilize the economy through the taxing, spending, and borrowing decisions made as part of the annual budget process.

**budget deficit** The result of the government spending more in any given year than it receives in revenues and making up the difference by borrowing money from citizens and noncitizens.

**gross domestic product (GDP)** The total value of goods and services produced in the economy.

**Keynesian economics** A set of countercyclical policy prescriptions proposed by British economist John Maynard Keynes at the time of the Great Depression, calling for the government to use taxes and expenditures to control economic recessions and expansions.

In the heat of the 2008 campaign, President Bush took the unusual step of inviting not only congressional leaders but also the Democratic and Republican nominees for president to the White House to discuss emergency measures to address the worsening recession.

FIGURE 15.7

## Total Federal Surpluses and Deficits as Percentage of GDP, 1965–2049

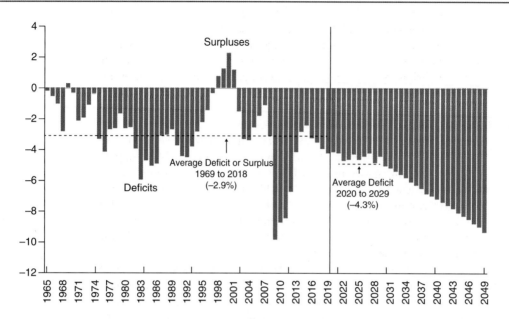

*Source: "Historical Budget Data" and "Long Term Budget Projections: 2019–2029," Congressional Budget Office, 2019, https://www.cbo.gov/about/products/budget-economic-data#2*

work, save, and invest. The Reagan and Trump administrations relied heavily on supply-side logic to guide their policies, and defenders point to the sustained growth of the economy during the 1990s and 2017–2018 as evidence that it works. Critics argue that this strategy creates ballooning and uncontrollable deficits and disproportionately benefits the wealthy.

When confronting the largest economic recession since the 1930s, in 2009, President Obama and Congress approved a large economic stimulus package of $789 billion designed to counter the worsening conditions. It included spending for many construction projects—that is, road, bridge, and public works projects that could be quickly started as a way to provide jobs and pump money into the economy. When this stimulus money was combined with the funds already spent under the Bush administration during the fall and winter of 2008 to 2009 to prevent the failure of banks, financial firms, and auto manufacturers General Motors and Chrysler, the government's budget year (fiscal year 2009) ended with the largest budget deficit in U.S. history—a staggering $1.42 trillion. President Obama's budget for 2010 produced an additional deficit of more than $1 trillion. Figure 15.7 expresses these deficits in terms of the percentage of GDP, showing the trend since 1968. Despite the countercyclical logic of Keynesian economic policy, presidents and members of Congress have had chronic difficulty avoiding annual budget deficits, with the notable exception of 1998–2001 under Clinton. When you add together all these annual budget deficits, you get the national debt.

## THE NATIONAL DEBT

**debt ceiling** The official limit set by Congress and the president on the federal government's ability to borrow funds through the sale of Treasury bonds.

In October 2008, the National Debt Clock located in midtown Manhattan, a public record of the federal government's total indebtedness, ran out of digits to record the total when it reached $10 trillion. To accommodate the growing total, the clock dropped the dollar sign from the display and added a "1." When the clock was unveiled in 1989, the debt stood at $2.7 trillion. In 20 years, the total more than quadrupled, but not inadvertently. Congress must approve government borrowing by setting a **debt ceiling**, the limit up to which the Treasury Department is authorized to borrow money, similar to the borrowing limit on a credit card. To combat the economic recession,

Congress raised that limit four times in 2008 and 2009. It has continued to rise with a political battle each time until 2018, when President Trump signed a bill that suspended the debt ceiling until March 2019; an additional compromise reached in 2019 extended the debt ceiling agreement to 2021. Until then, the ceiling would be whatever the national debt was. It stood at nearly $20.5 trillion (yes, with a *t*) at that point and hit $22 trillion a year later.[64]

A growing debt increases the interest payments that the government must pay to lenders, a mandatory expense that must be paid by the U.S. Treasury. Moreover, it means that current revenues have not been covering current spending, so future generations of Americans are responsible for paying off the current generation's debt. Congress established a debt ceiling for the first time in 1917, on the brink of the United States entering World War I. Until then, each time the United States wanted to issue bonds for the public to purchase and thereby loan money to the government, Congress had to approve. A debt ceiling gave the Treasury Department greater financial flexibility than having each bond sale approved separately. Most congressional votes on raising the debt ceiling (nearly 100) have been routine, but not so in 2011. As the federal government approached the approved ceiling, House Republicans, who believed that government spending was out of control, insisted that current spending be cut before they would approve an additional increase. After months of wrangling, only a last-minute agreement that further delayed the decision on spending cuts until later in the year prevented the wealthiest nation on earth from failing to pay its obligations.

The public was disgusted by the spectacle of their elected representatives unable to resolve such an important issue. The most frequent responses in a survey conducted by the Pew Research Center for the People and the Press were *ridiculous* followed by *disgusting, stupid, frustrating, childish,* and *terrible.*[65] Suspending the debt ceiling avoids such battles but it runs the danger of runaway borrowing. Republicans led the charge against additional borrowing in 2011, but once they gained control of both Congress and the White House, they passed a large tax cut and avoided the financial consequences by suspending the debt ceiling. The Democrats' record on the same issue is little better.

## MONETARY POLICY

Government spending and taxes are not the only way to influence economic conditions. The Federal Reserve Board (the Fed) uses a variety of techniques to shape monetary policy, the terms under which money and credit are made available to buyers and sellers in the market economy and so controls the supply of money circulating in the nation. The Fed tries to maintain steady and sustainable economic growth, full employment, and stable prices while ensuring the safety of bank practices. A seven-member Board of Governors, based in Washington, DC, coordinates the activities of 12 regional Federal Reserve Banks and 25 branches located in major cities throughout the nation.

> **Federal Reserve Board (the Fed)** An independent federal agency created in 1913 to regulate the banking industry and set monetary policy.
>
> **monetary policy** The terms under which money and credit are made available to buyers and sellers in the market economy.

Board members and regional bank presidents monitor conditions in their section of the nation's economy, and a subgroup (the Federal Open Market Committee) meets monthly to take actions that move interest rates up (called a *contractionary* policy because it reduces the supply of money) or down (an *expansionary* policy) as a way to influence consumer and business spending and borrowing. They can ease, tighten, or maintain the nation's money supply, resulting in interest rates that decrease, increase, or remain the same.

The Fed's designers hoped to remove politics from banking activities as much as possible. The Fed is self-financing; that is, Congress does not appropriate funding for it as part of the annual budget process, which insulates the Fed from political pressure. In addition, members of the Board of Governors each serve a single 14-year term that spans multiple presidential administrations. The Board's chair and vice chair serve four-year terms that straddle two administrations (they usually serve more than one term) and are nominated by the president, subject to Senate confirmation. The result is a highly independent agency whose leaders must coordinate their policies with

**Jerome Powell was sworn in as Chairman of the Federal Reserve in 2018. His term runs through 2022, at which time the president may choose to appoint him to another four-year term or replace him.**

Congress and the president but are not unduly controlled by either. Thus, the Fed chair reports to Congress at least twice a year and often more frequently in response to congressional requests for testimony. The chair also participates in meetings with other influential financial leaders in the administration, including the secretary of Treasury, members of the Council of Economic Advisers, and the director of OMB. Clearly, then, the Fed's leadership is well aware of the political context in which it must act, but the Fed is buffered from the most direct political pressures.

Just as Congress and the president tend to increase deficits during recessions, so too does the Fed seek to alter interest rates in response to changing economic conditions. The Fed can raise the interest rate that banks charge each other for short-term loans—the **federal funds rate**—as it did dramatically in the late 1970s and early 1980s to bring inflation under control, or it can reduce that rate to try to stimulate economic activity, as it did during recessionary periods. (The interest rates that banks charge to business and individual borrowers roughly parallel the federal funds rate.) Most recently, the Fed reduced effective interest rates to near zero in response to the severe recession beginning in 2008 and only began to raise them—slowly—beginning in 2015. In 2008, many central banks around the world adopted policies similar to those followed in the United States. Policy makers in several major economies took actions similar to the Fed's in order to stimulate economic activity in the face of the global recession. There were also nations reluctant to adopt such policies, including Germany, whose historical experience with uncontrollable inflation in 1923 made its economic and political leaders more likely to pursue "hard-nosed counter-inflationary policies."[66] Germany's experience with cheap money, low interest rates, and rising national debt had been so traumatic that later generations of decision makers were determined to avoid those policies' potential dangers.

## REGULATION

Both federal and state authorities regulate economic activity in the United States. The government seeks to prevent monopolies or near-monopolies from charging unfair prices to consumers and also creates an infrastructure that fosters economic growth. During its life, from 1887 to 1995, the Interstate Commerce Commission regulated railroads, interstate telephone service (until creation of the Federal Communications Commission in 1934), and trucking companies. In subsequent decades, Congress created similar agencies, including the following:

- Federal Trade Commission (1914) to regulate unfair business practices across a wide range of industries
- Federal Communications Commission (1934) to regulate radio, television, and telecommunications
- Securities and Exchange Commission (1934) to regulate stock trading
- Civil Aeronautics Board (1940) to regulate the airlines
- National Labor Relations Board (1935) to protect labor unions' organizing rights and to investigate unfair labor practices
- Consumer Product Safety Commission (1972) to protect citizens against injury caused by product defects

At the state and local level, public service and public utilities commissions regulate the cost and reliability of electricity, natural gas, telephone, TV (cable), water, and wastewater companies. Many states also have an insurance commissioner who oversees health, life, and auto insurance premiums. Originally, municipalities often gave companies exclusive service rights to guarantee the profits they needed for growth. But the commissions controlled these monopolies to prevent unfair pricing practices. AT&T grew to become the largest company in the world by 1970 because other companies could not gain entry into the local phone business dominated by its 18 "baby bells" that operated around the country and its monopoly on long-distance calling. The Interstate Commerce Commission and Federal Communications Commission had taken AT&T to court on several occasions for its monopolistic practices; after several years of litigation, an out-of-court settlement would limit some of the company's worst practices in exchange for the government's acceptance of the company's most profitable operations. But finally, a federal judge's decision issued in 1982 (the case began in 1974) forced AT&T to divest

**federal funds rate** The interest charges that banks collect from each other for loans, which are set by a committee of the Federal Reserve Board in order to influence economic activity through monetary policy.

itself of the local phone business. The result has been greater innovation in phone service and reduced prices as competitors jumped into the market.[67]

Those interests affected by regulation have many avenues to secure support from Congress, the president, and the bureaucrats who regulate them. This means that regulators often serve the interests of the businesses rather than the general public who are ostensibly being protected. There are, however, self-appointed public interest groups who claim to represent the best interests of the unorganized public, as discussed in Chapter 7.

## THE LIMITS OF DOMESTIC ECONOMIC POLICIES

In today's world, formulating economic policy is complicated by interdependence among nations. Policies in the United States are tightly connected to those of its major trading partners, financial partners, and creditors around the globe. Just as other nations are concerned about the health of the U.S. economy, U.S. business and government policy makers worry about conditions abroad. Financial problems starting in the United States mortgage market triggered a worldwide crisis in 2008. Developments in Ireland, Portugal, Greece, and Italy during 2010–2012 had ripple effects on the U.S. stock markets. A shift in exchange rates has immediate impacts on the price of goods being bought or sold. Speculation over the future supply of oil and other critical commodities can quickly drive up prices for consumers and stress family budgets. The unique role played by the United States in the world economy over the past 70 years has made the nation far more dependent on the policies and actions of others than it had been before.

Under these conditions, international coordination was the rule of the day—every day. Prime ministers and presidents, finance ministers, and central bankers met regularly and communicated daily, even more frequently during crises. Global markets responded to each other constantly, operating day and night. But globalism came under attack by President Trump and others around the world who believe that domestic policies should favor national priorities over global impacts. Thus, American farmers struggled with a sudden decline in soybean exports when China drastically reduced imports in retaliation for American tariffs that had reduced imports from China. Even the long-standing alliance with Canada came under stress when the Trump administration used trade restrictions as a way to pressure the Canadians to accept changes more favorable to U.S. interests in the North American Free Trade Association (NAFTA). After a bruising round of negotiations, the pact was renamed the United States–Mexico–Canada Agreement (USMCA). Canadians, still angry, refer to the agreement as the Canada–United States–Mexico Agreement (CUSMA). Until Congress adopts implementing legislation for the new agreement, NAFTA remains in effect, though President Trump has repeatedly threatened to scrap the new agreement entirely if Congress does not approve it on his schedule.

## CONSEQUENCES FOR DEMOCRACY

What do we learn about democracy in America from looking at its public policies? As we have seen, domestic policies reflect many features of the nation's politics—its fragmented decision-making structures, its highly individualistic political culture, and its responses to historical experiences from settling the frontier to fighting a civil war to contending with economic and environmental crises. Policies also reflect current thinking on how best to address the nation's needs: Put more power into the hands of Washington decision makers or decentralize programs to state capitals? Rely on markets to deliver health care or provide services from the state or national government? Help citizens meet their needs in retirement and health care or depend on citizens to meet their own needs?

Policy making in the United States is highly fragmented. State and federal governments share responsibilities; few areas of public policy are exclusively the concern of one or the other, and the precise mix of government responsibility varies along a spectrum from predominantly state to predominantly federal. In the cases we have examined, responsibilities for health care, energy, and the environment are fairly evenly shared; Social Security and Medicare are federal programs, but Medicaid is shared. Frequently, when officials at one level of government prove unresponsive to a problem, those at another level will take action. For example, California established rigorous state regulations for automobile emissions after the federal government failed to act, and several states (including Massachusetts) created universal health care coverage when the federal government would not meet the needs of the uninsured.

Policy making in the United States could scarcely be better structured to ensure that organized interests wield maximum influence. Officials in different branches of government typically share influence over agenda setting, policy formulation, adoption, and evaluation, and within those branches, there are sometimes multiple centers of decision making—for example, subcommittees and committees. With multiple centers of authority, groups seek to influence elected and unelected officials at local, state, and federal levels.

Similar situations are found in other nations. For example, the provinces are especially important centers for policy making in Canada, as are the länder (states) in Germany. But in most other political systems, state officials are either significantly less influential or the federal government is less internally fragmented. A more unified central government changes the dynamics of decision making. If leaders in parliamentary systems are confident of majority support, there is less need to build coalitions across party or ideological lines. The U.S. system, on the other hand, necessitates compromise and coalition building across party, ideological, and regional lines in order to create policies. During periods when such compromise is difficult to achieve, national policy is often frozen in place, as we see during the current period of partisan polarization. And when a majority decides to move ahead with major policy initiatives without buy-in from the minority party, we can expect the losing side to mount ongoing challenges, as in the case of the ACA.

Americans tend to prefer market solutions, distrust central authority, and resist intrusions on individual rights. This is particularly evident in the policies that have been proposed to deal with health care. When a solution seems to create a larger role for government or to shift influence from state to national control, resistance is virtually guaranteed. If citizens are ultimately responsible for providing their own health care in a market setting, for example, they will be less willing to assume shared responsibility to ensure that all citizens enjoy such benefits. Most other developed nations in the world regard health care as a basic right available to everyone, although the quality of those services varies.

Finally, why does the U.S. government have difficulty taking the long view of problems? Social Security is unusual in that it is a program that requires a 75-year time horizon. It would make sense to adopt such a long-term view on environmental problems. Problems that extend well beyond the two-, four-, or six-year time horizon of legislators' or executives' terms in office have less urgency. Do U.S. officials find it more difficult than policy makers in other nations to engage in long-term thinking? Or are there structural features that make the U.S. system different? While it may appear that France and Germany, for example, have adopted more coherent energy policies aimed to minimize environmental impact, they, too, have encountered problems in setting a consistent path.

Freedom of movement has always been a central feature of American life. Persons upset with the quality of health care, the cost of living, or the environmental quality can move someplace else—across town, elsewhere in the state, or elsewhere in the nation. For example, millions have moved from states in the Northeast to states in the rapidly growing Sun Belt to escape snowy winters and expensive heating costs. But not everyone can move, especially during an economic recession.

Which policies should become standardized, regardless of where people live? There is no right answer. Your list is likely to differ from the list of the student sitting next to you. If, for example, we said that a minimum quality of education, health care, and housing should prevail regardless of where you live, why not include other services such as police and fire protection? And do you have an obligation to provide persons less fortunate than yourself with housing, health care, or food? Do those more fortunate than you have an obligation to help you in a similar way? Where do we draw the line?

Questions of quality inevitably raise questions of money. Who pays, and how much do they pay for what services? Americans have accepted varying payment plans—federal taxes, state taxes, and local taxes pay for different services or are mixed in different proportions to pay for services. No one answer fits all times and all policies.

Ultimately, Americans hope that public policies reflect their long-term preferences at the local level, the state level, and the national level.

# Critical Thinking Questions

1. Which stage of the policy making process do you believe is most critical?

2. Why has it been so difficult for the United States to ensure that all residents, citizens and noncitizens alike, have access to affordable, high-quality health care? What issues of access and quality remain after the 2010 Affordable Care Act went into effect?

3. What makes an economic system socialist? How does such a system differ from capitalism?

4. Do the citizens of a nation collectively have responsibility for the well-being of its less fortunate citizens suffering from disability, ill health, old age, and other difficulties? What is your preferred solution to the problem of Social Security's financial solvency (that is, too many retirees and too few contributors)?

5. What balance would you strike between the nation's need for more energy and the desire for a healthy environment? Which sources of energy should be encouraged and discouraged for the future?

6. How does the federal government seek to use fiscal and monetary policies to maintain economic growth and full employment without inflation? Would you encourage more or less regulation of economic activity?

# Key Terms

agenda setting, 383

budget deficit, 405

capitalism, 386

debt ceiling, 406

delegation, 385

energy security, 398

entitlement program, 389

federal funds rate, 408

Federal Reserve Board (the Fed), 407

fiscal policy, 405

greenhouse gas, 399

gross domestic product (GDP), 405

Keynesian economics, 405

laissez-faire, 386

mixed economy, 388

monetary policy, 407

policy adoption, 384

policy evaluation, 385

policy formulation, 383

policy implementation, 385

public assistance program, 389

public policies, 383

regulated multi-payer system, 391

single-payer systems, 391

social insurance program, 394

socialism, 386

Visit edge.sagepub.com/maltese to help you accomplish your coursework goals in an easy-to-use learning environment.

# APPENDIX A
## The Declaration of Independence

## IN CONGRESS, JULY 4, 1776

The unanimous Declaration of the thirteen united States of America

When in the Course of human events, it becomes necessary for one people to dissolve the political bands which have connected them with another, and to assume among the powers of the earth, the separate and equal station to which the Laws of Nature and of Nature's God entitle them, a decent respect to the opinions of mankind requires that they should declare the causes which impel them to the separation.

We hold these truths to be self-evident, that all men are created equal, that they are endowed by their Creator with certain unalienable Rights, that among these, are Life, Liberty, and the pursuit of Happiness.—That to secure these rights, Governments are instituted among Men, deriving their just powers from the consent of the governed,—That, whenever any Form of Government becomes destructive of these ends, it is the Right of the People to alter or to abolish it, and to institute a new Government, laying its foundation on such principles and organizing its powers in such form, as to them shall seem most likely to effect their Safety and Happiness. Prudence, indeed, will dictate that Governments long established should not be changed for light and transient causes; and accordingly all experience hath shewn, that mankind are more disposed to suffer, while evils are sufferable, than to right themselves by abolishing the forms to which they are accustomed. But when a long train of abuses and usurpations, pursuing invariably the same Object evinces a design to reduce them under absolute Despotism, it is their right, it is their duty, to throw off such Government, and to provide new Guards for their future security.—Such has been the patient sufferance of these Colonies; and such is now the necessity which constrains them to alter their former Systems of Government. The history of the present King of Great Britain is a history of repeated injuries and usurpations, all having in direct object the establishment of an absolute Tyranny over these States. To prove this, let Facts be submitted to a candid world.

He has refused his Assent to Laws the most wholesome and necessary for the public good.

He has forbidden his Governors to pass Laws of immediate and pressing importance, unless suspended in their operation till his assent should be obtained; and, when so suspended, he has utterly neglected to attend to them.

He has refused to pass other Laws for the accommodation of large districts of people, unless those people would relinquish the right of Representation in the Legislature, a right inestimable to them and formidable to tyrants only.

He has called together legislative bodies at places unusual, uncomfortable, and distant from the depository of their public Records, for the sole purpose of fatiguing them into compliance with his measures.

He has dissolved Representative Houses repeatedly, for opposing with manly firmness his invasions on the rights of the people.

He has refused for a long time, after such dissolutions, to cause others to be elected; whereby the Legislative powers, incapable of Annihilation, have returned to the People at large for their exercise; the State remaining in the mean time exposed to all the danger of invasion from without, and convulsions within.

He has endeavoured to prevent the population of these States; for that purpose obstructing the Laws for Naturalization of Foreigners; refusing to pass others to encourage their migration hither, and raising the conditions of new Appropriations of Lands.

He has obstructed the Administration of Justice, by refusing his Assent to Laws for establishing Judiciary powers.

He has made Judges dependent on his Will alone, for the tenure of their offices, and the amount and payment of their salaries.

He has erected a multitude of New Offices, and sent hither swarms of Officers to harass our people, and eat out their substance.

He has kept among us, in times of peace, Standing Armies without the Consent of our legislatures.

He has affected to render the Military independent of and superior to the Civil power.

He has combined with others to subject us to a jurisdiction foreign to our constitution, and unacknowledged by our laws; giving his Assent to their Acts of pretended Legislation:

For Quartering large bodies of armed troops among us:

For protecting them, by a mock Trial, from punishment for any Murders which they should commit on the Inhabitants of these States:

For cutting off our Trade with all parts of the world:

For imposing Taxes on us without our Consent:

For depriving us in many cases, of the benefit of Trial by Jury:

For transporting us beyond Seas to be tried for pretended offences:

For abolishing the free System of English Laws in a neighbouring Province, establishing therein an Arbitrary government, and enlarging its Boundaries so as to render it at once an example and fit instrument for introducing the same absolute rule into these Colonies:

For taking away our Charters, abolishing our most valuable Laws, and altering, fundamentally, the Forms of our Governments:

For suspending our own Legislatures, and declaring themselves invested with power to legislate for us in all cases whatsoever.

He has abdicated Government here, by declaring us out of his Protection and waging War against us.

He has plundered our seas, ravaged our Coasts, burnt our towns, and destroyed the lives of our people.

He is at this time transporting large Armies of foreign Mercenaries to compleat the works of death, desolation and tyranny, already begun with circumstances of Cruelty & perfidy scarcely paralleled in the most barbarous ages, and totally unworthy of the Head of a civilized nation.

He has constrained our fellow Citizens taken captive on the high Seas to bear Arms against their Country, to become the executioners of their friends and Brethren, or to fall themselves by their Hands.

He has excited domestic insurrections amongst us, and has endeavoured to bring on the inhabitants of our frontiers, the merciless Indian Savages, whose known rule of warfare, is an undistinguished destruction of all ages, sexes and conditions.

In every stage of these Oppressions We have Petitioned for Redress in the most humble terms: Our repeated Petitions have been answered only by repeated injury. A Prince, whose character is thus marked by every act which may define a Tyrant, is unfit to be the ruler of a free people.

Nor have We been wanting in attention to our British brethren. We have warned them from time to time of attempts made by their legislature to extend an unwarrantable jurisdiction over us. We have reminded them of the circumstances of our emigration and settlement here. We have appealed to their native justice and magnanimity, and we have conjured them by the ties of our common kindred to disavow these usurpations, which, would inevitably interrupt our connections and correspondence. They too have been deaf to the voice of justice and of consanguinity. We must, therefore, acquiesce in the necessity, which denounces our Separation, and hold them, as we hold the rest of mankind, Enemies in War, in Peace Friends.

We, therefore, the Representatives of the united States of America, in General Congress, Assembled, appealing to the Supreme Judge of the world for the rectitude of our intentions, do, in the Name, and by the Authority of the good People of these Colonies, solemnly publish and declare, That these United Colonies are, and of Right ought to be Free and Independent States;

that they are Absolved from all Allegiance to the British Crown, and that all political connection between them and the State of Great Britain, is and ought to be totally dissolved; and that as Free and Independent States, they have full Power to levy War, conclude Peace, contract Alliances, establish Commerce, and to do all other Acts and Things which Independent States may of right do. And for the support of this Declaration, with a firm reliance on the protection of divine Providence, we mutually pledge to each other our Lives, our Fortunes, and our sacred Honor.

**The foregoing Declaration was, by order of Congress, engrossed, and signed by the following members:**

*John Hancock*

NEW HAMPSHIRE
*Josiah Bartlett*
*William Whipple*
*Matthew Thornton*

MASSACHUSETTS
*Samuel Adams*
*John Adams*
*Robert Treat Paine*
*Elbridge Gerry*

RHODE ISLAND
*Stephen Hopkins*
*William Ellery*

CONNECTICUT
*Roger Sherman*
*Samuel Huntington*
*William Williams*
*Oliver Wolcott*

NEW YORK
*William Floyd*
*Philip Livingston*
*Francis Lewis*
*Lewis Morris*

NEW JERSEY
*Richard Stockton*
*John Witherspoon*
*Francis Hopkinson*
*John Hart*
*Abraham Clark*

PENNSYLVANIA
*Robert Morris*
*Benjamin Rush*
*Benjamin Franklin*
*John Morton*
*George Clymer*
*James Smith*
*George Taylor*
*James Wilson*
*George Ross*

DELAWARE
*Caesar Rodney*
*George Read*
*Thomas McKean*

## MARYLAND
*Samuel Chase*
*William Paca*
*Thomas Stone*
*Charles Carroll of Carrollton*

## VIRGINIA
*George Wythe*
*Richard Henry Lee*
*Thomas Jefferson*
*Benjamin Harrison*
*Thomas Nelson, Jr.*
*Francis Lightfoot Lee*
*Carter Braxton*

## NORTH CAROLINA
*William Hooper*
*Joseph Hewes*
*John Penn*

## SOUTH CAROLINA
*Edward Rutledge*
*Thomas Heyward, Jr.*
*Thomas Lynch, Jr.*
*Arthur Middleton*

## GEORGIA
*Button Gwinnett*
*Lyman Hall*
*George Walton*

*Resolved,* That copies of the declaration be sent to the several assemblies, conventions and committees, or councils of the continental troops; that it be proclaimed in each of the United States, at the head of the army.

# APPENDIX B
## The Constitution of the United States of America[1]

We the People of the United States, in Order to form a more perfect Union, establish Justice, insure domestic Tranquility, provide for the common defence, promote the general Welfare, and secure the Blessings of Liberty to ourselves and our Posterity, do ordain and establish this Constitution for the United States of America.

## ARTICLE I

### SECTION 1

All legislative Powers herein granted shall be vested in a Congress of the United States, which shall consist of a Senate and House of Representatives.

### SECTION 2

The House of Representatives shall be composed of Members chosen every second Year by the People of the several States, and the Electors in each State shall have the Qualifications requisite for Electors of the most numerous Branch of the State Legislature.

No Person shall be a Representative who shall not have attained to the Age of twenty five Years, and been seven Years a Citizen of the United States, and who shall not, when elected, be an Inhabitant of that State in which he shall be chosen.

[Representatives and direct Taxes[2] shall be apportioned among the several States which may be included within this Union, according to their respective Numbers, which shall be determined by adding to the whole Number of free Persons, including those bound to Service for a Term of Years, and excluding Indians not taxed, three fifths of all other Persons.][3] The actual Enumeration shall be made within three Years after the first Meeting of the Congress of the United States, and within every subsequent Term of ten Years, in such Manner as they shall by Law direct. The Number of Representatives shall not exceed one for every thirty Thousand, but each State shall have at Least one Representative; and until such enumeration shall be made, the State of New Hampshire shall be entitled to chuse three, Massachusetts eight, Rhode-Island and Providence Plantations one, Connecticut five, New-York six, New Jersey four, Pennsylvania eight, Delaware one, Maryland six, Virginia ten, North Carolina five, South Carolina five, and Georgia three.

When vacancies happen in the Representation from any State, the Executive Authority thereof shall issue Writs of Election to fill such Vacancies.

The House of Representatives shall chuse their Speaker and other Officers; and shall have the sole Power of Impeachment.

### SECTION 3

The Senate of the United States shall be composed of two Senators from each State, chosen by the Legislature thereof, for six Years; and each Senator shall have one Vote.

Immediately after they shall be assembled in Consequence of the first Election, they shall be divided as equally as may be into three Classes. The Seats of the Senators of the first Class shall be vacated at the Expiration of the second Year, of the second Class at the Expiration of the fourth Year, and of the third Class at the Expiration of the sixth Year, so that one third may be chosen every second Year; and if Vacancies happen by Resignation, or otherwise, during the Recess of the Legislature of any State, the Executive thereof may make temporary Appointments until the next Meeting of the Legislature, which shall then fill such Vacancies.

No Person shall be a Senator who shall not have attained to the Age of thirty Years, and been nine Years a Citizen of the United States, and who shall not, when elected, be an Inhabitant of that State for which he shall be chosen.

The Vice President of the United States shall be President of the Senate, but shall have no Vote, unless they be equally divided.

The Senate shall chuse their other Officers, and also a President pro tempore, in the Absence of the Vice President, or when he shall exercise the Office of President of the United States.

The Senate shall have the sole Power to try all Impeachments. When sitting for that Purpose, they shall be on Oath or Affirmation. When the President of the United States is tried, the Chief Justice shall preside: And no Person shall be convicted without the Concurrence of two thirds of the Members present.

Judgment in Cases of impeachment shall not extend further than to removal from Office, and disqualification to hold and enjoy any Office of honor, Trust or Profit under the United States: but the Party convicted shall nevertheless be liable and subject to Indictment, Trial, Judgment and Punishment, according to Law.

## SECTION 4

The Times, Places and Manner of holding Elections for Senators and Representatives, shall be prescribed in each State by the Legislature thereof; but the Congress may at any time by Law make or alter such Regulations, except as to the Places of chusing Senators.

The Congress shall assemble at least once in every Year, and such Meeting shall be on the first Monday in December, unless they shall by Law appoint a different Day.

## SECTION 5

Each House shall be the Judge of the Elections, Returns and Qualifications of its own Members, and a Majority of each shall constitute a Quorum to do Business; but a smaller Number may adjourn from day to day, and may be authorized to compel the Attendance of absent Members, in such Manner, and under such Penalties as each House may provide.

Each House may determine the Rules of its Proceedings, punish its Members for disorderly Behaviour, and, with the Concurrence of two thirds, expel a Member.

Each House shall keep a Journal of its Proceedings, and from time to time publish the same, excepting such Parts as may in their Judgment require Secrecy; and the Yeas and Nays of the Members of either House on any question shall, at the Desire of one fifth of those Present, be entered on the Journal.

Neither House, during the Session of Congress, shall, without the Consent of the other, adjourn for more than three days, nor to any other Place than that in which the two Houses shall be sitting.

## SECTION 6

The Senators and Representatives shall receive a Compensation for their Services, to be ascertained by Law, and paid out of the Treasury of the United States. They shall in all Cases, except Treason, Felony, and Breach of the Peace, be privileged from Arrest during their Attendance at the Session of their respective Houses, and in going to and returning from the same; and for any Speech or Debate in either House, they shall not be questioned in any other Place.

No Senator or Representative shall, during the Time for which he was elected, be appointed to any civil Office under the Authority of the United States, which shall have been created, or the Emoluments whereof shall have been encreased during such time; and no Person holding any Office under the United States, shall be a Member of either House during his Continuance in Office.

## SECTION 7

All Bills for raising Revenue shall originate in the House of Representatives; but the Senate may propose or concur with Amendments as on other Bills.

Every Bill which shall have passed the House of Representatives and the Senate, shall, before it become a Law, be presented to the President of the United States; If he approve he shall sign it, but if not he shall return it, with his Objections to that House in which it shall have originated, who shall enter the Objections at large on their Journal, and proceed to reconsider it. If after such Reconsideration two thirds of that House shall agree to pass the Bill, it shall be sent, together with the Objections, to the other House, by which it shall likewise be reconsidered, and if approved by two thirds of that House, it shall become a Law. But in all such Cases the Votes of both Houses shall be determined by yeas and Nays, and the Names of the Persons voting for and against the Bill shall be entered on the Journal of each House respectively. If any Bill shall not be returned by the President within ten Days (Sundays excepted) after it shall have been presented to him, the Same shall be a Law, in like Manner as if he had signed it, unless the Congress by their Adjournment prevent its Return, in which Case it shall not be a Law.

Every Order, Resolution, or Vote to which the Concurrence of the Senate and House of Representatives may be necessary (except on a question of Adjournment) shall be presented to the President of the United States; and before the Same shall take Effect, shall be approved by him, or being disapproved by him, shall be repassed by two thirds of the Senate and House of Representatives, according to the Rules and Limitations prescribed in the Case of a Bill.

## SECTION 8

The Congress shall have Power To lay and collect Taxes, Duties, Imposts and Excises, to pay the Debts and provide for the common Defence and general Welfare of the United States; but all Duties, Imposts and Excises shall be uniform throughout the United States;

To borrow Money on the credit of the United States;

To regulate Commerce with foreign Nations, and among the several States, and with the Indian Tribes;

To establish a uniform Rule of Naturalization, and uniform Laws on the subject of Bankruptcies throughout the United States;

To coin Money, regulate the Value thereof, and of foreign Coin, and fix the Standard of Weights and Measures;

To provide for the Punishment of counterfeiting the Securities and current Coin of the United States;

To establish Post Offices and post Roads;

To promote the Progress of Science and useful Arts, by securing for limited Times to Authors and Inventors the exclusive Right to their respective Writings and Discoveries;

To constitute Tribunals inferior to the Supreme Court;

To define and punish Piracies and Felonies committed on the high Seas, and Offenses against the Law of Nations;

To declare War, grant Letters of Marque and Reprisal, and make Rules concerning Captures on Land and Water;

To raise and support Armies, but no Appropriation of Money to that Use shall be for a longer Term than two Years;

To provide and maintain a Navy;

To make Rules for the Government and Regulation of the land and naval Forces;

To provide for calling forth the Militia to execute the Laws of the Union, suppress Insurrections and repel Invasions;

To provide for organizing, arming, and disciplining, the Militia, and for governing such Part of them as may be employed in the Service of the United States, reserving to the States respectively, the Appointment of the Officers, and the Authority of training the Militia according to the discipline prescribed by Congress;

To exercise exclusive Legislation in all Cases whatsoever, over such District (not exceeding ten Miles square) as may, by Cession of particular States, and the Acceptance of Congress, become the Seat of the Government of the United States, and to exercise like Authority over all Places purchased by the Consent of the Legislature of the State in which the Same shall be, for the Erection of Forts, Magazines, Arsenals, dock-Yards, and other needful Buildings;—And

To make all Laws which shall be necessary and proper for carrying into Execution the foregoing Powers, and all other Powers vested by this Constitution in the Government of the United States, or in any Department or Officer thereof.

## SECTION 9

The Migration or Importation of such Persons as any of the States now existing shall think proper to admit, shall not be prohibited by the Congress prior to the Year one thousand eight hundred and eight, but a Tax or duty may be imposed on such Importation, not exceeding ten dollars for each Person.

The privilege of the Writ of Habeas Corpus shall not be suspended, unless when in Cases of Rebellion or Invasion the public Safety may require it.

No Bill of Attainder or ex post facto Law shall be passed.

No Capitation, or other direct, Tax shall be laid, unless in Proportion to the Census or Enumeration herein before directed to be taken.

No Tax or Duty shall be laid on Articles exported from any State.

No Preference shall be given by any Regulation of Commerce or Revenue to the Ports of one State over those of another: nor shall Vessels bound to, or from, one State, be obliged to enter, clear, or pay Duties in another.

No Money shall be drawn from the Treasury, but in Consequence of Appropriations made by Law; and a regular Statement and Account of the Receipts and Expenditures of all public Money shall be published from time to time.

No Title of Nobility shall be granted by the United States: And no Person holding any Office of Profit or Trust under them, shall, without the Consent of the Congress, accept of any present, Emolument, Office, or Title, of any kind whatever, from any King, Prince, or foreign State.

## SECTION 10

No State shall enter into any Treaty, Alliance, or Confederation; grant Letters of Marque and Reprisal; coin Money; emit Bills of Credit; make any Thing but gold and silver Coin a Tender in Payment of Debts; pass any Bill of Attainder, ex post facto Law, or Law impairing the Obligation of Contracts, or grant any Title of Nobility.

No State shall, without the Consent of the Congress, lay any Imposts or Duties on Imports or Exports, except what may be absolutely necessary for executing its inspection Laws: and the net Produce of all Duties and Imposts, laid by any State on Imports or Exports, shall be for the Use of the Treasury of the United States; and all such Laws shall be subject to the Revision and Controul of the Congress.

No State shall, without the Consent of Congress, lay any Duty of Tonnage, keep Troops, or Ships of War in time of Peace, enter into any Agreement or Compact with another State, or with a foreign Power, or engage in War, unless actually invaded, or in such imminent Danger as will not admit of delay.

# ARTICLE II

## SECTION 1

The executive Power shall be vested in a President of the United States of America. He shall hold his Office during the Term of four years, and, together with the Vice President, chosen for the same Term, be elected, as follows

Each State shall appoint, in such Manner as the Legislature thereof may direct, a Number of Electors, equal to the whole Number of Senators and Representatives to which the State may be entitled in the Congress: but no Senator or Representative, or Person holding an Office of Trust or Profit under the United States, shall be appointed an Elector.

[The Electors shall meet in their respective States, and vote by Ballot for two Persons, of whom one at least shall not be an Inhabitant of the same State with themselves. And they shall make a List of all the Persons voted for, and of the Number of Votes for each; which List they shall sign and certify, and transmit sealed to the Seat of the Government of the United States, directed to the President of the Senate. The President of the Senate shall, in the Presence of the Senate and House of Representatives, open all the Certificates, and the Votes shall then be counted. The Person having the greatest Number of Votes shall be the President, if such Number be a Majority of the whole Number of Electors appointed; and if there be more than one who have such Majority, and have an equal Number of Votes, then the House of Representatives shall immediately chuse by Ballot one of them for President; and if no Person have a Majority, then from the five highest on the List the said House shall in like Manner chuse the President. But in chusing the President, the Votes shall be taken by States, the Representation from each State having one Vote; A quorum for this Purpose shall consist of a Member or Members from two thirds of the States, and a Majority of all the States shall be necessary to a Choice. In every Case, after the Choice of the President, the Person having the greatest Number of Votes of the Electors shall be the Vice President. But if there should remain two or more who have equal votes, the Senate shall chuse from them by Ballot the Vice President.][4]

The Congress may determine the Time of chusing the Electors, and the Day on which they shall give their Votes; which Day shall be the same throughout the United States.

No Person except a natural born Citizen, or a Citizen of the United States, at the time of the Adoption of this Constitution, shall be eligible to the Office of President; neither shall any Person be eligible to that Office who shall not have attained to the Age of thirty five Years, and been fourteen Years a Resident within the United States.

In Case of the Removal of the President from Office, or of his Death, Resignation, or Inability to discharge the Powers and Duties of the said Office, the same shall devolve on the Vice President, and the Congress may by Law provide for the Case of Removal, Death, Resignation, or Inability, both of the President and Vice President, declaring what Officer shall then act as President, and such Officer shall act accordingly, until the Disability be removed, or a President shall be elected.

The President shall, at stated Times, receive for his Services, a Compensation, which shall neither be encreased nor diminished during the Period for which he shall have been elected, and he shall not receive within that Period any other Emolument from the United States, or any of them.

Before he enter on the execution of his Office, he shall take the following Oath or Affirmation:—"I do solemnly swear (or affirm) that I will faithfully execute the Office of President of the United States, and will to the best of my Ability, preserve, protect, and defend the Constitution of the United States."

## SECTION 2

The President shall be Commander in Chief of the Army and Navy of the United States, and of the Militia of the several States, when called into the actual Service of the United States; he may require the Opinion, in writing, of the principal Officer in each of the executive Departments, upon any Subject relating to the Duties of their respective Offices, and he shall have Power to grant Reprieves and Pardons for Offenses against the United States, except in Cases of Impeachment.

He shall have Power, by and with the Advice and Consent of the Senate, to make Treaties, provided two thirds of the Senators present concur; and he shall nominate, and by and with the Advice and Consent of the Senate, shall appoint Ambassadors, other public Ministers and Consuls, Judges of the supreme Court, and all other Officers of the United States, whose Appointments are not herein otherwise provided for, and which shall be established by Law: but the Congress may by Law vest the Appointment of such inferior Officers, as they think proper, in the President alone, in the Courts of Law, or in the Heads of Departments.

The President shall have Power to fill up all Vacancies that may happen during the Recess of the Senate, by granting Commissions which shall expire at the End of their next Session.

## SECTION 3

He shall from time to time give to the Congress Information of the State of the Union, and recommend to their Consideration such Measures as he shall judge necessary and expedient; he may, on extraordinary Occasions, convene both Houses, or either of them, and in Case of Disagreement between them, with Respect to the Time of Adjournment, he may adjourn them to such Time as he shall think proper; he shall receive Ambassadors and other public Ministers; he shall take Care that the Laws be faithfully executed, and shall Commission all the Officers of the United States.

## SECTION 4

The President, Vice President and all civil Officers of the United States, shall be removed from Office on Impeachment for, and Conviction of, Treason, Bribery, or other high Crimes and Misdemeanors.

# ARTICLE III
## SECTION 1

The judicial Power of the United States, shall be vested in one supreme Court, and in such inferior Courts as the Congress may from time to time ordain and establish. The Judges, both of the supreme and inferior Courts, shall hold their Offices during good Behaviour, and shall, at stated Times, receive for their Services, a Compensation, which shall not be diminished during their Continuance in Office.

## SECTION 2

The judicial Power shall extend to all Cases, in Law and Equity, arising under this Constitution, the Laws of the United States, and Treaties made, or which shall be made, under their Authority;—to all Cases affecting Ambassadors, other public Ministers and Consuls;—to all Cases of admiralty and maritime Jurisdiction;—to Controversies to which the United States shall be a Party;—to Controversies between two or more States;—between a State and Citizens of another State;[5]—between Citizens of different States—between Citizens of the same State claiming Lands under Grants of different States, and between a State, or the Citizens thereof, and foreign States, Citizens, or Subjects.

In all Cases affecting Ambassadors, other public Ministers and Consuls, and those in which a State shall be Party, the supreme Court shall have original Jurisdiction. In all the other Cases before mentioned, the supreme Court shall have appellate Jurisdiction, both as to Law and Fact, with such Exceptions, and under such Regulations as the Congress shall make.

The Trial of all Crimes, except in Cases of Impeachment, shall be by Jury; and such Trial shall be held in the State where the said Crimes shall have been committed; but when not committed within any State, the Trial shall be at such Place or Places as the Congress may by Law have directed.

## SECTION 3

Treason against the United States, shall consist only in levying War against them, or in adhering to their Enemies, giving them Aid and Comfort. No Person shall be convicted of Treason unless on the Testimony of two Witnesses to the same overt Act, or on Confession in open Court.

The Congress shall have power to declare the Punishment of Treason, but no Attainder of Treason shall work Corruption of Blood, or Forfeiture except during the Life of the Person attainted.

# ARTICLE IV
## SECTION 1

Full Faith and Credit shall be given in each State to the public Acts, Records, and judicial Proceedings of every other State. And the Congress may by general Laws prescribe the Manner in which such Acts, Records and Proceedings shall be proved, and the Effect thereof.

## SECTION 2

The Citizens of each State shall be entitled to all Privileges and Immunities of Citizens in the several States.

A Person charged in any State with Treason, Felony, or other Crime, who shall flee from Justice, and be found in another State, shall on Demand of the executive Authority of the State from which he fled, be delivered up, to be removed to the State having Jurisdiction of the Crime.

No Person held to Service or Labour in one State, under the Laws thereof, escaping into another, shall, in Consequence of any Law or Regulation therein, be discharged from such Service or Labour, but shall be delivered up on Claim of the Party to whom such Service or Labour may be due.

## SECTION 3

New States may be admitted by the Congress into this Union; but no new State shall be formed or erected within the Jurisdiction of any other State; nor any State be formed by the Junction of two or more States, or Parts of States, without the Consent of the Legislatures of the States concerned as well as of the Congress.

The Congress shall have Power to dispose of and make all needful Rules and Regulations respecting the Territory or other Property belonging to the United States; and nothing in this Constitution shall be so construed as to Prejudice any Claims of the United States, or of any particular State.

## SECTION 4

The United States shall guarantee to every State in this Union a Republican Form of Government, and shall protect each of them against Invasion; and on Application of the Legislature, or of the Executive (when the Legislature cannot be convened) against domestic Violence.

# ARTICLE V

The Congress, whenever two thirds of both Houses shall deem it necessary, shall propose Amendments to this Constitution, or, on the Application of the Legislatures of two thirds of the several States, shall call a Convention for proposing Amendments, which, in either Case, shall be valid to all Intents and Purposes, as part of this Constitution, when ratified by the Legislatures of three fourths of the several States, or by Conventions in three fourths thereof, as the one or the other Mode of Ratification may be proposed by the Congress; Provided that no Amendment which may be made prior to the Year One thousand eight hundred and eight shall in any Manner affect the first and fourth Clauses in the Ninth Section of the first Article; and that no State, without its Consent, shall be deprived of its equal Suffrage in the Senate.

# ARTICLE VI

All Debts contracted and Engagements entered into, before the Adoption of this Constitution, shall be as valid against the United States under this Constitution, as under the Confederation.

This Constitution, and the Laws of the United States which shall be made in Pursuance thereof; and all Treaties made, or which shall be made, under the Authority of the United States, shall be the supreme Law of the Land; and the Judges in every State shall be bound thereby, any Thing in the Constitution or Laws of any State to the Contrary notwithstanding.

The Senators and Representatives before mentioned, and the Members of the several State Legislatures, and all executive and judicial Officers, both of the United States and of the several States, shall be bound by Oath or Affirmation, to support this Constitution; but no religious Tests shall ever be required as a Qualification to any Office or public Trust under the United States.

# ARTICLE VII

The Ratification of the Conventions of nine States, shall be sufficient for the Establishment of this Constitution between the States so ratifying the Same.

Done in Convention by the Unanimous Consent of the States present the Seventeenth Day of September in the Year of our Lord one thousand seven hundred and Eighty seven, and of the Independence of the United States of America the Twelfth. In Witness whereof We have hereunto subscribed our Names.

These are the full names of the signers, which in some cases are not the signatures on the document.

GEORGE WASHINGTON
*President and deputy from Virginia*

NEW HAMPSHIRE
*John Langdon*
*Nicholas Gilman*

MASSACHUSETTS
*Nathaniel Gorham*
*Rufus King*

CONNECTICUT
*William Samuel Johnson*
*Roger Sherman*

NEW YORK
*Alexander Hamilton*

NEW JERSEY
*William Livingston*
*David Brearley*
*William Paterson*
*Jonathan Dayton*

PENNSYLVANIA
*Benjamin Franklin*
*Thomas Mifflin*
*Robert Morris*
*George Clymer*
*Thomas FitzSimmons*
*Jared Ingersoll*
*James Wilson*
*Gouverneur Morris*

DELAWARE
*George Read*
*Gunning Bedford, Jr.*
*John Dickinson*
*Richard Bassett*
*Jacob Broom*

MARYLAND
*James McHenry*
*Daniel of St. Thomas Jenifer*
*Daniel Carroll*

VIRGINIA
*John Blair*
*James Madison, Jr.*

NORTH CAROLINA
*William Blount*
*Richard Dobbs Spaight*
*Hugh Williamson*

SOUTH CAROLINA
*John Rutledge*
*Charles Cotesworth Pinckney*
*Charles Pinckney*
*Pierce Butler*

GEORGIA
*William Few*
*Abraham Baldwin*

*Articles in Addition to, and Amendment of the Constitution of the United States of America, proposed by Congress, and ratified by the Legislatures of the several States, pursuant to the fifth Article of the original Constitution.*[6]

# AMENDMENT I

Congress shall make no law respecting an establishment of religion, or prohibiting the free exercise thereof; or abridging the freedom of speech, or of the press; or the right of the people peaceably to assemble, and to petition the Government for a redress of grievances.

# AMENDMENT II

A well regulated Militia, being necessary to the security of a free State, the right of the people to keep and bear Arms, shall not be infringed.

# AMENDMENT III

No Soldier shall, in time of peace be quartered in any house, without the consent of the Owner, nor in time of war, but in a manner to be prescribed by law.

# AMENDMENT IV

The right of the people to be secure in their persons, houses, papers, and effects, against unreasonable searches and seizures, shall not be violated, and no Warrants shall issue, but upon probable cause, supported by Oath or affirmation, and particularly describing the place to be searched, and the persons or things to be seized.

## AMENDMENT V

No person shall be held to answer for a capital, or otherwise infamous crime, unless on a presentment or indictment of a Grand Jury, except in cases arising in the land or naval forces, or in the Militia, when in actual service in time of War or public danger; nor shall any person be subject for the same offence to be twice put in jeopardy of life or limb; nor shall be compelled in any criminal case to be a witness against himself, nor be deprived of life, liberty, or property, without due process of law; nor shall private property be taken for public use, without just compensation.

## AMENDMENT VI

In all criminal prosecutions, the accused shall enjoy the right to a speedy and public trial, by an impartial jury of the State and district wherein the crime shall have been committed, which district shall have been previously ascertained by law, and to be informed of the nature and cause of the accusation; to be confronted with the witnesses against him; to have compulsory process for obtaining witnesses in his favor, and to have the Assistance of Counsel for his defence.

## AMENDMENT VII

In Suits at common law, where the value in controversy shall exceed twenty dollars, the right of trial by jury shall be preserved, and no fact tried by a jury, shall be otherwise re-examined in any Court of the United States, than according to the rules of the common law.

## AMENDMENT VIII

Excessive bail shall not be required, nor excessive fines imposed, nor cruel and unusual punishments inflicted.

## AMENDMENT IX

The enumeration of the Constitution, of certain rights, shall not be construed to deny or disparage others retained by the people.

## AMENDMENT X

The powers not delegated to the United States by the Constitution, nor prohibited by it to the States, are reserved to the States respectively, or to the people.

## AMENDMENT XI [1795]

The Judicial power of the United States shall not be construed to extend to any suit in law or equity, commenced or prosecuted against one of the United States by Citizens of another State, or by Citizens or Subjects of any Foreign State.

## AMENDMENT XII [1804]

The Electors shall meet in their respective States, and vote by ballot for President and Vice-President, one of whom, at least, shall not be an inhabitant of the same state with themselves; they shall name in their ballots the person voted for as President, and in distinct ballots the person voted for as Vice-President, and they shall make distinct lists of all persons voted for as President, and of all persons voted for as Vice-President, and of the number of votes for each, which lists they shall sign and certify, and transmit sealed to the seat of the government of the United States, directed to the President of the Senate;—The President of the Senate shall, in the presence of the Senate and House of Representatives, open all the certificates and the votes shall then be counted;—The person having the greatest number of votes for President, shall be the President, if such number be a majority of the whole number of Electors appointed; and if no person have such majority, then from the persons having the highest numbers not exceeding three on the list of those voted for as President, the House of Representatives shall choose immediately, by ballot, the President. But in choosing the President, the votes shall be taken by states, the representation from each state having one vote; a quorum for this purpose shall consist of a member or members from two-thirds of the states, and a majority of all the states shall be necessary to a choice. And if the House of Representatives shall not choose a President whenever the right of choice shall devolve upon them, before the fourth day of March next following, then the Vice-President shall act as President, as in the case of the death or other constitutional disability of the President.—The person having the greatest number of votes as Vice-President, shall be the Vice-President, if such number be a majority of the whole number of Electors appointed, and if no person have a majority, then from the two highest numbers on the list, the Senate shall choose the Vice-President; a quorum for the purpose shall consist of two-thirds of the whole number of Senators, and a majority of the whole number shall be necessary to a choice. But no person constitutionally ineligible to the office of President shall be eligible to that of Vice-President of the United States.

## AMENDMENT XIII [1865]

Neither slavery nor involuntary servitude, except as a punishment for crime whereof the party shall have been duly convicted, shall exist within the United States, or any place subject to their jurisdiction.

Congress shall have power to enforce this article by appropriate legislation.

## AMENDMENT XIV [1868]

All persons born or naturalized in the United States, and subject to the jurisdiction thereof, are citizens of the United States and of the State wherein they reside. No State shall make or enforce any law which shall abridge the privileges or immunities of citizens of the United States; nor shall any State deprive any person of life, liberty, or property, without due process of law; nor deny to any person within its jurisdiction the equal protection of the laws.

Representatives shall be apportioned among the several States according to their respective numbers, counting the whole number of persons in each State, excluding Indians not taxed. But when the right to vote at any election for the choice of electors for President and Vice President of the United States, Representatives in Congress, the Executive and Judicial officers of a State, or the members of the Legislature thereof, is denied to any of the male inhabitants of such State, being twenty-one years of age, and citizens of the United States, or in any way abridged, except for participation in rebellion, or other crime, the basis of representation therein shall be reduced in the proportion which the number of such male citizens shall bear to the whole number of male citizens twenty-one years of age in such State.

No person shall be a Senator or Representative in Congress, or elector of President and Vice President, or hold any office, civil or military, under the United States, or under any State, who, having previously taken an oath, as a member of Congress, or as an officer of the United States, or as a member of any State legislature, or as an executive or judicial officer of any State, to support the Constitution of the United States, shall have engaged in insurrection or rebellion against the same, or given aid or comfort to the enemies thereof. But Congress may by a vote of two-thirds of each House, remove such disability.

The validity of the public debt of the United States, authorized by law, including debts incurred for payment of pensions and bounties for services in suppressing insurrection or rebellion, shall not be questioned. But neither the United States nor any State shall assume or pay any debts or obligation incurred in aid of insurrection or rebellion against the United States, or any claim for the loss or emancipation of any slave; but all such debts, obligations and claims shall be held illegal and void.

The Congress shall have the power to enforce, by appropriate legislation, the provisions of this article.

# AMENDMENT XV [1870]

The right of citizens of the United States to vote shall not be denied or abridged by the United States or by any State on account of race, color, or previous condition of servitude.

The Congress shall have power to enforce this article by appropriate legislation.

# AMENDMENT XVI [1913]

The Congress shall have power to lay and collect taxes on incomes, from whatever source derived, without apportionment among the several States, and without regard to any census or enumeration.

# AMENDMENT XVII [1913]

The Senate of the United States shall be composed of two Senators from each State, elected by the people thereof, for six years; and each Senator shall have one vote. The electors in each State shall have the qualifications requisite for electors of the most numerous branch of the State legislatures.

When vacancies happen in the representation of any State in the Senate, the executive authority of such State shall issue writs of election to fill such vacancies: Provided, That the legislature of any State may empower the executive thereof to make temporary appointments until the people fill the vacancies by election as the legislature may direct.

This amendment shall not be so construed as to affect the election or term of any Senator chosen before it becomes valid as part of the Constitution.

# AMENDMENT XVIII [1919]

After one year from the ratification of this article the manufacture, sale, or transportation of intoxicating liquors within, the importation thereof into, or the exportation thereof from the United States and all territory subject to the jurisdiction thereof for beverage purposes is hereby prohibited.

The Congress and the several States shall have concurrent power to enforce this article by appropriate legislation.

This article shall be inoperative unless it shall have been ratified as an amendment to the Constitution by the legislatures of the several States, as provided in the Constitution, within seven years from the date of the submission hereof to the States by the Congress.

# AMENDMENT XIX [1920]

The right of citizens of the United States to vote shall not be denied or abridged by the United States or by any State on account of sex.

Congress shall have power to enforce this article by appropriate legislation.

# AMENDMENT XX [1933]

The terms of the President and Vice President shall end at noon on the 20th day of January, and the terms of Senators and Representatives at noon on the 3d day of January, of the years in which such terms would have ended if this article had not been ratified; and the terms of their successors shall then begin.

The Congress shall assemble at least once in every year, and such meeting shall begin at noon on the 3d day of January, unless they shall by law appoint a different day.

If, at the time fixed for the beginning of the term of the President, the President elect shall have died, the Vice President elect shall become President. If a President shall not have been chosen before the time fixed for the beginning of his term or if the President elect shall have failed to qualify, then the Vice President elect shall act as President until a President shall have qualified; and the Congress may by law provide for the case wherein neither a President elect nor a Vice President elect shall have qualified, declaring who shall then act as President, or the manner in which one who is to act shall be selected, and such person shall act accordingly until a President or Vice President shall have qualified.

The Congress may by law provide for the case of the death of any of the persons from whom the House of Representatives may choose a President whenever the right of choice shall have devolved upon them, and for the case of the death of any of the persons from whom the Senate may choose a Vice President whenever the right of choice shall have devolved upon them. Sections 1 and 2 shall take effect on the 15th day of October following the ratification of this article.

This article shall be inoperative unless it shall have been ratified as an amendment to the Constitution by the legislatures of three-fourths of the several States within seven years from the date of its submission.

## AMENDMENT XXI [1933]

The eighteenth article of amendment to the Constitution of the United States is hereby repealed.

The transportation or importation into any State, Territory, or possession of the United States for delivery or use therein of intoxicating liquors, in violation of the laws thereof, is hereby prohibited.

This article shall be inoperative unless it shall have been ratified as an amendment to the Constitution by conventions in the several States, as provided in the Constitution, within seven years from the date of the submission hereof to the States by the Congress.

## AMENDMENT XXII [1951]

No person shall be elected to the office of the President more than twice, and no person who has held the office of President, or acted as President, for more than two years of a term to which some other person was elected President shall be elected to the office of the President more than once. But this Article shall not apply to any person holding the office of President when this Article was proposed by the Congress, and shall not prevent any person who may be holding the office of President, or acting as President, during the term within which this article becomes operative from holding the office of President or acting as President during the remainder of such term.

This article shall be inoperative unless it shall have been ratified as an amendment to the Constitution by the legislatures of three-fourths of the several states within seven years from the date of its submission to the states by the Congress.

## AMENDMENT XXIII [1961]

The District constituting the seat of Government of the United States shall appoint in such manner as the Congress may direct: A number of electors of President and Vice President equal to the whole number of Senators and Representatives in Congress to which the District would be entitled if it were a State, but in no event more than the least populous State; they shall be in addition to those appointed by the States, but they shall be considered, for the purposes of the election of President and Vice President, to be electors appointed by a state; and they shall meet in the District and perform such duties as provided by the twelfth article of amendment.

The Congress shall have power to enforce this article by appropriate legislation.

## AMENDMENT XXIV [1964]

The right of citizens of the United States to vote in any primary or other election for President or Vice President, for electors for President or Vice President, or for Senator or Representative in Congress, shall not be denied or abridged by the United States or any state by reason of failure to pay any poll tax or other tax.

The Congress shall have the power to enforce this article by appropriate legislation.

## AMENDMENT XXV [1967]

In case of the removal of the President from office or of his death or resignation, the Vice President shall become President.

Whenever there is a vacancy in the office of the Vice President, the President shall nominate a Vice President who shall take office upon confirmation by a majority vote of both Houses of Congress.

Whenever the President transmits to the President pro tempore of the Senate and the Speaker of the House of Representatives his written declaration that he is unable to discharge the powers and duties of his office, and until he transmits to them a written declaration to the contrary, such powers and duties shall be discharged by the Vice President as Acting President.

Whenever the Vice President and a majority of either the principal officers of the executive departments or of such other body as Congress may by law provide, transmit to the President pro tempore of the Senate and the Speaker of the House of Representatives their written declaration that the President is unable to discharge the powers and duties of his office, the Vice President shall immediately assume the powers and duties of the office as Acting President.

Thereafter, when the President transmits to the President pro tempore of the Senate and the Speaker of the House of Representatives his written declaration that no inability exists, he shall resume the powers and duties of his office unless the Vice President and a majority of either the principal officers of the executive departments or of such other body as Congress may by law provide, transmit within four days to the President pro tempore of the Senate and the Speaker of the House of Representatives their written declaration that the President is unable to discharge the powers and duties of his office. Thereupon Congress shall decide the issue, assembling within forty-eight hours for that purpose if not in session. If the Congress, within twenty-one days after receipt of the latter written declaration, or, if Congress is not in session, within twenty-one days after Congress is required to assemble, determines by two-thirds vote of both Houses that the President is unable to discharge the powers and duties of his office, the Vice President shall continue to discharge the same as Acting President; otherwise, the President shall resume the powers and duties of his office.

## AMENDMENT XXVI [1971]

The right of citizens of the United States, who are 18 years of age or older, to vote, shall not be denied or abridged by the United States or by any State on account of age.

The Congress shall have the power to enforce this article by appropriate legislation.

## AMENDMENT XXVII [1992]

No law varying the compensation for the service of Senators and Representatives shall take effect until an election of Representatives shall have intervened.

# APPENDIX C
## Federalist No. 10 (James Madison)

To the People of the State of New York:

Among the numerous advantages promised by a well-constructed Union, none deserves to be more accurately developed than its tendency to break and control the violence of faction. The friend of popular governments never finds himself so much alarmed for their character and fate, as when he contemplates their propensity to this dangerous vice. He will not fail, therefore, to set a due value on any plan which, without violating the principles to which he is attached, provides a proper cure for it. The instability, injustice, and confusion introduced into the public councils have, in truth, been the mortal diseases under which popular governments have everywhere perished; as they continue to be the favorite and fruitful topics from which the adversaries to liberty derive their most specious declamations. The valuable improvements made by the American constitutions on the popular models, both ancient and modern, cannot certainly be too much admired; but it would be an unwarrantable partiality to contend that they have as effectually obviated the danger on this side, as was wished and expected. Complaints are everywhere heard from our most considerate and virtuous citizens, equally the friends of public and private faith, and of public and personal liberty, that our governments are too unstable, that the public good is disregarded in the conflicts of rival parties, and that measures are too often decided, not according to the rules of justice and the rights of the minor party, but by the superior force of an interested and overbearing majority. However anxiously we may wish that these complaints had no foundation, the evidence, of known facts will not permit us to deny that they are in some degree true. It will be found, indeed, on a candid review of our situation, that some of the distresses under which we labor have been erroneously charged on the operation of our governments; but it will be found, at the same time, that other causes will not alone account for many of our heaviest misfortunes; and, particularly, for that prevailing and increasing distrust of public engagements, and alarm for private rights, which are echoed from one end of the continent to the other. These must be chiefly, if not wholly, effects of the unsteadiness and injustice with which a factious spirit has tainted our public administrations.

By a faction, I understand a number of citizens, whether amounting to a majority or minority of the whole, who are united and actuated by some common impulse of passion, or of interest, adversed to the rights of other citizens, or to the permanent and aggregate interests of the community.

There are two methods of curing the mischiefs of faction: the one, by removing its causes; the other, by controlling its effects.

There are again two methods of removing the causes of faction: the one, by destroying the liberty which is essential to its existence; the other, by giving to every citizen the same opinions, the same passions, and the same interests.

It could never be more truly said than of the first remedy, that it was worse than the disease. Liberty is to faction what air is to fire, an aliment without which it instantly expires. But it could not be a less folly to abolish liberty, which is essential to political life, because it nourishes faction, than it would be to wish the annihilation of air, which is essential to animal life, because it imparts to fire its destructive agency.

The second expedient is as impracticable as the first would be unwise. As long as the reason of man continues fallible, and he is at liberty to exercise it, different opinions will be formed. As long as the connection subsists between his reason and his self-love, his opinions and his passions will have a reciprocal influence on each other; and the former will be objects to which the latter will attach themselves. The diversity in the faculties of men, from which the rights of property originate, is not less an insuperable obstacle to a uniformity of interest. The protection of these faculties is the first object of government. From the protection of different and unequal faculties of acquiring property, the possession of different degrees and kinds of property immediately results; and from the influence of these on the sentiments and views of the respective proprietors, ensues a division of the society into different interests and parties.

The latent causes of faction are thus sown in the nature of man; and we see them everywhere brought into different degrees of activity, according to the different circumstances of civil society. A zeal for different opinions concerning religion, concerning government, and many other points, as well of speculation as of practice; an attachment to different leaders ambitiously contending for pre-eminence and power; or to persons of other descriptions whose fortunes have been interesting to the human passions, have, in turn, divided mankind into parties, inflamed them with mutual animosity, and rendered them much more disposed to vex and oppress each other than to co-operate for their common good. So strong is this propensity of mankind to fall into mutual animosities, that where no substantial occasion presents itself, the most frivolous and fanciful distinctions have been sufficient to kindle their unfriendly passions and excite their most violent conflicts. But the most common and durable source of factions has been the various and unequal distribution of property. Those who hold and those who are without property have ever formed distinct interests in society. Those who are creditors, and those who are debtors, fall under a like discrimination. A landed interest, a manufacturing interest, a mercantile interest, a moneyed interest, with many lesser interests, grow up of necessity in civilized nations, and divide them into different classes, actuated by different sentiments and views. The regulation of these various and interfering interests forms the principal task of modern legislation, and involves the spirit of party and faction in the necessary and ordinary operations of government.

No man is allowed to be a judge in his own cause, because his interest would certainly bias his judgment, and, not improbably, corrupt his integrity. With equal, nay with greater reason, a body of men are unfit to be both judges and parties at the same time; yet what are many of the most important acts of legislation, but so many judicial determinations, not indeed concerning the rights of single persons, but concerning the rights of large bodies of citizens? And what are the different classes of legislators but advocates and parties to the causes which they determine? Is a law proposed concerning private debts? It is a question to which the creditors are parties on one side and the debtors on the other. Justice ought to hold the balance between them. Yet the parties are, and must be, themselves the judges; and the most numerous party, or, in other words, the most powerful faction must be expected to prevail. Shall domestic manufacturers be encouraged, and in what degree, by restrictions on foreign manufacturers? [These] are questions which would be differently decided by the landed and the manufacturing classes, and probably by neither with a sole regard to justice and the public good. The apportionment of taxes on the various descriptions of property is an act which seems to require the most exact impartiality; yet there is, perhaps, no legislative act in which greater opportunity and temptation are given to a predominant party to trample on the rules of justice. Every shilling with which they overburden the inferior number, is a shilling saved to their own pockets.

It is in vain to say that enlightened statesmen will be able to adjust these clashing interests, and render them all subservient to the public good. Enlightened statesmen will not always be at the helm. Nor, in many cases, can such an adjustment be made at all without taking into view indirect and remote considerations, which will rarely prevail over the immediate interest which one party may find in disregarding the rights of another or the good of the whole.

The inference to which we are brought is, that the *causes* of faction cannot be removed, and that relief is only to be sought in the means of controlling its *effects*.

If a faction consists of less than a majority, relief is supplied by the republican principle, which enables the majority to defeat its sinister views by regular vote. It may clog the administration, it may convulse the society; but it will be unable to execute and mask its violence under the forms of the Constitution. When a majority is included in a faction, the form of popular government, on the other hand, enables it to sacrifice to its ruling passion or interest both the public good and the rights of other citizens. To secure the public good and private rights against the danger of such a faction, and at the same time to preserve the spirit and the form of popular government, is then the great object to which our inquiries are directed. Let me add that it is the great desideratum by which this form of government can be rescued from the opprobrium under which it has so long labored, and be recommended to the esteem and adoption of mankind.

By what means is this object attainable? Evidently by one of two only. Either the existence of the same passion or interest in a majority at the same time must be prevented, or the majority, having such coexistent passion or interest, must be rendered, by their number and local situation, unable to concert and carry into effect schemes of oppression. If the impulse and the opportunity be suffered to coincide, we well know that neither moral nor religious motives can be relied on as an adequate control. They are not found to be such on the injustice and violence of individuals, and lose their efficacy in proportion to the number combined together, that is, in proportion as their efficacy becomes needful.

From this view of the subject it may be concluded that a pure democracy, by which I mean a society consisting of a small number of citizens, who assemble and administer the government in person, can admit of no cure for the mischiefs of faction. A common passion or interest will, in almost every case, be felt by a majority of the whole; a communication and concert result from the form of government itself; and there is nothing to check the inducements to sacrifice the weaker party or an obnoxious individual. Hence it is that such democracies have ever been spectacles of turbulence and contention; have ever been found incompatible with personal security or the rights of property; and have in general been as short in their lives as they have been violent in their deaths. Theoretic politicians, who have patronized this species of government, have erroneously supposed that by reducing mankind to a perfect equality in their political rights, they would, at the same time, be perfectly equalized and assimilated in their possessions, their opinions, and their passions.

A republic, by which I mean a government in which the scheme of representation takes place, opens a different prospect, and promises the cure for which we are seeking. Let us examine the points in which it varies from pure democracy, and we shall comprehend both the nature of the cure and the efficacy which it must derive from the Union.

The two great points of difference between a democracy and a republic are: first, the delegation of the government, in the latter, to a small number of citizens elected by the rest; secondly, the greater number of citizens, and greater sphere of country, over which the latter may be extended.

The effect of the first difference is, on the one hand, to refine and enlarge the public views, by passing them through the medium of a chosen body of citizens, whose wisdom may best discern the true interest of their country, and whose patriotism and love of justice will be least likely to sacrifice it to temporary or partial considerations. Under such a regulation, it may well happen that the public voice, pronounced by the representatives of the people, will be more consonant to the public good than if pronounced by the people themselves, convened for the purpose. On the other hand, the effect may be inverted. Men of factious tempers, of local prejudices, or of sinister designs, may, by intrigue, by corruption, or by other means, first obtain the suffrages, and then betray the interests, of the people. The question resulting is, whether small or extensive republics are more favorable to the election of proper guardians of the public weal; and it is clearly decided in favor of the latter by two obvious considerations:

In the first place, it is to be remarked that, however small the republic may be, the representatives must be raised to a certain number, in order to guard against the cabals of a few; and that, however large it may be, they must be limited to a certain number, in order to guard against the confusion of a multitude. Hence, the number of representatives in the two cases not being in proportion to that of the constituents, and being proportionally greater in the small republic, it follows that, if the proportion of fit characters be not less in the large than in the small republic, the former will present a greater option, and consequently a greater probability of a fit choice.

In the next place, as each representative will be chosen by a greater number of citizens in the large than in the small republic, it will be more difficult for unworthy candidates to practice with success the vicious arts by which elections are too often carried; and the suffrages of the people being more free, will be more likely to centre in men who possess the most attractive merit and the most diffusive and established characters.

It must be confessed that in this, as in most other cases, there is a mean, on both sides of which inconveniencies will be found to lie. By enlarging too much the number of electors, you render the representatives too little acquainted with all their local circumstances and lesser interests; as by reducing it too much, you render him unduly attached to these, and too little fit to comprehend and pursue great and national objects. The federal Constitution forms a happy combination in this respect; the great and aggregate interests being referred to the national, the local and particular to the State legislatures.

The other point of difference is, the greater number of citizens and extent of territory which may be brought within the compass of republican than of democratic government; and it is this circumstance principally which renders factious combinations less to be dreaded in the former than in the latter. The smaller the society, the fewer probably will be the distinct parties and interests composing it; the fewer the distinct parties and interests, the more frequently will a majority be found of the same party; and the smaller the number of individuals composing a majority, and the smaller the compass within which they are placed, the more easily will they concert and execute their plans of oppression. Extend the sphere, and you take in a greater variety of parties and interests; you make it less probable that a majority of the whole will have a common motive to invade the rights of other citizens; or if such a common motive exists, it will be more difficult for all who feel it to discover their own strength, and to act in unison with each other. Besides other impediments, it may be remarked that, where there is a consciousness of unjust or dishonorable purposes, communication is always checked by distrust in proportion to the number whose concurrence is necessary.

Hence, it clearly appears, that the same advantage which a republic has over a democracy, in controlling the effects of faction, is enjoyed by a large over a small republic,—is enjoyed by the Union over the States composing it. Does this advantage consist in the substitution of representatives whose enlightened views and virtuous sentiments render them superior to local prejudices and to schemes of injustice?

It will not be denied that the representation of the Union will be most likely to possess these requisite endowments. Does it consist in the greater security afforded by a greater variety of parties, against the event of any one party being able to outnumber and oppress the rest? In an equal degree does the increased variety of parties comprised within the Union, increase this security. Does it, in fine, consist in the greater obstacles opposed to the concert and accomplishment of the secret wishes of an unjust and interested majority? Here, again, the extent of the Union gives it the most palpable advantage.

The influence of factious leaders may kindle a flame within their particular States, but will be unable to spread a general conflagration through the other States. A religious sect may degenerate into a political faction in a part of the Confederacy; but the variety of sects dispersed over the entire face of it must secure the national councils against any danger from that source. A rage for paper money, for an abolition of debts, for an equal division of property, or for any other improper or wicked project, will be less apt to pervade the whole body of the Union than a particular member of it; in the same proportion as such a malady is more likely to taint a particular county or district, than an entire State.

In the extent and proper structure of the Union, therefore, we behold a republican remedy for the diseases most incident to republican government. And according to the degree of pleasure and pride we feel in being republicans, ought to be our zeal in cherishing the spirit and supporting the character of Federalists.

PUBLIUS.

# APPENDIX D
## Federalist No. 51 (James Madison)

To the People of the State of New York:

To what expedient, then, shall we finally resort, for maintaining in practice the necessary partition of power among the several departments, as laid down in the Constitution? The only answer that can be given is, that as all these exterior provisions are found to be inadequate, the defect must be supplied, by so contriving the interior structure of the government as that its several constituent parts may, by their mutual relations, be the means of keeping each other in their proper places. Without presuming to undertake a full development of this important idea, I will hazard a few general observations, which may perhaps place it in a clearer light, and enable us to form a more correct judgment of the principles and structure of the government planned by the convention.

In order to lay a due foundation for that separate and distinct exercise of the different powers of government, which to a certain extent is admitted on all hands to be essential to the preservation of liberty, it is evident that each department should have a will of its own; and consequently should be so constituted that the members of each should have as little agency as possible in the appointment of the members of the others. Were this principle rigorously adhered to, it would require that all the appointments for the supreme executive, legislative, and judiciary magistracies should be drawn from the same fountain of authority, the people, through channels having no communication whatever with one another. Perhaps such a plan of constructing the several departments would be less difficult in practice than it may in contemplation appear. Some difficulties, however, and some additional expense would attend the execution of it. Some deviations, therefore, from the principle must be admitted. In the constitution of the judiciary department in particular, it might be inexpedient to insist rigorously on the principle: first, because peculiar qualifications being essential in the members, the primary consideration ought to be to select that mode of choice which best secures these qualifications; secondly, because the permanent tenure by which the appointments are held in that department, must soon destroy all sense of dependence on the authority conferring them.

It is equally evident, that the members of each department should be as little dependent as possible on those of the others, for the emoluments annexed to their offices. Were the executive magistrate, or the judges, not independent of the legislature in this particular, their independence in every other would be merely nominal. But the great security against a gradual concentration of the several powers in the same department, consists in giving to those who administer each department the necessary constitutional means and personal motives to resist encroachments of the others. The provision for defense must in this, as in all other cases, be made commensurate to the danger of attack. Ambition must be made to counteract ambition. The interest of the man must be connected with the constitutional rights of the place. It may be a reflection on human nature, that such devices should be necessary to control the abuses of government. But what is government itself, but the greatest of all reflections on human nature? If men were angels, no government would be necessary. If angels were to govern men, neither external nor internal controls on government would be necessary. In framing a government which is to be administered by men over men, the great difficulty lies in this: you must first enable the government to control the governed; and in the next place oblige it to control itself.

A dependence on the people is, no doubt, the primary control on the government; but experience has taught mankind the necessity of auxiliary precautions. This policy of supplying, by opposite and rival interests, the defect of better motives, might be traced through the whole system of human affairs, private as well as public. We see it particularly displayed in all the subordinate distributions of power, where the constant aim is to divide and arrange the several offices in such a manner as that each may be a check on the other—that the private interest of every individual may be a sentinel over the public rights. These inventions of prudence cannot be less requisite in the distribution of the supreme powers of the State. But it is not possible to give to each department an equal power of self-defense. In republican government, the legislative authority necessarily predominates. The remedy for this inconveniency is to divide the legislature into different branches; and to render them, by different modes of election and different principles of action, as little connected with each other as the nature of their common functions and their common dependence on the society will admit. It may even be necessary to guard against dangerous encroachments by still further precautions. As the weight of the legislative authority requires that it should be thus divided, the weakness of the executive may require, on the other hand, that it should be fortified.

An absolute negative on the legislature appears, at first view, to be the natural defense with which the executive magistrate should be armed. But perhaps it would be neither altogether safe nor alone sufficient. On ordinary occasions it might not be exerted with the requisite firmness, and on extraordinary occasions it might be perfidiously abused. May not this defect of an absolute negative be supplied by some qualified connection between this weaker department and the weaker branch of the stronger department, by which the latter may be led to support the constitutional rights of the former, without being too much detached from the rights of its own department? If the principles on which these observations are founded be just, as I persuade myself they are, and they be applied as a criterion to the several State constitutions, and to the federal Constitution it will be found that if the latter does not perfectly correspond with them, the former are infinitely less able to bear such a test.

There are, moreover, two considerations particularly applicable to the federal system of America, which place that system in a very interesting point of view. First. In a single republic, all the power surrendered by the people is submitted to the administration of a single government; and the usurpations are guarded against by a division of the government into distinct and separate departments. In the compound republic of America, the power surrendered by the people is first divided between two distinct governments, and then the portion allotted to each subdivided among distinct and separate departments. Hence a double security arises to the rights of the people. The different governments will control each other, at the same time that each will be controlled by itself. Second. It is of great importance in a republic not only to guard the society against the oppression of its rulers, but to guard one part of the society against the injustice of the other part. Different interests necessarily exist in different classes of citizens. If a majority be united by a common interest, the rights of the minority will be insecure.

There are but two methods of providing against this evil: the one by creating a will in the community independent of the majority that is, of the society itself; the other, by comprehending in the society so many separate descriptions of citizens as will render an unjust combination of a majority of the whole very improbable, if not impracticable. The first method prevails in all governments possessing an hereditary or self-appointed authority. This, at best, is but a precarious security; because a power independent of the society may as well espouse the unjust views of the major, as the rightful interests of the minor party, and may possibly be turned against both parties. The second method will be exemplified in the federal republic of the United States. Whilst all authority in it will be derived from and dependent on the society, the society itself will be broken into so many parts, interests and classes of citizens, that the rights of individuals, or of the minority, will be in little danger from interested combinations of the majority.

In a free government the security for civil rights must be the same as that for religious rights. It consists in the one case in the multiplicity of interests, and in the other in the multiplicity of sects. The degree of security in both cases will depend on the number of interests and sects; and this may be presumed to depend on the extent of country and number of people comprehended under the same government. This view of the subject must particularly recommend a proper federal system to all the sincere and considerate friends of republican government, since it shows that in exact proportion as the territory of the Union may be formed into more circumscribed Confederacies, or States oppressive combinations of a majority will be facilitated: the best security, under the republican forms, for the rights of every class of citizens, will be diminished; and consequently the stability and independence of some member of the government, the only other security, must be proportionately increased. Justice is the end of government. It is the end of civil society. It ever has been and ever will be pursued until it be obtained, or until liberty be lost in the pursuit. In a society under the forms of which the stronger faction can readily unite and oppress the weaker, anarchy may as truly be said to reign as in a state of nature, where the weaker individual is not secured against the violence of the stronger; and as, in the latter state, even the stronger individuals are prompted, by the uncertainty of their condition, to submit to a government which may protect the weak as well as themselves; so, in the former state, will the more powerful factions or parties be gradually induced, by a like motive, to wish for a government which will protect all parties, the weaker as well as the more powerful.

It can be little doubted that if the State of Rhode Island was separated from the Confederacy and left to itself, the insecurity of rights under the popular form of government within such narrow limits would be displayed by such reiterated oppressions of factious majorities that some power altogether independent of the people would soon be called for by the voice of the very factions whose misrule had proved the necessity of it. In the extended republic of the United States, and among the great variety of interests, parties, and sects which it embraces, a coalition of a majority of the whole society could seldom take place on any other principles than those of justice and the general good; whilst there being thus less danger to a minor from the will of a major party, there must be less pretext, also, to provide for the security of the former, by introducing into the government a will not dependent on the latter, or, in other words, a will independent of the society itself. It is no less certain than it is important, notwithstanding the contrary opinions which have been entertained, that the larger the society, provided it lie within a practical sphere, the more duly capable it will be of self-government. And happily for the *republican cause*, the practicable sphere may be carried to a very great extent, by a judicious modification and mixture of the *federal principle*.

PUBLIUS.

# GLOSSARY

**accountability:** The capacity to impose consequences on officials for their actions, including removal from office.

**administrative discretion:** The opportunity granted to bureaucrats by Congress to use their judgment in making decisions between alternative courses of action.

**administrative strategy:** A strategy to achieve the administration's goals by using the president's budget, personnel, reorganization, and regulatory powers.

**adversarial system:** The criminal justice system in which defendants are presumed innocent and guilt is determined when prosecutors face off against defense attorneys in a trial.

**affirmative action:** A policy intended to promote equal opportunities for members of previously disadvantaged groups in education and employment.

**agents of political socialization:** The people and institutions from whom we learn about politics.

**agricultural associations:** Organizations either of farmers in general or of a particular kind of farmer.

**American exceptionalism:** The idea that the political culture of the United States is distinctive in the world and that the United States has a special role to build democracy in the world.

**amicus curiae briefs:** "Friend of the court" briefs submitted by third parties who are not named in a case but who hope to influence the outcome of a particular case.

**Anti-Federalists:** States' rights advocates who opposed the ratification of the Constitution.

**appellate court:** A court that hears appeals from lower courts. Appeals involve questions of law rather than questions of fact.

**Articles of Confederation:** The first constitution of the United States (1781–1788), under which states retained sovereignty over all issues not specifically delegated to the weak central government, comprising a unicameral (one-house) legislature and no independent executive or judicial branch.

**attack ads:** Television ads criticizing the opponent, usually in terms of the opponent's positions on issues and his or her record in office.

**attitudinal model:** A model of judicial decision making that assumes that judges will decide cases according to their ideological preferences (or attitudes).

**Australian ballot:** A set of reforms introduced in the 1880s and 1890s to make elections more fair and secret.

**automatic registration:** Enrollment of voters done by the government automatically, without requiring the individual to take any particular action to be eligible to vote.

**bad tendency test:** The least protective free speech test, which allows government to restrict speech that merely poses a tendency or possibility to do harm (as opposed to a clear and present danger).

**bicameral legislature:** A legislature that has two chambers, with each chamber typically reflecting a different part of society or political grouping.

**bill:** A proposal for government action that is introduced in either the House or Senate and may result in a law.

**Bill of Rights:** The first ten amendments of the U.S. Constitution, which form the basis of civil liberties.

**Black Codes:** Post–Civil War laws passed by states that perpetuated discrimination against African Americans.

**block grants:** Funds from the national government to state and local governments that are earmarked for some general policy area, such as education, while giving the recipients flexibility to spend those funds within that policy area as they see fit.

**briefs:** Written statements of legal arguments submitted by the parties in a case and sometimes by outside groups.

***Brown v. Board of Education*:** The Supreme Court decision that overturned the "separate but equal" doctrine and declared racially segregated schools to be unconstitutional.

**bureaucracy:** A structure created to achieve complex goals through coordinated action undertaken either by governments (public bureaucracy) or corporations (private bureaucracy).

**cabinet:** A group of senior advisers to either a president or prime minister; these advisers each head a major department and meet collectively to discuss policy and political issues.

**categorical grants:** Funds from the national government to state and local governments that must be used to implement a specific federal regulation in a particular way, leaving recipients no flexibility regarding how to spend the money.

**caucuses:** Gatherings of party supporters at the neighborhood level who select delegates to a state nominating convention, which in turn selects delegates to the national nominating convention.

**central clearance:** The central coordinating practice established in the 1930s to review all legislative proposals arising from executive branch agencies in light of the president's agenda to determine whether they were consistent or inconsistent with those goals.

**checks and balances:** A method to protect against unrestrained governmental power by dividing and sharing powers among the legislative, executive, and judicial branches.

**citizen groups:** Membership organizations based on a shared set of policy goals; a group is open to all who agree with the policy goals of the organization.

**citizen journalist:** A nonprofessional who reports news via alternative outlets such as the Internet or other social media.

**citizens:** Members of a country's population who are legally recognized as subjects or nationals of the country.

**civil liberties:** The basic freedoms that citizens enjoy from governmental interference, such as the freedoms of speech, press, assembly, and religion, and the guarantees of due process and other specific protections accorded to criminal defendants.

**civil rights:** Freedom from governmental discrimination (unequal treatment) based on age, gender, race, or other personal characteristics.

**Civil Rights Act of 1964:** The most sweeping civil rights legislation since the 1870s; expanded civil rights and increased protections against various forms of discrimination.

*Civil Rights Cases*: Cases wherein the Supreme Court ruled that Congress did not have the authority to outlaw private discrimination in business establishments.

**classical liberalism:** The doctrine that a society is good only to the extent that all of its members are able to develop their capacities to the fullest and that to encourage this result, government should intervene as little as possible in people's lives.

**clear and present danger test:** A free speech test that allows government to restrict only speech that poses a clear and present danger of substantive evil; over time, it has become increasingly protective of speech.

**closed primary:** A primary election in which only those who have registered with a party designation may vote; they may vote only in that party's primary.

**closed rule:** Restrictive guidelines provided by the House Rules Committee that preclude amendments made from the floor during consideration of a bill.

**cluster sampling:** An approximation of a true random sample in which a sample of localities is randomly drawn and then a small random sample of individuals are interviewed in each locality.

**commerce clause:** Article I, Section 8 of the Constitution, which gives Congress the authority to "regulate Commerce with foreign Nations, and among the several States, and with the Indian Tribes."

**committee government:** The period during the mid-twentieth century when chairs of the standing committees were the most powerful figures in the Congress.

**committee jurisdictions:** Defined areas of standing committee responsibilities, comprising the policy areas, programs, and agencies that each committee oversees.

**committee of the whole:** A situation in which the whole House or whole Senate considers business rather than delegating work to committees.

**comparison:** Comparing aspects of a country's government and politics to those aspects in other countries to better understand their causes.

**concurrent powers:** Powers shared by the national government and the states (both, for example, have the power to tax).

**concurring opinion:** A written opinion by a judge who agrees with the outcome of a case but not with its legal reasoning.

**confederal system:** A system of government in which power rests primarily with regional entities that have banded together to form a league of independent governments.

**confederation:** A union of independent, sovereign states whose central government is charged with defense and foreign affairs but where the primary power—especially with regard to domestic politics—rests with the individual states.

**conference:** A meeting of Supreme Court justices in which they discuss cases and vote on how those cases should be decided.

**conference committee:** A temporary committee consisting of both House and Senate members, formed to resolve differences in versions of a bill approved by both chambers before it can be sent to the president.

**congressional campaign committees:** Four committees, one for each party in both the Senate and the House of Representatives, that recruit able candidates for Senate or House seats and raise money for congressional campaigns.

**conservatism:** In the United States, the ideology that supports government intervention on behalf of religious values but opposes intervention in the economic sphere.

**constituency service:** Assistance provided by representatives and senators to help residents of their districts or states resolve problems involving government programs and agencies.

**constitutional theory:** The view of the president's powers, elaborated by William Howard Taft, as strictly limited to those enumerated in the Constitution or conferred by congressional statutes.

**consumer interest:** A group of people consuming a product.

**conventional participation:** Routine behavior that occurs within the formal governmental process of a democracy, such as voting in elections, working for a candidate or party, putting a bumper sticker on your car, or contacting a member of Congress.

**cooperative federalism:** An interpretation of federalism that favors national supremacy and assumes that states will cooperate in the enforcement of federal regulations.

**coordinate construction:** Refers to constitutional interpretation by Congress or the president. Proponents of coordinate construction believe that all three branches of government (not only the judiciary) have the power and duty to interpret the Constitution.

**courts of general jurisdiction:** Courts that have broad authority to hear a wide range of cases.

**courts of limited jurisdiction:** Courts that hear a specialized type of case (such as traffic court).

**critical election:** An election that causes the bases of support for the two main parties to change fairly suddenly.

**crossover voting:** Voting in a primary election for a party other than the one with which you are registered.

**Declaration of Independence:** A statement written by Thomas Jefferson and approved by the Second Continental Congress on July 4, 1776, that asserted the independence of the American colonies from Great Britain.

**delegated authority:** The power to make decisions enjoyed by an agency or department that was approved by Congress.

**delegate model:** A form of representation in which legislators closely reflect the preferences and opinions of constituents in discharging their representative responsibilities—for example, voting the way constituents prefer on an issue.

**democracy:** Rule by the people.

**descriptive representation:** The belief that the extent to which a legislature reflects the demographic composition of the larger population is vitally important in determining the legislature's responsiveness to group needs.

**direct democracy:** Democracy in which all of the people of a community gather to decide policies for the community.

**direct primaries:** The elections to determine a party's nominee for a general election.

**discretionary spending:** One-third of the annual budget for which funding must be reapproved by Congress each year, which subjects programs using this funding to annual changes.

**dissenting opinion:** A written opinion by a judge who disagrees with the outcome of a case.

**divided government:** When political systems elect the president and legislature independently, conflict can easily arise if Congress is controlled by a party other than that of the presidency.

**docket:** A list of cases that a court is scheduled to decide.

**dual court system:** The existence of separate national and local courts in a federal system.

**dual federalism:** An interpretation of federalism that favors states' rights and regards states and the national government as "dual sovereigns" (two relative equals).

**due process clauses:** Clauses in the Fifth and Fourteenth Amendments that prevent the federal government (in the case of the Fifth) and states (in the case of the Fourteenth) from depriving people of life, liberty, or property without fair proceedings.

**earmarks:** Provisions in a bill that provide a benefit to a specific organization or for a specific project either through direct spending or a tax break.

**Electoral College:** The system by which presidents are elected in the United States. Voters vote for a set of electors, and the set that wins casts its vote for the candidate to which it is pledged.

**electoral mobilization:** An election strategy that relies on getting a candidate's supporters to the polls.

**electoral realignment:** A new and lasting rearrangement of the geographic and social bases of support for the parties, ushered in by a critical election.

**electoral system:** A set of rules to determine, based on the outcome of an election, which individuals will hold office.

**enumerated powers:** Powers specifically listed in the Constitution, such as congressional powers outlined in Article I, Section 8.

**Equal Pay Act:** Legislation that prohibits wage discrimination based on sex.

**Equal Rights Amendment (ERA):** A proposed constitutional amendment that would have guaranteed that the government could not deny or abridge the rights of women on account of their sex. It was not ratified.

**equal time rule:** An FCC regulation that requires a broadcast outlet that sells airtime for a political advertisement for one candidate to provide equal time for any other candidate who wishes to purchase it.

**Era of Good Feelings:** A brief period centering on the election of 1820 when the Federalists were in sharp decline and there was no organized opposition to the dominant Democratic-Republican Party.

**establishment clause:** The First Amendment provision that prevents government from imposing religion on citizens and is used to justify the separation of church and state.

**exclusionary rule:** The principle, created by the Supreme Court, that illegally seized evidence may not be introduced in criminal trials.

**Executive Office of the President (EOP):** A bureaucratic structure created in 1939 to house the personal staff and professional staff units created to help the president discharge a growing range of responsibilities.

**executive orders:** Unilateral decrees issued by presidents to deal with policy or procedural matters that fall under their authority.

**exit polls:** Polls conducted on Election Day at the voting places to provide television news stations with instantaneous analysis of what was moving the voters on that day.

**extradition clause:** A provision of Article IV, Section 2 of the Constitution that requires states to return (extradite), upon request, a fugitive who has fled the law to the state that has jurisdiction over the crime.

**527 committees:** Advocacy groups that are allowed to advertise on political issues and are not subject to regulation by the Federal Election Commission.

**Fairness Doctrine:** An FCC regulation in place from 1949 to 1987 that required broadcast licensees to devote a reasonable percentage of their broadcast time to conveying a balanced discussion of public issues of interest and importance to the community.

**fascism:** A nationalist, racist ideology of the 1930s that centered power on a single charismatic leader.

**Federal Communications Commission (FCC):** An independent U.S. government agency created by the Communications Act of 1934 to oversee and regulate the broadcast industry.

**Federalist Papers:** Essays by James Madison, Alexander Hamilton, and John Jay supporting ratification of the Constitution. Originally published in newspapers under the pseudonym "Publius" (Latin for "the people"), they were gathered together in 1788 and published in two volumes as *The Federalist*.

**Federalists:** Those who supported ratification of the Constitution and the stronger national government that it created.

**federal question:** A dispute over how to interpret the U.S. Constitution, acts of Congress, or a federal treaty. Cases involving a federal question can move from state court to federal court.

**federal system:** A system in which power is formally divided between the national government and regional entities such as states.

**Fifteenth Amendment:** The constitutional amendment guaranteeing that the right to vote will not be denied based on race, color, or previous condition of servitude.

**filibuster:** A delay tactic used in the Senate that rests on members' right to speak as long as they desire on a topic, thereby preventing a vote from being taken.

**filtering:** The process by which the media decides what constitutes "news"—what to cover and what not to cover.

**First Party System:** The period from 1800 to 1820, which was marked by the appearance of the new Democratic-Republican Party and the gradual decline of their opponents, the Federalists.

**fiscal year:** The period covered by the budget decisions made annually, running from October 1 to September 30 for the federal government and July 1 to June 30 for many state governments.

**focus group:** A small group of people who meet with campaign workers to discuss issues and a candidate.

**Fourteenth Amendment:** The constitutional amendment containing the guarantees that no state shall deprive any person of the equal protection of the law nor deprive any person of life, liberty, or property without due process of law.

**Fourth Estate:** A term used to describe the press as a social and political force independent of government.

**framing:** The way the media interprets or presents the news that it has decided to cover.

**free exercise clause:** The First Amendment provision that protects the right of citizens to practice their religion without governmental interference.

**free riders:** Those people who take advantage of the fact that a public good cannot possibly be denied to anyone by refusing to pay their share of the cost of providing the public good.

**frontload:** To move a state's primary or caucuses to the earliest date that the party's rules will permit.

**fugitive slave clause:** A provision of Article IV, Section 2 of the Constitution that required the return of escaped slaves to their owners even if they fled to a state where slavery was outlawed. Repealed by the Thirteenth Amendment (1865).

**full faith and credit clause:** The requirement of Article IV, Section 1 of the Constitution that requires states to recognize "the public Acts, Records, and judicial Proceedings of every other state."

**gatekeeping:** The role played by reporters in vetting and verifying information and news sources in order to prevent publication of inaccurate information.

**gender gap:** The difference between the percent of women and the percent of men voting for a candidate, which has been significant since about 1980.

**general election:** A regularly scheduled election at which voters make their final choices of public officials.

**generational effect:** A change in a whole generation's political viewpoint brought about by an event.

**generational replacement:** Change in overall attitudes caused by differences of opinion between young and old that gradually lead to a shift in overall opinion as older citizens pass from the scene.

**gerrymandering:** Drawing the boundaries of congressional or legislative districts with the deliberate intent to affect the outcomes of elections.

**going public:** A presidential strategy designed to influence Congress by appealing directly to the public, asking them to pressure legislators for passage of the president's proposals.

**government:** The set of people who make decisions that are binding for all people in the country and have the right to use force and coercion to implement their choices.

**government corporations:** Business enterprises wholly or partly owned by the government that Congress created to perform a public purpose or provide a market-oriented service but are designed to meet their costs by generating revenues through operations.

**government-sponsored enterprises (GSEs):** Financial services corporations created by Congress to provide credit to targeted areas of American life; for example, Fannie Mae and Freddie Mac specialize in home mortgages.

**grandfather clauses:** Exempted voters from literacy tests and poll taxes if they could prove that their grandfathers had voted before the end of the Civil War.

**Great Compromise:** The decision by the Constitutional Convention to resolve the debate over equal versus proportional representation by establishing a bicameral (two-house) legislature with proportional representation in the lower house, equal representation in the upper house, and different methods of selecting representatives for each house.

**head of state:** The role usually played by an elected president or a monarch who symbolizes the entire nation, is above politics, and, therefore, exercises very limited political powers, usually in only the most fundamental issues, such as forming a new cabinet.

**historical analysis:** Examining the way politics has developed over time in a country in order to understand how its development has helped to shape its current form.

**ideology:** An interconnected set of ideas.

**impeachment:** The power of Congress to remove a president from office before the elected term has expired. Technically, the House impeaches ("charges") a president with "high crimes and misdemeanors" and the Senate may find the president guilty or not guilty of the charges.

**implementation:** The process of carrying out the wishes of Congress as expressed in a policy through the creation and enforcement of programs and regulations by bureaucratic agencies.

**implied powers:** Powers that are not specifically enumerated in the Constitution but are considered "necessary and proper" to carry out the enumerated powers.

**incorporation:** The process by which the Supreme Court has made specific provisions of the Bill of Rights applicable to state and local governments as well as the federal government.

**independent regulatory commissions:** A type of federal government agency designed to allow experts, not politicians, to oversee and regulate a sector of the economy (for example, railroads) usually to protect consumers from unfair business practices but also to protect the businesses in that sector.

**indirect democracy:** Democracy in which the people do not decide policies for the community themselves but elect representatives to decide the policies.

**individualism:** The belief that people should have freedom to make decisions and act with as little government intervention or other control as possible.

**initiative:** A procedure by which a sufficient number of voters, by petition, can place a proposition on the ballot to be decided in a referendum.

**inquisitorial system:** The criminal justice system in which defendants are presumed guilty until proven innocent and guilt is determined by the judge (rather than a jury) who plays an active role in gathering evidence and questioning witnesses.

**institutional presidency:** A term applied to the staff support enjoyed by modern presidents, especially those staff units with relatively continuous operation such as the Office of Management and Budget, the National Security Council, and the cabinet.

**interest group:** A group of people organized to influence government policies.

**internet polling:** Drawing a truly random sample and getting the people in the sample to agree (in return for an incentive) to take part in surveys administered online.

**interstate compacts:** Contracts between two or more states that create an agreement on a particular policy issue.

**"introduce" ads:** Upbeat television ads, usually appearing early in a campaign, that are designed to create a positive first impression of a candidate.

**iron triangle:** The close relationship established and maintained among a trio of actors: the beneficiaries of a government policy (interest groups), the agency responsible for the beneficial programs (bureaucracy), and the congressional committees responsible for authorizing and funding the programs.

**Jim Crow laws:** State and local laws requiring the segregation of the races, including prohibition of interracial marriage and mandating of racially segregated schools.

**Joint Chiefs of Staff:** A structure created in 1947 to coordinate action among the separate military services and provide military advice to the president and the secretary of defense.

**judicial activism:** The idea that the Supreme Court should strictly scrutinize actions of other branches of government that restrict fundamental rights, such as free speech.

**judicial restraint:** The idea that the Supreme Court should defer to the actions of other branches of government as long as they have a rational basis.

**judicial review:** The power of courts, when confronted with a legitimate case, to review and strike down acts of government that violate the Constitution.

**judicial strategy:** A presidential strategy designed to achieve the administration's goals through the appointment of like-minded judges to the federal judiciary and the establishment of clear priorities for federal law enforcement.

**jurisprudence of original intent:** An approach to interpreting the Constitution that relies on the original intent of its framers to clarify the meaning of ambiguous clauses.

**lame ducks:** The description of presidents nearing the end of their fixed term in office who have little remaining leverage to accomplish their policy goals.

**legal model:** A model of judicial decision making that assumes that judges will decide cases according to the law (as opposed to the attitudinal model).

**legislative strategy:** A presidential strategy to achieve goals based on proposals presented to Congress for statutory action.

**libel:** Written defamation of character, which is not accorded First Amendment protection.

**liberalism:** In the United States, the ideology that opposes government intervention on behalf of religious values but supports intervention in the economic sphere to reduce inequality.

**libertarianism:** In the United States, the ideology that opposes government intervention in any area of people's lives.

**literacy tests:** A precondition for voting in some states, purportedly to verify a voter's ability to read or write but actually designed to prevent blacks from voting.

**majority-minority districts:** Congressional districts in which a majority of the electorate are of an ethnic minority. Sometimes these are deliberately created through gerrymandering.

**majority opinion:** A written opinion that expresses the legal reasoning used to justify an appellate court's ruling in a particular case.

**majority rule:** The principle that 50 percent plus one of the people should be able to elect a majority of elected officials and thereby determine the direction of policy.

**mandatory spending:** Spending set by statute rather than an annual vote by Congress, sometimes called *entitlement spending* because recipients qualify for benefits according to qualifications established by law.

***Marbury v. Madison:*** The 1803 Supreme Court case that serves as a precedent for the use of judicial review.

**margin of error:** Statistical measure of how much the sample estimate from a poll is likely to deviate from the true amount in the full population.

**mass media:** The wide array of organizations and outlets that collect and distribute information to the people.

**media effects:** Changes in public opinion based on the influence of the media.

**midterm election:** Elections held two years after a presidential election, in which all members of the House of Representatives and one-third of senators are elected and many states hold elections for governor and other state offices.

**minority rights:** Basic human rights that are considered important to guarantee for minorities in a democracy.

**Miranda warnings:** The list of rights that police must read to suspects at the time of arrest, including the right to remain silent and the right to request a lawyer. Absent such warnings, information obtained from suspects is inadmissible in court.

**mobilization:** The energizing of large numbers of people to act together.

**muckraking:** A type of journalism prevalent in the early part of the twentieth century that exposed corruption in business and government in order to promote reform.

**multiparty systems:** Party systems in which three or more parties regularly have a significant chance of gaining office.

**narrowcasting:** Programming designed to appeal to a particular segment of the population (as opposed to broadcasting, which is designed to appeal to as many people as possible).

**National Association for the Advancement of Colored People (NAACP):** An organization devoted to promoting the civil rights of African Americans.

**national committee:** A committee that oversees the day-to-day business of the political parties at the national level.

**national nominating convention:** A national gathering of delegates to choose a political party's presidential nominee, write a platform of policy positions, and transact other national party business.

**National Security Council (NSC):** A group created in 1947 to coordinate foreign, defense, financial, and intelligence policies for the president.

**natural rights:** Basic rights that all human beings are entitled to, whether or not they are formally recognized by the government.

**necessary and proper (elastic) clause:** The last clause of Article I, Section 8 of the Constitution, which authorizes Congress to make "all laws which shall be necessary and proper" for executing the Constitution's enumerated powers; sometimes called the *elastic clause* because it allows congressional powers to expand.

**net neutrality:** The unhindered flow of information over the Internet without interference by those who run or own the service providers.

**New Jersey Plan:** A plan, favored by small states, to amend (rather than replace) the Articles of Confederation. It would have retained the one-state/one-vote system of voting in the national legislature, with representatives chosen by state legislatures.

**new media:** Media, such as cable television and the Internet, that led to a vast increase in the amount of information available to the people and allowed targeting of particular segments of the population via specialized channels and websites.

**Nineteenth Amendment:** The constitutional amendment that guaranteed women the right to vote.

**nomination:** The designation of candidates among whom voters will choose in an election.

**nullification:** The concept that states can invalidate federal laws that they believe to be unconstitutional.

**objective journalism:** A type of journalism that embraces the idea that newspapers should report news in a fair and neutral manner, devoid of partisanship and sensationalism (as opposed to yellow journalism).

**Office of Management and Budget (OMB):** The successor agency to the Bureau of the Budget, created in 1970 and designed to perform management oversight that went beyond the traditional budget and central clearance functions performed by the Bureau of the Budget.

**Office of Personnel Management (OPM):** The agency created in 1978 as part of the Civil Service Reform Act to manage the civil service for presidents.

**open primary:** A primary election in which all voters may participate and may choose which party's primary they wish to vote in.

**open rule:** Guidelines provided by the House Rules Committee that allow germane amendments to be made from the floor during consideration of a bill.

**open seat:** A congressional seat whose sitting member retires, runs for some other office, or dies.

**oral arguments:** The opportunity for lawyers on both sides of a case to appear before the appellate courts to give a verbal argument and respond to questions from the judges about why their side should prevail.

**original jurisdiction:** The authority of the Supreme Court to hear a case that originates before it (as opposed to an appeal from a lower court).

**oversight:** Review and monitoring by Congress (particularly the relevant authorizing and appropriations committees) of executive branch activities to ensure that they are consistent with legislative intent.

**pack journalism:** A type of journalism conducted by groups (or "packs") of reporters who are assigned to cover the same institution and characterized by uniform coverage of issues, reliance on official channels of information, and lack of original research.

**paradox of voting:** The fact that one person's vote is highly unlikely to change the outcome of an election, so there is no concrete benefit for an individual who chooses to vote.

**parliamentary system:** A political system in which the legislature (parliament) selects the executive either through a single party majority or a majority coalition, providing for closer institutional coordination.

**partisan press:** A type of journalism associated with the late 1700s through the early 1800s when newspapers were affiliated with and controlled by a particular political party or emerging political party.

**party caucus:** A term used by House Democrats referring to the meeting of all party members.

**party conference:** A term used by House Republicans and both Democrats and Republicans in the Senate referring to the meeting of all party members.

**party identification:** A sense of belonging to one or another of the political parties.

**party in government:** The elected officials of a party, who organize themselves along party lines.

**party in the electorate:** The party's supporters in the electorate, including those who identify with the party and vote for it and activists who campaign for it.

**party organization:** A formal structure that conducts managerial and legal tasks for the party.

**party platform:** A set of policy positions adopted by a party at its national nominating convention.

**party polarization:** Increased feelings among partisans that their party is right and the other is wrong.

**party unity:** A measure of how often a majority of Republican legislators vote against a majority of Democratic legislators.

**patronage:** Financial rewards (especially public jobs) given to people in return for their political support.

**Pendleton Civil Service Reform Act:** Legislation approved in 1883 that created the U.S. civil service system, in which government employees are chosen based on expertise and experience rather than party loyalty.

**penny press:** Newspapers that emerged in 1830 and that, due to technological advances, sold for one penny—a sixth of what papers had previously sold for. This development made newspapers accessible to a wide array of people from all economic classes.

**photo opportunity:** A time period reserved for the media to photograph a public official, usually staged to reinforce a particular frame or theme that the official wishes to convey to the public.

*Plessy v. Ferguson*: A Supreme Court ruling that established the "separate but equal" doctrine, upholding state segregation laws.

**police powers:** The powers reserved to the states under the Tenth Amendment dealing with health, safety, public welfare, and morality.

**political action committees (PACs):** Organizations that donate money to political candidates and officeholders.

**political campaign:** The period during which candidates try to convince voters to support them.

**political consultant:** Professional political strategist who advises candidates on broad strategy as well as specific logistics.

**political culture:** A people's attitudes, beliefs, and factual assumptions about the basic nature of society and basic principles of politics.

**political identities:** The images of who you are, to the extent that your identity carries political content, such as your religion or your membership in a political party.

**political leader:** The role played by the U.S. president and, in parliamentary systems, by the prime minister in mobilizing political support behind major policy initiatives, requiring that the leader engage in explicitly political efforts.

**political machines:** Party organizations providing their supporters with benefits such as city jobs and other favors and, in return, controlling them politically.

**political participation:** All of the various actions that citizens can take to influence the government.

**political party:** An organization combining activists and potential officeholders, whose purpose is to determine who will hold office.

**political socialization:** The process of learning political values and factual assumptions about politics.

**politico model:** A form of representation in which legislators play different roles depending on whether constituents have strong views on an issue and the nature of that issue.

**politics:** The process by which decisions that are binding for everyone in the country are made, such as a law, a system of taxes, or a social program.

**poll:** A set of questions asked of a carefully constructed sampling of a population, selected in such a way that the people in the sample are likely to mirror the total population fairly accurately.

**poll taxes:** Tax payments required prior to voting; revived by states in the late nineteenth century as a way to prevent poor blacks from voting.

**popular legitimacy:** The belief among the citizens of a political system that the government's actions deserve to be obeyed because they reflect the will of the people.

**pork barrel:** The traditional way to preserve pork for gradual consumption; it refers more recently to public money used to meet local needs that lack a sound public purpose.

**position papers:** Documents prepared by candidates describing their stances on various issues in detail.

**precedent:** A previous court decision that is used to determine the outcome of subsequent cases involving a similar legal question.

**prerogative theory:** The view that justifies an executive using discretionary power to act in areas without congressional approval or even to violate the law if such action is for the public good and is consistent with the national interest.

**presidential system:** A political system distinguished by having an executive selected separately by the public rather than by the legislature; frequently characterized by fewer parties but higher levels of legislative–executive conflict.

**prime minister:** The executive officer in a parliamentary system who is supported in the legislature by a majority of his or her own party or a majority based on a coalition.

**prior restraint:** Censorship before publication (such as government prohibition against future publication).

**privileges and immunities clause:** A provision of Article IV, Section 2 of the Constitution that forbids a state from denying citizens of other states the rights it confers upon its own citizens.

**producer interest:** A group of people involved in producing a product.

**professional associations:** Organizations of members of a profession.

**Progressive movement:** A movement of mostly middle-class reformers in the early twentieth century who worked to eliminate machine politics.

**proportional representation (PR) electoral system:** An electoral system in which seats are allocated to parties in proportion to their shares of the vote.

**public good:** Something that benefits all members of the community and that no one can possibly be prevented from using.

**public opinion:** The collective opinion of citizens on a policy issue or a principle of politics.

**push poll:** A set of questions used by political campaigns to present negative information about an opposing candidate by taking advantage of the trust people feel for pollsters.

**quasi-governmental organizations ("quagos"):** Hybrid organizations that share some characteristics of public agencies and some features of private corporations, such as the Smithsonian Institution.

**quasi-nongovernmental organizations ("quangos"):** Private-sector organizations that fulfill some of the roles of government agencies, such as the disaster recovery activities of the American Red Cross.

**random digit dialing (RDD):** Drawing a roughly random sample by randomly dialing telephone numbers.

**random sample:** A sample drawn from the full population in such a way that every member of the population has an equal probability of belonging to the sample.

**redistricting:** Redrawing the boundaries of congressional or legislative districts because of population shifts that show up every 10 years after the U.S. Census has been conducted.

**referendum:** A provision of elections allowing citizens to vote directly on constitutional amendments or changes in law.

**registration:** A requirement by almost all states that citizens who wish to vote enroll prior to the election.

**republic:** An indirect democracy that particularly emphasizes insulation of its representatives and officials from direct popular pressure.

**republicanism:** A form of government in which power rests with the people but where the people rule only indirectly through elected representatives bound by the rule of law.

**reserved powers:** The powers not delegated to the national government by the Constitution that are retained by states under the Tenth Amendment.

**responsible party government:** Doctrine stating that parties should present clear alternative programs and enact them faithfully once in office.

**retrospective voting:** Voting to reelect an official if your life and the lives of those around you have gone well over the years that the person has been in office; if not, voting to oust the official.

**rule of four:** The requirement that four of the nine justices on the Supreme Court vote to grant a writ of certiorari.

**rule of law:** The idea that laws, rather than the whims or personal interests of officials, should determine the government's actions.

**safe seats:** Members of Congress who, election after election, win by large margins.

**secession:** The act of withdrawing from membership in a federation.

**Second Party System:** The period from the early 1830s until just before the Civil War, which was marked by rivalry between the Democratic Party and the Whigs.

**select committees:** Congressional committees formed for a specific purpose and limited period of time.

**Senate Majority Leader:** Leader of the majority party in the Senate who plays an important role in managing the business of the chamber.

**senatorial courtesy:** An informal rule that senators will refuse to confirm nominees to the lower federal courts who do not have the support of the senators from the state where the vacancy occurs.

**seniority rule:** A long-running practice followed in Congress in which the member of the majority party with the longest continuous service on a standing committee automatically becomes its chair.

**separate but equal doctrine:** Based on the *Plessy v. Ferguson* ruling that claimed that the equal protection clause of the Fourteenth Amendment allows the segregation of races.

**separation of powers:** The division of governmental powers among three separate and coequal branches—legislative, executive, and judicial.

**Shays' Rebellion:** An armed rebellion by farmers in Massachusetts who, facing foreclosure, tried using force to shut down courthouses where the foreclosures were issued. The national government's inability to quell the rebellion made the event a potent symbol of the weakness of the Articles of Confederation.

**single-member-district, plurality (SMDP) system:** An electoral system in which the country is divided into districts, each of which elects a single member to the Congress or parliament. The candidate receiving a plurality of votes wins the seat.

**slander:** Spoken defamation of character, which is not accorded First Amendment protection.

**social contract:** The idea, drawn from the writings of John Locke and others, that government is accountable to the people and bound to protect the natural rights of its citizens. If the government breaks this contract, the people have the right to rebel and replace the government with one that will enforce it.

socialism: An ideology that favors having the government take over most businesses and run them in the interest of social and economic equality.

social media: Technologies such as blogs, texting, video file sharing, and other Internet resources that enable people to exchange information. These technologies have helped to blur the line between news consumer and news producer.

social movements: Informally organized, often temporary groups that spring up around an issue or an event to advance a specific point of view.

solicitor general: A senior member of the Justice Department who is responsible for handling all appeals of cases in which the U.S. government is a party.

Speaker of the House: A constitutionally prescribed position of the presiding officer in the House, which became more partisan and more program-focused in the nineteenth century.

spin: Attempts by government officials to influence how the media will report an event by suggesting how a story should be framed.

split-ticket voting: When several candidates for different offices appear on a ballot, the practice of voting for a candidate of one party for one office and a candidate of another party for another office.

spoils system: A popular practice in the nineteenth century that allowed presidents to appoint party loyalists and campaign workers to government jobs as a reward for their support, establishing the adage of "to the victor belongs the spoils."

Stamp Act Congress: The first national meeting of representatives from the colonies in 1765. In response to duties (taxes) imposed by Parliament on the colonies through the Stamp Act, this Congress passed a Declaration of Rights that denounced taxation without representation—an important step toward the American Revolution.

standing committees: Permanent committees in the House or Senate whose responsibilities carry over from one Congress to the next, as does much of its membership.

State of the Union Address: The annual address delivered by the president in person to a joint session of Congress and other government leaders. Today, this address is broadcast to a prime-time television audience.

stewardship theory: The view of the president's role as a "steward" of the people who serves their interests because of the president's unique role as the representative of the entire nation and who is therefore empowered to define the position as broadly as necessary.

strategic model: A model of judicial decision making that assumes that judges are rational actors who will strategically try to get as close to their preferences as possible by building winning coalitions.

substantive due process: A judicially created concept whereby the due process clauses of the Fifth and Fourteenth Amendments can be used to strike down laws that are deemed to be arbitrary or unfair.

substantive representation: The capacity of a legislator or a legislature to represent the interests of groups despite not sharing the demographic characteristics of that group.

superdelegates: Delegates to the Democratic Party's national nominating convention who are not selected through a primary or caucus procedure but go to the convention because of the office they hold in the party or the government.

Super PAC: An independent campaign organization that may raise unlimited funds and spend them on overt attacks or support for candidates; it may not directly coordinate its strategy with campaigns.

Super Tuesday: The first Tuesday in a primary season on which parties allow states (except for early contests such as New Hampshire or Iowa) to schedule primaries or caucuses; large numbers of states usually schedule their contests for this day, which makes it "super."

supremacy clause: Article VI, Clause 2 of the Constitution specifying that federal laws and treaties passed pursuant to the Constitution trump contradictory state laws dealing with the same topic.

symbolic speech: Communication that is neither spoken nor written but is nonetheless accorded free speech protection under the First Amendment.

talk radio: A radio forum that opens the lines to listeners to discuss various topics of interest.

targeted marketing: Using consumer research to divide voters into tiny segments based on a wide variety of indicators so that different messages can be sent to various groups of voters.

Tenth Amendment: The amendment to the Constitution that says, "The powers not delegated to the United States by the Constitution, nor prohibited by it to the States, are reserved to the States respectively, or to the people."

third parties: Small political parties that are so greatly handicapped by the single-member, plurality electoral system in the United States and other obstacles that they have a low probability of winning office.

Thirteenth Amendment: The constitutional amendment that abolished slavery and other forms of involuntary servitude.

Three-Fifths Compromise: The decision by the Constitutional Convention to count slaves as three-fifths of a person for purposes of representation.

time, place, and manner restrictions: The stipulation that the freedoms of speech and assembly do not mean that people can assemble anytime, anywhere, and say whatever they want, however they want.

Title IX: One of the Education Amendments of 1972 designed to abolish all forms of sex discrimination in public education.

top-two primary: All candidates are listed on the same primary ballot, and the two candidates with the most votes go on to the general election.

tracking polls: Short, simple polls that are repeated day after day to allow a candidate to track exactly how a campaign is going on a daily basis.

**trade associations:** Organizations of businesses who share the same trade.

**trial courts:** Courts where cases originate and trials take place (as opposed to appellate courts).

**trustee model:** A form of representation in which legislators are not required to reflect the preferences and opinions of their constituents because voters expect them to use their own knowledge and good judgment.

**two-party system:** A party system with two—and only two—parties that regularly nominate candidates with a serious chance of winning office.

**unconventional participation:** Behavior that challenges the normal workings of government by disrupting it or by making people uncomfortable.

**unfunded mandate:** A legal requirement imposed on states by Congress to administer a program that comes with no federal money to pay for it.

**unified government:** Distinct from divided government; a situation in which the presidency and the two houses of Congress are controlled by the same political party, providing the basis for joint action.

**unitary system:** A system of government in which the national government has ultimate control over all areas of policy.

**unpledged delegates:** Delegates to the Republican Party's national nominating convention who are not selected through a primary or caucus procedure but go to the convention by right of the office they hold in the party or the government.

**U.S. courts of appeals:** An intermediate level of federal appellate courts.

**U.S. district courts:** Federal trial courts, where most federal cases are initiated.

**veto:** The constitutional power of a president to reject legislation passed by the legislature. In the United States, presidents have 10 days to act on legislation, which may be signed or returned with objections to the house in which it originated. Congress may override the veto and pass the bill by means of a two-thirds majority in both houses.

**Virginia Plan:** A plan, favored by large states, to replace (rather than amend) the Articles of Confederation and create a strong national government consisting of three branches. It also called for replacing the one-state/one-vote system used under the Articles of Confederation with proportional voting power in the legislature.

**Voting Rights Act of 1965:** Landmark legislation that outlawed literacy tests and took other steps to guarantee the voting rights of African Americans.

**War Powers Resolution:** Passed by Congress over Nixon's veto in 1973, this law establishes a framework for Congress to participate in presidential decisions to use force—short of a formal declaration of war—and to halt such a military deployment.

**Watergate:** The political scandals associated with Richard Nixon, triggered by the judicial, congressional, and media investigations into the illegal break-in at the Democratic National Committee's offices in the Watergate office complex in Washington, DC.

**Whig Party:** A party active from 1830 to the verge of the Civil War; it opposed the extension of presidential power and supported development of transportation and infrastructure.

**whips:** The members of the party leadership team charged with keeping the members in line—that is, getting them to cast votes in the way the party leaders would like.

**white primaries:** A Southern strategy for minimizing black voter influence that allowed only white voters to vote in the primary elections (the only ones that really mattered).

**women's suffrage movement:** The drive to grant women the right to vote.

**writ of certiorari:** An instruction to a lower court to send up the record in a particular case. This is the most common avenue for appeal to the U.S. Supreme Court.

**writ of habeas corpus:** A judicial order requiring that a prisoner be brought before a judge to determine whether there is a lawful justification for incarceration.

**yellow journalism:** A type of journalism that emerged in the late 1800s, characterized by scandalmongering and sensationalistic reporting.

# NOTES

## CHAPTER 1

1. R. Inglehart, C. Haerpfer, A. Moreno, C. Welzel, K. Kizilova, J. Diez-Medrano, M. Lagos, P. Norris, E. Ponarin & B. Puranen et al. (eds.). 2014. *World Values Survey: Round Four—Country-Pooled Datafile Version: www.worldvaluessurvey.org/WVSDocumentationWV4.jsp*. Madrid: JD Systems Institute.

2. Technically, we can speak of politics for any group of people—that is, making collective decisions for that group. We can speak of office politics or church politics, for example. For the sake of simplicity, we will confine ourselves here to the most usual kind of politics, the politics of an entire country.

3. Max Weber, "Politics as a Vocation," in *From Max Weber: Essays in Sociology*, eds. and trans. H. H. Gerth and C. Wright Mills (New York, NY: Oxford University Press, 1958), 77–128. The essay was first written in 1919.

4. Though all male citizens could participate in a city-state like Athens, this was actually a small fraction of the people living in Athens. Aside from female citizens, there were also large numbers of slaves and other noncitizens who were unable to participate.

5. Various editions of Freedom House's yearbook, *Freedom in the World*. Although we have noted that *democracy* is a matter of degree, here and in Figure 1.1 we dichotomize the concept, treating all countries as being either democracies or not democracies. We use Freedom House's category *electoral democracy*, which is rather loose and inclusive.

6. W. Phillips Shively, *Power and Choice: An Introduction to Political Science*, 12th ed. (New York, NY: McGraw-Hill, 2011), 160.

7. Angus Maddison, "A Comparison of Levels of GDP Per Capita in Developed and Developing Countries, 1700–1980," *Journal of Economic History* 43, no.1 (March 1983): 30.

8. *Public good* is a technical term that is defined and discussed on page 9.

9. Actually, this is a partial definition of the term. In economics, from which political scientists have borrowed the term, a *public good* is a good that is non-rival and non-excludable. *Non-rivalry* means that one person enjoying the good does not reduce the enjoyment of others. *Non-excludability* means that no one can be denied the good. We have left the first part out of our definition here, because we are interested in public goods in relation to the problem of free ridership, which often requires the intervention of government. The full definition is complicated for an introductory course and is not necessary for our purposes here.

10. The basic statement on the problem of public goods and free riders is found in Mancur Olson's *Logic of Collective Action* (Cambridge, MA: Harvard University Press, 1965).

11. Author's observation.

12. "OECD data," Organization for Economic Cooperation and Development (OECD), 2015, https://data.oecd.org/gga/general-government-spending.htm

13. Ibid.

14. Inglehart, R., C. Haerpfer, A. Moreno, C. Welzel, K. Kizilova, J. Diez-Medrano, M. Lagos, P. Norris, E. Ponarin & B. Puranen et al. (eds.). 2014. *World Values Survey: Round Five—Country-Pooled Datafile Version: www.worldvaluessurvey.org/WVSDocumentationWV5.jsp*. Madrid: JD Systems Institute.

15. Frederick Jackson Turner, "The Significance of the Frontier in American History." Paper presented to the American History Association meetings in Chicago, July 12, 1893. The essay is reprinted in Frederick Jackson Turner, *The Frontier in American History* (New York, NY: Holt, 1920).

16. John Locke (1632–1704) is often considered the father of liberalism. He argued in *Two Treatises of Government* that government is based on humans' natural, individual rights and that an unjust government that did not honor those rights should be overthrown. He also argued for the separation of church and state.

17. Massachusetts Constitution, Part the First, Article 30, written by John Adams in 1780.

18. Inglehart, R., C. Haerpfer, A. Moreno, C. Welzel, K. Kizilova, J. Diez-Medrano, M. Lagos, P. Norris, E. Ponarin & B. Puranen et al. (eds.). 2014. *World Values Survey: Round Six—Country-Pooled Datafile Version: www.worldvaluessurvey.org/WVSDocumentationWV6.jsp*. Madrid: JD Systems Institute.

19. Friedrich Engels, "Why There Is No Large Socialist Party in America," letter to Friedrich A. Sorge, December 2, 1893. In *German Essays on Socialism in the Nineteenth Century*, eds. Frank Mecklenburg and Manfred Stassen (New York, NY: Continuum, 1990), 75–76.

20. OECD, *"Panorama de la Société 2014,"* 153, https://read.oecd-ilibrary.org/social-issues-migration-health/panorama-de-la-societe-2014_soc_glance-2014-fr#page1

21. CIA World Factbook, accessed July 15, 2019, https://www.cia.gov/library/publications/the-world-factbook/

22. A good example is in Adam Przeworski et al., *Democracy and Development: Political Institutions and Well-Being in the World, 1950–1990* (New York, NY: Cambridge University Press, 2000).

23. Ibid., 230.

24. Inglehart, *World Values Survey.*

# CHAPTER 2

1. Wikipedia, "List of national constitutions," https://en.wikipedia.org/wiki/List_of_national_constitutions

2. Several websites offer detailed guidelines for drafting a constitution; see, for example, the Public International Law & Policy Group's *Post-Conflict Constitution Drafter's Handbook* at http://www.publicinternationallaw.org/areas/peacebuilding/consthandbook/

3. Joseph J. Ellis, *American Creation* (New York, NY: Random House, 2007), 3.

4. This section is drawn from material in Paul Soifer and Abraham Hoffman, *U.S. History I* (Hoboken, NJ: Wiley, 1998), 19–29.

5. "Text of the Magna Carta," Fordham University, accessed July 13, 2019, https://sourcebooks.fordham.edu/source/magnacarta.asp; Translations from the Latin vary slightly.

6. Quoted in Edmund Morgan, Joseph J. Ellis, and Rosemarie Zagarri, *The Birth of the Republic, 1763–89*, 4th ed. (Chicago, IL: University of Chicago Press, 2012), 18.

7. The full text of the Virginia Stamp Act Resolutions can be found at http://www.ushistory.org/declaration/related/vsa65.html.

8. The Massachusetts legislature issued the invitation in June 1765 for all colonies to send representatives to the Congress. The four colonies that did not send representatives were Georgia, New Hampshire, North Carolina, and Virginia.

9. The full text of the Declaration of Rights can be found at http://www.constitution.org/bcp/dor_sac.htm

10. The full text of the Declaratory Act can be found at http://www.constitution.org/bcp/decl_act.htm

11. David McCullough, *John Adams* (New York, NY: Simon & Schuster, 2001), 67–68.

12. Morgan, *The Birth of the Republic*, 58–59.

13. Merrill Jensen, *The Articles of Confederation: An Interpretation of the Social–Constitutional History of the American Revolution, 1774–1781* (Madison: University of Wisconsin Press, 1940), 56.

14. The full text of the Declaration and Resolves from the First Continental Congress can be found at http://www.historywiz.com/primarysources/declarationandresolves.htm

15. Ellis, *American Creation*, 41.

16. Ibid., 42.

17. This is the figure provided at https://brilliantmaps.com/population-density-1775/

18. When *Common Sense* was first published, 1 out of 5 people bought a copy. One-fifth of the current population (308,745,538 in the 2010 Census) is 62 million people.

19. Joseph J. Ellis, *American Sphinx: The Character of Thomas Jefferson* (New York, NY: Vintage Books, 1998), 57.

20. Jefferson originally wrote "certain inherent and inalienable rights." Congress deleted "inherent" and later printed versions changed "inalienable" to "unalienable." Both words mean the same thing, but there continues to be some debate about which is correct. Valerie Strauss, "Are Our Rights 'Inalienable' or 'Unalienable'?" *The Washington Post*, July 4, 2015, https://www.washingtonpost.com/news/answer-sheet/wp/2015/07/04/are-our-rights-inalienable-or-unalienable/

21. For an extended discussion of all of these debates, see Jensen, *The Articles of Confederation*, Chapter 6.

22. Morgan, *The Birth of the Republic*, 104–112.

23. Keith L. Dougherty, *Collective Action Under the Articles of Confederation* (Cambridge, UK: Cambridge University Press, 2001), 29.

24. Morgan, *The Birth of the Republic*, 126.

25. This requisition system was spelled out in Article VIII of the Articles of Confederation. For a detailed discussion of this and the collective action problems associated with such a system, see Dougherty, Collective Action Under the Articles of Confederation.

26. Jensen, *The Articles of Confederation*, 132.

27. David O. Stewart, *The Summer of 1787* (New York, NY: Simon & Schuster, 2007), 23.

28. Ibid., 19.

29. Morgan, *The Birth of the Republic*, 125.

30. Charles A. Beard, *An Economic Interpretation of the Constitution* (New York, NY: Macmillan, 1913).

31. Stewart, *The Summer of 1787*, 25, 68, 41, and 44.

32. Robert E. Brown, *Charles Beard and the Constitution: A Critical Analysis of "An Economic Interpretation of the Constitution"* (Princeton, NJ: Princeton University Press, 1956); Forrest McDonald, *We the People: The Economic Origins of the Constitution* (Chicago, IL: University of Chicago Press, 1958).

33. Stewart, *The Summer of 1787*, 49–51.

34. Ellis, *American Creation*, 103.

35. Stewart, *The Summer of 1787*, 57.

36. Ibid., 65.

37. Ibid., 66–78.

38. Forrest McDonald, *The American Presidency: An Intellectual History* (Lawrence: University Press of Kansas, 1994), 132–133.

39. Thomas Jefferson, *Notes on the State of Virginia*, quoted in Richard J. Ellis, ed., *Founding the American Presidency* (Lanham, MD: Rowman and Littlefield, 1999), 4.

40. McDonald, *The American Presidency*, 157.

41. Quoted in Ellis, *Founding the American Presidency*, 63.

42. Ibid., 64.

43. Quoted in Ellis, *Founding the American Presidency*, 64.

44. "Constitutional Convention Voting Record," Monticello Digital Classroom, accessd August 12, 2019, https://classroom.monticello.org/media-item/constitutional-convention-voting-record/

45. Ellis, *American Creation*, 114. The remainder of this section relies on pages 115–117.

46. Ibid., 120.

47. John R. Vile, *Encyclopedia of Constitutional Amendments, Proposed Amendments, and Amending Issues, 1789–2002*, 2nd ed. (Santa Barbara, CA: ABC-CLIO, 2003), xx.

48. Constitution of Alabama, 1901, http://alisondb.legislature.state.al.us/alison/codeofalabama/constitution/1901/toc.htm

49. *Marbury v. Madison*, 5 U.S. (1 Cranch) 137 (1803).

50. Louis Fisher, *Constitutional Dialogues* (Princeton, NJ: Princeton University Press, 1988), Chapter 7.

51. Charlie Savage, "Bush Challenges Hundreds of Laws, President Cites His Powers of Office," *Boston Globe*, April 30, 2006, A1. Although this article brought public attention to Bush's use of signing statements, political scientist Christopher S. Kelley had already written a doctoral dissertation on the topic: Christopher S. Kelley, "The Unitary Executive and the Presidential Signing Statement" (PhD diss., Miami University, 2003).

52. American Bar Association Task Force on Presidential Signing Statements, *Report* (August 2006), 32. The full text of the report is available at https://www.americanbar.org/content/dam/aba/publishing/abanews/1273179616signstatereport.authcheckdam.pdf

53. Charlie Savage, "Obama Looks to Limit Impact of Tactic Bush Used to Sidestep New Laws," *The New York Times*, March 10, 2009, A12.

54. Anne Flaherty, "Democrats Irked by Obama's Signing Statement," *Washington Examiner*, July 20, 2009, http://washingtonexaminer.com/politics/2009/07/democrats-irked-obama-signing-statement

55. Joyce A. Green, "Presidential Signing Statements," accessed July 14, 2019, http://www.coherentbabble.com/faqs.htm

56. Gregory Korte, "Trump Criticizes Some Russia Provisions of Defense Bill, Suggests in Signing Statement He May Ignore Them," *USA Today*, August 14, 2018, https://www.usatoday.com/story/news/politics/2018/08/14/trumps-signing-statement-defense-bill-objects-russia-provisions/986692002/

57. Learned Hand, *The Spirit of Liberty*, ed. Irving Dillard (New York, NY: Vintage Books, 1959), 144, quoted in William Van Alstyne, "Quintessential Elements of Meaningful Constitutions in Post-Conflict States," *William and Mary Law Review* 49 (March 2008): 1511.

# CHAPTER 3

1. Executive Order, "Enhancing Public Safety in the Interior of the United States," January 25, 2017, https://www.whitehouse.gov/presidential-actions/executive-order-enhancing-public-safety-interior-united-states/

2. For more about sanctuary schools, see https://www.nilc.org/wp-content/uploads/2018/08/sanctuary-schools-practice-advisory-2018.pdf

3. Gail Ablow, "Sanctuary Cities, Explained," billmoyers.com, April 25, 2017; Julie Davis, "Trump Calls Some Undocumented Immigrants 'Animals' in Rant," *The New York Times*, May 16, 2018, https://www.nytimes.com/2018/05/16/us/politics/trump-undocumented-immigrants-animals.html

4. Caroline Kelly, "9th Circuit Rules in DOJ's Favor in Sanctuary Cities Case," CNN Politics, https://www.cnn.com/2019/07/12/politics/ninth-circuit-doj-los-angeles-grants-sanctuary-city/index.html

5. Bryan Griffith and Jessica M. Vaughn, "Sanctuary Cities, Counties, and States," Center for Immigration Studies, April 16, 2019, https://cis.org/Map-Sanctuary-Cities-Counties-and-States

6. Jessica Bither and Paul Costello, "Cities Across the Atlantic Raise Their Voices for Migrants and Refugees," German Marshall Fund, February 28, 2017, http://www.gmfus.org/blog/2017/02/28/cities-across-atlantic-raise-their-voices-migrants-and-refugees

7. See, for example, the website for City of Sanctuary UK (https://cityofsanctuary.org/)

8. Mathilde Têcheur, "Across Europe, Cities of Sanctuary and Supportive Citizens Are Building a More Humane Migration Policy," *Equal Times*, July 25, 2018, https://www.equaltimes.org/across-europe-cities-of-sanctuary

9. Jason Horowitz, "Italy's Crackdown on Migrants Meets a Grass-Roots Resistance," *The New York Times*, February 1, 2019, https://www.nytimes.com/2019/02/01/world/europe/italy-mayors-migrants-salvini-security-decree.html

10. *New York State Ice Company v. Liebmann*, 285 U.S. 262 (1932), dissent by Justice Brandeis at 311.

11. Wendy Koch, "Biggest U.S. Tax Hike on Tobacco Takes Effect," *USA Today*, April 3, 2009, http://www.usatoday.com/money/perfi/taxes/2009-03-31-cigarettetax_N.htm

12. Ann Boonn, *State Cigarette Excise Tax Rates & Rankings* (Washington, DC: Campaign for Tobacco-Free Kids, 2019), https://taxfoundation.org/2019-state-cigarette-tax-rankings/

13. "Illinois Tax Increase on Cigarettes and E-Cigarettes Scheduled to Go Into Effect July 1," The Civic Federation, June 26, 2019, https://www.civicfed.org/civic-federation/blog/illinois-tax-increase-cigarettes-and-e-cigarettes-scheduled-go-effect-july-1

14. *Milwaukee County v. M.E. White Co.*, 296 U.S. 268 (1935), 277.

15. Robert Verbruggen, "Concealed-Carry 'Reciprocity' vs. Federalism," *National Review*, June 1, 2017, https://www.nationalreview.com/2017/06/concealed-carry-reciprocity-federalism-state-issue/

16. Council of State Governments—National Center for Interstate Compacts, *Understanding Interstate Compacts*, 2, http://www.gsgp.org/media/1313/understanding_interstate_compacts-csgncic.pdf

17. For a history of the Port Authority, see http://www.panynj.gov/about/history-port-authority.html

18. For a similar, expansive use of the term *cooperative federalism*, see Craig Ducat, *Constitutional Interpretation*, 9th ed. (Boston, MA: Cengage Learning, 2008), 270–272.

19. Justice Harlan Fiske Stone introduced this term to describe the Tenth Amendment in his opinion for a unanimous Supreme Court in *U.S. v. Darby*, 312 U.S. 100 (1941) at 124: "The Tenth Amendment states but a truism that all is retained which has not been surrendered."

20. To read Hamilton's opinion of the constitutionality of the First Bank of the United States, go to http://avalon.law.yale.edu/18th_century/bank-ah.asp

21. *McCulloch v. Maryland*, 17 U.S. 316 at 431.

22. *McCulloch v. Maryland*, 17 U.S. 316 at 436.

23. *Gibbons v. Ogden*, 22 U.S. 1 at 196 and 197.

24. Yale Law School, "South Carolina Ordinance of Nullification," *The Avalon Project*, November 24, 1832, http://avalon.law.yale.edu/19th_century/ordnull.asp

25. To view the text of the Force Bill of 1833, go to https://teachingamericanhistory.org/library/document/force-bill-of-1833/

26. *Texas v. White*, 74 U.S. 700 (1869).

27. To view the organization's website, go to http://www.texasnationalist.com/

28. Paul Starobin, "Divided We Stand," *Wall Street Journal*, June 13, 2009, http://online.wsj.com/article/SB10001424052970204482304574219813708759806.html

29. "Second Vermont Republic," Vermont Republic, accessed July 16, 2019, http://vermontrepublic.org/

30. "Alaskan Independence Party," 2010, http://www.akip.org/

31. *Kohlhaas v. State of Alaska*, 147 P.3d 714 (2006), http://caselaw.findlaw.com/ak-supreme-court/1497483.html

32. *The Slaughterhouse Cases*, 83 U.S. 36 (1873).

33. *Civil Rights Cases*, 109 U.S. 3 (1883).

34. *Plessy v. Ferguson*, 163 U.S. 537 (1896).

35. *U.S. v. E.C. Knight*, 156 U.S. 1 (1895).

36. For example, *Hammer v. Dagenhart*, 247 U.S. 251 (1918).

37. *Schechter Poultry Corp. v. United States*, 295 U.S. 495 (1935).

38. *Carter v. Carter Coal Company*, 298 U.S. 238 (1936).

39. Peter H. Irons, *A People's History of the Supreme Court* (New York, NY: Viking, 1999), 303–304.

40. The "Four Horsemen" were Justices Pierce Butler, Willis Van Devanter, James Clark McReynolds, and George Sutherland.

41. The "Three Musketeers" were Justices Louis Brandeis, Benjamin Cardozo, and Harlan Fiske Stone.

42. Chief Justice Charles Evans Hughes and Justice Owen Roberts.

43. One, Harlan Fiske Stone, was initially appointed as an associate justice by President Calvin Coolidge in 1925, but Roosevelt elevated him to the post of chief justice in 1941 to replace Charles Evans Hughes.

44. *National Labor Relations Board v. Jones & Laughlin Steel Corp.*, 301 U.S. 1 (1937).

45. *U.S. v. Darby*, 312 U.S. 100 (1941).

46. Kenneth Finegold, Laura Wherry, and Stephanie Schardin, "Block Grants: Historical Overview and Lessons Learned," *Urban Institute*, April 21, 2004, http://www.urban.org/publications/310991.html

47. President Bill Clinton, "State of the Union Address," January 23, 1996, https://clintonwhitehouse4.archives.gov/WH/New/other/sotu.html

48. Justin McCarthy, "Two in Three Americans Support Same-Sex Marriage," Gallup, May 23, 2018, https://news.gallup.com/poll/234866/two-three-americans-support-sex-marriage.aspx

49. Bruce Japsen, "Study Illustrates How Medicaid Expansion Can Pay For Itself," *Forbes*, March 18, 2018, https://www.forbes.com/sites/brucejapsen/2018/03/18/how-medicaid-expansion-pays-for-itself/#6f260e145fdd; see also Jesse Cross-Call, "Medicaid Expansion Continues to Benefit State Budgets, Contrary to Critics' Claims," Center on Budget and Policy Priorities, October 9, 2018, https://www.cbpp.org/health/medicaid-expansion-continues-to-benefit-state-budgets-contrary-to-critics-claims

50. For more about ACA's Medicaid expansion and its pros and cons, see Kip Piper, "Medicaid Eligibility Expansion: Arguments For and Against States Opting for ACA Medicaid Expansion," September 10, 2012, https://piperreport.com/blog/2012/09/10/medicaid-eligibility-expansion-arguments-for-and-against-states-opting-for-aca-medicaid-expansion/; "Medicaid: Changes Under the Affordable Care Act," http://www.healthreformtracker.org/medicaid-changes-under-the-affordable-care-act/

51. "Where the States Stand on Medicaid Expansion," Advisory Board, April 1, 2019, https://www.advisory.com/daily-briefing/resources/primers/medicaidmap

52. Ellen M. Gilmer, "Climate Rule Litigation: Here We Go Again?" *E&E News*, August 22, 2018, https://www.eenews.net/stories/1060094917

53. Wayne Parry, "States Fight Trump Drill Plan With Local Bans," *Chicago Tribune*, March 19, 2018, https://www.chicagotribune.com/news/nationworld/science/ct-states-oil-drill-bans-20180319-story.html

54. Jeremy Berke and Skye Gould, "Illinois Just Became the First State to Legalize Marijuana Sales Through the Legislature—Here Are All the States Where Marijuana Is Legal," *Business Insider*, June 25, 2019, https://www.businessinsider.com/legal-marijuana-states-2018-1

55. Dan Bilefsky, "Legalizing Recreational Marijuana, Canada Begins a National Experiment," *The New York Times*, October 17, 2018, https://www.nytimes.com/2018/10/17/world/canada/marijuana-pot-cannabis-legalization.html

## CHAPTER 4

1. "China Launches Platform to Stamp Out 'Online Rumors,'" *Reuters*, August 30, 2018, https://www.reuters.com/article/us-china-internet/china-launches-platform-to-stamp-out-online-rumors-idUSKCN1LF0HL

2. Sharon LaFraniere, Michael Wines, and Edward Wong, "China Reins In Entertainment and Blogging," *The New York Times*, October 26, 2011, http://www.nytimes.com/2011/10/27/world/asia/china-imposes-new-limits-on-entertainment-and-bloggers.html?hpw

3. This section is based on an interactive website, "China and Internet Censorship," that was hosted by CNN.com at http://www.cnn.com/interactive/world/0603/explainer.china.internet/frameset.exclude.html; see also "Chinese Government Cracks Down on Internet Free Speech," PBS NewsHour with Jim Lehrer, October 19, 2005, http://www.pbs.org/newshour/extra/features/july-dec05/china_10-19.html

4. See, for example, the website of the Congressional-Executive Commission on China, created by Congress in October 2000 to monitor human rights and the development of the rule of law in China (http://www.cecc.gov/pages/virtualAcad/exp/)

5. "China Defends Internet Regulation," *BBC News*, February 15, 2006, http://news.bbc.co.uk/2/hi/asia-pacific/4715044.stm

6. The text of the Virginia Declaration of Rights can be found in Gordon Lloyd and Margie Lloyd, eds., *The Essential Bill of Rights: Original Arguments and Fundamental Documents* (Lanham, MD: University Press of America, 1998), 188–196.

7. Delaware, Maryland, Massachusetts, New Hampshire, North Carolina, Pennsylvania, and Virginia

8. Robert Scigliano (Ed.), *The Federalist: A Commentary on the Constitution of the United States* (New York, NY: The Modern Library, 2001), 550.

9. Richard Labunski, *James Madison and the Struggle for the Bill of Rights* (New York, NY: Oxford University Press, 2006), 8.

10. Labunski, *James Madison*, 8.

11. Labunski, *James Madison*, 62; see also *Federalist* 38, 44, and 66.

12. Letter from James Madison to George Eve, January 2, 1789, quoted in Labunski, *James Madison*, 164.

13. The text of Madison's speech introducing his proposed amendments on June 8, 1789, along with the text of the 17 amendments initially approved by the House on August 24, 1789 and the final 12 amendments approved by the First Congress on September 25, 1789, can be found in Lloyd and Lloyd, *The Essential Bill of Rights*, 331–357.

14. Michael Kent Curtis, *No State Shall Abridge: The Fourteenth Amendment and the Bill of Rights* (Durham, NC: Duke University Press, 1986), 21.

15. In *Barron v. Baltimore*, 32 U.S. 243 (1833), Chief Justice John Marshall explained why this was so. In the original Constitution, whenever state action was limited (as in Article I, Section 10), there was unambiguous language that said, "No state shall." In contrast, the more general prohibitions of Article I, Section 9 (e.g., "No Bill of Attainder or ex post facto Law shall be passed") were clearly aimed at Congress and not the states. If the Bill of Rights was meant to limit the states, Marshall concluded, it would have explicitly said "No state shall."

16. *Barron v. Baltimore*, 32 U.S. 243 (1833), 243.

17. Curtis, *No State Shall Abridge*, 19.

18. Ibid., 30.

19. Ibid., 23.

20. Ibid., 28–32.

21. Justice Hugo Black was a leading exponent of this position on the Supreme Court. See his dissent in *Adamson v. California*, 332 U.S. 46 (1947) at 68–123. See also W. W. Crosskey, "Charles Fairman, 'Legislative History,' and the Constitutional Limitations on State Authority," *University of Chicago Law Review* 22, no. 1, and Curtis, *No State Shall Abridge*.

22. Charles Fairman, "Does the Fourteenth Amendment Incorporate the Bill of Rights?" *Stanford Law Review* 2, no. 5. See also Raoul Berger, *Government by Judiciary* (Cambridge, UK: Harvard University Press, 1977).

23. Curtis, *No State Shall Abridge*, 64–65.

24. *Butchers' Benevolent Association v. Crescent City Livestock Landing & Slaughterhouse Co.* [The Slaughterhouse Cases], 83 U.S. 36 (1873).

25. *Palko v. Connecticut*, 302 U.S. 319 (1937).

26. *Adamson v. California*, 332 U.S. 46 (1947), Black dissent, 89.

27. *McDonald v. Chicago*, 561 U.S. 3025 (2010).

28. *U.S. v. Cruikshank*, 92 U.S. 542 (1875); *Presser v. Illinois*, 116 U.S. 252 (1886); *U.S. v. Miller*, 307 U.S. 174 (1939).

29. *District of Columbia v. Heller*, 554 U.S. 570 (2008).

30. *Near v. Minnesota*, 283 U.S. 697 (1931).

31. *New York Times v. United States*, 403 U.S. 713 (1971).

32. Thomas Varela and David Gauthier-Villars, "France Urges Restraint From Media, Politicians," *The Wall Street Journal*, May 18, 2011, http://online.wsj.com/article/SB10001424052748703421204576328982375553362.html; François Quintard-Morénas, "The French Have a Legal Point," *The New York Times*, May 26, 2011, http://www.nytimes.com/roomfordebate/2011/05/26/can-strauss-kahn-get-a-fair-trial/the-french-have-a-legal-point

33. Maggie Haberman and Annie Karni, "Cliff Sims, White House Tell-All Author, Sues Trump for Going After Him Over Book," *The New York Times*, February 11, 2019, https://www.nytimes.com/2019/02/11/us/politics/cliff-sims-book-lawsuit.html

34. Christopher Mele, "Montana Republican Greg Gianforte Is Sentenced in Assault on Reporter," *The New York Times*, June 13, 2017, https://www.nytimes.com/2017/06/13/us/politics/greg-gianforte-sentenced.html

35. Seung Min Kim and Felicia Sonmez, "At Montana Rally, Trump Praises Congressman for Assaulting Reporter," *The Washington Post*, October 19, 2018, https://www.washingtonpost.com/politics/at-montana-rally-trump-praises-congressman-for-assaulting-reporter/2018/10/18/1e1d0d1e-d304-11e8-8c22-fa2ef74bd6d6_story.html?utm_term=.69d2eb050d77

36. Leonard W. Levy, *Emergence of a Free Press* (New Haven, CT: Yale University Press, 1985), 3–15.

37. Leonard Levy, *Origins of the Bill of Rights* (New Haven, CT: Yale University Press, 1999), 22.

38. Those convicted of conspiracy under the act could be fined $5,000 and sentenced to up to five years in prison.

39. Labunski, *James Madison*, 257.

40. Adjusted for inflation, $10,000 in 1917 would equal $176,502 in 2011.

41. The names of such men were routinely published in newspapers at that time.

42. *Schenck v. United States*, 249 U.S. 47 (1919).

43. *Schenck v. United States*, 249 U.S. 47 (1919) at 52.

44. *Abrams v. United States*, 250 U.S. 616 (1919).

45. Ibid., Holmes dissent at 629.

46. *Gitlow v. New York*, 268 U.S. 652 (1925) at 669.

47. *Whitney v. California*, 274 U.S. 357 (1927), Brandeis concurrence at 376 and 378 (emphasis added).

48. *U.S. v. Dennis*, 341 U.S. 494 (1951).

49. *Brandenburg v. Ohio*, 395 U.S. 444 (1969).

50. *Stromberg v. People of State of California*, 283 U.S. 359 (1931).

51. *Tinker v. Des Moines Independent Community School District*, 393 U.S. 503 (1969).

52. *Morse v. Frederick*, 551 U.S. 393 (2007).

53. *Texas v. Johnson*, 491 U.S. 397 (1989).

54. *Texas v. Johnson*, 491 U.S. 397 (1989) at 403; quoting *United States v. O'Brien*, 391 U.S. 367 (1968) at 376 and 409.

55. James McClure, "Trump Wants America to Join These 16 Countries That Prohibit Flag Burning," *Civilized*, December 1, 2016, https://www.civilized.life/articles/countries-where-you-cant-burn-the-flag/mp/4/

56. *Near v. Minnesota*, 283 U.S. 697 (1931).

57. *Jacobellis v. Ohio*, 378 U.S. 184 (1964), Justice Stewart's concurring opinion at 197.

58. *Regina v. Hicklin*, 3 Queen's Bench 360 (1868).

59. For a full discussion of this, see Lee Epstein and Thomas G. Walker, *Constitutional Law for a Changing America: Rights, Liberties, and Justice*, 5th ed. (Washington, DC: CQ Press, 2004), 363–367.

60. Nassim Hatam, "Iranian Women Threw Off the Hijab—What Happened Next", *BBC News*, May 19, 2018, https://www.bbc.com/news/world-middle-east-44040236

61. Saeed Kamali Dehghan, "Woman Arrested in Iran Over Instagram Video of Her Dancing," *The Guardian*, July 9, 2018, https://www.theguardian.com/world/2018/jul/08/iran-woman-arrested-instagram-video-dancing

62. *New York Times v. Sullivan*, 376 U.S. 254 (1964), at 280.

63. Erik Wemple, "President Trump Calls Libel Laws 'a Sham and a Disgrace,' Pledges Review," *The Washington Post*, January 10, 2018, https://www.washingtonpost.com/blogs/erik-wemple/wp/2018/01/10/president-trump-calls-libel-laws-a-sham-and-a-disgrace-pledges-review/?utm_term=.863d29cabb63

64. Epstein and Walker, *Constitutional Law*, 396.

65. *New York Times v. Sullivan*, 376 U.S. 254 (1964) at 271.

66. *Valentine v. Chrestensen*, 316 U.S. 52 (1942).

67. *Bates v. State Bar of Arizona*, 433 U.S. 350 (1977); *Bigelow v. Virginia*, 421 U.S. 809 (1975).

68. *Bolger v. Youngs Drugs Products Corp.*, 463 U.S. 60 (1983) at 74.

69. Quoted in Mary Beth Marklein, "On Campus: Free Speech for You but Not for Me?" *USA Today*, November 3, 2003, http://www.usatoday.com/news/washington/2003-11-02-free-speech-cover_x.htm

70. Kevin Freking and Collin Binkley, "Trump Vows Executive Order to Protect Campus Free Speech, but Critics, Including U. of C. President, Call It a Dangerous Move," *Chicago Tribune*, March 5, 2019, https://www.chicagotribune.com/news/local/breaking/ct-met-trump-campus-free-speech-executive-order-20190305-story.html; Susan Svrluga, "Trump Signs Executive Order on Free Speech on College Campuses," *The Washington Post*, March 21, 2019, https://www.washingtonpost.com/education/2019/03/21/trump-expected-sign-executive-order-free-speech/?utm_term=.118deb69dc86

71. *Doe v. Michigan*, 721 F.Supp. 852 (E.D. Mich. 1989).

72. *Adderley v. Florida*, 385 U.S. 39 (1966).

73. *Edwards v. South Carolina*, 372 U.S. 229 (1963).

74. *Smith v. Collin*, 439 U.S. 916 (1978).

75. *Chaplinsky v. New Hampshire*, 315 U.S. 568 (1942).

76. Josh Belzman, "Behind Their Hate, a Constitutional Debate: Anti-gay Group Targeting Military Funerals Sparks Free Speech Debate," MSNBC, January 24, 2008, http://www.msnbc.msn.com/id/12071434/

77. *Snyder v. Phelps*, Docket No. 09-751.

78. *Engel v. Vitale*, 370 U.S. 421 (1962).

79. Ducat, *Constitutional Interpretation*, 1049.

80. Anthony Lewis, "Mr. Meese's Freedom," *The New York Times*, September 30, 1985, A15.

81. Epstein and Walker, *Constitutional Law for a Changing America*, 202.

82. *Everson v. Board of Education*, 330 U.S. 1 (1947).

83. *Lemon v. Kurtzman*, 403 U.S. 602 (1971).

84. *Wallace v. Jaffree*, 472 U.S. 38 (1985).

85. *Edwards v. Aguillard*, 482 U.S. 578 (1987).

86. *The American Legion v. American Humanist Association*, 588 U.S. ___ (2019).

87. Loi du 9 décembre 1905 concernant la separation des Églises et de l'État.

88. Loi n8 2004-228 du 15 mars 2004 encadrant, en application du principe de laïcité, le port de signes ou de tenues manifestant une appartenance religieuse dans les écoles, collèges et lycées publics.

89. *Annual Report of the United States Commission on International Religious Freedom*, May 2007, 94–95.

90. Epstein and Walker, *Constitutional Law for a Changing America*, 114.

91. Tony Mauro, "Thank Jehovah's Witnesses for Speech Freedoms," *USA Today*, May 30, 2000; see also Shawn Francis Peters, *Judging Jehovah's Witnesses* (Lawrence: University Press of Kansas, 2000).

92. *Reynolds v. United States*, 98 U.S. 145 (1879).

93. *Employment Division, Department of Human Resources v. Smith*, 484 U.S. 872 (1990).

94. *Griswold v. Connecticut*, 381 U.S. 479 (1965).

95. *Eisenstadt v. Baird*, 405 U.S. 438 (1972).

96. *Griswold v. Connecticut*, 381 U.S. 479 (1965), Justice Black's dissent at 507.

97. Ibid., Justice Black's dissent at 510.

98. *Roe v. Wade*, 410 U.S. 113 (1973).

99. *City of Akron v. Akron Center for Reproductive Health*, 462 U.S. 416 (1983), Justice O'Connor's dissent.

100. *Planned Parenthood of Southeastern Pennsylvania v. Casey*, 505 U.S. 833 (1992).

101. Adam Liptak, "Supreme Court Blocks Louisiana Abortion Law," *The New York Times*, February 7, 2019, https://www.nytimes.com/2019/02/07/us/politics/louisiana-abortion-law-supreme-court.html

102. Ariana Eunjung Cha, "At Least 20 Abortion Cases Are in the Pipeline to the Supreme Court. Any One Could Gut Roe v. Wade," *The Washington Post*, February 15, 2019, https://www.washingtonpost.com/health/2019/02/15/least-abortion-cases-are-steps-us-supreme-court-any-one-could-gut-roe-v-wade/?utm_term=.f6a6d2886c71

103. Ronald Dworkin, *Life's Dominion: An Argument About Abortion, Euthanasia, and Individual Freedom* (New York, NY: Vintage Books, 1993), 6.

104. *Bowers v. Hardwick*, 478 U.S. 186 (1986).

105. *Lawrence v. Texas*, 539 U.S. 558 (2003).

106. *Lawrence v. Texas*, 539 U.S. 558 (2003), Justice Scalia's dissent at 605.

107. *Goodridge v. Department of Public Health*, 440 Mass. 309 at 344.

108. Rosamond Hutt, "This Is the State of LGBTI Rights Around the World in 2018," World Economic Forum, June 14, 2018, https://www.weforum.org/agenda/2018/06/lgbti-rights-around-the-world-in-2018/

109. *Cruzan v. Director, Missouri Department of Health*, 497 U.S. 261 (1990).

110. "Physician-Assisted Suicide Fast Facts," CNN, January 3, 2019, https://www.cnn.com/2014/11/26/us/physician-assisted-suicide-fast-facts/index.html

111. "Assisted Dying in Other Countries," My Death, My Decision, accessed July 19, 2019, https://www.mydeath-mydecision.org.uk/info/assisted-dying-in-other-countries/

112. *Palko v. Connecticut*, 302 U.S. 319 (1937); *Adamson v. California*, 332 U.S. 46 (1947).

113. *Duncan v. Louisiana*, 391 U.S. 145 (1968).

114. *Williams v. Florida*, 399 U.S. 78 (1970); *Apodaca v. Oregon*, 406 U.S. 404 (1972).

115. *Ballew v. Georgia*, 435 U.S. 223 (1978).

116. *Burch v. Louisiana*, 441 U.S. 130 (1979).

117. *Gideon v. Wainwright*, 372 U.S. 335 (1963).

118. *Miranda v. Arizona*, 384 U.S. 436 (1966).

119. *Dickerson v. United States*, 530 U.S. 428 (2000).

120. *Weeks v. United States*, 232 U.S. 383 (1914).

121. *Wolf v. Colorado*, 338 U.S. 25 (1949).

122. *Mapp v. Ohio*, 367 U.S. 643 (1961).

123. *United States v. Leon*, 468 U.S. 897 (1984).

124. Section 24 of the Canadian Charter of Rights and Freedoms, https://www.justice.gc.ca/eng/csj-sjc/rfc-dlc/ccrf-ccdl/check/art242.html

125. *Baze v. Rees*, 553 U.S. 35 (2008).

126. Amnesty International Global Report, *Death Sentences and Executions, 2018*, https://www.amnesty.org/download/Documents/ACT5098702019ENGLISH.PDF

127. "Death Penalty," Gallup, accessed July 19, 2019, https://news.gallup.com/poll/1606/death-penalty.aspx

128. *Furman v. Georgia*, 408 U.S. 238 (1972).

129. *Coker v. Georgia*, 433 U.S. 584 (1977).

130. *Atkins v. Virginia*, 536 U.S. 304 (2002).

131. *Roper v. Simmons*, 543 U.S. 551 (2005).

132. Adam Liptak and Michael D. Shear, "Trump's Travel Ban Is Upheld by Supreme Court," *The New York Times*, June 26, 2018, www.nytimes.com/2018/06/26/us/politics/supreme-court-trump-travel-ban.html

133. Richard Gonzales, "Supreme Court Broadens the Government's Power to Detain Criminal Immigrants," *NPR*, March 19, 2019, https://www.npr.org/2019/03/19/704953335/supreme-court-broadens-the-governments-power-to-detain-criminal-immigrants

134. Jennifer Steinhauer and Jonathan Weisman, "U.S. Surveillance in Place Since 9/11 Is Sharply Limited," *The New York Times*, June 2, 2015, https://www.nytimes.com/2015/06/03/us/politics/senate-surveillance-bill-passes-hurdle-but-showdown-looms.html

135. James Risen and Eric Lichtblau, "Bush Lets U.S. Spy on Callers Without Courts," *The New York Times*, December 16, 2005, A1.

136. *Hamdi v. Rumsfeld*, 542 U.S. 507 (2004).

137. *Hamdan v. Rumsfeld*, 126 S.Ct. 2749 (2006).

138. Richard M. Pious, "Obama's Use of Prerogative Powers in the War on Terrorism," in *Obama in Office*, ed. James A. Thurber (Boulder, CO: Paradigm Publishers, 2011), 258.

139. Jenna Johnson, "Trump Says 'Torture Works,' Backs Waterboarding and 'Much Worse,'" *The Washington Post*, February 17, 2016, https://www.washingtonpost.com/politics/trump-says-torture-works-backs-waterboarding-and-much-worse/2016/02/17/4c9277be-d59c-11e5-b195-2e29a4e13425_story.html?utm_term=.f06defc945ae; Erin Kelly, "Gina Haspel Promises Not to Allow Torture Program If Confirmed as CIA Director," *USA Today*, May 9, 2018, http://www.usatoday.com/story/news/politics/2018/05/09/gina-haspel-promises-not-restart-cia-torture-program-if-confirmed/591333002/

## CHAPTER 5

1. Becky Little, "How the U.S. Got So Many Confederate Monuments," History, August 17, 2017, https://www.history.com/news/how-the-u-s-got-so-many-confederate-monuments

2. Andrew Vanacore, "Among Contested New Orleans Monuments, Liberty Place Marker Has Always Been a Battleground," *The New Orleans Advocate*, April 14, 2017, https://www.theadvocate.com/new_orleans/news/article_bf24c1d6-1fe4-11e7-a6c1-8b5611a8c879.html

3. Andreas Preuss, "Flags, Cash and Medals Found Hidden Inside a 1913 Confederate Time Capsule," CNN, August 5, 2018, https://www.cnn.com/2018/08/05/us/new-orleans-beauregard-statue-time-capsule-trnd/index.html

4. Sarah Wildman, "Why You See Swastikas in America but Not Germany," Vox, August 16, 2017, https://www.vox.com/world/2017/8/16/16152088/nazi-swastikas-germany-charlottesville

5. *Prigg v. Pennsylvania*, 41 U.S. 539 (1842), 625.

6. *U.S. v. Amistad*, 40 U.S. 518 (1841).

7. *Dred Scott v. Sandford*, 60 U.S. 393, 405.

8. *Dred Scott v. Sandford*, 60 U.S. 393, 452.

9. Donald Lively, *The Constitution, Race, and Renewed Relevance of Original Intent* (Amherst, NY: Cambria Press, 2008), 45.

10. "Black Codes in the Former Confederate States," CivilWarHome.com, accessed July 20, 2019, http://www.civilwarhome.com/blackcodes.htm

11. Lively, *The Constitution, Race, and Renewed Relevance of Original Intent*, 44.

12. *Civil Rights Cases*, 109 U.S. 3 (1883).

13. John Anthony Maltese, *The Selling of Supreme Court Nominees* (Baltimore, MD: Johns Hopkins University Press, 1995), 95–97.

14. *Plessy v. Ferguson*, 163 U.S. 537 (1897), Justice Harlan's dissent, 559, 562.

15. *Breedlove v. Suttles*, 302 U.S. 277 (1937); *Harper v. Virginia State Board of Elections*, 383 U.S. 663 (1966).

16. *Guinn v. United States*, 238 U.S. 347 (1915).

17. Maltese, *The Selling of Supreme Court Nominees*, 101–104.

18. *Buchanan v. Warley*, 245 U.S. 60 (1917).

19. *Sweatt v. Painter*, 339 U.S. 629 (1950), 634, 635.

20. These included Felix Frankfurter and Robert Jackson.

21. *Brown v. Board of Education I*, 347 U.S. 483 (1954), 493–495.

22. Gerald N. Rosenberg, *The Hollow Hope: Can Courts Bring About Social Change?* (Chicago, IL: University of Chicago Press, 1991), 50, Table 2.1.

23. *Boynton v. Virginia*, 364 U.S. 454 (1960).

24. Raymond Arnsenault, *Freedom Riders: 1961 and the Struggle for Racial Justice* (New York, NY: Oxford University Press, 2006).

25. Thomas E. Patterson, *The Vanishing Voter: Public Involvement in an Age of Uncertainty* (New York, NY: Alfred A. Knopf, 2002), 5, 6.

26. *Shelby County v. Holder*, 570 U.S. 529 (2013).

27. Eugene Scott, "Stacey Abrams Showed Why Voting Rights Must Be a Key Issue for Democrats in 2020," *The Washington Post*, February 6, 2019, https://www.washingtonpost.com/politics/2019/02/06/stacey-abrams-showed-why-voting-rights-must-be-key-issue-democrats/?utm_term=.76a028e297bd

28. Vann R. Newkirk II, "The Georgia Governor's Race Has Brought Voter Suppression Into Full View," *The Atlantic*, November 6, 2018, https://www.theatlantic.com/politics/archive/2018/11/how-voter-suppression-actually-works/575035/

29. Jerry Markon, "Justice Department Rejects South Carolina Voter ID Law, Calling It Discriminatory," *The Washington Post*, December 21, 2011, http://www.washingtonpost.com/politics/justice-dept-rejects-south-carolina-voter-id-law-calling-it-discriminatory/2011/12/23/gIQAhLJAEP_story.html

30. Dan Merica, "Clinton: Trump Campaign Built on 'Prejudice and Paranoia'," CNN, August 25, 2016, https://www.cnn.com/2016/08/25/politics/hillary-clinton-alt-right-speech-donald-trump-kkk/index.html

31. Christal Hayes, "Here Are 10 Times President Trump's Comments Have Been Called Racist," *USA Today*, August 14, 2018, https://www.usatoday.com/story/news/politics/onpolitics/2018/08/14/times-president-trump-comments-called-racist/985438002/

32. Michael D. Shear and Maggie Haberman, "Trump Defends Initial Remarks on Charlottesville; Again Blames 'Both Sides,'" *The New York Times*, August 15, 2017, https://www.nytimes.com/2017/08/15/us/politics/trump-press-conference-charlottesville.html

33. Pia Katarina Jakobsson, "Daughters of Liberty: Women and the American Revolution," in *Women's Rights: People and Perspectives*, eds. Crista DeLuzio and Peter C. Mancall (Santa Barbara, CA: ABC CLIO, 2010), 36.

34. Susan Gluck Mezey, *In Pursuit of Equality: Women, Public Policy, and the Federal Courts* (New York, NY: St. Martin's Press, 1992), 9.

35. Sharon Hartman Strom, *Women's Rights* (Westport, CT: Greenwood Press, 2003), 55.

36. Kathleen S. Sullivan, *Constitutional Context: Women and Rights Discourse in Nineteenth-Century America* (Baltimore, MD: Johns Hopkins University Press, 2007), 9.

37. Strom, *Women's Rights*, 34–36.

38. Mezey, *In Pursuit of Equality*, 9.

39. For the full text of the Declaration of Sentiments, see Strom, *Women's Rights*, 66–68.

40. Charles C. Euchner and John Anthony Maltese, *Selecting the President: From Washington to Bush* (Washington, DC: CQ Press, 1992), 4–5.

41. Gayle Lemmon, "Now's the Time to Ratify the Equal Rights Amendment," CNN, November 24, 2018, https://www.cnn.com/2018/11/24/opinions/time-to-ratify-the-equal-rights-amendment-lemmon/index.html

42. The Supreme Court created intermediate scrutiny for gender classifications in *Craig v. Boren*, 429 U.S. 190 (1976).

43. *Rostker v. Golberg*, 453 U.S. 57 (1981).

44. *Wiliams v. Saxbe*, 413 F. Supp. 654 (D.D.C. 1976).

45. *Meritor Savings Bank v. Vinson*, 477 U.S. 57 (1986).

46. *Oncale v. Sundowner Offshore Services*, 523 U.S. 75 (1998).

47. Cassandra Santiago and Doug Criss, "An Activist, a Little Girl and the Heartbreaking Origin of 'Me Too,'" CNN, October 17, 2017, https://www.cnn.com/2017/10/17/us/me-too-tarana-burke-origin-trnd/index.html

48. Karla Adam and William Booth, "A Year After It Began, Has #MeToo Become a Global Movement?" *The Washington Post*, October 5, 2018, https://www.washingtonpost.com/world/a-year-after-it-began-has-metoo-become-a-global-movement/2018/10/05/1fc0929e-c71a-11e8-9c0f-2ffaf6d422aa_story.html?utm_term=.8f0bf3d96344

49. Emily Shugerman, "The #MeToo Movement Takes Office After Winning Elections Across the U.S.," *Daily Beast*, November 7, 2018, https://www.thedailybeast.com/the-metoo-movement-takes-office-after-winning-elections-across-the-us

50. Maya Salam, "A Record 117 Women Won Office, Reshaping America's Leadership," *The New York Times*, November 7, 2018, https://www.nytimes.com/2018/11/07/us/elections/women-elected-midterm-elections.html

51. *Wal-Mart Stores, Inc. v. Duke*, 564 U.S. (2011).

52. Felicia Sonmez, "Democrats React to Supreme Court Ruling on Wal-Mart," *The Washington Post*, June 20, 2011, http://www.washingtonpost.com/blogs/2chambers/post/congresswoman-reacts-to-supreme-court-ruling-on-walmart/2011/06/20/AGyHFzcH_blog.html

53. Sarah Gray, "It's Now Illegal to Pay Men More Than Women in Iceland," *Fortune*, January 2, 2018, http://fortune.com/2018/01/02/illegal-to-pay-men-more-than-women-iceland/

54. Cynthia Fuchs Epstein, *Women in Law*, 2nd ed. (Urbana, IL: University of Illinois Press, 1993), 5.

55. *United States v. Virginia*, 518 U.S. 515 (1996).

56. *Employment Division, Department of Human Resources of Oregon v. Smith*, 494 U.S. 872 (1990).

57. John D. McKinnon, "U.S. Offers an Official Apology to Native Americans," *The Wall Street Journal*, December 22, 2009, http://blogs.wsj.com/washwire/2009/12/22/us-offers-an-official-apology-to-native-americans/

58. *Korematsu v. U.S.*, 323 U.S. 214 (1944).

59. "Italian—Under Attack," Library of Congress, accessed July 20, 2019, http://www.loc.gov/teachers/classroommaterials/presentationsandactivities/presentations/immigration/italian8.html

60. Bryan Baker, "Population Estimates: Illegal Alien Population Residing in the United States: January 2015," Office of Immigration Statistics, U.S. Department of Homeland Security, December 2018, https://www.dhs.gov/sites/default/files/publications/18_1214_PLCY_pops-est-report.pdf

61. Amber Phillips, "'They're Rapists.' President Trump's Campaign Launch Speech Two Years Later, Annotated," *The Washington Post*, June 16, 2017, https://www.washingtonpost.com/news/the-fix/wp/2017/06/16/theyre-rapists-presidents-trump-campaign-launch-speech-two-years-later-annotated/?utm_term=.c6cf505d34ef

62. Lukas Mikelionis, "Trump Declares 'Country Is Full' in Fox News Interview, Says US Can No Longer Accept Illegal Immigrants," Fox News, April 6, 2019, https://www.foxnews.com/politics/trump-declares-the-country-full-in-fox-news-interview-says-american-can-no-longer-accept-illegal-immigrants

63. Colleen Long and Ricardo Alonso-Zaldivar, "Watchdog: Thousands More Children May Have Been Separated," *U.S. News & World Report*, January 18, 2019, https://www.usnews.com/news/politics/articles/2019-01-17/watchdog-many-more-migrant-families-may-have-been-separated

64. Caitlyn Oprysko, "Trump Backs Off Threat to Close the U.S.–Mexico Border," *Politico*, April 4, 2019, https://www.politico.com/story/2019/04/04/trump-backs-off-threat-to-close-the-southern-border-1255926

65. *Mendez v. Westminster*, 64 F. Supp. 544 (1946). For more information about the *Mendez* case, see http://mendezetalvwestminster.com/

66. *Westminster School District of Orange County v. Mendez*, 161 F.2d 774 (1947).

67. *Hernandez v. Texas*, 347 U.S. 475 (1954).

68. "About," MALDEF, 2018, http://www.maldef.org/about/mission/index.html

69. Alan Rappeport, "That Judge Attacked by Donald Trump? He's Faced a Lot Worse," *The New York Times*, June 3, 2016, https://www.nytimes.com/2016/06/04/us/politics/donald-trump-university-judge-gonzalo-curiel.html?module=inline

70. These numbers are continually updated at https://docs.google.com/spreadsheets/d/1O0ZUPKogqk1PMoJn50_gdbdBwyj54i-RqHUDFQ7Z5E8/edit#gid=1242775320

71. "10 Maps Show How Different LGBTQ Rights Are Around the World," *Business Insider*, April 4, 2019, https://www.businessinsider.com/lgbtq-rights-around-the-world-maps-2018-10; "Gay Sex Now Officially Punishable by Death by Stoning in Brunei," *CBS News*, April 3, 2019, https://www.cbsnews.com/news/brunei-gay-sex-punishable-death-stoning-islamic-sharia-laws-in-effect-

today-2019-04-03/; "Brunei Says It Will Not Enforce Gay Sex Death Penalty After Worldwide Protests of New Laws," *CBS News*, May 6, 2019, https://www.cbsnews.com/news/brunei-will-not-enforce-gay-sex-death-penalty-after-worldwide-protests/

72. Sheryl Gay Stolberg, "Obama Widens Medical Rights for Gay Partners," *The New York Times*, April 15, 2010, http://www.nytimes.com/2010/04/16/us/politics/16webhosp.html

73. Adam Liptak, "Supreme Court to Decide Whether Landmark Civil Rights Law Applies to Gay and Transgender Workers," *The New York Times*, April 22, 2019, https://www.nytimes.com/2019/04/22/us/politics/supreme-court-gay-transgender-employees.html?smid=nytcore-ios-share

74. *Romer v. Evans*, 517 U.S. 620 (1996), 635–36, 632.

75. Ryan C. Brooks, "Pete Buttigieg Is Not the First Openly Gay, Major Party Presidential Candidate. This Guy Was," *BuzzFeed*, April 2, 2019, https://www.buzzfeednews.com/article/ryancbrooks/fred-karger-mayor-pete-buttigieg-gay-2020

76. Emma Margolin, "With Transgender Military Ban Lifted, Obama Cements Historic LGBT Rights Legacy," *NBC News*, June 30, 2016, https://www.nbcnews.com/feature/nbc-out/transgender-military-ban-lifted-obama-cements-historic-lgbt-rights-legacy-n600541

77. Adam Liptak, "Supreme Court Revives Transgender Ban for Military Service," *The New York Times*, January 22, 2019, http://www.nytimes.com/2019/01/22/us/politics/transgender-ban-military-supreme-court.html

78. "'Bathroom Bill' Legislative Tracking," *National Conference of State Legislatures*, July 28, 2017, http://www.ncsl.org/research/education/-bathroom-bill-legislative-tracking635951130.aspx

79. Sandhya Somashekhar, Emma Brown, and Moriah Balingit, "Trump Administration Rolls Back Protections for Transgender Students," *The Washington Post*, February 22, 2017, https://www.washingtonpost.com/local/education/trump-administration-rolls-back-protections-for-transgender-students/2017/02/22/550a83b4-f913-11e6-bf01-d47f8cf9b643_story.html?utm_term=.4897b258a499

80. *Adarand Constructor's, Inc. v. Pena*, 515 U.S. 200 (1995).

81. *Grutter v. Bolling*, 539 U.S. 306 (2003).

82. *Fisher v. University of Texas*, 579 U.S. (2016).

83. Joan Biskupic, "Judge Hears Final Arguments in Harvard Case That Could Decide Future of Affirmative Action," CNN, February 13, 2019, https://www.cnn.com/2019/02/13/politics/harvard-asian-americans-affirmative-action-hearing/index.html

84. Alfred L. Brophy, *Reparations Pro and Con* (New York, NY: Oxford University Press, 2006), 74.

85. Ibid., 76–77.

## CHAPTER 6

1. International Monetary Fund, Government Finance Statistics Yearbook, accessed July 21, 2019, https://data.imf.org/?sk=89418059-d5c0-4330-8c41-dbc2d8f90f46&sId=1435762628665

2. Inglehart, R., C. Haerpfer, A. Moreno, C. Welzel, K. Kizilova, J. Diez-Medrano, M. Lagos, P. Norris, E. Ponarin & B. Puranen et al. (eds.). 2014. *World Values Survey: Round Six—Country-Pooled Datafile Version: www.worldvaluessurvey.org/WVSDocumentationWV6.jsp*. Madrid: JD Systems Institute.

3. Gordon S. Wood, "The Democratization of Mind in the American Revolution" in *The Moral Foundations of the American Republic*, 3rd ed., ed., Robert H. Horwitz (Charlottesville: University of Virginia Press, 1986), 129.

4. Alexis de. Tocqueville, *Democracy in America* (New York, NY: Knopf, 1980).

5. Smith, Tom W., Hout, Michael, and Marsden, Peter V. *General Social Survey, 1972–2016* [Cumulative File]. Ann Arbor, MI: Inter-university Consortium for Political and Social Research [distributor], National Opinion Research Center [distributor], 2017-11-14. https://doi.org/10.3886/ICPSR36797.v1

6. John L. Sullivan, Pat Walsh, Michal Shamir, David G. Barnum, and James L. Gibson, "Why Politicians Are More Tolerant: Selective Recruitment and Socialization Among Political Elites in Britain, Israel, New Zealand, and the United States," *British Journal of Political Science* 23 (January 1993): 51–76.

7. Samuel A. Stouffer, *Communism, Conformity, and Civil Liberties* (New York, NY: Doubleday, 1995), for the 1954 figure; for the figures after 1954, James Allan Davis, Tom W. Smith, and Peter V. Marsden, *General Social Surveys, 1972–2010: Cumulative Codebook*, Principal Investigator, James A. Davis; Director and Co-Principal Investigator, Tom W. Smith (Chicago, IL: National Opinion Research Center, 2010).

8. "The ANES Guide to Public Opinion and Electoral Behavior," ANES, 2017, https://electionstudies.org/resources/anes-guide/; in fact, this difference understates the decrease in efficacy somewhat, because the National Election Studies changed their question wording on this question from 1988 on to make it possible for people to reply more easily that they did not have an opinion on the question. Presumably, some people who in 2016 would have replied to the original question that they believed people do not have a say replied instead that they were unsure.

9. Inglehart, R., C. Haerpfer, A. Moreno, C. Welzel, K. Kizilova, J. Diez-Medrano, M. Lagos, P. Norris, E. Ponarin & B. Puranen et al. (eds.). 2014. *World Values Survey: Round Two—Country-Pooled Datafile Version: http://www.worldvaluessurvey.org/WVSDocumentationWV2.jsp*. Madrid: JD Systems Institute. The two countries closest to the United States were India and South Korea. To compare a couple of other countries, in Great Britain, 42 percent thought they could change an unjust law; in France, only 22 percent thought so. (This study was done at a time when efficacy was near an all-time low in the United States.)

10. The gizzard is an organ in birds that grinds up food for digestion. It is one of the entrails that is thrown out before eating a chicken or turkey and is tough, gristly, and generally unpleasant.

11. John R. Hibbing and Elizabeth Theiss-Morse, *Stealth Democracy: Americans' Belief About How Government Should Work* (New York, NY: Cambridge University Press, 2002).

12. "The ANES Guide to Public Opinion and Electoral Behavior," ANES, accessed July 21, 2019, https://electionstudies.org/resources/anes-guide/

13. "Likely Rise in Voter Turnout Bodes Well for Democrats," Pew Research Center, July 10, 2008, Section 2, https://www.people-press.org/2008/07/10/section-2-evaluating-the-candidates-and-campaigns/

14. Calculated from Table 2 of Richard G. Niemi and M. Kent Jennings, "Issues and Inheritance in the Formation of Party Identification," *American Journal of Political Science* 35 (November 1991): 970–988.

15. M. Kent Jennings and Richard G. Niemi, *The Political Character of Adolescence* (Princeton, NJ: Princeton University Press, 1974).

16. Ernest L. Boyer and May Jean Whitelaw, *The Condition of the Professoriate: Attitudes and Trends, 1989* (New York, NY: Harper and Row, 1989), cited in Robert S. Erikson and Kent L. Tedin, *American Public Opinion*, 5th ed. (Boston, MA: Allyn and Bacon, 1995), 134.

17. Mark D. Mariani and Gordon J. Hewitt, "Indoctrination U.? Faculty Ideology and Changes in Student Political Orientation," *PS: Political Science and Politics* 41, no. 4 (October 2008): 773–783.

18. Stephen Kull, Clay Ramsay, and Evan Lewis, "Misperceptions, the Media, and the Iraq War," *Political Science Quarterly* 118 (Winter, 2003–2004): 569–598. Cited in Gary C. Jacobson, *A Divider Not a Uniter: George W. Bush and the American People* (New York, NY: Pearson Longman, 2007), 251.

19. Jay D. Hmielowski, Lauren Feldman, Teresa A. Myers, Anthony Leiserowitz, and Edward Maibach, "An Attack on Science? Media Use, Trust in Scientists, and Perceptions of Global Warming," Public Understanding of Science (2013): 1–18. The authors used a multistage panel study that allowed them to sort out causality among their variables.

20. Robert S. Erikson and Kent L. Tedin, *American Public Opinion*, 7th ed. (New York, NY: Pearson Longman, 2007), 152.

21. George W. Bush, "Address to a Joint Session of Congress," History, Art & Archives: United States House of Representatives, September 20, 2001. President Bush made clear in the speech, however, that he was referring to Islamic terrorists, not to Islam in general.

22. "Americans Make Hard Choices on Social Security," National Academy of Social Insurance (2014): 20, https://www.nasi.org/sites/default/files/research/Americans_Make_Hard_Choices_on_Social_Security.pdf

23. "New Hampshire Democratic Entrance/Exit Poll," CBS Exit Polls, 2016, https://www.cbsnews.com/elections/2016/primaries/democrat/new-hampshire/exit/

24. ARD, Bundestagswahl, 2017, https://wahl.tagesschau.de/wahlen/2017-09-24-BT-DE/umfrage-alter.shtml

25. National Election Studies, 2016 presidential election survey.

26. Christine Fong, "Social Preferences, Self-Interest, and the Demand for Redistribution," *Journal of Public Economics* 88 (2001): 225–246.

27. CNN Exit Polls, 2018, https://www.cnn.com/election/2018/exit-polls

28. Darryl Fears, "Black Opinion on Simpson Shifts," *The Washington Post*, September 27, 2007, A03.

29. CNN Exit Polls, 2018, https://www.cnn.com/election/2018/exit-polls

30. John C. Green, *The American Religious Landscape and Political Attitudes: A Baseline for 2004* (Washington, DC: The Pew Forum on Religion and Public Life, 2004).

31. "Muslim Americans: Middle Class and Mostly Mainstream," Pew Research Center, 2007, 41.

32. Ibid., 41–46.

33. "Like Most Americans, U.S. Muslims Concerned About Extremism in the Name of Islam," Pew Research Center, 2017.

34. United Nations, Development Report 2018.

35. Evidence that there were no class differences before 1932 is offered by W. Phillips Shively, "A Reinterpretation of the New Deal Realignment," *Public Opinion Quarterly* 35, no. 4 (1971): 621–624.

36. National Election Studies.

37. "The ANES Guide to Public Opinion and Electoral Behavior."

38. "Two Years Later, the Fear Lingers," Pew Research Center, 2003, https://www.people-press.org/2003/09/04/two-years-later-the-fear-lingers/

39. "Katrina Has Only Modest Impact on Basic Public Values," Pew Research Center, 2005, https://www.people-press.org/2005/09/22/katrina-has-only-modest-impact-on-basic-public-values/

40. This is demonstrated in John Anthony Maltese, Joseph A. Pika, and W. Phillips Shively, *Government Matters* (New York, NY: McGraw-Hill, 2013), Figure 6.13.

41. National Election Studies.

42. Anne Hendershott, "How Support for Abortion Became Kennedy Dogma," *The Wall Street Journal*, January 2, 2009, W11.

43. More systematic evidence for the parties' role in defining liberalism and conservatism—beyond anecdotes such as this—is offered in Paul Goren, "Party Identification and Core Values," *American Journal of Political Science* 49 (October 2005): 882–897. In a causal analysis, Goren finds that voters' party identifications shape their ideologies but *not* vice versa. See also Paul Goren, Christopher M. Federico, and Miki Caul Kittilson, "Source Cues, Partisan Identities, and Political Value Expression," *American Journal of Political Science* 53 (October 2009): 805–820 and Matthew Levendusky, *The Partisan Sort* (Chicago, IL: University of Chicago Press, 2009), Chapter 6, esp. 113–114.

44. The question of whether parties structure ideology or whether ideologies are more central to people (and people therefore identify with the party that best fits their ideology) is difficult to answer definitively. We observe that conservatives tend to be Republicans, and Republicans tend to be conservative. But which causes which? When two phenomena are intertwined this tightly, it is difficult (but not impossible) to assess definitively which is the original cause. The interpretation we have given here (that ideologies take their structure in the United States largely on the basis of parties' positions) is our best judgment based on the evidence. But we must note for you that whereas at some points in this book we are giving you well established and agreed-upon facts, in this case, we are giving you our best call on a question of interpretation and judgment.

45. Richard H. Davis, "The Anatomy of a Smear Campaign," *The Boston Globe*, March 21, 2004.

46. Jonathon P. Schuldt, Sara H. Konrath, and Norbert Schwarz, "'Global Warming' or 'Climate Change'? Whether the Planet Is Warming Depends on Question Wording," *Public Opinion Quarterly* (Spring 2011): 115–124.

47. Scott Clement, "Public Support for Gun Restrictions Has Grown to the Highest Level in 25 Years," *The Washington Post*, March 14, 2018.

48. Larry M. Bartels, "Constituency Opinion and Congressional Policy: The Reagan Defense Build Up," *The American Political Science Review* 85, no. 2 (June 1991): 457–474. The next two paragraphs summarize his study.

49. Ibid.

50. Bartels had available poll data from more than 100 congressional districts, allowing him to measure public opinion on the question in each of those districts.

51. Martin Gilens, *Affluence and Influence* (Princeton, NJ: Princeton University Press, 2012), 75–76.

## CHAPTER 7

1. "Why the Communist Party Is Alive, Well, and Flourishing in China," *The Telegraph*, July 31, 2017.

2. "Membership of UK Political Parties," House of Commons Library Research Briefing, September 3, 2018, https://researchbriefings.parliament.uk/ResearchBriefing/Summary/SN05125

3. Mark P. Jones, "Explaining the High Level of Party Discipline in the Argentine Congress," in *Legislative Politics in Latin America*, eds. Scott Morgenstern and Benito Nacif (New York, NY: Cambridge University Press, 2002), 147–184.

4. Marty Cohen, David Carol, Hans Noel, and John Zaller, *The Party Decides: Presidential Nominations Before and After Reform* (Chicago, IL: University of Chicago Press, 2008), 57.

5. Good evidence that those of differing economic circumstances were not distinctly Republican or Democratic before 1932–1936 is offered by the *Literary Digest* poll. The *Literary Digest* was an important national magazine that ran an unscientific poll in the 1920s and 1930s, before statisticians had learned how to poll accurately. Their poll was limited to their subscribers and to names drawn from automobile registration lists and telephone books—sources that in the 1920s and 1930s consisted primarily of the upper class and upper middle class. In 1924, 1928, and 1932, the poll was almost exactly correct in predicting the presidential vote, which means that the upper class and upper middle class were not voting differently from other voters. In 1936, by which time the Republican and Democratic parties were realigned along New Deal lines, the poll proved disastrously wrong. It predicted that Roosevelt would lose in a landslide. What had happened is that between 1932 and 1936, the party sympathies of the upper class and upper middle class had shifted to the Republicans. See W. Phillips Shively, "A Reinterpretation of the New Deal Realignment," *Public Opinion Quarterly* 35 (1971): 621–624.

6. The Progressives stood especially for opening up government by making more decisions directly accessible to voters, but they also favored greatly expanded regulation of business corporations to prevent abuses.

7. The demise of the machines was also caused partly by the development of welfare programs, Social Security, and other measures of the New Deal. With the government now helping to ensure people's economic security, the poor were not as dependent on political machines as they had once been.

8. Megan Brenan, "Democrats Favor More Moderate Party; GOP, More Conservative," Gallup, December 12, 2018, https://news.gallup.com/poll/245462/democrats-favor-moderate-party-gop-conservative.aspx

9. See Figure 6.10.

10. Utah Foundation, "2016 Utah Priorities Project Part III: Survey of State Party Delegates," Research Report number 741, April 2016. Voters and delegates were asked a set of ten policy questions. *Strongly liberal* means that they took the liberal position on at least nine of the questions; *Strongly conservative* means they took the conservative position on at least nine of the questions.

11. The distinction is found in many sources but is presented well in John Aldrich, *Why Parties?* (Chicago, IL: University of Chicago Press, 1995), 7–12.

12. Austin Ranney, *Curing the Mischiefs of Faction: Party Reform in America* (Berkeley: University of California Press, 1975), 43.

13. *Government Affairs Yellow Book: Who's Who in Government Affairs* (New York, NY: Leadership Directories, Inc., Winter 2010).

14. "Microsoft Corp," OpenSecrets.org, accessed July 23, 2019, https://www.opensecrets.org/orgs/summary.php?id=D000000115

15. Calculated from O. Gokcekus, J. Knowles, and E. Tower, "Sweetening the Pot: How American Sugar Buys Protection" in *The Political Economy of Trade, Aid and Foreign Investment Policies*, eds. Devashish Mitra and Arvind Panagariaya (Amsterdam, The Netherlands: Elsevier, 2004), 178. Calculated for a family of four in 1998.

16. Martin Sebaldt, *Organisierter Pluralismus* (Opladen, Germany: Westdeutscher Verlag GmbH, 1997), 79–82.

17. This is not to say that there are *no* interest groups consisting of students or other young people. Public Interest Research Groups (PIRGs) often draw their membership primarily from students, for instance.

18. Martin Gilens, *Affluence and Influence* (Princeton, NJ: Princeton University Press, 2012), 77–85.

## CHAPTER 8

1. Inglehart, R., C. Haerpfer, A. Moreno, C. Welzel, K. Kizilova, J. Diez-Medrano, M. Lagos, P. Norris, E. Ponarin & B. Puranen et al. (eds.). 2014. *World Values Survey: Round Five—Country-Pooled Datafile Version: http://www.worldvaluessurvey.org/WVSDocumentationWV5.jsp*. Madrid: JD Systems Institute.

2. Pamela Paxton, "Women's Suffrage in the Measurement of Democracy: Problems of Operationalization," *Studies in Comparative International Development* 35, no. 3: appendix.

3. "Help America Vote Act," U.S. Election Assistance Committee, accessed August 12, 2019, from https://www.eac.gov/about/help-america-vote-act/

4. "New Voting Restrictions in America," Brennan Center for Justice, July 3, 2019, https://www.brennancenter.org/new-voting-restrictions-america

5. A small number of delegates are selected from United States territories, such as Guam and Puerto Rico.

6. There are numerous variants of the open primary, allowing voters to move between parties in varying ways.

7. Michael P. McDonald, "2016 Presidential Nomination Contest Rates," United States Election Project, http://www.electproject.org/Election-Project-Blog/2016presidentialnominationcontesturnoutrates; there is a question about whether the eligible voting population is the proper base for considering turnout in primary elections (David P. Redlawsk, Caroline J. Tolbert, and Todd Donovan, *Why Iowa?* [Chicago, IL: University of Chicago Press, 2001], 123), since the primaries or caucuses are intended solely for partisan voters but the eligible electorate includes independents as well. However, in both Iowa and New Hampshire, independents are free to participate if they choose, so considering turnout based only on the registered voters for either party could lead to misleading results. In New Hampshire in 2008, for instance, the number of voters in the Democratic primary equaled 110 percent of the registered Democratic voters, presumably because a large number of independents voted in that primary along with registered Democrats.

8. David P. Redlawsk, Caroline J. Tolbert, and Todd Donovan, *Why Iowa?* (Chicago, IL: University of Chicago Press, 2011), 131.

9. Alan Abramowitz, "Don't Blame Primary Voters for Polarization," *The Forum* 5, no. 4, http://www.bepress.com/forum/vol5/iss4/art4; John Sides, Chris Tausanovitch, Lynn Vavreck, and Christopher Warshaw, "On the Representativeness of Primary Electorates," *British Journal of Political Science*, published online March 13, 2018.

10. Des Moines Register archives. We have only counted here contests in which there was open competition among candidates. That eliminates contests in which a party had an incumbent president, such as the Republican contest in 1984 when Ronald Reagan ran unopposed. And it also eliminates the Democratic contest in 1992 when Iowa's Democratic Senator Tom Harkin ran for president and no other Democratic candidates mounted campaigns in his home state.

11. Several other democracies use primary elections to choose their candidates, so the United States is not unique in this regard. Mexico, for instance, uses primary elections. However, the majority of democracies keep nominations under the control of the party organization.

12. RealClearPolitics tracking polls.

13. RealClearPolitics tracking polls.

14. Theodore Landsman, "Shifts in Incumbency Advantage in the U.S. House," FairVote, https://www.fairvote.org, April 25, 2017; Nathaniel Rakich, "How Much Was Incumbency Worth in 2018?" fivethirtyeight.com, December 6, 2018.

15. This is necessary because the size of the House of Representatives was fixed by law in 1911 at 435 (including new states added since then).

16. Members of the House from states such as Wyoming or Delaware, which are small enough to have one House seat, are the exception to this. The boundaries of the state are the boundaries of the sole district in the state, and they never change. So, for these members, boundaries cannot be manipulated. But these are only 7 members in a House of 435.

17. Ron Lieber, "When to Call Your Elected Representative for Help," *The New York Times*, October 20, 2012, B1.

18. OpenSecrets.org.

19. The Electoral Commission, *UK Parliamentary General Election 2005*, March 2006. Turnover was no higher than this because many districts are very safe for one district or another, even without gerrymandering.

20. This is how elections for the House of Representatives are set up in the United States. Elections for the Senate are a variant of SMDP. There are two senators from each state, not one, so a senator is not quite a "single member"; however, only one senator runs at a time, so effectively, the races are "single-member." A more important difference is that since states obviously have different populations, senate "districts" do not have "roughly equal populations."

21. This may be why, as we noted earlier in this chapter, since 1864, third parties have won a limited number of seats in the House of Representatives (about 1 percent of seats, on the average) but have never won the presidency.

22. International IDEA Table of Electoral Systems Worldwide, http://www.idea.int; Elections Worldwide project, now administered by Wikipedia (http://en.wikipedia.org/wiki/Wikipedia:WikiProject_Elections_and_Referenda/Overview_of_results). *Two-party systems* are defined as countries in which the two largest parties hold at least 95 percent of the seats in Parliament or Congress; the electoral systems are as defined by International IDEA. Countries were included if they were identified by Freedom House as electoral democracies.

23. In 1824, Andrew Jackson received more votes than John Quincy Adams, but Adams became president. This is not a clear case, however, because at that time, it was still the case that in some states, the electors were chosen by the state legislature rather than by voters.

24. National Popular Vote, https://www.nationalpopularvote.com/campaign-events-2016

25. Cited on the website of National Popular Vote, http://www.nationalpopularvote.com/

26. "Women in National Parliaments," Inter-parliamentary Union, November 1, 2018, http://www.ipu.org/wmn-e/world.htm

27. Pippa Norris, "Women's Representation and Electoral Systems" in *Encyclopedia of Electoral Systems*, ed. Richard Rose (Washington, DC: CQ Press, 2000).

28. Majority-minority districts can also occur naturally, of course. An inner-city area might be heavily populated by a minority group so that any district, no matter how its boundaries were drawn, would have a majority from among the minority. In our discussion here, we are looking only at deliberate gerrymandering to create majority-minority districts.

29. Christopher Ingraham, "Somebody Just Put a Price Tag on the 2016 Election. It's a doozy," *The Washington Post*, April 14, 2017. (His source was OpenSecrets.org.)

30. The Electoral Commission, "Political Party Spending at Previous Elections," 2018, https://www

.electoralcommission.org.uk/find-information-by-subject/political-parties-campaigning-and-donations/political-party-spending-at-elections/details-of-party-spending-at-previous-elections

31. Peter Ferdinand, "Party Funding and Political Corruption in East Asia: The Cases of Japan, South Korea and Taiwan," in *Funding of Political Parties and Election Campaigns*, eds. Reginald Austin and Maja Tjernström (Stockholm, Sweden: International IDEA, 2003), 64.

32. Calculated from estimates in Center for Communication and Civic Engagement, "Assessment of US Senate Campaign Expenditure in 2000, 2002 and 2004, with Predictions for 2006" (working paper #2005-2, Department of Communication, University of Washington, Seattle, Washington, 2005).

33. *Buckley v. Valeo*, 424 U.S. 1 (1976).

34. Robert G. Boatright, "Campaign Financing in the 2008 Election," in *The American Elections of 2008*, eds. Janet M. Box-Steffensmeier and Steven E. Schier (New York, NY: Rowman & Littlefield, 2009), 145.

35. *Citizens United v. Federal Election Commission*, 130 S.Ct. 876 (2010).

36. US Court of Appeals for the District of Columbia: *SpeechNow.org v. Federal Election Commission*. No. 08-5223.

37. In practice, 527 committees and Super PACs have skirted very close to the line in coordinating with campaigns. "Independent" ads for Democrat Ben Nelson included an interview with the candidate (*The New York Times*, October 13, 2011, A17), and the website for Republican presidential candidate Rick Perry used some video that also appeared on the website of "Make Us Great Again," a Super PAC supporting his candidacy (*Politico*, November 26, 2011, http://www.politico.com/blogs/bensmith/1111/Perry_ad_features_SuprPAC_footage.html?showall).

38. Jeremy W. Peters, "'Super PACs', Not Campaigns, Do Bulk of Ad Spending," *The New York Times*, March 3, 2012, A10.

39. Mike McIntire and Michael Luo, "Fine Line Between 'Super PACs' and Campaigns," *The New York Times*, February 26, 2012, A1.

40. Torsten Persson and Guido Tabellini, "Electoral Systems and Economic Policy," in *Oxford Handbook of Political Economy*, eds. Barry Weingast and Donald Wittman (Oxford, England: Oxford University Press, 2008).

41. 52 U.S.C. § 30121, and 11 CFR 110.20.

42. The evidence for these conclusions is reviewed in Kathleen Hall Jamieson, *Cyber-War: How Russian Hackers and Trolls Helped Elect a President* (New York, NY: Oxford University Press, 2018), Chapter 2.

43. Elin Falguera, Samuel Jones, and Magnus Ohman, eds. *Funding of Political Parties and Election Campaigns* (Stockholm, Sweden: International IDEA, 2014), Annex I.

44. Library of Congress, "Regulation of Campaign Finance and Free Advertising: United Kingdom," https://www.loc.gov/law/help/campaign-finance-regulation/unitedkingdom.php

## CHAPTER 9

1. Rafael López Pintor and Maria Gratschew, *Voter Turnout Since 1945* (Stockholm, Sweden: International IDEA, 2002), 83, 84, 168.

2. World Values Surveys from 1990 to 2006, averaging results from several surveys. http://www.worldvaluessurvey.org

3. Laurie Chen, "Chinese Protesters Blame Fracking for Earthquakes That Killed Two People in Sichuan," *South China Morning Post*, February 26, 2019, https://www.scmp.com/news/china/society/article/2187718/chinese-demonstrators-rage-sichuan-government-and-blame-fracking

4. Inglehart, R., C. Haerpfer, A. Moreno, C. Welzel, K. Kizilova, J. Diez-Medrano, M. Lagos, P. Norris, E. Ponarin & B. Puranen et al. (eds.). 2014. *World Values Survey: Round Six—Country-Pooled Datafile Version: www.worldvaluessurvey.org/WVSDocumentationWV6.jsp*. Madrid: JD Systems Institute.

5. Percent voted is based on data from the U.S. Census Bureau, Current Population Survey, "Voting and Registration in the Election of November 2016." These statistics indicate the percent of citizens voting but do not take into account citizens who could not vote because they were disqualified as felons or for other reasons. Throughout this chapter, unless otherwise indicated, the United States Census reports will be our basic source on turnout. Figures for all other forms of participation in this table are from the National Election Studies, 2016 Presidential Election Survey.

6. Inglehart, *World Values Survey: Round Six*.

7. Also, of course, this suggests that some portion of the apparently high turnout before the 1890s might have consisted of fraudulent ballots.

8. US Census, "Educational Attainment in the United States 2018," CPS Historical Time Series Tables, https://www.census.gov/data/tables/time-series/demo/educational-attainment/cps-historical-time-series.html

9. United States Census Bureau reports, Voting and Registration in the Election of 2018.

10. Several states, however, allow citizens to register at the polls on Election Day if they have not registered beforehand.

11. G. Bingham Powell, Jr., "American Voter Turnout in Comparative Perspective," *American Political Science Review* 80 (March 1986): 17–43.

12. Campus Vote Project, http://campusvoteproject.org/administrators/student-id-as-voter-id/

13. Michael McDonald, United States Election Project, http://electproject.org

14. B. F. Skinner, *Walden Two* (New York, NY: Macmillan, 1948), 220–221.

15. For instance, Table 5.11 of Michael S. Lewis-Beck, William G. Jacoby, Helmut Norpoth, and Herbert F. Weisberg, *The American Voter Revisited* (Ann Arbor: University of Michigan Press, 2008).

16. Calculated from Michael McDonald, United States Election Project.

17. United States Census Bureau, "Voting and Registration in the Election of November 2018," https://www.census.gov/data/tables/time-series/demo/voting-and-registration/p20-583.html; Corporation for National and Community Service, Volunteering in America, https://www.nationalservice.gov/serve/via

18. Source for percent voting: United States Census, "Voting and Registration in the Election of November 2018."

Source for percent volunteering: Corporation for National and Community Service, Volunteering in America.

19. The exception was the 1992 election, but it is likely that this was a statistical quirk in the survey.

20. ANES, "The ANES Guide to Public Opinion and Electoral Behavior," accessed July 27, 2019, https://electionstudies.org/resources/anes-guide/

21. Information on the United States, France, and Italy from Jens Alber and Ulrich Kohler, "The Inequality of Electoral Participation in Europe and America and the Politically Integrative Functions of the Welfare State," in *United in Diversity? Comparing Social Models in Europe and America*, eds. Jens Alber and Neil Gilbert (New York, NY: Oxford University Press, 2008), 75. Information on India from Juan Linz, Alfred Stepan, and Yogendra Yadav, *Democracy and Diversity* (New York, NY: Oxford University Press, 2007), 99.

22. Sidney Verba, Norman H. Nie, and Jae-on Kim argue in *Participation and Political Equality* (Chicago, IL: University of Chicago Press, 1987) that there is less difference between participation rates of the poor and well-off in European countries than in the United States because in Europe, there are explicitly labor union-based socialist parties that directly mobilize workers to vote.

23. There are no fines for failing to vote, but a notation is made on the legal books that the person who did not vote has broken the law.

24. United States Census Bureau, "Voting and Registration in the Election of November 2018."

25. Ibid.

26. United States Census Bureau, "Voting and Registration in the Election of 2016," United States Census Bureau, "Voting and Registration in the Election of November 2018."

27. North Carolina State Board of Elections, accessed July 28, 2019, https://er.ncsbe.gov/?election_dt=11/06/2018&county_id=0&office=REF&contest=0.

28. American National Election Studies, Guide to Public Opinion and Electoral Behavior.

29. "Likely Rise in Voter Turnout Bodes Well for Democrats," Section 2, Pew Research Center, 2008, https://www.people-press.org/2008/07/10/section-2-evaluating-the-candidates-and-campaigns/

30. Michael S. Lewis-Beck, William G. Jacoby, Helmut Norpoth, and Herbert F. Weisberg, *The American Voter Revisited* (Ann Arbor: University of Michigan Press, 2008), 55–56. This study looks at presidential elections, but the four factors apply in races of all sorts.

31. Robert S. Erikson, "Economic Conditions and the Presidential Vote," *The American Political Science Review* 83 (June 1989): 567–573.

32. Michael S. Lewis-Beck and Guy D. Whitten, "Economics and Elections: Effects Deep and Wide," special issue of *Electoral Studies* 33 (September 2013): 391–562.

33. Christopher H. Achen and Larry M. Bartels, *Democracy for Realists* (Princeton, NJ: Princeton University Press, 2016), 118–128.

34. R.J. Reinhart, "Republicans More Positive on U.S. Relations With Russia," Gallup News, July 13, 2018, https://news.gallup.com/poll/237137/republicans-positive-relations-russia.aspx

35. "Positive Views of Economy Surge, Driven by Major Shifts Among Republicans," Pew Research Center, March 22, 2018.

36. Calculated from Michael S. Lewis-Beck, William G. Jacoby, Helmut Norpoth, and Herbert F. Weisberg, *The American Voter Revisited* (Ann Arbor: University of Michigan Press, 2008), Table 7.6. Only those who identify with a party are included in the figure.

37. CNN Exit Polls.

38. Calculated from 2008, 2016 CNN Exit Polls.

39. Donald E. Stokes and Gudmund R. Iversen, "On the Existence of Forces Restoring Party Competition," *Public Opinion Quarterly* 26 (1962): 159–171.

40. Dennis W. Johnson, *No Place for Amateurs* (New York, NY: Routledge, 2001), xiii.

41. See John Geer, *In Defense of Negativity: Attack Advertising in Presidential Campaigns* (Chicago, IL: University of Chicago Press, 2006).

42. Emily Stewart, "Donald Trump Rode $5 Billion in Free Media to the White House," The Street, November 20, 2016, https://www.thestreet.com/story/13896916/1/donald-trump-rode-5-billion-in-free-media-to-the-white-house.html

43. Noam Cohen, "Is Obama a Mac and Clinton a PC?" *The New York Times*, February 4, 2008.

44. W. Phillips Shively, "From Differential Abstention to Conversion: A Change in Electoral Change, 1864–1988," *American Journal of Political Science* 36 (May 1992): 309–330.

45. Much has been written on this topic, but see particularly Morris P. Fiorina, Samuel J. Abrams, and Jeremy C. Pope, *Culture War? The Myth of a Polarized America*, 2nd ed. (New York, NY: Pearson Longman, 2006); Barbara Sinclair, *Party Wars: Polarization and the Politics of the National Policy-Making Process* (Norman: University of Oklahoma Press, 2006); and Gary C. Jacobson, *A Divider Not a Uniter: George W. Bush and the American People* (New York, NY: Pearson Longman, 2007), Chapter 1.

46. Shanto Iyengar, Gaurav Sood, and Yphtach Lelkes, "Affect, Not Ideology: A Social Identity Perspective on Polarization," *Public Opinion Quarterly* 76, no. 3 (2012): 405–431.

47. "Partisanship and Political Animosity in 2016," Pew Research Center, June 22, 2016, https://www.people-press.org/2016/06/22/partisanship-and-political-animosity-in-2016/

48. Ibid.

49. "Political Segregation: The Big Sort," *The Economist*, June 21, 2008, 41.

50. Calculated from "Presidential Election Results—% Votes From the United States Election Results Database Shown in Percent: Date Type: Year; Political Party: All Parties," *Dave Leip's Atlas of US Presidential Elections* (Bethesda, MD: Data-Planet by Conquest Systems, 2018).

51. Iyengar, "Affect, Not Ideology," Table 4.

## CHAPTER 10

1. "The Story of Mohamed Bouazizi, the Man Who Toppled Tunisia," *International Business Times*, January 14, 2011, http://www.ibtimes.com/articles/101313/20110114/the-story-of-mohamed-bouazizi-the-man-who-toppled-tunisia.htm; Bob Simon, "How a Slap Sparked Tunisia's Revolution," *60 Minutes*, February 20, 2011, http://

www.cbsnews.com/stories/2011/02/20/60minutes/
main20033404.shtml

2. Robert M. Entman, "Foreword," in *Framing American Politics*, eds. Karen Callaghan and Frauke Schnell (Pittsburgh: University of Pittsburgh Press, 2005), viii.

3. Bill Carter and Brian Stelter, "In 'Daily Show' Role on 9/11 Bill, Echoes of Murrow," *The New York Times*, December 26, 2010, http://www.nytimes.com/2010/12/27/business/media/27stewart.html; Emily Cochrane, "9/11 First Responders Fund Clears Senate and Heads to Trump," *The New York Times*, July 23, 2019, https://www.nytimes.com/2019/07/23/us/politics/9-11-first-responders-fund-bill.html

4. David L. Paletz, *The Media in American Politics: Contents and Consequences* (New York, NY: Longman, 1999), 141.

5. "Media Watchdog Criticizes Coverage of Famine in Ethiopia," IJNET, May 24, 2001, http://ijnet.org/opportunities/media-watchdog-criticizes-coverage-famine-ethiopia

6. Rick Hampson, "Ethiopia's New Fame: 'A Ticking Time Bomb,'" *USA Today*, August 17, 2008, http://www.usatoday.com/news/world/2008-08-17-ethiopia_N.htm

7. Paletz, *The Media in American Politics*, 119.

8. U.S. Department of Justice, "Report on the Investigation Into Russian Interference in the 2016 Presidential Election, Volume I of II," 23; full text available at https://apps.npr.org/documents/document.html?id=5955997-Muellerreport

9. Ryan Broderick, "Here's Everything the Mueller Report Says About How Russian Trolls Used Social Media," BuzzFeed, April 18, 2019, https://www.buzzfeednews.com/article/ryanhatesthis/mueller-report-internet-research-agency-detailed-2016

10. Lauren Rosenthal, "Local Candidates Are the Subject of Political Tracking, Too," *NPR*, August 16, 2018, https://www.npr.org/2018/08/16/639149636/local-candidates-find-they-re-the-subject-of-political-tracking

11. Anthony M. DeStefano, "Body Cams Now Worn by All 20K New York City Police Officers," Government Technology, March 7, 2019, https://www.govtech.com/public-safety/Body-Cams-Now-Worn-by-All-20K-New-York-City-Police-Officers.html

12. "ACORN Officials Videotaped Telling 'Pimp,' 'Prostitute' How to Lie to IRS," Fox News.com, September 10, 2009, https://www.foxnews.com/story/acorn-officials-videotaped-telling-pimp-prostitute-how-to-lie-to-irs

13. Tom McCarthy, "James O'Keefe Agrees to Pay $100,000 Settlement to Fired Acorn Employee," *The Guardian*, March 8, 2013, https://www.theguardian.com/world/2013/mar/08/james-o-keefe-settlement-acorn

14. WikiLeaks can be found at http://www.wikileaks.org

15. Scott Shane and Andrew W. Lehren, "Leaked Cables Offer Raw Look at U.S. Diplomacy," *The New York Times*, November 28, 2010, http://www.nytimes.com/2010/11/29/world/29cables.html

16. Charlie Savage, "Assange Indicted Under Espionage Act, Raising First Amendment Issues," *The New York Times*, May 23, 2019, https://www.nytimes.com/2019/05/23/us/politics/assange-indictment.html

17. Andrew P. Thomas, "The CSI Effect: Fact or Fiction," *The Yale Law Journal Pocket Part* January 31, 2006, https://www.yalelawjournal.org/forum/the-csi-effect-fact-or-fiction

18. Frank Luther Mott, *American Journalism* (New York, NY: Macmillan, 1960), 251.

19. The first successful trans-Atlantic cable took place on August 5, 1858, between President James Buchanan of the United States and Queen Victoria of England, but that cable soon failed.

20. Eric Burns, *Infamous Scribblers: The Founding Fathers and the Rowdy Beginnings of American Journalism* (New York, NY: Public Affairs, 2006), 31–32.

21. Mott, *American Journalism*, 43.

22. Burns, *Infamous Scribblers*, 239.

23. Mott, *American Journalism*, 108.

24. Richard L. Rubin, *Press, Party, and Presidency* (New York, NY: Norton, 1981), 11.

25. Culver H. Smith, *The Press, Politics, and Patronage: The American Government's Use of Newspapers, 1789–1875* (Athens, GA: The University of Georgia Press, 1977), 13; Burns, *Infamous Scribblers*, 262–266.

26. Martin Mayes, *An Historical-Sociological Inquiry Into Certain Phases of the Development of the Press in the United States* (Richmond: Missourian Press, 1935), 48.

27. Mark Wahlgren Summers, *The Press Gang: Newspapers and Politics, 1865–1878* (Chapel Hill: The University of North Carolina Press, 1994), 12.

28. Mott, *American Journalism*, 525–526.

29. All of these figures are drawn from https://umdrive.memphis.edu/mbensman/public/history1.html

30. "Media Use and Evaluation," Gallup, accessed July 29, 2019, http://www.gallup.com/poll/1663/media-use-evaluation.aspx

31. "Tops of 2018: Radio," Nielsen, December 10, 2018, https://www.nielsen.com/us/en/insights/news/2018/tops-of-2018-radio.html

32. John P. Robinson and Leo W. Jeffres, "The Changing Role of Newspapers in the Age of Television," *Journalism Monographs* 63 (September 1979): 2.

33. National Institute of Mental Health, *Television and Behavior, Vol. 1* (Washington, DC: Government Printing Office, 1982), 1.

34. Steve M. Barkin, *American Television News: The Media Marketplace and the Public Interest* (Armonk, NY: M. E. Sharpe, 2003), 37.

35. Charles Franklin, "Walter Cronkite, Most Trusted Man in America," Pollster.com, July 17, 2009, http://www.pollster.com/blogs/walter_cronkite_most_trusted_m.php?nr51

36. White House press secretary George Christian used the term *shock waves* to describe the Johnson administration's reaction to Cronkite's report. See John Anthony Maltese, *Spin Control: The White House Office of Communications and the Management of Presidential News* (Chapel Hill: The University of North Carolina Press, 1992), 14.

37. "History of Cable," California Cable & Telecommunications Association, accessed August 12, 2019, https://www.calcable.org/learn/history-of-cable/

38. Amy Mitchell, "Americans Still Prefer Watching to Reading the News—and Mostly Still Through Television," Pew Research Center, December 3, 2018, https://www.journalism.org/2018/12/03/americans-still-prefer-watching-to-reading-the-news-and-mostly-still-through-television/

39. Elisa Shearer, "Social Media Outpaces Print Newspapers in the U.S. as a News Source," Pew Research Center, December 10, 2018, https://www.pewresearch.org/fact-tank/2018/12/10/

social-media-outpaces-print-newspapers-in-the-u-s-as-a-news-source/

40. "View of Press Values and Performance: 1985–2007," Pew Research Center, August 9, 2007, 15, https://www.pewresearch.org/wp-content/uploads/sites/4/legacy-pdf/348.pdf

41. Katerina Eva Matsa and Elisa Shearer, "News Use Across Social Media Platforms 2018," Pew Research Center, September 10, 2018, https://www.journalism.org/2018/09/10/news-use-across-social-media-platforms-2018/

42. Geoffrey A. Fowler, "I Fell for Facebook Fake News. Here's Why Millions of You Did, Too," *The Washington Post*, October 18, 2018, https://www.washingtonpost.com/technology/2018/10/18/i-fell-facebook-fake-news-heres-why-millions-you-did-too/?utm_term=.0f7ffd78abfc

43. Mike Wendling, "The (Almost) Complete History of 'Fake News,'" *BBC News*, January 22, 2018, https://www.bbc.com/news/blogs-trending-42724320

44. "Indicators of News Media Trust," Knight Foundation, September 11, 2018, https://www.knightfoundation.org/reports/indicators-of-news-media-trust

45. Jeffrey Gottfried, Galen Stocking, and Elizabeth Grieco, "Partisans Remain Sharply Divided in Their Attitudes About the News Media," Pew Research Center, September 25, 2018, https://www.journalism.org/2018/09/25/partisans-remain-sharply-divided-in-their-attitudes-about-the-news-media/

46. Kenneth C. Creech, *Electronic Media Law and Regulation*, 3rd ed. (Boston, MA: Focal Press, 2000), 54–56.

47. Ibid., 67.

48. Paul Weiss, "Cross-Ownership and Other Media Ownership Rules Eliminated by FCC," Lexology, November 17, 2017, https://www.lexology.com/library/detail.aspx?g=77a82235-de90-4014-a41d-c5fd1e6122d8

49. Joe Curtis, "The Pros and Cons of Net Neutrality," ITPro, July 31, 2018, https://www.itpro.co.uk/strategy/28115/the-pros-and-cons-of-net-neutrality

50. Harper Neidig, "Supreme Court Refuses to Take Up Challenge to Obama-Era Net Neutrality Rules," *The Hill*, November 5, 2018, https://thehill.com/regulation/court-battles/414902-supreme-court-refuses-to-take-up-challenge-to-obama-era-net

51. David Shepardson, "U.S. Appeals Court Hears Challenge to FCC Net Neutrality Repeal," *Reuters*, February 1, 2019, https://www.reuters.com/article/usa-internet/u-s-appeals-court-hears-challenge-to-fcc-net-neutrality-repeal-idUSL1N1ZW133

52. *Official Journal of the European Union*, L310, 58, November 26, 2015.

53. Quoted in Creech, *Electronic Media Law*, 42.

54. *Red Lion Broadcasting Co. v. Federal Communications Commission*, 395 U.S. 367 (1969).

55. Todd S. Purdum, "Terror in Oklahoma: The President; Shifting Debate to the Political Climate, Clinton Condemns 'Promoters of Paranoia,'" *The New York Times*, April 25, 1995, http://www.nytimes.com/1995/04/25/us/terror-oklahoma-president-shifting-debate-political-climate-clinton-condemns.html?pagewanted51

56. "Clinton Wants 'More Balance' on Airwaves," *Politico*, February 12, 2009, https://www.politico.com/blogs/michaelcalderone/0209/

Clinton_wants_more_balance_on_the_airwaves.html#; Steve Almond, "Want to Stop Fake News? Reinstate the Fairness Doctrine," *Boston Globe*, April 17, 2018, https://www2.bostonglobe.com/opinion/2018/04/17/want-stop-fake-news-reinstate-fairness-doctrine/BpMw4D3s9qLrDwA2geLywN/story.html

57. Creech, *Electronic Media Law and Regulation*, 118.

58. *Federal Communication Commission v. Pacifica Foundation*, 438 U.S. 726 (1978).

59. Amy Schatz, "Crying Foul: Supreme Court to Hear Challenge to FCC Cussing Crackdown," *The Wall Street Journal*, January 9, 2012, http://online.wsj.com/article/SB10001424052970203436904577148731524813906.html

60. *Reno v. American Civil Liberties Union*, 521 U.S. 844 (1997).

61. *ACLU v. Mukasey*, 534 F.3d 181 (2008), cert. denied 129 S.Ct. 1032 (2009).

62. *United States v. American Library Association*, 539 U.S. 194 (2003).

63. Damien Cave, "Countries Want to Ban 'Weaponized' Social Media. What Would That Look Like?" *The New York Times*, March 31, 2019, https://www.nytimes.com/2019/03/31/world/australia/countries-controlling-social-media.html

64. See, for example, Sue Halpern, "Mark Zukerberg, Elizabeth Warren, and the Case for Regulating Big Tech," *The New Yorker*, April 11, 2019, https://www.newyorker.com/tech/annals-of-technology/mark-zuckerberg-elizabeth-warren-and-the-case-for-regulating-big-tech; Editorial Board, "The Dark Side of Regulating Speech on Facebook," *The Washington Post*, April 3, 2019, https://www.washingtonpost.com/opinions/the-dark-side-of-regulating-speech-on-facebook/2019/04/03/73316af4-557a-11e9-814f-e2f46684196e_story.html?utm_term=.1b4d8bd0c8ad

65. W. Lance Bennett, *News: The Politics of Illusion*, 2nd ed. (New York, NY: Longman, 1988), xi.

66. Leon V. Sigal, *Reporters and Officials: The Organization and Politics of Newsmaking* (Lexington, MA: D. C. Heath and Company, 1973), 120.

67. Ibid., 121 (Table 6-1).

68. Samuel Kernell, *Going Public: New Strategies of Presidential Leadership* (Washington, DC: CQ Press, 1986).

69. Jeffrey K. Tulis, *The Rhetorical Presidency* (Princeton, NJ: Princeton University Press, 1987), see especially 64 (Table 3-1). Cf. Mel Laracey, *Presidents and the People: The Partisan Story of Going Public* (College Station: Texas A&M University Press, 2002).

70. Elmer J. Cornwell, Jr., *Presidential Leadership of Public Opinion* (Bloomington: Indiana University Press, 1965), 17.

71. Tucker Higgins and Kevin Breuninger, "White House Announces Press Briefing After Record Six Weeks Without One," *CNBC*, March 11, 2019, https://www.cnbc.com/2019/03/11/white-house-announces-press-briefing-after-record-time-without-one.html; Nancy Cook, "The President's Silent Spokeswoman," *Politico*, July 23, 2019, https://www.politico.com/story/2019/07/23/trump-spokeswoman-stephanie-grisham-1426697

72. Jordyn Phelps, "Trump White House hasn't held a traditional press briefing in 6 months," ABC News, September 11, 2019, https://abcnews.go.com/Politics/trump-white-house-held-traditional-press-briefing-months/story?id=65509975

73. Deanna Paul and Felicia Sonmez, "Sarah Sanders Lied, According to the Mueller Report. She's Calling It a 'Slip of the Tongue'," *The Washington Post*, April 19, 2019, https://www.washingtonpost.com/politics/2019/04/19/sarah-sanders-lied-according-mueller-report-shes-calling-it-slip-tongue/?utm_term=.03a52e1db874

74. Glenn Kessler, Salvador Rizzo, and Meg Kelly, "President Trump Has Made More Than 10,000 False or Misleading Claims," *The Washington Post*, April 29, 2019, https://www.washingtonpost.com/politics/2019/04/29/president-trump-has-made-more-than-false-or-misleading-claims/?utm_term=.6927fef7ec54

75. Martha Joynt Kumar, *Managing the President's Message: The White House Communications Operation* (Baltimore, MD: Johns Hopkins University Press, 2007); John Anthony Maltese, *Spin Control: The White House Office of Communications and the Management of Presidential News* (Chapel Hill: The University of North Carolina Press, 1992).

76. Summers, *The Press Gang*, 81.

77. David R. Mayhew, *Congress: The Electoral Connection* (New Haven, CT: Yale University Press, 1974).

78. David A. Fahrenthold, "27% of Communication by Members of Congress Is Taunting, Professor Concludes," *The Washington Post*, April 6, 2011, http://www.washingtonpost.com/politics/27percent-of-communication-by-members-of-congress-is-taunting-professor-concludes/2011/04/06/AF1no2qC_story.html

79. Jennifer Steinhauer, "The G.O.P.'s Very Rapid Response Team," *The New York Times*, October 25, 2011, A14.

80. For updated information, see https://www.mpsontwitter.co.uk/

81. Kyu Ho Youm, "Cameras in the Courtroom in the Twenty-First Century: The U.S. Supreme Court Learning From Abroad?" *Brigham Young University Law Review* 6 (December 18, 2012): Article 9, https://digitalcommons.law.byu.edu/cgi/viewcontent.cgi?article=2699&context=lawreview

82. Felipe Lopes, "Television and Judicial Behavior: Lessons From the Brazilian Supreme Court," *Economic Analysis of Law Review* 9, no. 1 (January–April 2018): 41.

83. Matthew C. Ingram, "Uncommon Transparency: The Supreme Court, Media Relations, and Public Opinion in Brazil," in *Justices and Journalists: The Global Perspective*, eds. Richard Davis and David Taras (Cambridge, UK: Cambridge University Press, 2017), 58.

84. David Taras, "Judges and Journalists and the Spaces In Between," in *Justices and Journalists: The Global Perspective*, eds. Richard Davis and David Taras (Cambridge, UK: Cambridge University Press, 2017), 1.

85. Elliot E. Slotnick and Jennifer A. Segal, "'The Supreme Court Decided Today . . .' or Did It?" in *Judicial Politics: Readings From Judicature*, 2nd ed., ed. Elliot E. Slotnick (Lanham, MD: Rowman & Littlefield, 1999), 449.

86. Jeremy W. Peters and Sapna Maheshwari, "Viral Videos Are Replacing Pricey Political Ads. They're Cheaper, and They Work," *The New York Times*, September 10, 2018, https://www.nytimes.com/2018/09/10/us/politics/midterm-primaries-advertising.html

87. David L. Paletz and Robert M. Entman, *Media Power Politics* (New York, NY: The Free Press, 1981), 48.

88. Ibid., 47.

89. Ibid., 45.

90. "Press Accuracy Rating Hits Two Decade Low," Pew Research Center, September 13, 2009, http://people-press.org/2009/09/13/press-accuracy-rating-hits-two-decade-low/; Jeffrey Gottfried, Galen Stocking, and Elizabeth Grieco, "Partisans Remain Sharply Divided in Their Attitudes About the News Media," Pew Research Center, September 25, 2018, https://www.journalism.org/2018/09/25/partisans-remain-sharply-divided-in-their-attitudes-about-the-news-media/

91. Michael Parenti, "Inventing Reality: The Politics of News Media" in *The Lanahan Readings in Media and Politics*, ed. Lewis S. Rangel (Baltimore, MD: Lanahan Publishers, 2009), 166, 171–172.

92. Bennett, *News*, 47.

93. Ibid., 45.

94. Ibid., 47.

95. Ibid., 47.

## CHAPTER 11

1. Government Printing Office, Public Law 107-40, accessed July 30, 2019, https://www.govinfo.gov/content/pkg/PLAW-107publ40/pdf/PLAW-107publ40.pdf

2. Austin Wright, "How Barbara Lee Became an Army of One," *Politico*, July 30, 2017, https://www.politico.com/magazine/story/2017/07/30/how-barbara-lee-became-an-army-of-one-215434

3. Bill French with John Bradshaw, "Ending the Endless War: An Incremental Approach to Repealing the 2001 AUMF," National Security Network, August 2014, Appendix A, https://www.justsecurity.org/wp-content/uploads/2014/08/ENDING-THE-ENDLESS-WAR_FINAL.pdf

4. Shoon Kathleen Murray, "Stretching the 2001 AUMF: A History of Two Presidencies," *Presidential Studies Quarterly*, February 2015; see the discussion at "Profile Authorization to Use Military Force (AUMF)," History Commons, http://www.historycommons.org/entity.jsp?entity=authorization_to_use_military_force__aumf__1 and the account of the drafting at Gregory D. Johnson, "60 Words and a War Without End: The Untold Story of the Most Dangerous Sentence in U.S. History," BuzzFeed, January 16, 2014, https://www.buzzfeed.com/gregoryjohnsen/60-words-and-a-war-without-end-the-untold-story-of-the-most

5. Stephanie Savell, "Where We Fight," *Smithsonian* 49, no. 9 (January–February 2019), https://smallwarsjournal.com/blog/smithsonian-magazines-special-januaryfebruary-issue-america-war

6. "Common Defense: More Members Mull the Parameters for War," *CQ Magazine*, July 24, 2017; "Anatomy of a Vote: War Powers Survive Attack, for Now," *CQ Magazine*, September 18, 2017.

7. Claire Mills, Parliamentary Approval for Military Action, House of Commons Library, CBP 7166 (May 8, 2018), https://researchbriefings.parliament.uk/ResearchBriefing/Summary/CBP-7166; Tom Whitehead, "Britain at War: A History of Parliamentary Votes and Debate," *The Telegraph*, December 1, 2015, https://www.telegraph.co.uk/news/worldnews/middleeast/syria/12028148/Britain-at-war-a-history-of-parliamentary-votes-and-debate.html

8. James Strong, "Why Parliament Now Decides on War: Tracing the Growth of the Parliamentary Prerogative Through Syria, Libya and Iraq," *British Journal of Politics and International Relations* 17, no. 4 (2015), https://journals-sagepub-com.udel.idm.oclc.org/doi/pdf/10.1111/1467-856X.12055

9. Michael L. Mezey, "The Functions of Legislatures in the Third World," *Legislative Studies Quarterly* 8, no. 4 (1983): 511–550.

10. By that time, 29 states were already using a form of popular participation in selecting senators rather than relying completely on state legislators. See the discussion on the website of the United States Senate: http://www.senate.gov/artandhistory/history/common/briefing/Direct_Election_Senators.htm

11. Research in Arizona has shown that in the House, where multimember districts are used, legislators are more ideological in their voting, while in the Senate, where a single-member district is used, constituency factors are more pronounced.

12. Heinz Eulau, John C. Wahlke, William Buchanan, and Leroy C. Ferguson, "The Role of Representation: Some Empirical Observations on the Theory of Edmund Burke." *The American Political Science Review* 53, no. 3 (1959): 742–756.

13. "Twenty Years of Televised Proceedings of the House of Commons," Parliament.uk, December 11, 2009, https://www.parliament.uk/business/news/2009/12/20-years-of-televised-proceedings-of-the-house-of-commons/

14. Deutscher Bundestag, "Parliamentary Television," accessed July 30, 2019, https://www.bundestag.de/en/press/tv; Inter-Parliamentary Union, "The Challenge of Broadcasting Parliamentary Proceedings," October 2006, http://archive.ipu.org/PDF/publications/ebu_en.pdf

15. Thomas Stratmann and Martin Baur, "Plurality Rule, Proportional Representation, and the German Bundestag: How Incentives to Pork-Barrel Differ Across Electoral Systems," *American Journal of Political Science* 46, no. 3 (July 2002), https://www.jstor.org/stable/3088395

16. David Denemark, "Partisan Pork Barrel in Parliamentary Systems: Australian Constituency-Level Grants," *The Journal of Politics* 62, no. 3, August 2000.

17. David J. Samuels, "Pork Barreling Is Not Credit Claiming or Advertising: Campaign Finance and the Sources of the Personal Vote in Brazil," *The Journal of Politics* 64, no. 3, August 2002.

18. Sean Kennedy, "All About Pork: The History, Abuse, and Future of Earmarks," *Citizens Against Government Waste* (2015). For the Democratic debate, see John Hudak, "Congress in 2019: Why the First Branch Should Bring Back Earmarks," Brookings: Congress in 2019, December 27, 2018, https://www.brookings.edu/blog/fixgov/2018/12/27/congress-in-2019-why-the-first-branch-should-bring-back-earmarks/; "Earmarks Could Be Making a Quiet Comeback," *CQ Magazine*, February 11, 2019.

19. Theresa Hebert, "Women in the 116th Congress," *Quorum*, November 7, 2018, https://www.quorum.us/data-driven-insights/women-in-116th-congress/401/

20. Kristen Bialik, "For the Fifth Time in a Row, the New Congress Is the Most Racially and Ethnically Diverse Ever," Pew Research Center, February 8, 2019, http://www.pewresearch.org/fact-tank/2019/02/08/for-the-fifth-time-in-a-row-the-new-congress-is-the-most-racially-and-ethnically-diverse-ever/

21. "Women in National Parliaments," Inter-Parliamentary Union, February 1, 2019, http://archive.ipu.org/wmn-e/classif.htm?month=6&year=2018

22. See David R. Mayhew, *Congress: The Electoral Connection* (New Haven, CT: Yale University Press, 1975).

23. Richard F. Fenno, "US House Members in Their Constituencies: An Exploration," *The American Political Science Review* 71, no. 3 (1977): 883–917.

24. Drew Desilver, "A Productivity Scorecard for the 115th Congress: More Laws Than Before, but Not More Substance," Pew Research Center, January 25, 2019, http://www.pewresearch.org/fact-tank/2019/01/25/a-productivity-scorecard-for-115th-congress/

25. "Statistics and Historical Comparison," GovTrack, accessed August 1, 2019, https://www.govtrack.us/congress/bills/statistics

26. Rowena Mason, "Intelligence and Security Committee Report: The Key Findings," *The Guardian*, March 12, 2015, https://www.theguardian.com/world/2015/mar/12/intelligence-security-committee-report-key-findings

27. "UK Spy Watchdog 'Taken In' by Security Agencies—MP," *BBC News*, February 27, 2015, https://www.bbc.com/news/election-2015-31665312

28. For a comprehensive review, see Richard F. Grimmett, "Instances of Use of United States Armed Forces Abroad, 1798–2010," CRS Report R41677 (March 10, 2011).

29. "Treaties," United States Senate, accessed August 1, 2019, https://www.senate.gov/artandhistory/history/common/briefing/Treaties.htm

30. Results of the survey by Erdos and Morgan as reported in *Foreign Affairs* 85, no. 6, November 30, 2006, https://www.foreignaffairs.com/issues/2006/85/6

31. Gary Fields and John R. Emshwiller, "As Criminal Laws Proliferate, More Are Ensnared," *The Wall Street Journal*, July 23, 2011, https://www.wsj.com/articles/SB10001424052748703749504576172714184601654

32. Elizabeth B. Bazan, "Impeachment: An Overview of Constitutional Provisions, Procedure, and Practices," Congressional Research Service Report, December 9, 2010, https://fas.org/sgp/crs/misc/98-186.pdf

33. "Nominations," United States Senate, accessed August 1, 2019, http://www.senate.gov/artandhistory/history/common/briefing/Nominations.htm

34. Yuki Noguchi, "Andrew Puzder Withdraws Nomination for Labor Secretary," *NPR*, February 15, 2017, https://www.npr.org/2017/02/15/515447105/andrew-puzder-withdraws-nomination-for-labor-secretary

35. "Supreme Court Nominations: Present–1789," United States Senate, accessed August 1, 2019, https://www.senate.gov/pagelayout/reference/nominations/Nominations.htm

36. Betty Drexhage, *Bicameral Legislatures: An International Comparison* (The Hague, The Netherlands: Ministry of the Interior and Kingdom Relations, 2015), 3.

37. John H. Aldrich and David W. Rohde, "Congressional Committees in a Partisan Era" in *Congress Reconsidered*, 8th ed., eds. Lawrence C. Dodd and Bruce I. Oppenheimer (Washington, DC: CQ Press, 2005), 249–270; Barbara Sinclair, "New World of US Senators" in *Congress Reconsidered*, 8th ed., eds. Lawrence C. Dodd

and Bruce I. Oppenheimer (Washington, DC: CQ Press, 2005), 1–22.

38. Casey Burgat and Charles Hunt, "Congress in 2019: The 2nd Most Educated and Least Politically Experienced House Freshman Class," Brookings, December 28, 2019, https://www.brookings.edu/blog/fixgov/2018/12/28/congress-in-2019-the-2nd-most-educated-and-least-politically-experienced-house-freshman-class/

39. Sarah J. Eckman, "Congressional Member Organizations and Informal Member Groups: Their Purpose and Activities, History, and Formation," Congressional Research Service, January 23, 2019, https://fas.org/sgp/crs/misc/R40683.pdf; data for individual legislators comes from the 114th Congress, 2015–2017.

40. "CQ Vote Studies: Key Senate Votes in 2017," *CQ Magazine*, March 12, 2018.

41. Chris Cilizza, "4 Major Lessons From Alexandria Ocasio-Cortez's Titanic Upset in New York," *CNN*, June 27, 2018, https://www.cnn.com/2018/06/26/politics/joe-crowley-alexandria-ocasio-cortez-new-york-upset/index.html

42. Simone Pathé and Bridget Bowman, "Why Republicans Aren't Sweating After 2 Incumbents Lose Primaries," *Roll Call*, June 14, 2018, https://www.rollcall.com/news/politics/republicans-not-sweating-primary-threats-after-two-incumbents-lose; David Jackson and John Fritze, "Trump Says Republican House Candidates Who Lost Should Have Embraced Him," *USA Today*, November 7, 2018, https://www.usatoday.com/story/news/politics/elections/2018/11/07/election-results-donald-trump-blames-gop-house-members-loss/1918936002/

43. "Presiding Officers: Speakers and Presidents of Legislatures," National Democratic Institute for International Affairs, Legislative Research Series, Paper #1, 1996, http://iknowpolitics.org/sites/default/files/ndi.20presiding20officers2c20speakers20and20presidents20of20legislat.pdf; the Speakers of the Australian and New Zealand House of Representatives are very similar to the British/Canadian model with the exception that a higher level of partisanship is allowed.

44. "Party Whips," United States Senate, accessed August 1, 2019, http://www.senate.gov/artandhistory/history/common/briefing/Party_Whips.htm

45. Kathryn Pearson, "Party Discipline in the Contemporary Congress: Rewarding Loyalty With Legislative Preference." Paper presented at the annual meeting of the American Political Science Association, August 28–31, 2003, in Philadelphia, PA.

46. Gebe Martinez, "DeLay's Conservatism Solidifies GOP Base for Bush," *CQ Weekly Online* (July 12, 2003): 1726–1733.

47. Ben Pershing, "Capitol Briefing: Pelosi, Harman Have Long History," *The Washington Post*, April 23, 2009, http://voices.washingtonpost.com/capitol-briefing/2009/04/pelosi_harman_have_long_histor.html?hpid5news-col-blog; David M. Herszenhorn, "Pelosi Now Remembers Harman Wiretap," *The New York Times*, April 22, 2009, https://thecaucus.blogs.nytimes.com/2009/04/22/pelosi-now-remembers-harman-wiretap/

48. Richard F. Fenno, *Congressmen in Committees* (Boston, MA: Little Brown, 1973).

49. John H. Aldrich and David W. Rohde, "Congressional Committees in a Partisan Era," in *Congress Reconsidered*, 8th ed., eds. Lawrence C. Dodd and Bruce I. Oppenheimer (Washington, DC: CQ Press, 2005), 249–270.

50. Daniel Diermeier and Roget B. Myerson, "Bicameralism and Its Consequences for the International Organization of Legislatures," *The American Economic Review* 89, no. 5 (December 1999), 1182–1196.

51. Ida A. Brudnick, "Congressional Salaries and Allowances," Congressional Research Service, accessed April 11, 2018, http://www.senate.gov/CRSReports/crs-publish.cfm?pid590E%2C*PL%5B%3D%23P%20%20%0A

52. "House of Representatives Staff Levels in Member, Committee, Leadership, and Other Offices, 1977–2016," Congressional Research Service, September 13, 2016, https://www.everycrsreport.com/files/20160913_R43947_da2c748f8678c287d55f1dc7ef1c843c6f25a93f.pdf; "Senate Staff Levels in Member, Committee, Leadership, and Other Offices, 1977-2016," Congressional Research Service, September 13, 2016, https://fas.org/sgp/crs/misc/R43946.pdf

53. David C. King, "The Nature of Congressional Committee Jurisdictions," *The American Political Science Review* 88, no. 1 (March 1994): 48–62.

54. "Former Members: 114th Congress Members," OpenSecrets.org, accessed August 2, 2019, https://www.opensecrets.org/revolving/top.php?display=Z

55. Peter Katel, "Lobbying Boom," *CQ Researcher*, July 22, 2005, 613–636.

56. Alexander Hertel-Fernandez, Matto Mildenberger, and Leah C. Stokes, "Legislative Staff and Representation in Congress," *American Political Science Review* 113, no. 1 (February 2019): 1–18.

57. Kevin M. Esterling, "Buying Expertise: Campaign Contributions and Attention to Policy Analysis in Congressional Committees," *American Political Science Review* 101, no. 1 (February 2007): 93–109.

58. Elaine K. Swift, "The Start of Something New: Clay, Stevenson, Polk and the Development of the Speakership, 1789–1869," in *Masters of the House: Congressional Leaders Over Two Centuries*, eds. Roger H. Davidson, Susan Webb Hammond, and Raymond Smock (Boulder, CO: Westview Press, 1998).

59. John Stanton, "Boehner's Style Weakened Hand in Negotiations," *Roll Call*, July 20, 2011, http://www.rollcall.com/issues/57_10/John-Boehner-Weakened-Hand-Negotiations-207474-1.html.

60. Mike Lillis, "Pelosi Cuts Deal With Problem Solvers on House Rules Overhaul," *The Hill*, November 28, 2018, https://thehill.com/homenews/house/418696-pelosi-cuts-deal-with-problem-solvers-on-house-rules-overhaul; Susan Davis, "Democrats Unveil Changes to House Rules on Debt Ceiling, Ethics," *NPR*, January 2, 2019, https://www.npr.org/2019/01/02/681547346/democrats-announce-major-changes-to-u-s-house-rules?fbclid=IwAR25jhYYu3xv600vDQohdI4Oz41rWhzYIAeGGz6PZdpzDD0XtLVBgExKFOc

61. "Liberals See 'Problem Solvers' as a Problem," *CQ Magazine*, January 14, 2019.

62. Charles W. Johnson, *How Our Laws Are Made* (Washington, DC: U.S. Government Printing Office, 2003). http://www.senate.gov/reference/resources/pdf/howourlawsaremade.pdf

63. See Valerie Heitshusen, "Introduction to the Legislative Process in the U.S. Congress" (updated November 15, 2018), Congressional Research Service, R42843.

64. Lee Hamilton, "What I Wish Political Scientists Would Teach About Congress," *PS: Political Science and Politics* 33, no. 4: 757–764.

## CHAPTER 12

1. C. Vann Woodward, ed. *Presidential Responses to Charges of Misconduct* (New York, NY: Dell Publishing Co., 1974).

2. "The Avalon Project," History of the Impeachment of Andrew Johnson, Chapter VII, 2008, http://avalon.law.yale.edu/19th_century/john_chap_07.asp#articles

3. Jeffrey Tulis, *The Rhetorical Presidency* (Princeton, NJ: Princeton University Press, 1987).

4. For Tulis's views of how Obama conducted the presidency with dignity, see his "Afterword" in the 2017 edition of *The Rhetorical Presidency*.

5. Trump's tweet of July 1, 2017. Also see Keith E. Whittington, "Trump's Rhetoric Is Offensive, but Is It Impeachable?" *Vox*, August 4, 2017, https://www.vox.com/mischiefs-of-faction/2017/8/4/16093946/trump-andrew-johnson-rhetoric-offensive; Jan Patja Howell, "Jeffrey Tulis on 'The Rhetorical Presidency' on Steroids," *Lawfare*, January 26, 2019, https://www.lawfareblog.com/jeffrey-tulis-rhetorical-presidency-steroids

6. Giovani Sartori, *Comparative Constitutional Engineering: An Inquiry Into Structures, Incentives and Outcomes*, 2nd ed. (New York, NY: New York University Press, 1997), 83–86. Elijah Ben-Zion Kaminsky also stresses the need for policy agreement between legislature and executive in a parliamentary system in "On the Comparison of Presidential and Parliamentary Governments," *Presidential Studies Quarterly* 27 (Spring 1997): 221–229.

7. Alfred Stepan and Cindy Skach, "Constitutional Frameworks and Democratic Consolidation: Parliamentarism Versus Presidentialism," *World Politics* 46, no. 1 (October 1993): 1–22.

8. Note that this includes Canada, which was a member of the British Commonwealth until recently and never made a sharp break with Britain.

9. Parts of this section are adapted, with permission, from W. Phillips Shively, *Power and Choice*, 11th ed. (New York, NY: McGraw-Hill, 2008).

10. Rebecca Shabad, "Democrats Blast Trump for Not Seeking Congressional Approval for Syria Air Strikes," *NBC News*, April 13, 2018, https://www.nbcnews.com/politics/congress/democrats-blast-trump-not-seeking-congressional-approval-syria-strike-n865981; Ben Jacobs, "Syrian Strikes: Democrats Demand Congressional Approval for Further Military Action," *The Guardian*, April 13, 2018, https://www.theguardian.com/us-news/2018/apr/14/syria-strikes-democrats-demand-congress-approval-for-further-military-action

11. Kevin Granville, "What Is TPP? Behind the Trade Deal That Died," *The New York Times*, January 23, 2017, https://www.nytimes.com/interactive/2016/business/tpp-explained-what-is-trans-pacific-partnership.html

12. Curtis A. Bradley and Jack L. Goldsmith, "Presidential Control Over International Law," *Harvard Law Review* 131, no. 5 (March 2018), https://harvardlawreview.org/wp-content/uploads/2018/03/1201-1297_Bradley-Goldsmith_Online.pdf

13. "Anne Burford, 62; Embattled EPA Chief for President Reagan," *Los Angeles Times*, July 22, 2004, http://articles.latimes.com/2004/jul/22/local/me-burford22

14. Michael Greshko, Laura Parker, Brian Clark Howard, Daniel Stone, Alejandra Borunda, and Sarah Gibbens, "A Running List of How President Trump Is Changing Environmental Policy," *National Geographic*, March 12, 2019, https://news.nationalgeographic.com/2017/03/how-trump-is-changing-science-environment/

15. "Leadership," The United States President's Emergency Plan for AIDS Relief, accessed August 2, 2019, https://www.pepfar.gov/about/c19569.htm

16. Fred I. Greenstein, *The Hidden Hand Presidency: Eisenhower as Leader* (New York, NY: Basic Books, 1981).

17. James Fallows, "Trump Refuses to Soothe a Wounded Nation," *The Atlantic*, January 13, 2019, https://www.theatlantic.com/politics/archive/2019/01/donald-trump-doesnt-console-the-nation/579799/

18. Gerard Baker, "Will the Issue of Character Be Trump's Undoing," *The Wall Street Journal*, March 8, 2019, https://www.wsj.com/articles/will-the-issue-of-character-be-trumps-undoing-11552070389?mod=searchresults&page=1&pos=1

19. Ronald Brownstein, "Trump Isn't Even Trying to Convince Voters on the Shutdown," *The Atlantic*, January 17, 2019, https://www.theatlantic.com/politics/archive/2019/01/trump-ignoring-voter-opinion-his-shutdown-fight/580687/

20. Interview with Richard Nixon by David Frost, televised May 19, 1977; quoted in Craig Ducat, *Constitutional Interpretation*, 7th ed. (Belmont, CA: West, 2000), 206.

21. Joseph A. Pika and John Anthony Maltese, *Politics of the Presidency*, 7th ed. (Washington, DC: CQ Press, 2008), 16.

22. Jeffrey Rosen, "Bush's Leviathan State: Power of One," *The New Republic*, July 24, 2006; Joel D. Aberbach, "Supplying the Defect of Better Motives? The Bush II Administration and the Constitutional System," in *The George W. Bush Legacy*, eds. Colin Campbell, Bert A. Rockman, and Andrew Rudalevige (Washington, DC: CQ Press, 2008), 112–133.

23. Richard E. Neustadt, *Presidential Power and the Modern Presidents: The Politics of Leadership From Roosevelt to Reagan* (New York, NY: The Free Press, 1990), 11.

24. Kenneth Mayer, *With the Stroke of a Pen: Executive Orders and Presidential Power* (Princeton, NJ: Princeton University Press, 2002); Samuel Kernell, *Going Public: New Strategies of Presidential Leadership* (Washington, DC: CQ Press, 1986).

25. "Trump Job Approval," Gallup, accessed August 2, 2019, https://news.gallup.com/poll/203207/trump-job-approval-weekly.aspx

26. Tony Saich, "Reflections on a Survey of Global Perceptions of International Leaders and World Powers," Ash Center for Democratic Governance and Innovation, December 2014, https://ash.harvard.edu/files/survey-global-perceptions-international-leaders-world-powers.pdf

27. William Mishler and John P. Willerton, "The Dynamics of Presidential Popularity in Post-Communist Russia: Cultural Imperative Versus Neo-Institutional Choice?" *The Journal of Politics* 65, no. 1 (February 2003).

28. See employee figures on page 1053 of *An American Budget, Appendix* (Washington, DC: Office of Management and Budget, 2019), https://www.whitehouse.gov/wp-content/uploads/2018/02/appendix-fy2019.pdf

29. Matthew J. Dickinson, "Neustadt, New Institutionalism, and Presidential Decision Making: A Theory and Test," *Presidential Studies Quarterly* 35 (June 2005): 259–288.

30. Kathryn Dunn Tenpas, "Tracking Turnover in the Trump Administration," *Brookings*, January 2019, https://www.brookings.edu/research/tracking-turnover-in-the-trump-administration/

31. "About Us," Gov.UK, accessed August 3, 2019, https://www.gov.uk/government/organisations/cabinet-office/about

32. George Jones, "The Power of the Prime Minister: 50 Years On," *The Constitution Society* (2016), 30, https://consoc.org.uk/wp-content/uploads/2016/10/The-Power-of-the-Prime-Minister-PDF.pdf

33. Andrew Blick and George Jones, "The Power of the Prime Minister," *History and Policy* (June 7, 2010), http://www.historyandpolicy.org/policy-papers/papers/the-power-of-the-prime-minister

34. The official website of the German Chancellor is https://www.bundeskanzlerin.de/bkin-en/chancellery/extension-of-the-federal-chancellery

35. The Cabinet Office's Role in the Cabinet Structure, Cabinet Office, Japan, https://www.cao.go.jp/en/pmf/pmf_about.pdf

36. See the four-part series on Vice President Cheney that ran from June 24 to June 27, 2007, starting with Barton Gelman and Jo Becker, "'A Different Understanding With the President,'" *The Washington Post*, June 24, 2007, A1.

37. *Court politics* refers to politics in a situation where a single leader is isolated and very powerful. This can lead to flattery, attempts to monopolize time with the single powerful leader, unwillingness to bring bad news to the leader, and special power to those—such as spouses, barbers, and so on—who unavoidably have hours of contact with the leader that others would give anything for. The term derives from the politics of the great royal courts of eighteenth-century Europe.

38. *Groupthink* refers to a psychological drive for consensus that suppresses dissent within decision-making groups. See Irving Janis, *Victims of Groupthink* (Boston, MA: Houghton Mifflin, 1972).

39. Paul Light, *The President's Agenda: Domestic Policy Choice From Kennedy to Carter* (Baltimore, MD: The Johns Hopkins University Press, 1982).

40. Fred I. Greenstein, *The Presidential Difference: Leadership Style From FDR to Barack Obama*, 3rd ed. (Princeton, NJ: Princeton University Press, 2009), 217–223.

41. When Nixon's vice president, Spiro T. Agnew, resigned in 1973 under charges of accepting bribes while he was governor of Maryland, Ford was nominated by Nixon and confirmed by Congress under the terms of the Twenty-Fifth Amendment. Ford became the nation's first unelected president in 1974 and, in turn, named Nelson Rockefeller to fill the vice presidential vacancy.

42. Chris Riotta, "GOP Aims to Kill Obamacare Yet Again After Failing 70 Times," *Newsweek*, July 29, 2017, https://www.newsweek.com/gop-health-care-bill-repeal-and-replace-70-failed-attempts-643832

43. Charles O. Jones, *The Presidency in a Separated System*, 2nd ed. (Washington, DC: Brookings Institution Press, 2005), 24.

44. "CQ Vote Studies: Presidential Support—Trump Conquered," *CQ Magazine*, February 12, 2018; "CQ Studies: Presidential Support—Trump's Last Hurrah," *CQ Magazine*, February 25, 2019.

45. "Vetoes," Ford Presidential Library and Museum, accessed August 3, 2019, https://www.fordlibrarymuseum.gov/library/document/factbook/vetoes.htm

46. Andrea Chandler, "Presidential Veto Power in Post-Communist Russia, 1994–1998," *Canadian Journal of Political Science* 34, no. 3 (September 2001): 487–516.

47. Rebecca Adams, "Lame Duck or Leap Frog?" *CQ Weekly Online*, February 12, 2007.

48. Charles S. Clark, "The Trump Administration's War on Regulations," *Government Executive* (undated), https://www.govexec.com/feature/trump-administrations-war-regulations/; also see Executive Order 13771 issued January 30, 2017, https://www.whitehouse.gov/presidential-actions/presidential-executive-order-reducing-regulation-controlling-regulatory-costs/

49. Kenneth R. Mayer, *With the Stroke of a Pen: Executive Orders and Presidential Power* (Princeton, NJ: Princeton University Press, 2002), 4.

50. Charlie Savage, "Korematsu, Notorious Supreme Court Ruling on Japanese Internment, Is Finally Tossed Out," *The New York Times*, June 26, 2018, https://www.nytimes.com/2018/06/26/us/korematsu-supreme-court-ruling.html; majority opinion written by Chief Justice Roberts on case of *Trump, President of the United States, et. al. v. Hawaii, et al.* (June 26, 2018), 38, https://www.supremecourt.gov/opinions/17pdf/17-965_h315.pdf

51. Neal Katyal, "Confession of Error: The Solicitor General's Mistakes During the Japanese-American Internment Cases," The United States Department of Justice Archives, May 20, 2011, https://www.justice.gov/archives/opa/blog/confession-error-solicitor-generals-mistakes-during-japanese-american-internment-cases

52. Kenneth R. Mayer, *With the Stroke of a Pen*, 75; also see the larger discussion on pages 39–80.

53. Sheldon Goldman, "Reagan's Judicial Legacy: Completing the Puzzle and Summing Up," *Judicature* 72 (April–May 1989): 319–320.

54. Personal communication with Susan Smelcer, an analyst on the federal judiciary at the Congressional Research Service, Library of Congress, May 19, 2011.

55. "Organization Chart," The United States Department of Justice, 2018, https://www.justice.gov/agencies/chart

56. On Trump, see Department of Justice, *Department of Justice Strategic Plan for 2018–2022*, https://www.justice.gov/jmd/page/file/1071066/download; on Obama, see U.S. Department of Justice, *Stewards of the American Dream: The Department of Justice Strategic Plan, Fiscal Years 2007–2012*, 1, https://www.justice.gov/archive/mps/strategic2007-2012/strategic_plan20072012.pdf

## CHAPTER 13

1. David E. Lewis, "FEMA's Politicization and the Road to Katrina," *The Politics of Presidential Appointments: Political Control and Bureaucratic Performance* (Princeton, NJ: Princeton University Press, 2008), 42. Also see Rebecca Adams, "FEMA Failure a Perfect Storm of Bureaucracy," *CQ Weekly Online* (September 12, 2005).

2. James Kendra, "Disaster Research Center 2011 Annual Report," University of Delaware, accessed August 3, 2019, http://udspace.udel.edu/bitstream/handle/19716/12899/2011%20DRC%20Annual%20Report.pdf?sequence=1&isAllowed=y; Arnold M. Howitt, "The Tohoku Disaster: Responding to Japan's 3/11 Earthquake, Tsunami, and Nuclear Accident," Harvard Kennedy School Program on Crisis Leadership, 2012, https://www.hks.harvard.edu/sites/default/files/centers/research-initiatives/crisisleadership/files/Tohoku%20Disaster_Taubman%20Center_2012%2011%2014_red_web_Part%202.pdf

3. "Disaster Statistics, United Nations Office for Disaster Risk Reduction (UNISDR), 2019, https://www.unisdr.org/we/inform/disaster-statistics

4. International Federation of Red Cross and Red Crescent Societies, *World Disasters Report 2005* (2005), 38, http://www.ifrc.org/publicat/wdr2005/chapter2.asp; Anita Snow, "Lesson From Ike: Nobody Does Evacuations Like Cuba," *Associated Press*, September 10, 2008; Martha Thompson and Izaskun Gaviria, *Cuba, Weathering the Storm: Lessons in Risk Reduction From Cuba* (Boston, MA: Oxfam America, 2004), https://www.preventionweb.net/educational/view/4585

5. August Nimtz, "Cuba and the Lessons of Katrina," *MR Online Monthly Review*, November 18, 2005, http://mrzine.monthlyreview.org/nimtz181105.html

6. Richard J. Stillman II, "The Constitutional Bicentennial and the Centennial of the American Administrative State," *Public Administration Review* 47, no. 1 (January/February 1987): 6.

7. First Inaugural Address of Ronald Reagan, January 20, 1981, https://www.reaganfoundation.org/ronald-reagan/reagan-quotes-speeches/inaugural-address-1/

8. William Jefferson Clinton's State of the Union Message, January 23, 1996, https://millercenter.org/the-presidency/presidential-speeches/january-23-1996-state-union-address

9. Barry Karl, "The American Bureaucrat: A History of a Sheep in Wolves' Clothing," *Public Administration Review* 47, no. 1 (January/February 1987): 34.

10. Harold J. Laski *The American Democracy* (New York: Viking Press, 1948), 167, as quoted in Harold Seidman and Robert Gilmour, *Politics, Position and Power: From the Positive to the Regulatory State*, 4th ed. (New York, NY: Oxford University Press, 1986), 259.

11. Rebeca Riffkin, "Americans Say Federal Government Wastes 51 Cents on the Dollar," Gallup, September 17, 2014, https://news.gallup.com/poll/176102/americans-say-federal-gov-wastes-cents-dollar.aspx

12. Directorate General for Communication, *Eurobarometer 73: Public Opinion in the European Union*, August 2010, http://ec.europa.eu/public_opinion/archives/eb/eb73/eb73_first_en.pdf

13. Norton Long, "Bureaucracy and Constitutionalism," *American Political Science Review* (September 1952): 808–818.

14. Ibid., 809.

15. Norton Long, "Power and Administration," *Public Administration Review* (Autumn 1949): 258.

16. Ralph Clark Chandler, "Public Administration Under the Articles of Confederation," *Public Administration Quarterly* 13, no. 4 (Winter 1990): 440–441.

17. Ibid., 443–448; "The History of the United States Postal System," United States Postal System, https://about.usps.com/publications/pub100/pub100_001.htm

18. Lynton K. Caldwell, "The Administrative Republic: The Contrasting Legacies of Hamilton and Jefferson," *Public Administration Quarterly* 13, no. 4 (Winter 1990): 470–493.

19. Stephen Minicucci, "Internal Improvements and the Union, 1790–1860," *Studies in American Political Development* 18 (Fall 2004): 160.

20. Stephen Skowronek, *Building a New American State: The Expansion of National Administrative Capacities, 1877–1920* (Cambridge, UK: Cambridge University Press, 1982), 23.

21. Richard T. Green, "Alexander Hamilton and the Study of Public Administration," *Public Administration Quarterly* 13, no. 4 (Winter 1990): 494–519.

22. Ibid., 9–12.

23. Matthew Crenson, *The Federal Machine* (Baltimore, MD: Johns Hopkins University Press, 1975).

24. Skowronek, *Building a New American State*, 47.

25. The Library of Congress Congressional Research Service, *History of Civil Service Merit Systems of the United States and Selected Foreign Countries* (Washington, DC: U.S. Government Printing Office, 1976), Table 1, 305–306, http://ufdc.ufl.edu/AA00024784/00001/3j

26. Organization for Economic Cooperation and Development (OECD), "Senior Civil Service," *Government at a Glance, 2009* (Paris, France, Author, 2009), https://doi.org/10.1787/9789264061651-20-en

27. There is no simple typology of government organizations. One influential classification scheme was suggested by Harold Seidman and Robert Gilmour, *Politics, Position and Power: From the Positive to the Regulatory State*, 4th ed. (New York, NY: Oxford University Press, 1986), 254–259.

28. "Report for Congress, Homeland Security: Department Organization and Management—Legislative Phase," Congressional Research Service CRS Report RL31493, February 25, 2003, https://www.everycrsreport.com/files/20030225_RL31493_098230b03b8ea99422e616feba2ade16817cab28.pdf

29. Ibid., 3–4.

30. *Homeland Security Act of 2002*, accessed August 4, 2019, https://www.dhs.gov/sites/default/files/publications/hr_5005_enr.pdf

31. For a list of these units, see Sharma, Amol. "Proposed Divisions and Duties of New Security Department," CQ Weekly (June 22, 2002): 1646–1647; "Who Became Part of the Department?" Homeland Security, 2006, https://web.archive.org/web/20120712192754/https://www.dhs.gov/xabout/history/editorial_0133.shtm

32. For a more comprehensive list, see https://www.usa.gov/federal-agencies/l

33. Seidman and Gilmour, *Politics, Position and Power*, 276.

34. Fabrizio Gilardi, "The Institutional Foundation of Regulatory Capitalism: The Diffusion of Independent Regulatory Agencies in Western Europe," *The Annals of the American Academy of Political and Social Science* 598 (March 2005): 84–101.

35. Peter Katel, "Future of the Airlines," *CQ Researcher* 18 (March 7, 2008): 217–240.

36. Ronald C. Moe "Federal Government Corporations: An Overview," Congressional Research Service CRS Report 98-954 (Nov. 24, 1998): 1.

37. David Randall Peterman, "Amtrak: Overview," Congressional Research Service CRS Report R44973, September 28, 2017, https://fas.org/sgp/crs/misc/R44973.pdf

38. Kevin R. Kosar, "The Quasi-Government: Hybrid Organizations With Both Government and Private Sector Legal Characteristics," *Congressional Research Service* CRS Report RL30533, February 13, 2007, http://www.fas.org/sgp/crs/misc/RL30533.pdf; also see Ronald C. Moe, "The Emerging Federal Quasi-Government: Issues of Management and Accountability," *Public Administration Review* 61, no. 3 (May/June 2001): 290–312.

39. There are at least five such entities, with more in the wings (Ibid., 9). The government definition of a GSE is found in Title 2, Chapter 17A, Section 8 of the 2 US Code Sec 622.8. The term *government-sponsored enterprise* refers to a corporate entity created by a law of the United States that (A)(i) has a Federal charter authorized by law; (ii) is privately owned, as evidenced by capital stock owned by private entities or individuals; (iii) is under the direction of a board of directors, a majority of which is elected by private owners; (iv) is a financial institution with power to (I) make loans or loan guarantees for limited purposes such as to provide credit for specific borrowers or one sector; and (II) raise funds by borrowing (which does not carry the full faith and credit of the Federal Government) or to guarantee the debt of others in unlimited amounts; and (B)(i) does not exercise powers that are reserved to the Government as sovereign (such as the power to tax or to regulate interstate commerce); (ii) does not have the power to commit the Government financially (but it may be a recipient of a loan guarantee commitment made by the Government); and (iii) has employees whose salaries and expenses are paid by the enterprise and are not Federal employees subject to Title 5.

40. Kate Pickert, "A Brief History of Fannie Mae and Freddie Mac," *Time*, July 14, 2008, http://content.time.com/time/business/article/0,8599,1822766,00.html; James R. Hagerty, *The Fateful History of Fannie Mae: New Deal Birth to Mortgage Crisis Fall* (Charleston, SC: The History Press, 2012).

41. "Federally Funded Research and Development Centers (FFRDCs): Background and Issues for Congress," Congressional Research Service CRS Report R44629, December 1, 2017, https://www.everycrsreport.com/files/20171201_R44629_ea1b350293c759e9ee734fbdf2fbf497bd42d3c4.pdf

42. "Master Government List of Federally Funded R&D Centers," National Science Foundation, May 2019, https://www.nsf.gov/statistics/ffrdclist/

43. Paul C. Light, *The Government-Industrial Complex: The True Size of the Federal Government, 1984–2018* (New York, NY: Oxford University Press, 2019).

44. Paul Light, "The Fog of Government: What to Do About Bureaucratic Overlap," Light on Leadership [blog], *The Washington Post* March 3, 2011, http://views.washingtonpost.com/leadership/light/2011/03/fog-of-government-bureaucratic-overlap.html; "Opportunities to Reduce Potential Duplication in Government Programs, Save Tax Dollars, and Enhance Revenue," Government Accountability Office, March 2011, https://www.gao.gov/assets/320/315920.pdf

45. "2018 Annual Report: Additional Opportunities to Reduce Fragmentation, Overlap and Duplication and to Achieve Other Financial Benefits," Government Accountability Office (GAO), April 26, 2018, https://www.gao.gov/products/GAO-18-371SP

46. The published list of positions in the federal government subject to noncompetitive appointment is referred to as the "plum book," officially known as *United States Government Policy and Supporting Positions*, and is published shortly after a presidential election so that everyone knows the potential spoils from the campaign.

47. Bonnie Berkowitz and Kevin Uhrmacher, "It's Not Just the Cabinet: Trump's Transition Team May Need to Find About 4,100 appointees," *The Washington Post*, December 5, 2016, https://www.washingtonpost.com/graphics/politics/trump-transition-appointments-scale/; James P. Pfiffner, "The Office of White House Presidential Personnel," White House Transition Project 1997–2017, http://whitehousetransitionproject.org/wp-content/uploads/2016/10/WHTP2017-27_Office_of_Presidential_Personnel.pdf; We have used the slightly lower total provided by Pfiffner in a personal communication: "Presidential appointees with consent of the Senate (1054), presidential appointees not requiring Senate consent (527), non-career Senior Executive Service (680), and Schedule C appointments (1,392)."

48. "Nominations: A Historical Overview," United States Senate, accessed August 4, 2019, http://www.senate.gov/artandhistory/history/common/briefing/Nominations.htm

49. Clifford L. Berg, "Lapse of Reorganization Authority," *Public Administration Review* 35, no. 2 (March/April 1975): 195–199.

50. Text of the National Security Act of 1947 can be found at https://www.cia.gov/library/readingroom/docs/1947-07-26.pdf

51. "Who We Are," Office of the Director of National Intelligence, accessed August 4, 2019, https://www.dni.gov/index.php/who-we-are

52. GlobalChange.gov, U.S. Global Change Research Program, accessed August 4, 2019, https://www.globalchange.gov/

53. Brian Friel, "Unshackled," *Government Executive*, November 15, 2002, https://www.govexec.com/magazine/2002/11/unshackled/12865/

54. Tanya N. Ballard, "Back to the Future," *Government Executive*, October 16, 2003, https://www.govexec.com/pay-benefits/2003/10/back-to-the-future/15185/; Shawn Zeller, "Smashing the System," *Government Executive*, November 1, 2003, https://www.govexec.com/magazine/2003/11/smashing-the-system/15420/

55. J. Edward Kellough, Lloyd G. Nigro, and Gene A. Brewer, "Civil Service Reform Under George W. Bush: Ideology, Politics and Public Personnel Administration," *Review of Public Personnel Administration* 30 (December 2010): 4.

56. David L. Dillman, "Enduring Values in the British Civil Service," *Administration and Society* 39, no. 7 (November 2007): 883–900.

## CHAPTER 14

1. Amy B. Wang, "Trump Lashes Out at 'So-Called Judge' Who Temporarily Blocked Travel Ban," *The Washington Post*, February 4, 2017, https://www.washingtonpost.com/news/the-fix/wp/2017/02/04/trump-lashes-out-at-federal-judge-who-temporarily-blocked-travel-ban/?utm_term=.d74d9fa665fb

2. Eric Bradner and Jeff Zeleny, "Trump: 'If Something Happens Blame' the Judge," *CNN*, February 5, 2017, https://www.cnn.com/2017/02/05/politics/trump-twitter-attacks-judge/index.html

3. Adam Liptak, "Trump Takes Aim at Appeals Court, Calling It a 'Disgrace,'" *The New York Times*, November 20, 2018, https://www.nytimes.com/2018/11/20/us/politics/trump-appeals-court-ninth-circuit.html

4. Matthew Choi, "Trump Hits Back at Chief Justice Roberts, Escalating an Extraordinary Exchange," *Politico*, November 21, 2018, https://www.politico.com/story/2018/11/21/supreme-court-chief-justice-john-roberts-calls-out-trump-for-his-attack-on-a-judge-1011203

5. "In His Own Words: The President's Attacks on the Courts," Brennan Center for Justice, June 5, 2017, https://www.brennancenter.org/analysis/his-own-words-presidents-attacks-courts

6. Tony Mauro, "Roberts, Gonzales Speak on Judicial Independence," *Legal Times*, October 2, 2006, http://www.law.com/jsp/article.jsp?id51159567621347; see also Tony Mauro, "O'Connor Fires Back on Judicial Independence," *Legal Times*, November 28, 2005, http://www.law.com/jsp/article.jsp?id51132740311603, and the transcript of a PBS NewsHour interview with O'Connor and Breyer discussing judicial independence on September 26, 2006, https://www.pbs.org/newshour/show/supreme-court-justices-reflect-on-judicial-independence

7. "Judicial Independence Under Threat in Nigeria, Warns UN Rights Expert," *UN News*, February 11, 2019, https://news.un.org/en/story/2019/02/1032391

8. Stephanie Busari and Rob Picheta, "Buhari Dismisses Criticism Following Suspension of Country's Top Judge," CNN, January 28, 2019, https://www.cnn.com/2019/01/26/africa/buhari-nigeria-judge-elections-intl/index.html

9. Marc Santora, "Amid Growing Uproar, Poland to Remove 27 Supreme Court Justices," *The New York Times*, July 3, 2018, https://www.nytimes.com/2018/07/03/world/europe/poland-supreme-court-judiciary.html

10. Joanna Berendt and Marc Santora, "Poland Reverses Supreme Court Purge, Retreating From Conflict With E.U.," *The New York Times*, December 17, 2018, https://www.nytimes.com/2018/12/17/world/europe/poland-supreme-court.html

11. Thomas Paine, *Rights of Man* (New York, NY: Everyman's Library/Knopf, 1994), 41.

12. *Constitution of the People's Republic of China*, English.gov.cn, August 23, 2014, http://english.www.gov.cn/archive/laws_regulations/2014/08/23/content_281474982987458.htm

13. *Marbury v. Madison*, 5 U.S. (1 Cranch) 137 (1803).

14. *Dr. Bonham's Case*, 77 Eng. Rep. 646 (1610), 652.

15. Leonard W. Levy, *Original Intent and the Framers' Constitution* (New York, NY: Macmillen, 1988), 91; Edward S. Corwin, *Doctrine of Judicial Review* (Princeton, NJ: Princeton University Press, 1914); Charles Warren, *Making of the Constitution* (Boston, MA: Little, Brown, 1928); Raoul Berger, *Congress v. the Supreme Court* (Cambridge, MA: Harvard University Press, 1969).

16. Levy, *Original Intent*, 99; Louis B. Boudin, *Government by Judiciary* (New York, NY: William Godwin, 1932); William W. Crosskey, *Politics and the Constitution in the History of the United States* (Chicago, IL: University of Chicago Press, 1953).

17. For a more thorough discussion of this topic, see Levy, *Original Intent*, 108–110.

18. Alexander Hamilton, "Federalist No. 78," in *The Federalist: A Commentary on the Constitution of the United States*, ed. Robert Scigliano (New York, NY: The Modern Library, 2000), 500.

19. Arguably, the Court engaged in a form of judicial review of congressional action in *Hylton v. United States*, 3 U.S. (3 Dall.) 171 (1796), when the Court upheld a federal tax on carriages, but unlike *Marbury*, that case invalidated nothing.

20. At that time, there was no separate ticket for president and vice president; electors simply cast two votes. As a result, Thomas Jefferson and Aaron Burr (unofficially recognized as the vice presidential candidate for the Democratic-Republicans) tied. After 36 ballots, the House elected Jefferson president and Burr vice president.

21. Some have suggested that the Court may have misinterpreted the relevant portion of the Judiciary Act and argued that the Act was not, in fact, unconstitutional. See, for example, William Van Alstyne, "A Critical Guide to *Marbury v. Madison*," *Duke Law Journal* (1969): 1.

22. *Marbury v. Madison*, 5 U.S. (1 Cranch) 137 (1803).

23. *Eakin v. Raub*, Supreme Court of Pennsylvania, 12 S. & R. 330 (1825), Justice Gibson's dissent.

24. Craig R. Ducat, *Constitutional Interpretation*, 9th ed. (Boston, MA: Wadsworth, 2009), 14; see *Norris v. Clymer*, 2 Pa. 277 (1845) at 281.

25. Walter F. Murphy, C. Herman Pritchett, Lee Epstein, and Jack Knight (Eds.), *Courts, Judges, and Politics: An Introduction to the Judicial Process*, 6th ed. (New York, NY: McGraw Hill, 2006), 48–49.

26. Alec Stone Sweet, *Governing With Judges: Constitutional Politics in Europe* (Oxford, UK: Oxford University Press, 2000), 94.

27. Ibid., 113.

28. Harry P. Stumpf, *American Judicial Politics*, 2nd ed. (Upper Saddle River, NJ: Prentice-Hall, 1998), 94.

29. Saul Cornell, *The Other Founders: Anti-Federalism and the Dissenting Tradition in America, 1788–1828* (Chapel Hill, NC: University of North Carolina Press, 1999), 31, 90.

30. A list of judgeships can be found at https://www.uscourts.gov/sites/default/files/allauth.pdf

31. Henry J. Abraham, *The Judicial Process*, 7th ed. (New York, NY: Oxford University Press, 1998), 360, quoting Justice Brandeis in *Barnet v. Coronado Oil & Gas Co.*, 2285 U.S. 293 (1932).

32. Since justices have life tenure, no justice was removed when the size of the Court was reduced; rather, when a justice left, he was not replaced.

33. *Goodridge v. Department of Public Health*, 798 N.E.2d 941 (Mass., 2003).

34. "The Justices' Caseload," Supreme Court of the United States, accessed August 5, 2019, https://www.supremecourt.gov/about/justicecaseload.aspx

35. G. Alan Tarr, *Judicial Process and Policymaking*, 2nd ed. (New York, NY: West/Wadsworth, 1999), 40.

36. Prior to legislation passed by Congress in 1988 (102 Stat. 662), cases reached the Supreme Court in one of three ways: by appeal, by certification, and by certiorari. Since 1988, the Court has become an almost all certiorari tribunal. See Ducat, *Constitutional Interpretation*, 27.

37. For more on the history and function of law clerks, see Todd C. Peppers, *Courtiers of the Marble Palace: The Rise and Influence of the Supreme Court Law Clerk* (Palo Alto, CA: Stanford University Press, 2006); Artemus Ward and David Weiden, *Sorcerers' Apprentices: 100 Years of Law Clerks at the United States Supreme Court* (New York: New York University Press, 2006).

38. Ducat, *Constitutional Interpretation*, 31.

39. Rebecca Mae Salokar, *The Solicitor General: The Politics of Law* (Philadelphia, PA: Temple University Press, 1992), 3.

40. Kevin T. McGuire, "Explaining Executive Success in the U.S. Supreme Court," *Political Research Quarterly* 51 (June 1998), 522.

41. Adam Feldman, "Empirical SCOTUS: Supreme Court All-stars 2013–2017," SCOTUSblog, September 13, 2018, https://www.scotusblog.com/2018/09/empirical-scotus-supreme-court-all-stars-2013-2017/

42. Stephen L. Wasby, *The Supreme Court in the Federal Judicial System*, 3rd ed. (Chicago, IL: Nelson-Hall, 1988), 223–224.

43. Lawrence Baum, *The Supreme Court*, 6th ed. (Washington, DC: CQ Press, 1998), 136.

44. Quoted in Baum, *The Supreme Court*, 21.

45. For example, Stuart Taylor, Jr., and Benjamin Wittes, "Of Clerks and Perks," *Atlantic* (July/August 2006), http://www.theatlantic.com/doc/200607/supreme-court-clerks; but cf. Emily Bazelon and Dahlia Lithwick, "Endangered Elitist Species: In Defense of the Supreme Court Law Clerk," *Slate*, June 13, 2006, https://slate.com/news-and-politics/2006/06/defending-the-supreme-court-law-clerk.html

46. The Eleventh, Thirteenth, Sixteenth, and Twenty-Seventh Amendments.

47. 558 U.S. 310 (2010). Byron Tau, "Obama Calls for Constitutional Amendment to Overturn Citizens United," *Politico*, August 29, 2012.

48. Alan Silverleib, "Gloves Come Off After Obama Rips Supreme Court Ruling," CNN, January 28, 2010, http://www.cnn.com/2010/POLITICS/01/28/alito.obama.sotu/index.html

49. Rachel Frazin, "Schiff Introduces Constitutional Amendment to Overturn Citizens United," *The Hill*, May 8, 2019, https://thehill.com/homenews/house/442697-schiff-introduces-constitutional-amendment-to-overturn-citizens-united

50. *Ex Parte McCardle*, 74 U.S. 506 (1869).

51. "Impeachments of Federal Judges," Federal Judicial Center, https://www.fjc.gov/history/judges/impeachments-federal-judges

52. The case in question was *Worcester v. Georgia*, 31 U.S. (6 Pet.) 515 (1832).

53. Baum, *American Courts*, 295.

54. Robert A. Dahl, "Decision Making in a Democracy: The Supreme Court as a National Policy Maker" in *Courts, Judges, and Politics*, 6th ed., eds. Walter F. Murphy, C. Herman Pritchett, Lee Epstein, and Jack Knight (New York, NY: McGraw Hill, 2006), 69.

55. Allan Ashman and Malia Reddick, "Methods of Judicial Selection," in *Legal Systems of the World*, ed. Herbert M. Kritzer (Santa Barbara, CA: ABC Clio, 2002), 800.

56. Richard L. Vining, Jr., Amy Steigerwalt, and Susan Navarro Smelcer, "Bias and the Bar: Evaluating the ABA Ratings of Federal Judicial Nominees," Paper presented at the annual meeting of the Midwest Political Science Association, Chicago, Illinois, April 2009.

57. Allan Smith, "Trump Is Bypassing Judicial Ratings Agencies Before Making His Nominations," *Business Insider*, November 15, 2017, https://www.businessinsider.com/trump-judicial-nominees-increase-in-aba-not-qualified-ratings-2017-11

58. Melody E. Valdini and Christopher Shortell, "Women's Representation in the Highest Court: A Comparative Analysis of the Appointment of Female Justices," *Political Research Quarterly* 69, no. 4 (2016): 865.

59. David Montgomery, "Conquerors of the Courts," *Washington Post Magazine*, January 2, 2019, https://www.washingtonpost.com/news/magazine/wp/2019/01/02/feature/conquerors-of-the-courts/?utm_term=.586fe4fbf19d

60. Ashman and Reddick, "Methods of Judicial Selection" in *Legal Systems of the World*, ed. Herbert M. Kritzer (Santa Barbara, CA: ABC Clio, 2002), 799.

61. Ottavio Campanella, "The Italian Legal Profession," *The Journal of the Legal Profession* 19 (1995): 81.

62. For a more complete account of these developments, see John Anthony Maltese, *The Selling of Supreme Court Nominees* (Baltimore, MD: Johns Hopkins University Press, 1995), especially Chapter 6.

63. Lee Epstein, René Lindstädt, Jeffrey A. Segal, and Chad Westerland, "The Changing Dynamics of Senate Voting on Supreme Court Nominees," *The Journal of Politics* 68 (May 2006): 296ff.

64. For a detailed discussion of the Rutledge nomination, see Maltese, *The Selling of Supreme Court Nominees*, 26–31.

65. P.S. Ruckman, Jr., "The Supreme Court, Critical Nominations, and the Senate Confirmation Process," *The Journal of Politics* 55 (August 1993): 794.

66. Ann E. Marimow, "Two Years In, Trump's Appeals Court Confirmations at a Historic High Point," *The Washington Post*, February 4, 2019, https://www.washingtonpost.com/local/legal-issues/two-years-in-trumps-appeals-court-confirmations-at-a-historic-high-point/2019/02/03/574226e6-1a90-11e9-9ebf-c5fed1b7a081_story.html?utm_term=.4e9004ebbe69; for an updated tally of appointments, see https://en.wikipedia.org/wiki/List_of_federal_judges_appointed_by_Donald_Trump

67. Elliot Slotnick, Sara Schiavoni, and Sheldon Goldman, "Obama's Judicial Legacy: The Final Chapter," *Journal of Law and Courts* (Fall 2017): 376.

68. Larry C. Berkson and Susan B. Carbon, *The United States Circuit Court Nominating Commissions: Their Members, Procedures, and Candidates* (Chicago, IL: American Judicature Society, 1980).

69. Alan Neff, *The United States District Court Nominating Commissions: Their Members, Procedures, and Candidates* (Chicago, IL: American Judicature Society, 1981).

70. Sheldon Goldman, "Reagan's Judicial Legacy: Completing the Puzzle and Summing Up," *Judicature* 72 (April–May 1989): 319–320.

71. Alex Swoyer and Stephen Dinan, "Lindsey Graham Says 'Blue Slips' Won't Derail Trump Appeals Court Picks," *The Washington Times*, February 7, 2019, https://www.washingtontimes.com/news/2019/feb/7/lindsey-graham-blue-slips-wont-derail-trump-picks/

72. Deanna Paul, "'Damaging Precedent': Conservative Federal Judge Installed Without Consent of Home-State Senators," *The Washington Post*, February 28, 2019, https://www.washingtonpost.com/politics/2019/02/27/dangerous-first-conservative-judge-installed-after-vetting-by-only-two-senators/?utm_term=.85b322cadb43

73. Edward M. Chen, "The Judiciary, Diversity, and Justice for All," *California Law Review* 91 (July 2003): 1112; "How Women Lawyers Fare," *U.S. News & World Report*, January 15, 1996, 14.

74. Based on Tables 9.1 and 9.2 in Sheldon Goldman, *Picking Federal Judges: Lower Court Selection From Roosevelt Through Reagan* (New Haven, CT: Yale University Press, 1997), 350, 356.

75. "Judicial Diversity Statistics 2018," Lord Chief Justice of England and Wales, 2 and 5, July 12, 2018, https://www.judiciary.uk/wp-content/uploads/2018/07/judicial-diversity-statistics-2018-1.pdf

76. "Judicial Diversity Committee of the Judges' Council—Report on Progress and Action Plan 2018," Courts and Tribunals Judiciary, 2019, https://www.judiciary.uk/about-the-judiciary/who-are-the-judiciary/diversity/judicial-diversity-committee-of-the-judges-council-report-on-progress-and-action-plan-2018/

77. Rhode Island is one state that gives its judges life tenure.

78. "Gubernatorial Appointment of Judges," Ballotpedia, accessed August 6, 2019, https://ballotpedia.org/Gubernatorial_appointment_of_judges

79. "Legislative Election of Judges," Ballotpedia, accessed August 6, 2019, https://ballotpedia.org/Legislative_election_of_judges

80. Tarr, *Judicial Process and Policymaking*, 63.

81. For an up-to-date compendium of all the judicial selection methods for all the different types of judges at the state level, see "Judicial Selection in the States," Ballotpedia, accessed August 6, 2019, https://ballotpedia.org/Judicial_selection_in_the_states

82. For a sympathetic treatment of lay judges, see Doris Marie Provine, *Judging Credentials: Nonlawyer Judges and the Politics of Professionalism* (Chicago, IL: University of Chicago Press, 1986). Not surprisingly, professional organizations, such as the American Bar Association, are more critical of nonlawyer judges.

## CHAPTER 15

1. "Cannabis Act," Canada Justice Laws Website, June 20, 2019, https://laws-lois.justice.gc.ca/eng/acts/C-24.5/

2. "Designated Smoking Areas on Municipal Property," Halifax, accessed August 6, 2019, https://www.arcgis.com/apps/View/index.html?appid=f0474231f1594d5db31906207a9379f3; Ian Austin, Catherine Porter, and Dan Bilefsky, "Canada Is Legalizing Marijuana. Here Are Some Questions, Answered," *The New York Times*, October 16, 2018, https://www.nytimes.com/2018/10/16/world/canada/marijuana-legalization-explainer.html

3. Rob Gillies, Gene Johnson, and Tracey Lindeman, "Jubilant Customers Light Up As Pot Sales Begin in Canada," *AP News*, October 17, 2018, https://www.apnews.com/af182242261340c8a337d7fc61a644a5

4. Ian Austen, "Trudeau Unveils Bill Legalizing Recreational Marijuana in Canada," *The New York Times*, April 13, 2017, https://www.nytimes.com/2017/04/13/world/canada/trudeau-marijuana.html

5. Jody Wilson-Raybould, Jane Philpot, and Ralph Goodale, "A Framework for the Legalization and Regulation of Cannabis in Canada: The Final Report of the Task Force on Cannabis Legalization and Regulation," Government of Canada, November 30, 2016, https://www.canada.ca/en/health-canada/services/drugs-medication/cannabis/laws-regulations/task-force-cannabis-legalization-regulation/framework-legalization-regulation-cannabis-in-canada.html?utm_source=news.gc&utm_medium=report_link_en&utm_campaign=mj_task_force_16&_ga=1.99667228.388580584.1489681942#es

6. Press Release, National Academies of Science, Engineering and Medicine, January 12, 2017, http://www8.nationalacademies.org/onpinews/newsitem.aspx?RecordID=24625; Christopher Ingraham, "How Many Americans Regularly Use Pot? The Number Is, Errr, Higher Than You Think," *The Washington Post*, April 20, 2017, https://www.sacbee.com/news/nation-world/national/article145681414.html

7. Hannah Hartig and Abigail Geiger, "About Six-in-Ten Americans Support Marijuana Legalization," Pew Research Center, October 8, 2018, http://www.pewresearch.org/fact-tank/2018/10/08/americans-support-marijuana-legalization/

8. Malcolm Gladwell, "Is Marijuana as Safe as We Think?" *The New Yorker*, January 14, 2019, https://www.newyorker.com/magazine/2019/01/14/is-marijuana-as-safe-as-we-think?reload=true

9. Uki Goni, "Uruguay, the First Country Where You Can Smoke Marijuana Wherever You Like," *The Guardian*, May 27, 2017, https://www.theguardian.com/society/2017/may/27/marijuana-legalisation-uruguay-seen-half-measure-users

10. Aisha Hassan, "All the Places in the World You Can (Legally) Smoke Weed," Quartz, October 17, 2018, https://qz.com/1427177/where-is-marijuana-legal-around-the-world/

11. Andrew Christie, "Rethinking Wildfires," Sierra Club, November 19, 2018, https://www.sierraclub.org/santa-lucia/blog/2018/11/rethinking-wildfires; "Governor Brown Signs Legislation to Strengthen Wildfire Prevention and Recovery," YubaNet, September 21, 2018, https://yubanet.com/regional/governor-brown-signs-legislation-to-strengthen-wildfire-prevention-and-recovery/; Julia Gheorghiu, "Edison Electric Institute Takes on Wildfire Challenges With New CEO Task Force," Utility Dive, January 25, 2019, https://www.utilitydive.com/news/edison-electric-institute-takes-on-wildfire-challenges-with-new-ceo-task-fo/546809/

12. Niall McCarthy, "The Countries With the Most Think Tanks Worldwide," *Forbes*, August 13, 2018, https://www.forbes.com/sites/niallmccarthy/2018/08/13/the-countries-with-the-most-think-tanks-worldwide-infographic/#41c7fa319234

13. "About the Office of Water," Environmental Protection Agency, July 8, 2019, https://www.epa.gov/aboutepa/about-office-water

14. "The World Factbook," Central Intelligence Agency, August 6, 2019, https://www.cia.gov/library/publications/resources/the-world-factbook/index.html

15. Price Fishback, "Government and the Economy" in *Government and the American Economy: A New History*, ed. Price V. Fishback (Chicago, IL: University of Chicago Press, 2007).

16. Paul Krugman, "Trump Versus the Socialist Menace," *The New York Times*, February 7, 2019, https://www.nytimes.com/2019/02/07/opinion/trump-socialism-state-of-the-union.html; Council of Economic Advisers, *The Opportunity Costs of Socialism*, October 2018, https://www.whitehouse.gov/wp-content/uploads/2018/10/The-Opportunity-Costs-of-Socialism.pdf

17. "The Condition of Education," National Center for Education Statistics, accessed August 6, 2019, https://nces.ed.gov/programs/coe/indicator_cgb.asp

18. PricewaterhouseCoopers, "Public-Private Partnerships in the U.S.: The State of the Market and the Road Ahead," November 2016, https://www.pwc.com/us/en/capital-projects-infrastructure/publications/assets/pwc-us-public-private-partnerships.pdf

19. "Health at a Glance 2017," OECD iLibrary, Table 5.1, November 10, 2017, https://www.oecd-ilibrary.org/docserver/health_glance-2017-24-en.pdf?expires=1543783318&id=id&accname=guest&checksum=430D6136ADB03F776B413F6D9657F658

20. Ibid.

21. Anne-Emanuelle Birn, Theodore M. Brown, Elizabeth Fee, and Walter J. Lear, "Struggles for National Health Reform in the United States," *American Journal of Public Health* 93, no. 1 (January 2003): 86–91.

22. Atul Gawande, "Getting There From Here: How Should Obama Reform Health Care?" *The New Yorker*, January 26, 2009.

23. "Health Insurance Coverage of the Total Population," Henry J. Kaiser Family Foundation, 2017, https://www.kff.org/other/state-indicator/total-population/

24. Ibid.

25. "Who Is Eligible for Medicaid?" U.S. Department of Health and Human Services, accessed August 4, 2017, https://www.hhs.gov/answers/medicare-and-medicaid/who-is-eligible-for-medicaid/index.html

26. Jeanine Skowronski, "A State-by-State Guide to Medicaid: Do I Qualify?" Policygenius, January 26, 2018, https://www.policygenius.com/blog/a-state-by-state-guide-to-medicaid/

27. "Health at a Glance 2015, How Does the United States Compare?" OECD, www.oecd.org/unitedstates/Health-at-a-Glance-2015-Key-Findings-UNITED-STATES.pdf

28. Irene Papanicolas, Liana R. Woskie, and Ashish K. Jha, "Health Care Spending in the United States and Other High-Income Countries," *JAMA (Journal of the American Medical Association)* (March 13, 2018): 1024–1039.

29. Jeffrey A. Rhodes, "The Uninsured in America, 2004: Estimates for the U.S. Civilian Noninstitutionalized Population Under Age 65," *Medical Expenditure Panel Survey Statistical Brief #83*, June 2005, Agency for Health Care Research and Quality.

30. Marilyn Moon, "The Future of Medicare as an Entitlement Program," *The Elder Law Journal* 12, no. 1: 228.

31. "Key Facts About the Uninsured Population," Kaiser Family Foundation, December 7, 2018, https://www.kff.org/uninsured/fact-sheet/key-facts-about-the-uninsured-population/

32. "The Requirement to Buy Coverage Under the Affordable Care Act," Kaiser Family Foundation, August 2, 2017, https://www.kff.org/infographic/the-requirement-to-buy-coverage-under-the-affordable-care-act/

33. "Infant Mortality Rates," OECD Health Statistics: Health Status, 2018, https://data.oecd.org/healthstat/infant-mortality-rates.htm#indicator-chart

34. Papinocolas, "Health Care Spending," 1034.

35. Jonathan Weisman, "Health Law Puts Governors in Pickle," *The Wall Street Journal*, August 26, 2011.

36. Timothy S. Jost, "The Affordable Care Act Under the Trump Administration," The Commonwealth Fund, August 30, 2018, https://www.commonwealthfund.org/blog/2018/affordable-care-act-under-trump-administration; a group of Republican attorneys general mounted another court challenge that produced a ruling in late 2018 declaring the entire law unconstitutional: Amy Goldstein, "Federal Judge in Texas Rules Entire Obama Healthcare Law Is Unconstitutional," *The Washington Post*, December 14, 2018, https://www.washingtonpost.com/national/health-science/federal-judge-in-texas-rules-obama-health-care-law-unconstitutional/2018/12/14/9e8bb5a2-fd63-11e8-862a-b6a6f3ce8199_story.html?noredirect=on&utm_term=.b83515be09b9

37. Karen Pollitz and Gary Claxton, "Proposals for Insurance Options That Don't Comply With ACA Rules: Trade-offs in Cost and Regulation," Kaiser Family Foundation, April 18, 2018, https://www.kff.org/health-reform/issue-brief/proposals-for-insurance-options-that-dont-comply-with-aca-rules-trade-offs-in-cost-and-regulation/

38. Chris Lee, "Implications of 'Medicare for All' and 'Public Plan Strategies,'" Kaiser Family Foundation, October 10, 2018, https://www.kff.org/medicare/press-release/implications-of-medicare-for-all-and-public-plan-strategies-new-brief-and-interactive-tool-summarize-legislative-proposals-and-key-issues/

39. Niv Elis and Peter Sullivan, "House GOP 2019 Budget Calls for Deep Medicare, Medicaid Spending Cuts," *The Hill*, June 19, 2018, https://thehill.com/policy/finance/393028-house-gop-2019-budget-calls-for-deep-medicare-medicaid-spending-cuts

40. "Frequently Asked Questions," Q19, Social Security Administration, https://www.ssa.gov/history/hfaq.html

41. "Old-Age, Survivors, and Disability Trust Funds 1957–2018," Social Security Administration, accessed August 7, 2019, https://www.ssa.gov/oact/STATS/table4a3.html; also see "Trust Fund Operations," Social Security Administration, accessed August 7, 2019, http://ssa.gov/history/tftable.html

42. "Policy Basics: Top Ten Facts About Social Security," Center on Budget and Policy Priorities, August 14, 2018, https://www.cbpp.org/research/social-security/policy-basics-top-ten-facts-about-social-security

43. "Ratio of Covered Workers to Beneficiaries," Social Security Administration, accessed August 7, 2019, https://www.ssa.gov/history/ratios.html

44. OECD, "Figure 5.10: Expected Years After Labor Market Exit by Gender in 2016," *Pensions at a Glance: OECD and G20 Indicators*, 2017, https://www.oecd-ilibrary.org/docserver/pension_glance-2017-25-en.pdf?expires=1565224218&id=id&accname=guest&checksum=2DED56925A04DFF6A6EE811C2D704D41

45. Ibid.; "Figure 4.2 Gross Pension Replacement Rates by Earnings," *Pensions at a Glance*, https://www.oecd-ilibrary.org/docserver/pension_glance-2017-12-en.pdf?expires=1565224555&id=id&accname=guest&checksum=54341B6359FE73889974F52BDC8A37D6

46. The Trustees of the Old Age and Survivors Insurance and Federal Disability Trust Fund report annually to Congress with their 75-year projections. For the report made in 2018 see https://www.ssa.gov/OACT/TR/2018/tr2018.pdf

47. Congressional Budget Office, *Options for Reducing the Deficit: 2019 to 2028*, December 13, 2018 https://www.cbo.gov/budget-options/2018/54743

48. Sarah Gibbens, "15 Ways the Trump Administration Has Changed Environmental Policies," *National Geographic*, February 1, 2019, https://www.nationalgeographic.com/environment/2019/02/15-ways-trump-administration-impacted-environment/; also see "A Running List of How President Trump Is Changing Environmental Policy," *National Geographic*, May 3, 2019, https://news.nationalgeographic.com/2017/03/how-trump-is-changing-science-environment/

49. "Breakdown of Electricity Generation by Energy Source," The Shift Project, accessed August 7, 2019, http://www.tsp-data-portal.org/Breakdown-of-Electricity-Generation-by-Energy-Source#tspQvChart

50. "Changes in Coal Sector Led to Less SO2 and NOx Emissions From Electric Power Industry," U.S. Energy Information Administration, December 11, 2018, https://www.eia.gov/todayinenergy/detail.php?id=37752

51. "Frequently Asked Questions: How Much of U.S. Carbon Dioxide Emissions Are Associated With Electricity Generation?" U.S. Energy Information Administration, 2017, https://www.eia.gov/tools/faqs/faq.php?id=77&t=11

52. Jeff Brady, "Trump's EPA Plans to Ease Carbon Emissions Rule for New Coal Plants," *NPR*, December 6, 2018, https://www.npr.org/2018/12/06/674255402/trumps-epa-plans-to-ease-carbon-emissions-rule-for-new-coal-plants

53. "Nuclear Power in France," World Nuclear Association, June 2019, http://www.world-nuclear.org/information-library/country-profiles/countries-a-f/france.aspx

54. "Nuclear Power in Germany," World Nuclear Association, March 2019, http://www.world-nuclear.org/information-library/country-profiles/countries-g-n/germany.aspx

55. "Disposal of High Level Nuclear Waste," U.S. Government Accountability Office, accessed August 7, 2019, https://www.gao.gov/key_issues/disposal_of_highlevel_nuclear_waste/issue_summary

56. U.S. Department of Energy, *The Smart Grid: An Introduction*, accessed August 7, 2019, https://www.energy.gov/sites/prod/files/oeprod/DocumentsandMedia/DOE_SG_Book_Single_Pages%281%29.pdf

57. "Frequently Asked Questions: What Is the United States' Share of World Energy Consumption?" U.S. Energy Information Administration, December 26, 2018, https://www.eia.gov/tools/faqs/faq.php?id=87&t=1

58. Bruce Stokes, Richard Wike, and Jill Carle, "Global Concern About Climate Change, Broad Support for Limiting Emissions," Pew Research Center, November 5, 2015, http://www.pewglobal.org/2015/11/05/1-concern-about-climate-change-and-its-consequences/

59. U.S. Department of Energy, *2008 Renewable Energy Book* (July 2009), 7.

60. Tom DiChristopher, "Trump Wants America to Be 'Energy Dominant.' Here's What That Means," *CNBC*, June 28, 2017, https://www.cnbc.com/2017/06/28/trump-america-energy-dominant-policy.html

61. Michael Greshko, Laura Parker, Brian Clark Howard, Daniel Stone, and Alejandra Borunda, "A Running List of How President Trump Is Changing Environmental Policy," *National Geographic*, https://news.nationalgeographic.com/2017/03/how-trump-is-changing-science-environment/; Alisa Barba, "Trump Administration's Slow but Sure Energy Dominance Agenda," *Inside Energy*, December 22, 2017, http://insideenergy.org/2017/12/22/trump-administrations-slow-but-sure-energy-dominance-agenda/

62. "Summary for Policymakers of IPCC Special Report on Global Warming of 1.5C Approved by Governments," IPCC, October 8, 2018, https://www.ipcc.ch/2018/10/08/summary-for-policymakers-of-ipcc-special-report-on-global-warming-of-1-5c-approved-by-governments/

63. Carolynn Kormann, "The False Choice Between Economic Growth and Combatting Climate Change," *The New Yorker*, February 4, 2019, https://www.newyorker.com/news/news-desk/the-false-choice-between-economic-growth-and-combatting-climate-change?utm_campaign=aud-dev&utm_source=nl&utm_brand=tny&utm_mailing=TNY_Daily_020519&utm_medium=email&bxid=5be9ec8c24c17c6adf0a3931&user_id=30158558&utm_term=TNY_Daily

64. Jeanne Sahadi, "The Sneaky Way Congress Plans to Raise the Debt Ceiling," CNN, February 9, 2018, https://money.cnn.com/2018/02/08/news/economy/debt-limit/index.html; Bill Chappell, "U.S. National Debt Hits Record $22 Trillion," *NPR*, February 13, 2019, https://www.npr.org/2019/02/13/694199256/u-s-national-debt-hits-22-trillion-a-new-record-thats-predicted-to-fall

65. Bill McInturff, "A Pivot Point in American Opinion," *Public Opinion Strategies*, September 1, 2011, http://www.foxandhoundsdaily.com/2011/09/9381-a-pivot-point-american-opinion-the-debt-ceiling-negotiation-and-its-consequ/

66. Lothar Funk, "The German Economy During the Financial and Economic Crisis Since 2008/2009," *Konrad Adenauer Stiftung*, 2012, 9, https://www.kas.de/c/document_library/get_file?uuid=effcf59f-84bc-2a10-1e13-97dd022312b4&groupId=252038

67. See the fascinating discussion of regulation on a site maintained by the Smithsonian Institution (http://americanhistory.si.edu/powering/).

## APPENDIX B

1. This version, which follows the original Constitution in capitalization and spelling, was published by the United States Department of the Interior, Office of Education, in 1935.
2. Altered by the Sixteenth Amendment.
3. Negated by the Fourteenth Amendment.
4. Revised by the Twelfth Amendment.
5. Qualified by the Eleventh Amendment.
6. This heading appears only in the joint resolution submitting the first ten amendments, which are collectively known as the Bill of Rights. They were ratified on December 15, 1791.

# INDEX

Tenth Amendment, 40, 41, 54, 58, 59, 61, 62, 66, 68. *See also* States' rights

*Texas v. Johnson*, 87

*Texas v. White*, 65

Think tanks, 384 (figure)

Third Amendment, 80, 95. *See also* Bill of Rights

Thirteenth Amendment, 58, 65, 112, 113

*THOMAS* (computerized database), 272

Thomas, Clarence, 87

Thoreau, Henry David, 142

Three-Fifths Compromise, 36, 109

Thurmond, Strom, 179

*Tinker v. Des Moines Independent Community School District*, 86

Title IX, 126, 132

Tocqueville, Alexis de, 139

Tolerance, political, 139–140, 140 (figure)

Townshend, Charles, 28

Townshend Acts, 28

Tracking polls, 156

Trade associations, 183–184

Trans-Pacific Partnership, 306

Treasury Department, 249

Treaties, 278, 307–308

Trial courts, 360

Truman, Harry S., 346, 372

Trump, Donald J., 13, 178, 189, 192, 197, 198
    administrative strategy of, 321
    after convention, 199
    attempted repeal of ACA, 2, 393
    bureaucracy and, 330, 331, 337, 344, 349
    campaign promises, 182
    as chief administrator, 309
    as chief diplomat, 306, 308
    as chief magistrate, 309
    civil liberties and, 103–104
    Congress and, 319, 320
    credibility of, 260
    deregulation and, 321
    economic policy and, 409
    environmental policies and, 72, 309, 400, 403
    executive orders and, 322 (table), 322–323
    experience of, 318
    fake news and, 254
    far-right nationalist parties and, 120
    fiscal policy and, 406, 407
    on flag desecration laws, 87
    free speech concerns and, 83, 88, 89
    as head of state, 310–311
    health care and, 2, 393
    on Hispanics, 128, 130
    immigration policies and, 103–104, 128–129
    intelligence community and, 349
    judicial strategy of, 323
    judiciary and, 70, 96, 130, 354, 373, 375, 376, 377
    Justice Department and, 349
    LGBT rights and, 132
    media and, 141, 254
    nomination of, 195
    party identification and, 236
    presidential communication and, 302, 303, 324
    press and, 260
    public approval of, 313
    relation with Republican party, 177
    sanctuary cities and, 53–54
    signing statements and, 312
    social media and, 302, 303, 324, 344–345
    Social Security and, 397
    staff of, 314, 315 (table)
    support for, 165, 232, 233 (figure)
    trade agreements and, 306
    use of force and, 305, 306

Trustee model, 272

Trust in government, 140–141, 141 (figure), 149–150, 332 (figure)

Tulis, Jeffrey, 302

Turnout, voter. *See* Voter turnout

Twenty-First Amendment, 47, 180

Twitter, 246. *See also* Internet/social media

Two-party system, 177–180

*Two Treatises of Government* (Locke), 30

Unemployment insurance, 10

Unfunded mandates, 69

Unified government, 319

Unitary system, 39, 54, 55, 56 (figure)

United Kingdom. *See* Great Britain

*United States v. Leon*, 101

*University of California v. Bakke*, 134

Unpledged delegates, 193

Unreasonable searches and seizures, 48, 99. *See also* Fourth Amendment

*Unsafe at Any Speed* (Nader), 250

*U.S. v. Lopez*, 70

Values, 12–16, 139
    American compared to Iranian, 148 (table)
    American exceptionalism, 146–148
    conflicts in, 16, 16 (figure)
    Confucian, 143
    German, 20
    political culture and, 147–148
    *See also* Fairness; Freedom; Individualism; Political culture; Political socialization; Religion; Rule of law

Van Buren, Martin, 166

Vavreck, Lynn, 194

Veto, 40, 320

Vice president, 315–316

Vietnam War, 140, 145, 146, 153, 169

Vinson, Fred, 115, 116

Vinson, Mechelle, 123

Volunteerism, 19 (figure), 19–20, 223 (figure)

Voter identity
    age, 224–225
    ethnicity, 225
    income, 225
    overview, 223–224

Voter suppression, 118–119

Voter turnout
    age and, 225 (figure)
    in congressional elections, 226, 227 (figure)
    convenience and, 222
    decline of, 221–222
    education and, 221 (figure)
    ethnicity and, 225 (figure)